Legislative

Congressional
Deskbook

The Practical and Comprehensive Guide to Congress

FIFTH EDITION

Michael L. Koempel

Judy Schneider

Contributing Authors

Eugene Boyd, Peggy Garvin, Bill Heniff Jr.,
Henry B. Hogue, and Robert Keith

TheCapitol.Net

Alexandria, VA

2007

TheCapitol.Net, Inc. is a non-partisan firm that annually provides continuing professional education and information for thousands of government and business leaders that strengthens representative government and the rule of law.

Our publications and courses, written and taught by *current* Washington insiders who are all independent subject matter experts, show how Washington works.™ Our products and services can be found on our web site at <*www.TheCapitol.Net*>.

Additional copies of the *Congressional Deskbook* can be ordered online: <*www.CongressionalDeskbook.com*>.

The Legislative Series from TheCapitol.Net includes the *Congressional Directory,* which is updated annually, *Legislative Drafter's Deskbook*, and the Congressional Operations Poster. The spiral-bound *Directory* of the members of the U.S. Senate and the U.S. House of Representatives includes color photos, room, phone and fax numbers, committee and subcommittee listings, a fold-out map of Capitol Hill, and much more. See <*www.CongressionalDirectory.com*> for more information.

Citation Form—URLs: We use a standard style for all web addresses, also known as Uniform Resource Locators (URLs). URLs appear in text next to the first mention of the resource being described, and are surrounded with open and close angle brackets.

For URLs that have the standard web addressing form at the beginning of the URL of "http://www." we show only the initial "www." For example, the URL "http://www.domainname.com" will appear in text and tables as "<*www.domainname.com*>".

For URLs that begin with anything other than "www.", such as "http://thomas.loc.gov", the URL will appear in text and tables as "<*http://thomas.loc.gov*>". For example, the URL "http://www3.domain.gov" will appear in text and tables as "<*http://www3.domain.gov*>".

Design and production by Zaccarine Design, Inc., Evanston, IL; 847-864-3994.

v 5.0

ISBN: 1587330970
ISBN 13: 978-1-58733-097-1

Summary Table of Contents

Table of Contents

Chapter Six
Supporting Congress: The Capitol Complex 159

Chapter Seven
Organizing Congress:
Members, Leaders, and Committees 189

Chapter Fourteen
**Legislative Research:
How to Monitor and Research Congress**

    14.11 House Floor Plan

    14.12 View of the Speaker's Dais and Wall of the House

    14.13 View of the Speaker's Dais, Floor of the House, and Galleries

    14.21 Senate Floor Plan

    14.22 View of the Senate Rostrum, or Presiding Officer's Dais

Chapter Fifteen
Putting It All Together: A Working Example

    15.01a Bill as Introduced in the House

    15.02a Bill as Reported

    15.03a Banking and Financial Services Committee Report

    15.04a Banking and Financial Services
            Committee Supplementary Report

    15.05a Commerce Committee Report

    15.06a Special Rule from the Rules Committee

    15.07a Rules Committee Report

Back of the Book

Acknowledgments

As we worked on the fifth edition of the *Congressional Deskbook*, we again reflected on our debt to family, friends, and colleagues who assisted us in numerous ways in writing the first edition of this book, and who have continued to support us in the work of revising for subsequent editions. We once again must thank especially Dianne Hunt, Mike's wife, and Jean Yavis Jones, a dear friend, who assisted us in every phase of the writing. They helped get us back on track whenever we began to lose sight of our goal. We are also especially thankful to Bob Keith, a colleague at the Congressional Research Service, who contributed generously to the chapter on the federal budget process in the first, second, and current editions. Mike also thanks Gabriel Koempel for his patience in sharing his dad with the evening, weekend, and holiday demands of writing and updating a book.

We are fortunate to have worked at the Congressional Research Service with exceptional people whose daily concern is service to Congress. We also are fortunate to have friends and colleagues in the media, government affairs, executive agencies, congressional offices, policy organizations, and universities. The experiences and knowledge of these people are certainly reflected in our perspective in writing this book. Some friends and colleagues whom we would like to thank specifically for their roles in this book over the years are Mildred Amer, Joe Cantor, Bob Cuthriell, Paul Dwyer, Eric Fischer, Peggy Garvin, Sharon Gressle, Nancy Kervin, Jennifer Manning, Jack Maskell, Lynne McCay, Mary Mulvihill, Ilona Nickels, Walter Oleszek, Charlotte Preece, Harold Relyea, Mort Rosenberg, Steve Rutkus, Jim Saturno, Steve Stathis, Jeffrey Weinberg, Clay Wellborn, Leneice Wu, and Linda Zappasodi. Each has helped make this book better.

We could not have written or revised this book without the experiences we shared with members of Congress and congressional staff for more than thirty years. We began our professional careers working on Capitol Hill as congressional staffers. From the beginning, we learned important lessons from members and staff. Those lessons became the focus of this book, and continue to inform this book as Congress evolves and members and staff conduct their work differently as each new Congress unfolds. Our affection and respect for the men and women who serve the nation in Congress and the staff who work in committees, personal offices, and administrative offices is constant. We are grateful to members and staff for information used in this book. For their assistance on several editions of the book, we must specifically thank former-Representative Karen Thurman and Representative Jan Schakowsky and congressional staffers Cathy Hurwit, Nora Matus, and Ellen McCarthy.

For the fourth and fifth editions of the *Congressional Deskbook*, we invited knowledgeable, wonderful people to join us. Peggy Garvin completely claims as hers Chapter 13, on legislative research, which she completely revised in the third edition. This chapter continues to change rapidly as research methods and sources change, and it shares some of the wealth of knowledge Peggy has about conducting research on Congress in the dynamic world of electronically stored information. Bill Heniff Jr. updated and added to the procedurally rich chapter on the federal budget process in the third edition, and he played the same role in the fourth edition. He continued the lucid explanation and writing begun by Bob Keith, and enriched the chapter with his own insights into what is important to know. Bob has now rejoined us to update the budget chapter for the fifth edition.

For the fourth and fifth editions, we invited two more contributing authors to join us to enrich sections of the book with their expertise. Henry B. Hogue has tackled the sections of Chapter 10 dealing with Congress and the executive, adding a new level of knowledge to the key institutional relationship in national policymaking. Eugene Boyd has taken over the sections of Chapter 10 dealing with federalism, that complex, ever-changing relationship between Congress and the states and localities. It is a subject to which Eugene has devoted years of study and work.

Finally, and most importantly, this book would probably not have been written without the encouragement of Chug Roberts of TheCapitol.Net. Chug is serious about serving people inside and outside Washington who wish to understand Congress at a very practical level. The challenges of the first, second, third, fourth, and fifth editions of this graphically complex book were ably handled by production editor Catherine Zaccarine. We are very grateful to TheCapitol.Net for its encouragement, support, and vision, and for the opportunity to continue this book to its fifth edition.

Michael L. Koempel
Judy Schneider
May 2007

About the Authors

Michael L. Koempel is a senior specialist in American national government at the Congressional Research Service, a department of the Library of Congress. He worked previously for Congressional Quarterly Inc., and on the staffs of a U.S. representative and a state governor. Mr. Koempel holds a bachelor's degree from Georgetown University and a law degree from The Catholic University of America, and is admitted to practice law in the District of Columbia.

Judy Schneider is a specialist on Congress at the Congressional Research Service, a department of the Library of Congress, and an adjunct scholar at The Brookings Institution. She worked previously for Senate and House committees, including the Senate Select Committee to Study the Senate Committee System. Ms. Schneider was selected as a Stennis Fellow for the 108th Congress, and received the Women in Government Relations (WGR) Distinguished Member Award in 2004. Ms. Schneider is a frequent speaker and lecturer on Congress and legislative procedures. She holds bachelor's and master's degrees from The American University.

Chapter 10 (Congress and federalism)

Eugene Boyd is a public policy analyst at the Congressional Research Service, where he specializes in issues relating to federalism, intergovernmental relations, the federal grant system, and urban policy. He has also published articles on congressional actions affecting state and local governments. Mr. Boyd holds a bachelor's degree in urban studies from Virginia Commonwealth University and has undertaken graduate studies in city and regional planning at Howard University.

Chapters 13

Peggy Garvin is an information consultant and author of *The United States Government Internet Manual*, an annual reference book from Bernan Press, and *Real World Research Skills*, published in 2006 by TheCapitol.Net. She has worked with government information, libraries, and information technology over her twenty-year career with the Congressional Research Service and in the private sector. Ms. Garvin earned her Master of Library Science degree from Syracuse University.

Chapter 9

Bill Heniff Jr. is an analyst in American national government at the Congressional Research Service, where he specializes in the budget and legislative processes. He holds a doctorate in government and politics from the University of Maryland.

Robert Keith, who has worked at the Congressional Research Service since 1974, is a Specialist in American National Government. He specializes in legislative procedure and the federal budget process, focusing particularly on the development and consideration of budget resolutions, reconciliation bills, authorization and appropriation acts, revenue and debt-limit legislation, and proposals to change the budget process.

Chapter 10 (Congress and the executive)

Henry B. Hogue earned his doctorate in public administration from The American University. His subsequent areas of study and publication have included the presidential appointment process, presidential recess-appointment authority, electronic government, and topics related to federal executive organization and management. Dr. Hogue is an analyst at the Congressional Research Service.

The views expressed in this book are those of the individual authors. They do not represent the views of their employers or of TheCapitol.Net.

Preface

In its physical presence, the Capitol symbolizes our national political life. In this magnificent building, one senses the history of the nation. Paintings depict historical events. Visitors listen to whispers at the location of John Quincy Adams's desk in the Old House Chamber, now National Statuary Hall. Busts of the vice presidents, who served as presidents of the Senate, line the Senate chamber and corridors. Presidents are inaugurated at the Capitol, and they deliver their State of the Union addresses in the House chamber. When one walks the Capitol corridors, one feels the presence of presidents, of renowned and nearly forgotten members of Congress, and of millions of visitors. It is in the Capitol Rotunda that a few Americans have lain in state, most recently President Ford. This is the place where national and foreign dignitaries have come to witness history or to be a part of it, from the Marquis de Lafayette to Julia Ward Howe to Frederick Douglass to Winston Churchill to the Apollo astronauts to Nelson Mandela.

Most importantly, the Capitol houses Congress. The Congress that the founding fathers designed over 200 years ago has been a strong and vibrant institution throughout its history. More than 11,800 members have served in the House and Senate. They have come from all walks of life, from privileged backgrounds and from lives of hardship, and at different ages and times in their careers and lives. Each member comes to Congress with parochial concerns, but, as a legislature, Congress acts for the entire nation.

While many Americans might think first of the president when they think of the federal government, the founding fathers placed Congress first in the Constitution, in Article I. They gave it authority "To make all Laws which shall be necessary and proper for carrying into Execution the foregoing Powers [enumerated in Article I], and all other Powers vested by this Constitution in the Government of the United States, or in any Department or Officer thereof." (Art. I, sec. 8, cl. 18.) Our democratic system of representative government is centered on a strong, independent legislative branch. Our government is not a parliamentary democracy with a party's or coalition's control of both the executive and legislature and the prime minister and cabinet drawn from the parliamentary majority.

The founding fathers created an open institution, and the men and women who have served in Congress have fostered that openness. The Capitol and congressional office buildings are physically open to visitors every day. Even with the increased security concerns following the tragic events in the fall of 2001, Congress has tried to accommodate its own and the citizenry's desire to meet and visit and observe in the Capitol and the congressional office buildings.

All but a few committee meetings are open to anyone who wishes to attend, and the rules of the House and Senate essentially require meetings to be open. One can sit in the House and Senate visitors' galleries and watch floor proceedings, or stay at home or at the office and watch the proceedings live on television. Journalists have ready access to members, committee meetings, and floor proceedings, and report news in every medium. Votes cast by individual members in committee and on the House floor are readily available to the public in both congressional documents and private print and electronic publications. Anyone can request a meeting with his or her representative or senator, and will be accommodated if at all possible. With its openness, Congress mediates between the federal government and the American people.

The founding fathers and the men and women who have served in Congress have also created a system of parliamentary procedures that values political consensus and, thus, makes legislation difficult to enact into law. The Constitution requires majority support on a measure in each chamber before the measure is sent to the president, who can then veto it. Unless a two-thirds majority in each chamber votes to override a president's veto, the measure dies. House rules generally enable a majority to work its will, but the rules still protect the minority party or minority viewpoint in many ways. Senate rules protect individual senators' prerogatives in nearly all instances, making it difficult for Senate leaders to process legislation.

Because of this openness, difficulty in enacting legislation, and Congress's political nature, it is easy to criticize Congress. In the best American tradition, we satirize politicians for their human and political foibles. Mark Twain long ago commented, "It could probably be shown by facts and figures that there is no distinctly native American criminal class except Congress." Will Rogers also satirized Congress; yet, his statue stands today in the Capitol. It faces the center doors to the House of Representatives where he could "keep an eye on Congress" for the country. *(See § 6.10.)*

But, for its foibles, it is in Congress that slavery was debated, the West was opened to homesteaders, a national economy was fostered, war was declared on five occasions, the rights of labor were secured, GIs returning from World War II were given new opportunities, the vote was extended step-by-step to every adult American, and federal financial support for education at all levels, health care, retirement security, and other programs of national welfare were enacted. Demagogues and bad public policy have held sway at times, but other forces in Congress arose ultimately to defeat them. The ability of Congress to correct course, usually because it has heard the voice of the people, is a unique and valuable part of our political heritage.

Is it possible for members of Congress, congressional staff, Capitol Hill visitors, and congressional critics to understand all that Congress has been and can be? It is easy to lose that perspective when mired in daily toil and daily headlines. Who fully appreciates the continuity of the Constitution and of Congress as its enduring embodiment? Few probably reflect regularly or at all on the Constitution. One has a sense that many think of the Constitution as a document from long ago rather than as the beacon that guides government day after day. Who outside Congress learns more than a few facts about the legislative process or tries to understand its impact on lawmaking? Even the number of scholars who study the legislative process is small. How do members, staff, visitors, and critics think about the complexities of the relationship among the three branches of government? Do they know the many options and opportunities available? It is tempting to focus, as the media often do, on who is "up" and who is "down" on a given day or political topic, as though each day of policymaking in Congress is part of a baseball season rather than an ongoing constitutional activity.

In this book we share our observations and experiences with readers who study Congress, who work there as members or staffers, who cover the institution as journalists, or who try to influence it as advocates, lobbyists, or citizens. Scores of books and studies about Congress are published each year. Some address legislative or budget procedures. Others detail documents that are generated on Capitol Hill or catalogue available Internet resources. Some explore an aspect of congressional history, or tell the story of Congress through a biography, voting patterns, leadership styles, or individual legislation. This book owes much to earlier books and studies. In some ways, it is a synthesis of these publications; in other ways, it is a complementary volume.

We decided that another book on Congress was not superfluous, but should provide as much practical information on the operations of this institution as possible in one volume. In this book, we cover legislative, budget, and special procedures; how various procedures relate to each other; the forms and impact of political competition on Capitol Hill; overviews of the election, lobbying, and ethics laws and rules that regulate congressional behavior; the work of congressional, committee, and administrative offices; the variety of congressional documents; and how to conduct research on Congress.

Young and idealistic, we came to the Congress as staffers over thirty years ago. We wanted to make a difference and take part in the next evolution of a 200-year tradition. Between us, we worked for individual members and committees and for different parties. Both of us now work for a nonpartisan legislative support agency. Thirty years later, we are still excited to be working in the Capitol and congressional office buildings and assisting members and staff in their work.

Experience has not tempered our idealism or awe. It has added realism. We appreciate Congress's greatness, in part because we understand its weaknesses. One must see Congress as a whole and in its parts, and recognize that understanding comes in knowing the relationship between them. One must look not only at a member's committee assignments, but at what those assignments may mean for policy outcomes. One must consider not only rules and procedures, but what strategic and tactical choices members face each day. Dozens of documents are generated daily, and one must know their significance. As this book explains, beginning on the first page, when Congress acts, it is a complex process that has four indivisible aspects—people, politics, policy, and procedure.

Michael L. Koempel
Judy Schneider
May 2007

Introduction

As the name *Congressional Deskbook* implies, this book is meant to be kept close at hand for answering the variety of questions that arise daily in monitoring, interacting with, and studying Congress. The book is organized for daily use in answering questions, but it may be read in sections, by chapters, or in its entirety, as the reader chooses.

Chapter One attempts to create an image of what it is like to be a member of Congress. It describes the competition that imbues every aspect of the institution and the fragmented life of a member.

Chapters Two, Three, and Four guide the reader through some of the major pressures affecting members of Congress. These pressures come from campaigns and elections, constituency, media, the president and executive branch, the courts, lobbyists, and the ethics environment. The chapters provide an overview of the laws and congressional rules that affect members, staff, and the individuals who interact with them.

Chapters Five and Six explain the support structures of Congress. They identify components of the expense allowance system, staff positions and responsibilities, the work of support offices, and features of the Capitol and congressional office buildings. These chapters orient the reader to congressional staff roles and offer a guide to finding one's way around Capitol Hill.

Chapter Seven describes the organization of Congress. It addresses not only the structures of the committee system and of the leadership hierarchy, but also how committee assignments are made and leaders are selected. It describes the early organization activities of the House and Senate following a general election.

Chapter Eight describes the legislative process in detail. It explains hearings and committee markup strategies and methods of obtaining floor consideration of legislative initiatives. Amendments between the chambers and conference procedures are explained. The chapter describes options available to leaders and members throughout the legislative process, and provides guides for keeping track of events at each major stage of the legislative process.

Chapter Nine demystifies the federal budget process. It includes discussion of the president's role in budgeting, the congressional budget process, authorizations, and appropriations. It explains the terminology, concepts, and procedures of the budget process, such as reconciliation.

Chapter Ten discusses procedures and powers in Congress's relations with the executive, the judiciary, and the states and localities. It also explains some of the ways in which Congress deals procedurally with defense and foreign policy. Topics in this chapter include confirmation of presidential appointees to executive and judicial posts, the role of legislative history, fast-track procedures, the War Powers Act, alternative procedures for selection of a president and vice president, constitutional amendments, and unfunded mandates.

Chapters Eleven and Twelve identify and explain the use of congressional documents. Subjects include the forms and versions of legislation, laws and implementing executive documents, official rules and procedure manuals, and party and administrative publications.

Chapter Thirteen identifies numerous private and governmental information resources, and provides descriptions of print and electronic resources, web addresses, and telephone contacts for obtaining additional information on resources. Numerous tips on research will facilitate a reader's work.

Chapter Fourteen guides the reader in researching members and committees, monitoring floor action, and tracking legislative action.

A case study in Chapter Fifteen ties the legislative process, legislative documents, and other topics in the book together as it takes a measure enacted into law in the 106th Congress through the legislative steps from inception to public law. Document excerpts are displayed, and explanatory texts and annotations accompany each excerpt.

A cumulative, expanded glossary complements the individual glossaries and definitions that appear in individual chapters. Appendices One through Seven provide extensive telephone and room listings for members, committees, and leaders on Capitol Hill. All of the web sites listed throughout the book are cumulated in a table. This list is followed by an index to the book.

Chapter One

Being a Member
of Congress

1

Analysis

1

§1.00 Introduction

The purpose of this book is to provide government affairs professionals, government officials, journalists, students of Congress, librarians, and other interested people, including members of Congress and congressional staff, particularly those new to Congress or seeking or taking on more senior roles, with a practical guide to Congress. The book offers an orientation to Congress, assisting the reader in understanding how Congress works and why it works the way it does.

The authors each have over thirty-five years' experience in American government. First as congressional staff, and then as analysts, writers, and educators, we have worked to understand and explain Congress to members and to congressional staff and to people whose profession requires a solid understanding of Congress. Based on our experiences, we designed this book to answer the variety of questions about Congress that arise daily in the work of individuals with a professional interest in Congress.

§1.10 Who . . . Gets . . . What!

Walter Kravitz, our late colleague at the Congressional Research Service (CRS), began his lectures and speeches by asserting the immediately and comfortably obvious: "Congress is a political institution." Then he would pause a long time, and silently watch discomfort gradually but relentlessly take hold of his listeners. Their faces showed they were becoming very uncertain about the meaning of the word *political*.

Kravitz would finally ask, "What do I mean by that?" Answering his own question, he would practically shout, "WHO . . . GETS . . . WHAT!" He would pause again briefly and then begin a litany: "Who gets what in terms of benefits, preferences, advantages? Who gets what in terms of North versus South? City versus rural areas? Rich versus poor? Business versus labor? Republican versus Democrat? Who gets dams or highways or research? That's what I mean by political—who gets what!" And on he would continue with more examples until it was painfully obvious to all listening that *political* means *who gets what*.

§1.20 Congress, the Political Institution

A member of Congress takes to Washington all the aspirations, desires, and conflicted sentiments of his or her constituency, and serves as one of 435 representatives, four delegates, one resident commissioner, and one hundred senators, all of whom have their own constituencies, each with its own aspirations, desires, and conflicted sentiments. It is worth noting the number of Democratic freshmen elected in 2006 who had experience as servicemen in Iraq—a war still underway—who ran in opposition to the war. Yet other Democratic and Republican freshmen ran and won on positions in support of the war or in support of a change in mission without necessarily endorsing an immediate withdrawal. Somehow, these 540 men and women make national policy. *(See Chapter Three, Pressures on Congress: Constituents, Media, President, and Courts.)*

The policymaking process in Congress—the means for determining who gets what—is not easy. It can be partisan, fractious, slow, cumbersome, and frustrating. It can even seem craven as each member seeks advantages for his or her constituency. If we find it difficult to settle differences in our daily lives, how much more difficult must it be for members of Congress to make policy as they represent all 300-plus million of us?

The framers of the Constitution well understood competition between groups of people and regions, and created Congress to provide an outlet for debating and deciding the common good, balancing one interest against others in the process.

The rules of procedure and organization that each chamber has developed exist equally for the use of proponents and opponents of any proposition. At each step of the legislative process, proponents must build a new majority to get to the next step. Or, opponents may try to build a new majority to stop a proposition that they have not yet been able to stop. Outside groups—constituents, lobbyists, the president and his administration, and the media—are never far from the fray, and they pressure, pressure, pressure to influence the outcome. *(See Chapter Three, Pressures on Congress: Constituents, Media, President, and Courts.)* Finally, it is important always to recognize that not just one proposition at a time is moving in Congress, but many propositions, offering individual members and groups of members numerous opportunities to trade for support or opposition on more than one of these. These multiple propositions also restrain members—the colleague one alienates on one vote may be the colleague one needs on another vote.

At each step of the legislative process, proponents and opponents must build their majorities within larger groups. A committee is larger than a subcommittee, a chamber is larger than a committee, and the two houses voting on a conference report are larger still.

Winning a majority in Congress is not usually based on denying members—and thereby their constituents—a stake in the outcome of a piece of legislation. Winning a majority is more likely based on giving as many members as needed for a majority a stake in the outcome—by compromising, old-fashioned logrolling, papering over differences, trading for legislative support elsewhere, or exchanging favors within or outside Congress. To become a law, a measure must pass the House and Senate in identical form.

A piece of legislation must also pass the test of having sufficient political support to gain the president's signature to become law. The president, however, might *veto* a measure for any number of reasons, including a different sense of what the nation wants or needs. For Congress then to override a presidential veto requires a two-thirds supermajority in each chamber. On those infrequent occasions when a veto is overridden, political consensus in Congress must be very high.

It is in the power of the presidential veto that one can clearly see what the phrase "co-equal branches of government" means. Unless there are two-thirds of the members of each chamber willing to vote to override a veto, almost the equivalent of Congress speaking with one voice, the power of the sole executive—the president—is equal to the votes of more than 280 representatives and more than 60 senators, assuming all members are present and vote overwhelmingly for a measure. But, few controversial measures pass Congress by majorities within striking distance of the two-thirds required for a veto override. The president's exercise of the veto should be seen as a constitutional action first and a political action second.

Two examples illustrate the power of the president in lawmaking. The Republican-controlled Congress was frustrated by President Bill Clinton's vetoes of appropriations bills in late 1995 as Congress tried to dictate the terms of achieving a balanced budget. Two shutdowns of the federal government ensued, for a total of twenty-seven days, and the public by wide margins blamed Congress. Congress ultimately responded with appropriations measures that the president was willing to sign. In 2007, Democrats in Congress and their supporters believed voters put Democrats back in the majority in Congress to stop funding for the war in Iraq, and Congress in May sent President George W. Bush an appropriations bill with a troop withdrawal or redeployment time frame. The president vetoed the measure, and a majority of the House, but only 222 of 425 representatives present, cast their votes for an override. Congress responded with an appropriations measure that nearly all Republicans voted for and a large majority of Democratic representatives voted against.

At every stage of the legislative process, and in every alliance made during the legislative process, Congress is a political institution, deciding who, including the president, gets what.

§1.30 A Member of Congress as Politician, Policymaker, and Parliamentarian

To be a successful member of Congress, a person must be a politician, policymaker, and parliamentarian. In the role of politician, a member must have the self-confidence to represent a large, diverse constituency. A constituency, in turn, expects its member of Congress, in the role of policymaker, to advance its interests and vote on the major issues of the day. Less visible to a constituency is the member of Congress in the role of parliamentarian, acting within the rules, precedents, and practices of the House or Senate to represent the constituency's interests and sentiments, and make policy for the entire nation. All three roles are constantly in play, thereby shaping the work of a member of Congress.

Politician

As a politician, a prospective or elected member of Congress can look in the mirror and see a person with a gift that most of us do not have—the capacity to campaign for and win a congressional election. He or she knows how to raise money; how to manage a campaign operation; how to rally a crowd; how to debate; how to listen; how to learn what issues matter to an individual, a constituency group, or a constituency generally; and how to advocate for himself or herself and for key issues. *(See Chapter Two: Pressures on Congress: Campaigns and Elections.)*

Once elected, the member of Congress can put the same skills to work in committee and on the House or Senate floor representing a congressional district or a state. The goal is to make policy—who gets what. The member's interests might be parochial or national or both; they might be simple or complex; they might be quite focused or fairly broad. The member has to be the same self-confident advocate with congressional colleagues as with constituents, able to speak persuasively one-on-one to a committee chair or ranking minority member and equally able to speak persuasively to the House or Senate in session.

Each member of Congress looks out for his or her own political interests in party and leadership meetings. A member wants to follow party leaders, unless they lead in a direction that would create political problems back home. The member must balance personal political needs against any stance taken by party leaders. A member might even want to have a role in the leadership, perhaps within the party's whip structure, but still maintain some flexibility in the relationship so he or she can speak for a different point of view or vote against the party leadership when necessary politically.

A principal challenge for any member is to be successful in a group. A *group* in Congress is not a *team*, as we might think of a sports team with everyone working together in various support roles to accomplish the clear goals of offense, defense, and winning. A group in Congress also lacks the formal system of direction or command that exists in business, the military, or even executive agencies, where a superior can give an order to subordinates with some degree of assurance that it will be carried out.

A member of Congress, in contrast, constantly functions within groups of different sizes, composition, like-mindedness, partisanship, purpose, role, structure, and so on. While some members of a group might have positions of power or discretion, such as the chair of a committee or a leader of a chamber, members are largely equal in many circumstances. No one is, or will be allowed to be, fully in charge since each state or district and set of supporters and other conditions are different for each member. A member must be skillful and adaptive in a variety of group structures to be a successful politician and policymaker.

Policymaker

As a policymaker, a member must be in command of facts, arguments, perspectives on a problem, and the advantages of particular policy or legislative solutions and the disadvantages of others. A member of Congress must also be able to manage his or her relationships with party and committee leaders. A member will need his or her leaders' assistance and even indulgence on matters critical to the member's constituency or political well-being.

Members of Congress might say that their views are rarely swayed by a colleague's speech. That may be true. However, it is equally true that their views are never positively swayed by a colleague who is unprepared or uninformed. More experienced members might be tolerant of

1

a junior member learning a new policy issue. They are not accepting of another member who is not in command of facts and arguments for a point of view, who speaks loudly in ignorance, or who makes implausible arguments.

As policymakers, members introduce bills, ask questions in hearings, offer amendments in committee markup and in the chamber, debate and vote in committee and in the chamber, and maneuver inside and outside of conferences to protect or kill provisions in measures submitted to conference. All their actions are intended to advance to the degree possible their constituents' interests and their own policy and legislative positions.

In leading a chamber of policymakers, party leaders have the tough job of putting together majorities (or even supermajorities in the instance of veto override attempts or, in the Senate, motions to invoke cloture). They need to put together these majorities without compromising core party positions. Leaders must also stop opposing viewpoints from gathering momentum. To build a majority on some matter within a chamber, leaders first seek a majority within their parties. Leaders try to enforce party discipline through favors, threats, or even a member's isolation. *(See Chapter Seven, Organizing Congress: Members, Leaders, and Committees.)*

Parliamentarian

As a parliamentarian, a member of Congress must understand chamber structure and the procedures through which members try to advance or impede policy in the form of legislation. Does the member introduce a bill or offer an amendment? If an amendment, should it be offered in a committee or on the floor? When? Is one committee more receptive to a policy solution than another? What opportunities or limitations will exist in committee because of the markup vehicle chosen? How does a member get time to speak on the floor? What can he or she do during that time? What is the optimal time? All these questions, options, and choices come into play as a member works within a chamber's procedures to realize a policy goal through the legislative process.

Congress has a formal structure. Each house of Congress follows laws, rules, precedents, and practices that apply in its chamber. Each chamber is very different. The strategies that work in the House, a majoritarian institution, are different from those that work in the Senate, an institution where the individual senator reigns supreme. Representatives who are elected to the Senate often find the first year or so to be a frustrating experience. It seems so difficult to get anything done in the Senate, compared with the practices of the House. *(See Chapter Eight, Legislating in Congress: Legislative Process; Chapter Nine, Legislating in Congress: Federal Budget Process; and Chapter Ten, Legislating in Congress: Special Procedures and Considerations.)*

To be effective and realize policy goals, a member of Congress must use all his or her skills and abilities as a politician, policymaker, and parliamentarian—both inside and outside committees and chambers, and at all stages of the legislative process.

Congress and Its 540 Members

In contrast to the roles of politician, policymaker, and parliamentarian, what images do Americans carry of members of Congress? Most citizens have images of a teacher in a classroom, a businessman or woman in an office, a programmer at a computer, a carpenter building a house, a therapist helping a patient, or an entertainer on stage. They have strong, largely accurate images of people at work. They generally think well of people in various professions, even if they have had a bad experience with an individual in any profession.

With members of Congress, Americans might very well have somewhat or largely positive images of their own representatives and senators, yet dismiss Congress as a whole because it is made up of "politicians." Even worse, they might dismiss it because it represents America too well—a lack of consensus in Congress often reflects a lack of consensus in the country.

To avoid the cynical view of Congress held by many Americans, how might someone interacting regularly with Congress try to imagine it as a whole, as a working institution? One possible way is to imagine Congress as a living organism, with a skeleton, nervous system, and muscular system. The skeleton is legislative procedure and the organization of Congress for processing legislation, which gives each chamber an enduring structure. The nervous system is complex, and involves all the avenues for information to reach members, committees, and leaders, such as the stimuli of elections, constituents, the president, lobbyists, the media, perceptions of problems, dissatisfaction with the status quo, events at home, events abroad, and the individual interests of members. The muscular system of Congress, which gives it the capacity to act, results in policymaking. Competing legislation is drafted, hearings are held, information is gathered, arguments are devised, and advocacy takes place inside and outside Congress. This image offers a way one might view Congress as a whole, in its capacity to act and to change.

The framers did not create Congress to achieve specific legislative results. They created it to process (or stop) legislation and to make law, whatever the outcome might be. A Congress that was largely controlled by Democrats for forty years until the 1994 elections worked just as well as a policymaking institution for Republicans who controlled it for twelve years until the 2006 elections. The policy results for Congress under Democratic control may be different from the policy results under Republican control. The framers, in fact, could not have anticipated modern political parties, but created a legislature where a majority, however composed, could win—in passing or stopping legislation. The stimulus of issues, the making of policy, and the procedural structure are just as important and evident today as they were in 1994, 1894, or 1794.

A member of Congress works as a politician, policymaker, and parliamentarian within a complex structure. He or she is one of 540 members motivated by different constituencies and personal and professional interests. To be successful, a member must combine roles skillfully within this complex structure.

§1.40 Obligations and Perquisites

With election come obligations to constituents, one's chamber, and the public and interests affected by one's role, and to the next election campaign.

If a member intends to seek reelection, he or she must be attentive to a constituency—through case work, visits home, prompt response to mail, and so on. Sometimes, proposed legislation could have a direct, adverse impact on a district or state. Constituents expect their members of Congress to defeat the legislation—not just do everything possible to defeat it, but defeat it. Think of how hard and how long the Nevada delegation, no matter what party or chamber, has fought the storage of civilian nuclear reactor waste in its state.

The obligations to a representative's constituency nowadays also require the member's presence in the home district every weekend. The demand of this kind of obligation is felt more keenly by representatives than senators, but no member who will seek reelection can afford to spend many weekends in Washington.

A member might also serve on as many as three or four committees and many more subcommittees. However, meetings often conflict so that a member might spend a morning running from one important markup to another as well as fitting in other commitments. Floor votes occur regularly on Tuesday, Wednesday, and Thursday afternoons and often well into those nights. Floor votes may occur on other days as well. Meetings on specific legislation with chamber leaders, other party members, or allied members might take place at any time to try to work out problems, get commitments, or strategize. Formal party meetings are regularly scheduled, but informal party meetings can occur at any time. To participate in the politics of Congress, a member must be present and working.

The members' appearances and participation in events contribute significantly to their workloads. A member must choose which events to attend (and for how long), which to respond to with more than regrets (and how to respond), and which to decline. Home state and Washington lobbyists, interest group representatives, important constituents such as business or labor leaders, and constituent delegations or deputations want meetings. A member's staff needs to schedule time to discuss legislative initiatives. A member's family would like to be remembered somewhere in the schedule.

Another important consideration in daily, weekly, and monthly schedules is the need to focus on reelection. A reelection campaign starts as soon as an election is won, and neither party now waits for an election year or the selection of an opposition candidate to begin targeting members whom they perceive to be vulnerable or whom they wish to test for vulnerability. Negative attacks on freshmen members might start with their swearing-in. Representatives and delegates must face the electorate again in just two years. (The Puerto Rican resident commissioner has a four-year term.) Senators have six years between elections, but they cannot rest on their laurels for long. Each member must raise money for each campaign. Nearly every representative must set aside some time each week just to keep in touch with principals in his or her campaign organization, campaign contributors, and politicians back home. Members might go as often as once or twice a week to the Democratic or Republican headquarters in Washington to telephone their political advisors back home and their campaign contributors.

Senators' reelection campaigning is much less visible than that of representatives during the first three or four years of their terms. Yet, senators also must keep in touch with principals in their campaign organizations, raise money, and speak with home-state politicians. Senators seek to build large campaign funds by the fourth year of their terms, to ward off challengers or to ensure that a challenger knows a race will be hard-fought.

Many activities are important, and all must be accommodated somehow. Private time or "think time" is rare once a day starts. A plane or train ride home to the state or district becomes catch-up time for reading—so long as another member, an administration official, a lobbyist, or an important constituent is not also on the plane and desiring a conversation.

It is all too common for a member's workday in Washington to begin before 8:00 a.m. and continue well into the night. A day in the district or state might be just as long or even longer. A member of Congress almost always has one eye on a watch, frequently rechecks his or her daily schedule, cannot be separated from a cell phone or BlackBerry®, and is often accompanied by a staffer who seems to be urging the member to leave wherever they are only moments after their arrival. On foot or by car, staffers are always picking up or dropping off a member and assisting with some aspect of the member's personal life as well as attending to the official one. *(See Chapter Five, Supporting Congress: Allowances and Staff.)*

One must imagine holding the job of a member of Congress to appreciate the attributes required. To be effective—to ensure that one's constituency is well served—requires exceptional skills and endurance.

The Honorable. . .

Election and congressional service also bring recognition and perhaps even adulation. Congratulatory letters and phone calls flow in after an election. Past and potential contributors want to associate with a successful candidate. People want to work in a congressional office; hundreds of résumés arrive in the temporary congressional mailboxes of members-elect. Party leaders are eager to get relations off to a good start. In less than two months after the election, the member's swearing-in ceremony is carried on C-SPAN, and dozens of well-wishers join the member in swearing-in festivities in Washington.

Subsequent speeches in floor and committee proceedings are carried on C-SPAN, and excerpts might be broadcast elsewhere. National newspapers and news services seek comments from senators on everything, and state and local newspapers want the views of representatives as well. Congressional leaders, administration officials, and the president seek the support of members of Congress on important votes. Lobbyists also want members' support, and all sorts of home-state and national organizations want members to give speeches, meet their boards of directors, and shake hands with their employees. Invitations to events, including perhaps a state dinner at the White House, arrive by the bagful. Constituents visiting Washington cannot leave town without taking the opportunity to say hello. These activities, largely flattering, are part and parcel of the politics of Congress.

For members, there are a number of smaller perquisites that accompany election and further indicate a change in status. Members of Congress and their spouses receive pins when the members are sworn in. The pins have the practical effect of facilitating the members' and their spouses' movement throughout the Capitol complex. *(See Chapter Six, Supporting Congress: The Capitol Complex.)* But, they are also the mark of an elite fraternity. There are also VIP parking lots for members of Congress and other dignitaries set aside at the Washington, DC, airports, Reagan Washington National and Dulles International. Again, it is a practical and cost-effective arrangement to deal with VIPs' cars, but, out of the millions of passengers who pass through those two airports each year, members are some of the few who are treated specially.

There are many flattering aspects and emotional rewards to being a member of Congress. Whether in Washington or traveling, a member of Congress is generally extended every courtesy. Most simply stated, being a member of Congress makes others pay attention.

§1.50 Ever-Changing and Unpredictable Schedules

Daily and weekly schedules in Washington, as well as district or state schedules, are major preoccupations of every congressional office. Scheduling a member's time is a job that often involves a scheduling assistant, a chief of staff, and a district or state director, in addition to the member. The watchword is *contingency*.

The first item to consider is whether the chamber in which the member serves is in session, when it is in session, and when there will be votes. The next item involves when the committees, subcommittees, and groups on which the member serves will meet and what their business will be. The legislative assistants and committee staff provide the scheduling team with information to assist them in setting priorities and ensuring the member's legislative interests are accommodated. The member's personal staff might want to reserve time, and there might be personal events or family needs and plans to be protected in a schedule.

Most of the staff know the flight and train options for going to the district or state and returning. Possible events in the home district or state over a weekend are factored in. There are town hall meetings, breakfasts, lunches, receptions, dinners, events, and requests for meetings for which RSVPs are waiting, and quasi-official activities such as party conference or caucus meetings, briefings by legislative branch or administration staff, various meetings of like-minded members, and legislative strategy meetings that compete for a specific place on the schedule. No matter how senior or junior they may be, all members are very, very busy. *(See § 1.51, Example of a Senior House Member's Daily Schedule; and § 1.52, Example of a Freshman House Member's Daily Schedule.)*

Example of a Senior House Member's Daily Schedule

November 9 (Tuesday)

8:00a–9:30a	Democratic Women Candidates Networking Breakfast to promote Democratic agenda regarding education and children Location: Capital Hilton, Congressional Meeting Room, 1001 16th St., NW
9:00a	Democratic Caucus to discuss the budget and appropriations Notes: special guest—White House Chief of Staff John Podesta Location: B-339 Rayburn
9:00a	Morning Hour
10:00a	Ways and Means Committee (W&M)—full committee hearing on President Clinton's new Social Security plan Location: 1100 Longworth
10:00a	House convenes—measures under suspension
11:00a	Prescription drug press conference with Hillary Clinton, Leader Gephardt, Whip Bonior, others Notes: staff—Helen Location: Rayburn Gold Room (2168)
11:30a	Democratic Women Candidates' Networking Lunch Notes: keynote speaker—Hillary Clinton Location: Capital Hilton, Congressional Meeting Room, 1001 16th St., NW
12:30p	Joint Health/Medicare task force meeting on Medicare prescription drug benefits Notes: staff—Jeff; pizza and drinks to be served Location: HC-9, Capitol
1:30p–2:00p	W&M Democrats to discuss minimum-wage bill Location: 1129 Longworth
2:00p	Sue Esserman to brief W&M Democrats and Democratic advisory group on World Trade Organization (WTO) Ministerial Notes: staff—Nora Location: H-137, Capitol
2:30p	Bob Quaine of the Kidnapped & Hostage program in Spring Hill to discuss silent survival signals Notes: staff—Bob
2:30p	White House ceremony giving the Congressional Gold Medal to the Little Rock Nine, the nine black students to integrate Little Rock's Central High School Notes: Members asked to arrive at 2:30; ceremony in the East Room from 2:45–3:45; reception in State Dining Room from 3:45-4:45

Continued on page 13

§ 1.51 (continued)

3:00p W&M markup on minimum-wage bill
Notes: staff—Bob
Location: 1100 Longworth

3:30p W&M Democrats and WTO labor advisory group Democrats' briefing on WTO Ministerial
Notes: staff—Nora
Location: H-137, Capitol

4:00p Major Walker and various representatives from the Marine Corps Liaison to follow up
on last week's meeting, answer Member's previous questions
Notes: staff—Nora

4:30p New Democratic Coalition "top of the week" meeting
Notes: featuring John Podesta
Location: HC-8, Capitol

5:00p Members only briefing on WTO Ministerial
Location: H-137, Capitol

6:30p–8:30p Congressional Black Caucus reception to honor the Little Rock Nine
Location: Great Hall, Jefferson Building, Library of Congress

A scheduling assistant's work does not end when he or she puts a schedule for the next day in a member's hands. The schedule rarely works as planned, and much of the day might be spent rearranging meetings and other commitments to accommodate changes.

Changes can result from additions to or deletions from agendas in committees or on the floor. Party leaders might also require a member's presence on short notice—a member does not say "I'm unavailable" to the Speaker or to party leaders. An event inside Congress or outside anywhere in the world—such as party leaders announcing an agreement with the White House on an important matter, a foreign crisis that leaves American citizens in harm's way, the sudden death of a member of Congress, or similar events—can have an immediate effect on every member's activities and schedule. A chamber might adjourn or recess early for the week or stay in session longer than announced. Many occurrences can scramble plans. *(See § 1.53, Excerpt from House's Daily Schedule (GOP Source); and § 1.54, Excerpt from House's Daily Schedule (Democratic Source).)*

Planning weekend and weeklong visits to the home district or state can also be fraught with anxiety when chamber leaders are unable to give commitments on an adjournment or recess or when members are required to return earlier than anticipated. *(See § 1.55, Floor Discussion of Schedule Changes.)* Weather can also upset travel plans for leaving or returning to Washington, and for maintaining a schedule at home. Compared with Washington schedules, however, members at home are better able to make and stick to schedules. Principal schedul-

Example of a Freshman House Member's Daily Schedule

Thursday, March 18

7:59a–9:14a	Breakfast for another Member—National Democratic Club
8:00a–9:00a	Breakfast reception for another Member—National Democratic Club
9:00a–9:45a	Copanelist with another Member opening the 1999 Consumer Assembly; two staffers to accompany—Washington Plaza Hotel, 10 Thomas Circle, NW
9:00a–9:45a	WHIP Meeting—HC-9
9:01a–10:01a	GOVERNMENT REFORM SUBCOMMITTEE HEARING (preventing and treating drug abuse, government witnesses)—2247 Rayburn
9:30a–10:00a	SPEAKER'S CLOSED MEETING OF THE HOUSE to discuss highly classified material relating to emerging ballistic missile threats, followed later today by House action on HR 4—House Chamber
10:00a–10:30a	SMALL BUSINESS COMMITTEE MARKUP: HR 536 (SBA district offices)—2360 Rayburn
11:00a–11:30a	Meet with representative of American Immigration Lawyers' Association from Member's district to discuss immigration matters; staffer present—Member's office
12:00 noon	HOUSE convenes: HR 4 scheduled (missile defense policy), votes expected
12:00p–1:15p	Luncheon with National Newspaper Association editors and publishers; staffer to accompany—Montpelier Room, 6th floor, Madison Building, Library of Congress
2:00p–2:15p	Meet with parent of a campaign volunteer; staffer present—Member's office
2:30p–3:00p	Meet with a representative of State Podiatric Medical Association—Member's office
3:00p–3:45p	Meet with representative of Indo-American Democratic Organization; two staffers present—Member's office
4:00p–4:15p	Meet with representative of State Press Association—Member's office
4:30p–5:00p	Staff meeting on upcoming recess activities—Member's office
5:00p–9:00p	Reception at 5:00 followed by dinner and awards presentation 6:00p–9:00p for Center for Women Policy Studies; Member to speak and make presentation (business attire)—Hyatt Regency Washington on Capitol Hill, 400 New Jersey Ave., NW

1

§ 1.53

Excerpt from House's Daily Schedule
(GOP Source)

One of the principal jobs of the party whips in both parties in both chambers is to keep party members apprised of the floor schedule. The parties' whips' web sites in both chambers are listed in § 11.10, Finding and Obtaining Congressional Documents. On any day, a reader will find different and useful supporting information available through the two parties' whip notices.

THE WHIPPING POST
✦ FROM THE OFFICE OF REPUBLICAN WHIP ROY BLUNT ✦

WWW.REPUBLICANWHIP.HOUSE.GOV	**MONDAY, APRIL 16, 2007**	PHONE: (202) 225-0197

REVISED

Anticipated Floor Schedule
On Monday, the House will meet at 2:00 p.m. for legislative business. Votes will be postponed until 6:30 p.m.

One Minutes

Suspensions (6 bills):

1) **H.R. 988** - To designate the facility of the United States Postal Service located at 5757 Tilton Avenue in Riverside, California, as the "Lieutenant Todd Jason Bryant Post Office" *(Sponsored by Rep. Calvert / Oversight and Government Reform Committee)*
2) **H.Res.273** - Supporting the goals and ideals of Financial Literacy Month, and for other purposes *(Sponsored by Rep. Hinojosa / Oversight and Government Reform Committee)*
3) **H.Con.Res.71** - Commemorating the 85th Anniversary of the founding of the American Hellenic Educational Progressive Association (AHEPA), a leading association for the Nation's 1.3 million American citizens of Greek ancestry, and Philhellenes *(Sponsored by Rep. Maloney / Oversight and Government Reform Committee)*
4) **H.Res.179** - Expressing support for a National Foster Parents Day *(Sponsored by Rep. Boyda / Oversight and Government Reform Committee)*
5) **H.Con.Res.88** - Honoring the life of Ernest Gallo *(Sponsored by Rep. Cardoza / Oversight and Government Reform Committee)*
6) **H.Con.Res.76** - Honoring the 50th Anniversary of the International Geophysical Year (IGY) and its past contributions to space research, and looking forward to future accomplishments *(Sponsored by Rep. Udall (CO) / Science and Technology Committee)*

Special Orders

Tuesday's Forecast
On Tuesday, the House will meet at 10:30 a.m. for morning hour and 12:00 p.m. for legislative business.

Suspensions (15 bills):

1) **H.R. 886** - Wild Sky Wilderness Act of 2007 *(Sponsored by Rep. Larsen / Natural Resources Committee)*
2) **H.Res.217** - Expressing the sense of the House of Representatives concerning the 50th anniversary of Celilo Falls *(Sponsored by Rep. Wu / Natural Resources Committee)*
3) **H.R. 609** - To amend the Reclamation Wastewater and Groundwater Study and Facilities Act to authorize the Secretary of the Interior to participate in the Central Texas Water Recycling and Reuse Project, and for other purposes *(Sponsored by Rep. Edwards / Natural Resources Committee)*
4) **H.R. 786** - To amend the Reclamation Wastewater and Groundwater Study and Facilities Act to authorize the Secretary of the Interior to participate in the Los Angeles County Water Supply Augmentation Demonstration Project, and for other purposes *(Sponsored by Rep. Linda Sanchez / Natural Resources Committee)*
5) **H.R. 309** - To direct the Secretary of the Interior to establish a demonstration program to facilitate landscape restoration programs within certain units of the National Park System established by law to preserve and interpret resources associated with American history, and for other purposes *(Sponsored by Rep. Pearce / Natural Resources Committee)*
6) **H.R. 815** - To provide for the conveyance of certain land in Clark County, Nevada, for use by the Nevada National Guard *(Sponsored by Rep. Porter / Natural Resources Committee)*
7) **H.R. 865** - To grant rights-of-way for electric transmission lines over certain Native allotments in the State of Alaska *(Sponsored by Rep. Don Young / Natural Resources Committee)*
8) **H.R. 1191** - To authorize the National Park Service to pay for services rendered by subcontractors under a General Services Administration Indefinite Deliver/Indefinite Quantity Contract issued for work to be completed at the Grand Canyon National Park *(Sponsored by Rep. Renzi / Natural Resources Committee)*
9) **H.R. 1677** - Tax Payer Protection Act *(Sponsored by Rep. Rangel / Ways and Means Committee)*
10) **H.Res.125** - Expressing deep concern over the use of civilians as "human shields" in violation of international humanitarian law and the law of war during armed conflict, including Hezbollah's tactic of embedding its forces among civilians to use them as human shields during the summer of 2006 conflict between Hezbollah and the State of Israel *(Sponsored by Rep. Ros-Lehtinen / Foreign Affairs Committee)*
11) **H.Res.196** - Supporting the goals and ideals of World Water Day *(Sponsored by Rep. Blumenauer / Foreign Affairs Committee)*
12) **H.Con.Res.100** - Condemning the recent violent actions of the Government of Zimbabwe against peaceful opposition party activists and members of civil society *(Sponsored by Rep. Lantos / Foreign Affairs Committee)*
13) **H.R. 1681** - To amend the Congressional Charter of The American National Red Cross to modernize its governance structure, to enhance the ability of the board of governors of The American National Red Cross to support the critical mission of The American National Red Cross in the 21st century, and for other purposes *(Sponsored by Rep. Lantos / Foreign Affairs Committee)*
14) **H.Res.293** - Supporting the goals and ideals highlighted through National Volunteer Week *(Sponsored by Rep. Shea-Porter / Education and Labor Committee)*
15) **H.R. 1515** - To amend the Housing and Community Development Act of 1974 to treat certain communities as metropolitan cities for purposes of the community development block grant program *(Sponsored by Rep. Costello / Financial Services Committee)*

§ 1.54

Excerpt from House's Daily Schedule (Democratic Source)

Party entities in the House and Senate provide various forms of information on their respective chamber's daily, weekly, and long-term schedules. The parties' scheduling web sites in both chambers appear in § 11.10, Finding and Obtaining Congressional Documents. The starting point with party-provided information on floor action begins with whip information, shown here.

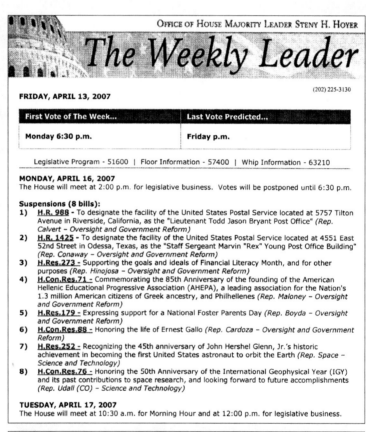

1

Floor Discussion of Schedule Changes

The negotiation of schedules is a time-consuming but important activity on Capitol Hill. Everyone desires predictability, but it is difficult for congressional leaders to deliver it.

The excerpt below is representative of congressional concerns over unpredictability in scheduling. The excerpt was taken from a House floor colloquy between House Majority Leader Dick Armey, R-TX, and House Appropriations Committee Ranking Member David Obey, D-WI, on Thursday, June 15, 2000. The House was considering amendments to the fiscal year 2001 Interior appropriations bill. The Republican leadership expressed its hope on Wednesday, June 14, to complete all floor votes by 6:00 p.m. Thursday. As Thursday afternoon wore on, representatives became anxious about making evening airline flights to their home districts. Finally, Obey raised the scheduling question with Armey in formal debate, and ultimately offered a preferential motion for the *Committee of the Whole to rise. (See § 8.120, Committee of the Whole: Amendment Process.)*

The motion was defeated on a recorded vote, 183 to 218. The Obey-Armey colloquy began about 5:20 p.m. The colloquy and vote on the motion consumed about thirty minutes. The House worked late and finally adjourned for the week on Friday morning, June 16 at 1:25 a.m.

Mr. Obey: . . . I would simply like to ask if the leadership intends to keep the commitment which was announced to the House (to take no votes after 6:00 p.m. today) or whether the rumors are true that we hear that they now intend to be in until 9:00.

Mr. Armey: . . . We worked out an agreement last night that we thought would give us good progress. We had high hopes of continuing this work and completing it by 6:00 today. But as we can see, we are approaching that hour; and we are not near completion.

Mr. Obey: . . . Let me simply say that the problem, as has been brought to my attention by a number of members, is that the schedule published by the leadership indicates legislative business, no votes after 6:00 p.m. . . . But I regret that the leadership has seen fit to upset the ability of each individual member to get back to their district. . . .

Mr. Armey: . . . [O]ur agreement that we made last night was in full understanding of the need and the commitment to complete this, where the floor manager said, and I think in good faith and with all good intention, that they would do everything they could to finish by 6:00. Unfortunately, given their best efforts, they have not been able to achieve that. . . .

Mr. Obey: . . . We were told that the intention of the leadership was that we were leaving at 6, that the committee should do its best to be done by 6, but there was a clear understanding that the members would be allowed to leave as scheduled at 6:00.

ing problems at home tend to result from overcommitment, insufficient travel time between event locations, and weather conditions affecting travel.

Mindful of the problems of alienation and exhaustion caused by congressional schedules, leaders and members have discussed a variety of scheduling options since the 1990s, but none of the alternatives has taken hold. Both chambers looked at options such as three weeks in session and one week not in session each month. The House looked at the possibility of eliminating evening votes, and went so far as to build a "family room" for members' children near the House floor, just off Statuary Hall.

Nothing has happened to make congressional committee and floor schedules more predictable. Members have also not changed their behavior in traveling routinely to their districts or states, and constituents have not changed their expectations for members to be physically present in their districts or states as often as possible.

Within this demanding and shifting framework, a member's time and attention are resources that must be strategically and tactically deployed. Effectiveness in Congress is oftentimes based on a member taking the right step at the right time and being in the right place at the right time. Committee markups, floor debate and votes, constituent visits, calls to campaign contributors, purposeful chats with party leaders, and other important activities must be accommodated in the swirl of ever-changing and unpredictable schedules.

§ 1.60 Family Life

In addition to public and institutional pressures and demands, a member faces the challenge of balancing public and private lives. The demands of congressional service take a toll on a member's family and family life.

Just a little over a generation ago, most members' families lived in the Washington area. Today, a significant number of members' families live in the home district or state. It is a key difference in congressional life. Washington is a very expensive city compared with many of the places that members call home. To relocate a family and provide comparable housing, schools, and lifestyle is beyond many members' means. In Washington, spouses and children are cut off from the network of family and friends in their hometowns. Members, therefore, end up maintaining two residences, even if one is a tiny or shared apartment on Capitol Hill. Some members with families back home even stay in their Washington office rather than rent another place to live, although the House and Senate discourage that.

Whether a member's family lives in Washington or elsewhere, the toll on family and personal life is high. A spouse can become a stranger when one is a member of Congress. The time it takes to be a member of Congress can be a factor in a marriage's breakup. Even when a family is in Washington and a member goes to his or her district or state a bit less frequently or for a shorter period of time, the schedule of the House or Senate in session seems to preclude a regular home life. As mentioned in § 1.50, there has been discussion of "family friendly scheduling" in the last several Congresses, but no identifiable changes have endured.

Moreover, congressional families reflect changes in American life. Many spouses work. Delayed childbearing has affected members, too, with many of them, including an increasing number of women members, having young children at the same time they are building their congressional careers. For these and other reasons, Congress in session has become the temporary location for many members. A family and the constituents back home make the district or state the member's principal residence and workplace. Members are in Washington three or four days a week and not at all when there is a week-long recess.

A generation ago, members of Congress got to know each other fairly well. Members, spouses, and families socialized together. Members themselves would also socialize at activities such as weekly poker games. That is much less common among junior members today. Some representatives, in reaction, have attempted to create some common ground. Two bipartisan family "retreats" were organized at Hershey Park, PA, just after the convening of the 105th and 106th Congresses, to enable House members and their families to socialize together. The 107th and 108th Congresses' retreats were held at the Greenbrier resort in White Sulphur Springs, WV, but no subsequent bipartisan or family retreats have been held since then. Congressional spouse organizations also attempt to provide a common ground. *(See § 5.191, Congressional Spouse Organizations.)*

Senators' lives seem to have been affected somewhat less dramatically than those of representatives. A senator is somewhat more likely to have older grown children rather than be a parent of young children during his or her Senate service, and the relentless travel to the home state is principally a feature of the last two years of a term. It is also somewhat less common for a senator's spouse and family to reside in the home state rather than in the Washington area.

Like the trade-offs between obligations and perquisites, the honor and rewards of serving in Congress come at a price. A member's family might be unprepared for its new status and regular separation from one parent. A member might be unprepared for the loneliness of having family far away.

§1.70 Staying in Congress

Another change in congressional service involves members' departures from Congress after a few terms.

The median number of terms or years that a member might be expected to serve in Congress declined for some time. A generation ago, a newly elected member could reasonably expect to be reelected. Members frequently served twenty years or more before retirement. Reelection rates for the House—members choosing to run for reelection—are historically over 90 percent. At the beginning of the 110th Congress, the median number of terms served by representatives was five (ten years). Reelection rates for the Senate are historically below those for the House, but are still high. At the beginning of the 110th Congress, the median number of years served in the Senate was ten.

However, members whose seats are safe, who have no problem raising campaign funds, who hold positions of influence within Congress, and who contribute substantially to legislation regularly decide not to run for reelection. Why is this commitment to a career in Congress eroding?

Members of Congress cite many dissatisfactions with the congressional way of life as it has evolved over a generation. Some of these are as follows:

- high toll on personal and family life
- living with guilt over trying and being unable to be all things to all people, especially loved ones
- life in a fishbowl
- backbreaking schedule
- loss of time to think and be expert
- partisanship of Congress
- anonymity among colleagues that goes with a three-and-one-half-day-a-week presence in Washington
- endless fund-raising and the cost of campaigns
- undue influence of special interests
- negative campaigning, which has become year-round and includes groups affiliated with one's own party as well as the opposition party
- perceived irrelevance and intransigence of Congress in solutions to national problems
- vacuous, symbolic, and partisan legislation and votes on the congressional agenda
- perception of parties' lack of interest in governing
- low salary for the work and high cost of being a member of Congress
- need for a higher salary to provide family needs, such as college costs
- decline of interest in public service
- term limits as a political issue and as a reality in committee and subcommittee chairmanships
- stronger interest in other careers

The hardship of congressional life is undeniable. Even the most self-confident and politically gifted member might choose to make a change after a few terms.

However, turnover might also reflect generational changes in how Americans view their jobs. Many workers today hold several jobs in the course of a lifetime, in contrast to the norm in their parents' generation, when a successful career might have meant working for just one or two employers. In part, the shorter tenure of members of Congress could simply reflect larger national trends.

Whatever the reason for a member departing after a few terms, the departure means a loss of expertise and of political experience in Congress. National problems are complex and not easily mastered in a short time. Even with knowledge or expertise, members need political experience to identify and engineer legislative solutions. For the professional interacting with Congress, the shorter tenure presents both opportunities and challanges in developing working relationships, understanding congressional dynamics, and advocating and facilitating legislative solutions. (*See Chapter Four, Pressures on Congress: Lobbying and Congressional Ethics.*)

Chapter Two

Pressures on Congress:

Campaigns and Elections

Analysis

§ 2.00 Introduction

From the moment of his or her first election to Congress until the last day of service, a member is subjected to pressures from numerous sources, including constituents, media, executive officials, and lobbyists. A major pressure present is that the next election is always right around the corner.

This chapter briefly describes campaigns and elections as a pressure on Congress, and summarizes key aspects of federal campaign law related specifically to congressional campaigns. (*See also § 4.30, Congressional Ethics, and § 10.220, Congress and Federalism: Extending the Franchise.*)

§ 2.10 Campaigns and Elections

A member of Congress is an independent entrepreneur whose business is advancing his or her political career. An individual might have many motives for seeking a seat in Congress. These motives may include looking after the public good or tackling a tough policy problem in the public interest. An individual must have political skills to act on those motivations, get elected to Congress, achieve his or her goals as a member of Congress, and communicate achievements to the public and the media.

The Democratic and Republican Parties (and sometimes other parties) try to recruit candidates to run for *open seats* and seats occupied by incumbent members of Congress running for reelection. But, the parties must rely on people motivated to run and politically skillful in doing so. The parties offer many forms of help, but a candidate for Congress is largely in charge of building his or her own volunteer and paid campaign organization, raising money, and developing a campaign strategy. This is true the first time a candidate runs for office and every time thereafter. To attract volunteers, media attention, and financial support, a candidate must project confidence that he or she can win. To remain attractive, a candidate must back up that confidence with evidence that he or she is running a campaign that can succeed. The goal is to get elected in the first place and to get reelected until the member resigns or retires voluntarily.

The advantages of incumbency—better fund-raising ability, more-automatic media attention, an existing corps of campaign volunteers, and so on—sometimes make it hard for the parties to attract candidates willing to take on incumbents. And, for some open House seats, the key fight is for the Democratic or Republican nomination: the party tilt of some districts typically makes one party's nominee a favorite in the general election. (*See § 2.11, 2008 Congressional Election Information.*)

Still, in any election, many House seats and most Senate seats are considered competitive to some degree, and incumbent members of Congress running for reelection have learned not to take anything for granted. In the 2006 election, two representatives were defeated in primaries, and twenty-one representatives and six senators were defeated in the general election.

§ 2.11

2008 Congressional Election Information

Election Day is November 4, 2008. Before then, states' parties will have held various kinds of conventions and many states will have held major-party primaries and perhaps even runoffs. In addition to candidacies and candidate fund-raising that commence in 2007, the earliest filing deadlines begin in December 2007 in Illinois, unless state law is changed.

Announcements of incumbent members' plans and of challengers can occur early. As of March 2007, two representatives and a senator had announced their retirements or resignations from Congress. In 2005–2006, thirty-nine representatives and senators retired or resigned from office or sought another office.

The methods by which major-party and independent- or third-party candidates get their names on the general-election ballot are different in each state. Minimally, registration dates will differ from state-to-state, and congressional primary dates in some states may be different in years in which the state holds a presidential primary than in the non-presidential election years. In addition, between each general election, some number of states amend their election laws.

The web sites of the secretaries of state's election divisions or the independent state election boards provide a variety of information: important dates for registration and primaries, links to state and federal laws, past election statistics, and candidate lists, among other election-related information and links. For the reader's convenience, a telephone number for each state's election authority is provided below, in addition to each state's election authority's web site. Information is also provided for the District of Columbia and the four territories' election authorities.

State	Phone	Website
Alabama	334-242-7210	www.sos.state.al.us/election/index.cfm
Alaska	907-465-4611	www.elections.state.ak.us
American Samoa	684-633-4116	http://americansamoa.gov
Arizona	602-542-8683	www.azsos.gov/election
Arkansas	501-682-3419	www.arelections.org
California	916-657-2166	www.ss.ca.gov/elections/elections.htm
Colorado	303-894-2200	www.elections.colorado.gov
Connecticut	800-540-3764	www.sots.ct.gov/ElectionsServices/ElectionIndex.html
Delaware	302-739-4277	http://elections.delaware.gov
District of Columbia	202-727-2525	www.dcboee.org
Florida	850-245-6200	http://election.dos.state.fl.us
Georgia	404-656-2871	www.sos.state.ga.us/elections
Guam	671-477-9791	www.guamelection.org
Hawaii	808-453-8683	www.hawaii.gov/elections
Idaho	208-334-2852	www.idsos.state.id.us/elect/eleindex.htm
Illinois	217-782-4141	www.elections.state.il.us
Indiana	317-232-3939	www.state.in.us/sos/elections
Iowa	515-281-0145	www.sos.state.ia.us/elections/index.html
Kansas	785-296-4561	www.kssos.org/elections/elections.html

For live links, see <*www.CongressionalDeskbook.com*>, § 2.11.

Continued on page 25

Kentucky	502-573-7100	http://sos.ky.gov/elections
Louisiana	225-922-0900	www.sec.state.la.us/elections/elections-index.htm
Maine	207-624-7736	www.maine.gov/sos/cec/elec
Maryland	800-222-8683	www.elections.state.md.us
Massachusetts	800-462-8683	www.sec.state.ma.us/ele/eleidx.htm
Michigan	517-373-2540	www.michigan.gov/sos/0,1607,7-127-1633- - -,00.html
Minnesota	877-600-8683	www.sos.state.mn.us/home/index.asp?page=4
Mississippi	601-359-6359	www.sos.state.ms.us/elections/elections.asp
Missouri	573-751-2301	www.sos.mo.gov/elections
Montana	406-444-4732	http://sos.state.mt.us/ELB/index.asp
Nebraska	402-471-2555	www.sos.state.ne.us/elec
Nevada	775-684-5705	http://sos.state.nv.us/nvelection
New Hampshire	603-271-3242	www.sos.nh.gov/electionsnew.html
New Jersey	800-292-0039	www.state.nj.us/lps/elections/electionshome.html
New Mexico	505-827-3620	www.sos.state.nm.us/displayContent.asp?id=17
New York	518-474-8100	www.elections.state.ny.us
North Carolina	919-733-7173	www.sboe.state.nc.us
North Dakota	701-328-4146	www.state.nd.us/sos/electvote
Ohio	614-466-2585	www.sos.state.oh.us/sos/ElectionsVoter/ohioElections.aspx
Oklahoma	405-521-2391	www.state.ok.us/~elections
Oregon	503-986-1518	www.sos.state.or.us/elections
Pennsylvania	717-787-5280	www.dos.state.pa.us/bcel
Puerto Rico	787-777-8675	www.ceepur.org
Rhode Island	401-222-2345	www.elections.state.ri.us
South Carolina	803-734-9060	www.state.sc.us/scsec
South Dakota	605-773-3537	www.sdsos.gov/electionsvoteregistration/elections voteregistration_overview.shtm
Tennessee	615-741-7956	www.state.tn.us/sos/election/index.htm
Texas	800-252-8683	www.sos.state.tx.us/elections/index.shtml
Utah	801-538-1041	www.elections.utah.gov
Vermont	800-439-8683	www.vermont-elections.org/soshome.htm
Virginia	800-552-9745	www.sbe.virginia.gov/cms
Virgin Islands	340-773-1021	www.vivote.gov
Washington	800-448-4881	www.secstate.wa.gov/elections
West Virginia	866-767-8683	www.wvsos.org/elections/main.htm
Wisconsin	608-266-8005	http://elections.state.wi.us
Wyoming	307-777-7186	http://soswy.state.wy.us/election/election.htm

For live links, see <www.CongressionalDeskbook.com>, § 2.11.

An incumbent member tries to act preemptively to reduce the chances of a tough reelection campaign. By raising as much money as possible as early as possible, responding quickly to any criticism, and not allowing a primary or general election opponent to characterize his or her record without response, an incumbent attempts to control public perceptions of his or her popularity and political strength. Further, by putting a "spin" on his or her own record and an opponent's, and not being reluctant to use "negative advertising" if it is expected to work, an incumbent attempts to influence public and media perceptions. An incumbent must also be conscious of what is being posted on web sites and web logs, or blogs, and other information being captured and distributed electronically as another avenue of attack, pressure, or support. Many members have begun their own blogs to have a stronger, more active presence on the Internet than just their official and campaign web sites. *(See § 13.50, Media, Policy, and Opinion on the Web.)* As an entrepreneur in the business of advancing a political career, a member is always vigilant to an opponent trying to "take market share."

These preemptive moves serve other purposes as well. They motivate campaign volunteers and likely supportive voters. They also send a message of confidence to home-district or home-state elected officials of the same party, both warding off potential primary challengers and motivating these other political professionals to affiliate with and support a successful member of the party team. They counteract advertising by interest groups intended to arouse constituents against a member or against his or her stand on a particular issue. A member needs to prevent openings for opponents within his or her party as well as from the other parties.

One of the biggest concerns for congressional candidates is fund-raising. With over 120 House primary and general election candidates spending $1 million–$1.5 million and over 170 House candidates spending over $1.5 million in the 2005–2006 election cycle, and with over forty of the major-party Senate primary and general election candidates spending over $5 million, the money chase is perhaps a candidate's greatest test. Some members and candidates relish fund-raising, and raise large sums of money for their parties as well as for themselves. Many others resent the time it takes and the distraction it presents. The political parties and interest groups raise and spend hundreds of millions more in support of or opposition to specific candidates and specific election issues. Critics believe the system of fund-raising contributes to legislative stalemate. *(See § 2.20, Election Laws.)*

A member of Congress might spend part of a week in Washington using telephones at Democratic or Republican offices on Capitol Hill to call financial supporters. For any candidate, fund-raising via the Internet is also rapidly growing to compete with direct mail and other fund-raising methods a candidate might use. A member might well attend several fundraisers each month for his or her party, its leadership, various colleagues, or several like-minded political committees as well as for himself or herself. A member needs to make appearances in his or her own behalf, and to make personal appearances both in Washington and in the home districts or states of at least some party colleagues.

2

§ 2.12

Members' Support for Candidates

Please Join Honorary Chairs
Congressman Jesse Jackson, Jr., Congressman Harold Ford, Jr.,
Congressman Kendrick Meek, Congressman Artur Davis

National Chairs
Gabriel Barry * Dhamian Blue * Lyndon Boozer * Joyce Brayboy * Shaun Butler * Rob Byrd *
Richard Chew * Megan Cosby * DC Crenshaw * Megan Crosly * Mike Davis * Stan Fendley * Sean
Ford * Michael A. Graves * Nkenge Harmon * Kim Hassan * Milagros Hill * Toni Irving * Hiram
Jackson * Kenneth Johnson * Jake Jones * Oscar Joyner * Mayor Kuame Kilpatrick *
Martin King * Vivienne LaBorde * Tonia Lee * Bob Maloney * Lamell McMorris *
Mike McQuerry * Tiffany Moore * Dana & Damon Munchus * Narda Newby * Spencer Overton
John C. Peoples * Irwin Persuad * Mark Persaud * Michael Persaud * William Persaud * Jaques
Philippe-Piverger * Kevin Powell * Juliett Pryor * Angela & Hans Riemer * Darren Riley * Michelle
Robinson * Joi Sheffield * Robert Smith * Tiffany Moore * Michael Strautmanis *
Denia Tapscott * Francine Terrell * Juan Thomas * Darrel Thompson * Nicole Venable *
Muthoni Wambu * Ervin Webb * Jimmie Williams * Joanne Yoo

Hosts
Tom Adams - Saundra Andrews- Lew Baker- Katreice Banks- Pamay Bassey- Wilfredo Benitez- Steve Benjamin- Kanya
Bennett- Wes Bizzell- Tia Breakley- Kirsten Brecht- Michael Brown- Chellee Cephas- Imani Crawford- Ed Dandridge-
Amy Demske- Karl Douglass- Larry Duncan- Eric Easter- Marshall Edwards- Mary Elliott- Jamellah & Malik Ellis-
Rodney Emery- Anita Estell- Fran Fattah- Isaac Fordjour- Tracy Fortson- Latoya Foster- Craig Galloway- Cecilio Gill-
Ulysses Glen, Jr.- Benjamin Guy II- Marc J Harrington- Rahman Harrison- Emil Hill- James Ingram- Antar Johnson-
Lolita Justice- John King- Crystal Kuykendall- Marvin Lawrence- Atiba Madyun- Flo McAfee- Tiffany McConnell-
Howard Menell- Katherine Miller- Aisha Mills- Jeff Murray- Charisse Nunes- Rob Pearson- Aquila Powell- Jesse Price-
Philip Pulliam- Sharon Randolph- Lenny Rayford- Josh Raymond- Tamara Richardson- Jon Samuels- Angela Scott-
David Sutphen- Marie Sylla- Dominique Rougeau- Yelberton Watkins- Arlene Williams- Yvette Williams- Keirston
Woods

At a Fundraising reception on the occasion of the CBC ALC for

Barack Obama

(Democratic Candidate for US Senate-Illinois)

Friday, September 10, 2004
8:00PM-10:00PM
Pearl
901 9th Street, NW

$2,000 National Chair (write/raise), $1,000 Host (write/raise), $50 Requested Contribution
To purchase tickets on-line, please go to: http://www2.obamaforillinois.com/dcyp
Please mail and make personal checks payable to: "Obama for Illinois." P.O. Box 802799, Chicago, IL 60680-2799. For
more information or to RSVP, please call Vera Baker at 202-628-3344 or vbaker@obamaforillinois.com

Authorized and paid for by Obama for Illinois. Candidates are required to report the name, mailing address, employer and occupation for individuals
with aggregate contributions over $200 in a calendar year. Contributions to federal candidates are not deductible for income tax purposes. Corporate
checks are not acceptable for federal campaigns. Contributions are limited to $2,000 per individual for each election cycle. This material was
authorized and paid for by Obama for Illinois.

A member is expected to raise money and make appearances for the party's other candidates for Congress if the member has leadership ambitions within his or her chamber. (*See § 2.12, Members' Support for Candidates.*) Congressional leaders and many individual members maintain political action committees (PACs), which they use to support their party's candidates for Congress, and members are expected to support their parties' congressional campaign committees—the National Republican Congressional Campaign Committee, the

Democratic Congressional Campaign Committee, the National Republican Senatorial Committee, and the Democratic Senatorial Campaign Committee. These committees are headed by members, and many of their colleagues participate not just as contributors but as chairs of special fund-raising and outreach efforts. The congressional campaign committees may levy "dues" on their party's members, expecting higher payments from chamber and committee leaders than from rank-and-file members. One of the first chores of a freshman member is raising money to retire campaign debt and get a start on the first reelection campaign, especially where there was a narrow win.

As part of his or her fund-raising effort, a member of Congress must interact with lobbyists, PAC representatives, and home-district or home-state interests. Those back-home interests are every bit as critical to successful fund-raising and reelection as donations from Washington-based organizations. In addition, the back-home interests more often represent voters. Because of the need for campaign cash, however, more candidates are turning to out-of-state areas of wealth as well, participating in fund-raisers in places such as Los Angeles, New York, and Silicon Valley. In some races, the amount of money a candidate raises in the state versus the amount raised outside the state can become an issue.

As described in § 3.10 (*Constituency Pressure*), constituents seem to have ever greater expectations of a member of Congress. They expect his or her regular presence in the district or state, and they expect a member to play an ombudsman role in dealing with their local and personal matters at the federal level. A member must be vigilant in service to constituents and *case work*, and must set standards for congressional office staff in ensuring quick and responsive attention to mail, phone calls, visits, and other contacts. A member is expected to "bring home the bacon," both in helping local entities with their federal *grantsmanship* and in obtaining *earmarks* through legislation. (See § 3.16, "*Pork Barrel Politics*.")

To deliver for constituents and enhance his or her political profile, a member of Congress seeks committee assignments that support career ambitions. An assignment to a key committee can also open larger fund-raising opportunities. A member might also seek to cast a wider net of interests and influence by obtaining appointments to task forces and party committees dealing with specialized subjects. A member might also join one or more congressional special-interest caucuses, or even organize a caucus, to demonstrate commitment to an interest or to the solution to a policy problem.

A member must be conscious of the public record he or she builds—what bills and amendments to sponsor or cosponsor, what to say in debate, and how to cast votes in committee and on the floor. In recent Congresses, members cast politically difficult votes on trade; Democrats risked alienating labor backers and Republicans from textile-manufacturing areas risked alienating constituents. Votes on so-called omnibus bills can be particularly troublesome, because an opponent might try to tie a member's vote to just one item out of the several hundred that appear in an omnibus measure. How will constituents receive each bill introduced or cosponsored or each vote cast? How will interests at home or in Washington react?

How might an opponent attack an initiative or a vote? Is the record being built consistent with the past, and can that consistency be sustained in the future?

Come election day, the national mood also matters. The electorate was genuinely angry when it went to the polls in 1994 and ended forty years of Democratic control of the House. Members who seemed to be in tune with their constituents were tossed out of office along with those who had "bounced" checks at the "House bank" or had other political problems. In 2002, for example, candidates backed by business or farm interests did relatively well, while those backed by labor or environmental interests did relatively poorly. In 2006, the congressional elections seemed to be as much a referendum on the war in Iraq and the perceived failures of the Bush administration as a decision on individual Republican and Democratic candidates.

Presidents also know how to apply pressure and how to reward allies. President Bush, for example, showed his attractiveness as a fund-raiser throughout every election cycle. He also began his presidency by taking his campaign for congressional enactment of his tax-cut proposal to the home states of then-Senate Democratic leader Tom Daschle, wavering Democrats, and senators representing states where Bush had done well. He ended the 2001–2002 cycle making numerous appearances on behalf of Republican candidates for both chambers. By the 2006 election, the president continued to be a strong fund-raiser, but he was asked to make fewer appearances in behalf of his party's congressional candidates.

It is difficult for members to make commitments on a measure or a future vote early in the legislative process. Who knows what might end up in legislation on the floor? Who knows before the moment of a vote what the alternatives might be, if any? For this and other reasons, "absolutely," "never," "definitely," and similar words are rarely part of the vocabulary of a member of Congress in this context. Members of Congress expect their party leaders to protect their interests in the votes that arise. Can a divisive or difficult vote be prevented from occurring, diluted in its difficulty, or handled indirectly through a procedure that avoids a direct vote?

Like most people, a member of Congress wishes to be successful in his or her job—to be thought well of, to have influence, to win reelection, and so on. A member might also have ambitions beyond the current office. A representative might want to become a senator or governor at some future point, or a member might want to be president, a Cabinet secretary, an ambassador, or a Supreme Court justice. These career ambitions must also be weighed in a member's political conduct.

Reapportionment and Redistricting

Every ten years, an additional election pressure is added for incumbent candidates for House seats. As required by the Constitution, seats in the House are reapportioned among the states, based on each state's population relative to all other states. After the House seats are reapportioned, state legislatures, commissions created by state law, or state or federal courts take

§ 2.13

Reapportionment and Redistricting

Reapportionment

Reapportionment following the 2000 census was completed and court challenges settled. In the 108th through the 112th Congresses, four states gained one seat each in the U.S. House of Representatives—California, Colorado, Nevada, and North Carolina. Four states gained two seats—Arizona, Florida, Georgia, and Texas. On the other hand, eight states lost one seat—Connecticut, Illinois, Indiana, Michigan, Mississippi, Ohio, Oklahoma, and Wisconsin. Two states—New York and Pennsylvania—each lost two seats. The seats apportioned to all of the other states remained the same.

Under the Constitution, seats in the House of Representatives are *apportioned* among the states. They are reapportioned every ten years following the decennial census. Every state is entitled to one seat under the Constitution, and seven states, because of their relatively small population in the 2000 census, have just one seat. These states are Alaska, Delaware, Montana, North Dakota, South Dakota, Vermont, and Wyoming. (These same seven states also were apportioned one seat each following the 1990 census.) California, the largest state, was apportioned fifty-three seats.

State representation in the U.S. Senate is not affected by reapportionment. Under the Constitution, each state has two senators, no matter how large or small a population it has. Nonvoting representation of American Samoa, the District of Columbia, Guam, Puerto Rico, and the Virgin Islands in the House is also not affected by reapportionment. Puerto Rico has one resident commissioner, and the other four jurisdictions have one delegate each. *(See § 7.10, Members of Congress.)*

The usual explanation for a shift of seats is the more rapid growth of some states in relation to other states. A state might lose population from one decennial census to the next, but none did in the 2000 census. The table below shows the apportionment population of each state in the 1990 and 2000 censuses, the numeric and percent change from 1990, and the total seats and change in seats following reapportionment. The map that follows the table illustrates the relative growth of the fifty states.

In 2005, the Census Bureau released its projection of states' populations in 2010. While at best an approximation of what the 2010 census populations will be, the projection can be used by demographers and others to also project seat changes in the House. Past population trends seem to be continuing so that Northeastern and Midwestern states, such as New York and Ohio, will likely lose seats, while Southern, Southwestern, and Western states, such as Florida, Texas, and Arizona, will likely gain seats. (See *<www.census.gov/Press-Release/www/releases/archives/population/004704.html>*.)

Apportionment is based on the *total resident population* of each of the fifty states, but also includes federal employees (principally military personnel) stationed abroad. The combined total is called the *apportionment population*. Excluded from the calculation are foreign officials such as other nations' ambassadors, nonresident citizens of other nations, and residents of the District of Columbia, commonwealths, and territories.

Congress in 1911 first set the number of seats in the House at 435; this size was made permanent in 1929. When seats in the House are reapportioned following a census, each state is first allocated one seat (to meet constitutional requirements), and the remaining 385 seats (with fifty states) are

Continued on page 31

§ *2.13 (continued)*

apportioned according to each state's population in the latest census. Several formulas have been used over the past 200 years, but, since the 1940 census, the *method of equal proportions* has been used. *(See an explanation of the method of equal proportions and other useful information on reapportionment at, <www.census.gov/population/www/censusdata/apportionment.html>.)*

The 2000 census date, following the practice for most twentieth-century censuses, was April 1. Federal law required the Census Bureau within nine months (no later than December 31, 2000) to deliver to the president the population totals and allocation of U.S. House seats for each state. The Census Bureau released this information to the public December 28. Within a week of the convening of the 107th Congress, the president was required to transmit this information to the clerk of the House, who then, within fifteen days, was required to notify each state governor of the number of representatives to which the state was entitled.

Redistricting

Using census data within the guidelines established by federal and state laws and federal and state court decisions, the states followed their own procedures to draw new congressional districts for the 2002 elections. That is the second step, following reapportionment, in determining representation in the U.S. House of Representatives. ("Redistricting" also refers to procedures employed at the state and local level to obtain population equality in state legislative districts and local representational units. Those procedures are not covered here.)

Federal law requires single-member districts. The federal Voting Rights Act, among its provisions, requires some states to obtain "pre-clearance" of redistricting plans from the U.S. Justice Department. (States covered in whole or in part by the pre-clearance provisions of the Voting Rights Act are Alabama, Alaska, Arizona, California, Florida, Georgia, Louisiana, Michigan, Mississippi, New Hampshire, New York, North Carolina, South Carolina, South Dakota, Texas, and Virginia.) Congress has not chosen to exercise its constitutional authority *(art. I, sec. 4, cl. 1)* to prescribe other criteria for state legislatures to use in redistricting. *(See § 10.220, Congress and Federalism: Extending the Franchise.)*

Federal court decisions applicable to state redistricting include "one person, one vote," the requirement of equal district populations (not voting populations) within a state. Other court decisions have interpreted the Constitution—particularly the Fourteenth Amendment's Equal Protection Clause—and the Voting Rights Act to offer guidance to the states on creating "majority-minority districts," the use of race as a factor in redistricting to remedy past discrimination, the "compactness" of districts, and other factors. Once a state has adopted a redistricting plan, it is subject to court challenge and possibly to legislative or court revision.

Many states also have laws that govern redistricting. These laws discourage splitting political units, favor compact districts, and set forth other goals.

In most states, the legislatures enact redistricting plans, which are then submitted to the governor for approval or veto. Other states use commissions to create redistricting plans. In some states, failure by the legislature to act can send responsibility for redistricting to a commission.

Under federal law, the Census Bureau, by April 1, 2001, was to provide the governors and state legislatures with the population data that their states needed to redistrict. States have some discretion in what data they may request, and they receive data by political jurisdiction, such as

Continued on page 32

county; by census geographical units, such as census tracts; and by other geographical units, such as voting precincts.

Although laws and court decisions govern redistricting decisions, redistricting is a political process. It is particularly painful to congressional incumbents in states that have lost seats. Unless one or more incumbents retire, two incumbents are likely to face each other in a primary if they are of the same party, or in a general election if they are of opposing parties.

However, redistricting is also viewed as an opportunity by Democrats and Republicans to strengthen their respective party's representation in Congress. A party might attempt to add its party's voters to a marginal district to shore up its strength in that district, or it might add its party's voters to a district that has favored the other party's candidates in an attempt to destabilize the district's voting pattern. The parties might make a deal to create an equal number of districts favorable to each party or to favor each party's incumbents. Influential state legislators facing term limits and having political ambitions of their own might try to create districts favorable to their own future campaign for Congress. Some congressional incumbents are very popular or very unpopular with state legislators, and might reap the rewards or agonies of their standing.

Even in states that gain seats, redistricting can be a problem for incumbents. Where a party controls both houses of the legislature and the governorship, it often uses this power to increase the likelihood of winning additional districts, both existing, albeit revised, and new. In states with commission redistricting, there can be a sense of unpredictability and lack of influence by politicians over the outcome. And, the addition of districts due to reapportionment offers additional opportunities for drafting district lines to favor a party, a racial or ethnic group, a socioeconomic group, or another set of voters.

It is no wonder that U.S. representatives are actively involved in redistricting. Some hire lobbyists to represent them in their state's capital while they are working in Washington, DC, and their districts. Others spend time and effort keeping up contacts from their time in their state's legislature. Some support their party's state legislators and legislative candidates politically.

Still, incumbent representatives must be circumspect in another way. U.S. House rules proscribe the use of official funds for redistricting activities.

A new wrinkle following the 2002 elections, in which one major party or the other increased its control of a state's elective offices, has been the discussion of a legislative re-opening of the state's congressional districts. In a challenge to Texas's mid-decade redistricting, the U.S. Supreme Court did not find anything "inherently suspect" in the action. (*League of Latin American Citizens (LULAC) v. Perry*, No. 05-204, slip op. (June 28, 2006).) Texas successfully redistricted for the 2004 election, but the court challenge resulted in an additional change for the 2006 election, based on a Voting Rights Act violation. Georgia successfully redistricted in early 2005.

The possibility of redistricting was discussed in other states as well, with California Governor Arnold Schwarzenegger having proposed a new redistricting process, removing the state legislature from the process, for implementation before the 2006 elections. The governor's plan was defeated by the voters. *(To view district maps, see the Census Bureau's web site at <www.census.gov/geo/www/maps/cd109/cd109_mainPage.htm>, and the U.S. Geological Survey's web site at <www.nationalatlas.gov/printable/congress.html>. Some secretaries of state's election divisions or independent state election boards also have district maps on their web sites. See the URLs for these web sites at § 2.11.)*

Continued on page 33

2

Change in States' Population and Seats in the House of Representatives

State	1990 Census Apportionment population	2000 Census Apportionment population	Change from 1990 Total	Percent	Seats	Seat change from 1990
AL	4,040,587	4,461,130	420,543	10.41	7	
AK	550,043	628,933	78,890	14.34	1	
AZ	3,665,228	5,140,683	1,475,455	40.26	8	+2
AR	2,350,725	2,679,733	329,008	14.00	4	
CA	29,760,021	33,930,798	4,170,777	14.01	53	+1
CO	3,294,394	4,311,882	1,017,488	30.89	7	+1
CT	3,287,116	3,409,535	122,419	3.72	5	-1
DE	666,168	785,068	118,900	17.85	1	
FL	12,937,926	16,028,890	3,090,964	23.89	25	+2
GA	6,478,216	8,206,975	1,728,759	26.69	13	+2
HI	1,108,229	1,216,642	108,413	9.78	2	
ID	1,006,749	1,297,274	290,525	28.86	2	
IL	11,430,602	12,439,042	1,008,440	8.82	19	-1
IN	5,544,159	6,090,782	546,623	9.86	9	-1
IA	2,776,755	2,931,923	155,168	5.59	5	
KS	2,477,574	2,693,824	216,250	8.73	4	
KY	3,685,296	4,049,431	364,135	9.88	6	
LA	4,219,973	4,480,271	260,298	6.17	7	
ME	1,227,928	1,277,731	49,803	4.06	2	
MD	4,781,468	5,307,886	526,418	11.01	8	
MA	6,016,425	6,355,568	339,143	5.64	10	
MI	9,295,297	9,955,829	660,532	7.11	15	-1
MN	4,375,099	4,925,670	550,571	12.58	8	
MS	2,573,216	2,852,927	279,711	10.87	4	-1
MO	5,117,073	5,606,260	489,187	9.56	9	

Source: Bureau of the Census, Congressional Research Service

Continued on page 34

§ 2.13 (continued)

State	1990 Census Apportionment population	2000 Census Apportionment population	2000 Census Change from 1990 Total	2000 Census Change from 1990 Percent	Seats	Seat change from 1990
MT	799,065	905,316	106,251	13.30	1	
NE	1,578,385	1,715,369	136,984	8.68	3	
NV	1,201,833	2,002,032	800,199	66.58	3	+1
NH	1,109,252	1,238,415	129,163	11.64	2	
NJ	7,730,188	8,424,354	694,166	8.98	13	
NM	1,515,069	1,823,821	308,752	20.38	3	
NY	17,990,455	19,004,973	1,014,518	5.64	29	-2
NC	6,628,637	8,067,673	1,439,036	21.71	13	+1
ND	638,800	643,756	4,956	0.78	1	
OH	10,847,115	11,374,540	527,425	4.86	18	-1
OK	3,145,585	3,458,819	313,234	9.96	5	-1
OR	2,842,321	3,428,543	586,222	20.62	5	
PA	11,881,643	12,300,670	419,027	3.53	19	-2
RI	1,003,464	1,049,662	46,198	4.60	2	
SC	3,486,703	4,025,061	538,358	15.44	6	
SD	696,004	756,874	60,870	8.75	1	
TN	4,877,185	5,700,037	822,852	16.87	9	
TX	16,986,510	20,903,994	3,917,484	23.06	32	+2
UT	1,722,850	2,236,714	513,864	29.83	3	
VT	562,758	609,890	47,132	8.38	1	
VA	6,187,358	7,100,702	913,344	14.76	11	
WA	4,866,692	5,908,684	1,041,992	21.41	9	
WV	1,793,477	1,813,077	19,600	1.09	3	
WI	4,891,769	5,371,210	479,441	9.80	8	-1
WY	453,588	495,304	41,716	9.20	1	
Total:	**248,102,973**	**281,424,177**	**33,321,204**	**13.43**	**435**	

Continued on page 35

Percent Change in States' Resident Population, 1990–2000

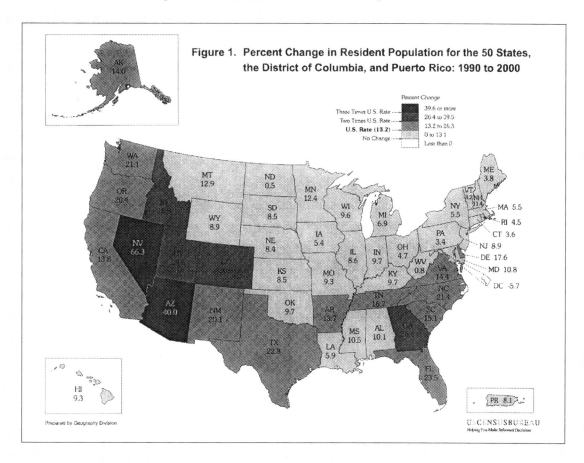

Figure 1. Percent Change in Resident Population for the 50 States, the District of Columbia, and Puerto Rico: 1990 to 2000

over and redraw congressional district boundaries. Subject to federal and state laws and court decisions, including Supreme Court decisions, the body doing the redistricting tries to obtain an equal population in each district in the state. Redistricting goals might include favoring a political party in some of the districts, or trying to accomplish other purposes, such as the creation of districts with a majority of minority population or with geographical compactness. Court cases are used to challenge districting decisions, and several states have redistricted or considered redistricting during the decade. *(See § 2.13, Reapportionment and Redistricting.)*

Term Limits

In recent years, Congress was under pressure to enact *term limits* applicable to members of Congress. A number of states have enacted limits on the number of terms a person may serve or serve consecutively in the state legislature. The attempt by some states to extend term limits to members of Congress, however, was stopped by a Supreme Court decision, *U.S. Term*

Limits Inc. v. Thornton, 514 U.S. 779 (1995), which found an Arkansas congressional term-limits statute unconstitutional. Nevertheless, some members of Congress have voluntarily pledged to their constituents not to run for reelection after serving a certain number of terms. As time has gone on, fewer members or candidates for Congress seem to have made a pledge, and some members seem to be repudiating it and doing so without losing significant votes in reelection.

Election Challenges

The House and Senate are empowered by the Constitution to be ". . . the Judge of the Elections, Returns and Qualifications of [their] own Members. . . ." *(Art. I, sec. 5, cl. 1.)* Following each election, the House Administration Committee on behalf of the House, and the Rules and Administration Committee on behalf of the Senate, consider election challenges. Most of these are disposed of expeditiously by the committees. However, investigations into challenges can go on for a long time, and even result in a seat being declared vacant and a new election ordered.

In the contemporary Congress, the House is likely to choose to employ the procedures established for resolving contested House elections established in the Federal Contested Elections Act *(P.L. 91-138; 83 Stat. 284)*, whereby a candidate for a House seat may challenge the election for that seat. (A member or member-elect or another person could also challenge the seating of a member-elect, although not under the provisions of the contested elections act, and the House could refer the matter to the House Administration Committee for its consideration and recommendations.)

After a winner has been declared by the appropriate state authority, the candidate challenging the election initiates House action by filing a notice with the clerk of the House and by serving the notice on the member-elect. The notice is to state "with particularity the grounds" on which the election is contested. The member-elect must respond, and may do so with defenses; with a motion to dismiss, based on various assertions, which will be decided by the House Administration Committee; or with a motion for a more definite statement of notice, which the House Administration Committee would rule on.

While these proceedings are unfolding, the new Congress might convene. Normally, the member-elect, possessing "credentials" from the state election authority—an election certificate considered to be prima facie evidence of the outcome of an election—is seated. The member-elect may be sworn in with other members-elect, or asked to stand aside and be sworn in separately. In either case, the House retains the authority to decide the contested election at a future date. In addition, further proceedings, either administrative or judicial, may take place in the state where the contested election occurred. The House Administration Committee, which has jurisdiction over contested elections, might be inclined to wait for these proceedings to conclude before undertaking its own consideration of the contested election.

The Federal Contested Elections Act, in addition to governing the notice, response, and motions, contains provisions dealing with time limits or deadlines, depositions, affidavits, subpoenas, default, penalties, and dismissal, and requires that all documents developed in the course of state and Federal Contested Elections Act proceedings be filed with the clerk of the House. This documentation provides the basis under the act for the committee's consideration of a contested election.

The House Administration Committee might discharge its consideration in a number of ways, with the end result of a simple resolution (H. Res.) reported from the committee for the consideration of the House. The committee might form a task force to do the committee's preliminary work, hold hearings, or conduct its own field work, in addition to or as a supplement to considering the documentary record. Although it has normally been reluctant to do so, the committee might undertake a full or partial recount.

Upon the completion of its work, the House Administration Committee makes its recommendation to the House. The committee might recommend dismissal of the challenge, the seating of a specific candidate, an investigation of fraud and other problems with the election, a declaration that the seat is vacant and a new election is to be held, or a variation on these choices. The resolution is privileged in the House, and the House might decide it with or without debate, with or without amendment, and by voice or recorded vote.

Following the 1996 general election, for example, a challenge in the House was not settled until early 1998. In the House, the incumbent, Republican Bob Dornan, was defeated for reelection by just under 1,000 votes, and challenged the election under the provisions of the Federal Contested Elections Act. Dornan alleged that noncitizens had voted illegally in the election in favor of Democrat Loretta Sanchez. The House Oversight Committee (now House Administration) appointed a task force to investigate. The challenge continued until the House voted, 378 to 33, on February 12, 1998, to end the investigation.

As a later example, when the 110th Congress convened January 4, 2007, an election challenge had been noticed for Florida's Thirteenth Congressional District. Vern Buchanan, a Republican, had been certified as the winner of the election by the Florida election authority, the secretary of state, and, following normal House practice even for a contested seat, Buchanan was sworn in with the other members-elect.

Prior to the swearing-in of the members-elect, Rep. Rush Holt, D-NJ, posed a parliamentary inquiry to the Speaker, asking whether the losing candidate, Democrat Christine Jennings, had filed a notice of contest with the clerk and what effect Buchanan's seating had on the contested election. The Speaker responded that the notice had been filed with the clerk, that the "House remains the judge of the elections of its Members," and that the seating was "without prejudice to the contest over the final right to that seat that is pending under the statute. . . ." (The central argument in the contested election involved an apparent undervote by 18,000 voters in Sarasota County, which Jennings claimed was caused by a malfunction of the electronic voting machines used there.)

A further parliamentary inquiry was then posed by Rep. Adam Putnam, R-FL, asking whether Buchanan "has been certified by the Secretary of State as duly elected from the 13th District of Florida." The Speaker stated that Putnam was correct.

At the time the *Deskbook's* update was completed, judicial proceedings were ongoing in Florida, and the House Administration Committee had created a task force to investigate "possible voting rights violations."

In contrast to the House, the Senate does not act on contested elections pursuant to a statute. The Senate tends to consider each election contest uniquely, although precedents, such as having the Senate Rules and Administration Committee conduct an investigation and make a recommendation to the Senate, may play an important role. Two modern cases of contested elections illustrate the structure and flexibility of the Senate's consideration of election challenges.

In a Senate race in Louisiana in 1996, Mary Landrieu, a Democrat, and Woody Jenkins, a Republican, fought for an open seat, which Landrieu won by fewer than 6,000 votes out of more than 1.7 million cast. Jenkins charged voter fraud, and asked that the seat be declared vacant and a new election ordered. The Senate seated Landrieu "without prejudice" to the Senate's constitutional right to make a later decision on dismissing Jenkins' petition, seating Jenkins, setting aside the election, or taking another action. The Rules and Administration Committee's investigation, which began with a bipartisan adoption of supplementary committee rules to govern the investigation, became a partisan investigation, from which the Democratic committee members withdrew. The investigation lasted until the committee voted unanimously on October 1, 1997, to end it.

In an earlier instance, following a New Hampshire Senate race in 1974, the Senate voted to declare the seat vacant and seek a new election. Although several ballot counts emerged in New Hampshire following the election, the final count, which was used to certify the winner, provided only a two-vote win to the Republican candidate, former Rep. Louis Wyman. The Democratic candidate, former state insurance commissioner John Durkin, filed a petition to contest the election with the Senate, and sought to have the Senate seat him based on one of the earlier ballot counts. When the Senate convened, it voted against a proposal to seat Wyman and another proposal to declare the seat vacant, and voted instead to refer the matter to the Senate Rules and Administration Committee.

The Rules and Administration Committee agreed on a procedure to review about 3,500 ballots from the more than 32,000 that were questioned by one or both candidates. The committee ultimately agreed on how voters had cast all but twenty-seven of these ballots, and reported to the Senate a resolution that allowed the full Senate to vote on each of the twenty-seven ballots and on eight questions of procedure related to recounts of certain precincts, voting machines that allegedly malfunctioned, and other matters. For each item, the Senate would be choosing between Wyman and Durkin, and presumably by its votes deciding the winner, or at least pointing the way for the Rules and Administration Committee to determine a winner.

Deadlock ensued on the Senate floor for six weeks as the parties largely voted as blocs, with just enough Democrats voting with Republicans to defeat motions to invoke cloture. This situation continued until Durkin reversed his position of opposition to a new election, on which Senate Democrats had supported him. The Senate voted July 30, 1975, to declare the seat vacant. A new election was held September 16, which Durkin won with just over 53 percent of the vote. He was sworn in September 18.

While these examples deal with House and Senate judging elections of their members, either house might need to determine the constitutional qualifications of a member-elect to serve. In a landmark decision, the Supreme Court enunciated a limitation on congressional judgments on seating a member-elect related to these qualifications. The case stemmed from the House's refusal to seat a member-elect, but the court's opinion presumably applies to the Senate as well. Rep. Adam Clayton Powell, D-NY, was reelected to his House seat in the 1966 election. Rather than seat Powell, the Speaker directed him to step aside while the other members-elect were sworn. The House did not seat Powell but agreed to a resolution to establish a select committee to consider Powell's qualifications, his involvement in a civil case in New York in which he had been held in contempt, and his alleged misconduct involving a misappropriation of funds that was the subject of an investigation at the end of the preceding 89th Congress. The resolution also disallowed Powell from being seated pending House action on the select committee's report. The select committee subsequently recommended seating Powell, but censuring and fining him and depriving him of his seniority.

When the House considered the resolution embodying the select committee's recommendations, it approved an amendment to the resolution, and then agreed to the resolution as amended. The resolution as amended excluded Powell from the House and declared his seat vacant. Powell sued Speaker John McCormack and other House officers. Powell argued that he must be seated if he met the constitutional qualifications for a representative—twenty-five years of age, a citizen for seven years, and a resident of the state from which elected. Following lower-court decisions, the Supreme Court granted certiorari, settled arguments against the federal courts' jurisdiction and the matter's justiciability, and supported Powell's claim to his seat. The Court held that "in judging the qualifications of its members Congress is limited to the standing qualifications prescribed in the Constitution." (*Powell v. McCormack*, 395 U.S. 486 (1969)).

§ 2.20 Election Laws

Election campaigns for the House and Senate are subject to numerous laws and regulations. These include federal election, tax, communications, and criminal laws; Federal Election Commission (FEC), Internal Revenue Service (IRS), and Federal Communications Commission (FCC) regulations and rulings; chamber rules and their interpretations by the House and Senate ethics committees; and state laws and regulations. The general intent of the proscriptions in these laws and regulations is to prevent or minimize conflicts of interest by candidates for Congress, protect the integrity of citizens' exercise of the franchise, and prevent diversion of public funds to political purposes.

Campaign Finance

The costs of congressional campaigns are high. Preliminary reporting to the FEC showed that candidates for Congress—House and Senate—spent at least $1.4 billion in the 2005–2006 election cycle.

It takes money, organization, ideas, media attention, and other resources to rise above the din of commercial and other messages and the activities and distractions in voters' lives. A winning congressional candidate must attract a plurality or majority of votes in a general election and possibly also in an earlier primary and primary runoff. In the 2005–2006 election cycle, the FEC reported that over 1,800 Democratic, Republican, and third-party candidates for the House disclosed *receipts* of at least $844.8 million. In the same election cycle, the FEC reported that over 200 Democratic, Republican, and third-party candidates for the Senate disclosed receipts of at least $565.7 million.

The FEC's preliminary reports showed that individuals contributed 61 percent of funds to congressional candidates; political action committees (PACs) contributed 28 percent; and candidates themselves lent or contributed 8 percent. (In 2006, the FEC reported that there were at least 4,200 registered PACs, although registration does not necessarily mean there was financial activity.)

The total receipts by House and Senate candidates are independent of the campaign activities of political parties, businesses, labor unions, individuals, and various interest groups that spend money on congressional elections in legal ways other than through contributions to individual candidates' campaign committees. In recent election cycles, much attention was paid to so-called section 527 political organizations, which are partly tax-exempt under section 527 of the Internal Revenue Code. While these organizations reportedly spent several hundred million dollars to influence various campaigns in the 2006 elections, they were able to legally operate exempt from federal election law. (The Internal Revenue Code may completely or partially restrict the election activity of organizations that are completely or partially exempt from federal income taxes.)

The federal campaign laws applicable to congressional campaigns reflect several principles:
- private financing, not public financing
- no ceilings on candidates' expenditures from their campaign or their personal funds
- periodic disclosure of receipts and expenditures as the principal means of enabling the public to assess candidates' campaign-finance activities
- ceilings on contributions made by individuals, parties, and PACs to House and Senate candidates
- prohibitions on entities that may contribute to House and Senate candidates

Campaign funding fully covered by federal laws and regulations, such as an individual's donation to a congressional candidate's campaign, is called *hard money*. Campaign funding that is legal but only partially or immaterially regulated is called *soft money*.

While there have been numerous proposals for public financing of congressional campaigns, Congress has not enacted such a proposal. The system of private financing and unlimited expenditures remains intact, although the costs of congressional campaigns, the time consumed by fund-raising, and the role of wealthy contributors (and candidates) invite frequent criticism. The current system seems to prevail because of concerns about the advantages of incumbency that a challenger's fund-raising might overcome, potential electoral distortions in a public-funding system, limitations on spending as a direct or indirect limitation on constitutionally protected speech, and other matters.

A frequent complaint of congressional candidates is the significant amount of time they must spend on fund-raising because of both the high costs of campaigns and the ceilings that exist on individual and other contributions. When Congress passed the Federal Election Campaign Act Amendments of 1974 (*88 Stat. 1263*), it enacted limits on candidates' campaign expenditures. The ceiling for a House primary or general election was set at $70,000, adjusted by a cost-of-living allowance. (The expenditure ceilings were subsequently struck down as part of the Supreme Court's ruling in *Buckley v. Valeo*, 424 U.S. 1 (1976).) In the 2005–2006 campaign cycle, over 290 House candidates spent over $1 million, and at least thirteen candidates (other than congressional leaders) spent over $4 million in winning and losing campaigns.

In contrast, the ceilings on campaign contributions were not raised from the ones set in the 1974 law until the 2003–2004 election cycle. In the 1974 law, contribution limits were set at not more than $1,000 from an individual to a candidate and not more than $5,000 from a PAC to a candidate, per election. Pursuant to the Bipartisan Campaign Reform Act of 2002 (*116 Stat. 81*), these limits were raised to $2,000 for contributions by individuals, and rise due to indexing to $2,300 for the 2007–2008 election cycle. The indexed cumulative limit for the 2007–2008 election cycle was set at $42,700 for all of an individual's candidate contributions. (Other contribution ceilings, indexed for inflation, exist for other forms of political committees and contributors and in specific circumstances.) Squeezed between high campaign costs and low campaign contribution ceilings, House candidates have conducted fund-raising year-round; for Senate candidates, fund-raising is no longer confined to the last one or two years of a six-year term.

Moreover, lest bad publicity and legal sanctions harm a congressional candidate, a candidate's campaign-finance operation must ensure that contribution ceilings are honored and that other prohibitions and requirements of law are observed. Contributions may not be made from corporate or union treasuries. Foreign nationals may not contribute, although permanent resident aliens are exempt as are, under certain conditions, U.S. subsidiaries of foreign corporations. A candidate's campaign may not coordinate activities with an outside group that *independently* spends money in support of the candidate or in opposition to the candidate's opponent; otherwise, the expenditure would be subject to contribution limits. (Political parties are permitted to make both independent expenditures and limited coordinated expenditures in behalf of their candidates.) Certain information must be obtained and then disclosed about the donor of any contribution of more than $200.

In response to concerns over wealthy candidates who have been able to spend large amounts from personal fortunes, the Bipartisan Campaign Reform Act of 2002 (BCRA) allowed opponents of such candidates to increase their fund-raising according to a set of thresholds. For House elections, the threshold was a dollar amount, $350,000 in personal campaign spending. For Senate elections, there were a series of thresholds, beginning with $150,000 plus four cents times the voting-age population in a state in personal campaign spending. As multiples of this spending are reached, an opponent may increase fund-raising through specified increases on individual and party support limits. This BCRA provision was first activated in the 2004 Colorado Senate race in which Peter Coors, a family member of Coors Brewing Co., used personal resources in his campaign against Ken Salazar, who ultimately prevailed in the general election.

Another change related to the new law as implemented by the FEC allowed a candidate for federal office to receive a salary from his or her principal campaign committee. For congressional candidates, the salary was limited to the lesser of a member of Congress's salary or what the candidate received as earned income in the previous year. An incumbent member of Congress may not receive a salary payment from campaign funds.

The Bipartisan Campaign Reform Act of 2002 contained provisions dealing with soft money, issue advocacy, and many more aspects of campaign finance law than have been described here. Its policies on soft money very directly affect the fund-raising and spending programs used by the Democratic and Republican Parties' national committees, including the four congressional committees. The law also prohibited members of Congress and candidates for Congress, among others, from raising soft money except in very narrow, specific instances; for example, a member or candidate for Congress would seem to be able to be a featured guest at a state or local party fundraiser. And, it augmented sponsorship disclosure laws to make disclaimers more prominent in campaign advertising, including a requirement that candidates' broadcast ads include an image of the candidate and a statement of his or her approval.

BCRA was subject to First and Fifth Amendment court challenges, but the U.S. Supreme Court largely upheld the constitutionality of key provisions in *McConnell v. FEC*, 540 U.S. 93 (2003).

House candidates' disclosure reports are available for public inspection at the FEC and the clerk of the House's Legislative Resource Center. Senate candidates' disclosure reports are available for public inspection at the FEC and secretary of the Senate's Public Records Office. *(For information on the FEC, see the FEC web site at <www.fec.gov>; the home page is shown in § 2.21, Federal Election Commission Web Site. For information on the House's Legislative*

§ 2.21

Federal Election Commission Web Site

The Federal Election Commission (FEC) web site *(<www.fec.gov>)* provides access to FEC legal and advisory documents, forms, certain campaign-finance reports, and other information. The monthly FEC newsletter, *Record*, also appears on the web site. The FEC also offers informational programs, including ones of interest to potential contributors; the dates of these programs are listed on the web site. The FEC maintains an office where a visitor may conduct research on the voluminous reports not included on the web site. The FEC's information number is 202-628-0618.

Additional sources of campaign finance information include the Center for Responsive Politics *(<www.opensecrets.org>)* and PoliticalMoneyLine *(<www.politicalmoneyline.com>)*, publications such as *Campaigns and Elections* magazine, and various legal and loose-leaf services.

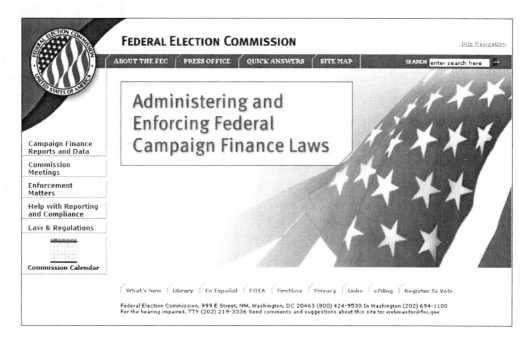

Resource Center and the Senate's Public Records Office, see § 13.10, Legislative-Branch Agencies and Offices.)

Various other laws also affect congressional candidates' campaign-finance activities. For example, it is illegal for a congressional candidate to solicit a contribution from an individual on public assistance or to solicit specifically from a federal employee. Cash contributions over $100 are prohibited, as are contributions in another's name. It is also illegal for a member of Congress to solicit or accept a contribution from employees of his or her congressional office. A candidate for Congress may not solicit campaign contributions on federal property, although member-to-member solicitations are exempt from this law. A congressional candidate may not designate a federal facility as the location for receiving contributions. Should a donor send a contribution to a congressional office, the contribution must be forwarded promptly, not using the frank, to the member's campaign committee.

Congressional candidates also have some privileges. For example, broadcasters, including cable systems, must make advertising time available to congressional and other candidates for what is known as the "lowest unit broadcast rate." The purpose of this prerogative is to make available to candidates the same rates as are available to a broadcaster's most-favored advertisers. The rate requirement is in effect forty-five days before a primary election and sixty days before a general election.

Other Election Laws and Rules

A theme of both federal law and the rules of the House and Senate is to segregate official and political activity. (*Political activity* is used here in a popular, not legal, sense to describe an array of activities, political or campaign-related, that are described in federal law, regulation, and chamber rules and their interpretations.) In general, a member of Congress may not use his or her office, its staff, its equipment, or official funds for political activity. He or she may not use campaign funds to support official activities, such as operating a congressional office, or convert campaign funds to personal use.

While congressional staff may not, in general, engage in political work in congressional offices or in the course of performing their congressional office duties, they might "volunteer" their time to congressional campaigns at other locations and at other times. Nonetheless, an office scheduler may coordinate a member's schedule with a campaign office. On some occasions, a congressional staffer might go off the congressional payroll while performing extensive campaign work or might reduce his or her official hours and salary commensurate with reduced official duties and increased campaign duties. A congressional staffer may also concurrently draw a congressional salary and, for campaign work, a campaign salary. A senator may, in addition, designate up to three of his or her congressional staff, at least one of whom is in the senator's Washington, DC, office, to handle campaign funds for the senator's or a group of senators' campaign committee.

Laws and rules also attempt to reduce some of the advantages of incumbency. As mentioned in § 5.50 (*Franking Privilege*), mass mailings—500 pieces or more, largely identical in content—must be postmarked not fewer than ninety days before an election in which a representative is a candidate for any public office and not fewer than sixty days before an election in which a senator is a candidate for any public office. The House prohibition pertains to all mass communications, for example, announcements of "town hall" meetings. In addition, both the House and Senate regulate and monitor the use of the frank in recognition of its purposes in the conduct of congressional business rather than for campaign activities.

Also, for a representative, official travel must be paid from official funds. Travel cannot be designated as official if it originates or ends at a campaign event, and official travel may not be combined with or related to travel paid with campaign funds. For a senator's travel, reimbursement is allowed for actual transportation and disallowed for other travel-related expenses during the sixty days before a primary or general election in which the senator is a candidate, unless the candidacy is uncontested. Allocation of travel expenses between campaign funds and official funds is permitted when a trip has a "mixed purpose" of both official and campaign-related activities.

Campaign-related restrictions also exist, among others, for using House and Senate recording studios, video and audio from the House and Senate floors, mobile offices, and House and Senate office equipment, as well as for making campaign advertisements in congressional offices. In addition, the House considers redistricting to be a political activity, and, for the most part, disallows use of official funds related to a member's redistricting expenses. (*See also* § *4.30, Congressional Ethics;* § *5.30, House Allowances for Staff, Office, and Other Expenses; and* § *5.40, Senate Allowances for Staff, Office, and Other Expenses.*)

Chapter Three

Pressures on Congress:

Constituents, Media, President, and Courts

Analysis

§ 3.00 Introduction

Members are subjected to numerous demands and pressures. Constituents, the news media, the president and executive branch, and the judicial branch all affect how members do their jobs. An understanding of the pressures exerted by these groups can help explain members' interests in and positions on a public-policy issue.

§ 3.10 Constituency Pressure

Congress was designed by the founding fathers as a representative body—two equal chambers whose job is to make laws that reflect the interests of members' constituents. Members might also feel pulled in different directions by the views of their parties or by their perceptions of national interest. These views might sometimes conflict with sentiment in their home districts or states.

Some issues resonate more in one district or state than in another. Some members know that they will be reelected by a comfortable margin while others know every election campaign will be a close race. A member with a secure seat may be able to take the lead on an issue, even at the risk of alienating some voters, or might be able to spend more time on national concerns. A member in a competitive district or state may need to put his or her representational role ahead of a legislative role. Attention to constituent concerns often accelerates as elections approach, a phenomenon especially noticeable in the Senate, where it is six years between elections. The tendency to emphasize local concerns also often increases with the competitiveness of a race.

Members of the House represent districts that, after the 2001 redistricting, included an average of over 645,000 people. District sizes in 2001 ranged from Wyoming's single district with just under 500,000 people to Montana's single district with over 900,000 people. In 2006, senators represented states ranging in population from just over 500,000 (Wyoming) to over 36 million (California). Large and diverse constituencies make it difficult for members to gauge constituent opinion on every issue. Few districts or states are solely rural, suburban, or urban. Most areas now contain a cross-section of these kinds of interests. Most districts and states are heterogeneous—they include citizens, immigrants, schoolchildren, parents, and retirees, and people with diverse ethnic backgrounds, occupations, educational levels, and socioeconomic status.

No member of Congress seeking reelection can afford to take his or her constituency for granted. The levels of expectations for service, for reflecting a constituency's views, for being home often, and for being responsive are very high. (See § 3.11, *Example of Constituent Outreach.*) Members try their best to meet those expectations. Failure to do so may provide an opening for a challenge within a member's own party in a primary, from the other major party, or even from a third party in a general election. (See § 3.12, *Example of Member's Newsletter.*)

§ 3.11

Example of Constituent Outreach

FOR IMMEDIATE RELEASE

Congressman **Rahm Emanuel**

FOR IMMEDIATE RELEASE
February 23, 2005

Emanuel to Host Free Tax Preparation & Federal Student Aid Assistance Sessions

CHICAGO, IL - Congressman Rahm Emanuel (D-IL) will host free tax preparation services as well as provide assistance for families exploring financial aid options for college on Saturdays in February, March & April—February 26, March 12, March 19, March 26, April 2 and April 9 from 8:30–11:30 a. m. The tax preparation services and financial aid help are provided by the Tax Assistance Program's trained volunteers.

The Tax Assistance Program is a non-profit service authorized by the IRS that helps families with incomes of $35,000 or less file for the tax credits, refunds and other tax benefits to which they are entitled. In the past ten years of operation, the Tax Assistance Program has helped more than 35,000 families recoup more than $45 million in tax refunds and financial help.

"The Earned Income Tax Credit and other benefits can return hundreds of dollars or more to eligible families – if they are able to apply for it," Emanuel said. "These important tax benefits can be complicated, so I am pleased to provide families with the help they need."

Families can also get help with the Free Application for Federal Student Aid (FAFSA). "I encourage families to take advantage of student aid opportunities that will help make college more affordable," Emanuel said.

Who:

- Experienced tax preparation volunteers.
- Tax filers with incomes of $35,000 or below. Bring W-2's and other proofs of income, and if possible, earlier tax returns.
- Any family is eligible for free FAFSA application assistance. Families seeking FAFSA assistance whose income exceeds $35,000 should bring completed tax returns.
- Office of Congressman Rahm Emanuel hosting with the Tax Assistance Program

What:

Tax preparation and FAFSA assistance sessions

Where:

Congressman Emanuel's District Office
3742 W. Irving Park Rd.
Chicago, IL 60618
(773) 267-5926 or Tax Assistance Program Client Hotline—(312) 409-1555

When:

9 Saturday mornings, all from 8:30 – 11:30 a.m.
February: 26
March: 12, 19, 26 (no session March 5)
April: 2, 9

###

Example of Member's Newsletter

2005 ANNUAL REPORT

U.S. SENATOR

CHUCK HAGEL

February, 2006

Senator Hagel visited Nebraska troops in Iraq while leading a Congressional Delegation to the Middle East in December. Pictured are Lt. Col. Gary Krupa, USAF, Senator Hagel and Lt. Col. Stephen Graf, USAF.

Dear Friends,

Nebraska continues to play a critical role in the many events that shape America's future. In 2005, President Bush named Nebraska Governor Mike Johanns as U.S. Secretary of Agriculture. Afghan President Hamid Karzai visited West Point and received an honorary degree from the University of Nebraska at Omaha, and Nebraska's servicemen and women and their families continue to make great sacrifices on behalf of our nation.

Since my first year in the Senate, I have compiled an annual report to keep you informed of the actions taken the previous year on issues of importance to our state and nation. Meeting the challenges of 2006 and the 21st century will require continued hard work and principled, disciplined leadership.

I look forward to meeting with many of you this year in Nebraska and Washington and receiving your thoughtful suggestions as my staff and I work to responsibly address your concerns. Thank you.

Sincerely,

MAJOR ISSUES IN CONGRESS IN 2005

National Security

Iraq, Afghanistan and the Greater Middle East

In December, I led a bipartisan congressional delegation to the Middle East. We met the leaders of Israel, the Palestinian Authority, Jordan, Saudi Arabia, Iraq, Lebanon and Egypt. In Iraq, we met with the Iraqi Prime Minister, our U.S. Ambassador, the U.S. Commander of the Multinational Force and other U.S. and Iraqi officials. We also met with American troops, including men and women from Nebraska. All of Nebraska can be proud of our troops who are fighting bravely and working tirelessly in Iraq.

In the Fiscal Year 2006 Foreign Operations Appropriations bill, we secured continued funding for the Afghanistan Young Leaders Program at UNO, which brings outstanding young leaders from Afghanistan to Nebraska for leadership training.

Intelligence Reform

In 2005, Congress addressed challenging legal issues that have emerged during the war on terror. In July, I traveled to Guantanamo Bay, Cuba, to inspect U.S. detention facilities and methods of interrogations. I was an original cosponsor of an amendment, which passed as part of the Fiscal Year 2006 Defense Appropriations bill, that prohibits the cruel and inhumane treatment of detainees in U.S. custody.

As a member of the Senate Intelligence Committee, I devoted significant attention to ensuring responsible congressional oversight of U.S. intelligence activities, and helped lead the Committee's effort to examine the accuracy of pre-war intelligence regarding Iraq. I am pleased that the new Director of National

Intelligence began implementing reforms of the intelligence community mandated by Congress during the past year.

Oversight of the intelligence community will continue to be a priority in 2006 and the Intelligence Committee began hearings in February.

Immigration Reform

America cannot continue to defer making tough choices about its immigration policy. I agree with President Bush that it is not in our national security interests to have 10-12 million undocumented individuals living inside our borders. In March, I visited the Mariposa Port of Entry in Nogales, Arizona to observe border crossing operations between the U.S. and Mexico with Department of Homeland Security officials.

In October, after meeting with many Nebraska law enforcement officials, community leaders, business owners and immigration lawyers, I reintroduced a comprehensive package of immigration reform bills.

My legislation will enhance America's national security, protect our workforce, and bring accountability to those living in America illegally. In 2006, I will work with the President and Congress to ensure passage of comprehensive immigration reform.

Agriculture and Rural Development

BSE - Beef Trade

In December 2003, the first case of Bovine Spongiform Encephalopathy (BSE) was discovered in the United States, causing several foreign countries to ban U.S. beef from their

markets. Since that time, I have worked with the U.S. Department of Agriculture, foreign diplomats and my Senate colleagues to regain market access for beef producers. In October, I hosted Japanese Ambassador Ryozo Kato on a visit to Nebraska to discuss the reopening of the Japanese border to American beef. In December, Japan officially announced they would lift their ban on U.S. beef. Since that time, Hong Kong, Singapore and Taiwan's markets have reopened, and South Korea, Thailand, and other foreign markets have taken steps toward reopening their markets to U.S. beef.

This year, Japan announced that it would suspend the importation of U.S. beef until the causes of banned beef parts in a shipment from New York are known. The incident being investigated is an isolated technical violation, not a beef safety issue. I will continue to push for worldwide market access for beef producers from the U.S.

Arsenic Regulation Compliance

The Environmental Protection Agency's (EPA) new Arsenic Rule went into effect in January. Many Nebraska communities will be required to install water treatment systems that lower arsenic levels in public drinking water. The Nebraska Department of Health and Human Services estimates that the cost for Nebraska communities to comply with the new standard will exceed $120 million over the next ten years. This is an unacceptable burden on our communities.

In an effort to address these costs, Senator Domenici (R-NM) and I reintroduced the Community Drinking Water Assistance Act, which proposes federal funding of $1.9 billion annually to assist small communities in complying with drinking water standards.

continued ...

PREPARED, PUBLISHED AND MAILED AT TAXPAYER EXPENSE

§ 3.13

Example of Privacy Act Release Form

In order to facilitate the exchange of information with federal agencies on case work and to protect the privacy of an individual's records held by the federal government, congressional offices use a Privacy Act release form.

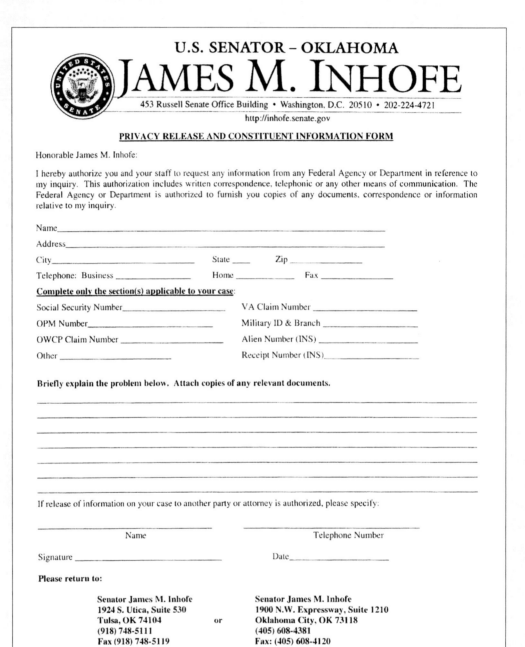

U.S. SENATOR – OKLAHOMA

JAMES M. INHOFE

453 Russell Senate Office Building • Washington, D.C. 20510 • 202-224-4721

http://inhofe.senate.gov

PRIVACY RELEASE AND CONSTITUENT INFORMATION FORM

Honorable James M. Inhofe:

I hereby authorize you and your staff to request any information from any Federal Agency or Department in reference to my inquiry. This authorization includes written correspondence, telephonic or any other means of communication. The Federal Agency or Department is authorized to furnish you copies of any documents, correspondence or information relative to my inquiry.

Name_____

Address_____

City_____ State ____ Zip _____

Telephone: Business _____ Home _____ Fax _____

Complete only the section(s) applicable to your case:

Social Security Number_____ VA Claim Number _____

OPM Number_____ Military ID & Branch _____

OWCP Claim Number _____ Alien Number (INS) _____

Other _____ Receipt Number (INS)_____

Briefly explain the problem below. Attach copies of any relevant documents.

_____

_____

_____

_____

_____

_____

If release of information on your case to another party or attorney is authorized, please specify:

_____   _____
        Name   Telephone Number

Signature _____   Date_____

Please return to:

Senator James M. Inhofe		**Senator James M. Inhofe**
1924 S. Utica, Suite 530		**1900 N.W. Expressway, Suite 1210**
Tulsa, OK 74104	**or**	**Oklahoma City, OK 73118**
(918) 748-5111		**(405) 608-4381**
Fax (918) 748-5119		**Fax: (405) 608-4120**

§ 3.14

Constituent Service Reflected in Member's Newsletter

The excerpt from Rep. Chris Van Hollen's newsletter shows two good examples of case work, one in behalf of individuals and one to assist a local organization. In the former instance, Van Hollen cites his intervention with the president.

Getting Things Done for the 8th District

Securing Local Investments

Working with state and local officials, we have brought important funding to our community for transportation projects, education programs and public safety efforts. In July I had the privilege of presenting a $1.3 million Head Start grant to the Lourie Center for Infants and Children in Rockville.

Chris speaks with a family about Head Start at the Lourie Center in Rockville.

Helping the Disabled

This fall I visited the Bethesda Naval Hospital, which has developed an innovative and successful program hiring disabled individuals from our local community to work in its kitchen and cafeteria. Many of these individuals have worked there for more than twenty years. They are hard-working, reliable and beloved by the naval officers and staff. The Administration had selected these positions to be bid out to private contractors, leaving these disabled employees on the verge of losing their jobs. I wrote to the President about this injustice and am pleased that as a result of our timely intervention, these disabled individuals have been able to keep their jobs and the sense of dignity that comes with them.

Case Work and Grants

Case work refers to helping individuals or small groups of constituents, including local governments, in their dealings with federal government agencies. How well a member conducts case work can be key to reelection. A congressional office may perform advocacy or referral functions for as many as several thousand *cases* a year, ranging from tracking down missing Social Security checks to expediting a passport application to clearing up immigration cases to facilitating consideration of a community's grant application for some public project. *(See § 3.13, Example of Privacy Act Release Form.)* Constituents have been known to forgive a member for a controversial vote. However, they can be less forgiving when case work is ignored or mishandled. *(See § 3.14, Constituent Service Reflected in Member's Newsletter, and § 3.15, Case Work Outreach.)*

Pork barrel politics is often used to describe what members do to try to obtain federal funds for public-works projects, federal installations, grants, and other benefits for their districts or states. The federal government also buys goods and services from private suppliers, and government contracts are let to companies around the country. Federal research and development programs disburse billions of dollars to universities, federal laboratories, and private companies. Members try to obtain allocations of these kinds of funds for their districts or states

Case Work Outreach

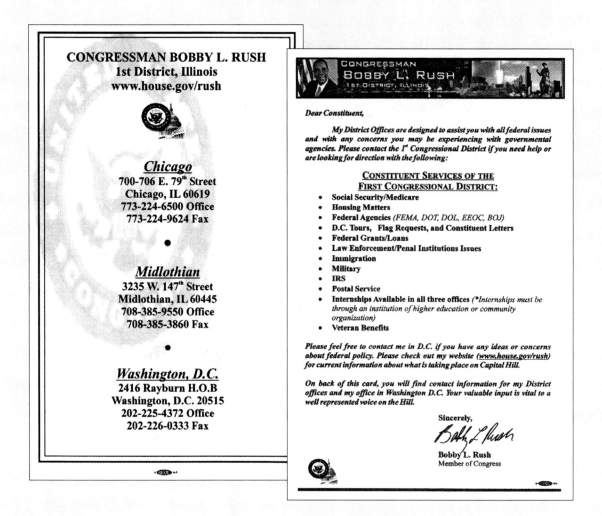

in both the legislative process and the grant-making process. (*See § 3.16, "Pork Barrel Politics."*)

Members of Congress attempt to assist their constituents with information and links on their web sites to federal, private, and other grants resources. For example, many link to the Catalog of Federal Domestic Assistance, <*www.cfda.gov*>.

Mail from Home

Constituent pressure manifests itself in the form of millions of letters, postcards, faxes, emails, phone calls, and personal visits to members each year, asking assistance or urging support or opposition on issues before Congress. Although many contacts are the result of advocacy-group activity, many are in the form of individual letters, calls, and other communications sent by individual constituents on particular matters important to them.

Most offices have policies on responding to constituent mail. Mail from the district or state is always answered, usually on a one-week or two-week turnaround. (However, following the delivery of anthrax spores to Capitol Hill via the U.S. mail in fall 2001, letters to members and committees of Congress are delayed by irradiation and inspection procedures.) Mail from outside the district or state may be answered if a member aspires to statewide or national office or has become associated with an issue. Or, mail from outside a member's district or state might be referred to a member representing that other district or state. *(See § 5.50, Franking Privilege.)*

Mail from constituents, lobbyists, and other members serves as a barometer of opinion on a particular issue. Most offices pay particular attention when incoming mail is heavy on an issue, especially when that mail comes from the home district or state. *(See § 3.17, Tips for Contacting Members of Congress; and § 3.18, Addressing Correspondence to Members of Congress.)*

Members' Travel to the District and State

Representatives' districts are statewide in only seven states. Most representatives, therefore, are better known to their con-

§ 3.16

"Pork Barrel Politics"

When a member of Congress secures funds for federal projects or government benefits for a specific district or state, those funds are often referred to as *pork*. Whether one thinks pejoratively or happily about pork-barrel spending might depend on principles or perspective. Congress has the constitutional power to establish specific spending programs and activities, but debate within Congress and outside of it surrounds how Congress exercises this power in favor of members' local interests. Examples of so-called pork include the following:

- dams, highways, and other federally funded public works
- federal building or courthouse construction
- Corps of Engineers projects
- locations of federal facilities
- economic-development aid
- creation of parks and recreation areas, including land purchases
- retention or expansion of military bases
- federal water projects
- naming federal buildings after prominent citizens
- establishment of endowments or research, educational, or other centers, named after former members of Congress or prominent Americans connected to a location or purpose
- naming highways or federal roads
- naming scholarships or educational grants
- participation in *pilot programs*
- federal government contracts

stituents than the senators representing a state. Representatives are often more involved in local affairs, or in local affairs with a federal dimension. They also run for reelection every two years, and are almost always campaigning. Representatives usually do not receive the same level of media coverage as their counterparts in the Senate. Moreover, because they usually share a media market with other representatives, they must work harder to make themselves known and stay in the public eye. Add these and other factors together and one understands why members of the House return home much more frequently than senators.

On average, representatives make about forty trips to their home districts each year. Some

§ 3.17

Tips for Contacting Members of Congress

Common sense probably tells us that hateful, insulting, or threatening communications do not work. Vague, unfocused, or nebulous requests for action or assistance are also ineffective.

Types of Communication

1. Letters, Faxes, and Email
   - Be brief and to the point
   - Write at the proper time in the legislative process
   - Use your own language
   - Stick to one issue for each communication
   - Personalize the issue
   - Write to your own representative or senator
   - Clearly identify the legislation, using bill numbers if possible
   - Know your facts
   - Be polite and positive
   - Speak for yourself
   - Ask for a reply and include your phone number and postal address, even on email
   - Write on personal stationery, if a letter

2. Telephone Calls
   - Be brief, to the point, and considerate of the member's time constraints
   - Identify yourself as a concerned constituent
   - Indicate the issue
   - Be specific about the action you want
   - Be courteous and polite
   - Compose your thoughts before the call
   - Follow up with a thank-you note

3. Personal Visits
   - Be brief, to the point, and considerate of the member's time constraints
   - Thank the staffer or member by name
   - Put a human face on your issue
   - Begin the meeting by thanking the office for any prior help
   - Respect member's or staffer's opinion
   - "Connect the dots" for the member or staff: explain why the member's help is needed and what specifically the member can do to help

may fly across the continent nearly every weekend, and House schedules try to accommodate the flight schedules to the West Coast. For example, votes are not generally held before 6:30 p.m. on Mondays or Tuesdays, because one flight popular with members from California arrives at Washington, DC's Dulles International Airport at 5:00 p.m.

Senators generally do not return home as often as representatives, although that usually depends on the distance of a state from Washington, DC, the convenience of airline flight schedules, the Senate's schedule, and the balance of time until the next election. There are always exceptions, however—Delaware's senators return home by train nearly every night.

As an acknowledgment of the importance of going home, the House schedules *district work periods*, and the Senate schedules *nonlegislative periods*, to allow "long weekends" or full weeks to be spent in home districts and states.

Members in Their Home Offices. At home, members usually maintain several district or state offices. The staff in those offices have responsibility for much of an office's case work

§ 3.18

Addressing Correspondence to Members of Congress

Addressing Letters to an Individual Member

Honorable [name of representative]
[room number, building]
e.g., 1111 Longworth House Office Building
U.S. House of Representatives
Washington, DC 20515

Dear Representative [last name]:

Honorable [name of senator]
[room number, building]
e.g., 123 Russell Senate Office Building
U.S. Senate
Washington, DC 20510

Dear Senator [last name]:

Addressing Letters to a Committee Chair

Committee on [name]
[room number, building]
e.g., 2222 Rayburn House Office Building
U.S. House of Representatives
Washington, DC 20515

Dear Chairman [last name]:

Committee on [name]
[room number, building]
e.g., 123 Dirksen Senate Office Building
U.S. Senate
Washington, DC 20510

Dear Chairman [last name]:

and day-to-day contact with constituents. Although all offices do outreach to constituents, some offices hire a designated staffer to do outreach for the member. When in the district or state, a member usually works at one or more of his or her offices at least part of the time. *(See § 3.19, Constituent Outreach Meetings.)*

A member may also convene town meetings to obtain the views of voters and generate goodwill publicity. It is important to demonstrate interest in and awareness of local sentiment. Some members have instituted regular practices to achieve this goal. For instance, for *supermarket Saturdays*, a member goes to a different supermarket in his or her district each Saturday at an announced time. Between a lot of visiting and a little grocery shopping, a member of Congress is seen by constituents to be engaged in a normal activity, down-to-earth, and in touch—not having "gone Washington." *(See § 3.110, Advertising Constituents' Access to a Member, and § 3.111, Example of Community Holiday Event.)*

Constituents Come to Washington

From Memorial Day to Labor Day, Washington, DC, is one of the most-visited cities in the world. Families come to see the sights, and often wish to see their representatives and senators in Congress. They might come to discuss legislative issues of national importance, to discuss parochial concerns about their communities, or just to get visitors' gallery passes to the House

§ 3.19

Constituent Outreach Meetings

U.S. Congresswoman
Ginny Brown - Waite
Representing Florida's Fifth District

As part of her commitment to keeping open lines of communication between Washington and the Fifth Congressional District and providing the highest level of constituent service, Congresswoman Ginny Brown-Waite will hold constituent outreach meetings each month, following the schedule below.

At these meetings, staffers from Brown-Waite's office will explain how to get in touch with the Congresswoman to remedy a problem, offer general assistance and information, and outline what services are available through the office.

First Tuesday of Each Month

Lakeland
9:00 to 10:00 a.m.
Bethel Baptist Church's Fellowship
Building
3125 Socrum Loop Road West

Clermont
10:30 a.m. – 11:30 a.m.
Cooper Memorial Library's Florida Room
620 W. Montrose Ave

Crystal River
11:00a.m. - 12:00 p.m.
City Council Chambers
Crystal River City Hall, 123 NW Hwy. 19

Inverness
City Council Chambers
1:30 p.m. – 2:30 p.m.
Inverness City Hall, 212 W. Main St.

First Wednesday of Each Month

Chiefland
City Council Chambers
8:30 a.m. - 9:30 a.m.
Chiefland City Hall, 214 E Park Ave

Dunnellon
2:00 p.m. - 3:30 p.m.
City Council Chambers City Hall
20750 River Dr.

First Thursday of Each Month
Bushnell
9:00 a.m. - 10:00 p.m.
City Council Chambers
Bushnell City Hall, 219 N. Market St

The Villages
9:00 a.m. - 10:00 a.m.
The Villages Government Annex
8033 E. County Rd., Oxford

Wildwood
10:30 a.m. – 11:30 a.m.
City Hall Meeting Room
Wildwood City Hall, 100 N. Main St.

Second Wednesday of Each Month
Hudson
10:30 a.m. – 12:00 p.m.
Hudson Library
8012 Library Road

###

Advertising Constituents' Access to a Member

§ 3.111

Example of Community Holiday Event

Congressman Xavier Becerra
and his family

invite you to attend
The 31st Congressional District's 14th Annual

Holiday Party and Toy Drive

Monday, December 11, 2006
6:30 to 8:30 pm

featuring
Live Music • Festive Food
Door Prizes • Crafts for Kids

Center for the Arts, Eagle Rock
2225 Colorado Boulevard
Eagle Rock, California 90041

Bring the kids!
Please bring a new unwrapped toy to brighten the holidays
for a local child in need.

Call (213) 484-8961 to RSVP

Parking on nearby streets and in Bank of America's parking lot
(2263 Colorado Blvd.)

and Senate chambers and information about Washington's museums. Washington, DC, is also the destination of choice of school groups across the country, particularly in the spring of each year. In addition to class trips, many students participate in programs run by the Close-Up Foundation, American Youth Scholarship Foundation, and other organizations promoting civic education or public service. Members regularly make presentations to student groups.

Whatever the reason and whatever the time of day or time of year, members and their staff are expected to meet with visiting constituents and respond to their concerns and needs. Ideally, of course, a constituent should leave the office feeling that he or she was treated specially. Part of that special treatment comes from home-state offerings of snacks and beverages stocked by members' offices, from peanuts to candy to juice to soft drinks.

Congressional offices provide passes to the chambers' visitors' galleries and brochures on museums and other tourist attractions. When possible, special tours to Washington sights (such as the Capitol or the White House) are arranged. Generally, constituents are met by staff. Walking through the Capitol complex, one regularly sees a staffer showing around a family or group of students. A staffer might also take visitors to a committee meeting to see a member, or may accompany them to the chamber's gallery. This enables visitors not only to see the member but also to see the legislative process in action. For visitors, meeting with a staffer is always nice, but they generally want to meet the member. Whenever possible, a visit with the member is arranged. *(See § 3.112, Constituent Services and Courtesies.)*

§ 3.20 Media Pressure

One of the most pervasive pressures on a member is the local and national media. The media's choice of what to report and how to report it, their ferreting out of problems from city hall to the White House, and their editorializing create public perceptions and public demands for action or change. Twenty-four hour news cycles and the proliferation of "news" formats on the World Wide Web have only added to media pressure on members. The media's treatment of a politician and his or her political, official, and personal lives contributes indirectly and sometimes directly to longevity and effectiveness in office. Local media do not nec-

§ 3.112

Constituent Services and Courtesies

Members' offices provide a wide range of services to constituents in addition to assisting with case work and obtaining grants. A member can distribute numerous government publications, obtain presidential greetings for some occasions, arrange tours in Washington, DC, and nominate worthy students to serve as pages or to receive appointments to the U.S. service academies. *(See § 5.113, Congressional Pages.)* This section lists some of these services.

Flags Flown over the Capitol

Flags can be flown over the Capitol at the request of a member of Congress to acknowledge the civic contributions of a constituent or simply for a constituent's honor of possessing such a flag. Hundreds or thousands of flags can be flown over the Capitol each day to carry out this program. The single-day record was set on July 4, 1976, when 10,471 flags flew over the Capitol.

Flags are purchased by a member with funds provided by the requesting constituent. The cost to the requester is based on the cost of the flag plus the cost of shipping and handling. The requester receives a flag and a certificate, which states the date it was flown, the name of the honoree (recipient), and the event for which it was flown. *(For U.S. flag information, see TheCapitol.Net at <www.capitolflags.us>.)*

Service Academy Appointments

The majority of appointments to the U.S. service academies are congressional appointments. Members of Congress can nominate constituents for appointments to the U.S. Military Academy, U.S. Naval Academy, U.S. Air Force Academy, and U.S. Merchant Marine Academy. Each office is allocated a specific number of appointments, but the academies can select additional appointees from among a representative's or senator's applicants. Applications are available from a member's office, or, in many cases, a member's web site. Within guidelines set by the service academies, each member's office establishes its own procedures and deadlines for processing the applications of prospective appointees. These procedures can be very elaborate and involve dozens of citizens volunteering their time to interview and make recommendations to a member.

Tours in Washington, DC

Many historic and unique sites are open to the public in Washington, DC. Most congressional offices arrange "VIP" tours for individuals and groups from a member's district or state. These tours are very popular, and reservations for busy seasons may need to be obtained months in advance. Some of the sites for which a congressional office might arrange a tour are listed below, along with their public-tour hours.

Capitol: If the Capitol is open to the public, timed, ticketed, 30-minute public tours are available from 9:00 a.m. to 4:30 p.m. Monday–Saturday, except Thanksgiving and Christmas. Tickets are free and are given away beginning at 9:00 a.m. at the ticket kiosk on First Street, S.W., across from the U.S. Botanical Garden. One ticket per person. Gallery passes for both chambers are available from members of either the House or the Senate, to be used when the House or Senate is meeting or between 9:00 a.m. and 4:00 p.m., Monday–Friday. It is a good idea to confirm tour information by checking the Capitol Guide Service's recording, 202-225-6827. *(See additional information at § 6.20, Guide to Public Buildings on Capitol Hill.)* Member offices may also arrange guided Capitol tours for their constituents.

Continued on page 62

§ 3.112 *(continued)*

Bureau of Engraving and Printing: Public tours are available between 9:00 a.m. and 2:00 p.m. on weekdays, with extended summer hours. Tickets are required March–August, and may be picked up beginning at 8:00 a.m. *(See <http://moneyfactory.gov>.)*

Holocaust Museum: First-come, first-served passes are distributed at 10:00 a.m. for tours that day. *(See <www.ushmm.org>.)*

John F. Kennedy Center for the Performing Arts: Tours are available weekdays 10:00 a.m.– 5:00 p.m., and Saturdays and Sundays 10:00 a.m.–1:00 p.m. *(See <www.kennedy-center.org/visitor/ tours.html>.)*

Library of Congress: Public tours on Monday through Friday occur at 10:30 and 11:30 a.m., and 1:30, 2:30, and 3:30 p.m. There is no 3:30 p.m. tour on Saturday, and buildings are closed Sundays and federal holidays. Reserved group tours can be arranged. *(See <www.loc.gov/visit>.)*

Mount Vernon: A 45-minute guided tour of the gardens is offered at 8:45 a.m. daily, after which guests may take a self-guided tour of the mansion. Admission is charged. *(See <www.mountvernon. org>.)*

Smithsonian Institution: Comprising 13 museums and the National Zoo in the Washington, DC, area, the Smithsonian has something to offer nearly every visitor. Check the Smithsonian's web site for hours and locations, *<www.si.edu>*.

State Department: The Diplomatic Receptions Rooms are available for 45-minute guided tours weekdays 9:30 and 10:30 a.m. and 2:45 p.m. *(See <http://receptiontours.state.gov>.)*

Supreme Court: Public-tour lectures are available every hour on the half-hour, on weekdays from 9:30 a.m. to 3:30 p.m. when the Court is not in session. The Court can be observed in session from 10:00 a.m. to noon and 1:00 p.m. to 3:00 p.m. during the days cases are being heard. Seats are available on a first-come basis. *(See <www.supremecourtus.gov/visiting/visiting.html>.)*

Treasury Department: One-hour building tours are available Saturdays at 9:00, 9:45, 10:30, and 11:15 a.m. Reservations must be made through the office of a member of Congress. *(See <www. ustreas.gov/offices/management/curator/tours.shtml>.)*

United States Marine Corps Evening Parade: Friday evenings in summer at 8:00 p.m. at the Marine Barracks, Eighth and Eye Streets SE. *(See <www.mbw.usmc.mil/parades.asp>.)*

Washington National Cathedral: Ninety-minute tours are available Mondays and Wednesdays at 9:15 a.m. *(See <www.cathedral.org/cathedral>.)*

White House: Public tours for groups of ten or more must be requested through the office of a member of Congress. Some members attempt to make larger groups to accommodate constituents with groups of under 10 individuals. *(See <www.whitehouse.gov/history/tours>.)*

For links to the web sites of these entities and other memorials, monuments, and museums in Washington, DC, see TheCapitol.Net's web site, *<www.TheCapitol.Net>*, and click on *Visiting Washington, DC.*

§ 3.21

Member's Web Site

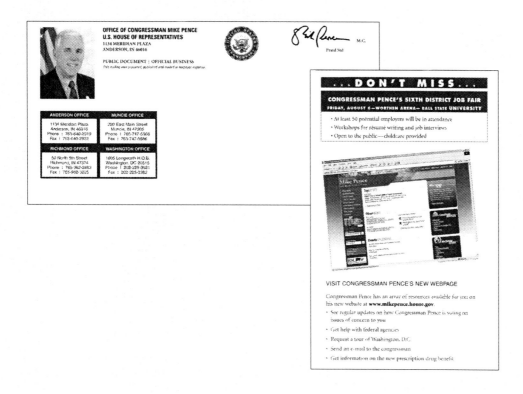

essarily make it their responsibility to report on a member's every word and deed, but they do report a great deal and tend to publicize missteps.

Just as the media seek out members, members reach out to the media. Members generate press coverage or attention by sending out press releases and audio and video recordings. Members keep the local press—and, in turn, their constituents—informed about legislative and representational accomplishments. Some members have even tried their hand at "journalism" by hosting their own local cable television shows or by contributing regular "columns" to local newspapers. Members' web sites and web logs, or blogs, are becoming more sophisticated in their outreach to the media and constituents. *(See § 3.21, Member's Web Site.)*

Today more than 5,000 reporters and broadcast technicians hold credentials in the House and Senate press galleries. They represent daily and other newspapers, news services, periodicals, newsletters, radio, television, and new forms of media. *(See § 3.22, Media Galleries.)*

In response to both a large media presence and members' own needs to generate press coverage, every member employs a press assistant, often a former journalist. A press assistant handles contacts with reporters, brings together journalists and the member or appropriate staff for a comment, and arranges formal interviews between the member and one or more

Media Galleries

A Standing Committee of Correspondents, a panel of journalists elected by their peers, issues credentials for admittance to the media galleries.

House Media Galleries

A portion of the observation galleries in the chamber is reserved for use by reporters. Reporters are also provided adjacent office space.

House Press Gallery provides access and information to the daily newspaper and news service press corps, and assists members and staff with press-related inquiries and events. The press gallery also maintains a filing center for information on daily committee and chamber meetings, and serves as a distribution point for congressional press releases. Located in H-315 of the Capitol; *<www.house.gov/daily/hpg.htm>*.

Periodical Press Gallery serves magazine, newsletter, and online reporters as a press release distribution point, information resource, and work area. Located in H-304 of the Capitol; *<http://periodical.house.gov>*.

Radio-Television Correspondents Gallery facilitates electronic media coverage of the House. The gallery provides facilities, information, and services to broadcasters and members of the House. Located in H-321 of the Capitol; *<http://radiotv.house.gov>*.

Senate Media Galleries

A portion of the observation galleries in the chamber is reserved for use by reporters. Reporters are also provided adjacent office space.

Senate Press Gallery, in addition to its services for the daily newspaper and news service press corps, handles accreditation for daily newspapers and news services to cover both the House and Senate. Located in S-316 of the Capitol; *<www.senate.gov/galleries/daily>*.

Senate Periodical Press Gallery serves magazine, newsletter, and online reporters as a press release distribution point, information resource, and work area. Located in S-320 of the Capitol; *<www.senate.gov/galleries/pdcl>*.

Senate Press Photographers Gallery serves photographers covering Capitol Hill. Located in S-317 of the Capitol; *<www.senate.gov/galleries/photo>*.

Senate Radio and Television Gallery facilitates electronic media coverage of the Senate. Located in S-325 of the Capitol; *<www.senate.gov/galleries/radiotv>*.

journalists. Appearances on "Sunday talk shows" are also scheduled to maximize a member's visibility. Typically, at least twenty-five press releases and other communications, such as audio recordings, are generated every month by a member's office. (See § 3.23, Sample Senate Press Release.)

Most members maintain close ties with newspapers and broadcast stations in their home districts or states. Many deal regularly with local reporters, developing close relationships that

§3.23

Sample Senate Press Release

United States Senator
JIM BUNNING

McCONNELL AND BUNNING PUSH FOR INVESTIGATION INTO ALLEGED EUROPEAN DUMPING OF ENRICHED URANIUM

WASHINGTON, D.C.
DECEMBER 19, 2000 – Kentucky's two U.S. Senators, Mitch McConnell and Jim Bunning today called on the U.S. Department of Commerce to conduct an investigation into allegations that overseas suppliers of enriched uranium are causing significant damage to the U.S. industry by driving down the price of enriched uranium through unfair trade practices, known as "dumping".

In a letter to Commerce Secretary Norm Mineta, Senators McConnell and Bunning, along with Congressmen Ed Whitfield (R-KY) and Ted Strickland (D-OH), pointed out that the United States Enrichment Corporation (USEC), the U.S.'s sole source of enriched uranium, supplies 70% of the U.S. nuclear power plant market. Earlier in December, USEC filed a petition with the Department of Commerce indicating that foreign dumping was inflicting serious damage to the U.S. uranium enrichment industry.

"If foreign suppliers are using unfair trade practices to drive USEC out of business, they must be stopped," said Bunning. "As a nation, we currently receive 20% of our power from nuclear energy sources. If USEC stops producing enriched uranium, we will be forced to look to foreign producers in order to keep our nuclear plants running. At a time when the United States already maintains an unhealthy dependence on foreign oil, it would be a disaster to also become reliant on foreign sources for our enriched uranium."

"The Paducah Plant has always been a top priority for me," said McConnell. "I call on the Administration to take USEC's complaint seriously, and undertake an investigation into trading practices that may further damage the domestic enrichment industry and its workforce."

The United States Enrichment Corporation, Inc., headquartered in Bethesda, MD currently operates the nation's only uranium enrichment facilities, one in Paducah, KY and the other Piketon, OH. In June of 2000, USEC announced that it would be closing the Piketon facility by July, 2001.

###

may help them sway local coverage. Senators and party or committee leaders in both houses deal with the national media as well.

The relationship between members and the press can be symbiotic. Journalists need members and their staffs to obtain information and report stories. Members, in turn, want the media to amplify their points of view, party goals, and criticisms of other members' or the administration's policy initiatives and perspectives. For example, the Senate Radio-Television

Media Guidance for a Major Committee Hearing

MEDIA GUIDELINES FOR THE NOMINATION HEARING OF SAMUEL A. ALITO, JR., OF NEW JERSEY, TO BE AN ASSOCIATE JUSTICE OF THE SUPREME COURT OF THE UNITED STATES

WHO: Members of the Media: Reporters, Photographers, and Producers

WHAT: Media Access and Accreditation for the Supreme Court Nomination Hearing of Samuel A. Alito, Jr.

WHEN: Week of January 9, 2006

WHERE: Hart Room 216

NOTE: Members of the Media planning to cover the hearing MUST PRE-REGISTER with the United States Senate Press and Media Galleries in order to obtain the proper access and accreditation for the hearing.

Due to a LIMITED amount of seats in the hearing room, Members of the Media MUST RESERVE A SEAT with the United States Senate Press and Media Galleries.

CONTACT INFORMATION:

Accreditation and pre-registration for Members of the Media interested in covering the Supreme Court Nomination Hearing are being coordinated by the United States Senate Press and Media Galleries. Their contact information is as follows:

Daily Press Gallery: (202) 224-0241
Periodical Press Gallery: (202) 224-0265
Press Photographer's Gallery: (202) 224-6548
Radio Television Gallery: (202) 224-6421

For more information on and the guidelines of the United States Senate Press and Media Galleries, please go to: http://www.senate.gov/galleries

For general information regarding the Supreme Court Nomination Hearing please contact the Senate Committee on the Judiciary at (202) 224-5225 or visit our website at: http://www.judiciary.senate.gov

FREQUENTLY ASKED QUESTIONS:

I am a reporter, producer, or photographer interested in covering the hearing. How do I obtain the appropriate accreditation to gain access into the hearing room?

Members of the Media planning to cover the hearing MUST PRE-REGISTER with the United States Senate Press and Media Galleries. In addition to pre-registration, individuals will need a "hard" credential in order to obtain access to the hearing room.

Due to a LIMITED amount of seats in the hearing room, Members of the Media MUST RESERVE A SEAT with the United States Senate Press and Media Galleries.

I am a reporter from out of town or a foreign journalist that does not have a "hard" credential. How do I obtain the appropriate "hard" credential for the hearing?

Members of the Media that meet the appropriate guidelines and rules for obtaining a "hard" credential should contact their respective Gallery. This should be done in advance of the hearing to allow for the adequate time required to obtain a "hard" credential.

I am doing a documentary or I am an independent photographer interested in getting still photos or video coverage of the hearing. How do I obtain access to the hearing?

Only Members of the Media that have obtained the appropriate "hard" credential and have pre-registered with the United States Senate Press and Media Galleries will be allowed access to the hearing.

Video coverage for the hearing is being coordinated by the Radio/Television Gallery. Still photography for the hearing is being coordinated by the Senate Press Photographer's Gallery. In order to obtain access, Members of the Media should contact their respective Gallery.

How early should I get to the hearing and where should I go?

Members of the Media are encouraged to arrive at the hearing far in advance of the scheduled start time. Access into the hearing room will be available for Members of the Media with a "reserved" space and appropriate credential approximately 1 hour before the hearings are scheduled to begin.

What will I be able to bring into the hearing room?

Due to the limited amount of space available in the hearing room, Members of the Media are not allowed to bring articles such as jackets, briefcases, and other cumbersome materials into the hearing room. Members of the Media will be allowed to bring a laptop computer into the hearing room (wireless access will be available). Members of the Media will also be allowed the use of a voice recorder in the hearing. ONLY still photographers will be allowed the use of cameras in the hearing room. All communication devices must be in the off or silent mode. Use of cell phones is strictly prohibited, except by authorized staff. Failure to comply with this rule could result in removal from the hearing.

What type of resources will be available to Members of the Media at the hearing?

The Judiciary Committee will provide a filing center for Members of the Media to use throughout the hearing. To reserve a space in the filing center, Members of the Media must reserve a space with their respective Gallery. The filing center will have desk space, televisions, and phones available for use.

The filing center is located in:
- Hart SH30X (Hart 216 hearing room, upper level)

The filing center will become operational on January 9, 2006 at 10:00 AM.

There are no longer any reserved spaces available for Members of the Media in the hearing room. How do I cover the hearing?

Members of the Media MUST RESERVE A SEAT with the United States Senate Press and Media Galleries. In the event that all reserved space is used, Members of the Media will be required to cover the hearings from the filing center that is provided.

NOTE: Due to safety concerns, standing will NOT be allowed in the hearing room. Failure to follow this rule could result in removal from the hearing.

How will information such as Senators' statements and relevant documents be distributed to Members of the Media?

Only Senators' statements and relevant documents will be allowed for distribution in the hearing room. Distribution will be performed by the Judiciary Committee staff. In addition, copies of relevant materials will be provided at the filing centers.

I am not a Member of the Media, but my organization or group would like to distribute informational materials to Members of the Media covering the hearing. Where would I be able do to that?

Outside organizations and groups will NOT be allowed to distribute information inside the hearing room. A table will be provided outside the filing center for any organization or group wishing to distribute materials at the hearing.

Gallery reported for July 2000 that sixty-nine broadcast organizations had covered eighteen Senate hearings; that Senators had come to the gallery fifty-one times for seventy-four television and twenty-eight radio interviews; that ten live television appearances occurred in the gallery; and that six news conferences were conducted before forty-seven broadcast organizations. *(See § 3.24, Media Guidance for a Major Committee Hearing.)*

Members are wary, however, of contributing a basis to a story suggesting that the member has "gone Washington" and forgotten where he or she came from.

In addition, the media and members need each other to learn what is happening in the executive branch. The media draw on congressional hearings, interviews with members, and other Capitol Hill sources to get leads or gain insights into the executive. Members of Congress and their staffs sometimes first learn of executive initiatives or scandals from the media. In the United States, the branches of government often communicate with each other through the media as well as by official or formal routes.

Televised Coverage of Congressional Proceedings

Regular televised sessions of House proceedings began in 1979; televising of the Senate began in 1986. Routine coverage of committee sessions began in the 1980s, and today many committee meetings are webcast. Televised proceedings have made the House and Senate and the individual members more visible to constituents and the media. All members can be seen by constituents back home and by a national audience while they address issues on the floor of the House or Senate.

Members are conscious of how their speeches on the floor are received by viewers and of the news potential of televised speeches and debate. They have also become more sophisticated about television news schedules. *One-minute speeches* at the beginning of a House session, *morning business speeches* during a Senate session, and follow-up media activities are often timed to coordinate with press deadlines or the early evening television news. The parties, groups of members, and even individual members employ a communications strategy in daily sessions in each chamber, on party priorities, and for members' use on weekends and during recesses. For example, party "theme teams" sometimes coordinate House one-minute speeches and communications guidance for recesses.

Public controversy and congressional investigations frequently capture the attention of the national press and generate a national audience. For example, many Americans were riveted by the Clarence Thomas/Anita Hill hearings. Television broadcast the hearings, in whole or in part, over and over. Citizens were able to see and hear for themselves what the nominee and his accuser had to say. Over the past few years, problems with the savings and loan industry and the House bank, as well as various ethics scandals, reverberated in the media for months or weeks. Coverage of President Clinton's House impeachment and Senate trial dominated all forms of media. The clever staging of Senate hearings and compelling stories of citizens told there about "abuses" by the Internal Revenue Service led directly to passage of IRS reform legislation. President George W. Bush's nomination of former Senator John Ashcroft was on trial in the court of public opinion as he was subjected to Senate committee deliberations. During spring training in 2005, the House held hearings on steroid use in Major League Baseball that generated blanket media coverage, including live coverage by television and cable networks beyond C-SPAN. Witnesses included not only the commissioner of baseball but several current and former star players. These events were covered by the print media, but television coverage of Congress and its committees in session sustained public interest.

The increase in "celebrity witnesses" at hearings has furthered the public's interest in Congress and fostered greater media coverage. For example, hearings on health-related issues featuring citizens with specific diseases or conditions have not attracted the same media attention or public interest as the hearing featuring actor Michael J. Fox discussing his fight with Parkinson's disease or actress Mary Tyler Moore addressing diabetes. While the State Department has testified repeatedly on China issues, with limited or no media coverage, actor Richard Gere attracted intense media interest when he testified on Tibet. (*See § 8.44, Celebrity Witnesses.*)

§ 3.30 Executive-Branch Pressure

Congress and the executive must work together to achieve their respective policy goals. Congress makes laws, including appropriations laws, with the approval of the president. The executive branch then carries out those laws. One branch generally cannot achieve its policy goals without the other branch. Yet, the two branches view each other warily across an institutional divide.

A president, Cabinet secretary, or regulatory agency official might view Congress and its members as meddlesome, ignorant, small-minded, parochial, or in any other number of unflattering terms. The president or member of the administration might also envy the ability of Congress to require the executive's attention, compliance, and, in some circumstances, even obeisance. Executive officials often have difficulty dealing with the decentralization, collegiality, partisanship, tit-for-tat, and relative equality within Congress. It is a dismaying thought to them that no one is really in charge and there is no set schedule. An administration official might also feel unduly constrained by a "Captain, may I?" relationship with Congress, especially with particular members of Congress.

Members of Congress, for their part, might view the president, his appointees, and federal bureaucrats as arrogant, unrealistic, out-of-touch, rigid, or in any other number of unflattering terms. A member of Congress might also envy the ability of the president to speak on behalf of the executive branch—and even, on occasion, the American people—and of a Cabinet secretary or head of an agency to speak on behalf of a department or agency. A member might enviously perceive the discretion and command of resources at the disposal of the president and his appointees, and wish to have the kind of power that the discretion and resources represent. A member of Congress might also want someday to be president, perhaps because

Members of Congress Who Served as President

Although only one sitting representative, James A. Garfield, has been elected to the presidency, many presidents have served in the House. Although senators are often thought of as potential presidential candidates, only two have been elected to the White House while serving in the Senate, Warren G. Harding and John F. Kennedy. John Quincy Adams and Andrew Johnson were the only presidents to serve in Congress after serving as president. Adams served in the House from 1831 to 1848, Johnson served in the Senate in 1875. A number of sitting or former senators and representatives have been candidates or party nominees.

In addition, several early presidents served in the Continental Congress: George Washington (1774–1775); John Adams (1774–1778); Thomas Jefferson (1775, 1776, 1783–1784); James Madison (1780–1783, 1787–1788); and James Monroe (1783–1786).

Name	Years in House	Years in Senate	Years as President
James Madison	1789–1797		1809–1817
James Monroe		1790–1794	1817–1825
John Quincy Adams	1831–1848	1803–1808	1825–1829
Andrew Jackson	1796–1797	1797–1798; 1823–1825	1829–1837
Martin Van Buren		1821–1828	1837–1841
William Henry Harrison	1799–1800,[1] 1816–1819	1825–1828	1841
John Tyler	1817–1821	1827–1836	1841–1845
James K. Polk	1825–1839[2]		1845–1849
Millard Fillmore	1833–1835, 1837–1843		1850–1853
Franklin Pierce	1833–1837	1837–1842	1853–1857
James Buchanan	1821–1831	1834–1845	1857–1861
Abraham Lincoln	1847–1849		1861–1865
Andrew Johnson	1843–1853	1857–1862; 1875	1865–1869
Rutherford B. Hayes	1865–1867		1877–1881
James A. Garfield	1863–1880		1881
Benjamin Harrison		1881–1887	1889–1893
William McKinley	1877–1883; 1885–1891		1897–1901
Warren G. Harding		1915–1921	1921–1923
Harry S. Truman		1935–1945[3]	1945–1953
John F. Kennedy	1947–1953	1953–1960	1961–1963
Lyndon B. Johnson	1937–1949	1949–1961[4]	1963–1969
Richard M. Nixon	1947–1950	1951–1953	1969–1974
Gerald R. Ford	1949–1973[5]		1974–1977
George H. W. Bush	1967–1971		1989–1993

1. Delegate to U.S. Congress.
2. Speaker (1835–1839).
3. Elected vice president in 1944.
4. Senate Democratic leader (1953–1961); elected vice president in 1960.
5. House Republican leader (1965–1973); appointed vice president in 1973.

§ 3.32

Former Members of Congress Appointed by President Bush to Executive Positions

As noted in § 3.33 *(White House Legislative Affairs)*, the president maintains a legislative liaison office to work with Congress. Many of the staff in that office worked in congressional offices before their executive-branch service. In addition to liaison staff, the president often appoints former members of Congress to executive-branch positions—in the Cabinet, as ambassadors, and in other executive positions. Former members have also served as chief of staff to the president.

Many of the members appointed to executive-branch positions are from the same party as the president. They may have retired or lost reelection bids; they might also be sitting members at the time of their appointment. Their years of congressional service make them particularly knowledgeable about the legislative process. They are also effective negotiators with their former colleagues, an important skill for a president to have at his disposal. Similarly, presidents without congressional service themselves might select members of Congress as their running mates.

For example, President George W. Bush selected Richard B. Cheney, a former House member (1979–1989), as his vice-president. He selected four former members of Congress to serve in his first-term Cabinet; one continued to serve early in his second-term Cabinet. The Senate confirmed Bush's nominations of Spencer Abraham (Senate, 1995–2001) as secretary of energy; John Ashcroft (Senate, 1995–2001) as attorney general; Norman Y. Mineta (House, 1975–1995) as secretary of transportation; and Tom Ridge (House, 1983–1995) as secretary of homeland security. In his second term, Bush nominated former Senator Dirk Kempthorne (1993–1999) to serve as secretary of the interior. He also chose Representative Rob Portman (1993–2005) to serve as the U.S. trade representative and later nominated him as director of the Office of Management and Budget (OMB). Bush has also selected current and former members and congressional staff for Cabinet-level, subcabinet, and other positions.

of these perceptions about the executive. The member might be confident of his or her ability to do a better job than the incumbent and to have learned from past presidents' mistakes. *(See § 3.31, Members of Congress Who Served as President.)*

In the end, the two branches must and do work together. Neither branch wants the electorate to see an utter stalemate unresponsive to its needs and desires. If the electorate is sufficiently dissatisfied with relations between Congress and the president, it can express that dissatisfaction at the polls. In the words of President Lyndon Johnson, a master of legislative leadership as Senate majority leader and a master of legislative relations as president, "Without constant attention from the administration, most legislation moves through the congressional process at the speed of a glacier." (Lyndon Johnson, *The Vantage Point* (New York: Holt, Rinehart and Winston, 1971), p. 448.)

The president needs majorities in Congress to create a legacy approximating his goals. There is only so much that a president can achieve through speech making, executive orders, congressionally delegated authority, regulatory changes, lawsuits, foreign-policy initiatives, and other activities. To govern, a president needs Congress to make laws, including appropri-

§ 3.33

White House Legislative Affairs

Every president since Dwight Eisenhower has maintained a full-time legislative liaison officer. Organized as an Office of Legislative Affairs, this staff is an important component of the executive office of the president.

As the eyes and ears of the White House, the legislative affairs staff read how members may respond to key presidential initiatives and report back to the White House. As the time for floor votes approaches, this intelligence might guide the White House in determining if a Cabinet official, the vice president, or the president himself needs to be involved in helping to sway any individual members to the president's position. Legislative liaison staff can often be seen outside the party cloakrooms during debates and votes that are particularly important to the president.

By dispensing personal gestures and presidential invitations, the White House lobbying team can have a strong influence with members of Congress. An invitation to a state dinner for a visiting head of state or a seat on Air Force One on an official trip is perceived as very important by most members and as quite persuasive by the White House.

Because knowing the legislative players—both members and staff—is so important, the White House office is often staffed by people who have had experience working on Capitol Hill. The positions in the office in early 2007 were as follows:

- assistant to the president and director of legislative affairs
- special assistant to the assistant to the president for legislative affairs
- deputy assistant to the president for legislative affairs
- deputy assistant to the president for legislative affairs—Senate
- four special assistants to the president for legislative affairs—Senate
- deputy assistant to the president for legislative affairs—House
- five special assistants to the president for legislative affairs—House

---

ations laws. He needs to obtain the Senate's consent on nominations and treaties, and to consult the congressional leadership, specific committees, and appropriate members of Congress on matters in the national interest.

To facilitate a relationship with Congress, a president often chooses former members of Congress to serve in the administration, for the same reasons that former members are sought by Washington lobbying entities, law firms, and associations. Former members have better access to sitting members of Congress and a better understanding of the institution. *(See § 3.32, Former Members of Congress Appointed by President Bush to Executive Positions.)* Presidents also sometimes select sitting members for key administration positions, as President George W. Bush did when he selected Representative Rob Portman, R-OH, in 2005 to serve as the U.S. trade representative and later to serve as director of the Office of Management and Budget (OMB). The White House also maintains a top-notch congressional affairs office, often populated by former congressional staff and by individuals successful in party organizations or private lobbying operations. *(See § 3.33, White House Legislative Affairs.)* Presidents also develop close friendships with some members of each chamber, who look out for a president's interests and provide honest advice on congressional politics.

Departments and agencies maintain large congressional affairs operations under a senior official, such as an assistant secretary for legislative and public affairs in a department. An entity such as the Department of State, Department of the Army, or the Social Security Administration might handle tens of thousands of congressional inquiries a year. Those inquiries are in addition to a secretary's, agency head's, or other departmental or agency official's attendance at hearings, and phone calls and meetings with members and staff. *(See § 5.170, Congressional Liaison Offices.)*

For their part, individual members of Congress and groups of members, such as each party's leadership in each chamber, want the president to solicit their views and be solicitous of their concerns. They want to be associated with the importance and symbolism of the presidency and to share in the perquisites—small-group or private meetings with the president, phone calls from him, invitations to state dinners, sharing the dais with the president at events in their districts or states, and assistance in fund-raising if the president is of the same party. *(See § 3.34, Presidential Support for His Party's Members.)* In other words, members wish to be courted by the president and be treated like the successful politicians they are in their districts or states and in the House or Senate. But, a member of Congress also wants to be able to say "no" to the president or to keep a distance from him if the administration pursues a course on some issue that is unpopular in the representative's district or senator's state.

Members of Congress expect attention from Cabinet secretaries and agency heads and their representatives whose departments, agencies, and programs the members deal with in committees. Members want their input to departments and agencies to be solicited and accommodated. They want to know in advance about initiatives in departments and agencies that affect their districts and states or the issues and legislation that most concern them. Members of Congress want to know about grants, contracts, and other benefits given or denied to home-state beneficiaries before the media and the potential beneficiaries find out. They expect their communications to departments and agencies to be treated expeditiously, seriously, and responsively.

President's Advantages in Relations with Congress

In his relations with Congress, the president has many advantages. Some of the following aspects of being president contribute to those advantages and enable the president to wield influence with Congress.

Chief Executive and Commander in Chief. As the head of the executive branch, the president commands a cadre of several thousand political loyalists at the top layers of executive departments and agencies. A president uses his power of appointment to reward his party as well as to ensure, within the law, that departments and agencies will support his political goals, develop and carry out policies compatible with those goals, and defend the presi-

§ 3.34

Presidential Support for His Party's Members

"...I very much admire the work that Congresswoman Jane Harman has done in the United States Congress. She is, I think, the best of a new breed of political leaders who want to see our country go beyond the old division of stale, partisan, political debates...to find creative ways for government to work with you...to create better jobs and a brighter future for all Americans."

President Bill Clinton
Northridge, CA
March 8, 1996

Please Join

Former Congresswoman Jane Harman
(CA-36)
and Special Guest

President Bill Clinton

at a reception to help regain her seat in the
U.S. House of Representatives

Thursday, February 3, 2000
6:30-8:30 p.m.

at the home of
The Honorable Molly Raiser
3318 O Street N.W.
Washington, D.C.

RSVP-Kimball or Elizabeth at (202)543-9700
Paid for and Authorized by Friends of Jane Harman

dent's and administration's programs on Capitol Hill. (*See § 10.80, Congress and the Executive: Appointments.*)

The president has constitutional powers to establish administration policy. He can issue executive orders, and use the State of the Union address, legislative proposals, and the veto or threat of a veto to exercise great influence over the congressional agenda. In numerous statutes, Congress has also granted discretion to the president and to departmental and agency officials. That discretion can be exploited to make a difference in how the administration approaches regulations, grants, and other activities; consider, for example, the different approach of regulations that one might expect from Democratic and Republican administrations.

Discretion also carries over into how an administration might approach enforcement of laws. What view does the administration take of antitrust? Of white-collar crime? Of civil rights? How do administration views affect inspection programs under certain laws? How will those views affect enforcement actions? What lawsuits will be filed? What will the administration argue in amicus briefs? The discretion that Congress grants the executive may lead to tensions between the two branches, between the administration and members of the other party in Congress, or between the administration and a particular region's representatives and senators. Hearings, legislation, and a public war of words might result from conflicting views between Congress and the executive.

The president also seeks to make an impact on the judiciary that will outlive his administration through his nominations to all levels of federal courts. *(See § 10.121, Nominations to Federal Courts.)*

In his roles as commander in chief and leader of American foreign policy, the president is accorded broader discretion by Congress than is generally conferred or allowed in other policy fields. He is at the top of the civilian leadership of the military under the Constitution. His foreign-policy authority emanates from his treaty-making power and his appointment of ambassadors and top military officials under the Constitution. Congress exercises its powers in defense and foreign policy in numerous ways; congressional exercise of power limits and directs the president. Nonetheless, in practical terms, the president is the leader of the military, most pointedly in immediate decisions on committing troops, and is the leader of foreign policy in negotiating treaties and executive agreements and in managing foreign relations. *(See §§ 10.130–10.170, Congress and Foreign Policy.)*

One Voice. Congress is usually a cacophony of 540 members speaking as senators or representatives from specific states, districts, and other jurisdictions. Members of Congress act in their roles as leaders of their chambers, congressional parties, committees, or subcommittees. Members act as advocates for specific legislation, issues, and causes. In contrast, there is one president, who is elected by the nation as a whole. When he speaks, he speaks authoritatively and unquestionably for the executive branch. His appointees in the departments and agencies echo or amplify his views.

The president controls the form and timing of his communications. If he chooses to make a speech or hold a news conference, it is likely to be broadcast, allowing anyone wishing to do so to learn directly from the president what he wants for America and what he thinks about issues of the day. Through the Cabinet and other political appointees, the Office of Management and Budget, the Executive Office of the President, and other entities, the president controls policymaking in the executive branch and communication of policy to Congress and the public. If he wishes to talk informally with a member of Congress, he might call the member or invite him or her to the White House for a personal meeting.

In the annual State of the Union address to Congress in late January, the president describes many of his legislative and budget priorities, explains some of the executive initiatives he is taking based on his authority as president, and makes a political appeal to Congress and the public. Subsequently, the president makes other speeches, sends other communica-

§ 3.35

State of the Union Address

In contemporary practice, the president appears before a joint session of Congress in late January to deliver a speech popularly referred to as the State of the Union address or message, laying out his legislative program, explaining his policies on the major issues of the time, and exhorting Congress to take specific actions in support of his vision and program. The address emanates from a constitutional provision *(art. II, sec. 3, cl. 1)*: "He [the president] shall from time to time give to the Congress Information on the State of the Union, and recommend to their Consideration such measures as he shall judge necessary and expedient[.]"

After consultation with the White House, the House and Senate pass a concurrent resolution setting a day and time for a joint session "for receiving such communication as the President of the United States shall be pleased to make to them." When the day arrives, a special security sweep is made of the Capitol, and other security measures are triggered. The senators are escorted to the House chamber by the Senate sergeant at arms. Other dignitaries are also seated in the chamber— former members, justices of the Supreme Court, the joint chiefs of staff, Cabinet secretaries and Cabinet-rank officials, and ambassadors to the United States. Traditionally, one Cabinet secretary and several members of Congress, representing both parties, do not attend the joint session, to ensure succession should a catastrophe happen at the Capitol while the president is there. The first lady and guests of the president are allocated seats in the gallery. Other gallery guests must obtain tickets.

The Speaker presides over the joint session, but shares the dais with the vice president in his role as president of the Senate. A group of senators and representatives that was previously selected escorts the president into the chamber. The president is announced first at the House door by the House sergeant at arms and then again by the Speaker after the president takes his place on the dais. The group of members also escorts the president out of the chamber after he completes his address.

President Truman's 1947 address was the first to be televised. President Johnson was the first to make his address during prime-time television viewing hours, recognizing the opportunity to speak to the nation that the event presented. A formal opposing-party response was first made in 1966. The State of the Union address has now become an important media event, and both parties use it to publicize their positions on issues covered or not covered in the address.

In 2002, Democrats began formally challenging President Bush's program the day before his address. Appearing at the National Press Club in Washington, DC, then-Senate Minority Leader Tom Daschle and House Minority Leader Nancy Pelosi criticized the president's tax-cut proposals and spending policies. Democrats continued to expound their messages the day of the State of the Union address, and later that evening in the opposing-party response to the address by Washington Governor Gary Locke. At the same time, the president's press secretary, Republican members of Congress, administration officials, and Republican Party organizations transmitted their own messages of support for the president's proposals and policies. These practices have continued.

Immediately following a State of the Union address, members of Congress meet the press in National Statuary Hall to put their "spin" on it. The day after the State of the Union address, the president might travel to several states to publicize his program and to build public support for his proposals.

In years in which a new president takes office, the outgoing president might choose not to deliver an address in person, or might choose to make a televised address at a place other than the Capitol, and the incoming president might choose to make a more focused address several months into office to seek action by Congress on a specific presidential initiative.

tions to Congress, and offers draft legislation or outlines of legislation that represent his positions. Again, executive-branch officials work in concert to promote the president's legislative and budget program in Congress and to explain it to the media and the public. *(See § 3.35, State of the Union Address.)*

In another of his quasi-legislative roles, the president sets the agenda for Congress. Each year in late January or early February, the president transmits the executive budget to Congress. Although Congress needs to pass appropriations and other legislation to implement the federal budget, it begins from the president's budget, which is the culmination of thousands of budget decisions made in various executive agencies over the course of eighteen months or more. In addition, executive-branch officials support the president's recommendations in their dealings with Congress. *(See Chapter Nine, Legislating in Congress: Federal Budget Process.)*

The president can also use bill-signing ceremonies to trumpet legislative achievements, even when legislation originated in Congress or was primarily fashioned by it. Moreover, he can use the threat of a veto or, if a measure he disapproves of is sent to him, a veto message, to make Congress aware of how strongly he holds a position. *(See § 8.290, Presidential Action on Enacted Measures.)*

Commanding Public Attention. A presidential appearance or utterance is nearly always newsworthy. If the president wants to make an address to the nation or hold a press conference, it will be broadcast live. Reporters are present at the White House, and a large entourage of reporters accompanies the president wherever he goes. Daily press briefings and later, follow-up answers to reporters' questions keep the president's press office busy.

When the president travels, his appearance in a city or other location is always newsworthy in that area, and throngs of people turn out to see his motorcade or hear a public address. In a time of crisis or catastrophe, people want to know what the president thinks or will do or will request of Congress. The presidency is a highly symbolic office, as well as the nation's most important and powerful office.

Presidents often use their automatic newsworthiness for political advantage. A president might address the nation in a prime-time televised appearance on the eve of a crucial vote in Congress, knowing that this will likely motivate thousands of people to contact their members of Congress. He might use a well-publicized veto threat to influence congressional deliberations, or travel to a school, factory, impoverished neighborhood, or place of scenic beauty or historical significance to give graphic illustration to a policy initiative. The president attempts to reach and influence Congress by persuading the electorate to support his views and to act on that support, such as by communicating with their members of Congress.

Cabinet secretaries and heads of important agencies like the Environmental Protection Agency also command media attention. They are not as automatically newsworthy as the president, but they communicate the president's and administration's policies and views to the media and the public. Their appearances in Washington and around the country at public events, conventions, conferences, and other forums are carefully monitored by the national and trade press for news. Knowledge of Cabinet secretaries' and agency heads' views and actions are of critical importance to congressional committees and individual members.

Presidential Favors. A president has at his disposal a vast array of favors that he can bestow on members of Congress—a weekend invitation to Camp David, a gift of one of the pens used to make one letter in his name in signing a bill, a photo of a member and the president with a personal inscription, a ride on Air Force One to the home district or state or a ride back to Washington, a round of golf, an evening in the presidential box at Washington, DC's Kennedy Center for the Performing Arts, and so on. Representatives and senators suggest names of individuals for presidential appointments. Senators might work closely with the administration on choices for executive departments' and agencies' state directors and on judicial, U.S. attorney, and U.S. marshal appointments in their states.

By granting the president, Cabinet secretaries, agency heads, and other officials discretion in implementing numerous laws, Congress affords the president and his administration the opportunity to make many decisions on how to distribute federal largesse. Presidents use this discretion to recognize loyalty, build support, and withhold favors. Presidents, Cabinet secretaries, and others might also participate in fund-raising for congressional candidates by serving as star attractions at fund-raising events and by other means.

§ 3.40 Judicial-Branch Pressure

As one of the coequal branches of the federal government and possessor of checks and balances vis-à-vis Congress, the judicial branch has a major influence on the work of Congress. In committee, on the House and Senate floors, and on the hustings back home, members of Congress regularly speak about decisions of the courts. They must contend with public reaction to controversial judicial rulings. In the last half century, the impact of judicial rulings on abortion rights, school desegregation and school busing, civil rights, rights of an accused, federalism, separation of powers, public prayer and religious freedom, and flag burning, among other constitutional and statutory issues, has landed squarely on members' legislative and political agendas. What follows is a brief description of some of the ways in which the exercise of judicial power pressures Congress.

Interpretation and Application of Laws

The executive, other governmental bodies, and private entities and citizens, within their roles and rights in society, turn to the courts for the prosecution of crimes, adjudication of civil cases arising from the execution of laws, settlement of disputes, vindication of constitutional and civil rights, and other matters for which there is a judicial remedy. The federal district courts interpret and apply thousands of laws in many more thousands of cases each year. The Supreme Court, an appellate court, disposes of approximately seventy to ninety cases a year with full opinions. Some cases and the interpretation and application of laws to those cases generate controversy, public defense and criticism, and calls for congressional action. An example is described briefly in § 10.123 (*Congressional Response to Court Decisions*), dealing with congressional response to a series of rulings between 1986 and 1991 on employment discrimination under civil-rights statutes.

Interpretation of the Constitution

The courts, along with Congress and the president, are interpreters of the Constitution. Congress's decision to legislate and presidential reasons for signing or vetoing legislation often make reference to constitutional authority. (The House requires committee reports to include, "A statement citing the specific powers granted to Congress in the Constitution to enact the law proposed by the bill or joint resolution." *(Rule XIII, cl. 3(d)(1).)*

The courts are frequently called upon to make constitutional as well as statutory decisions. Although the courts will usually attempt to decide cases by interpreting statutes, they must often interpret the Constitution itself in light of a set of facts, and fashion an appropriate remedy. These constitutional rulings and judicial remedies often generate public controversy. Debate and controversy, for instance, have arisen when courts decided cases involving the following issues:

- application of various parts of the Bill of Rights to state and local investigations of criminal suspects and prosecution of defendants during the 1960s
- school busing to achieve public-school desegregation in the 1970s
- abortion rights, beginning in 1972
- affirmative action and civil rights in the 1980s and 1990s
- religious freedom and federalism beginning in the 1990s
- the "war on terrorism" in the first decade of the new century

In each of these subject areas, there was public pressure for congressional action. Every member of Congress needed to have politically sound positions on these issues.

Judicial Review of Laws

Beginning with *Marbury v. Madison*, 5 U.S. 137 (1803), there has been an understanding that the courts may review statutes for their constitutionality. While courts try to construe statutes so that they are constitutional and even try to avoid dealing with constitutional issues, courts regularly find it necessary to decide the constitutionality of statutes.

In recent years, for example, the courts have sometimes questioned Congress's use of the Commerce Clause as constitutional justification for enacting a law. The Supreme Court struck down the Gun-Free School Zones Act in *United States v. Lopez*, 514 U.S. 549 (1995), finding that Congress had exceeded the powers granted to it through the Commerce Clause of the Constitution. *(See also § 10.190, Congress and Federalism: Exercising Congressional Powers.)*

Of immediate impact on Congress are decisions in recent years related to the separation of powers. For example, the Supreme Court struck down the Line Item Veto Act as a violation of the Constitution's Presentment Clause in *Clinton v. City of New York*, 524 U.S. 417 (1998). The Supreme Court in *Bowsher v. Synar*, 478 U.S. 714 (1986), found a provision of the Gramm-Rudman-Hollings deficit-reduction law unconstitutional because it vested part of the execution of the law in the comptroller general, an officer of Congress. In *INS v. Chadha*, 462 U.S. 919 (1983), the Supreme Court held the one-house congressional veto in the federal immigration law unconstitutional as a violation both of the bicameralism scheme of Article I and the Presentment Clause.

A district court decision in late 2002 might have implications for congressional authority vis-à-vis the executive branch (*Walker v. Cheney*, 230 F. Supp. 2d 51 (D.D.C. 2002)). After the refusal by the vice president to turn over documents sought by the comptroller general, the comptroller general sued, pursuant to statute, to obtain the documents. The district court dismissed the suit, finding the comptroller general did not have a personal or institutional stake in obtaining the documents and that his principal, Congress, had not endorsed his "investigatory and enforcement efforts" so as to indicate its own stake. The decision raised separation of powers questions, including over Congress's delegation of investigative and enforcement authority to the comptroller general.

Nonetheless, for every statute or statutory provision found to be unconstitutional, many more pass judicial review, if constitutionality is even considered by a court.

(See § 7.19, Former Judges Serving in the 110th Congress.)

Chapter Four

Pressures on Congress:
Lobbying and Congressional Ethics

Analysis

4

§ 4.00 Introduction

Along with the campaign-finance laws summarized in § 2.20 (*Election Laws*), lobbying and congressional ethics laws and rules form a regulatory triad circumscribing the behavior of members of Congress. Whether they apply to members of Congress or congressional staff on the one hand or to individuals outside Congress on the other hand, these laws and rules are intended to regulate relationships between the two groups. Therefore, it is just as important for a government affairs professional to be aware of these laws and rules as it is for a member of Congress and congressional staffer.

§ 4.10 Lobbying Pressures

After the federal government, a feature of Washington that most Americans would probably call to mind is *special interests* or, simply, *lobbyists*. Self-representation or representation of an interest predates the Constitution, was anticipated by James Madison in *Federalist No. 10*, and was enshrined in the Bill of Rights as part of the First Amendment set of freedoms.

A lobbyist's role is straightforward—to contact and persuade one or more members of Congress to take a legal action. A lobbyist might seek to obtain or prevent a member's sponsorship of a bill or amendment. A lobbyist might seek a member's support on a vote in committee or on the floor in comprising a majority for or against a measure or amendment, or might request the member phone a committee chair or subcommittee chair to alert the chair regarding a matter before the panel that affects a segment of the population or the economy. A lobbyist might suggest a member contact a department or agency to request that fair consideration be given to a problem, or might request any other number of actions. The first issue for a lobbyist is access.

Citizens and even members of Congress themselves can lose track of the value of lobbying. People may deplore the means often associated with lobbying, such as high-priced meals, entertainment, travel that appears more involved with pleasure than work, and campaign contributions. All are appalled when greed overtakes the judgment of a member of Congress, such as the criminal conduct that led to convictions during the 109th Congress of Representatives Bob Ney and Randy "Duke" Cunningham and the alleged behavior of other Democratic and Republican representatives that has led to ongoing investigations and interim House actions, such as depriving members under an ethical cloud of certain committee assignments. Yet, for lobbyists and the interests they represent, critical matters are at stake. The means of influence that some lobbyists use, which Congress once again was seeking to change through legislation pending early in the 110th Congress, should not be confused with the purposes for which lobbyists work. For a corporation, the business's ability to make a profit, conduct its operations, control costs, or compete may be a major issue. For a labor union, governmental and business decisions might have eroded previously enjoyed worker rights. For a group of individuals sharing similar physical traits, having equal opportunities in all phases of life might still be a goal rather than a reality. For a group of citizens united by an idea, these citizens might see their highest calling as having that idea validated in law. For a small business, not-for-profit organization, or local government, a federal grant or loan may be perceived as the difference between failure and success. For a government contractor, Congress's or the administration's choice of what to buy and how to buy it can affect the company's profitability and competitiveness for years. If lobbyists do not inform members of Congress of the stakes of a decision, the opportunities for members to be well-informed may be limited.

Congress in its constitutional role is a mediating institution, the place in the national government where those competing interests foreseen by Madison could battle without bloodshed over the public interest. A special-interest organization's Washington presence probably includes at least the monitoring of the executive departments, regulatory agencies, and the courts, and, nationally, might include state and even local representation. Some organizations might focus on regulatory policy or court challenges as their principal means of influencing the direction of public policy. But most special-interest organizations concerned with public policy lobby Congress. Access to Congress is open to all individuals and groups.

On nearly any issue, however, the work of the lobbyist today involves more members with more diverse backgrounds. The old concept of the "iron triangle" between committees or subcommittees, executive agencies, and interest groups does not adequately explain lobbying relationships today. More players participate inside and outside of Congress.

Inside, Congress is decentralized, and members look out for their own political needs. Members are well-educated. They are diverse, not only in the numbers of women and minority-group members now serving in Congress but also in their backgrounds, accomplishments, and pre-Congress careers. Among the membership, there is a broad array of knowledge and experience to draw on. Senators represent states that seem to be growing more heterogeneous in their populations each year, providing senators with even more perspectives to be accommodated. Many House districts seem less heterogeneous than whole states as "majority-minority" districts are created, suburban areas are large enough to comprise their own districts distinct from cities, and districts are created that have a strong partisan tilt.

Outside Congress, many groups participate in policymaking. They do direct lobbying, share information with like-minded group members, stimulate grass-roots actions, engage in media strategies, manage political action, and undertake other activities, such as conducting or supporting research and conducting public opinion surveys. At any one time, many groups and lobbying coalitions are at work on the many legislative issues active, or possibly to become active, on Capitol Hill. No one group seems to have a clear shot at attaining any policy goal. Attaining a goal or a compromise, or even trying and falling short, results from multi-faceted lobbying, grass roots, political action, public relations, and media activities orchestrated by very smart, organizationally skilled people, some of whom never go to Capitol Hill and some of whom are not even located in Washington. The media, likewise, comprise well-educated, aggressive reporters and editors who can define issues in ways critical to the success or failure of a lobbying campaign and who quickly blow the whistle on congressional favors to special interests.

The political parties also have realigned so that the Democratic Party in Congress is more consistently the party of "liberal" members and the Republican Party is more consistently the party of "conservative" members. There still are members from along the political spectrum in each party in Congress, but the parties as a whole are more partisan than they have been in much of the last fifty years. Their backers are also more partisan and more vocal on an array of issues, and either become engaged or are invited by party leadership to become engaged in rallying support for or opposition to legislative issues.

Regarding access in its most literal sense, lobbyists, just like everyone, have been affected by security measures on Capitol Hill. Mail and deliveries are diverted to a facility for processing. A lobbyist must make a personal delivery to assure timely delivery of materials. Also, entities such as the American League of Lobbyists and individuals are working to institute easy Capitol access through a mechanism such as a "frequent visitors' access card."

Congress as an Open Institution

Congress is open through its individual members and their Washington and district or state staffs. A constituent, a lobbyist, or an administration representative will be received; virtually no caller is turned away. A staff member will meet with a visitor. Most lobbying contacts with a congressional office are initially and often principally with staff members. A lobbyist can build relationships with members through staff over the course of time, becoming known for the information and other services he or she can provide.

With the high turnover of congressional staff, a lobbyist might even find an advantage in the effort that this change in contacts entails. If a staff member simply changes offices, the lobbyist might end up with a contact in another congressional office. In the office that lost the staff member, the lobbyist might have an advantage in providing continuity for a new staff member. A lobbyist quickly learns that it is important to be gracious to all members of a congressional staff—the lobbyist will want the scheduler as well as the chief of staff and the legislative aides to know him or her.

Lobbyists have another longer-range purpose in getting to know members and staff—identifying potential future lobbyists. Lobbying is an alternative career to working on Capitol Hill, in the executive branch, or elsewhere, and many members and staff decide at some point to parlay their contacts, issue knowledge, and political acumen into lobbying. (In the 110th Congress, the House adopted a rules change intended to prevent representatives from intervening in private entities' hiring decisions so that a decision would be made on a partisan basis, under a threat to take, withhold, or influence an official act.)

Every member of Congress, except one retiring from elective office, needs campaign funds. A portion of nearly every member's campaign fund-raising for reelection is based on contributions from political action committees (PACs). Another substantial percentage is

Grass-roots Training

Nearly all associations engage in some type of rallying or training of an association's members to ensure that members of Congress have heard firsthand about the association's legislative concerns and priorities from one or more constituents—the *grass roots*. Members are attentive to constituents. While they cannot possibly satisfy all the competing legislative desires of each constituent or group of constituents, they will usually do everything they can to appear interested and not alienate anyone. Associations, whether located in Washington, DC, a state capital, or another major city, understand this, and attempt to get the "grass roots" to articulate the association's positions to their own members of Congress.

The American Dietetic Association held a "legislative symposium" in 1997, which included training on grass-roots action. It is representative of many associations' efforts. The following is an excerpt from one of the training materials handed out at the symposium:

How to Play the Grass-roots Game

Do you think of yourself as a political leader? You should! To understand why, first we'll take a look at what political people say about politics.

All Politics Is...

All Politics Is Local

The favorite saying of the late House Speaker Thomas P. "Tip" O'Neill (D-MA) was "all politics is local." Because "all politics is local," the voice of the American Dietetic Association will not be heard without **Grass-roots Communication**.

Here are some applications of the "all politics is local" principle. **All politics is local** means:

- It isn't an issue in Washington until it's an issue back home.
- Constituents can have more influence over elected officials than party leaders do. Even if there is a Republican or Democratic position on an issue, individual elected officials frequently tell their party leaders, "I have to vote my district."
- A local example of how something works will have more influence than a national statistic.
- Elected officials tend to believe that what is best for their district is in the national interest.
- Elected officials measure communications by how many people the communicator knows locally.
- Elected officials measure communications by how much effort is involved locally.
- The oldest rule in politics is flatter the king; in a democracy the voter is king.

All Politics Is Personal

All politics is personal means that in **Grass-roots Communication**:

- The credibility of the messenger determines the credibility of the message.
- A story involving people is more memorable than an argument based on logic.
- Put your personal endorsement behind your message.
- Different people can tell different stories.
- Elected officials sometimes take a position simply because they have been asked.
- Elected officials see every person as a potential voter, contributor, and campaign volunteer.

Continued on page 87

All Politics Is Competitive

Finally, "all politics is competitive." To govern is to choose, and each governmental choice affects some people better than others.

During the health-care reform debate, dozens of organizations involving millions of citizens attempted to make their voices heard.

All politics is competitive means:

- The political process is dominated by people who make an effort to make their voices heard.
- People and groups who have the most to gain or lose by legislation usually make the most effort to influence the process.
- Even a compromise is usually the result of competition.

For information on grass-roots training from TheCapitol.Net, see <*www.CapitolHillDay.com*> and <*www.AdvocacyCampaigns.com*>.

4

based on contributions from people of means inside and outside a district or state, including individual lobbyists in Washington, DC, all of whom have a political interest in supporting a member financially. A lobbyist might have a role in an organization's PAC, engage in other political activities, some of which may directly support one member's or several members' political campaigns, and be a contributor himself or herself. *(See § 2.20, Election Laws.)*

A lobbyist's contribution to a member's campaign fund, or a contribution by the lobbyist's employer's or client's PAC, is not a claim to the member's allegiance. The breadth of individuals and PACs that contribute to a winning campaign reduces the influence of any one contributor. It can be a means of obtaining access and a hearing from the member on a matter of concern to a lobbyist. Contributions are closely related to a member's position in Congress. The committees on which the member serves will generate additional contributions from certain PACs and individual contributors with interests before those committees. Members generally in accord with a PAC's or individual contributor's positions might receive relatively more contributions.

Congress is also open to lobbyists through individual member's constituents. Members are attuned to contacts from their constituents, even if those contacts have been orchestrated as part of a lobbying campaign. Members take seriously the letters, postcards, faxes, emails, phone calls, visits, remarks at town meetings, and other contacts they have with constituents. While several individual letters or individual office visits might make a compelling case on some issue, members also take cognizance of the volume of constituent calls and letters as part of their decision making on an issue, even when a lobbyist's *grass-roots campaign* stimulated an outpouring of constituent mail.

The multiplication in the variety of forms by which constituents can contact members, the inexpensiveness of these communications, and their ubiquitousness make it easy for a constituent to initiate contact with a member of Congress. Computer databases coupled with the different communication forms also make it easy for a lobbyist to conduct a grass-roots campaign and to get the right messages to the right members at the right time in the right volume. Members, too, use computer databases to target particular constituents. *(See § 4.11, Grass-roots Training, and § 4.12, Example of Grass-roots Campaign.)*

The increasing population of districts and states and the expectations of constituents for members' presence have also meant that members have turned to additional methods for keeping in touch with constituents, such as *town meetings* and *supermarket Saturdays*. In addition to traditional events such as plant visits, speeches to local organizations, and appearances at events such as fairs and parades, these forums provide another avenue for grass-roots activity by lobbyists. The lobbyist, or the constituent sharing the lobbyist's perspective, can express views in a diverse public forum, question a member of Congress, and inform fellow constituents at the same time. *(See § 3.10, Constituency Pressure.)*

In this same vein, a lobbyist can encourage a committee or specific members to conduct field hearings. The lobbyist can provide local witnesses to bolster the members' understanding of a specific perspective on an issue, and turn out an audience for the hearing.

Congress is open to lobbyists in that it is decentralized. Party leaders rely mostly on persuasion to work their will, and they must accommodate the sentiments of individual or small groups of members to put together majorities. In addition to the formal committee structure, there are *congressional member organizations*, party task forces, leadership task forces, and other entities concerned with policy. There are thus many access points and opportunities where a lobbyist's concerns might be shared and where the lobbyist's information is welcome. In this decentralized environment, where voting majorities can be difficult to assemble, lobbying coalitions can be effective, or even essential, to reaching members.

This decentralization can also mean hard work for lobbyists because committee leaders or party leaders are limited in what they can do to bring or keep their members in line. On key votes, for example, negotiations might proceed with little advance knowledge of what the winning political and policy combination might be, or how and when it might be implemented procedurally. In such instances, many members' votes might remain in play until the last moment. A lobbyist has an opportunity to play a role at all stages of the legislative process, whether or not the lobbyist's position accords with majority sentiment.

Congress is open to lobbyists in the equality of its members. Freshman representatives are courted by their leadership for their votes just as much as other members are courted. A representative in the majority party might chair a subcommittee by his or her third term (or even sooner); in the minority party, he or she might be the ranking member on a subcommittee in that same short time. Term limits on committee and subcommittee chairs are providing members with additional opportunities to diversify their expertise and influence. Representatives

§ 4.12

Example of
Grass-roots Campaign

In 2000, the Juvenile Diabetes Foundation organized and gave a name to its "grass-roots advocacy movement run by the volunteers" of the foundation. It was called the "Promise to Remember Me Campaign." To simplify as much as possible what the grass-roots advocates were supposed to do in meeting with members of Congress, which included having their photos taken with their members, the foundation provided the following guidance:

JDF Promise to Remember Me Campaign
TALKING POINTS for Congressional Meetings

- Thank the Member for the meeting and for posing for the photograph with you

- Tell your PERSONAL STORY about diabetes and that you are a JDF advocate

- Ask for increased funding for diabetes research

- Ask for a doubling of the National Institutes of Health (NIH) budget

---

interested in serving in the Senate are likely to attempt Senate election after just a short time in the House. The Senate, because of its rules, has always been a more egalitarian chamber than the House. Today it is even more so, with some freshman senators of the majority party chairing subcommittees in their first year. A lobbyist, therefore, has the opportunity to build relationships at the beginning of a member's career that can prove useful over time.

Congress is open to lobbyists in that its members and staff are voracious consumers of information. Even if a member begins with a firm opinion on an issue, he or she is always looking for additional, plausible justifications for that position and new persuasive arguments to raise with colleagues. If a justification is based on a positive or negative impact on the member's constituents, it is a justification worth knowing. A principal job for any lobbyist is purveying information—preferably reliable and authoritative information. It may, of course, be biased to support the lobbyist's position, but it must be credible. (*See § 4.13, Meeting Tips for a Lobbyist.*) A lobbyist or knowledgeable officials in his or her client organization might also convey information formally as witnesses at committee hearings.

This voracious need for information includes national and local media and public relations. Along with a grass-roots strategy, a full lobbying effort today must include media and

§ 4.13

Meeting Tips for a Lobbyist

The following tips for a lobbyist conducting a meeting with a member of Congress or congressional staffer appeared in the August 1989 issue of *Association Management,* the monthly periodical of the American Society of Association Executives. The tips remain as timely today as they were when published.

Thou Shalt Lobby
It's an association commandment—
so learn how to do it right
By Steve Charton

As simple as they seem, the following 10 guidelines are the keys to successful lobbying. They have served me well for more than 20 years.

1. Never tell a lie.
Your reputation is everything. If you don't know the answer to a question, pledge to get one as soon as possible. You lose your credibility permanently if you lie.

2. Be patient.
Public officials, whether elected or appointed, have many parties vying for their attention. Use your time constructively to work on your presentation while you wait your turn.

3. Be courteous.
Public officials and their employees and representatives are human and expect common courtesy. Plus, they may be more helpful if you treat them with respect.

4. Be brief.
Get in and out of an official's office quickly. Show that you know how valuable his or her time is.

5. Get to the point.
Don't beat around the bush. Keep embellishments to a minimum.

6. K.I.S.S.
Keep it simple, stupid. Don't be too technical, too detailed, too complex, or too oblique. Get to the point, cover the basics, and make sure the official understands your main point. Don't be condescending either.

7. Keep your group small.
An unwieldy group can make everyone uncomfortable,

distract from your message, and waste valuable time getting set up.

8. Plan your pitch.
Make sure that a great deal of consideration goes into your positions. Develop, rework, and refine your stance in advance— not in front of the official you want to impress.

9. Practice, practice, practice.
Repeat your presentation over and over until it is a work of art. Nothing is more impressive to a public official than a smooth and professional presentation. Nothing is less impressive than to go in unprepared and stumble through your case. Involve all participants in practice sessions to avoid dissension and duplication among your delegation.

10. Don't forget to close.
Always ask for the official's vote or support.

Steve Charton is executive vice president, Arkansas Telephone Association, Little Rock.

public relations strategies. What happens to sway public opinion and convey that opinion to Congress can make a difference. For example, advertising against President Clinton's early health-care initiative (the widely seen "Harry and Louise" ads) is credited for its part in stopping the initiative in Congress. Since public concern over health care was a major issue, opponents of the president's initiative needed to convince constituents that his initiative was not the answer. From the lobbyist's perspective, members and constituents must read and hear about the lobbyist's concerns or perspectives both in Washington and in the home districts or states.

Since the public and media relations campaign against the Clinton health-care proposal, the intensity and approaches of national lobbying campaigns for and against legislation and nominations has increased. Lobbying campaigns outside of Washington using public relations; media relations; ingenious symbols, ideograms, events, and other devices; and grassroots organization have been directed at broad matters of national significance and narrow matters of regional or local interest. More specifically, they have been directed at specific members of Congress who are viewed as persuadable, or at variance with their constituents in their apparent position, or politically vulnerable, or soon facing re-election. These lobbying campaigns, occurring year-round as different issues come to the fore, have been financed by national and state political parties, interest and advocacy groups, and individuals or groups of individuals of all political stripes.

For example, to coincide with the introduction in the Senate in the 109th Congress of a bill to repeal the federal estate tax, a group bought hundreds of thousands of dollars of radio and television advertisements in Maine, South Dakota, and Montana to arouse constituents to put pressure on senators from those states. As a Senate test vote on estate tax repeal approached, a group opposing repeal spent over a million dollars on media purchases in Arizona, Arkansas, Maine, Ohio, Rhode Island, and Washington, where it perceived one or both of the senators from those states to be sitting on the fence. Another group bought millions of dollars in media advertising in Arkansas, Montana, Nebraska, and Washington, DC, and its environs to coincide with the Senate Judiciary Committee's markup of legislation to resolve claims by victims suffering injuries from asbestos exposure; the group opposed curtailing victims' rights to sue.

An administration can also do a full-court press on its highest priorities. With complementary media buys and public relations activities by the national political party and well-funded, supportive private groups, an administration can deploy the president, vice president, Cabinet officers, and other officials across the country to speak directly to regional and local media, interested groups such as business or labor organizations, and citizens.

These two forms of intense national lobbying merged during the 109th Congress in the administration's campaign for changes to Social Security and for the nominations to the U.S. Supreme Court of John G. Roberts Jr. and Samuel A. Alito Jr. Republicans and Democrats organized wide-ranging, in-depth national campaigns using dozens of tactics in support of their strategy to prevail in the Social Security debate. The president personally campaigned across the country for changes to Social Security. The administration dispatched supporters to television and radio programs. The Republican National Committee, other party entities, and supportive groups were active with public and media relations. And so on. On the other side, Democrats turned to "town-hall" meetings and other local fora to press their case against the president's ideas. They also dispatched spokesmen to television and radio programs, and the Democratic National Committee, other party entities, and supportive groups were active with public and media relations. The process was repeated with the Supreme Court nominations, including sending teams of people, such as then-appeals court judge Alito's former law clerks, to states with senators viewed as persuadable for or against the nominations.

In the 110th Congress, another lobbying trend seems to be coming into maturity. Existing groups and new groups that support Democrats politically are focusing on the positions and votes of Democratic members of Congress. These groups seem to be seeking to ensure a political orthodoxy among Democratic members and in legislative outcomes in Congress. For example, CODEPINK, a women's peace organization, has established a permanent presence on Capitol Hill and has targeted Democratic members throughout the country both before and after votes to try to stop funding for the war in Iraq. Republican members continue to be pressured by groups on the right to adhere to certain positions. Members of both parties straying from a group's perception of the right position or vote on a matter may find themselves the subject of radio and television advertising, harsh questioning at local constituent meetings, insistent visitors in their Washington and home offices, e-mail and letter-writing campaigns, World Wide Web log ("blog") attacks, threats of primary challenges, and other forms of lobbying pressure. These actions are current and immediate; they are not being saved for a member's reelection campaign.

§ 4.20 Lobbying Laws

With recognition of First Amendment freedoms, Congress has chosen to regulate lobbying to reduce or minimize possible corruption. The following description characterizes aspects of this regulation; it does not offer specific professional advice on compliance with federal law.

Lobbying is regulated principally by the Lobbying Disclosure Act of 1995 (*109 Stat. 691; 112 Stat. 38; 2 U.S.C. § 1601 et seq.*) and the Foreign Agents Registration Act (FARA) (*22 U.S.C. § 611 et seq.*), but it is also subject to tax, appropriations, and criminal laws, House and Senate rules, and other rules. The Lobbying Disclosure Act requires registration with the clerk of the House and the secretary of the Senate. FARA requires registration with the Justice Department. The Lobbying Disclosure Act requires semiannual reporting. FARA requires registrants to file "informational material" generated by the foreign interest and to keep records for inspection. (*See § 4.21, Resources on Lobbying.*)

At the time of publication, both the House and Senate have passed bills changing lobby

§ 4.21

Resources on Lobbying

Text of law and forms:

The Lobbying Disclosure Act, *Lobbying Disclosure Act Guidance*, the registration and reporting forms in PDF format, and other information is available from the clerk of the House web site *(<http://lobbyingdisclosure.house.gov/register.html>)* and the Senate web site *(<www.senate.gov/pagelayout/legislative/g_three_sections_with_teasers/lobbyingdisc.htm>)*.

The clerk of the House's Legislative Resource Center (B-106 Cannon HOB; 202-225-5200) receives and maintains the registration and reporting forms. The secretary of the Senate's Office of Public Records (SH-232 Hart Building; 202-224-0758) performs the same function for the Senate.

Registration under the Foreign Agents Registration Act occurs in the Foreign Agents Registration Unit, U.S. Department of Justice, 1400 New York Ave., NW, Suite 100, Washington, DC 20005; 202-514-1145. *(See <www.usdoj.gov/criminal/fara>.)*

The House Ethics Committee's advisory memoranda, or pink sheets, and other information are available on the committee's web site, *<www.house.gov/ethics>*, which is accessible through the House web site, *<www.house.gov>*.

The *Senate Ethics Manual* (S.Pub. 108-1) is available online on the site of the Senate Select Committee on Ethics at *<http://ethics.senate.gov>*.

For a guide to lobbying laws, see publications such as:

- William V. Luneburg and Thomas M. Susman, *The Lobbying Manual: A Complete Guide to Federal Law Governing Lawyers and Lobbyists*, 3rd ed. (Chicago: American Bar Association, 2005)
- Trevor Potter, ed., *Political Activity, Lobbying Laws, and Gift Rules Guide,* 2d ed. (Eagan. MN: Thomson West, 1999)

Organizations interested in the profession of lobbying include:

- American League of Lobbyists *(<www.alldc.org>)*
- American Society of Association Executives *(<www.asaecenter.org>)*
- Public Affairs Council *(<www.pac.org>)*
- Women in Government Relations *(<www.wgr.org>)*

For training, see:

- TheCapitol.Net's Communication and Advocacy training *(<www.CommunicationAndAdvocacy.com>)*

laws. These changes are not described here. Should lobby legislation be enacted—passed in identical form by both houses of Congress and signed into law by the president—it could have a large impact on members of Congress, on requirements placed on lobbyists, and on the manner in which lobbying is conducted. Both measures contain additional disclosure requirements, including disclosure of "bundled" political contributions collected by a lobbyist for a congressional candidate and other political committees. The Senate-passed bill doubles the post-employment lobbying restrictions on members of Congress to two years from one year. Both measures also amend respective chamber rules to disallow a member of Congress from negotiating post-congressional private employment, except under prescribed conditions. The Senate-passed bill contained changes to Senate ethics rules. Changes to House ethics rules were contained in the House rules package agreed to the opening day of the 110th Congress, a subsequent House resolution agreed to as of May 2007, and guidance issued by the Standards of Official Conduct Committee; these changes have already taken effect. (*See* § 4.30, *Congressional Ethics.*)

Factors Affecting Application of Laws and Rules

Criteria and Thresholds. The Lobbying Disclosure Act establishes criteria and thresholds for registration, reporting, and termination of a registration. In general, the thresholds require registration for a "lobbying firm" for each client from whom the lobbying firm expects income to exceed $6,000 in a six-month period. For an organization employing in-house lobbyists, registration generally must occur if expenses for lobbying activities are expected to exceed $24,500 during a six-month period. (The six-month periods are January through June and July through December.) These thresholds are adjusted every four years, beginning from a base set in 1997: the amounts here reflect the January 2005 adjustments. Reporting continues as long as the registration is active, whether or not the thresholds are met. (*See* § 4.22, *Lobbying Disclosure Form.*)

A lobbyist is defined as an individual who is employed or retained by a client entity for compensation. The services provided include more than one "lobbying contact," and "lobbying activities" constitute 20 percent or more of the individual's services during a six-month period. "Lobbying contact" and "lobbying activities" are also defined in the Lobbying Disclosure Act.

Foreign interests generally must register under FARA, except for foreign commercial or other private interests that meet the registration criteria of the Lobbying Disclosure Act. Those interests do not register under FARA, but must register with the clerk and the secretary under the Lobbying Disclosure Act. The official activities of foreign diplomats are exempt from either registration.

Context. The application of the Lobbying Disclosure Act and other laws regulating lobbying often depends on context in addition to criteria and thresholds. For example, in providing guidance on the Lobbying Disclosure Act, the clerk of the House and the secretary of the Senate use an example of a former congressional chief of staff who leaves congressional employment and enters private law practice. The former chief of staff waits more than a year before contacting her former office (thus honoring post-employment restrictions), and then calls that office to speak to a staff member about the status of legislation affecting the interests of one of her clients. Although the law would normally exempt this kind of communication as

§ 4.22

Lobbying Disclosure Form

There are two forms, one for registration (shown here) and one for reporting. Both are available online. *(See § 4.21, Resources on Lobbying.)*

Clerk of the House of Representatives   Secretary of the Senate
Legislative Resource Center   Office of Public Records
B-106 Cannon Building   232 Hart Building
Washington, DC 20515   Washington, DC 20510

LOBBYING REGISTRATION
Lobbying Disclosure Act of 1995 (Section 4)

Check if this is an Amended Registration ☐   1. Effective Date of Registration_____

2. House Identification Number_____ Senate Identification Number_____

REGISTRANT
3. Registrant name

Address

City   State   Zip

4. Principal place of business (if different from line 3)
City   State/Zip (or Country)

5. Telephone number and contact name
( )   Contact   E-mail (optional)

6. General description of registrant's business or activities

---

CLIENT *A Lobbying firm is required to file a separate registration for each client.* **Organizations employing in-house lobbyists should check the box**
labeled "Self" and proceed to line 10.   ☐ *Self*

7. Client name

Address

City   State   Zip

8. Principal place of business (if different from line 7)
City   State/Zip (or Country)

9. General description of client's business or activities

LOBBYISTS
10. Name of each individual who has acted or is expected to act as a lobbyist for the client identified on line 7. If any person listed in this section has served as a "covered executive branch official" or "covered legislative branch official" within two years of first acting as a lobbyist for the client, *state the executive and/or legislative position(s) in which the person served.*

Name	Covered Official Position (if applicable)

Form LD-1 (Rev. 06/98)   Page 1

Continued on page 96

Lobbying Disclosure Form

Registrant Name_____ Client Name_____

LOBBYING ISSUES

11. General lobbying issue areas. Select all applicable codes listed in instructions and on the reverse side of Form LD-1, page 1.

_____   _____   _____   _____   _____   _____   _____   _____   _____

12. Specific lobbying issues (current and anticipated)

AFFILIATED ORGANIZATIONS

13. Is there an entity other than the client that contributes more than $10,000 to the lobbying activities of the registrant in a semiannual period **and** in whole or in major part plans, supervises or controls the registrant's lobbying activities?

☐ No ⇨ Go to line 14.   ☐ Yes ↓ Complete the rest of this section for each entity matching
                                         the criteria above, then proceed to line 14.

Name	Address	Principal Place of Business (city and state or country)

FOREIGN ENTITIES

14. Is there any foreign entity that:

    a) holds at least 20% equitable ownership in the client or any organization identified on line 13; **or**

    b) directly or indirectly, in whole or in major part, plans, supervises, controls, directs, finances or subsidizes
       activities of the client or any organization identified on line 13; **or**

    c) is an affiliate of the client or any organization identified on line 13 and has a direct interest in the outcome
       of the lobbying activity?

☐ No ⇨ Sign and date the registration.   ☐ Yes ↓ Complete the rest of this section for each entity
                                                          matching the criteria above, then sign and date the
                                                          registration.

Name	Address	Principal place of business (city and state or country)	Amount of contribution for lobbying activities	Ownership percentage in client

Signature_____ Date_____

Printed Name and Title _____

Form LD-1 (Rev. 06/98)   Page 2

Continued on page 97

§ 4.22 *(continued)*

Lobbying Disclosure Form

GENERAL LOBBYING ISSUE AREAS: Select those from the following list that most closely match the client's lobbying issue areas. Enter the corresponding codes on line 11.

ACC	Accounting	HOU	Housing
ADV	Advertising	IMM	Immigration
AER	Aerospace	IND	Indian/Native American Affairs
AGR	Agriculture	INS	Insurance
ALC	Alcohol & Drug Abuse	LBR	Labor Issues/Antitrust/Workplace
ANI	Animals	LAW	Law Enforcement/Crime/Criminal Justice
APP	Apparel/Clothing Industry/Textiles	MAN	Manufacturing
ART	Arts/Entertainment	MAR	Marine/Maritime/Boating/Fisheries
AUT	Automotive Industry	MIA	Media (Information/Publishing)
AVI	Aviation/Aircraft/Airlines	MED	Medical/Disease Research/Clinical Labs
BAN	Banking	MMM	Medicare/Medicaid
BNK	Bankruptcy	MON	Minting/Money/Gold Standard
BEV	Beverage Industry	NAT	Natural Resources
BUD	Budget/Appropriations	PHA	Pharmacy
CHM	Chemicals/Chemical Industry	POS	Postal
CIV	Civil Rights/Civil Liberties	RRR	Railroads
CAW	Clean Air & Water (Quality)	RES	Real Estate/Land Use/Conservation
CDT	Commodities (Big Ticket)	REL	Religion
COM	Communications/Broadcasting/Radio/TV	RET	Retirement
CPI	Computer Industry	ROD	Roads/Highway
CSP	Consumer Issues/Safety/Protection	SCI	Science/Technology
CON	Constitution	SMB	Small Business
CPT	Copyright/Patent/Trademark	SPO	Sports/Athletics
DEF	Defense	TAX	Taxation/Internal Revenue Code
DOC	District of Columbia	TEC	Telecommunications
DIS	Disaster Planning/Emergencies	TOB	Tobacco
ECN	Economics/Economic Development	TOR	Torts
EDU	Education	TRD	Trade (Domestic & Foreign)
ENG	Energy/Nuclear	TRA	Transportation
ENV	Environmental/Superfund	TOU	Travel/Tourism
FAM	Family Issues/Abortion/Adoption	TRU	Trucking/Shipping
FIR	Firearms/Guns/Ammunition	URB	Urban Development/Municipalities
FIN	Financial Institutions/Investments/Securities	UNM	Unemployment
FOO	Food Industry (Safety, Labeling, etc.)	UTI	Utilities
FOR	Foreign Relations	VET	Veterans
FUE	Fuel/Gas/Oil	WAS	Waste (hazardous/solid/interstate/nuclear)
GAM	Gaming/Gambling/Casino	WEL	Welfare
GOV	Government Issues		
HCR	Health Issues		
HOM	Homeland Security		

an "administrative request," the guidance comments that the identity of the person asking questions and that person's relationship to the office are important factors. In the example, the guidance states, "Presumably [the law firm's client] will expect the call to have been part of an effort to influence the member, even though only routine matters were raised at that particular time."

Kind of Organization. The kind of organization engaged in lobbying or wishing to engage in lobbying affects the application of various lobbying laws. Organizations exempt from taxation under the Internal Revenue Code may be restricted in their lobbying activities. Different criteria apply to different kinds of tax-exempt organizations. Special rules apply to religious organizations under the Lobbying Disclosure Act, and certain IRC § 501(c)(3) tax-exempt organizations have the option of using IRC definitions of lobbying or definitions under the Lobbying Disclosure Act. The criteria of the Lobbying Disclosure Act are meant to apply to lobbying that is compensated so that the law reaches professional lobbyists and their activities. Lobbying firms and organizations with in-house lobbyists that meet the criteria and thresholds of the Lobbying Disclosure Act must register and report. Because of the criteria for registering and reporting, a group of homegrown volunteers should still be aware of the law.

Federal Funds. If an organization receives federal funds, lobbying laws might apply if the organization lobbies or desires to lobby. For the most part, congressionally appropriated funds may not be used for lobbying so that federal officers and employees may not lobby. Federal contractors, grantees, borrowers, and parties to cooperative agreements may not use federal funds for lobbying, and certain tax-exempt organizations ("§ 501(c)(4)" organizations) may not lobby if they wish to receive federal grants, loans, or other awards.

Individual Lobbyist. Officials in both Congress and the executive branch are covered by post-employment restrictions once they leave federal service. A former member of Congress may not lobby either house of Congress for one year after leaving office. (Moreover, a former member who is a registered lobbyist or foreign agent is disallowed certain perquisites available to former members, such as access to the Hall of the House.) In general, a highly paid staffer of a member's office may not lobby his or her former office for one year after leaving the member's office. Similarly, a highly paid committee staffer may not lobby his or her former committee or its members and their staff for one year after leaving the committee staff. Various restrictions in law and executive orders apply to former executive-branch employees. A lawyer who is engaged in lobbying would also be covered by rules of professional conduct.

Kind of Activity. Some activities undertaken by certain kinds of people are not covered as lobbying activities, for example, public officials acting in an official capacity and journalists gathering news. Hearings testimony is also exempted, as is a response to a specific request for information from a member of Congress. The Lobbying Registration Act clearly covers "lobbying contacts," but an organization's efforts to get others to contact members of Congress, such as the kind of activity that is often called *grass-roots lobbying*, is not generally considered a lobbying contact for an organization unless it is in support of lobbying contacts. As was seen in the example above involving the former congressional chief of staff, an activity not normally characterized as a lobbying contact might be converted to one, based on the attributes of the person engaging in the activity.

Gifts. Aspects of Congress's *gift rules* are summarized in § 4.30 (*Congressional Ethics*), but some aspects of these rules apply in specific ways to lobbyists. Unlike the Lobbying Disclosure Act, the gift rules are not laws but House and Senate rules that are applicable to members and staff. They are also complex. Nonetheless, lobbyists should be aware of the chambers' gift rules so that they do not compromise members or staff or embarrass themselves. Some applications of the gift rules affecting lobbyists include the following:

- Gifts of under $50 in value, including meals, may be accepted, but a member or staff may not accept gifts exceeding a value of $100 a year from a single source. Beginning in the 110th Congress, the House eliminated this so-called de minimis exception.
- A member or staff may accept gifts from a personal friend, including a lobbyist, if that person qualifies under criteria defining that relationship. A gift exceeding $250 in value, however, must be approved by the House or Senate Ethics Committee for members and staff of the respective chambers.
- A member or staff may not generally accept a gift of personal hospitality in a lobbyist's home.
- A member or staff may not generally accept a travel reimbursement from a lobbyist. Beginning in the 110th Congress, the House disallowed travel by a member planned by a lobbyist or accompanied by a lobbyist.
- Lobbyists are permitted to make campaign contributions, with no distinction based on their occupation under federal campaign-finance laws.

The lobbyist must also beware of gifts and campaign contributions that might be construed as having an intent or connection related to an official act by a member or staff. This could trigger the application of the federal bribery or illegal-gratuities statute. Reporting requirements might also apply to gifts, such as those applicable to gifts to members and some highly paid congressional staff when filing their annual financial disclosure forms.

§ 4.30 Congressional Ethics

A member of Congress works in an environment with numerous ethical standards, and with constraints on official, political, and personal activities. These limits exist in laws, regulations, chamber rules, interpretations, and practices. The expectations of members' constituents also contribute to the ever-tightening acceptable norms of behavior.

There are a number of places where one can begin research on congressional ethics, including the following:

- House *Ethics Manual*, formally the *Ethics Manual for Members, Officers, and Employees of the U.S. House of Representatives*, last published in 1992 by the Committee on Standards of Official Conduct (popularly referred to as the House Ethics Committee), and available on the committee's web site, *<www.house.gov/ethics>*
- House Ethics Committee's advisory memoranda, or pink sheets, and other information available on the committee's web site, *<www.house.gov/ethics>*
- *Members' Congressional Handbook*, available through the web site of the Committee on House Administration, *<http://cha.house.gov/index.php?option=com_content&task =view&id=49&Itemid=37>*
- *Committees' Handbook*, available through the web site of the Committee on House Administration, *<http://cha.house.gov/index.php?option=com_content&task=view&id =50&Itemid=37>*

- *Constitution, Jefferson's Manual, and Rules of the House of Representatives of the United States* (H. Doc. 108-241), the 110th Congress update of which was expected to be published in 2007
- *Senate Ethics Manual* (S. Pub. 108-1), published in 2003 by the Senate Select Committee on Ethics, available on the committee's web site, <*http://ethics.senate.gov*>
- interpretive rulings and other forms of advice to the Senate on specific ethics matters
- *United States Senate Handbook* (S. Prt. 109-70), updated in November 2006 and available internally on the Senate web site
- *Senate Manual* (S. Doc. 107-1)
- instruction booklets prepared annually by the House and Senate Ethics Committees and provided to members and highly paid congressional staff to assist them in preparing their financial disclosure forms
- Congressional Management Foundation, *Setting Course: A Congressional Management Guide* (Washington, DC: Congressional Management Foundation, 2006), Chapter 16, Managing Ethics.

The House Ethics Committee attempts to respond to organizations and individuals from outside the House after serving House members and staff. The committee may be contacted by telephone, 202-225-7103, or in writing, Committee on Standards of Official Conduct, HT-2, U.S. Capitol, U.S. House of Representatives, Washington, DC 20515. *(For explanation of the availability of committee advice to the public, see the committee's web site, <www.house.gov/ethics/ CommitteeAddress.htm>.)*

The Senate Ethics Committee also attempts to respond to organizations and individuals from outside the Senate after serving senators and staff. The telephone number is 202-224-2981. The committee is located at SH-220 Hart Building, Washington, DC 20510.

There are many aspects and considerations involved in the application of ethics laws and rules in a particular situation. There are laws that apply to both representatives and senators, yet different chamber rules, interpretations, and practices apply in the House and Senate. Differing rules may apply to members' spouses, children, and staff. Therefore, it is prudent to get a professional opinion on a specific activity before it is undertaken. A government affairs professional might have every good intention in offering a service or courtesy to a member of Congress. However, he or she may inadvertently be running afoul of a well-established ethics norm.

Members are not exempt from civil or criminal liability. They are subject to prosecution for violations of federal, state, and local criminal law. In addition, they are subject to disciplinary procedures in their respective chambers. The Constitution states *(art. I, sec. 5, cl. 2)*: "Each House may . . . punish its Members for disorderly Behaviour, and, with the Concurrence of two thirds, expel a Member." Each chamber has disciplined members for violations of law and congressional rules, including ethics rules. Each has also disciplined members for actions that are not explicitly disallowed in law or rules, but that bring discredit or disrepute on the House or Senate. However, the jurisdiction of the House and Senate is over sitting members, not former members. The most serious disciplinary action that a chamber may take is expulsion, which, as the Constitution provides, requires a two-thirds vote. Each chamber has a variety of other responses to "disorderly Behaviour," including censure, reprimand, and lesser disciplinary actions, which the chambers and their ethics committees tend to shape and name to suit the offense and the response that is desired to be made to it.

In the 107th Congress, the House expelled Rep. James Traficant, D-OH, following his criminal conviction for conspiracy to violate the federal bribery statute, receiving an illegal gratuity in violation of the federal bribery statute, violating the federal obstruction of justice statute, conspiracy to defraud the United States, and filing a false tax return (<*www.house. gov/ethics/Traficant_Report_Cover.htm*>). The House Standards of Official Conduct Committee conducted an investigation and reported a resolution to expel Traficant, which the House agreed to.

In the 108th and 109th Congress, the Standards of Official Conduct Committee resolved other investigations, about which it announced a culmination, in a variety of ways. For example, in the 108th Congress, following allegations by Representative Nick Smith, R-MI, that other members had linked his vote on the proposed Medicare prescription drug benefit to support for the congressional candidacy of his son, the committee appointed an investigative subcommittee and ultimately adopted the report of the subcommittee. The committee stated that its report "will serve as a public admonishment by the Committee" of Representative Smith, Representative Candice Miller, R-MI, and then-Majority Leader Tom DeLay, R-TX, and recommended no further action. (Report available online at <*www.house.gov/ethics/ Medicare_Report_Cover.htm*>.) The committee also in the 108th Congress issued a letter of admonishment on two matters to Representative DeLay, concerning the appearance of giving special access to political donors regarding pending energy legislation and the use of governmental resources for a political undertaking, which involved contacts with the Federal Aviation Administration over the whereabouts of a plane carrying Democratic members of the Texas legislature engaged in a partisan dispute in the legislature over redistricting. (Letter and other documents available online at <*www.house.gov/ethics/DeLay_Cover.htm*>.)

In the 109th Congress, the Standards of Official Conduct Committee resolved investigations and other inquiries involving:

- Representative John Conyers, D-MI, recommending no further action so long as he implemented prescribed policies in his office to ensure that congressional staff and resources were not used for political or personal purposes. (*See* <*www.house.gov/ ethics/Press_Statement_Conyers.htm*>.)
- Representative Tom Feeney, R-FL, recommending no further action so long as he paid the cost of a trip to the U.S. Treasury, noting that the purpose and payment for the trip had violated House rules. (*See* <*www.house.gov/ethics/Press_Statement_ Feeney.htm*>.)

- Representative Curt Weldon, R-PA, recommending no further action so long as he reimbursed donors for a trip for himself and family members, which the committee found to be officially related and not subject to a gift rule exception. *(See <www. house.gov/ethics/Press_Statement_Weldon.htm>.)*
- Representative Jim McDermott, D-WA, recommending no action beyond publication of the committee's report on the matter of his disclosure, while serving as ranking minority member of the ethics committee, of a tape of an intercepted telephone call between Representative John Boehner, R-OH, and other members; the committee did not reach a conclusion on questions arising from a possible violation of a provision of federal law on intercepted electronic communications but found that McDermott's behavior "risked undermining the ethics process" and was "not consistent with the spirit of the Committee's rules." *(See <www.house.gov/ethics/McDermott_Report_ Cover.htm>.)*
- Publication of the committee's report, recommending no further action, following its investigation into the actions of members, House officers, and staff over improper conduct between Representative Mark Foley, R-FL, and House pages; the committee found "a pattern of conduct" exhibited by members, officers, and staff "to remain willfully ignorant of the potential consequences of former Representative Foley's conduct with respect to House pages," but did not find that current members or employees violated the Code of Official Conduct. *(See <www.house.gov/ethics/Page_ Report_Cover.htm>, and § 5.113, Congressional Pages.)*

In the 107th Congress, the Senate Ethics Committee issued a "letter of admonition" *(<http://ethics.senate.gov/downloads/pdffiles/torricelli.pdf>)* to Sen. Robert Torricelli, D-NJ, for "poor judgment," violation of the Senate gift rule, and, consequently, violation of financial disclosure requirements, based on a relationship between the senator and an individual, David Chang, who, as the committee stated, "was attempting to ingratiate himself, in part through a pattern of attempts to provide you (Sen. Torricelli) and those around you with gifts over a period of several years when you and your Senate office were taking official action of benefit to Mr. Chang. . . ." Torricelli, at the time the committee released the letter, was in the midst of a reelection campaign. He subsequently ended his campaign, and was replaced on the ballot.

Regulated Activities

What follows is a description of some of the types of activities regulated by congressional ethics laws, rules, interpretations, and practices. Each activity is accompanied by a characterization of the norm regulating the activity, but these characterizations are neither exhaustive nor statements or interpretations of specific laws or rules. *(See also §§ 5.10–5.50 in Chapter Five, Supporting Congress: Allowances and Staff.) (Beginning in the 100th Congress, the House Standards of Official Conduct Committee was required by House rules to offer ethics training to representatives and House staff.)*

This list also does not necessarily describe the norms applicable to party conferences and caucuses, congressional staff, family members, the vice president in his role as president of the Senate, or others whose activities might be covered by congressional ethics norms. In general, however, laws and rules applicable to members are often applicable to their staffs as well.

The descriptions below include some of the key changes made by the House in adopting ethics rules changes at the beginning of the 110th Congress, in a subsequent House resolution agreed to as of May 2007, and in guidance from the Standards of Official Conduct Committee. At the time of publication, the Senate had passed a bill containing changes to the Senate's ethics rules that corresponded to the House changes, such as elimination of the so-called de minimis exception to the prohibition on gifts, further restrictions on lobbyist support for travel, curtailing senators' attempts to influence private hiring for partisan purposes, and prohibiting senators from requesting earmarks in which they had a financial interest. The proposed Senate ethics rules changes are not included in the descriptions below. While the Senate could have made changes to its ethics rules through a simple resolution or perhaps by other means, it chose to couple these changes in a bill with proposed changes to lobby laws. As of May 2007, the House has also passed a bill containing proposed changes to lobby laws. The two chambers will need to reconcile differences in the legislation and both agree to the reconciled version, and President George W. Bush will need to sign the legislation Congress passes for this set of Senate ethics rules and changes to lobby laws to take effect. Finally, the Speaker and House minority leader appointed members to a bipartisan task force to examine the question of whether an ethics mechanism in addition to the Standards of Official Conduct Committee is needed.

Office Expenses. Members may not use their official allowances or federal property for political purposes, and campaign contributions may not be used to support official activities or to defray official expenses. In general, neither money nor in-kind contributions may be accepted to support official activities, but there are exceptions to this principle, such as the loan or display of a home-state product or artifact.

Campaign Activities. A congressional staffer might engage in limited forms of political work on his or her own time, but a staffer engaging only nominally in official duties and performing political work might trigger the operation of various antifraud statutes against a member. Members are also proscribed under law from a number of campaign-related activities, such as promising assistance in obtaining federal employment in exchange for a political contribution and, in general, soliciting or receiving political contributions in a federal building.

Gifts. The House and Senate have broad, general prohibitions on members' receipt of gifts, with specific enumerated exceptions, such as the permissibility of accepting any gift valued at less than $50 as long as the total value of gifts from any one source does not exceed $100 in a calendar year. Through a House rules change, this so-called de minimis exception was eliminated in the 110th Congress for lobbyists' gifts to representatives. The rules change disallowed small-value gifts from registered lobbyists, foreign agents, and private entities employing registered lobbyists, although gifts of nominal value, such as a baseball cap, may still be accepted. A representative could accept a ticket to a sports and entertainment event only if the member paid the face value of the ticket. In addition, if a private entity—not a lobbyist or one employing a lobbyist—gives a sports or entertainment ticket to a representative, the ticket's value is its face value and may be accepted only if the face value does not violate the de minimis exception.

Solicitation or acceptance of a gift related to an official act can trigger the federal bribery or illegal-gratuity statute, and solicitation of a gift is not allowed under any circumstances.

Gifts of Travel. Members may accept privately sponsored travel covering food, lodging, and transportation expenses for trips of specifically limited duration under limited conditions. This travel is subject to restrictions, such as a prohibition on a lobbyist, lobbying organization, or foreign agent paying for travel and a limitation paying for recreational activities as part of such travel. A gift of travel must be related to official duties. Members must disclose gifts of travel on their financial disclosure statements and must also report them to their chamber within thirty days of a trip (now fifteen days in the House).

In addition, beginning in the 110th Congress as a consequence of changes to its rules adopted by the House, new restrictions were placed on lobbyist participation in travel. In addition to representatives being disallowed from receiving travel paid for by a lobbyist, they may not travel accompanied by a lobbyist or make a trip planned by a lobbyist. The prohibition on a lobbyist paying for a trip was extended to private entities employing a registered lobbyist or foreign agent. The rules changes allowed two exceptions: when the travel is paid for by a qualified institution of higher education or when the travel is for a one-day event and the participation of a lobbyist in the travel is de minimis. A member receiving paid travel must make certain certifications in advance to the Standards of Official Conduct Committee, such as the travel will not be paid for by a registered lobbyist, foreign agent, or private entity employing a registered lobbyist or foreign agent, and receive the committee's approval. Such documents are to be made publicly available. Expenses for the travel are also to be "reasonable," which the committee has defined in perhaps most circumstances to be such expenses as coach or business-class air fare and the federal government per diem for food and lodging.

Representatives in most circumstances are also prohibited from flying on private, corporate aircraft, although members who own a plane may continue to use it for congressionally related purposes.

Charitable Events. Members and staff may accept attendance at charitable events where fees are waived and food and entertainment provided. In the 108th Congress, the House changed a previous prohibition on reimbursement for transportation and lodging to allow a charity to provide transportation and lodging under certain conditions, although the sponsoring entity may not be a registered lobbyist, foreign agent, or private entity that employs them. The Senate allows reimbursement, under certain conditions, when the charitable event is not substantially recreational.

Gifts of Food and Refreshments. Gifts in the form of food and refreshments occupy a substantial part of the exceptions and rulings involving gifts. In addition to the exception for meals under $50, not totaling more than $100 from one source in a year, there is an exception for food and refreshments that are not part of a meal and are of nominal value. (Again, the House in the 110th Congres ended this so-called de minimis exception when the gift was made by a registered lobbyist, foreign agent, or private entity employing a registered lobbyist.) Hence, members and staff may attend receptions. There is an exception for "personal hospitality" where an individual, not a lobbyist, entertains in his or her home at personal expense. Another exception exists in the form of "widely attended" events, such as conventions or conferences. The fee may be waived, and food and other expenses, such as convention or conference materials, may be provided free. The member or staff should be a participant in the event, or the event should be "appropriate to the performance of the (member's) official duties." The House changed another exception in the 108th Congress so that the value of perishable food sent to a congressional office would be allocated among individual recipients and not allocated as one sum to the member. Additional exceptions exist.

Honoraria. Honoraria are prohibited, but an event sponsor may pay up to $2,000 to a charity in lieu of an honorarium. Payment of such an honorarium must be made directly to the charity by the provider of the honorarium. Neither the member nor a relative of the member may receive a financial or tax benefit from the donation. Neither an employee of the member nor a relative of an employee may receive a financial or tax benefit from the donation. In addition, if a charitable contribution in lieu of an honorarium is made for a representative by a registered lobbyist or registered foreign agent, then the representative must file a report with the clerk of the House. Travel expenses, however, may be covered or reimbursed.

Outside Earned Income. Certain categories of outside earned income are proscribed; for example, paid professional services such as law, real estate sales, and insurance sales, and compensation for services as an officer or board member of an organization. A member may not represent a person or entity in a private capacity before a federal agency or a federal court, whether compensated or not, and, in general, may not contract or benefit from a contract with the federal government. Outside earned income is limited to 15 percent of a member's pay.

Financial Disclosure. Members and some highly paid congressional staff must file financial disclosure forms each year, usually by May 15, providing extensive information on earned and unearned income, assets, liabilities, and other financial and quasi-financial interests. The disclosure form is not a net-worth financial statement. *(See § 4.31, House Financial Disclosure Form.)*

Interns, Fellows, and Volunteers. In general, private interns, fellows, and volunteers may work in congressional offices, with consideration in their hiring being given to their affiliation with organizations having an interest in matters before Congress, the educational benefit such individuals will receive, the potential displacement of paid employees, and other factors. *(See § 5.100, Congressional Fellowships and Internships.)*

House Financial Disclosure Form

UNITED STATES HOUSE OF REPRESENTATIVES 2007 FINANCIAL DISCLOSURE STATEMENT	FORM A For use by Members, officers, and employees	

(Full Name)

(Mailing Address)　　　　Daytime Telephone:

(Office Use Only)

Filer Status	☐ Member of the U.S. House of Representatives　State: _____ District: _____	☐ Officer or Employee	Employing Office:	**A $200 penalty shall be assessed against anyone who files more than 30 days late.**
Report Type	☐ Annual (May 15)	☐ Amendment	☐ Termination　Termination Date: _____	

PRELIMINARY INFORMATION — ANSWER EACH OF THESE QUESTIONS

I. Did you or your spouse have "earned" income (e.g., salaries or fees) of $200 or more from any source in the reporting period? **If yes, complete and attach Schedule I.**	Yes ☐　No ☐	VI. Did you, your spouse, or a dependent child receive any reportable gift in the reporting period (i.e., aggregating more than $305 and not otherwise exempt)? **If yes, complete and attach Schedule VI.**　Yes ☐　No ☐
II. Did any individual or organization make a donation to charity in lieu of paying you for a speech, appearance, or article in the reporting period? **If yes, complete and attach Schedule II.**	Yes ☐　No ☐	VII. Did you, your spouse, or a dependent child receive any reportable travel or reimbursements for travel in the reporting period (worth more than $305 from one source)? **If yes, complete and attach Schedule VII.**　Yes ☐　No ☐
III. Did you, your spouse, or a dependent child receive "unearned" income of more than $200 in the reporting period or hold any reportable asset worth more than $1,000 at the end of the period? **If yes, complete and attach Schedule III.**	Yes ☐　No ☐	VIII. Did you hold any reportable positions on or before the date of filing in the current calendar year? **If yes, complete and attach Schedule VIII.**　Yes ☐　No ☐
IV. Did you, your spouse, or dependent child purchase, sell, or exchange any reportable asset in a transaction exceeding $1,000 during the reporting period? **If yes, complete and attach Schedule IV.**	Yes ☐　No ☐	IX. Did you have any reportable agreement or arrangement with an outside entity? **If yes, complete and attach Schedule IX.**　Yes ☐　No ☐
V. Did you, your spouse, or a dependent child have any reportable liability (more than $10,000) during the reporting period? **If yes, complete and attach Schedule V.**	Yes ☐　No ☐	**Each question in this part must be answered and the appropriate schedule attached for each "Yes" response.**

EXCLUSION OF SPOUSE, DEPENDENT, OR TRUST INFORMATION — ANSWER EACH OF THESE QUESTIONS

TRUSTS—Details regarding "Qualified Blind Trusts" approved by the Committee on Standards of Official Conduct and certain other "excepted trusts" need not be disclosed. Have you excluded from this report details of such a trust benefiting you, your spouse, or dependent child?	Yes ☐　No ☐
EXEMPTION—Have you excluded from this report any other assets, "unearned" income, transactions, or liabilities of a spouse or dependent child because they meet all three tests for exemption?	Yes ☐　No ☐

CERTIFICATION — THIS DOCUMENT MUST BE SIGNED BY THE REPORTING INDIVIDUAL AND DATED

This Financial Disclosure Statement is required by the Ethics in Government Act of 1978, as amended. The Statement will be available to any requesting person upon written application and will be reviewed by the Committee on Standards of Official Conduct or its designee. Any individual who knowingly and willfully falsifies, or who knowingly and willfully fails to file this report may be subject to civil penalties and criminal sanctions (*See* 5 U.S.C. app. 4, § 104 and 18 U.S.C. § 1001).

Certification	Signature of Reporting Individual	Date *(Month, Day, Year)*
I CERTIFY that the statements I have made on this form and all attached schedules are true, complete and correct to the best of my knowledge and belief.		

Case Work. Members are to avoid ex parte communications in departments' and agencies' adjudicatory proceedings, and may make recommendations for federal employment based only on personal knowledge. There are other situations involving departments and agencies, however, where a member might express judgment, such as when a proceeding is not adjudicatory or when a prospective employee is vying for a political appointment.

Members also sometimes attempt to promote a business or not-for-profit entity that they believe has an important product, technology, idea, or service. They might promote the entity to a federal agency as a good procurement opportunity or in legislation, such as through an earmark. If members fail to keep an arms-length relationship, or become overly zealous in assisting the entity, the relationship can become a basis for investigation by the respective chamber's ethics committee and a political problem for the affected members.

Members could also run into ethical trouble if they attempt to bestow official action, such as case-work assistance or access to a member, on political supporters, party members, or campaign contributors, while discriminating in extending or withholding the same official action from others, or even in taking punitive action. Both the House Committee on Standards of Official Conduct in 1999 and the Senate Committee on Ethics in 2002 sent communications to all members of their respective chambers reminding them of rules and guidance disallowing preferential treatment for a member's supporters and contributors.

Earmarks. In the 110th Congress, the House adopted rules regulating earmarks enforceable by points of order made on the House floor. The earmarks affected were congressional earmarks related to spending, limited tax benefits, and limited tariff benefits. *(See § 9.80, Authorization and Appropriation Processes (Additional Congressional Controls in Appropriations Acts).)* It also adopted related ethics rules changes. A representative is disallowed from conditioning the inclusion of an earmark on the vote of another member. A representative requesting an earmark was also required to disclose certain information to the chair and ranking minority member of the committee from which the member was making the earmark request. This information includes a certification that the member has no financial interest in the earmark. Each committee must make information related to earmark requests publicly available.

Support of Noncongressional Entities. Members may not support outside organizations by lending or giving them franked envelopes, letterhead, or valuable items purchased with official funds.

Lobbying after Leaving Office. Post-employment restrictions on lobbying and advising foreign government interests apply for one year after a member leaves office. Similar one-year bans apply to highly paid personal staff, who may not lobby their former employer's office, and highly paid committee staff, who may not lobby their former committee.

4

Chapter Five

Supporting Congress:
Allowances and Staff

5

Analysis

5

§ 5.00 Introduction

The work of Congress depends on thousands of people in addition to the members. Congressional staffers work in members' personal offices and in their district or state offices. Staffers are employed by committees, subcommittees, and leadership offices in a variety of professional and clerical positions. Additional employees work for limited periods as a result of numerous internships and fellowships sponsored by both government and private groups.

Support offices, such as the architect of the Capitol, the clerk of the House, and the secretary of the Senate, are integral to the work of Congress. Agencies that provide specialized information are known as support agencies and include the Library of Congress, the Congressional Research Service (CRS), the Congressional Budget Office (CBO), and the Government Accountability Office (GAO).

This chapter describes the allowances for members, committee offices, and the staff that support Congress.

§ 5.10 Pay and Allowances of Members

Like executives hired in many other positions, members, including the resident commissioner for Puerto Rico and the four delegates in the House, receive salaries, employee benefits, office space, supplies, and expense accounts to perform their jobs. They hire staff to assist them in discharging their responsibilities in office. Members operate fairly independently in managing their offices, but their management is subject to many laws, rules and regulations, and practices. *(See also § 4.30, Congressional Ethics.)* A chair or ranking minority member on a committee or subcommittee also wears a second hat as manager of resources for that entity. A vast bureaucracy, answerable to House and Senate officers and oversight committees, services members' offices and the committees on which members serve. Part of this bureaucracy keeps up the nation's premier public building, the U.S. Capitol, and the grounds and other buildings that surround it, in which members, their staff, the Supreme Court, and others work.

§ 5.20 Salary, Earned Income, and Benefits

The Constitution empowers Congress to set its own compensation, and the Twenty-Seventh Amendment provides that a variance in compensation voted by one Congress will not take effect until after the next intervening election. Congress last specifically voted to increase its pay in 1989 and 1991. It first adopted the Ethics Reform Act of 1989 (*P.L. 101-194; 103 Stat. 1716*), which raised representatives' and senators' salaries. (Representatives' salaries were raised by a greater amount than senators' in this legislation.) In 1991, Congress approved a Senate amendment to the fiscal 1992 legislative appropriations bill raising senators' salaries to equal those of representatives (*P.L. 102-90; 105 Stat. 447*).

As enacted, these two laws were also important in linking a pay increase to two changes affecting members' income. Receipt of *honoraria* was barred and other, *outside earned income* was limited to 15 percent of a congressional salary. The changes for representatives were included in the Ethics Reform Act, and the changes for senators were begun in the Ethics Reform Act and completed in the fiscal 1992 legislative branch appropriations bill.

House and Senate rules implement the honoraria ban and outside earned-income limit. Ethics laws and chamber rules allow a payment of up to $2,000 to be made to a charity in lieu of an honorarium. Payment of such an honorarium must be made directly to the charity by the provider of the honorarium. Neither the member nor a relative of the member may receive a financial or tax benefit from the donation. Neither an employee of the member nor a relative of an employee may receive a financial or tax benefit from the donation. These donations must also be reported on a member's financial disclosure statement.

Ethics laws and chamber rules proscribe certain categories of outside earned income, for example, compensation for professional services such as real estate and insurance sales, the practice of law, and service as an officer or board member of an organization. Any outside income and service as an officer or board member must be reported on a member's financial disclosure statement.

The Ethics Reform Act also created a revised means of automatic, annual salary increases for members of Congress and other highly paid federal officials, which has become the basis for congressional pay increases. (Another means of salary increases exists in law, which requires a congressional vote.) Under the Ethics Reform Act, the pay-increase formula is based in part on components of the Bureau of Labor Statistics' employment cost index. It is limited both by a 5-percent ceiling and by the size and effective date of adjustments to general schedule federal employees' base pay. Unless Congress votes to prohibit an increase, it automatically takes effect. (Congress under law might also modify the increase, but a question exists about whether that would trigger the operation of the Twenty-Seventh Amendment, thus postponing the increase to after the next election.)

Within the formula and limitations, members' pay increased on January 1, 2006, by 1.9 percent, to $165,200. The changes appear in the table on the next page. (Congress nullified a scheduled salary increase by including a provision in the Revised Continuing Appropriations Resolution, 2007 (P.L. 110-5, § 115). The next automatic, annual salary increase would take place in January 2008, unless Congress acts to nullify it.)

Like other federal employees, members of Congress may participate in the Federal Employees Health Benefits program, the Federal Employees Group Life Insurance program, and the federal retirement system. Members' pension contributions, benefit formulas, and years of service and retirement age for receiving an unreduced pension are different from other federal employees. In general, they contribute more in exchange for more generous retirement income. Social Security participation is mandatory. Free outpatient care is available to members at the Naval Medical Center in Bethesda, MD, and Walter Reed Army Hospital in Washington, DC, a long-standing privilege also available to the president, vice president, and other government officials.

Office Held	Salary on Jan. 1, 2006*
Vice President (President of the Senate) and Speaker of the House	$212,100
President Pro Tempore of the Senate, Senate Majority and Minority Leaders, and House Majority and Minority Leaders	$183,500
Senators, Representatives, and, in House, Delegates and Resident Commissioner	$165,200

These rates of pay continued in effect in 2007 since Congress rejected the annual salary increase, as explained above.

Upon retirement, resignation, or defeat for reelection, a member of Congress continues to enjoy certain perquisites. For example, floor privileges are allowed with certain limitations; access to reports of the Congressional Research Service continues; and a limited franking privilege exists for ninety days.

Finally, a member is entitled to an annual income tax deduction of up to $3,000 for living expenses while away from his or her home district or state.

§5.30 House Allowances for Staff, Office, and Other Expenses

In the House, a "member's representational allowance" (MRA) in 2007 averaged $1,357,733. The maximum amount in an MRA was $1,899,744, and the minimum amount was $1,262,065. The MRA is used by representatives, delegates, and the resident commissioner for staff salaries in Washington and district offices, office expenses in both locales, rent of district offices, and use of the *frank* for mail.

Each member receives the same amount in his or her MRA for staff salaries—$842,244 in 2007. An MRA does not include salary overhead. A member may not employ more than eighteen permanent staff in his or her Washington, DC, office and any district offices. Up to four other staffers may be employed if their positions are in classifications such as temporary or paid intern. The top salary that a member may pay a staffer in 2007 was $159,828.

The amount included in an MRA for office expenses varies because the allocation includes money for travel and for district office rent. In 2007, each member received in this account a base of $210,189. In addition, each member received money for travel based on a formula that included the distance from Washington, DC, to the point in his or her district farthest from Washington; a minimum amount of $6,200 was provided. Finally, using a formula based on the applicable per-square-foot rental charge the General Services Administration might incur in a district, money is provided for a total of 2,500 square feet in one or more district offices.

In addition to travel and district office rental, office expenses include office equipment, furnishings for district offices, computer equipment, office supplies, and telephone services, and perhaps lease charges for a car, "mobile district office" expenses, mailing-list purchases (as long as addresses are in the member's district, result from an arm's length transaction, and do not contain campaign-related or political party information), and subscriptions. There are a number of prohibitions on use of this allowance as well; for example, expenses for professional association and membership dues, holiday greeting cards, and relocation costs are not allowed.

Funds are included in an MRA to cover the costs of all franked mail from a member's Washington and district offices, including mass mailings, which are defined as 500 pieces or more, largely identical in content. This allocation is calculated individually for each member, based on the number of nonbusiness addresses in a district, and, in 2007, averaged $157,523. (*Some of the procedures and prohibitions applicable to use of the franking privilege are discussed in § 5.50, Franking Privilege.*)

Money is largely—but not completely—fungible among these three funds.

A separate allocation, not part of an MRA, provides *public document envelopes* to each representative.

A travel expense allowance is available for reelected and newly elected members and, for each, one staff member to travel to Washington to attend early organization meetings following a general election. For newly elected members, this allowance includes a per diem.

A number of ethics laws, rules, and guidelines surround the MRA and office operations. (*See § 4.30, Congressional Ethics.*) Some of these are as follows:

- A member is personally responsible for expenses that exceed his or her MRA.
- Funds in the MRA cannot be reallocated or transferred between years. (A year runs from January 3 of one year through January 2 of the next year.)
- A member may not use campaign or private funds to support his or her office, and a member may not pay for personal, social, or political expenses from an MRA.
- A member may not use committee resources for his or her office, or use an MRA for committee expenses.
- Neither the member nor a relative may benefit from spending from an MRA.
- Employees must perform duties commensurate with their compensation.
- With some exceptions that deal with changes of status after a person is employed, a member may not employ a relative.

Separate from the MRAs, all representatives, the resident commissioner, and delegates are provided with furnished office suites in one of the House office buildings. Parking for members and a portion of their staffs is provided in garages and other locations on Capitol Hill. In addition, other services are available:

- Numerous service providers operate in the "small city" on the House side of the Capitol and in the House office buildings: post offices; a credit union; a stationery shop and a gift shop; restaurants and cafeterias; private meeting rooms; a members' gymnasium; a staff fitness center; a travel reservation and ticketing service; beauty and barber shops; a drycleaner; housekeeping, maintenance, and repair services; parking garages and parking areas for representatives and staff; a shuttle-bus service; in-house television and radio feeds; and the Capitol police. Many services charge normal retail rates or, in the case of the gymnasium, levy an annual fee. Services such as the post offices, dining halls, and beauty and barber shops are open to the public.

- The Chief Administrative Officer (CAO) staff supports the telecommunications, automation, finance, and personnel needs of a modern-day office environment. The General Services Administration assists members in obtaining and furnishing district office space. The House recording studio provides radio and television services for a fee and the photographic studio also provides services for a fee. Numerous government documents flow into a representative's office for office use or redistribution to constituents.

- Department and agency congressional liaison offices, and department and agency regional or state office contacts, facilitate the handling of *congressional case work* in the executive branch. Intern, volunteer, and fellowship programs support students and professionals in Washington and district offices. The Legislative Resource Center provides legislative documents and other services.

- The House general counsel may assist individual representatives on official matters. The House employment counsel provides assistance on employment law, and the House administrative counsel assists with questions on administrative issues. The House legislative counsel provides legislative drafting services, and the House parliamentarian provides procedural advice.

- Legislative and administrative staffs work under the management of the clerk of the House. Administrative staffs under the management of the House sergeant at arms, the CAO, and the architect of the Capitol assist with or facilitate the needs, concerns, or questions of any representative's office.

- The attending physician's office, health units in the office buildings, and the House chaplain serve the needs of representatives and staff. An annual fee is charged to members for regular use of the attending physician's services.

- The Congressional Budget Office and Government Accountability Office principally serve congressional committees with a variety of reports. The Congressional Research Service assists both committees and members with research and policy analyses. The Government Printing Office serves Congress's extensive document needs.

- Reporters from all media are present in the Capitol, providing ready access if a representative wishes to distribute a press release or hold a press conference.

§ 5.40 Senate Allowances for Staff, Office, and Other Expenses

In the Senate, the total allocation for personnel, office, and other expenses varies with the population of the state that a senator represents and its distance from Washington. Thus, senators from populous states like California, the largest state with a population of over 36 million, have more financial resources available to them than senators from small-population states like Wyoming, the smallest state with a population of just over 500,000.

A senator has three funds available for the operation of his or her Washington and state offices. Two accounts support personnel: the administrative and clerical assistance allowance, which is based on population, and the legislative assistance allowance, which is the same for all senators. (Salary overhead is not included in these funds.) The third fund, with components based on population and distance of the home state from Washington, is the official office expense allowance, which covers travel, stationery, and other expenses. Money is largely—but not completely—fungible among these three funds.

A senator's administrative and clerical assistance allowance ranged in 2007 from $2,043,223 for a senator from a state with a population of less than 5 million to $3,329,671 for a senator from a state with a population of 28 million or more. The allowance covers staff in Washington and state offices. The top salary that could be paid in 2006, the latest year for which a figure was officially available, was $157,559.

The second personnel fund, the legislative assistance allowance, in 2007 provided each senator with $481,977 to hire up to three legislative assistants. The primary purpose of this fund is to ensure that senators have sufficient legislative staff to support their committee work. The top salary that could be paid in 2007 was $160,659.

The third fund is the official office expense allowance, which has several components that are determined by formula. Compared with the House's equivalent allocation, this Senate fund covers fewer items. The Senate does not charge an individual senator's offices for some of the office expenses that are covered by a representative's allowance. For example, most of the costs of a representative's district office are charged against the individual member's representational allowance, while most costs of a senator's state office are not charged against the senator's official office expense allowance. In 2007, the official office expense allowance for a senator ranged from $128,607 to $467,873. (See § 5.41, *Senators' Official Personnel and Office Expense Account.*)

Some items covered by this allowance illustrate its components and, in some cases, the complexity of its administration:

- Telecommunications equipment and services, including both charges for standard equipment and services supplied or paid for by the Senate and additional costs and charges incurred by an individual senator.
- Stationery and office supplies purchased from the Senate stationery room as well as supplies purchased from commercial outlets or General Services Administration (GSA) stores, mailing lists, regular postage, and subscriptions.

- Expenses for state offices not otherwise covered, for example, cable television service charges, and additional office equipment for the Washington or a state office not included in the standard equipment supplied by the Senate.
- Travel expenses for senators and their staff, and, if a senator chooses, for individuals who are not Senate employees but who serve a limited time on an advisory group assisting a senator with nomination recommendations for federal judgeships, U.S. attorneys, U.S. marshals, or the U.S. service academies. Travel costs for a senator and his or her staff are also limited to "actual transportation expenses" in the sixty days preceding any election in which the senator's name appears on a ballot, unless the candidacy is uncontested and that fact is attested to by an appropriate state official.
- Recording and photographic services performed by the Senate recording and photographic studios or by commercial services.
- The "official mail account," which is totaled with the official office expense allowance and is based on the number of addresses in a senator's state. A senator may supplement official mail costs that exceed his or her allotment from other funds in the senator's official office expense allowance. In addition, $50,000 is available within a senator's official office expense allowance for "mass mailings"—that is, mailings of 500 or more pieces, largely identical in content. A senator may not increase the amount of money allotted for mass mailings.

Senators-elect are provided with allowances for travel for themselves and two staff persons for attending early organization meetings, for telecommunications expenses, and for stationery expenses.

In addition to a furnished and equipped office in one of the Senate office buildings, separate allowances and perquisites cover many other office needs of a senator:

- Space for state offices in federal buildings or privately owned buildings, with the total amount of space allowed increasing with a state's population, to a maximum of 8,200 square feet for a state with a population of 17 million or more. GSA furnishes state offices, and the expense allocation available for that also increases with a state's population, from a minimum amount of $45,000. The Senate sergeant at arms provides standard office equipment for each state office.
- One mobile state office, including lease and operating costs (but not personnel).
- Blank stationery, letterhead, white envelopes, and public-document envelopes, allocated on the basis of state population, with a minimum of 180,000 pieces of letterhead and 180,000 white envelopes.
- An allocation from a computer services fund for lease or purchase of computer hardware and software and related training and support.
- With a senator's election or reelection, an allowance of $5,000 for furnishing the senator's personal office, reception area, and conference room. A senator entitled to a Capitol office is allowed $2,500 each term to purchase nonstandard furnishings for that office.

§ 5.41

Senators' Official Personnel and Office Expense Account

In its report on the legislative branch appropriations bill for fiscal year 2007 (S. Rept. 109–267), the Senate Appropriations Committee included a table showing the proposed state-by-state allowances for senators' administrative and clerical assistance allowances, legislative assistance allowances, and official office expense allowances. That table is reproduced here.

State	Administrative and Clerical Assistance Allowance	Legislative Assistance Allowance	Official Office Expense Allowance	Total Allowance
Alabama	$2,043,223	$481,977	$184,707	$2,709,907
Alaska	2,043,223	481,977	253,289	2,778,489
Arizona	2,107,422	481,977	205,051	2,794,450
Arkansas	2,043,223	481,977	170,014	2,695,214
California	3,329,671	481,977	467,873	4,279,521
Colorado	2,043,223	481,977	192,063	2,717,263
Connecticut	2,043,223	481,977	160,851	2,686,051
Delaware	2,043,223	481,977	128,607	2,653,807
Florida	2,877,848	481,977	313,946	3,673,771
Georgia	2,364,228	481,977	220,420	3,066,625
Hawaii	2,043,223	481,977	280,409	2,805,609
Idaho	2,043,223	481,977	165,745	2,690,945
Illinois	2,556,837	481,977	266,157	3,304,971
Indiana	2,171,625	481,977	196,114	2,849,716
Iowa	2,043,223	481,977	171,119	2,696,319
Kansas	2,043,223	481,977	169,248	2,694,448
Kentucky	2,043,223	481,977	178,557	2,703,757
Lousiana	2,043,223	481,977	186,417	2,711,617
Maine	2,043,223	481,977	148,986	2,674,186
Maryland	2,107,422	481,977	172,178	2,761,577
Massachusetts	2,171,625	481,977	195,590	2,849,192
Michigan	2,428,435	481,977	235,168	3,145,580
Minnesota	2,107,422	481,977	189,369	2,778,768
Mississippi	2,043,223	481,977	169,869	2,695,069
Missouri	2,107,422	481,977	198,097	2,787,496
Montana	2,043,223	481,977	162,848	2,688,048
Nebraska	2,043,223	481,977	161,328	2,686,528
Nevada	2,043,223	481,977	176,174	2,701,374
New Hampshire	2,043,223	481,977	143,723	2,668,923
New Jersey	2,300,030	481,977	205,875	2,987,882

Continued on page 119

State	Administrative and Clerical Assistance Allowance	Legislative Assistance Allowance	Official Office Expense Allowance	Total Allowance
New Mexico	$2,043,223	$481,977	$167,730	$2,692,930
New York	2,959,995	481,977	320,398	3,762,370
North Carolina	2,300,030	481,977	218,971	3,000,978
North Dakota	2,043,223	481,977	150,616	2,675,816
Ohio	2,492,637	481,977	255,868	3,230,482
Oklahoma	2,043,223	481,977	181,800	2,707,000
Oregon	2,043,223	481,977	191,018	2,716,218
Pennsylvania	2,556,837	481,977	262,604	3,301,418
Rhode Island	2,043,223	481,977	139,158	2,664,358
South Carolina	2,043,223	481,977	175,453	2,700,653
South Dakota	2,043,223	481,977	152,477	2,677,677
Tennessee	2,107,422	481,977	195,458	2,784,857
Texas	3,083,223	481,977	366,643	3,931,843
Utah	2,043,223	481,977	171,285	2,696,485
Vermont	2,043,223	481,977	137,093	2,662,293
Virginia	2,235,827	481,977	196,864	2,914,668
Washington	2,171,625	481,977	216,021	2,869,623
West Virginia	2,043,223	481,977	148,870	2,674,070
Wisconsin	2,107,422	481,977	192,598	2,781,997
Wyoming	2,043,223	481,977	153,754	2,678,954

5

- Parking is provided to senators and a portion of their staffs in garages and other Capitol Hill locations.
- A limited number of plants available on loan from the Botanic Garden for a senator's office, two framed reproductions from a limited selection available on loan from the National Gallery of Art, and unmounted maps available on loan (or possibly free) from the U.S. Geological Survey.
- Numerous service providers operate in the "small city" on the Senate side of the Capitol and in the Senate office buildings: post offices; a credit union; a packaging service; a stationery shop and gift shop; restaurants and cafeterias; private meeting rooms; a travel reservation and ticketing service; beauty and barber shops; a members' gymnasium; storage lockers; housekeeping, maintenance, and repair services; parking garages and parking areas for senators and staff; a shuttle-bus service; in-house television and radio feeds; and the Capitol police. Many services charge normal retail rates or, in the case of

the gymnasium, levy an annual fee. Services such as the post offices, dining halls, and beauty and barber shops are open to the public.

- The Senate sergeant at arms supports the telecommunications needs of a modern-day office environment. The Senate computer center provides an array of services. The Senate recording studio offers radio and television services for a fee, and the photographic studio also provides services for a fee. The General Services Administration assists senators in obtaining and furnishing state offices. Numerous government documents flow into a senator's office for office use or for redistribution to constituents.

- Department and agency congressional liaison offices, and department and agency regional or state office contacts, facilitate the handling of *congressional case work* in the executive branch. Intern, volunteer, and fellowship programs support students and professionals in Washington and home-state offices. The Senate historian's office and Senate library provide research and other services.

- The Senate legal counsel may assist individual senators, and the Senate chief counsel for employment provides assistance on employment law. The Senate legislative counsel provides legislative drafting services, and the Senate parliamentarian provides procedural advice.

- Legislative, administrative, and executive staffs work under the management of the secretary of the Senate. Administrative staff under the management of the Senate sergeant at arms and architect of the Capitol assist with or facilitate the needs, concerns, or questions of any senator's office.

- The attending physician's office, health units, and the Senate chaplain serve the needs of senators and their staffs. An annual fee is charged to senators for regular use of the attending physician's services.

- The Congressional Budget Office and Government Accountability Office principally serve congressional committees with a variety of reports. The Congressional Research Service assists both committees and members with research and policy analyses. The Government Printing Office serves Congress's extensive document needs.

- Reporters from all media are present in the Capitol, providing ready access if a senator wishes to distribute a press release or hold a press conference.

As with their House counterparts, senators spend from their allowances pursuant to a number of laws, Senate rules and regulations, and interpretations. Funds provided by the Senate must be used for official—not personal or political—purposes. Additional restrictions begin within sixty days of an election in which a senator's name appears on a ballot. The federal antinepotism law applies to hiring for a senator's office.

Both houses generally allow the use of only appropriated or personal funds for official expenses. Both houses also generally allow a third party to reimburse for expenses for services a member provided to the outside entity, such as travel expenses in conjunction with a speech at a conference or a fact-finding trip. (*See § 4.30, Congressional Ethics.*)

§ 5.50 Franking Privilege

Members of Congress by law are given the privilege of sending official mail under their signatures; members-elect and specified officers of each chamber, such as the clerk of the House and the secretary of the Senate, are also extended the franking privilege. "It is the policy of the Congress that the privilege of sending mail as franked mail shall be established under this section in order to assist and expedite the conduct of the official business, activities, and duties of the Congress of the United States." *(39 U.S.C. § 3210(a)(1).)* In its annual legislative-branch appropriations bill, Congress defrays postal charges for the costs of members exercising this privilege of office.

The use of the frank is regulated in the House and the Senate, respectively, by the House Commission on Congressional Mailing Standards (popularly called the "Franking Commission") and the Senate Select Committee on Ethics. Members are encouraged to consult the Franking Commission and the Select Ethics Committee with questions on use of the frank; representatives must seek clearance from the Franking Commission for mass mailings before they are mailed. Additional authority resides with the House Administration Committee and the Senate Rules and Administration Committee.

Numerous provisions of law, rules and regulations of the House and Senate, and advisory and interpretative opinions govern the use of the frank or affect its use. Following are some of these limits:

- Mail may not be personal, such as holiday greetings.
- Mail may not seek political support, mention candidacy, solicit funds, or electioneer (for example, advocate someone's election or defeat).
- The frank may not be lent to another person or organization or generally be used for the benefit of a third party.
- The frank may generally be used for newsletters, questionnaires, news releases, and the distribution of some types of publications (for example, the *Congressional Record*).
- Mass mailings—500 pieces or more, largely identical in content—must be postmarked not fewer than ninety days before an election in which a representative's name appears on any ballot and not fewer than sixty days before an election in which a senator's name appears on any ballot.
- Mass mailings must carry the disclaimer, "This mailing was prepared, published, and mailed at taxpayer expense."
- Representatives must get clearance for mass mailings (and other mass communications) from the Franking Commission. Mass mailings may not be mailed to addresses outside representatives' districts.
- Senators must register their mass mailings with the secretary of the Senate. Senate mass mailings must be handled by the Senate service department, which certifies the cost of each mailing so that it can be charged against the $50,000 mass-mailing ceiling applicable to each senator's official office expense allowance.

§ 5.61

Staff Salary Data

2006 House and Senate Staff Salary Data

Position in Washington, DC, Office of Representativeor Senator	Average Salary	Average Years in House Position	Years in Position in Senate
House Administrative Assistant/ Chief of Staff	$129,736	5.2	
Senate Chief of Staff	$151,767		3–6
House Legislative Director	$76,490	3.1	
Senate Legislative Director	$116,952		1–3
House Press Secretary	$58,756	3.0	
Senate Press Secretary	$66,027		1–3
House Legislative Assistant	$43,433	1.8	
Senate Legislative Assistant	$66,789		1–3
House Systems Administrator	$39,898	3.7	
Senate Systems Administrator	$60,955		3–6
House Office Manager	$52,922	5.1	
Senate Office Manager	$78,266		3–6
House Scheduler	$48,394	3.6	
Senate Scheduler	$63,634		3–6

Source of data: U.S. House, Chief Administrative Office, *2006 House Compensation Study*, and U.S. Senate, Office of the Secretary of the Senate, *2006 U.S. Senate Employment, Compensation, Hiring and Benefits Study.*

• Overseas mail, express mail, and some other specific types of mail are not frankable.

• Former members may use the frank for limited purposes for up to ninety days following the end of their term.

A member whose mailing violates franking rules may be required to pay for the mailing. Recipients of mailings may complain to the House Franking Commission or the Senate Select Ethics Committee.

§ 5.60 Personal Staff

The first paid staff on Capitol Hill were hired by committees before the Civil War. By World War II, there were approximately 2,000 people in the personal offices of members of the House and Senate. In the 110th Congress, that number was approximately 14,000.

Being a staffer is not a nine-to-five job. Members can require staffers to work ten or more hours a day, often six days a week. Each member decides office policies on vacation and sick leave. Each staffer individually negotiates salary with the member, the member's chief of staff, or, possibly, an office manager. According to the Congressional Management Foundation, most personal staff are young and white, and a substantial portion are female. Senior positions are held predominantly by men. Many staff are recent college graduates with little previous full-time job experience.

As described in § 5.30 (*House Allowances for Staff, Office, and Other Expenses*), each House member has a member's representational allowance (MRA), which allows a member to hire up to eighteen permanent and four other staff, such as paid interns. Staff are divided between the Washington and district offices. The maximum House personal staff salary in 2007 was $159,828. Each employee must be paid at least minimum wage.

A senator's administrative and clerical assistance allowance varies with the size of a senator's state. For 2007, the proposed allowance ranged from $2,043,223 for a senator representing a state with a population of less than 5 million people, to $3,329,671 for a senator representing a state with a population of 28 million people or more. The maximum staff salary in a senator's office in 2006, the latest year for which a figure was officially available, was $157,559. In addition, in 2007, the legislative assistance allowance authorized for each senator for the appointment of three legislative assistants was proposed at $481,977.

There is not a limit on the number of staff that a senator may hire with the administrative and clerical assistance allowance. Depending on a state's population, a senator might employ 30–50 staff, or even more for a larger state.

Staff from across Capitol Hill who serve in the National Guard or reserves are being called up for active duty. Pursuant to law, they are entitled to leave without loss in pay, time, or performance rating.

Personal Office Staff Functions

Personal staff work for a member in his or her representative and legislative capacities. They contact executive-branch agencies to assist constituents with bureaucratic tangles that affect the constituents' Social Security or veterans' benefits. Personal staff help private and governmental entities in their home states or districts secure grants or special-project funds, answer constituent mail, and, in many offices, initiate mail to constituents.

Personal staff monitor legislation and issues to assist a member in his or her committee, floor, and constituency activities. They meet with constituents and representatives from interest groups on behalf of a member. Press staff work with the national and local media to keep them apprised of a member's activities. (*See also § 5.62, Congressional Staff Organizations.*)

Personal Staff Positions

Some of the principal positions and functions that appear in members' offices include the following:

§ 5.62

Congressional Staff Organizations

In addition to informal groups of staff, such as teams in the congressional softball leagues (<*www.congsoftball.com*>, <*www.housesoftball.com*>, and <*www.senatesoftball.org*>), staff belong to numerous Hill-based membership organizations. (For an extensive list, see the Commitee on House Administration web site, <*http://cha.house.gov*>.) Here is a representative list:

- Administrative Assistants/Chiefs of Staff Association
- Capitol Hill Chapter, Federal Bar Association
- Capitol Hill Toastmasters Club
- Congressional Asian Pacific American Staff Association
- Congressional Black Associates
- Congressional Chorus
- Congressional Hispanic Staff Association
- Congressional Jewish Staff Association
- Congressional Legislative Staff Association
- Congressional Staff Dive Club
- Democratic Press Secretaries Association
- Democratic Women of Capitol Hill
- Equestrian Society
- Federalist Society–Capitol Hill
- Lesbian and Gay Congressional Staff Association
- Professional Administrative Managers
- Rotary Club of Capitol Hill

- *Administrative Assistant (AA)* or *Chief of Staff (COS)*: The chief of staff coordinates and supervises the work of the entire staff and frequently serves as a political (not campaign) adviser to a member.
- *District/State Director*: The district/state director is the senior staffer in a state or district office, and supervises field representatives and other non-Washington staff.
- *Legislative Director (LD)*: The LD is usually the senior legislative assistant and supervisor of the legislative staff.
- *Legislative Assistant (LA)*: The LA drafts legislation and amendments (usually working with the Office of Legislative Counsel), monitors committee and floor action, and deals with constituents and lobbyists. In some offices, the LA also answers constituent correspondence. In most Senate offices, the LA works with a legislative correspondent.
- *Legislative Correspondent (LC)*: The LC drafts responses to letters and other communications sent to the member.
- *Case Worker*: A case worker is responsible for dealing with constituent problems with agencies, such as requesting compassionate leave for enlisted persons, or assisting homeowners and small businesses in obtaining aid after after natural disasters. Case workers might also assist localities and nonprofits with grantsmanship and concerns arising in the course of participating in grant programs. In some offices, case workers do "outreach" to meet constituents on behalf of members.

- *Press Secretary or Press Assistant:* A press secretary is the member's chief spokesperson to the media. A press secretary composes press releases, writes newsletters, organizes press conferences, and undertakes other media-relations activities.
- *Systems Manager/Web Master:* The systems manager is responsible for computer hardware, software, and applications, and may also be responsible for maintaining a member's web site.
- *Office Manager:* Sometimes called executive assistant, the office manager deals with staff recruitment, pay, vouchers, use of space and equipment, and coordination between Washington and district or state offices.
- *Scheduler:* The scheduler manages competing demands for a member's time. *(See § 1.50, Ever-Changing and Unpredictable Schedules.)*

Although job titles usually connote a likely set of responsibilities, they do not necessarily indicate who is the most influential staffer in an office. For example, a member might rely on an AA to manage an office, but rely on a press secretary or district director for political advice that affects all aspects of the member's conduct and issue positions.

§ 5.70 Committee and Subcommittee Staff

Although the first full-time committee staff were hired in 1865 by the House Ways and Means Committee and the Senate Finance Committee, there were not many committee staff until relatively recently. The Legislative Reorganization Act of 1946 established a system of permanent professional staff for each standing committee; however, there were fewer than 400 committee staff in both chambers at that time. Since then, that number has risen sharply. Today there are approximately 1,300 House committee staff and nearly twice as many Senate committee staff.

There is great variation in the organization of committee staffs. Some committees are highly centralized, where all staff work for the full committee and help subcommittees as needed. Other committees are decentralized, with each subcommittee having its own staff.

A few committees employ a single nonpartisan staff. Most committees, however, divide their funds for hiring staff between the majority and minority parties, with the largest share accorded to the majority. Each party hires its own staff, although even the most partisan committees may share some administrative staff. The degree of bipartisanship between majority and minority staffs depends largely on the tone set by members: on some committees staff from both parties work closely with each other, while on other committees the relationship is more adversarial.

When there are separate majority and minority staffs, each party generally employs a top staff person called a staff director or minority staff director. A chief or general counsel may also be employed. (A staffer can wear more than one hat, so that, for instance, a chief counsel might also serve as staff director.) On behalf of the respective chair or ranking minority member, a staff director manages the party's staff and acts as liaison between the staff and the committee leader.

Staff are often classified into two groups—the professional staff and the administrative staff. Professional staff draft legislation, plan hearings, write committee reports, conduct investigations, prepare for floor action, and assist conference committees. Some professional staff titles include—in addition to staff director and chief counsel—counsel, specialist, investigator, professional staff assistant, press coordinator, and associate staff.

Administrative staff perform tasks such as keeping the schedule of hearings and meetings, controlling committee meeting rooms, getting committee documents published, maintaining files, and providing general support services. Some common administrative staff titles include chief clerk, staff assistant, clerk, and receptionist.

Job titles on committees can be misleading. For example, clerks on the Appropriations Committees are the top staff. Also, the staff director probably manages a committee staff but might not be the closest adviser to the committee chair or ranking member. Members might also rely on committee staff for some committee matters and personal staff for other committee matters.

§ 5.80 House of Representatives Committee Funding

Each standing and select committee of the House, except the Appropriations Committee, is required to submit an operating budget request for expenses over the two years of a Congress to the Committee on House Administration. The budget includes estimated staff salary needs and the cost of consulting services, detailees, printing, office equipment and supplies, travel for committee members and staff, and other administrative expenses. The House Administration Committee may hold hearings on each request and ask committee leaders to testify on behalf of their committees. The House Administration Committee marks up each request and packages the individual requests into an omnibus *primary expense resolution*.

The minority party is required to be "treated fairly in the appointment" of committee staff. Both parties as majority parties have oftentimes interpreted "fairly" to mean one-third of a committee's staff and resources for the minority.

The maximum committee staff salaries in 2007 were $163,700 a year for up to three staff (two majority and one minority), $161,997 a year for up to nine staff (six majority and three minority), and $159,828 a year for other committee staff.

§ 5.90 Senate Committee Funding

By January 31 of the first session of a Congress, each Senate committee, except the Appropriations and Ethics Committees, reports a resolution requesting funding for staff and expenses for a Congress. The Appropriations and Ethics Committees have permanent authorizations for staff salaries and expenses.

Each *committee funding resolution* is referred to the Committee on Rules and Administration. The committee may hold hearings on each request and ask other committees' leaders to testify on behalf of their committees. The Rules and Administration Committee marks up each request and packages all the requests into an omnibus funding resolution. The resolution recommends funding levels for the entire Congress, but allocates funding in two portions. In recent years, funding has been allocated for nineteen months in the first portion and twelve months in the second portion. The seven-month overlap allows committees to carry over to the second period any unexpended funds from the first period.

Each committee establishes a maximum level of staff that its budget can accommodate. By resolution, however, a majority of the minority party members of a committee may request at least one-third of the funds for hiring minority staff. Committees may also hire consultants or request that staff be detailed from federal agencies if they receive approval to do so from the Committee on Rules and Administration. Each senator also receives a legislative assistance allowance, separate from a committee's budget, to hire personal staff who handle committee work for the senator.

The maximum committee staff salary in 2006, the latest year for which a figure was officially available, was $159,415 a year.

§ 5.100 Congressional Fellowships and Internships

College students, graduate students, and professionals on sabbatical have opportunities to work on Capitol Hill. Executive agencies and private organizations sponsor fellowships and internships (the terms are often used interchangeably) in congressional offices. The following inventory lists some entities sponsoring major fellowship programs and highlights key information on each fellowship. The applications for many of these programs can be obtained on the appropriate web site.

Internship opportunities, generally unpaid, can also be explored through individual congressional offices.

Fellowship Name and Sponsor	Duration	Qualifications	Comments
American Planning Association Congressional Fellowship for Urban Planning and Community Livability (*<www.planning.org/fellowships>*)	Six months	Graduate or post-graduate students in urban planning	$4,000 stipend
Capitol Hill Fellowship Program, Government Affairs Institute, Georgetown University (*<www3.georgetown.edu/grad/gppi/gai/programscourses/program/fellowship.html>*)	Twelve months, or seven months	GS-13 or uniformed service equivalent, minimum of two years in executive branch	

Fellowship Name and Sponsor	Duration	Qualifications	Comments
Congressional Black Caucus Congressional Fellows Program and Louis Stokes Urban Health Public Policy Fellows Program (and also internships) (<www.cbcfinc.org/Leadership%20Education/Fellowships/congressional.html>)	Nine months	Full-time graduate or law students, recent college graduates, professionals with five or more years of experience pursuing part-time graduate studies, and faculty members interested in legislative process	$25,000 stipend and health and dental benefits for nine-month Congressional Fellows; $35,000 stipend and health and dental benefits for twelve-month Stokes Fellowship
Congressional Fellows, American Political Science Association (<www.apsanet.org/section_165.cfm>)	Ten months, November–August	Political scientists, journalists, federal and foreign affairs executives, health policy executives, and international scholars	$38,000 and travel allowance (political scientists)
Congressional Fellowship Program, U.S.D.A. Graduate School (<www.grad.usda.gov/index.php?option=com_content+task=view+id=214+Itemid=306>)	Six months, or one year	Senior-level federal employees (GS-13–15)	Graduate school credit
Congressional Hispanic Caucus Institute Fellowship Program (and also internships) (<www.chci.org/chciyouth/fellowship/fellowship.htm>)	Eight weeks during summer, or nine months	College undergraduates, graduate students, and recent graduates	$2,200 a month, or $2,600 with graduate degree
Congressional Science and Technology Fellowships, coordinated by American Association for the Advancement of Science (<http://fellowships.aaas.org/02_Areas/02_Congressional.shtml>)	One year, September–August	Ph.D. or equivalent doctoral-level degree, or master's degree in engineering and three years of post-degree professional experience	$64,000 stipend and allowances for health insurance and relocation

Fellowship Name and Sponsor	Duration	Qualifications	Comments
LEGIS Fellows Program, Brookings Institution and Congressional Fellowship for Corporate Executives (*<www.brookings.edu/execed/fellows/legis_fellows.htm>*)	Twelve months beginning in January, or seven-month winter or spring assignment (beginning in January or April)	GS-13 or uniformed service equivalent, two years of federal service in executive branch, and corporate executives with seven years management experience, respectively	
Native American Congressional Summer Internship Program, Morris K. Udall Foundation (*<www.udall.gov/udall.asp?link=300>*)	Ten weeks	Native American college students	$1,200 educational stipend
Public Leadership Education Network (*<www.plen.org/internships.html>*)	Spring session (four months), summer session (two months), fall session (three months)	Women undergraduate or graduate students	Course credit granted
Robert Wood Johnson Health Policy Fellowships, sponsored by National Academy of Sciences, Institute of Medicine (*<www.healthpolicyfellows.org>*)	One year, September–August	Midcareer health professionals	Grants up to $84,000
Truman Scholars (*<www.truman.gov>*)	Ten-week summer institute in Washington	Undergraduate students pursuing careers in public service	Up to $30,000 merit-based grant toward graduate school
Washington Semester Fellows, American Politics Semester, sponsored by American University (*<www.american.edu/washingtonsemester>*)	One semester	College juniors or seniors	
Women's Research and Education Institute—Fellowship on Women and Public Policy (*<www.wrei.org/Fellows.htm>*)	January–September	Women graduate and post-graduate students	$1,300 per month stipend; $500 for health insurance, and up to $1,500 for tuition reimbursement

§ 5.110 Administrative Offices of the House

An administrative structure of legislative and nonlegislative staff supports the House in its legislative and representational roles and as a large, operating governmental entity. *(See also § 5.121, Architect of the Capitol; and § 5.122, Office of the Attending Physician.)*

Chaplain

(<http://chaplain.house.gov>)

The chaplain is elected by the House, and serves the pastoral needs of members, their families, and congressional staff. The chaplain offers a prayer at the opening of each day's session. *(See § 5.111, Chaplains and Guest Chaplains.)*

Chief Administrative Officer

(<www.house.gov/cao>)

(For procurement opportunities, <www.house.gov/cao-opp>)

(For support office employment opportunities, <www.house.gov/cao-hr>)

(For congressional office vacancy announcements, 202-226-4504)

(For House and Hill access only, <http://housenet.house.gov>)

The chief administrative officer (CAO) is elected by the House to supervise its nonlegislative support services. The CAO may be removed by the Speaker or by the House. The CAO's staff, largely administrative and technical, is organized into five units in addition to the CAO's "immediate office," which oversees the media galleries in the Capitol:

- Finance provides financial management and financial services to the House, such as processing expenses, offering advice on expenses, and preparing the monthly financial statements and the quarterly *Statement of Disbursements*.
- House Information Resources coordinates technology and communications products and services, including offering advice on technology purchases and integration, troubleshooting, contacting vendors, and managing computer security.
- Human Resources provides a variety of human resource management services, such as administering the House payroll and benefits, maintaining an employee assistance office, organizing training, and assisting offices with Americans with Disabilities Act services.
- House Support Services offers a number of services, including furnishing House offices, providing office equipment (including equipment and furnishings purchases for district offices), providing office supplies, managing the House office supply service and gift shop, managing the House postal operations and other specific services contracts, operating a child care center, and maintaining video, audio, and photography services.
- Procurement and Purchasing supports the purchase of supplies and services, evaluates major purchase proposals, and manages contracts. *(See § 5.112, Selling Products and Services to Congress.)*

§ 5.111

Chaplains and
Guest Chaplains

Rev. Daniel Coughlin, a Roman Catholic priest, was sworn in as the House chaplain on March 23, 2000. The Senate chaplain, Rear Admiral Dr. Barry C. Black (Ret.), a Seventh-day Adventist minister, was elected June 27, 2003. The chaplains are elected by their respective chamber to open the daily session with a prayer; serve as spiritual counselor to members, families, and staff; conduct Bible studies and discussion sessions; and officiate at weddings and funerals of members and on other special occasions.

Guest chaplains often deliver the daily invocation. Members contact their respective chamber chaplain to request approval to invite a guest chaplain. Guest chaplains are usually clergy from a member's home state or district. The guest chaplain may meet with the chamber chaplain before his or her appearance, to discuss the length—and often the tenor—of the daily prayer.

All 121 chaplains (59 in the House and 62 in the Senate) have been Protestant, except two: a Catholic priest who served in the Senate for one year, and now Father Coughlin. Guest chaplains have represented many faiths.

5

The administrative counsel within the CAO's immediate office reviews district office leases and car leases for compliance with House rules, and provides legal advice on administrative matters. The CAO manages relations with the media galleries.

Clerk of the House

(<http://clerk.house.gov>)

At the convening of a new Congress, the clerk is elected by the House as its chief legislative officer. The clerk may be removed by the Speaker or the House. On the first day of a new Congress, the clerk presides over the House until the Speaker is elected. Throughout a Congress, the clerk has numerous powers and responsibilities. The clerk does the following, among other duties:

- receives and authenticates certificates of election
- maintains the *Journal of the House of Representatives of the United States*
- certifies the passage of bills and joint resolutions
- prints and distributes the calendars of the House
- lists reports due to Congress from executive departments and agencies
- receives messages from the president and Senate when the House is not in session
- attests to and affixes the House seal to documents issued by an order of the House
- manages the House's institutional records
- supervises the staff and manages the office of a member, delegate, or resident commissioner who dies, resigns, or is expelled, or in the event the House declares a vacancy in a congressional district

§ 5.112

Selling Products and Services to Congress

The House and Senate operate separately in vendor and procurement operations.

The House chief administrative officer (CAO) through the Office of Procurement is responsible for House procurement activities. Information on procurement policy and current procurement opportunities are listed on the CAO's web site, *<www.house.gov/cao-opp>*.

The House has "privatized" some of its support services, increasing the number of procurement opportunities available in particular to services vendors. Some of the privatized services include restaurants, internal mail operations, and the beauty and barber shops.

The Senate sergeant at arms manages procurement activities through the Financial Office, Procurement. Information on procurement policy is available at 202-224-2547.

The architect of the Capitol (AOC) is also a purchaser of goods and services, with information available online at the AOC's web site, *<www.aoc.gov/business>*.

Some congressional procurement opportunities are advertised on the Federal Business Opportunities web site, *<www.fedbizopps.gov>*.

Other congressional officers also procure goods and services. For example, the clerk of the House publicizes "solicitations" on the clerk's web site at *<http://clerk.house.gov/about/solicit.html>*.

Following are some of the principal units of the clerk's office:

- Legislative Operations comprises the various clerks who support the House's legislative activities. They are present working on the Speaker's dais when the House is in session. They also work behind the scenes processing the legislation introduced in and considered by the House, and preparing other documents.
- Official Reporters record the proceedings of the House for the *Congressional Record*, and also record the proceedings of House committees.
- Publication Services provides liaison with the Government Printing Office, among other services.
- Legislative Computer Systems manages the functioning of the electronic voting system, among other responsibilities.
- Capitol Service Groups support the Democratic and Republican cloakrooms and other rooms set aside for special purposes for members, such as the Prayer Room.
- The House page program is managed by the clerk, who is a member of the Page Board. *(See § 5.113, Congressional Pages.)*
- The Legislative Resource Center (LRC) distributes documents to the House and the public, providing the services of the former House Document Room. It also provides some library and research services to House offices. In its public-disclosure function, the LRC makes available for public review financial disclosure statements, foreign travel reports, gift and travel filings, mass mailings under members' franks, Federal Election Commission reports, the *Statement of Disbursements*, and lobbying registrations and

§ 5.113

Congressional Pages

Both the House and Senate are served by pages, high-school juniors of at least 16 years age who serve as messengers and assistants in the House or in the Senate. Pages may be boys or girls; must be appointed to the House or Senate page program by a representative or senator, respectively; and serve for a semester or for a summer session, although pages are sometimes reappointed for two semesters, two summer sessions, or both a school year and a summer.

The House authorized seventy-two pages, with up to forty-eight positions allocated to the majority and up to twenty-four to the minority. In the Senate, thirty pages were authorized, with up to eighteen positions allocated to the majority and up to twelve to the minority.

In addition to carrying messages and documents to or from member and committee offices from or to other locations in the Capitol complex, pages work in the House and Senate chambers. They assist each chamber's officers in setting up the House and Senate chambers for each day's activities, such as placing documents relevant to the day's agenda on each senator's desk. They also respond to representatives and senators on the floor by carrying documents to the dais, or carrying messages outside of the chamber.

Each house has a page board that acts as the governing body for its page program. The clerk of the House supervises House pages, and the sergeant at arms of the Senate supervises Senate pages. The pages live in dormitories supervised by the page programs' staff. They take grade-level classes in page schools operated by the page programs. The House page school is located at the Library of Congress, and the Senate page school is located at the Senate pages' residence hall. Pages receive a salary, and pay a housing and meals fee.

5

reports. The LRC also distributes in print and on the clerk's web site official lists (for example, members and committee assignments), and, on the web site, copies of discharge petitions. *(See also the entries for the National Archives and Records Administration and the Federal Election Commission in §13.30, Information Sources: A Selective List.)*

• Office of History and Preservation curates the House collection of art and artifacts, and is responsible for archiving and maintaining the official records of the House and its committees, and for giving advice to members on the archiving of their papers.

• The Employment Counsel offers legal advice to members and represents House offices in employment matters, including those arising under the Congressional Accountability Act.

(For additional information on the services of the clerk's office, see § 11.10, Finding and Obtaining Congressional Documents; and § 13.10, Legislative-Branch Agencies and Offices.)

General Counsel

Appointed by the Speaker, the general counsel provides legal advice to members, committees, officers, and employees on matters pertaining to their official duties, and represents them in litigation related to their official duties. The general counsel offers support to committees in their oversight and investigatory roles. Under the House rules establishing the Office of General Counsel, the Speaker consults on the office's direction with a bipartisan legal advisory group consisting of the majority leader, majority whip, minority leader, and minority whip.

Inspector General

(<www.house.gov/IG>)

Appointed jointly by the Speaker and the House majority and minority leaders, the inspector general conducts periodic audits of the financial and administrative activities of the House and of joint entities. (Joint entities are legislative-branch agencies and offices shared by the House and the Senate, such as the architect of the Capitol.)

Law Revision Counsel

(<http://uscode.house.gov>)

Appointed by the Speaker, the law revision counsel and counsel's staff codify public laws into the U.S. Code and prepare titles of the U.S. Code for enactment. *(See also § 11.50, Laws and Their Implementation by the Executive; and § 13.10, Legislative-Branch Agencies and Offices.)*

Legislative Counsel

(<http://legcoun.house.gov>)

Appointed by the Speaker, the legislative counsel and counsel's staff provide legislative drafting services and advice to leaders, committees, and members of the House.

Parliamentarian

Appointed by the Speaker, the parliamentarian and parliamentarian's staff advise the House's presiding officer on parliamentary procedure when the House is in session. On a nonpartisan and confidential basis, the parliamentarian also advises House leaders and members on parliamentary procedure at all other times. A very important function is to advise the Speaker on referral of measures, rulings on points of order, and responses to parliamentary inquiries. The parliamentarian compiles the precedents of the House, prepares the parliamentarian's notes for the *Constitution, Jefferson's Manual, and Rules of the House of Representatives of the United States*, and authors documents such as *How Our Laws Are Made*. *(See also § 12.40, Official Rules Publications of the House; and § 12.60, Other Congressional Sources of Information on Rules and Procedures.)*

Sergeant at Arms

(For Hill and House access only, <http://sgtatarms.house.gov>)

Elected by the House as chief protocol and law enforcement officer, the sergeant at arms maintains order in the House at the direction of the Speaker; executes orders of the Speaker;

ensures that only individuals privileged to be on the House floor enter when the House is in session; and regulates the House galleries. The sergeant at arms also leads ceremonial processions at events such as joint sessions or meetings of Congress and presidential inaugurations. The mace, the symbol of the authority of the House and of the office of the sergeant at arms, is in the custody of the sergeant at arms.

The sergeant at arms has extensive responsibility for security for the House side of the Capitol, the House office buildings, and House garages and parking areas. This House officer provides various forms of support for major events in the Capitol and House office buildings. The sergeant at arms may investigate threats to members and crimes, and provide protective details. The sergeant at arms also bears security and other responsibilities for traveling congressional delegations. The sergeant at arms issues IDs to congressional staff. With the Senate sergeant at arms and the architect of the Capitol, the House sergeant at arms serves on the Capitol Police Board and the Capitol Guide Board. *(See § 5.123, Capitol Police.)*

The sergeant at arms may make funeral arrangements for representatives who die in office.

§ 5.120 Administrative Offices of the Senate

An administrative structure of legislative and nonlegislative staff supports the Senate in its legislative and representational roles and as a large, operating governmental entity. *(See also § 5.121, Architect of the Capitol; and § 5.122, Office of the Attending Physician.)*

Chaplain

(<www.senate.gov/reference/office/chaplain.htm>)
(<www.senate.gov/artandhistory/history/common/briefing/Senate_Chaplain.htm>)

The chaplain is elected by the Senate, and serves the pastoral needs of members, their families, and congressional staff. The chaplain offers a prayer at the opening of each day's session. *(See § 5.111, Chaplains and Guest Chaplains.)*

Legal Counsel

Appointed by the president pro tempore on the recommendation of the majority and minority leaders and "confirmed" by adoption of a Senate resolution, the legal counsel provides legal advice to members, committees, officers, and employees on matters pertaining to their official duties, and represents them in litigation related to their official duties. The legal counsel offers support to committees in their oversight and investigatory roles. Under the law establishing the Office of Legal Counsel, the legal counsel is responsible to the bipartisan joint leadership group consisting of the majority and minority leaders, president pro tempore, and the chairs and ranking minority members of the Judiciary and Rules and Administration Committees.

Architect of the Capitol

(<www.aoc.gov>)

The architect of the Capitol operates in a broad, complex web of responsibilities, is involved in numerous entities, and is accountable to several officers and committees of the House and Senate.

The buildings and grounds under the architect's authority include the Capitol and its grounds, which include the Taft Memorial, fountains, and other structures; the House and Senate office buildings, including the subways to the Capitol; the Library of Congress buildings and grounds; the Supreme Court building and grounds; the Thurgood Marshall Federal Judiciary Building and grounds; the Capitol police headquarters; the Botanical Garden and the adjoining outdoor National Garden; the Capitol power plant; and other buildings. The architect's duties in relation to these buildings include planning, operations, structural improvements and upkeep, construction and renovation, systems upgrades and maintenance, historic preservation, preservation of art and artifacts, landscaping and groundskeeping, and installation of physical security and life safety systems. The architect also operates the Senate restaurants and furnishes Senate offices, and serves as civil defense coordinator for the Capitol complex.

Major projects include the rehabilitation of the Capitol dome, improvements to security within the Capitol complex, including a perimeter security system, and construction of the Capitol Visitor Center. The architect also bears partial responsibility for the arrangement of presidential inaugurations and other ceremonies held in the Capitol or on its grounds. *(See § 6.12, Current Projects at the Capitol.)*

With the Capitol arguably the most important structure in Washington, DC, and with the extent of the federal presence on Capitol Hill, the architect plays an important role in District of Columbia planning. The architect is responsible for the master plan for the Capitol complex, and serves on the District of Columbia Zoning Commission, the Advisory Council on Historic Preservation, the National Capital Memorial Commission, and the Art Advisory Committee to the Washington Metropolitan Area Transit Authority, among various regional entities. Within the confines of the Capitol complex, the architect is an ex officio member of the U.S. Capitol Preservation Commission, and a member of the Capitol Police Board and the Capitol Guide Board, among various congressional entities. The architect's duties intertwine with those of the House's chief administrative officer, the Senate sergeant at arms, and other officers of the House and Senate.

In connection with his duties for the House, the architect is subject to the oversight of the House Administration Committee and the House Appropriations Committee. In connection with duties for the Senate, the architect is subject to the oversight of the Senate Rules and Administration Committee and the Senate Appropriations Committee. The Speaker, House Office Building Commission, Joint Committee on the Library, and other entities also play key policy and oversight roles.

At the time of publication, a search was underway for an architect of the Capitol to replace Alan Hantman, who was the first architect to be appointed under a 1989 law that established an appointment process and a ten-year term, with eligibility for reappointment. Mr. Hantman did not seek reappointment. The law provides that a congressional commission recommend three names to the president, who then chooses an appointee. The appointment is subject to Senate confirmation. Upon confirmation, the architect is an officer of the legislative branch. *(See also § 13.10, Legislative-Branch Agencies and Offices.)*

§ 5.122

Office of the
Attending Physician

During normal weekday working hours and whenever the House or Senate is in session, emergency and nonemergency medical care is available from the Office of the Attending Physician and health units located in the Capitol and several of the congressional office buildings. The attending physician maintains an emergency response team to provide emergency care until a patient can be taken to an appropriate medical facility. The health units are staffed by registered nurses, who provide first aid and emergency nursing services.

The health units also provide services such as flu shots, injections of allergy medications, blood pressure screening and monitoring, some occupational-health nursing services, and other nonemergency services.

These services are available to members, congressional staff, Capitol police, and pages. Emergency responses are made for Capitol visitors as well. An annual fee is charged to members for regular use of the office's services. Staffing and funding for the office have traditionally been shared by Congress and the Department of the Navy.

When mail containing anthrax spores was delivered to the office of then-Majority Leader Tom Daschle, the Office of the Attending Physician coordinated response for both the eradication of the contaminants and the testing and care of members and staff.

Legislative Counsel

(<http://slc.senate.gov>)

Appointed by the president pro tempore, the legislative counsel and counsel's staff provide legislative drafting services and advice to leaders, committees, and members of the Senate.

Parliamentarian

Appointed by the secretary of the Senate with the approval of the majority leader, the parliamentarian and parliamentarian's staff advise the Senate's presiding officer on parliamentary procedure when the Senate is in session. During a session, the parliamentarian or a member of his staff sits on the dais directly below the presiding officer. A very important function of the parliamentarian is to advise the presiding officer on referral of measures, rulings on points of order, and responses to parliamentary inquiries. On a nonpartisan and confidential basis, the parliamentarian also advises Senate leaders and senators on parliamentary procedure at all other times. The parliamentarian compiles the precedents of the Senate and prepares other documents such as *Enactment of a Law. (See § 12.50, Official Rules Publications of the Senate; and § 12.60, Other Congressional Sources of Information on Rules and Procedures.)*

Capitol Police

<www.uscapitolpolice.gov>

Created in the early 1800s, the U.S. Capitol Police today exercises jurisdiction throughout the complex of congressional buildings and surrounding streets and parks. It protects life and property; prevents, detects, and investigates crimes; and enforces traffic regulations. It is called on to protect members and officers of Congress and their families throughout the United States in addition to its principal work on Capitol Hill. Assignments include protective services, investigations, drug enforcement, emergency response, hazardous devices, patrol, communications, K-9, and other activities. The police are overseen by the Capitol Police Board, which comprises the sergeants at arms of the House and Senate and the architect of the Capitol.

Congress has authorized an increase in the size of the police force in light of the increased security challenges and workload the force has confronted, particularly since the terrorist and anthrax attacks of 2001. Police personnel needs are also affected by the numbers of members of Congress who run for president, which can trigger the addition of security details beyond those normally accorded special protection, such as the Speaker. Like other Capitol Hill workers, the police force has had to confront personnel reductions caused by call-ups of National Guard and reserve units.

Secretary for the Majority

(<www.senate.gov/reference/common/person/martin_paone.htm>)

The secretary for the majority, selected by the majority leader, is an elected officer of the Senate. The secretary supervises the majority party's cloakroom, assigns chamber seats for majority-party senators, and works on and off the Senate floor to keep majority-party senators apprised of pending business. The secretary polls senators if requested by the leadership, monitors nominations on the *Executive Calendar*, performs other duties for the leadership as directed, and obtains *pairs* on votes for senators. The secretary for the majority is the repository of official minutes of majority-party conference meetings and of meetings of its policy and other committees. The secretary staffs the committee that arranges majority-party committee assignments, and maintains a file of senators' requests for committee assignments. The secretary also recommends to the leadership majority-party appointees to boards, commissions, and international conferences, and keeps records of those appointments.

Secretary for the Minority

(<www.senate.gov/reference/common/person/dave_schiappa.htm>)

The secretary for the minority, selected by the minority leader, is an elected officer of the Senate. The secretary performs similar duties for the minority-party leadership and senators as the secretary for the majority performs for the majority party in the Senate.

Secretary of the Senate

(*<www.senate.gov/reference/office/secretary_of_senate.htm>*)

(*<www.senate.gov/artandhistory/history/common/briefing/secretary_senate.htm>*)

Elected by the Senate to provide legislative, financial, and administrative support to the Senate, the secretary of the Senate plays a key role in the Senate's operations. In addition, the secretary presides over the Senate in the absence of the vice president of the United States and pending election of a president pro tempore, and has custody of the Senate seal. The secretary is aided by an assistant secretary.

In a legislative role, the secretary's office comprises the various clerks, including the official reporters of debate, who support the Senate's legislative activities. They are present working on the dais when the Senate is in session. They also work behind the scenes processing the legislation introduced in and considered by the Senate and preparing other documents. One clerk position that exists in the Senate but not the House is the executive clerk, who prepares the *Executive Journal* and the *Executive Calendar,* recording activity on nominations, treaties, and resolutions pertaining to the Senate's executive business.

The secretary is the Senate's chief financial officer, responsible for accounting for all funds appropriated to the Senate and managing the disbursing office, headed by a financial clerk, which handles the Senate payroll, employee benefits, and all Senate appropriated funds. The secretary also audits Senate financial activities, and issues the semiannual *Report of the Secretary of the Senate*, showing all disbursements over a six-month period.

The administrative offices under the secretary of the Senate, which include the following, serve the Senate or the public or both:

- Conservation and Preservation coordinates programs for the preservation of Senate records and materials.
- Security protects classified information.
- The Historical Office assists senators and committees with archives, performs research for use by senators and the public, assists researchers in access to Senate records, maintains senators' profiles in the online *Biographical Directory of the United States Congress*, and offers other services.
- The Library offers legislative, legal, and reference services to Senate offices, and makes its enormous collection of congressional and government documents available to senators and other authorized users.
- Public Records provides public access to financial disclosure forms, travel reports, Federal Election Commission reports, registrations of mass mailings, lobbying registration and reports, and other records. *(See also the entries for the National Archives and Records Administration and the Federal Election Commission in § 13.30, Information Sources: A Selective List.)*
- Printing and Document Services serves as liaison with the Government Printing Office.

- The Senate Curator administers museum programs of the Senate for the Capitol and Senate office buildings.
- Interparliamentary Services assists interparliamentary conferences and Senate delegations traveling overseas.
- The Stationery Room provides stationery and other office supplies, and the Gift Shop offers a variety of items.
- The Senate Page School is managed by the secretary, who serves as a member of the Page Board. *(See § 5.113, Congressional Pages.)*
- The Chief Counsel for Employment offers legal advice to members and represents Senate offices in employment matters, including those arising under the Congressional Accountability Act. The secretary of the Senate also administers other human resources programs.

In the event of a senator's death, the secretary manages the senator's staff until a successor is chosen. *(For additional information on services of the secretary's office, see § 11.10, Finding and Obtaining Congressional Documents; and § 13.10, Legislative-Branch Agencies and Offices.)*

Sergeant at Arms

(<www.senate.gov/reference/office/sergeant_at_arms.htm>)
(<www.senate.gov/artandhistory/history/common/briefing/sergeant_at_arms.htm>)
(For Senate employment opportunities, <www.senate.gov/visiting/resources/pdf/Placement_Brochure_2005.pdf>, and <www.senate.gov/visiting/resources/pdf/seb.pdf>)

Elected by the Senate as chief protocol and law enforcement officer and administrative manager, the sergeant at arms supervises the Senate floor and galleries. *Doorkeepers* ensure that only individuals privileged to be on the Senate floor enter when the Senate is in session. The sergeant at arms also regulates the Senate galleries and supervises Senate pages and other workers who serve the Senate. *(See § 5.113, Congressional Pages.)* The Senate gavel is entrusted to the care of the sergeant at arms.

In a protocol role, the sergeant at arms escorts official guests to the Senate, may make funeral arrangements for senators who die in office, and provides various forms of support for major events in the Capitol and Senate office buildings. The sergeant at arms leads the Senate wherever it goes as a body, such as to the House for a joint session or meeting or to the presidential inaugural platform.

The sergeant at arms has responsibility for security for the Senate side of the Capitol and its grounds, the Senate office buildings and grounds, and the senators themselves. The sergeant at arms enforces all rules governing the Senate side of the Capitol and the Senate office buildings, and may arrest violators. The sergeant at arms also bears security and other responsibilities for traveling congressional delegations. The sergeant at arms issues IDs to Senate staff. With the House sergeant at arms and the architect of the Capitol, the Senate sergeant at arms serves on the Capitol Police Board and the Capitol Guide Board. *(See § 5.123, Capitol*

Police.) The sergeant at arms is also custodian of property of the Senate. *(See also § 5.112, Selling Products and Services to Congress.)*

As an administrative manager, the sergeant at arms has the largest staff and budget in the Senate and supports the Senate in numerous ways. Following are some of the organizational units of the sergeant at arms office:

- The Capitol Division includes an executive office and is responsible for security and emergency preparedness.
- The Operations Division assists Senate offices with the production of mass mailings and the Senate mail system. It also operates the Senate post office, and administers parking and automobile fleet maintenance. It manages the Senate's furnishings, including their repair and moving; equipment repair; services such as housekeeping and barber and beauty shops; auto leasing for Senate officers; and recording and photographic services, including operation of television cameras that record the Senate in session.
- Two units deal with the variety of services needed to provide technology in as complex an organization as the Senate. Their services range from network engineering to information security to Internet services to software acquisition to user support.
- The Support Services Division includes offices for financial management and human resources, which administers various employment programs, such as employee assistance, workers' compensation, and training.

The sergeant at arms also has jurisdiction over the media galleries, and assists senators in establishing and maintaining their state offices. Pages are supervised by the sergeant at arms.

§ 5.130 Legislative-Branch Support Agencies

A handful of agencies within the legislative branch assist Congress in both its lawmaking and representational or informational roles. Some, like the Congressional Research Service, work exclusively for Congress, and their work products traditionally must be obtained through congressional offices. Others, such as the Government Accountability Office, make many of their work products available directly to the public in both print and electronic form, although the public release of some work might be delayed to give the requesting committee or member a first chance to read or release it.

Congressional Budget Office

(<www.cbo.gov>)

The Congressional Budget Office (CBO) explains its nonpartisan role in congressional policymaking as "helping the Congress formulate a budget plan, helping it stay within that plan, helping it assess the impact of federal mandates, and helping it consider issues related to the budget and to economic policy." CBO's mandate originated in the Congressional Budget and

Impoundment Control Act of 1974. Its director is appointed jointly by the Speaker of the House and the president pro tempore of the Seante to a four-year term.

In fulfilling its role, CBO works first and foremost for the House and Senate Budget Committees. Its next priority is service to the four "money" committees—the House and Senate Appropriations Committees, which have jurisdiction over the discretionary portion of the federal budget, and the House Ways and Means and Senate Finance Committees, which have jurisdiction over taxation and full or partial jurisdiction over programs that are tax-based, such as Social Security and Medicare. It then serves Congress's authorizing committees, such as the House Agriculture Committee and the Senate Agriculture, Nutrition, and Forestry Committee. CBO handles individual member requests to the extent it can. (In its work with the tax committees, CBO uses revenue projections prepared by the congressional Joint Committee on Taxation, a bicameral study committee without legislative authority.)

In assisting the Budget Committees in preparing the annual *congressional budget resolution*, CBO prepares economic forecasts and projections, *baseline budget projections*, an analysis of the president's budget, and policy options. For most bills reported from committee, CBO prepares a *cost estimate*. It then tracks those bills and performs *scorekeeping*, a tabulation of the cumulative impact of congressional spending and revenue decisions. It also performs other economic and budget analyses and prepares policy options, often at the request of a specific committee. *(See Chapter Nine for an explanation of the federal budget process and CBO's role in it.)*

Finally, under the Unfunded Mandates Reform Act of 1995 *(109 Stat. 48)*, CBO is required to provide committees with a determination of whether a reported measure contains a *federal mandate*, make an estimate of the direct costs of the mandate if specific criteria are met, and assess funding provided or needed to cover the mandate's costs. *(See § 10.202, Unfunded Mandates; see also § 13.10, Legislative-Branch Agencies and Offices.)*

Congressional Research Service

(<www.loc.gov/crsinfo/whatscrs.html#about>)

The nonpartisan Congressional Research Service (CRS) provides information services in many forms to all congressional offices—reports, confidential memoranda and briefings, seminars, a web site, audio and video programs, and research in a variety of formats. CRS performs legislative research and analysis and policy analysis within a legislative context; provides research and analytical services related to legislative, budget, and other processes; and offers legal and constitutional research and analyses on legal issues. (Unlike the Government Accountability Office, CRS does not evaluate federal programs.) Through its research centers in the congressional office buildings and the Library of Congress's Madison Building and its staff of librarians, CRS also provides library research, reference, bibliographic, and other services. CRS responds to more than 500,000 congressional inquiries annually.

None of these services is available directly to the public. CRS reports may be obtained in print form through a member or committee office or, selectively, online through a member or committee web site. (A CRS product online through a member or committee web site may not be the latest version.) Members and committees also often release CRS confidential analyses in the course of hearings, floor debate, or press conferences, and CRS staff often testify at congressional hearings.

Organizationally, CRS is a department of the Library of Congress, and CRS is headed by a director appointed by the librarian of Congress. *(See also § 13.10, Legislative-Branch Agencies and Offices.)*

Government Accountability Office

(<www.gao.gov>)

In response to requests from committees or members or in fulfilling its legal and legislative responsibilities, the nonpartisan Government Accountability Office (GAO) provides reports, testimony, and briefings based on its *audits* and *evaluations* of government agencies, programs, and activities. Its work is often used by congressional committees in their *oversight* and *investigatory* roles, and GAO's work might well be the source of legislative provisions in *reauthorization* and other legislation. GAO also provides Congress with legal analyses and advice related to legislative proposals, legislative drafting, and potential policy changes to specific government agencies, programs, and activities. *(For an explanation of the criteria and procedures used by GAO to undertake work for Congress, see GAO's Congressional Protocols, available online at <www.gao.gov/special.pubs/d04310g.pdf>. See also § 5.131, Requesting GAO Assistance.)*

The laws under which GAO operates provide it with broad investigatory powers and broad access to agencies' information. Its authority and the interdisciplinary expertise that its audit and evaluation teams bring together enable GAO to measure the achievement of goals and objectives in federal programs, determine whether federal funds are being spent efficiently, and ensure compliance with federal law.

In addition to responsibilities for special investigations, accounting standards, and other work affecting the executive branch, GAO reports to Congress pursuant to specific laws. For example, under the Congressional Review Act, the comptroller general reports to the committees of jurisdiction of both houses of Congress on major rules proposed by federal agencies. Under the Government Performance and Results Act, GAO plays a lead role in monitoring executive departments and agencies in their implementation of the law and reports its findings to Congress. And, in assisting Congress under the Congressional Budget and Impoundment Control Act of 1974, GAO reviews *rescissions* and *deferrals* of spending proposed by the president. *(See § 10.41, Congressional Review of Agency Rule Making; § 10.61, Program Performance Information Resources; and Chapter Nine, Legislating in Congress: Federal Budget Process.)*

GAO is headed by the comptroller general. After receiving a list of candidates from a special bicameral, bipartisan commission, the president nominates the comptroller general to a

§ 5.131

Requesting GAO Assistance

Committees and individual members regularly turn to the Government Accountability Office to request a variety of assistance. Here is a letter written in the 109th Congress from the then-chair and ranking member of the House Judiciary Committee and chair and ranking member of its Constitution Subcommittee seeking a GAO investigation of government contracts with database companies and of related questions.

F. JAMES SENSENBRENNER, JR., Wisconsin
CHAIRMAN

HENRY J. HYDE, Illinois
HOWARD COBLE, North Carolina
LAMAR S. SMITH, Texas
ELTON GALLEGLY, California
BOB GOODLATTE, Virginia
STEVE CHABOT, Ohio
DANIEL E. LUNGREN, California
WILLIAM L. JENKINS, Tennessee
CHRIS CANNON, Utah
SPENCER BACHUS, Alabama
BOB INGLIS, South Carolina
JOHN N. HOSTETTLER, Indiana
MARK GREEN, Wisconsin
RIC KELLER, Florida
DARRELL ISSA, California
JEFF FLAKE, Arizona
MIKE PENCE, Indiana
J. RANDY FORBES, Virginia
STEVE KING, Iowa
TOM FEENEY, Florida
TRENT FRANKS, Arizona
LOUIE GOHMERT, Texas

JOHN CONYERS, JR., Michigan
RANKING MINORITY MEMBER

HOWARD L. BERMAN, California
RICK BOUCHER, Virginia
JERROLD NADLER, New York
ROBERT C. SCOTT, Virginia
MELVIN L. WATT, North Carolina
ZOE LOFGREN, California
SHEILA JACKSON LEE, Texas
MAXINE WATERS, California
MARTIN T. MEEHAN, Massachusetts
WILLIAM D. DELAHUNT, Massachusetts
ROBERT WEXLER, Florida
ANTHONY D. WEINER, New York
ADAM B. SCHIFF, California
LINDA T. SÁNCHEZ, California
ADAM SMITH, Washington
CHRIS VAN HOLLEN, Maryland

ONE HUNDRED NINTH CONGRESS

Congress of the United States
House of Representatives
COMMITTEE ON THE JUDICIARY

2138 RAYBURN HOUSE OFFICE BUILDING

WASHINGTON, DC 20515–6216

(202) 225–3951

http://www.house.gov/judiciary

March 9, 2005

The Honorable David M. Walker
Comptroller General of the United States
U.S. Government Accountability Office
441 G Street, NW
Washington, DC 20548

Dear Mr. Walker:

We are writing to request that the Government Accountability Office investigate issues arising from the federal government's reliance on and contributions to commercially available databases to provide information for use by law enforcement and in other important domestic functions Specifically, we request an investigation of the legality of data acquisition, verification, and security procedures and the overall magnitude of government contracts with ChoicePoint Inc. and similar database companies.

In April, 2001, the Wall Street Journal reported that ChoicePoint provided personal information to at least thirty-five government agencies and was the largest of the data suppliers. The accuracy of such data being relied upon by federal agencies must be of the highest caliber. Accurate data enhances national security, while inaccurate data can be both dangerous and personally destructive. In fact, the Transportation Security Administration (TSA) relied on erroneous private contractor data in hiring personnel to secure our nation's airports and, as a result, failed to flag background issues with 161 of 504 applicants to the air marshal program.

As private firms participate in the modernization of routine security checks, such as those at our nation's airports, the security procedures employed by private dataminers merit close scrutiny. This month, ChoicePoint disclosed that thieves may have stolen the personal data of more than 35,000 people in the state of California and up to 145,000 people nationwide. Before this information became public, however, TSA announced a pilot program for privatization of the "registered traveler" program at Orlando International Airport involving Verified Identity Pass, Inc., a partner of ChoicePoint. For a fee, frequent fliers would disclose personal information to a Verified Identity database for faster clearance through airport security.

Continued on page 145

The Honorable David M. Walker
March 9, 2005
Page Two

We are concerned about the government's reliance on, and possible contributions to, private contractors that may not have accurate or secure data, especially as it relates to the role these companies play in providing data for law enforcement and national security decision-making. For these reasons, we request that the GAO examine and report on the following:

(1) the contracts between commercial data suppliers and any federal agency, the variety of information supplied, including the form of the information (e.g, website), the term and compensation arrangements;

(2) the guidelines of the federal agencies governing the use and acquisition of personal information from commercial data suppliers and all oversight, quality control, or verification procedures for said data (including assessments on the quality of commercial databases); and

(3) internal data acquisition guidelines, quality controls, oversight, and security procedures used by the commercial data suppliers.

We thank you for your immediate attention to this matter and look forward to meeting with you as soon as possible to discuss our proposal. Please contact Keenan Keller of the Democratic staff of the Committee on the Judiciary at 202-225-6906 and Mindy Barry of the Republican at 202-226-7687 with any inquiries concerning this request.

Sincerely,

F. JAMES SENSENBRENNER, JR.
Chairman

JOHN CONYERS, JR.
Ranking Member

STEVE CHABOT
Chairman
Constitution Subcommittee

JARROLD NADLER
Ranking Member
Constitution Subcommittee

fifteen-year term; the presidential appointment is subject to the Senate's confirmation. Until July 2004, the agency's name was the General Accounting Office. *(See also § 13.10, Legislative-Branch Agencies and Offices.)*

Library of Congress

(<www.loc.gov>)

The Library of Congress is the most publicly oriented of the legislative-branch support agencies. Indeed, the number of domestic and foreign visitors, researchers, librarians with business at the Library of Congress, copyright registrants, guests for public events, visitors to its ever-expanding web resources, and so on vastly exceeds the number of congressional requests the library receives. Yet, the Library of Congress is also a vital resource for members and committees of Congress.

In terms of subject matter, the library's collections are vast and comprehensive. It is only in the fields of technical agriculture and clinical medicine "where it yields precedence to the National Agricultural Library and the National Library of Medicine, respectively." Books and other items from the library's collections are available for lending to congressional offices, and research assistance related to special collections can be obtained. The Library of Congress makes its public rooms available to members for official events, and maintains a members' reading room in the Jefferson Building. And, the library serves members' constituents with *THOMAS*, the web-based legislative information system, *<http://thomas.loc.gov>*.

Finally, the Library of Congress maintains the world's largest law library, the collection of which includes both domestic and foreign legal materials available for use by the public. The law library staff serves Congress primarily with foreign-law research, *<www.loc.gov/law/public/law.html>*. Domestic legal research and analysis is performed by the Congressional Research Service's American Law Division, another part of the Library of Congress.

The Library of Congress is headed by the librarian of Congress, who is nominated by the president; the appointment is subject to Senate confirmation. *(See also § 13.10, Legislative-Branch Agencies and Offices.)*

§ 5.140 Government Printing Office

(<www.gpoaccess.gov>)

As the principal producer and disseminator of congressional documents, the Government Printing Office (GPO) is a key source of information—in both print and electronic (online and CD-ROM) formats—about Congress and its activities. As a legislative body, Congress needs fast, accurate printing services to assist it in the processing of legislation. GPO was established in 1860 to do just that.

The congressional documents that GPO prints are distributed to the House Legislative Resource Center, the Senate Document Room, congressional committees, and elsewhere within Congress. Most documents are redistributed by those offices to members and congressional staff and to the public, but some are printed for the specific use of a committee or other congressional entity. In addition, most congressional documents are also available free online, for examination in depository libraries, or for purchase from GPO's superintendent of documents.

In addition to the printing of bills and resolutions and other legislative documents, GPO provides each congressional office with specific printed documents, as authorized by law, resolution, or regulation. These include the following:

- *Congressional Record*
- *Statutes at Large*
- *Congressional Directory* and *Congressional Pictorial Directory*
- *Federal Register* and *Presidential Papers*
- *U.S. Treaties and Other International Agreements*

Senators each receive a permanent edition of the *Congressional Record*, the *Senate Manual*, and other documents. Representatives each receive the *Constitution, Jefferson's Manual, and Rules of the House of Representatives of the United States*, a set of the U.S. Code, and other documents.

GPO provides members with franked, public-document envelopes, reprints from the *Congressional Record* (for a nominal fee), estimates of the cost of insertions exceeding two pages into the Extensions of Remarks section of the *Congressional Record*, and other services.

GPO also serves Congress and the public through its web site, GPO Access. Many congressional web sites, the Library of Congress's THOMAS service, and other government and private web sites link to GPO Access. It provides online access to congressional bills and resolutions, committee reports (including conference committee reports), public laws, the *Congressional Record*, the *Congressional Directory*, and a variety of other congressional documents. It also provides online access to the *Federal Register, Code of Federal Regulations*, and other executive-branch publications essential to the work of a government-relations professional. *(See also § 11.10, Finding and Obtaining Congressional Documents; and § 13.10, Legislative-Branch Agencies and Offices.)*

As the administrator of the federal depository libraries program, GPO also makes these and other congressional, executive, and judicial documents available to federal depository libraries, *<www.gpoaccess.gov/fdlp.html>*. *(See also § 11.10, Finding and Obtaining Congressional Documents.)*

§ 5.150 Congressional Accountability Act

Office of Compliance

(<www.compliance.gov>)

A key provision of the House Republican's 1995 "Contract with America" and the first new law of the Republican-controlled Congress, the Congressional Accountability Act *(P.L. 104-1; 109 Stat. 3)*, extended application of eleven federal labor and nondiscrimination laws to Congress and the legislative branch. It superseded existing practices and regulations, and afforded legislative-branch staff with rights and redress provided to other government and private workers.

The laws made applicable by the Congressional Accountability Act were the following:
- Age Discrimination in Employment Act of 1967
- Americans with Disabilities Act of 1990

- Civil Rights Act of 1964
- Employee Polygraph Protection Act of 1988
- Fair Labor Standards Act of 1938
- Family and Medical Leave Act of 1993
- Labor-Management Dispute Procedures (part of Title 5 of the U.S. Code)
- Occupational Safety and Health Act of 1970
- Rehabilitation Act of 1973
- Veterans Reemployment Act of 1993
- Worker Adjustment and Retraining Notification Act of 1988

The law established the Office of Compliance, with authority over the legislative branch, to enforce the statutes and handle complaints of employees. It is headed by an executive director, hired by a board of directors that is appointed jointly by the Speaker, House minority leader, and Senate majority and minority leaders. Oversight is exercised by the House Administration Committee, Senate Rules and Administration Committee, and Senate Homeland Security and Governmental Affairs Committee. Congress created the office to avoid a potential separation-of-powers problem caused by executive administration of the act in the legislative branch.

For resolution of a grievance, an employee must bring his or her grievance to the Office of Compliance and follow a formal process of counseling, mediation, and hearing. After the mediation process, an employee can file a formal complaint and request an administrative hearing with the office or file a civil suit in U.S. district court. The act also provides for an appeals process from a decision made by a hearing officer. Members of Congress may not be held personally liable for any damage awards, and punitive damages are disallowed.

The Office of Compliance is also given authority to determine unionization rights of employees. However, unionization is not allowed for staffs of member, committee, and leadership offices, or for staff in other specified legislative-branch agencies and offices. The general counsel investigates OSHA, disability access, and other matters under the Congressional Accountability Act.

The House and Senate Ethics Committees retained authority to discipline members, officers, and employees for violations of rules on nondiscrimination in employment. However, members of Congress were allowed to continue to consider party affiliation, residence, and "political compatibility" in making employment decisions.

Issues continuing to the 110th Congress from past Congresses include members raising the Speech and Debate Clause to seek dismissal of suits. The Supreme Court was expected to rule in 2007 on a case that onvolved the Speech and Debate Clause, the Congressional Accountability Act, and mootness since the senator being sued retired at the end of the 109th Congress.

§5.160 General Services Administration

(<www.gsa.gov>, and in box for "GSA Organizations," choose "OCIA")

The General Services Administration (GSA) has congressional services representatives in each GSA region who serve over 1,400 House district and Senate state offices. The congressional services representatives coordinate requests for space, furnishings and equipment, and other office services (such as moving, custodial, and security services).

The congressional services representatives work under the policies and guidance provided by GSA's Office of Congressional and Intergovernmental Affairs, which works to ensure that GSA services for district and state offices are carried out in accordance with House and Senate rules and policies. GSA, in turn, works through the House's Office of the Chief Administrative Officer (under the policy guidance of the House Administration Committee) and the Senate Office of the Sergeant at Arms (under the policy guidance of the Senate Rules and Administration Committee). The House chief administrative officer and the Senate sergeant at arms provide the points of contact for congressional offices in obtaining GSA services. They also review leases for offices not in federal buildings.

In another service useful to both members of Congress and their constituents, GSA maintains online a searchable *Catalog of Federal Domestic Assistance*, facilitating research on grants and other federal funding available to governments, nonprofits, individuals, and other entities *(<www.cfda.gov>)*. GSA also compiles the print version of the *Catalog. (See also <www.grants. gov>, managed by the Department of Health and Human Services.)* GSA maintains both online and other services to the American public, services for business, and services for government agencies that are useful to members of Congress and their constituents. These services include the consumer information center and the federal information centers. *(In box for "GSA Organizations," choose "OCSC.")*

§5.170 Congressional Liaison Offices

Congressional liaison offices in executive departments and agencies are vital to congressional-executive relations. They might also be called congressional affairs offices, legislative relations offices, or some other appropriate name. A congressional liaison office responds to congressional requests for information and coordinates case work for congressional offices with an agency. It might coordinate an agency's legislative program and some or many aspects of appropriations requests. It also works with the Office of Management and Budget on legislative clearance. *(See § 5.180, Office of Management and Budget.)* Several agencies that handle congressional requests numbered in the thousands each year maintain offices in the House and Senate office buildings. *(See § 5.171, Liaison Offices on Capitol Hill.)*

The General Services Administration (GSA) Office of Congressional and Intergovernmental Affairs and Department of Health and Human Services Assistant Secretary for Legislation provide a good description of a liaison office's work. *(Excerpts appear in § 5.172, Duties of a Congressional Liaison Office.)*

§ 5.171

Liaison Offices on Capitol Hill

All departments and many agencies maintain congressional affairs offices, a point of contact for congressional offices with a specific department or agency. In addition, some of the departments and agencies that handle among the highest volume of congressional inquiries maintain offices within the House and Senate office buildings. These Capitol Hill offices are listed below. All area codes are 202.

Department or Agency	House		Senate	
	Room	Phone	Room	Phone
Air Force	B322 Rayburn	225-6656	SR-182 Russell	224-2481
Army	B325 Rayburn	225-3853	SR-183 Russell	224-2881
Coast Guard	B320 Rayburn	225-4775	SR-183 Russell	224-2913
Marine Corps	B324 Rayburn	225-7124	SR-182 Russell	224-4681
Navy	B324 Rayburn	225-7124	SR-182 Russell	224-4682
Office of Personnel Management	B332 Rayburn	225-4955	B332 Rayburn	225-4955
Social Security Administration	G3-L1, Rayburn	225-3133	G3-L1, Rayburn	225-3133
Department of State	B330 Rayburn	226-4640	B330 Rayburn	226-4640
Department of Veterans' Affairs	B328 Rayburn	225-2280	SH-321 Hart	224-5351

The general counsel's office in departments and agencies is also involved in legislative relations, working closely with both the congressional liaison office and the head of the department or agency. *(Excerpts describing the responsibilities of two general counsel offices appear in § 5.173, General Counsel Offices.)*

Heads of departments and agencies and their personal staffs, budget offices, and program offices might all become involved at one time or another in liaison with Congress. Cabinet secretaries and other departmental officials and agency officials might testify at legislative, appropriations, oversight, and investigatory hearings. Responses to congressional case work might include policy decisions that require review by a senior departmental or agency official. Requests for information might involve regional, state, or field offices assisting in a response. When a congressional office is the client, departments and agencies tend to be responsive.

§ 5.172

Duties of a Congressional Liaison Office

General Services Administration's Office of Congressional and Intergovernmental Affairs

(<www.gsa.gov>, and in box for "GSA Organizations," choose "OCIA")

The following excerpt from the General Services Administration (GSA) web site offers a good summary of the work and responsibilities of a congressional liaison office.

General Information

The Office of Congressional and Intergovernmental Affairs serves as advisor to the Administrator and supervises and maintains agency liaison with all Members of Congress and Congressional committees.

The Office of Congressional and Intergovernmental Affairs: prepares and coordinates GSA's annual legislative program; communicates GSA's legislative program to the Office of Management and Budget (OMB), Congress, and other interested parties; works closely with OMB in the coordination and clearance of all proposed legislation impacting GSA and its programs; prepares comments and makes recommendations on all bills submitted by GSA to the President for final action; and initiates, coordinates, and presents briefings to Members of Congress and their staff on GSA programs and initiatives.

The Office also prepares, circulates, and finalizes agency reports/recommendations on GSA's position concerning bills (including drafts) which affect GSA's mission and responsibilities; coordinates and clears with OMB and other agencies GSA reports, positions on legislative initiatives, testimony, follow-up questions, and answers submitted to congressional committees; coordinates all activities associated with GSA's appearances before congressional committees including the development of strategy, designation of witnesses, and preparation of testimony; represents GSA in meetings and discussions with other agencies on all legislative matters; and coordinates and approves all written responses to congressional correspondence.

The Office also: develops periodic mailings to the Congress on significant agency initiatives; coordinates preparation of reports mandated by statute to be forwarded to the Congress as required; serves as liaison with state and local government officials and their official national organizations on items concerning GSA; and prepares weekly GSA intergovernmental affairs report for the White House Director of Intergovernmental Affairs.

General Services Administration's Office of Congressional and Intergovernmental Affairs

The GSA web site previously listed procedures applicable to agency work with congressional offices, which remain of interest in understanding an agency's congressional liaison procedures:

5. Procedures. The following procedures will be followed in dealings with the Congress:

a. Hearing statements to be presented by GSA witnesses must first be submitted to the Office of Congressional Affairs for review. The congressional statements also require

Continued on page 152

approval from the Office of Management and Budget before submission to the Congress; therefore, enough time must be allowed for both GSA and OMB to review the statements.

b. Congressional hearings dealing with matters of direct interest to GSA, whether or not GSA witnesses are involved, must be monitored by a member of the office of Congressional Affairs, and a brief memorandum listing the major issues covered at the hearing and the commitments made on behalf of the agency will be forwarded to the program office involved. The Office of Congressional Affairs will track and follow up on these commitments.

c. Associate Administrators and Heads of Services and Staff Offices are expected to take initiative and work diligently with the committee staffs on issues. Their dealings should be coordinated through the Office of Congressional Affairs, which will take the lead in contacting the Congress and will maintain the agency record. If legislative issues arise or requests are received for technical assistance in contacts between GSA's Office of Budget and the Congress, the Office of Congressional Affairs must be notified regarding the nature of the issues and of any further action needed.

d. Any GSA employee dealing directly with a Member of Congress and staff on policy issues or a subject involving an agency commitment must inform the Office of Congressional Affairs and the next higher level of management within the affected Service or Staff Office. When regional GSA congressional support representatives contact a Member or staff in providing and outfitting State and district offices, the Office of Congressional Affairs does not need to be contacted. Regional congressional support representatives must report to the Office of Administrative Services any situations that are not routine. The Office of Administrative Services will, when necessary, inform the Office of Congressional Affairs. Direct contacts that result in a meeting being scheduled that involves policy issues and agency commitments must be reported to the Office of Congressional Affairs before the meeting takes place.

e. All congressional correspondence, background material, and factsheets, whether initiated by GSA or in reply to an inquiry, whether for signature by the Administrator or a Service Head (excluding Regional Administrators), must be routed through the Office of Congressional Affairs for concurrence. Congressional correspondence signed by Regional Administrators must include a copy to the Office of Congressional Affairs.

f. Deadlines on requests for comment on legislation sent out by the Office of Congressional Affairs are to be honored by the Services and Staff Offices, which are expected to give the deadlines top priority. Normally, extensions to deadlines will not be granted by the Office of Congressional Affairs. The Office of Congressional Affairs will keep the Administrator informed of each service's compliance with deadlines.

g. When meetings are held to discuss legislation, projects, inquiries, or matters of congressional interest, a representative from the Office of Congressional Affairs must be invited to attend.

Continued on page 153

U.S. Department of Health and Human Services Assistant Secretary for Legislation

(<www.hhs.gov/asl>)

Cabinet departments have an assistant secretary charged with congressional liaison and often other responsibilities, as shown in this example:

Mission

The Office of the Assistant Secretary for Legislation (ASL) is responsible for the development and implementation of the Department's legislative agenda.

It provides advice on legislation and facilities communication between the Department and Congress. The office also informs the Congress of the Department's views, priorities, actions, grants and contracts. ASL is the Department liaison with Members of Congress, staff, Committees, and with the Government Accountability Office (GAO).

The office provides support to the Secretary of Health and Human Services by:

- developing, transmitting, providing information about, and working to enact the Department's legislative and administrative agenda;

- supporting implementation of legislation passed by Congress;

- working closely with the White House to advance Presidential initiatives relating to health and human services;

- responding to Congressional inquiries and notifying Congressional offices of grant awards (GrantsNet, TAGGS) made by the Department;

- providing technical assistance regarding grants and legislation to Members of Congress and their staff and facilitating informational briefings relating to Department programs and priorities;

- managing the Senate confirmation process for the Secretary and the fourteen other Presidential appointees (HHS) who must be confirmed by the Senate;

- preparing witnesses and testimony for Congressional hearings;

- coordinating meetings and communications of the Secretary and other Department officials with Members of Congress;

- notifying and coordinating with Congress regarding the Secretary's travel and event schedule;

- coordinating Department response to Congressional oversight and investigations;

- acting as Departmental liaison with the Government Accountability Office (GAO) and coordinating responses to GAO inquiries; and

- serves as liaison to external organizations, including public and private interest groups, with respect to the legislative agenda.

§ 5.173

General Counsel Offices

The following two examples show the support that a general counsel's office gives an executive department in its relations with Congress.

U.S. Department of Transportation Office of the General Counsel

(<www.dot.gov/ost/ogc/org/legislation/index.html>)

The Office of Legislation, U. S. Department of Transportation, serves as legislative counsel to the Office of the Secretary in all modes of Transportation.

Its areas of responsibility include:
- Departmental legislation to be transmitted to Congress
- Departmental analysis of legislation pending before Congress
- Departmental analysis of legislation under consideration in the Administration
- Confirmation hearings of the Secretary, Deputy Secretary, and General Counsel
- Departmental testimony to be given by departmental witnesses before Congressional Committees
- Departmental analysis of testimony to be given by Administration witnesses before Congressional Committees
- Executive Orders
- Presidential Memoranda
- Proclamations

U.S. Department of Commerce Office of General Counsel

(<www.ogc.doc.gov/legis_reg_main.html>)

Office of the Assistant General Counsel for Legislation and Regulations
The Legislative Division works with various bureaus to develop the Department's legislative initiatives and is the focal point within the Department for coordinating the analysis of legislation, developing and articulating the views of the Department on pending legislation. This office is the principal legal liaison with the Office of Management and Budget, working to obtain required clearances and interagency consensus on departmental letters, reports, testimonies, and legislative proposals for delivery to the Congress. The office also represents the Department's views in interagency deliberations on legislative proposals and expression of legislative views advanced by other agencies.

§ 5.180 Office of Management and Budget

<www.whitehouse.gov/omb>

The Office of Management and Budget plays many roles of interest to Congress and important to the operation of the executive branch, but two roles in particular stand out as of interest to Congress: coordinating preparation and defense of the annual budget, and *legislative coordination and clearance.*

OMB organizes the preparation of the annual budget in the executive branch, and works to implement the president's guidance and decisions during that process. The OMB director and his staff bring all decisions together in the budget documents that the president submits to Congress. The OMB director is also one of the leadoff executive witnesses each year before several committees to explain the president's budget recommendations to Congress and to defend them, and continues to play a key role throughout the year as congressional committees draft appropriations, tax, and other budgetary legislation. *(For more information on OMB's budget role, see § 9.40, Presidential Budget Process.)*

OMB also seeks to ensure that the administration speaks with one voice through the system of legislative coordination and clearance. OMB Circular A-19 describes policies and procedures *(see <www.whitehouse.gov/omb/circulars/a019/a019.html>)*; it is supplemented occasionally by memoranda to department and agency heads from the OMB director *(see, for example, <www.whitehouse.gov/omb/memoranda/m01-12.html>)*. Legislative clearance and coordination covers legislation that agencies wish to transmit to Congress. The process allows other interested agencies to have input and for OMB to consider the draft legislation's compatibility with the president's legislative program. If the legislation is cleared, there will be "no objection" to the legislation, or it will be "in accord with the president's program," that is, it implements a portion of the president's legislative program. The agency makes this information known to Congress with its transmittal.

Legislative coordination and clearance similarly covers agency testimony and reports, critical to the committee stage of the legislative process.

As legislation moves to the floor of the House or Senate, OMB regularly prepares "statements of administration policy," or SAPS, on major legislation. Interested agencies, White House offices, and OMB each contribute to these documents, which are then made available to Congress. *(See examples of SAPs at §§ 15.08 and 15.13.)*

Finally, the president needs advice once legislation is submitted to him for his signature or veto. Agencies usually have forty-eight hours to submit their views, in the form of a letter signed by a presidential appointee in the agency, to OMB, which then prepares a memorandum for the president on the views submitted and its own analysis of the legislation. Agencies are also tasked with first drafts of signing or veto statements. *(For more information on these processes and OMB's role, see § 10.20, Congress and the Executive: Legislation.)*

§ 5.190 Outside Groups

Several outside groups maintain close relationships with members and staff because of services these groups provide. Congressional spouses also organize for social and other purposes. *(See § 5.191, Congressional Spouse Organizations.)*

Center for Democracy & Citizenship Program

(<www.excelgov.org/index.php?keyword=a432929c8e1952>)

Associated with the Council for Excellence in Government, the Center for Democracy & Citizenship Program exists to "improve the performance of America's representative democ-

§ 5.191

Congressional Spouse Organizations

- Congressional Club (Democratic and Republican spouses)

- Democratic Spouses Club

- Meager Means Investment Club (bipartisan)

- Spouses Club (Republican spouses)

racy." It has managed the bipartisan congressional retreats *(see § 1.60, Family Life)*. With the Stennis Center for Public Service, the center manages the "Congress to Campus" program of the U.S. Association of Former Members of Congress.

Congressional Institute

(<www.conginst.org>)

The Congressional Institute was established in 1987 to provide information about Congress to the general public, and to encourage dialogue between Congress and the public on issues of national importance.

The institute conducts conferences, briefings, and seminars for members of Congress, congressional staff, and private-sector leaders. The institute has also assisted in the bipartisan House retreats.

Congressional Management Foundation

(<www.cmfweb.org>)

The Congressional Management Foundation (CMF) was founded in 1977 to assist members and staff in improving office management.

CMF provides management training programs for senior staff and consulting services for individual offices. CMF also conducts training for new senior staff during the early organization meetings. It publishes management books and reports, and provides advisory research services for staff.

National Academy of Public Administration

(<www.napawash.org>)

The National Academy of Public Administration undertakes studies for Congress and the executive "upon any subject of government." The academy comprises 550 fellows, both scholars and government practitioners, who serve on project panels and undertake other activities to aid government in improving its efficiency, effectiveness, and accountability.

National Academy of Sciences

(<www.nationalacademies.org>)

The National Academy of Sciences has a "mandate that requires it to advise the federal government on scientific and technical matters." The academy comprises about 2,000 members and 350 foreign associates who are engaged in scientific and engineering research. Members volunteer their time to work on committees created by Congress and the executive to conduct studies on science, technology, and medicine.

Stennis Center for Public Service

(<*www.stennis.gov*>)

Created by Congress as a legislative branch agency in honor of the late Senator John Stennis, D-MS, the Stennis Center's mandate is to "attract young people to careers in public service, to provide training for leaders in or likely to be in public service, and to offer development opportunities for senior congressional staff." Programs for congressional staff include the Congressional Staff Fellows Program and the Emerging Congressional Staff Leadership Program.

U.S. Association of Former Members of Congress

(<*www.usafmc.org*>)

The Former Members of Congress Association was founded in 1970 as a bipartisan and non-profit educational, research, and social organization.

The association promotes public understanding of Congress, both domestically and internationally. The former members group, through its "Congress to campus" program, conducts education programs in high schools and colleges. Through its foreign policy seminars, the association travels throughout the world to meet with legislators from other countries to address common concerns.

The former members also routinely return to Washington for special events, such as a day on Capitol Hill honoring their service. A biennial seminar on "life after Congress" is conducted for new former members to assist them in adjusting to life outside Congress. A number of former members also contributed to a book, *Inside the House: Former Members Reveal How Congress Really Works,* edited by Lou Frey Jr. and Michael T. Hayes (Lanham, MD: University Press of America, 2001).

Former members of Congress are extended certain privileges and courtesies by the House and Senate. They continue to have floor privileges, including to joint sessions or meetings, with some restrictions if they are now lobbyists. They have access to the Congressional Research Service and Library of Congress, priority after sitting members in testifying at hearings, seating in the members' dining rooms, and other courtesies. Departing members are allowed to make some purchases of office furnishings and equipment, may use the frank for certain purposes for ninety days, and are provided guidance on archiving correspondence and other print and nonprint items.

U.S. Capitol Historical Society

(<*www.uschs.org*>)

The Capitol Historical Society was founded in 1962 as a nonprofit, nonpartisan educational organization chartered to "enhance and perpetuate the history and heritage of the Capitol, its institutions and the individuals who have served in Congress and the Capitol."

The society holds programs on Congress for elementary and secondary schools and scholarly symposia. It works for the enhancement of the Capitol's collection of art and artifacts, and supports research on the art and architectural history of the Capitol and the careers of members of Congress. The society is publisher of *We the People: The Story of the U.S. Capitol.*

Woodrow Wilson International Center for Scholars

(<www.wilsoncenter.org>)

(Congress Project, <www.wilsoncenter.org/index.cfm?fuseaction=topics.home&topic_id=1412>)

The Wilson Center is a think tank created by Congress that sponsors scholars for extended periods of time in Washington, DC, so that policymakers might interact with them and benefit from diverse views presented in written work, seminars, and other formats. The Wilson Center sponsors the Congress Project, which "fosters a dialogue between scholars who study Congress and policymakers who have experience with how Congress works."

Chapter Six

Supporting Congress:
The Capitol Complex

Analysis

6

§6.00 Introduction

The Capitol complex includes the Capitol and House and Senate office buildings, where members of Congress, committees, leaders, and other congressional entities have offices. The House and Senate meet in chambers in the Capitol itself. The Library of Congress, the Supreme Court, and other buildings and grounds on and near Capitol Hill are also part of the Capitol complex.

§6.10 U.S. Capitol and Grounds

The year 2000 was significant for more than being a millennial year—it is also the bicentennial of Congress's move to Washington, DC, from Philadelphia. On November 17, 1800, the House and Senate convened in the U.S. Capitol for the first time.

Moreover, 2000 was a year of preparation for the presidential inauguration on January 20, 2001. Beginning in 1801 with Thomas Jefferson's inaugural, the Capitol has been the primary site of presidential inaugurations. While most of these events have been held on the East Front of the Capitol, they have also been held on the West Front as well as inside the Capitol. President George W. Bush's first and second inaugurations were held on the West Front, the fifty-first and fifty-second times that the presidential oath of office has been administered at the Capitol.

History of Construction

The Capitol building today covers approximately four acres of ground and contains over sixteen acres of floor space. Its length exceeds 751 feet, and its greatest width is nearly 350 feet. The distance from the base of the East Front to the top of the Statue of Freedom is nearly 288 feet. The area under the Capitol Dome, the Rotunda, is 96 feet in diameter and rises 180 feet, 3 inches. The Capitol is a beautiful manifestation of nineteenth-century neoclassical architecture. Its immediate grounds cover fifty-eight acres, but the architect of the Capitol is responsible for over 280 acres on Capitol Hill.

The Constitution in Article I, Section 8, Clause 17 provided for one or more states to cede land not exceeding ten miles square for the seat of government, over which Congress would have legislative authority. Maryland and Virginia ceded land, and, pursuant to the Residence Act of 1790, President Washington selected the area that is now the District of Columbia. (The land ceded by Virginia was returned in 1846.) President Washington also chose commissioners to survey and oversee the design and construction of the District and of government buildings. They, in turn, selected French engineer Pierre Charles L'Enfant to plan the city. The location chosen for the Capitol was on the brow of what was called Jenkins' Hill, a site that L'Enfant described as "a pedestal waiting for a monument."

The commissioners announced a competition for the Capitol's design, with an award of $500 and a city lot for the design chosen. The competition ended in July 1792 without a selection. In October, a physician living in the British West Indies, Dr. William Thornton, requested the opportunity to present a design, which the commissioners granted. The design—a central section with a low dome flanked by two rectangular wings—was accepted by the commissioners and approved by President Washington on July 25, 1793. The president laid the cornerstone on September 18, 1793.

Because of funding and other problems, Congress and the Library of Congress moved into an incomplete north wing in 1800. (The Supreme Court, another Capitol occupant, remained in Philadelphia until 1801.) A temporary building known as *The Oven* was subsequently constructed within the unfinished walls of the south wing as the meeting place for the House of Representatives. Benjamin Henry Latrobe was appointed architect; he modified the Thornton design, and oversaw completion of the south wing and partial reconstruction of the north wing. A temporary wooden passageway connected the two wings. On August 24, 1814, during the War of 1812, the British burned the Capitol.

A building, later known as the *Old Brick Capitol*, was constructed on the site of today's Supreme Court building, and was used by Congress from 1815 to 1819. Latrobe oversaw reconstruction of the Capitol through most of 1817, when he resigned in a dispute over his authority. Charles Bulfinch was appointed his successor in 1818, and completed the Capitol and some of its grounds by 1829, when his position ended. From 1816–1867, supervision of the Capitol was directed by the federal commissioner of public buildings. Running water was added in the Capitol in 1832, and gas lighting was added in the 1840s.

Because of the growth of the United States and the increase in the number of members, Congress was in need of more room by 1850, and another design competition was held. President Fillmore selected Thomas U. Walter as architect and the plan he had submitted. The cornerstone of the House wing was laid on July 4, 1851, and, beginning in early 1853, Captain Montgomery C. Meigs of the Corps of Engineers was named superintendent of construction. The House was able to meet in its new chamber on December 16, 1857, and the Senate in its new chamber on January 4, 1859. The Supreme Court moved from its chamber to the Old Senate Chamber in 1860.

In construction of the Capitol before the Civil War, slaves worked as artisans and laborers in the Capitol's construction.

With the onset of the Civil War, work on the Capitol, including its new dome, was suspended in 1861 and resumed in 1862. The Statue of Freedom, created by sculptor Thomas Crawford, was placed atop the Capitol Dome in 1863, with completion on December 2. (*See § 6.11, The Lantern and Flags.*) In 1866, Italian-born Constantino Brumidi finished the canopy fresco in the Rotunda, *The Apotheosis of George Washington*. (By the time Brumidi died in 1880, he had worked for more than twenty-five years creating frescoes, murals, other art, and decoration in the Capitol.) The Capitol wings were completed in 1868.

Edward Clark, an assistant to Walter, oversaw construction following Walter's resignation over a contract dispute in 1865, and served as architect of the Capitol until his death in 1902.

During Clark's tenure, steam heating was gradually added throughout the Capitol. Electrical lighting was installed beginning in 1885. In 1874, the first elevator was installed. By 1894, modern plumbing had been installed throughout the building, and, by 1902, following a gas explosion and fire in the original north wing, fireproofing of the old House and Senate wings was completed. The Library of Congress moved to its new quarters, now the Thomas Jefferson Building, in 1897, and the Supreme Court moved to its new building in 1935. The designation, duties, and relationship to Congress of the architect of the Capitol developed during this period; formal control over the Capitol was transferred by Congress to the architect in 1867.

It was during Clark's tenure as well that landscape designer Frederick Law Olmsted, creator of New York City's Central Park, Brooklyn's Prospect Park, and many other public and private spaces, was commissioned to design the Capitol grounds. The project was carried out between 1874 and 1892. In addition to landscaping, Olmsted's plan included terraces for the north, west, and south sides of the Capitol building, and a grotto and other structures on the grounds.

§6.11

The Lantern and Flags

The Capitol Dome is topped by twelve columns encircling a lantern. The lantern is lit when one or both houses of Congress meet in night session. Although there is not a legal requirement for the night lighting or a record of when the lighting began, it is believed that the practice started in about 1864, when members lived in boarding-houses and hotels near the Capitol.

Moreover, when either the House or Senate is in session, a flag flies over the respective chamber. If a chamber recesses rather than adjourns, the flag remains flying until the next adjournment.

Flags also fly over the East and West Fronts twenty-four hours a day, a tradition that started during World War I. They are lowered and removed only when they are worn. *(For information on flags flown over the Capitol that may be obtained through the office of a member of Congress, see § 3.112, Constituent Services and Courtesies.)*

The U.S. Botanic Garden has been located on the Capitol grounds since 1850; it moved to its current site in 1933. The Bartholdi Fountain, created for the 1876 Centennial Exposition in Philadelphia, was moved to the Capitol grounds in 1877 and to its current location at Independence Avenue and First Street, SW, in 1932. Its surrounding gardens are associated with the U.S. Botanic Garden. The Peace Monument, commemorating naval deaths at sea during the Civil War, was erected during 1877 and 1878 at the foot of Capitol Hill at Pennsylvania Avenue and First Street. The James A. Garfield Monument at Maryland Avenue and First Street, SW, was unveiled in 1887. The massive, expressive Ulysses S. Grant Memorial, on First Street at the foot of Capitol Hill, was dedicated on April 27, 1922, the 100th anniversary of Grant's birth. The Robert A. Taft Memorial, a bell tower northwest of the Senate side of the Capitol and on the Capitol grounds across Constitution Avenue, was dedicated in 1959. Senator Taft, R-OH, served from 1939 until his death in 1953; he served as Senate majority leader in 1953. In addition, before construction began on the Capitol Visitor Center, there were ninety-nine "memorial trees" commemorating people, organizations, and events, and other trees contributed by states. Many are marked by plaques. (With the construction, eight memorial trees were transplanted and six were planned to be replaced.)

Clark was succeeded by Elliott Woods, who served as architect of the Capitol until his death in 1923. This was a period of relatively little change in the Capitol itself. However, it was during this time that the House abandoned desks for chairs because it had grown to 435 members. Most significantly, Woods oversaw the construction of the first House (Cannon) and Senate (Russell) office buildings. The tunnel between the Capitol and the Senate office building, later named the Russell Building, was completed, and motorized transport began between the two buildings via the tunnel in 1912. Woods's successor, David Lynn, served until retirement in 1954, and oversaw the 1949 to 1951 renovation of the Capitol, which included remodeling of the House and Senate chambers; structural, safety, and other improvements; and the addition of modern air conditioning to replace the systems first installed before 1930. During Lynn's tenure, he supervised construction of the Longworth House Office Building, the Supreme Court, the Adams Library of Congress building, and the Botanic Garden.

J. George Stewart served as architect of the Capitol from 1954 until his death in 1970; he oversaw the extension of the East Front, which added ninety rooms to the Capitol. Stewart also oversaw construction of the Rayburn House Office Building and completion of the second Senate office building. The East Front project included a new subway system to the two Senate office buildings, then called the Old and New Senate Office Buildings and later renamed the Russell and Dirksen Buildings, respectively *(see § 6.20)*, reconstruction of the Senate steps, repairs to the Dome, and other changes. (The sandstone columns removed from the old East Front now form an imposing sculpture in the landscape of the National Arboretum, in Washington, DC.) When the Rayburn House Office Building was completed and occupied in 1965, subway service was also opened to the House side via this new building.

During the 1971 to 1995 tenure of Architect of the Capitol George M. White, work in the Capitol looked both forward and back. Electronic voting equipment was installed in the House chamber in 1973. Facilities for television coverage of the chambers were added in the House in 1979 and in the Senate in 1986. Improved climate control, modern computer and communications systems, and electronic surveillance systems were added. Looking back, the Old Senate Chamber, National Statuary Hall (the former House chamber), and the Old Supreme Court Chamber were restored to nineteenth-century appearances in time for the nation's bicentennial.

White supervised construction of the Hart Senate Office Building, the Madison Library of Congress building, and the Thurgood Marshall Federal Judiciary Building. Among other projects, the West Front was restored between 1983 and 1987, and the Olmsted terraces were also renovated, adding several thousand square feet of office and meeting space by 1993. The Statue of Freedom was removed from the Capitol Dome, refurbished, and reinstalled on the Dome in 1993. On the Capitol's interior, among other projects, the ceiling murals in the House first-floor corridors were completed by artist Allyn Cox. Alan M. Hantman was appointed the tenth architect of the Capitol in January 1997, and did not seek reappointment to the office in 2006. *(See § 5.121, Architect of the Capitol.)* Hantman oversaw extensive security and life-safety improvements throughout the Capitol complex, and saw construction of the Capitol Visitor Center nearly to completion. *(See § 6.12, Current Projects at the Capitol.)*

Some of the Prominent Rooms in the Capitol

Beginning at the south end of the second (principal) floor, the *chamber of the House of Representatives* is one of the largest legislative chambers in the world. It is the room in which the House and Senate assemble for joint sessions and joint meetings. Full-length portraits of George Washington, by John Vanderlyn, and the Marquis de Lafayette, by Ary Scheffer, flank the Speaker's dais. Off the House floor to the south is the Speaker's Lobby, a place for representatives to work off the floor; beyond the Speaker's Lobby are the Members' Reading Rooms, private chambers for reading and consultation. At the rear of the House chamber are doors to the Democratic and Republican Cloakrooms. The visitors' gallery has seating for 624 in addition to the desks in the press gallery, which are located overlooking the Speaker's dais. The electronic voting display is in the wall panels above the press gallery seats. Above twenty-three of the twenty-four gallery doors are relief portraits of great lawgivers through history, from Hammurabi to Jefferson. Around the ceiling are the seals of the fifty states and the territories. *(See a floor plan and illustrations of the House chamber in § 14.10, How to Follow Floor Proceedings in the House.)*

The *Rayburn Room*, across the corridor and near the main entrance to the House chamber, is a place for members to talk together or to meet with staff and guests. A full-length portrait of George Washington by Gilbert Stuart hangs in this room. The Lindy Claiborne Boggs Congressional Women's Reading Room, a suite available to women House members, is near the Rayburn Room.

National Statuary Hall was created by statute in 1864, pursuant to which each state could submit two statues of illustrious citizens for display in the redesignated old House chamber. In 1933, Congress limited the number of statues in the old House chamber to one for each state, with second statues to be located elsewhere in the Capitol. *(See § 6.13, Statues in National Statuary Hall.)* Above the north doorway of the chamber is the "Franzoni Clock," named for its sculptor, Carlo Franzoni; it is also called the "Car of History" because History (the muse Clio) stands in a winged car recording events in a book as time passes.

Some of the additional statues submitted by the states are located in other corridors, such as the corridor between Statuary Hall and the House chamber. In this latter corridor, all but one of the statues face into the corridor. The statue of Oklahoma's Will Rogers faces the main House door because, he stated, he wanted to "keep an eye on Congress."

States have begun to replace statues in the collection with new statues. For example,

§ 6.12

Current Projects at the Capitol

As the history of the Capitol's construction in § 6.10 suggests, there are nearly always major and minor preservation, modernization, expansion, or other projects underway. Conservation of the Brumidi Corridors in the Capitol continues, as does replacement of the Minton tiles. In addition, congressional leaders and individual members have supported studies and steps to reduce the environmental impact of congressional operations, adherence to so-called green principles and standards. Other developments have revealed the need for other changes. The largest number of women ever elected to the House, ninety in the 110th Congress, has brought a demand for more women's restrooms convenient to the House chamber. Evacuations of the Capitol have shown a need for egress better suited to disabled individuals' needs. *(See the architect of the Capitol's web site for a variety of information on the Capitol. Major projects are described at <www.aoc.gov/projects/index.cfm>.* Current or ongoing major projects include:

This artist's rendering shows how the Capitol Visitor Center will appear when complete. The viewpoint is approximately from above the Jefferson Building of the Library of Congress, looking in northwesterly direction across First Street N.E./S.E.

Capitol Visitor Center: With the ceremonial groundbreaking on June 20, 2000, construction planning and then construction of the visitor center began, a structure that is three-fourths the size of the Capitol itself. At the culmination of more than a decade of planning and debate, Congress approved construction of an underground, 580,000 square-foot, three-level visitor center outside the East Front of the Capitol. The visitor center space includes 170,000 square feet of expansion space for the House and Senate. The visitor center was expected to open to the public in late 2008 or early 2009. The visitor center was planned to maintain the openness of the Capitol, provide appropriate visitor facilities for the now-more-than 3 million visitors a year to the Capitol, and enhance Capitol security.

As described by the architect of the Capitol, the visitor center includes space for exhibits, reception and services, food service, security, connections to existing buildings, service tunnels and loading docks for underground vehicle access to the Capitol, mechanical facilities, and storage. It will accommodate about 5,000 visitors at any given time, allowing about 1,500 people an hour to tour the central portions of the Capitol and another 700 an hour to visit the House and Senate visitors' galleries. *(See <www.aoc. gov/cvc/index.ctm>.)*

Plans for the visitor center also call for redesign of the plaza outside the East Front, providing a more attractive setting compatible with the Frederick Law Olmsted design prevalent everywhere else on the Capitol's grounds.

While visitors have had to put up with temporary entrances to the Capitol, members and staff have been inconvenienced in trying to do their work. Because the center connects to the Capitol's East Front, precious Capitol office space has been lost during construction. Staff have been dispersed to other congressional buildings and elsewhere. Members and leaders have lost Capitol office space, and some of the so-called Capitol hideaways have had to be abandoned. Temporary parking has also had to be found.

The cost of the visitor center could exceed $600 million. There are presently three sources of funds: appropriations made by Congress, receipts from sales of a coin commemorating the bicentennial of

Continued on page 167

Congress's move to Washington in 1800, and private funds raised by a section 501(c)(3) foundation set up by The Pew Charitable Trusts.

The much-higher-than-expected costs and the much-longer-than-anticipated construction level are reminiscent of the $100,000 appropriation in 1855 for the construction of the Capitol dome, which was thought by some to need only a few months for construction. The dome cost over $1 million, and took eight years to finish, but without Brumidi's art work.

Security: The murder of two Capitol police officers in the line of duty in 1998 further heightened congressional concerns with Capitol security. Planning and implementation accelerated after the September 11, 2001, terrorist attacks and the October anthrax-contaminated mailings to Congress. Plans call for creating a secure perimeter around the Capitol's immediate grounds that include police-activated vehicle barriers, card-activated parking, steel bollards, landscaped islands, planters compatible with the Olmsted walls, cameras and other security devices, and other security elements. Security enhancements within Capitol complex buildings range from surveillance systems to protective window film. (Other security measures, such as those involving personnel, organization, and tactics, are being taken by the U.S. Capitol Police.) The Capitol Visitor Center is an integral part of security improvements planned for the Capitol.

Fire Safety: Another congressional concern in recent years has been fire safety, which it has supported with designated appropriations to the architect of the Capitol. Work is occurring in the Capitol, the congressional office buildings, and the Library of Congress buildings. Different strategies must be employed in nearly every building because of their differing ages and the differing fire-safety codes and practices that were in place when a building was built or renovated. Work has included installation of smoke detection systems, replacement of sprinkler heads, installation of new sprinkler systems, upgrades of electrical wiring, egress improvements, and compartmentalization of building floors.

Utility Tunnels: In the course of construction of the Capitol Visitor Center, Congress and the Office of Compliance gave added attention to the state of the approximately five miles of "steam tunnels" that serve the Capitol complex. The Office of Compliance found extensive health and safety violations in the tunnels, endangering employees of the architect of the Capitol working there. The architect's office and Office of Compliance agreed in 2007 to a plan of at least five years' duration to abate the hazardous conditions in the tunnels.

Supreme Court Modernization: Beginning in 2003, the architect undertook a modernization effort at the Supreme Court building consisting of two large projects. The first project was construction of a two-story underground annex to support Supreme Court police and other uses. The second project was the first modernization of the court building's infrastructure since 1935 when the Supreme Court moved into its then-new building. This project includes mechanical and electrical work, life-safety improvements, asbestos abatement, structural repairs, and renovation activities.

Other Projects: Some of the other important projects planned or underway in the Capitol complex include rehabilitation of the Capitol dome; completion of expansion of the Capitol Power Plant's West Refrigeration Plant; development of an alternate computing facility; extensive repairs to the Bartholdi fountain; upgrades to the House and Senate legislative call systems; upgrades to HVAC, electrical, and communications systems in the Capitol and congressional office buildings; and egress improvements throughout the Capitol complex.

§ 6.13

Statues in National Statuary Hall

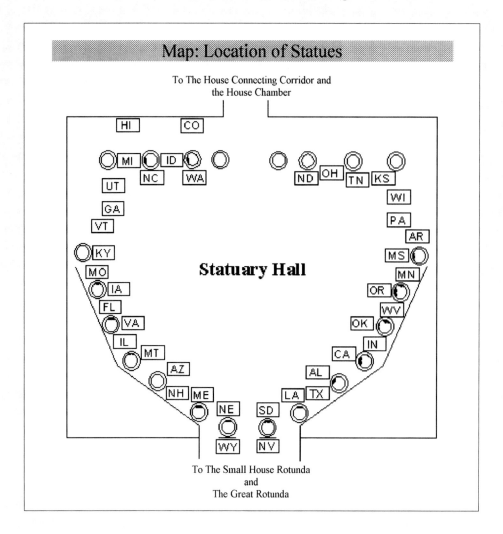

Map: Location of Statues

To The House Connecting Corridor and
the House Chamber

Statuary Hall

To The Small House Rotunda
and
The Great Rotunda

Continued on page 169

Kansas replaced Governor George Washington Glick's statue, which was returned for display in Kansas, with a statue of native son, President Dwight David Eisenhower.

National Statuary Hall has also been refurbished to a nineteenth-century appearance. The location of John Quincy Adams's desk is marked and is popular with visitors. Standing there, one can hear a loud whisper from the other side of the room. Adams was the only president to serve in the House after his presidency. It was in this room that Adams suffered a paralyzing stroke in 1848 and, too ill to be moved, died two days later in the Speaker's office just off the chamber. Seven other floor markers show the location of desks of representatives who served while the House met in this chamber and who went on to become president. (Andrew

Statues in National Statuary Hall

State	Statue	Sculptor
Alabama	General Joseph Wheeler	Berthold Nebel
Arizona	John Campbell Greenway	Gutzon Borglum
Arkansas	Uriah M. Rose	Federic W. Ruckstuhl
California	Junipero Serra	Ettore Cadorin
Colorado	Dr. Florence Rena Sabin	Joy Flinsch Buba
Florida	John Gorrie	Charles Adrian Pillars
Georgia	Alexander H. Stephens	Gutzon Borglum
Hawaii	King Kamehameha I	Thomas R. Gould
Idaho	George L. Shoup	Federick Ernst Triebel
Illinois	Frances E. Willard	Helen Farnsworth Mears
Indiana	General Lew Wallace	Andrew O'Connor
Iowa	Samuel J. Kirkwood	Vinnie Ream
Kansas	John J. Ingalls	Charles H. Niehaus
Kentucky	Henry Clay	Charles H. Niehaus
Louisiana	Huey P. Long	Charles Keck
Maine	Hannibal Hamlin	Charles E. Tefft
Michigan	Lewis Cass	Daniel Chester French
Minnesota	Henry M. Rice	Frederick Ernst Triebel
Mississippi	Jefferson Davis	Augustus Lukeman
Missouri	Thomas H. Benton	Alexander Doyle
Montana	Charles Marion Russell	John B. Weaver
Nebraska	William Jennings Bryan	Rudulph Evans
Nevada	Patrick A. McCarran	Yolande Jacobson
New Hampshire	Daniel Webster	Carl Conrads
North Carolina	Zebulon B. Vance	Gutzon Borglum
North Dakota	John Burke	Avard Fairbanks
Ohio	William Allen	Charles H. Niehaus
Oklahoma	Sequoyah (Sequoya)	Vinnie Ream
Oregon	Rev. Jason Lee	Gifford MacG. Proctor
Pennsylvania	Robert Fulton	Howard Roberts
South Dakota	Gen. William Henry H. Beadle	H. Daniel Webster
Tennessee	John Sevier	Belle K. and L. F. Scholz
Texas	Samuel Houston	Elisabet Ney
Utah	Brigham Young	Mahonri Young
Vermont	Ethan Allen	Larkin G. Mead
Virginia	Robert E. Lee	Edward V. Valentine
Washington	Marcus Whitman	Avard Fairbanks
West Virginia	Francis H. Pierpont	Franklin Simmons
Wisconsin	Robert M. La Follette, Sr.	Jo Davidson
Wyoming	Esther H. Morris	Avard Fairbanks

6

§ 6.14

Those Who Have Lain in State or in Honor in the Capitol Rotunda

The Rotunda of the Capitol, completed in 1824, is considered a suitable place for the nation to pay final tribute to eminent citizens. To lay in state or honor, the congressional leadership authorizes the use of the Rotunda or both chambers agree to a concurrent resolution. The deceased's survivors must grant permission. Following are the names of those who have lain in state or in honor, showing the dates they lay in state or in honor and their principal offices or positions.

July 1, 1852	**Henry Clay**: member of House, Speaker of House, senator, secretary of state
April 19–21, 1865	**Abraham Lincoln**: member of House, president of United States
August 13–14, 1868	**Thaddeus Stevens**: member of House
March 13, 1874	**Charles Sumner**: senator
November 25–26, 1875	**Henry Wilson**: senator, vice president
September 21–23, 1881	**James A. Garfield**: member of House, president of United States
December 30–31, 1886	**John A. Logan**: member of House, senator
September 17, 1901	**William McKinley**: member of House, governor of Ohio, president of United States
April 28, 1909 (on reinterment)	**Pierre Charles L'Enfant**: planner of Washington, DC
January 20, 1917	**George Dewey**: admiral
November 9–11, 1921	**Unknown soldier** of World War I
August 8, 1923	**Warren G. Harding**: senator, president of United States
March 11, 1930	**William Howard Taft**: secretary of war, president of United States, chief justice of Supreme Court
July 18–19, 1948	**John Joseph Pershing**: general
August 2–3, 1953	**Robert A. Taft**: senator
May 28–30, 1958	**Unknown soldiers** of World War II and Korean War
November 24–25, 1963	**John F. Kennedy**: member of House, senator, president of United States
April 8–9, 1964	**Douglas MacArthur**: general
October 23–25, 1964	**Herbert Hoover**: secretary of commerce, president of United States
March 30–31, 1969	**Dwight D. Eisenhower**: general, president of United States
September 9–10, 1969	**Everett M. Dirksen**: member of House, senator
May 3–4, 1972	**J. Edgar Hoover**: first director of Federal Bureau of Investigation (FBI)
January 24–25, 1973	**Lyndon B. Johnson**: member of House, senator, vice president, president of United States
January 14–15, 1978	**Hubert H. Humphrey**: senator, vice president
May 25–28, 1984	**Unknown soldier** of Vietnam era
June 1–2, 1989	**Claude Pepper**: senator, member of House
July 28, 1998	**Jacob Joseph Chestnut** and **John Michael Gibson**: Capitol police officers killed in line of duty
June 9–11, 2004	**Ronald Reagan**: governor of California, president of the United States
October 30–31, 2005	**Rosa Parks**: civil rights pioneer
December 30, 2006– January 2, 2007	**Gerald R. Ford**: member and minority leader of the House, vice president, president of the United States

In addition, funerals and memorial services for members of Congress and other persons have been held in other rooms of the Capitol. A memorial service was held in National Statuary Hall on January 5, 2005, for Representative Robert Matsui, D-CA, who died January 1, 2005.

Johnson served briefly in the Senate in 1875, six years after his presidency ended.) *(See also § 3.31, Members of Congress Who Served as President.)*

The massive *Rotunda* is in the center of the building, midway between the entrances to the House and Senate chambers. In its canopy is Brumidi's *The Apotheosis of George Washington*—Washington in the center attended by Liberty and Victory and surrounded by thirteen female figures representing the thirteen original states and, in an outer circle, by six allegorical groupings representing War (with Freedom in the center), Sciences (Minerva), Marine (Neptune), Commerce (Mercury), Mechanics and Art (Vulcan), and Agriculture (Ceres). Famous Americans such as Benjamin Franklin and Samuel F.B. Morse also appear in the allegorical groupings, as do technological advances of the time, such as the transatlantic telegraph cable in the grouping with Neptune.

The Rotunda Frieze, seventy-five feet above the floor, contains nineteen historical scenes, beginning with the landing of Columbus and ending with the birth of aviation. Massive historical paintings hang on the walls of the Rotunda, and include the *Baptism of Pocahontas*, by John Chapman, and *Washington Resigning His Commission as Commander-in-Chief of the Army*, by John Trumbull (one of four by Trumbull commissioned for the Rotunda).

In bas-relief carvings over the four entrances to the Rotunda, encounters between white settlers and Native Americans are portrayed: the Pilgrims at Plymouth, Pocahontas seeking to spare John Smith's life, William Penn's treaty with the Indians, and Daniel Boone in the wilderness.

Statuary and other art and artifacts also adorn the Rotunda. Recent additions to Rotunda statuary include a bust of the Rev. Martin Luther King, Jr., and the *Memorial to the Pioneers of the Women's Suffrage Movement,* a portrait monument of Elizabeth Cady Stanton, Susan B. Anthony, and Lucretia Mott, by Adelaide Johnson, received by Congress in 1921 and previously displayed in the Crypt. The Rotunda is also the place where a small number of Americans have lain in state or in honor. *(See § 6.14, Those Who Have Lain in State or in Honor in the Capitol Rotunda.)*

The *Prayer Room,* just off the Rotunda, is a nondenominational chapel for members and staff to use for prayer and meditation. Its stained-glass window shows George Washington kneeling at prayer. A Bible always lies open on an altar, and two prie-dieu sit in front of candelabrum on either side of the altar.

The *Old Senate Chamber* was used by the Senate until 1859, and by the Supreme Court from 1860 to 1935. It has been restored to a nineteenth-century appearance. The great debates about slavery, states' rights, and union occurred in this room. The Old Senate Chamber is still used on occasion by the Senate for both official and ceremonial meetings, such as the executive meetings of the Senate during its trial of President Clinton. A significant feature of this room is the "porthole portrait" of George Washington by Rembrandt Peale. This room is open to the public.

The current *chamber of the Senate* is a model of simplicity. Individual desks facing the rostrum are assigned to each senator; it is a tradition for a senator to carve his or her name into the senator's desk. Senators maneuver to obtain specific desks with historic connections to their states' predecessors. Off the Senate floor to the north is the Senate Lobby, a place for senators to work off the floor; beyond the Senate Lobby is the Marble Room, a private chamber for reading and consultation. At the rear of the chamber are doors leading to the Democratic and Republican Cloakrooms. Busts of twenty vice presidents line the gallery walls; other vice presidential busts are located outside the Senate chamber. (The vice president is president of the Senate.) In addition to the desks in the press gallery, there are 611 seats in the Senate gallery. *(For a floor plan and illustration of the Senate floor, see § 14.20, How to Follow Floor Proceedings in the Senate.)*

The *Reception Room* at the east end of the Senate Lobby is where senators may meet visitors. Pursuant to a Senate resolution, a committee chaired by then-Senator John F. Kennedy, who had recently written *Profiles in Courage*, chose five outstanding senators whose likenesses should fill the empty medallions in the room. The committee's choices were Henry Clay, Daniel Webster, John C. Calhoun, Robert M. La Follette, and Robert A. Taft. Dedication ceremonies took place on March 12, 1959.

Pursuant to instructions in a subsequent Senate resolution, the Senate Commission on Art recommended the addition of Senators Arthur H. Vandenberg and Robert F. Wagner in two of the remaining six portrait spaces in the Senate Reception Room. The new portraits were unveiled September 14, 2004. Pursuant to a 2003 resolution, the commission was directed to commemorate the Great Compromise, or Connecticut Compromise, proposed by Roger Sherman and Oliver Ellsworth, Connecticut delegates to the Constitutional Convention. The compromise proposed a bicameral legislature, with representation by population in one house and equal representation by state in the other house. The portrait of Sherman and Ellsworth was unveiled September 12, 2006.

The *President's Room* is the most ornate room in the Capitol. Until adoption of the Twentieth Amendment changing the beginning dates of the terms of the president and Congress, a president would use this room on March 3–4 in the fourth year of his term, when he would go there to sign legislation before his term ended on March 4 at noon. Immediately following his first inauguration ceremony, President George W. Bush went to this room to sign his Cabinet nominations, three of which the Senate confirmed that afternoon.

The *Vice President's Room,* also a beautiful and ornate room, is the vice president's ceremonial office in the Capitol. Among the room's furnishings is Rembrandt Peale's portrait of George Washington. (The vice president has more typical office space on the Senate side of the Capitol and in one of the Senate office buildings.)

On the first floor of the Capitol, the *Old Supreme Court Chamber* has been refurbished to its appearance before the Supreme Court moved to the Old Senate Chamber in 1860. It is open to the public. It was in this room that Chief Justice John Marshall led the court in numerous critical decisions under the new Constitution, where Daniel Webster established his legal reputation in *Trustees of Dartmouth College v. Woodward* (1819), and where the court under Chief Justice Roger B. Taney decided the *Dred Scott Case* (1857). Near the Supreme Court chamber in 1844, Samuel F.B. Morse sent the first telegraph message, "What hath God wrought," from Washington to Baltimore over lines for which Congress had appropriated construction funds.

The *Crypt* is located directly beneath the Rotunda. A white stone in the pavement marks the Capitol's mathematical center. Informative displays in this room show visitors the history of the Capitol in drawings and models. In a vault below the Crypt is the black-draped catafalque used as the funeral couch for individuals who lie in state or in honor in the Rotunda. (It has been used in other locations in Washington, such as at the Supreme Court for the viewing of Associate Justice Thurgood Marshall, upon his death in 1993.) The vault was intended to house the remains of George and Martha Washington, but the Washington family objected to their removal from Mount Vernon.

The *Brumidi Corridors*, including the *Patent Corridor*, on the first floor of the Senate wing demonstrate Brumidi's command of the decorative arts in a paean to American history, personages, and flora and fauna. At the opposite end of the Capitol's first floor, Allyn Cox painted murals in the House corridors that depict the history of buildings where Congress met and historical events involving the U.S. Capitol. Cox's projects were undertaken through the House's acceptance of donations from the U.S. Capitol Historical Society and the Daughters of the American Revolution, and were completed in the early 1970s.

Interior Art and Artifacts

The Capitol is rich in the quality and quantity of paintings, sculpture, furnishings, and other art and artifacts that Congress possesses.

In addition to works of art already mentioned in the course of describing the history and prominent rooms of the Capitol, paintings include Charles Willson Peale's *George Washington at Princeton*, Thomas Sully's portrait of Thomas Jefferson, John Singer Sargent's portrait of Speaker Thomas B. Reed, Mathew Brady's oil-tinted photograph of House Appropriations Chair Thaddeus Stevens, Albert Bierstadt's *Discovery of the Hudson River*, John Trumbull's *Declaration of Independence in Congress*, which hangs in the Rotunda, and a number of Seth Eastman paintings of American forts and Native American scenes.

The four grand staircases in the Capitol are dominated by huge paintings commemorating events in American history:
- House wing, east staircase—*Scene of the Signing of the Constitution of the United States*, by Howard Chandler Christy
- House wing, west staircase—*Westward the Course of Empire Takes Its Way*, by Emanuel Leutze
- Senate wing, east staircase—*Battle of Lake Erie*, by William H. Powell
- Senate wing, west staircase—*First Reading of the Emancipation Proclamation*, by Francis Bicknell Carpenter

§ 6.15

Resources on the Capitol

Information on many aspects of the Capitol, including its history, specific elements, and current projects, is available at the architect of the Capitol's web site, *<www.aoc.gov>*. This site also contains a bibliography of books on the Capitol. Additional information on the Capitol is available through the House and Senate's web sites, *<www.house.gov>* and *<www.senate.gov>*, respectively.

The Library of Congress has an "online exhibit" about the Capitol at *<www.lcweb.loc. gov/exhibits/us.capitol/s0.html>*.

The United States Capitol Historical Society comprises individuals interested in the preservation of the history of the Capitol; see *<www.uschs.org>*.

Some of the basic references on the Capitol include the following:

- William C. Allen, *The Dome of the United State Capitol: An Architectural History* (Washington, DC: Government Printing Office, 2002)

- William C. Allen, *History of the United States Capitol: A Chronicle of Design, Construction, and Politics* (Washington, DC: Government Printing Office, 2001) *(Available online through GPO, at <www.access.gpo.gov/congress/senate/capitol/index.html>.)*

- William C. Allen, *"In the Greatest Solemn Dignity": The Capitol's Four Cornerstones* (Washington, DC: Government Printing Office, 1995)

- William C. Allen, *The United States Capitol: A Brief Architectural History* (Washington, DC: Government Printing Office, 1990)

- Architect of the Capitol, *Art in the United States Capitol* (Washington, DC: Government Printing Office, 1978)

- Congress, *The Capitol: A Pictorial History of the Capitol and of the Congress,* 9th ed. (Washington, DC: Government Printing Office, 1988)

- Donald R. Kennon and Thomas P. Somma, eds., *American Pantheon: Sculptural and Artistic Decoration of the United States Capitol* (Athens, Ohio: Ohio University Press, 2004)

- William Kloss and Diane K. Skvarla, *United States Senate Catalogue of Fine Art,* S.Doc. 107-11 (Washington, DC: Government Printing Office, 2002) *(Available online through GPO, at <www.gpoaccess.gov/serialset/cdocuments/sd107-11/browse.html>.)*

- Marty LaVor, *The Capitol: See It Again for the First Time—Looking Up.* (Alexandria, VA: The LaVor Group, 2002)

- Montgomery C. Meigs, *Capitol Builder: The Shorthand Journals of Montgomery C. Meigs, 1853-1859, 1861: A Project to Commemorate the United States Capitol Bicentennial, 1800-2000.* Wendy Wolff, ed. (Washington, DC: Government Printing Office, 2001)

- Henry Hope Reed, *The United States Capitol: Its Architecture and Decoration* (New York: W.W. Norton & Co., 2005)

- Pamela Scott, *Temple of Liberty: Building the Capitol for a New Nation.* (New York: Oxford University Press, 1995)

- United States Capitol Historical Society, *We, the People: The Story of the United States Capitol, Its Past and Its Promise* (Washington, DC: United States Capitol Historical Society, 2002)

Continued on page 175

§ 6.15 *(continued)*

- United States Capitol Historical Society, *Where the People Speak: The United States Capitol and Its Place in American History*. (Washington, DC: United States Capitol Historical Society, 2004)

- United States Senate, *Art and Historic Objects in the Senate Wing of the Capitol and Senate Office Buildings,* S. Doc. 106-25. (Washington, DC: GPO, 2000)

- United States Senate, *United States Senate Catalogue of Graphic Art,* S. Doc. 109-2. (Washington, DC: Government Printing Office, 2006). *(Available online through GPO, at www.gpoaccess.gov/serialset/cdocuments/sd109-2.)*

- George M. White, *Under the Capitol Dome.* (Washington, DC: American Institute of Architects Press, 1997)

- Barbara Wolanin, *Constantino Brumidi: Artist of the Capitol* (Washington, DC: Government Printing Office, 1998) *(Available online through GPO, at <www.access. gpo.gov/congress/senate/brumidi>.)*

6

Over the staircases are "lay lights" with decorative painting. Numerous marble, bronze, and plaster busts and statues are located throughout the Capitol. Sculptors include Gutzon Borglum (best known for the carvings at Mount Rushmore), Daniel Chester French (who also created the Lincoln statue in the Lincoln Memorial), Augustus Saint-Gaudens (known in Washington as well as the sculptor of *Peace of God*, Henry Adams's memorial to his wife in Rock Creek Cemetery), and Jean Antoine Houdon, the renowned French sculptor whose statue of George Washington, located in the Rotunda, is an image of Washington familiar to many Americans. (The marble original of Houdon's statue stands in the Virginia state capitol.)

Other art, furnishings, artifacts, and decorations are found throughout the Capitol and in its office buildings. For example, the bronze "Columbus Doors" depict events in the life of Christopher Columbus, and portray contemporaries of Columbus, historians who wrote of his voyages, and allegorical figures. The doors are also called the "Rogers Doors" after their creator, Randolph Rogers, who designed and modeled them in Rome in 1858. The doors have been hung between National Statuary Hall and the House wing and on both the former and current East Front entrances to the Rotunda. They are now displayed inside the Capitol, on the first floor near the central ground-level entrance.

In recent years, Congress and donors of artworks have sought to diversify the individuals represented and memorialized in Congress's collections of paintings, sculpture, and other art. Paintings added to the collections have included those of Joseph Rainey, R-SC, the first elected black representative; Romualdo Pacheco, R-CA, the first elected Hispanic representative; Jeanette Rankin, R-MT, the first elected woman representative; and Rep. Dalip Saund Singh, D-CA, the first elected Asian American and Indian American representative. States donating statues to the National Statuary Hall collection have given statues of Sarah Winnemucca, a Paiute, whose statue was donated by Nevada; Po'Pay, a Pueblo, whose statue was donated by New Mexico; and Sakakawea, a Shoshone, whose statue was donated by North Dakota.

The House, Senate, and United States Capitol Historical Society have also sought to identify artifacts of earlier Congresses that have passed into private or other public possession and artifacts identified with Congress, such as movie properties. In addition, needless to say, conservatorship is a large, ongoing activity throughout the Capitol and its office buildings.

Exterior Art and Artifacts

The Capitol's neoclassical architecture, fountains, sculpture, and other artifacts engage the visitor in walking around the Capitol and its grounds and in viewing the building from many vantages. One of the most prominent features is the *Statue of Freedom*, facing east atop the Capitol Dome. The statue, designed in Rome in 1856 by sculptor Thomas Crawford and cast in Washington, is nineteen feet, six inches tall. The figure is of a woman clad in flowing robes, with a brooch at her waist inscribed with the letters *U S*. On her head sits a helmet circled with stars and topped with large feathers and talons and an eagle's head. Her right hand rests on the hilt of a sheathed sword. In her left hand, she holds a wreath and shield with thirteen stripes. She stands on a globe circled with a band bearing the insignia *E Pluribus Unum*. The statue sits on a base decorated with fasces and wreaths.

The tympanums (the triangle-shaped pediments) over the East Front porticoes are odes in sculpture to America as an ideal. The House tympanum, *Apotheosis of Democracy*, was modeled in Paris by Paul Wayland Bartlett and carved by the Piccirilli brothers in New York City. The central allegorical group is two figures, Peace Protecting Genius. A grouping representing Agriculture appears to Peace's left, and a grouping representing Industry appears on Peace's right. Waves at either end of the tympanum symbolize the Atlantic and Pacific Oceans.

The central tympanum is *Genius of America*. First executed in sandstone by Luigi Persico after a design suggested by John Quincy Adams, the badly deteriorated figures were removed and repaired, and casts were made of them as part of the East Front extension. Reproductions in marble were executed by Bruno Mankowski from 1959 to 1960. The central figure, America, grasps in her right hand a shield inscribed *USA*, which rests on an altar, inscribed *July 4 1776*. An eagle stands on her left side. America points to her right at Justice, who bears the scales of justice in one hand and a scroll in the other, inscribed *Constitution 17 September 1787*. America looks to her left at Hope, who rests an arm on an anchor.

The Senate tympanum, *Progress of Civilization*, was designed in Rome by Thomas Crawford and carved at the Capitol. The central figure is again America, with an eagle at her side and the sun at her back. To her left is a tableau representing the early days in America—a woodsman, a hunter, a Native American chief, a Native American mother and child, and a Native American grave. On her right side are a soldier, a merchant, two youths, a schoolmaster and child, and a mechanic. Sheaves of wheat, symbolic of fertility, and an anchor, symbolic of hope, complete this side of the tympanum. *(See also § 6.15, Resources on the Capitol.)*

§ 6.20 Guide to Public Buildings on Capitol Hill

The Capitol and surrounding congressional buildings are accessible by Metro (subway), bus, taxi, and car. The Metro station closest to the Capitol and the House office buildings is Capitol South; the station closest to the Senate office buildings is Union Station. Public parking is very limited, with Union Station north of the Senate office buildings being the closest place where parking is nearly always available. Visitors with disabilities who have appointments at the Capitol may request parking; the congressional office with whom the visitor has an appointment should contact the Congressional Special Services Office to reserve a parking space. Street spaces are restricted to permit holders or to short-term parking (neighborhood zone and meters).

Public and barrier-free entrances to the Capitol and other public Capitol Hill buildings are shown on the Capitol Hill map. *(See § 6.21, Capitol Hill Map.)* The Congressional Special Services Office assists congressional staff and visitors with disabilities. It provides guided tours, wheelchairs, TDD-TTY support, interpreting, FM systems, and special assistance at events. *(Call 202-224-4048 or, TDD-TTY, 202-224-4049.)*

Visitor entrances to the Capitol are limited during construction of the Capitol Visitor Center, which is being built on the East Front. Visitors must obtain timed-entry tickets at a kiosk on First Street, SW, between Independence and Maryland Avenues (across from the Botanical Garden), and queue up near the House south door. *(For information, call the Capitol Guide Service, 202-225-6827. See also § 3.112, Constituent Services and Courtesies.)* Guided tours can also be arranged in advance through the office of a member of Congress. The House south door, House steps, and carriageway door are open, as are the Senate north door, Senate steps, and carriageway door. Visitors to the House and Senate galleries, which are open when the respective chamber is in session and during business hours Monday through Friday, must obtain gallery passes from a member of Congress; admission is through the House south door and Senate north door. *(See § 6.22, Capitol Security.)*

The West Front faces The Mall, with its terraces providing sweeping views of Pennsylvania Avenue, the Smithsonian buildings, and other museums, monuments, and federal office buildings.

In elevator lobbies in the Capitol and House and Senate office buildings, a visitor finds wall directories for the offices of representatives, senators, committees, and other officials, including both office and telephone numbers. Often there are floor plans in the elevator lobbies, as well, to orient visitors.

Many rooms in the Capitol and congressional office buildings are available for meals, receptions, meetings, and other activities. A person or organization wishing to arrange a Capi-

Capitol Hill Map

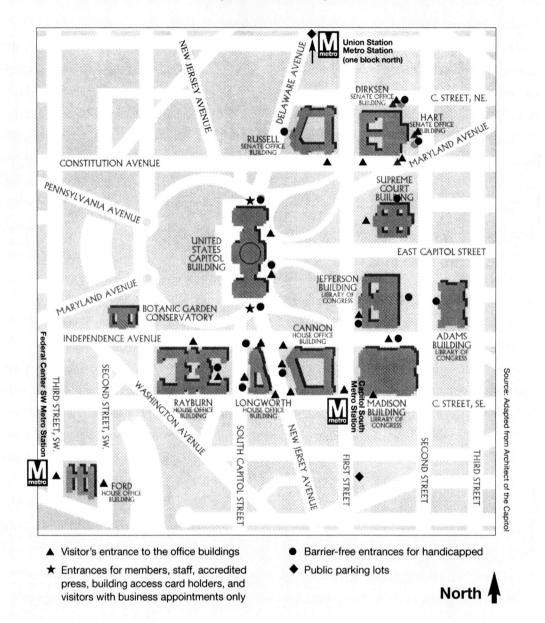

▲ Visitor's entrance to the office buildings

★ Entrances for members, staff, accredited press, building access card holders, and visitors with business appointments only

● Barrier-free entrances for handicapped

◆ Public parking lots

North ↑

Source: Adapted from Architect of the Capitol

tol Hill event must work through the office of a member of Congress, a congressional committee or a congressional leader.

Capitol

The chambers of the House and Senate, National Statuary Hall, and the Rotunda are located on the second ("principal") floor of the Capitol. *(See § 6.23, The Capitol's Second (Principal) Floor.)*

§ 6.22

Capitol Security

To Capitol visitors, perhaps the five most noticeable components of increased Capitol security are construction of the Capitol Visitor Center, inability to enter the Capitol without a guide, metal detectors and other security measures at building entrances, implementation of timed, ticketed tours of the Capitol, and street closures. These changes are part of a larger array of security-related activities, including:

- off-site irradiation and inspection of mail and other packages before delivery to congressional offices
- evacuation planning and training for office emergency coordinators, and allocation of emergency supplies and equipment
- security planning for state and district offices
- increased perimeter security with both police presence and barriers around the Capitol grounds and congressional office buildings, in addition to street closures
- restrictions on truck and bus traffic around the Capitol and congressional office buildings
- construction of permanent perimeter security structures aesthetically compatible with the Capitol and Olmsted landscape architecture
- increased police hiring and special training, and policies on use of lethal force
- conduct of evacuation drills and security sweeps
- installation of notification systems
- installation of chemical and biological agents detection systems
- access of members to the federal government's emergency telephone system
- military transport for the Speaker
- implementation of security plans as threat levels change, such as the increased threat level following the London transit bombings in July 2005
- identification of alternate meeting sites for House and Senate
- continuity of operations planning
- changes in House rules, adopted at the beginning of the 108th and 109th Congresses, to provide the Speaker with additional authority in the event of an emergency

On a daily basis, the Capitol police, members and staff, and visitors must respond to the sudden implementation of security plans in response to real or potential emergencies and to changes resulting from other developments. Spontaneous events have included suspicious packages, suspicious substances, violations of airspace, computer attacks, discovery of weapons, weapons-wielding individuals, practical jokes, unauthorized demonstrations, power outages, and loss of water pressure, while planned events have included presidential visits to Capitol Hill, authorized demonstrations, addition of construction sites, and sidewalk closures.

The Capitol's Second (Principal) Floor

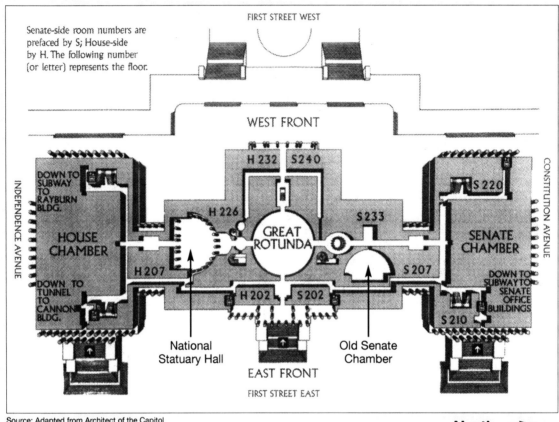

Source: Adapted from Architect of the Capitol

North ➡

Entrances to the visitor galleries for each chamber are located on the third floor. A visitor must have separate House and Senate gallery passes (both available from a representative's or senator's office), or be accompanied by a guide, or a person with a congressional ID to be admitted to the galleries. Members, congressional staff, the credentialed media, and other staff have IDs that provide them with access to various parts of the Capitol. Special events, such as the president's State of the Union address, generally are not open to guests without event tickets. *(For floor plans and illustrations of the House and Senate chambers, see § 14.10, How to Follow Proceedings in the House, and § 14.20, How to Follow Proceedings in the Senate.)*

Rooms in the Capitol are numbered with an H or an S, such as S-228, the Old Senate Chamber. H rooms are located on the House side of the Capitol, and S rooms on the Senate side. One room on the first (ground) floor in the middle of the East Front is numbered EF-

100. On the basement level, there are rooms designated *HB, HC,* and *HT* on the House side of the Capitol, and *SB, SC,* and *ST* on the Senate side.

From the Capitol, there is underground access to the House and Senate office buildings. From the southwest elevators on the House side of the Capitol, a visitor can reach the subway and walkway to the Rayburn House Office Building. From the southeast elevators on the House side, a visitor can reach the underground walkway to the Cannon House Office Building, which connects to underground walkways to the Longworth and Rayburn Buildings and, via the Cannon Building, to the Library of Congress's Madison Building. Current security measures restrict self-guided tours from use of these connections to the Capitol. *(See § 6.22, Capitol Security.)*

From the northeast elevators on the Senate side of the Capitol, a visitor can reach the subways and walkways to the Senate's Russell, Dirksen, and Hart Office Buildings. Underground walkways also connect the Russell to the Dirksen and Hart Buildings. Again, current security measures restrict self-guided tours from use of these connections to the Capitol.

Some elevators in the Capitol and the congressional office buildings are reserved for members. When bells ring to summon members to the House or Senate floor, the respective subways and additional elevators are reserved for members.

At street level, when the bells ring summoning members, the police operate the traffic lights at corners next to the congressional office buildings to provide priority to members crossing Independence Avenue on the House side and Constitution Avenue on the Senate side. At evening rush hour, this activity can lead to traffic backups.

House Office Buildings

There are four House office buildings. The three principal buildings—Rayburn, Longworth, and Cannon—accommodate member, most committee, and most subcommittee offices; they line Independence Avenue from First Street, SW, to First Street, SE. The fourth building, Ford, is located at Third and D Streets, SW.

Beginning at the foot of Capitol Hill, the westernmost building is the Rayburn Building, named for Representative Sam Rayburn, D-TX (1913–1961; Speaker, 1940–1947, 1949–1953, 1955–1961). Rooms in this building are indicated by four digits, beginning with a *2,* such as 2120 Rayburn HOB, the main office of the Armed Services Committee. The second digit indicates the floor—2120 is on the first floor. (A *B* or *SB* preceding a number indicates a location on the basement or subbasement floor.)

Across South Capitol Street from the Rayburn Building is the Longworth Building, named for Representative Nicholas Longworth, R-OH (1903–1913, 1915–1931; Speaker, 1925–1931). Rooms in this building are indicated by four digits, beginning with a *1,* such as 1301 Longworth HOB, the main office of the Agriculture Committee. The second digit indicates the floor—1301 is on the third floor. (A *B* or *SB* preceding a number indicates a location on the basement or subbasement floor.)

House Office Buildings

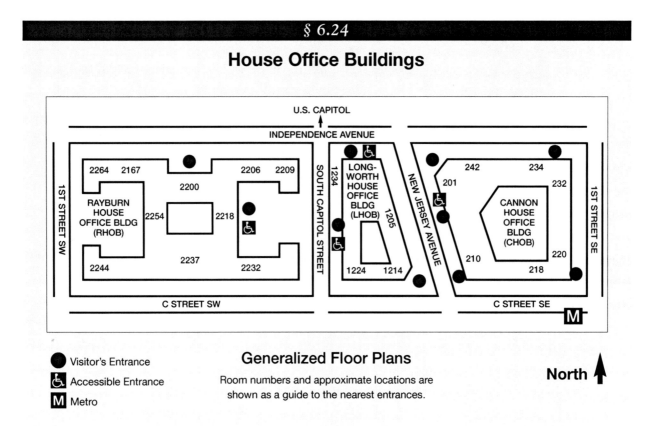

● Visitor's Entrance

♿ Accessible Entrance

Ⓜ Metro

Generalized Floor Plans

Room numbers and approximate locations are
shown as a guide to the nearest entrances.

North ↑

Across New Jersey Avenue from the Longworth Building is the Cannon Building, named for Representative Joseph G. Cannon, R-IL (1873–1891, 1893–1913, 1915–1923; Speaker, 1903–1911). Rooms in this building are indicated by three digits, such as 207 Cannon HOB, the main office of the Budget Committee, located on the second floor. (A *B* preceding a number indicates a location on the basement floor.)

The Ford Building, west of the Rayburn Building and past an entrance to I-395, is named for former Republican representative from Michigan, vice president, and president, Gerald R. Ford (House, 1949–1973; minority leader, 1965–1973; vice president, 1973–1974; president, 1974–1977). Rooms in this building are indicated by an *H2*, followed by a three-digit number, such as H2-405, the Congressional Budget Office, located on the fourth floor.

Senate Office Buildings

There are three Senate office buildings, which line Constitution Avenue, NE. Closest to the Capitol is the Russell Building, named for Senator Richard B. Russell, D-GA (1933–1971). Rooms in this building are indicated by an *SR*, such as SR-328A Russell Building, the main office of the Agriculture, Nutrition, and Forestry Committee. (A *B* preceding a number indicates a location on the basement floor.)

Across First Street, NE, is the Dirksen Building, named for Senator Everett McKinley

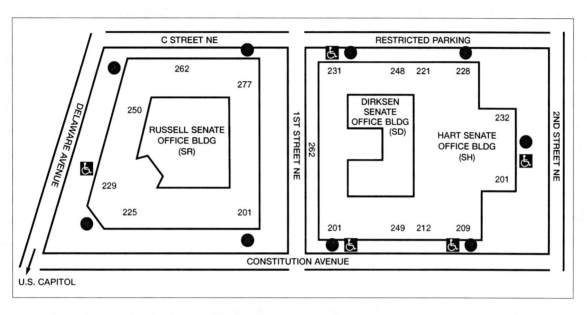

§ 6.25

Senate Office Buildings

Visitor's Entrance
 Accessible Entrance

Generalized Floor Plans

Room numbers and approximate locations are
shown as a guide to the nearest entrances.

North

Dirksen, R-IL (House: 1933–1949; Senate: 1951–1969; Republican leader, 1959–1969). Rooms in this building are indicated by an *SD*, such as SD-624 Dirksen Building, the main office of the Budget Committee. (A *B* preceding a number indicates a location on the basement floor.)

Connected to the Dirksen Building is the third Senate office building, the Hart Building, named for Senator Philip Hart, D-MI (1959–1976). Rooms in this building are indicated by an *SH*, such as SH-838 Hart Building, the main office of the Indian Affairs Committee. (A *B* preceding a number indicates a location on the basement floor.)

Members' and Committees' Office Locations

Representatives' and senators' offices are located in the House and Senate office buildings. Addresses for current office locations are provided in directories at the back of this book. Members' office locations currently remain the same until the end of a Congress. A new representative elected or new senator appointed to replace a member who resigns from Congress or dies in office before the end of a Congress occupies his or her predecessor's office.

Shortly after a general election, through the period of the early organization meetings, members bid on vacant offices, based on seniority. Any reelected members who wish to bid on vacant offices, all members filling vacancies and now elected to a new term, and all newly elected members bid on vacant offices. A chain reaction ensues as more senior members decide to move due to a myriad of reasons—such as the availability of offices closer to Capitol subways and walkways, or closer to their principal committees. A reelected member might also decide *not* to move because a better office is unavailable or because the disruption of moving is undesirable.

By the end of November or early December, new office assignments are completed. Retiring members and those defeated for reelection are given a deadline by which they must vacate their offices. Members-elect work in shared or temporary quarters with temporary mail drops. Space must also be found for retiring or defeated representatives if a lame-duck session lasts past the vacate date. The architect of the Capitol, other congressional support offices, and telephone company and other services then go into action and execute moves in December, right through the holidays, to try to get every representative into his or her new, repainted, cleaned, furnished, functioning office before the next Congress convenes. New senators might reside in temporary offices for as long as several months after the convening of a Congress. Freshman members in both chambers generally take the phone numbers of the members they are replacing.

In addition, about 70 senators have offices in the Capitol. These small rooms are colloquially referred to as "hideaways."

Committee offices change less frequently. The principal majority and minority offices and main meeting rooms tend to stay the same from Congress to Congress, although the allocation of staff and other resources in both chambers may have an impact on committee room assignments. However, subcommittee rooms often change because subcommittees are regularly abolished, reorganized, or created with the convening of each new Congress and the organizing of the House and Senate committees. Temporary committees also must be accommodated when they are created. Space is freed when a temporary committee expires.

Other Government Buildings

The Supreme Court Building is located on First Street, NE, between East Capitol Street and Maryland Avenue, NE. Visitors are not free to tour this building on their own, but public lecture tours are available. *(See § 3.112, Constituent Services and Courtesies.)*

The Library of Congress has three buildings on Capitol Hill, each named for a president and all connected by underground walkways. The Jefferson Building (named for Thomas Jefferson, the third president), where rooms are designated with an *LJ* followed by a number, is located at the corner of Independence Avenue and First Street, SE. (A new tunnel connects the Jefferson Building to the Capitol Visitor Center.) Directly across First Street is the Madison Building (named for James Madison, the fourth president), where rooms are designated with an *LM* followed by a number. (The Madison Building is also connected to the Cannon

House Office Building by an underground walkway, not open to visitors.) At Independence Avenue and Second Street, SE, is the Adams Building (named for John Adams, the second president), where rooms are designated with an *LA* followed by a number. *(For tour information, see § 3.112, Constituent Services and Courtesies.)*

The Botanic Garden conservatory is located at the corner of Independence Avenue and First Street, SW. It was renovated to reopen in 2001. The outdoor National Garden, completed in 2006 to the west of the conservatory, comprises a rose garden, a butterfly garden, a lawn terrace, the First Ladies Water Garden, a Mid-Atlantic regional garden, and a small amphitheater. Bartholdi Park, with the 1876 Centennial Exposition fountain created by Frédéric Auguste Bartholdi, designer of the Statute of Liberty, lies across Independence Avenue from the conservatory.

§ 6.30 Bells and Lights: Senate and House Signals

The House and Senate use a system of "bells" and "buzzers," respectively, to announce a vote or quorum call on the chamber floor; the convening, recess, or adjournment of the chamber; and, in the Senate, the conclusion of Morning Business. House bells and lights operate only on the House side of the Capitol and in House office buildings, and Senate buzzers and lights operate only on the Senate side of the Capitol and in Senate office buildings. There are also lights circling many wall clocks throughout the House and Senate, which complement the bells or buzzers. For example, two rings and two illuminated lights on the Senate side of the Capitol and in the Senate office buildings would indicate a quorum call on the Senate floor.

As soon as the bells or buzzers sound, personal and committee staffers check the floor proceedings on television, or BlackBerries®, or by a call to the members' party floor recordings or cloakrooms to find out what is happening in the chamber, and alert members as necessary. The parties in each chamber also use telecommunications systems to notify members of floor action.

The House bells and Senate buzzers are tested early in the day on days in which a chamber will be in session.

In addition, the chandeliers outside the facing entrances of the House and Senate—the north entrance to the House chamber and the south entrance to the Senate chamber—are equipped with bulbs to indicate that a chamber is in session. Beneath the House chandelier hang two red bulbs that are illuminated when the House is in session. Beneath the Senate chandelier hang a white bulb and a red bulb. The white bulb is illuminated when the Senate is in regular session; the red one is lit when the Senate is in executive session.

Senate Buzzer and Light Signals

1. One long ring at hour of convening	• One red light remains lighted at all times while the Senate is in session.
2. One ring	• Yeas and nays.
3. Two rings	• Quorum call.
4. Three rings	• Call of absentees.
5. Four rings	• Adjournment or recess (end of daily session).
6. Five rings	• Seven and one-half minutes remaining on yea-or-nay vote.
7. Six rings	• Morning Business concluded, with lights shut off immediately; or recess during daily session, with lights staying on during period of recess.
8. Twelve rings rung at two-second intervals	• Civil Defense Warning.

House Bell and Light Signals

1. One long ring	• Occurs fifteen minutes before the House convenes, with one ring at the time of convening. One red light remains lighted at all times while the House is in session.
2. One long ring, pause, followed by three rings	• Signals the start or continuation of a notice quorum call. It is terminated if and when 100 members appear.
3. One long ring	• Termination of a notice quorum call.
4. Two rings	• Fifteen-minute electronically recorded vote.
5. Two rings, pause, followed by two rings	• Manual roll-call vote. The bells are sounded again when the clerk reaches the letter R in the roster of representatives. Manual roll-call votes are rare.
6. Two rings, pause, followed by five rings	• First vote under suspension of the rules or on clustered votes. Two rings occur five minutes later. The first vote of a set of clustered votes takes fifteen minutes. Successive votes are taken at intervals of not less than five minutes, and each successive vote is signaled by five rings.

House Bell and Light Signals

7. Three rings	• Quorum call, either initially or after a notice quorum has been converted to a regular quorum call. The bells are repeated five minutes after the first ring. Members have fifteen minutes to be recorded.
8. Three rings, pause, followed by three rings	• Manual quorum call. The bells are sounded again when the clerk reaches the letter R in the roster of representatives. Manual quorum calls are rare.
9. Three rings, pause, followed by five rings	• Quorum call in Committee of the Whole, which may be immediately followed by a five-minute recorded vote.
10. Four rings	• Adjournment of the House.
11. Five rings	• Five-minute electronically recorded vote.
12. Six rings	• Recess of the House.
13. Twelve rings rung at two-second intervals	• Civil Defense Warning.

6

Chapter Seven

Organizing Congress:
Members, Leaders, and Committees

Analysis

7

§7.00 Introduction

The structure and organization of Congress can have a tremendous impact on how policy decisions are reached. The selection of party leaders influences the legislative agenda. The selection of committee and subcommittee chairs and committee and subcommittee members can determine committees' policy outcomes. The choice of individuals in charge of the administrative organs of Congress can affect the services that a chamber provides its members.

The Constitution outlines the structure of Congress and places some constraints on membership qualifications and administration. Largely, however, the House of Representatives and the Senate are free to establish their own rules, create their own structures, and form their own systems of administration. In addition, the federal courts have generally found cases

---

§ 7.01

Constitutional Provisions Related to the Composition and Organization of Congress

Guide	Article I
Bicameral legislature	**Section 1.** All legislative Powers herein granted shall be vested in a Congress of the United States, which shall consist of a Senate and House of Representatives.
Two-year term in House	**Section 2.** [1] The House of Representatives shall be composed of Members chosen every second Year by the People of the several States, and the Electors in each State shall have the Qualifications requisite for Electors of the most numerous Branch of the State Legislature.
Age, citizenship, and residency requirements for House	[2] No person shall be a Representative who shall not have attained to the Age of twenty five Years, and been seven Years a Citizen of the United States, and who shall not, when elected, be an Inhabitant of that State in which he shall be chosen.
Decennial census	[3] *[Part of original Constitution on counting for the census changed by section 2 of the Fourteenth Amendment.]* . . . The actual Enumeration shall be made within three Years after the first Meeting of the Congress of the United States, and within every subsequent Term of ten Years, in such Manner as they shall by Law direct. The Number of Representatives shall not exceed one for every thirty Thousand, but each State shall have at Least one Representative. . . . *[Specifies original number of representatives for each state.]*

Continued on page 192

Guide	Article I
Vacancies in House	[4] When vacancies happen in the Representation from any State, the Executive Authority thereof shall issue Writs of Election to fill such Vacancies.
House officers	[5] The House of Representatives shall chuse their Speaker and other Officers. . . .
Two senators for each state, and a six-year term for senators	**Section 3.** [1] The Senate of the United States shall be composed of two Senators from each State . . . for six Years; and each Senator shall have one Vote. *[Ellipses represent original text changed by first clause of the Seventeenth Amendment, which provided for direct popular election of senators.]*
Senate classes	[2] Immediately after they shall be assembled in Consequence of the first Election, they shall be divided as equally as may be into three Classes. The Seats of the Senators of the first Class shall be vacated at the Expiration of the second Year, of the second Class at the Expiration of the fourth Year, and of the third Class at the Expiration of the sixth Year, so that one third may be chosen every second Year. . . . *[Part of original Constitution on filling vacancies changed by second clause of the Seventeenth Amendment.]*
Age, citizenship, and residency requirements for senators	[3] No Person shall be a Senator who shall not have attained to the Age of thirty Years, and been nine Years a Citizen of the United States, and who shall not, when elected, be an Inhabitant of that State for which he shall be chosen.
Vice president is Senate president	[4] The Vice President of the United States shall be President of the Senate, but shall have no Vote, unless they be equally divided.
Senate officers	[5] The Senate shall chuse their other Officers, and also a President pro tempore, in the Absence of the Vice President, or when he shall exercise the Office of President of the United States.
Congress to assemble annually	**Section 4.** [2] The Congress shall assemble at least once in every Year, and such Meeting shall [be on the first Monday in December,] unless they shall by Law appoint a different Day. *[Original text in brackets was changed by Section 2 of the Twentieth Amendment.]*

Continued on page 193

Guide

Article I

Each house judges its own elections, returns, and qualifications

Section 5. [1] Each House shall be the Judge of the Elections, Returns and Qualifications of its own Members, and a Majority of each shall constitute a Quorum to do Business; but a smaller Number may adjourn from day to day, and may be authorized to compel the Attendance of absent Members, in such Manner, and under such Penalties as each House may provide.

Each house creates its own rules

[2] Each House may determine the Rules of its Proceedings, punish its Members for disorderly Behaviour, and, with the Concurrence of two thirds, expel a Member.

Journal of each house, and provision for vote requested by one-fifth of those present

[3] Each House shall keep a Journal of its Proceedings, and from time to time publish the same, excepting such Parts as may in their Judgment require Secrecy; and the Yeas and Nays of the Members of either House on any question shall, at the Desire of one fifth of those Present, be entered on the Journal.

Consent of both houses to adjourn

[4] Neither House, during the Session of Congress, shall, without the Consent of the other, adjourn for more than three days, nor to any other Place than that in which the two Houses shall be sitting.

Compensation, privilege from arrest, Speech and Debate clause

Section 6. [1] The Senators and Representatives shall receive a Compensation for their Services, to be ascertained by Law, and paid out of the Treasury of the United States. They shall in all Cases, except Treason, Felony and Breach of the Peace, be privileged from Arrest during their Attendance at the Session of their respective Houses, and in going to and returning from the same; and for any Speech or Debate in either House, they shall not be questioned in any other Place.

Limitation on holding an executive office

[2] No Senator or Representative shall, during the Time for which he was elected, be appointed to any civil Office under the Authority of the United States, which shall have been created, or the Emoluments whereof shall have been encreased during such time; and no Person holding any Office under the United States, shall be a Member of either House during his Continuance in Office.

Continued on page 194

Guide	Article II

Article II

President may
convene Congress

Section 3. . . . he *[the president]* may, on extraordinary Occasions, convene both Houses, or either of them, and in Case of Disagreement between them, with Respect to the Time of Adjournment, he may adjourn them to such Time as he shall think proper. . . .

Article VI

Oath of office

[3] The Senators and Representatives before mentioned . . . shall be bound by Oath or Affirmation, to support this Constitution; but no religious Test shall ever be required as Qualification to any Office or public Trust under the United States. *[Text represented by ellipses refers to executive and judicial officers of the United States and the states.]*

Fourteenth Amendment

Apportionment

Section 2. Representatives shall be apportioned among the several States according to their respective numbers, counting the whole number of persons in each State, excluding Indians not taxed. But when the right to vote at any election for the choice of electors for President and Vice President of the United States, Representatives in Congress, the Executive and Judicial officers of a State, or members of the Legislature thereof, is denied to any of the male inhabitants of such State, being twenty-one years of age, *[provision affected by Twenty-Sixth Amendment]* and citizens of the United States, or in any way abridged, except for participation in rebellion, or other crime, the basis of representation therein shall be reduced in the proportion which the number of such male citizens shall bear to the whole number of male citizens twenty-one years of age in such State.

Disqualification from
service in Congress
for certain acts

Section 3. No person shall be a Senator or Representative in Congress . . . who, having previously taken an oath, as a member of Congress, or as an officer of the United States, or as a member of any State legislature, or as an executive or judicial officer of any State, to support the Constitution of the United States, shall have engaged in insurrection or rebellion against the same, or given aid or comfort to the enemies thereof. But Congress may by a vote of two-thirds of each House, remove such disability. *[Text represented by ellipses deals with other office holders.]*

Continued on page 195

Guide	**Seventeenth Amendment**

Popular election of senators

The Senate of the United States shall be composed of two Senators from each State, elected by the people thereof, for six years; and each Senator shall have one vote. The electors in each State shall have the qualifications requisite for electors of the most numerous branch of the State legislatures.

Vacancies in the Senate

When vacancies happen in the representation of any State in the Senate, the executive authority of such State shall issue writs of election to fill such vacancies: *Provided,* That the legislature of any State may empower the executive thereof to make temporary appointments until the people fill the vacancies by election as the legislature may direct.

This amendment shall not be so construed as to affect the election or term of any Senator chosen before it becomes valid as part of the Constitution.

Twentieth Amendment

New congressional term begins at noon on January 3 in odd-numbered years

Section 1. The terms of the President and Vice President shall end at noon on the 20th day of January, and the terms of Senators and Representatives at noon on the 3d day of January, of the years in which such terms would have ended if this article had not been ratified; and the terms of their successors shall then begin.

Annual congressional session

Section 2. The Congress shall assemble at least once in every year, and such meeting shall begin at noon on the 3d day of January, unless they shall by law appoint a different day.

Twenty-Seventh Amendment

Congressional compensation

No law varying the compensation for the services of the Senators and Representatives shall take effect until an election of Representatives shall have intervened.

7

involving the internal affairs of the House and Senate to be nonjusticiable. *(See § 7.01, Constitutional Provisions Related to the Composition and Organization of Congress.)*

This chapter addresses the organization of Congress. It describes the decisions reached before the swearing-in of a new Congress, the leadership and administrative structures, and the committee and subcommittee systems.

§7.10 Members of Congress

The Constitution in Article I established a bicameral (two-house) legislature comprising the House of Representatives and the Senate. Article I tells us that there must be at least one representative from each state in the House and exactly two senators from each state in the Senate. With fifty states, there are one hundred senators. *(See § 7.01, Constitutional Provisions Related to the Composition and Organization of Congress.)*

Seven states have just one representative, but, as a result of the 2000 census, the most populous state, California, has fifty-three representatives in the 110th Congress, one for each of its fifty-three congressional districts. Seats in the House of Representatives are apportioned according to population, and Congress by law has provided that the total number of representatives is 435. In addition there are four delegates—one each from American Samoa, the District of Columbia, Guam, and the Virgin Islands—and a resident commissioner from Puerto Rico, as explained later in this section. *(See § 2.13, Reapportionment and Redistricting.)*

§ 7.11

Senate Classes

The Constitution provides that senators are elected to six-year terms. The Constitution also provides that one-third of the senators are to be elected every two years, and that after the first election of the Senate "they shall be divided as equally as may be into three Classes." *(Art. I, sec. 3, cl. 2.)* As states joined the union, a state's two new senators were assigned to two classes in keeping with the constitutional requirement of near equal numbers of senators in each class.

Senators Whose Terms End in 2009

Republicans

Lamar Alexander, TN	Larry Craig, ID	Mitch McConnell, KY
Wayne Allard, CO	Elizabeth Dole, NC	Pat Roberts, KS
Saxby Chambliss, GA	Pete Domenici, NM	Jeff Sessions, AL
Thad Cochran, MS	Mike Enzi, WY	Gordon Smith, OR
Norm Coleman, MN	Lindsay Graham, SC	John Sununu, NH
Susan Collins, ME	Chuck Hagel, NE	Ted Stevens, AK
John Cornyn, TX	James Inhofe, OK	John Warner, VA

Continued on page 197

Democrats

Max Baucus, MT	Tim Johnson, SD	Carl Levin, MI
Joseph Biden, Jr., DE	John Kerry, MA	Mark Pryor, AR
Richard Durbin, IL	Mary Landrieu, LA	Jack Reed, RI
Tom Harkin, IA	Frank Lautenberg, NJ	John Rockefeller, IV, WV

Senators Whose Terms End in 2011

Republicans

Robert Bennett, UT	Jim DeMint, SC	Richard Shelby, AL
Christopher Bond, MO	Chuck Grassley, IA	Arlen Specter, PA
Sam Brownback, KS	Judd Gregg, NH	John Thune, SD
Jim Bunning, KY	Johnny Isaakson, GA	David Vitter, LA
Richard Burr, NC	Mel Martinez, FL	George Voinovich, OH
Tom Coburn, OK	John McCain, AZ	
Mike Crapo, ID	Lisa Murkowski, AK	

Democrats

Evan Bayh, IN	Daniel Inouye, HI	Barack Obama, IL
Barbara Boxer, CA	Patrick Leahy, VT	Harry Reid, NV
Christopher Dodd, CT	Blanche Lincoln, AR	Ken Salazar, CO
Byron Dorgan, ND	Barbara Mikulski, MD	Charles Schumer, NY
Russell Feingold, WI	Patty Murray, WA	Ron Wyden, OR

Senators Whose Terms End in 2013

Republicans

Bob Corker, TN	Kay Bailey Hutchison, TX	Richard Lugar, IN
John Ensign, NV	Jon Kyl, AZ	Olympia Snowe, ME
Orrin Hatch, UT	Trent Lott, MS	Craig Thomas, WY

Democrats

Daniel Akaka, HI	Hillary Rodham Clinton, NY	Robert Menendez, NJ
Jeff Bingaman, NM	Kent Conrad, ND	Ben Nelson, NE
Sherrod Brown, OH	Dianne Feinstein, CA	Bill Nelson, FL
Robert Byrd, WV	Edward Kennedy, MA	Bernard Sanders, VT*
Maria Cantwell, WA	Amy Klobuchar, MN	Debbie Stabenow, MI
Benjamin L. Cardin, MD	Herb Kohl, WI	Jon Tester, MT
Thomas Carper, DE	Joseph Lieberman, CT*	Jim Webb, VA
Bob Casey, PA	Claire McCaskill, MO	Sheldon Whitehouse, RI

* Independent who caucuses with Democrats.

§ 7.12

Membership Changes, 110th Congress, First Session[1]
(as of April 30, 2007)

House

State and District	Former Member and Party	Date of Death or Resignation
California, 37th District	Juanita Millender-McDonald, D	Died April 22, 2007[2]
Georgia, 9th District	Charlie Norwood, R	Died February 13, 2007[3]

1. On April 2, 2007, Rep. Martin T. Meehan, D-MA (5), announced that he would resign from the House May 9 to become the chancellor of the University of Massachusetts at Lowell and leave the House on July 1.
2. A special primary election was scheduled for June 26, 2007. If no candidate received more than 50 percent of the vote, a special election between the top two primary vote recipients was scheduled for August 22.
3. A special primary election was scheduled for June 19, 2007. If no candidate received more than 50 percent of the vote, a special election between the top two primary vote recipients was scheduled for July 17.

Different rules for proceedings evolved in the House and Senate—in part because of their difference in size, in part because senators were appointed by their state legislatures until ratification of the Seventeenth Amendment in 1913, in part because of an earlier perspective of senators as "ambassadors" from their states, and for other reasons. The House is a *majoritarian institution* where majority sentiment on an issue is usually able to work its will and, at least on the floor, to do so in a relatively short time. Senate rules, on the other hand, provide numerous protections to the individual senator and to minority points of view; hence, the *filibuster*—the use of extended debate and dilatory motions—is a feature of the Senate.

In addition to the difference in size and constituency between the House and the Senate, representatives face elections every two years while senators serve six-year terms. The Constitution provided that there would be three "classes" of senators so that one-third of seats in the Senate (a class) would be up for election every two years. *(See § 7.11, Senate Classes.)*

In the event of a House seat vacancy, a special election is held unless the date of the general election is so close that the state's governor decides to hold the special election concurrent with the general election. *(See below for additional information on House vacancies.)*

In the event of a Senate seat vacancy, all states except Alaska, Massachusetts, Oregon, and Wisconsin allow a governor to make a temporary appointment to a vacancy until the next general election. The individual elected serves the balance remaining in that Senate class's term. Alaska, Massachusetts, Oregon, and Wisconsin allow a vacancy to be filled only by election. Oklahoma is a special case. The governor may appoint if the vacancy occurs after March 1 of an even-numbered year, and the term expires the next year; otherwise, the vacancy must be filled by election. In Arizona, Hawaii, Utah, and Wyoming, state law limits the governor's range of choice of persons when making a temporary appointment. *(See § 7.12, Membership Changes, 110th Congress, First Session.)*

While it is clear that a vacancy due to a death occurs after an election has taken place, there was concern over what was state law and, despite that, what should be done in the 2000 and 2002 elections following deaths *before* the election. Senate candidate Mel Carnahan (Missouri in 2000), and Senate candidate, Sen. Paul Wellstone, D-MN, and House candidate, Rep. Patsy Mink, D-HI, both in 2002, died before the respective elections but after ballots had been printed. The practice in nearly all states in the interest of orderly election administration has been to set a cutoff date for replacing candidates, and to proceed after that date even if a candidate should die. The practice in Congress, in judging elections, has been to consider a seat vacant if the deceased candidate obtains the greatest number of votes in the election. Laws for filling the vacancy are then followed, and that is what happened in filling the vacancies caused by Carnahan's and Mink's deaths. In Minnesota, a replacement candidate was named for the general election.

Following the terrorist attacks of September 11, 2001, members of Congress and others have become concerned over *continuity of government* for the legislative branch should many members be killed or disabled in a terrorist attack. Plans for continuity of government and *continuity of operations* exist or are being further developed, but attention continues to focus on succession for representatives. Governors are able to act quickly in most states to name replacement senators. However, the Constitution requires House vacancies to be filled by special election. A number of proposals have been made, including a constitutional amendment to allow governors to appoint representatives under certain circumstances. As an interim step, the House amended its rules at the beginning of the 108th Congress to deal with some contingencies: enabling the Speaker to secretly designate his successors should his office become vacant, allowing the Speaker to declare an emergency recess, and codifying the practice of adjusting the whole number of the House in the case of vacancies. The House amended its rules again at the beginning of the 109th Congress, providing a method for establishing a "provisional quorum" in the case of a catastrophic event. Under the rule, if the House is without a quorum due to a catastrophic circumstance, a quorum would be a majority of the "provisional number" of the House.

During the 109th Congress, Congress passed legislation that was signed by the president to provide an expedited time table in "extraordinary circumstances" for filling House vacancies through special elections *(P.L. 109-55, Title III)*. These extraordinary circumstances were

---

§ 7.13

Party Switchers

House

Rodney Alexander, LA—became Republican, Aug. 6, 2004

Virgil Goode, VA—became Republican, Aug. 1, 2002

Nathan Deal, GA—became Republican, Apr. 10, 1995

Senate

Richard Shelby, AL—became Republican, Nov. 9, 1994

Joseph Lieberman, CT—became Independent Democrat, January 12, 2007

7

§ 7.14

Selected Characteristics of the 110th Congress

(Data were current as of March 31, 2007)

Party Alignment[1]

	Democrats	Republicans	Independents
House	233	202[2]	0
Senate	49	49	2[3]

1. For history of party control from the 80th Congress through the 109th Congress, see § 7.41. For current party alignment see TheCapitol.Net web page <www.PartyNumbers.com>.
2. Includes one vacancy resulting from the death Feb. 13, 2007, of Charlie Norwood, R-GA.
3. The independent senators caucus with the Democrats.

Median Age, and Oldest and Youngest Members

	Median Age	Oldest Democratic and Republican Members	Youngest Democratic and Republican Members
House	56	**John D. Dingell,** D-MI, b. July 8, 1926	**Patrick Murphy,** D-PA, b. Oct. 19, 1973
		Ralph M. Hall, R-TX, b. May 3, 1923	**Patrick McHenry,** R-NC, b. Oct. 22, 1975
Senate	62	**Robert Byrd,** D-WV, b. Nov. 20, 1917	**Mark Pryor,** D-AR, b. Oct. 10, 1963
		Ted Stevens, R-AK, b. Nov. 18, 1923	**John Sununu,** R-NH, b. Sept. 10, 1964

Median Service, and Most Senior Members

	Median Service	Most Senior Democratic and Republican Members, and Date Current Service Began
House	Service beginning 1997	**John D. Dingell,** D-MI, Dec.13, 1955 (twenty-six consecutive terms)
		Ralph Regula, R-OH, Jan. 3, 1973 (seventeen consecutive terms)
Senate	Service beginning 1997	**Robert Byrd,** D-WV, Jan. 3, 1959
		Ted Stevens, R-AK, Dec. 24, 1968

Members Serving from States with One Representative

Don Young, R-AK
Michael N. Castle, R-DE
Denny Rehberg, R-MT

Earl Pomeroy, D-ND
Stephanie Herseth Sandlin, D-SD

Peter Welch, D-VT
Barbara Cubin, R-WY

Continued on page 201

Other Information

Professions: More members of Congress are lawyers than any other profession. Business is the second most represented profession for representatives as public service is for senators.

Education: Nearly all senators and representatives have bachelor's degrees. Members have also collected 274 advanced degrees—doctorates, and degrees in law and medicine.

Religion: The majority of members of Congress claim affiliation with Protestant denominations, but the largest representation of a religious denomination is Roman Catholic.

Women Members: Seventy-four women (53 Democrats and 21 Republicans) serve in the House, and 3 of the women members are delegates; 16 women (11 Democrats and 5 Republicans) serve in the Senate.

Minority Members: There are 42 African-American members in the House (all Democrats) and 1 in the Senate; 14 of the African-American members are women, 2 of whom are delegates. There are 27 Hispanic members of the House, 1 of whom is the resident commissioner from Puerto Rico, and 3 Hispanic Senators. Seven Hispanic members are women. All but 5 of the Hispanic members are Democrats. There are 6 representatives, 1 delegate, and 2 senators whose heritage is Asian, native Hawaiian, or Pacific Islander. All but 1 are Democrats. One Republican representative is Native American.

Military Service: There are 102 representatives and 29 senators who have served in the military, including the reserves and national guard. In a sign of the times, the number of veterans of World War II in Congress is declining, but it is also a sign of the resiliency of that generation that 5 senators and 3 representatives continue as key legislators. The senators are Daniel Akaka, D-HI; Daniel Inouye, D-HI; Frank Lautenberg, D-NJ; Ted Stevens, R-AK; and John Warner, R-VA. The representatives are John Dingell, D-MI; Ralph Hall, R-TX; and Ralph Regula, R-OH. In addition, Rep. Tom Lantos, D-CA, who was born in Budapest, was active in the anti-Nazi underground.

New Members of the 110th Congress: In the 2006 general election, 55 new representatives were elected—42 Democrats and 13 Republicans. Three representatives, Baron Hill, Nick Lampson, and Ciro Rodriguez, had previous House service.

In the 2006 general election, 10 new senators were elected—8 Democrats, 1 Republican, and 1 independent. Three had previous House service.

defined as existing when the Speaker of the House announced that there were over one hundred vacancies in the House. If the Speaker makes such an announcement, the governor of any state with a vacancy must schedule a special election within forty-nine days, unless a general election or a special election for that vacancy has already been scheduled to occur within seventy-five days of the Speaker's announcement. Candidates are to be chosen by political parties within ten days of the Speaker's announcement, or states may prescribe another

Senators in the 110th Congress
Who Previously Served in the House of Representatives

Service in the House is often a political stepping-stone to the Senate. Nearly half the Senate in the 110th Congress had previous House service. Because of its small size relative to the House, the Senate's political dynamics can be affected by small changes in its membership. Some observers, for example, think that the influx of former House members—thirty-one just since 1995 serving in the 110th Congress—has made the Senate more partisan and more oriented toward constituent service, attributes more often associated with the House than the Senate. The last member to serve in the House after serving in the Senate was Claude Pepper, D-FL (House, 1963–1989; Senate, 1936–1951).

Senator	Service in House	Year Entered Senate	Senator	Service in House	Year Entered Senate
Daniel Akaka	1977–1990	1990	Tom Harkin	1975–1985	1985
Wayne Allard	1991–1997	1997	James Inhofe	1987–1994	1994
Max Baucus	1975–1978	1978	Daniel Inouye	1959–1963	1963
Barbara Boxer	1983–1993	1993	Johnny Isakson	1999–2005	2005
Sherrod Brown	1993–2007	2007	Tim Johnson	1987–1997	1997
Sam Brownback	1995–1996	1996	Jon Kyl	1987–1995	1995
Jim Bunning	1987–1999	1999	Blanche Lincoln	1993–1997	1999
Richard Burr	1995–2005	2005	Trent Lott	1973–1989	1989
Robert C. Byrd	1953–1959	1959	John McCain	1983–1987	1987
Maria Cantwell	1993–1995	2001	Barbara Mikulski	1977–1987	1987
Benjamin L. Cardin	1987–2007	2007	Bill Nelson	1979–1991	2001
Thomas Carper	1983–1993	2001	Jack Reed	1991–1997	1997
Saxby Chambliss	1995–2003	2003	Harry Reid	1983–1987	1987
Tom Coburn	1995–2001	2005	Pat Roberts	1981–1997	1997
Thad Cochran	1973–1978	1978	Bernard Sanders	1991–2007	2007
Larry Craig	1981–1991	1991	Charles Schumer	1981–1999	1999
Mike Crapo	1993–1999	1999	Richard Shelby	1979–1987	1987
Jim DeMint	1999–2005	2005	Olympia Snowe	1979–1995	1995
Christopher Dodd	1975–1981	1981	Debbie Stabenow	1997–2001	2001
Byron Dorgan	1981–1992	1992	John Sununu	1997–2003	2003
Richard Durbin	1983–1997	1997	Craig Thomas	1989–1995	1995
John Ensign	1995–1999	2001	John Thune	1997–2003	2005
Lindsay Graham	1995–2003	2003	David Vitter	1999–2005	2005
Charles Grassley	1975–1981	1981	Ron Wyden	1981–1996	1996
Judd Gregg	1981–1989	1993			

§ 7.16

Former Governors Serving
in the 110th Congress

Governors often seek election to the Senate. Having won a statewide office already, they are able to mount another statewide campaign. One former governor also serves in the House in the 110th Congress, from a single-district state. A former governor is likely to be conversant with the range of policy issues confronting Congress.

Member	Party and State	Service as Governor
Sen. Lamar Alexander	R-TN	1979–1987
Sen. Evan Bayh	D-IN	1989–1997
Sen. Christopher Bond	R-MO	1973–1977; 1981–1985
Sen. Thomas Carper	D-DE	1993–2001
Sen. Judd Gregg	R-NH	1989–1993
Sen. Ben Nelson	D-NE	1991–1999
Sen. John Rockefeller	D-WV	1977–1985
Sen. George Voinovich	R-OH	1991–1999
Rep. Michael N. Castle	R-DE	1985–1993

method of choosing candidates, including a primary. Additional provisions of the law dealt with expedited judicial review of a challenge to the Speaker's announcement; accommodation of military and overseas voters voting absentee; and the continuing applicability of various federal statutes protecting the franchise.

More routinely, members can also change their party affiliations after election to Congress. One party might well seek to attract potential defectors from the other party. *(See § 7.13, Party Switchers.)*

From time to time, the outcome of an election might be challenged because two candidates obtained nearly the same number of votes or because some irregularity is alleged. In any case, the Constitution provides that the House and Senate "shall be the Judge of the Elections, Returns and Qualifications of its own Members." *(Art. I, sec. 5, cl. 1.)* Investigatory work is usually conducted in the House by the House Administration Committee and in the Senate by its Rules and Administration Committee. *(See § 2.10, Campaigns and Elections.)*

The Constitution also provides that representatives and senators must be residents of the states from which they are elected, and that representatives must be twenty-five years of age or older and senators thirty years of age or older to take office. Foreign-born individuals can serve in Congress. However, a representative must have been a citizen for seven years; a sen-

§ 7.17

Numbers of Former State and Local Elected Officials Serving in the 110th Congress

State legislatures and state, regional, county, city, and other local offices are the political training grounds of many members of Congress, including delegates. Because of the number of federal aid and regulatory programs affecting states and localities, former state and local officials elected to Congress are often able to take part quickly in many policy debates in Congress. Many members with experience in state legislatures held leadership positions in their chamber or key legislative committees. In addition to these officials, the 110th Congress includes former Cabinet secretaries, executive officials from all levels of government, White House staff, presidential and congressional campaign staff, not-for-profit and think-tank officials, and national, state, and local party officials. Sen. John Kerry, D-MA, was his party's 2004 presidential nominee, and other members have run active campaigns for their party's presidential nomination. Many members, before or since being elected to Congress, have served as delegates to their parties' national political conventions.

Former Local and Regional Elected Officials	Former State Legislators	Former State Officials Elected Statewide
House: 137	House: 233	House: 16
Senate: 25	Senate: 40	Senate: 25

§ 7.18

Members of Congress Who Subsequently Served on the Supreme Court

Congressional service has been a route to appointment to the Supreme Court.

Served in House of Representatives and on Supreme Court	Served in Senate and on Supreme Court	Served in Both House of Representatives and Senate, and on Supreme Court
John Marshall	William Paterson	John McKinley
Joseph Story	Oliver Ellsworth	Lucius Q.C. Lamar
Gabriel Duvall	Levi Woodbury	George Sutherland
John McLean	Salmon P. Chase	James F. Byrnes
Henry Baldwin	Stanley Matthews	
James Wayne	Howell Jackson	
Philip Barbour	Edward D. White	
Nathan Clifford	Hugo L. Black	
Mahlon Pitney	Harold Burton	
William Strong	Sherman Minton	
Joseph McKenna	David Davis (resigned	
William Moody	from Supreme Court	
Fred M. Vinson	to serve in Senate)	

§ 7.19

Former Judges Serving in the 110th Congress

Because state and local judgeships are often elective, members of the judiciary are sometimes attracted to congressional service.

Member	Party and State	Type of Judge
Sen. John Cornyn	R-TX	Justice, Texas Supreme Court
Rep. Robert B. Aderholt	R-AL	Municipal judge
Rep. G. K. Butterfield	D-NC	Superior court judge; justice, North Carolina Supreme Court
Rep. John Carter	R-TX	Municipal judge; district court judge
Rep. Nathan Deal	R-GA	Juvenile court judge
Rep. Lloyd Doggett	D-TX	Justice, Texas Supreme Court
Rep. John J. Duncan Jr.	R-TN	County criminal court judge
Rep. Louie Gohmert	R-TX	District court judge; Texas Court of Appeals, chief justice
Rep. Charles A. Gonzalez	D-TX	Municipal judge; judge, county court at law; district court judge
Rep. Al Green	D-TX	Justice of the peace
Rep. Ralph M. Hall	R-TX	County judge
Rep. Alcee L. Hastings	D-FL	U.S. district court judge
Rep. Sheila Jackson-Lee	D-TX	Municipal judge
Rep. Hank Johnson	D-GA	Magistrate court judge
Rep. Stephanie Tubbs Jones	D-OH	Municipal judge; judge, court of common pleas
Rep. Paul E. Kanjorski	D-PA	Workers' compensation administrative law judge
Rep. Gregory W. Meeks	D-NY	State workers' compensation judge
Rep. Ted Poe	R-TX	District court judge
Rep. Deborah Pryce	R-OH	Municipal judge
Rep. Steven R. Rothman	D-NJ	Surrogate court judge
Rep. Roger F. Wicker	R-MS	Municipal judge

7

§ 7.110

Members of the 110th Congress
Who Were Pages

Pages are high-school juniors, at least sixteen years old, both male and female, who serve members of the House and Senate by delivering packages and messages throughout the Capitol complex. They also serve on the floor of each house. *(See § 5.113, Congressional Pages.)*

House		Senate
Dan Boren, D-OK	John D. Dingell, D-MI	Christopher Dodd, D-CT
Jim Cooper, D-TN	Rush D. Holt, D-NJ	Mark Pryor, D-AR
Ander Crenshaw, R-FL	Paul E. Kanjorski, D-PA	
Thomas M. Davis, R-VA	Roger F. Wicker, R-MS	

ator, for nine years. *(See § 7.14, Selected Characteristics of the 110th Congress; additional characteristics appear in §§ 7.15–7.112.)*

Members and, by interpretation, their aides, have a limited protection in what they say because of the Speech and Debate Clause of the Constitution, but both chambers have rules and practices of decorum to which their members must adhere. The Constitution also protects members from arrest under certain circumstances, but the provision is obsolete because the circumstances to which it applied no longer exist. However, each house may punish its members and, on a two-thirds vote, even expel a member.

Finally, a member may not hold another federal office while serving in Congress.

For a further explanation of clauses of the Constitution applicable to Congress and its members, see *Constitution of the United States of America: Analysis and Interpretation*, available in print from the Government Printing Office and online through GPO Access, <*www.gpo access.gov/constitution/*>.

Delegates in the House of Representatives

In addition to 435 representatives, the House's membership includes four delegates—one each from American Samoa, the District of Columbia, Guam, and the Virgin Islands—and one resident commissioner from Puerto Rico. There are no practical differences between the positions of delegate and resident commissioner.

In a 1902 law, Puerto Rico was granted representation in the House; the position of resident commissioner was created. In a 1970 law, the District of Columbia was authorized to elect a delegate to the House. This same privilege was extended by law to Guam and the Virgin Islands in 1972 and to American Samoa in 1978. Delegates and the resident commissioner are treated equally with representatives in the allocation of members' representational allowances, salary, and other perquisites available to representatives.

§ 7.111

Members of the 110th Congress
Who Have Served as Congressional Staff

Numerous members of the 110th Congress served in congressional staff positions before their election. Some senators served on Senate staffs; others served on House staffs. One senator served on the Capitol police force. Some House members served on Senate staffs; others served on House staffs.

This list was compiled from information in the *Congressional Directory,* the *Biographical Directory of the United States Congress (online version),* official and campaign web sites, and press sources. Included are members who served as either permanent staff or fellows. If the source provided the name of the office for whom a member worked, it is included; if the office was not provided, the term "congressional staff" is noted. Some members listed here and others not listed also served as interns and campaign workers; this list does not show those relationships.

Many congressional staff who seek election to Congress fail in the attempt. However, service on Capitol Hill offers great political training and unparalleled exposure to national issues. As is evident from the list below, many former congressional staff have been successful in seeking election to Congress.

Current Member	Staff on Which Member Served
Sen. Lamar Alexander	Sen. Howard Baker
Sen. Robert Bennett	Rep. Sherman Lloyd
Sen. Barbara Boxer	Rep. John Burton
Sen. Hillary Rodham Clinton	House Committee on the Judiciary
Sen. Susan Collins	Sen. William Cohen; Senate Committee on Governmental Affairs
Sen. Chuck Hagel	Rep. John McCollister
Sen. Tom Harkin	Rep. Neal Smith
Sen. Joseph Lieberman	Sen. Abraham Ribicoff
Sen. Blanche Lincoln	Rep. Bill Alexander
Sen. Trent Lott	Rep. William Colmer
Sen. Mitch McConnell	Sen. Marlow Cook
Sen. Harry Reid	Capitol Police
Sen. Pat Roberts	Sen. Frank Carlson; Rep. Keith Sebelius
Sen. Olympia Snowe	Rep. William Cohen
Sen. John Thune	Sen. James Abdnor
Rep. Tom Allen	Sen. Edmund Muskie
Rep. Jason Altmire	Rep. Pete Peterson
Rep. Gus Bilirakis	Rep. Don Sundquist
Rep. Jo Bonner	Rep. Sonny Callahan

Continued on page 208

Current Member	Staff on Which Member Served
Rep. Dan Boren	Rep. Wes Watkins
Rep. Ken Calvert	Rep. Victor Veysey
Rep. Dave Camp	Rep. Bill Shuette
Rep. Dennis Cardoza	Rep. Gary Condit
Rep. Julia Carson	Rep. Andrew Jacobs
Rep. William Lacy Clay, Jr.	Congressional staff
Rep. Tom Cole	National Republican Congressional Committee
Rep. John Conyers, Jr.	Rep. John D. Dingell
Rep. Jim Costa	Rep. John Krebs
Rep. Peter A. DeFazio	Rep. James Weaver
Rep. Rosa L. DeLauro	Sen. Christopher Dodd
Rep. Charlie Dent	Rep. Don Ritter
Rep. Norman D. Dicks	Sen. Warren Magnuson
Rep. Chet Edwards	Rep. Olin Teague
Rep. Vernon J. Ehlers	Rep. Gerald Ford
Del. Eni F.H. Faleomavaega	House Committee on Interior and Insular Affairs
Rep. Jeff Fortenberry	Senate Subcommittee on Intergovernmental Relations
Rep. Barney Frank	Rep. Michael Harrington
Rep. Bob Goodlatte	Rep. M. Caldwell Butler
Rep. Phil Hare	Rep. Lane Evans
Rep. Jane Harman	Senate Committee on the Judiciary; Sen. John Tunney
Rep. Jeb Hensarling	National Republican Senatorial Committee; Sen. Phil Gramm
Rep. Mazie Hirono	Sen. Spark Matsunaga
Rep. Rush D. Holt	Rep. Bob Edgar
Rep. Steve Israel	Rep. Richard Ottinger
Rep. Sheila Jackson-Lee	House Select Committee on Assassinations
Rep. William Jefferson	Sen. J. Bennett Johnston
Rep. Mark Kirk	Rep. John Edward Porter; House Committee on International Relations
Rep. Ray LaHood	Rep. Robert Michel; Rep. Thomas Railsback
Rep. Tom Lantos	Senate Committee on Foreign Relations
Rep. Barbara Lee	Rep. Ron Dellums
Rep. Daniel Lipinski	Rep. Rod Blagojevich; Rep. Richard Gephardt

Continued on page 209

§ 7.111 *(continued)*

Current Member	Staff on Which Member Served
Rep. Zoe Lofgren	Rep. Don Edwards
Rep. Dan Lungren	Rep. Bill Colmer; Sen. Bill Brock
Rep. Kevin McCarthy	Rep. Bill Thomas
Rep. Jim McCrery	Rep. Buddy Roemer
Rep. James P. McGovern	Rep. John Moakley; Sen. George McGovern
Rep. Martin Meehan	Rep. James Shannon
Rep. John L. Mica	Sen. Paula Hawkins
Rep. James P. Moran	Senate Committee on Appropriations
Rep. James L. Oberstar	Rep. John Blatnik; House Committee on Public Works
Rep. Charles W. (Chip) Pickering	Rep. Trent Lott
Rep. Jim Ramstad	Rep. Thomas Kleppe
Rep. Denny Rehberg	Rep. Ron Marlenee; Sen. Conrad Burns
Rep. Rick Renzi	Sen. Jon Kyl; Rep. Jim Kolbe
Rep. Peter Roskam	Rep. Tom DeLay; Rep. Henry Hyde
Rep. Paul Ryan	Sen. Robert Kasten/Senate Committee on Small Business; Rep. and Sen. Sam Brownback
Rep. Tim Ryan	Rep. James Traficant
Rep. James Sensenbrenner	Rep. J. Arthur Younger
Rep. Mark E. Souder	Rep. and Sen. Daniel Coats; House Select Committee on Children, Youth, and Families
Rep. Mac Thornberry	Rep. Tom Loeffler; Rep. Larry Combest
Rep. Pat Tiberi	Rep. John Kasich
Rep. Fred Upton	Rep. David Stockman
Rep. Chris Van Hollen	Senate Committee on Foreign Relations; Sen. Charles Mathias
Rep. Nydia M. Velázquez	Rep. Edolphus Towns
Rep. Peter J. Visclosky	Rep. Adam Benjamin/ House Committee on Appropriations
Rep. Greg Walden	Rep. Denny Smith
Rep. Anthony D. Weiner	Rep. Charles Schumer
Rep. Jerry Weller	Rep. Thomas Corcoran
Rep. Roger F. Wicker	Rep. Trent Lott/House Committee on Rules
Rep. Frank R. Wolf	Rep. Ed Biester
Rep. John Yarmuth	Sen, Marlow Cook
Rep. C.W. Bill Young	Rep. William Cramer

7

§ 7.112

Vice Presidents Elected to Senate

Five individuals have been elected to the Senate after serving as vice president. One, Andrew Johnson, was vice president to Abraham Lincoln and became president upon Lincoln's assassination.

John Calhoun, SC

Hannibal Hamlin, ME

Andrew Johnson, TN

Alben Barkley, KY

Hubert Humphrey, MN

Delegates and the resident commissioner may do any of the following:

- introduce bills and resolutions
- speak on the House floor
- serve on committees and accrue seniority in the same manner as other members of their party on those committees
- fully participate in committee activities, including offering amendments and motions, and voting during markups
- chair subcommittees

The House on January 24, 2007, agreed to a House resolution (H. Res. 78) permitting delegates and the resident commissioner to vote in the Committee of the Whole. (*See § 8.110, Committee of the Whole: Debate, and § 8.120, Committee of the Whole: Amendment Process*). However, the resolution stated that such votes could not provide the margin of victory or defeat on any amendment. The delegates and resident commissioner were also not allowed to vote on final passage or on procedural motions. After similar voting rights were extended to the delegates and resident commissioner in the 103rd Congress, there was an unsuccessful court challenge to the House procedures. A challenge might again be expected to the 110th Congress procedures. The 103rd Congress change was repealed in the 104th Congress.

In the 110th Congress, at the time of publication, the House passed legislation to award one representative in the House to the District of Columbia; to award a fourth representative in the House to Utah, which would have received the next apportioned seat following the 2000 census if the House had 436 seats; and to increase the number of House seats to 437 from 435 beginning in the 110th Congress. (*See § 2.13, Reapportionment and Redistricting, and § 7.41, Party Control of Congress, 80th through 110th Congresses.*) While the Constitution provides that the House of Representatives comprises members chosen by the people of the "several States" (*art. I, sec. 2, cl. 1*), proponents argued that the Constitution also gives Congress plenary power over the District of Columbia, including power to provide representation in Congress (*art. I, sec. 8, cl. 17*). No provision was included in the bill passed by the House to provide senators for the District of Columbia. To become law, any legislation, including providing a representative's seat in the House for the District of Columbia, would need to pass both houses of Congress in identical form and to be signed by the president or, in the event of a veto, to become law through an override by two-thirds of the members voting in each house. Should legislation become law granting the District of Columbia a representative in the House, a challenge in the federal courts to the constitutionality of the statute would be likely.

§ 7.21

Terms of Congress

Congress	Years	Congress	Years	Congress	Years
80th	1947–1949	94th	1975–1977	108th	2003–2005
81st	1949–1951	95th	1977–1979	109th	2005–2007
82nd	1951–1953	96th	1979–1981	110th	2007–2009
83rd	1953–1955	97th	1981–1983	111th	2009–2011
84th	1955–1957	98th	1983–1985	112th	2011–2013
85th	1957–1959	99th	1985–1987	113th	2013–2015
86th	1959–1961	100th	1987–1989	114th	2015–2017
87th	1961–1963	101st	1989–1991	115th	2017–2019
88th	1963–1965	102nd	1991–1993	116th	2019–2021
89th	1965–1967	103rd	1993–1995	117th	2021–2023
90th	1967–1969	104th	1995–1997	118th	2023–2025
91st	1969–1971	105th	1997–1999	119th	2025–2027
92nd	1971–1973	106th	1999–2001	120th	2027–2029
93rd	1973–1975	107th	2001–2003	121st	2029–2031

7

§ 7.20 Terms and Sessions of Congress

A term of Congress lasts for two years, beginning at 12:00 noon on January 3 of odd-numbered years, about two months after the latest general election. Congress might decide to convene a new term and swear in members on another day, but members of the previous Congress cease collecting their pay at noon on January 3, and members of the new Congress begin collecting theirs at that time. The 110th Congress convened on January 4, 2007. (*See § 7.21, Terms of Congress.*)

A term of Congress in contemporary practice comprises first and second sessions. The first session occurs within the first calendar year covered by the term—2007 for the first session of the 110th Congress. The second session occurs in the second calendar year—2008 for the second session of the 110th Congress. When the 110th Congress convened on January 4, it convened its first session. There is not usually any legislative significance attached to the sessions, but they fulfill the Twentieth Amendment requirement that Congress assemble "at least once in every year."

A session of Congress continues until Congress adjourns the session *sine die,* that is, without (*sine*) any day (*die*) to return or reconvene. When the second session of a Congress convenes, legislative work picks up where it left off in the first session; for example, a bill on

Lame-Duck Sessions of Congress, 1935–2006

Congress	Date Pre-Election Session Ended	Date Post-Election Session Began	Date Post-Election Session Adjourned Sine Die
76th Congress, 3rd Session (1940–1941)	Congress stayed in session		Jan. 3, 1941
77th Congress, 2nd Session (1942)	Congress stayed in session		Dec. 16, 1942
78th Congress, 2nd Session (1944)	Sept. 21, 1944	Nov. 14, 1944	Dec. 19, 1944
80th Congress, 2nd Session (1948)	Aug. 7, 1948	Dec. 31, 1948	Dec. 31, 1948
81st Congress, 2nd Session (1950–1951)	Sept. 23, 1950	Nov. 27, 1950	Jan. 2, 1951
83rd Congress, 2nd Session (1954)	Aug. 20, 1954	Senate: Nov. 8, 1954	Senate: Dec. 2, 1954
91st Congress, 2nd Session (1970–1971)	Oct. 14, 1970	Nov. 16, 1970	Jan. 2, 1971
93rd Congress, 2nd Session (1974)	Oct. 17, 1974	Nov. 18, 1974	Dec. 20, 1974
96th Congress, 2nd Session (1980)	Senate: Oct. 1 House: Oct. 2, 1980	Nov. 12, 1980	Dec. 16, 1980
97th Congress, 2nd Session (1982)	Oct. 1, 1982	Senate: Nov. 29 House: Nov. 21, 1982	Senate: Dec. 23 House: Dec. 21, 1982
103rd Congress, 2nd Session (1994)	Oct. 8, 1994	Nov. 28, 1994	Senate: Dec. 1 House: Nov. 29, 1994
105th Congress, 2nd Session (1998)	Oct. 21, 1998	House: Dec. 17, 1998	House: Dec. 19, 1998
106th Congress, 2nd Session (2000)	Senate: Nov. 2 House: Nov. 3, 2000	House: Nov. 13 Senate: Nov. 14, 2000	House: Dec. 15 Senate: Dec. 15, 2000
107th Congress, 2nd Session (2002)	House: Nov. 4 Senate: Nov. 4, 2002	House: Nov. 7 Senate: Nov. 7, 2002	Senate: Nov. 20 House: Nov. 22, 2002
108th Congress, 2nd Session (2004)	House: Oct. 9 Senate: Oct. 11, 2004	House: Nov. 16, Dec. 6 Senate: Nov. 16, Dec. 7, 2004	House: Nov. 24, Dec. 7 Senate: Nov. 24, Dec. 8, 2004
109th Congress, 2nd Session (2006)	House: Sept. 29 Senate: Sept. 29, 2006	House: Nov. 13, Dec. 5 Senate: Nov. 13, Dec. 4, 2006	House: Nov. 15, Dec. 8 Senate: Nov. 16, Dec. 8, 2006

§ 7.23

Résumé of Congressional Activity, 109th Congress

Every measure introduced in Congress has a two-year life cycle. Legislation to be enacted into law must pass in identical form both the House and Senate and be signed by the president. Some measures must be introduced in several Congresses before sufficient political support is generated for them to be enacted into law. Other measures authorize programs for several years, and Congress does not need to consider another authorization bill until the end of that period. Although it is difficult to assess the workload of a given Congress, scholars generally base a Congress's success on certain factors, including workload, time in session, and legislation enacted.

This table identifies some common measures of legislative activity in the 109th Congress.

Activity	House	Senate
Days in session	241	297
Public bills enacted into law	294	123
Measures passed	1,425	1,259
Bills introduced	6,438	4,122
Joint resolutions introduced	102	41
Concurrent resolutions introduced	504	123
Recorded votes, including yeas and nays	1,206	645
Congressional Record pages of proceedings	22,391	26,274

which there were subcommittee hearings and markup could be considered in full committee markup and be reported to the committee's parent chamber.

When Congress adjourns *sine die* at the end of a second session, the uncompleted work of that Congress remains uncompleted. Legislation at any stage of the legislative process dies. Work must begin again with the introduction of legislation after the new Congress convenes. (See § 7.23, *Résumé of Congressional Activity, 109th Congress.*)

It is possible for Congress to convene other sessions within its two-year term. It is also possible under the Constitution for the president to reconvene Congress within or between sessions. The threat of the president calling Congress back is sometimes used tactically to extract an extra effort from Congress toward completing a specific legislative action. With the first session of a Congress comprising nearly a full calendar year and the second session often concluding just a few weeks before the next general election, it is somewhat unlikely that there would be another session within a two-year term.

If Congress considers the need to reconvene following a general election possible or prob-

Joint Meetings and Joint Sessions

In 1789 and 1790, meetings of the two chambers were held in the Senate chamber in Federal Hall in New York. From 1790 to 1793, such meetings were held in the Senate chamber in Congress Hall in Philadelphia. From 1794 to 1799, meetings of the two chambers were held in the hall of the House chamber. When the Congress moved to Washington in 1800, the Senate chamber hosted the two houses. Since 1809, with few exceptions, these meetings have been held in the House chamber.

There are four terms that are used to describe times when the House and Senate meet together. The distinction among the four is not always clear or consistent.

A **joint session** is a formal meeting that occurs when both houses adopt a concurrent resolution. A joint session, for example, is usually what the sessions are called to count electoral votes and receive the State of the Union message.

A **joint meeting** occurs when each chamber agrees by unanimous consent to meet with the other chamber. Addresses by foreign dignitaries or special guests, as well as commemorative gatherings, occur in joint meetings.

- Joint meetings for foreign dignitaries have included Winston Churchill, Clement Atlee, Haile Selassie, Charles de Gaulle, Anwar Sadat, Yitzhak Rabin, Margaret Thatcher, Lech Walesa, Vaclav Havel, Nelson Mandela, Hamid Karzai, Ayad Allawi, Ellen Johnson Sirleaf, and King Abdullah.
- Joint meetings for special guests have included General Douglas MacArthur, the Apollo astronauts, and General William Westmoreland.
- Joint meetings for commemorative gatherings have included the fiftieth anniversary of World War II, Friendship 7, the first orbital space flight, the first lunar landing, the centennial of Harry Truman's birth, and the bicentennial of the 1st Congress.
- Joint meeting in New York City to honor the city on its recovery from the September 11, 2001, terrorist attack.

A **joint reception** occurs when a concurrent resolution calls for the Senate to recess to meet with the House, but the Senate adjourns instead. For example, a joint reception was held for the 1939 visit of King George VI of England.

The inauguration of the president is referred to as a **joint gathering**, although in recent years it has been held pursuant to concurrent resolution and thus would be a joint session.

The Speaker of the House presides over both joint sessions and joint meetings, with one exception: the vice president as the president of the Senate or the president pro tempore of the Senate presides over the counting of electoral votes.

able, it does not adjourn *sine die* before the election. If it reconvenes following an election, the ensuing work period is referred to colloquially as a *lame-duck session*. (See § 7.22, *Lame-Duck Sessions of Congress, 1935–2006.*)

During a session, the House and Senate might adjourn or recess during a day or at the end of a day, setting the next day and time of their meeting. The House might recess during a day to take a break from its proceedings for some reason, and it then will adjourn at the end of a day. The Senate, however, sometimes prefers to recess at the end of a day so as not to trigger a new legislative day the next day. *(The reasons for this Senate practice are explained in § 8.160, Senate Scheduling. See also § 7.24, Joint Meetings and Joint Sessions.)*

Secret Sessions

Secret sessions, also called closed or executive sessions, are held in the House and Senate chambers, with the galleries closed to the press and the public. *(An executive session of the Senate should not be confused with executive business, as explained in § 8.180, Senate Calendars and Legislative and Executive Business before the Senate.)* Secret sessions are held at the request of any member, and are convened to discuss issues of national security, confidential information, and sensitive executive communications. Senate deliberations during impeachment trials may be held in secret session.

To convene in secret session, a member makes a nondebatable motion to resolve into secret session. Proceedings in secret session are not published in the *Congressional Record* unless the chamber votes to release them.

Secret sessions are rare. Since 1929, when the Senate ended its practice of considering treaties and nominations behind closed doors, it has held fifty-four secret sessions, including six in 1999 to discuss impeachment proceedings against President Clinton. Since 1830, the House has met in secret session three times, the most recent in 1983 to discuss U.S. support for paramilitary operations in Nicaragua.

§ 7.30 Early Organization Meetings

Since the mid-1970s, both chambers have convened early organization meetings in November or December of even-numbered years to prepare for the start of the new Congress in January. These meetings serve educational, organizational, and social purposes.

The educational sessions range from meetings on legislative procedures and staff hiring to seminars on current policy issues. These sessions are taught by current members of Congress, former members, government practitioners, and academic experts. Issue sessions generally focus on the substance of issues, previous attempts at legislative changes, administration policy, and the outlook for action in the new Congress.

The organizational sessions serve new members as their first introduction to Congress and to each other. Some meetings are conducted for all freshmen and some for all members of the incoming Congress. Some meetings are organized by party affiliation. At these early organization meetings, class officers are elected, party leaders selected, and chamber officers chosen. Regional representatives to steering committees are named. Candidates for chair of selected committees are interviewed or elected, and members of those committees might be chosen. Each of these actions involving committees is then subject to official ratification by the House or Senate at the start of the Congress.

Room selection drawings and room assignments are also accomplished during the early organization meetings. *(See § 6.20, Guide to Public Buildings on Capitol Hill.)*

A Representative Early Organization Schedule: 108th Congress

Overview: Schedule of Events

Monday, November 11

All day	Registration
6:00pm	Welcome Reception hosted by Representative Steny H. Hoyer
6:00pm	Majority Whip's Dinner
8:00pm	Welcome Reception hosted by House Administration Chairman Robert W. Ney

Tuesday, November 12

8:00–8:45am	Members and Family Room Continental Breakfast for Members-Elect and Spouses
8:45–9:00am	Class Picture at Capitol Steps
9:15am–1:00pm	Committee on House Administration Program for Members-Elect
12:00–2:00pm	Luncheon hosted by Rep. Steny Hoyer, Ranking Minority Member, Committee on House Administration
1:00–2:00pm	Republican Member Lunch and Discussion
2:30–4:30pm	Members-Elect Meeting with Speaker, Majority Leader, Majority Whip, House Republican Conference and Deputy Majority Whip
2:30–5:00pm	Democratic Leadership Orientation Program
6:30–10:00pm	Dinner Hosted by Rep. Nancy Pelosi, Minority Whip Dinner Hosted by Rep. Martin Frost, Chairman, Democratic Caucus
6:00–10:00pm	Speaker's Dinner at Statuary Hall–Capitol
6:00–7:00pm	Reception and Candlelight Tour of Capitol
7:00–10:00pm	Dinner

Wednesday, November 13

7:00–8:00am	Breakfast for Republican New Members with Conference Vice Chair, Congresswoman Deborah Pryce
7:00–8:00am	Breakfast hosted by Rep. Nancy Pelosi, Minority Whip
7:30–10:00am	Breakfast hosted by Rep. Robert Menendez, Vice Chairman, Democratic Caucus
7:30–8:30am	Democratic Members-Elect Breakfast at Hyatt Regency on Capitol Hill
8:15am–12:00pm	Committee on House Administration Members-Elect Program
8:15am–4:15pm	Spouses Program
12:00–12:30pm	Members-Elect Meeting with Speaker and Minority Leader
12:30–1:30pm	Lunch Sponsored by Congressman Tom Reynolds
12:30–1:45pm	Lunch Hosted by Rep. Steny Hoyer, Ranking Minority Member, Committee on House Administration
2:00–5:00pm	Democratic Leadership Orientation Program
2:00–4:00pm	Conference Activities Begin
6:00–9:00pm	Minority Leader's Dinner, Statuary Hall, The Capitol
6:30–9:00pm	Representative Roy Blunt Reception and Dinner
Time TBD	Tour of West Wing of White House
8:30–10:30pm	Dessert Reception hosted by Representative Nancy Pelosi, Minority Whip

Thursday, November 14

9:00am	Democratic Caucus
7:00–8:30am	Republican Policy Committee Breakfast sponsored by Congressman Chris Cox
8:30–9:00am	Rain Date for Class Picture
10:00am–2:00pm	Conference Activities
8:00am–4:15pm	Designated-Aide Program Sponsored by Congressional Management Foundation (CMF)
3:00–6:00pm	NRCC Activities
7:00–9:00pm	Committee on House Administration Reception
Time TBD	Reception Hosted by Congressman Rogers

Friday, November 15

Time/Place TBD	Begin NRCC Activities
9:00am	Democratic Caucus

Committee on House Administration • 2002 New Member Orientation

The House Administration Committee and the Senate majority and minority leaders organize the chamber-specific official orientation programs for members-elect and their families. Orientation handbooks are provided, which describe the official rules of the chamber relating to staff hiring, ethics regulations, office equipment (including computer hardware and software), roles of the chamber officers, services of the legislative support agencies, and the like. Several sessions are devoted to these topics.

Separate, simultaneous programs are held for spouses and designated staff of members-elect. Spouse organizations are responsible for the spouse sessions. The spouse sessions, in addition to being social in nature, help spouses understand the congressional schedule and pressures on family life.

The Congressional Management Foundation, in conjunction with the House Administrative Assistants Association, has conducted the sessions for House staff of newly elected members for the last several Congresses. These sessions are designed to assist the new chiefs of staff, or individuals designated by the newly elected members to lead the set-up of their offices, in planning, budgeting, and setting up an office. The Congressional Management Foundation often conducts similar programs for Senate staff of newly elected senators.

Following orientation sessions for members-elect, the returning members join the members-elect for party organization meetings. At these sessions, the parties generally meet separately, although dinners are often hosted by the respective leadership for all members. Other evening events are held for members of only one party. (*See § 7.31, Representative Early Organization Schedule: 108th Congress.*)

In addition to the formal House and Senate programs, other orientation sessions are available to new members. Several outside organizations have in recent years held policy seminars. Harvard University's Institute of Politics presents a several-days-long policy program for newly elected House members soon after the official organization concludes. The Heritage Foundation holds a several-days-long seminar on policy issues for both Senate and House members-elect. In January, soon after the swearing-in, the Congressional Research Service conducts a several-days series of policy and procedural briefings for newly elected House members and their families. A one-day program conducted by the Congressional Research Service for new senators is sometimes held soon after the orientation meetings.

§7.40 Party Leadership

The party leadership is responsible for bringing order and efficiency in a body comprising individualistic legislators. Former Speaker of the House Dennis Hastert said his job was to "keep the trains moving on time." A former Senate leader once described his job as "janitor," and another said it was like "herding cats."

Party leaders serve both institutional and partisan functions. The majority leadership sets the agenda, determines legislative priorities and political strategies, schedules measures for floor action, assesses support for legislation, and rounds up votes for passage. The minority

Party Control of Congress, 80th through 110th Congresses

Party control of Congress indicates the party that has the majority of members in each chamber.

Membership may change throughout a Congress, due to deaths, resignations, or party switching by members. Twice in history, in the 65th Congress (1917–1919) and in the 72nd Congress (1931–1933), party control in the House changed from that based on the election results. In the 65th Congress, there were 210 Democrats, 216 Republicans, and 7 members of other parties. These 7 members affiliated with the Democrats, thereby making the Democrats the majority party in the 65th Congress. In the 72nd Congress, the election yielded 216 Democrats, 218 Republicans, and 1 member of a third party. By the time the 72nd Congress met on December 7, 1931, 14 representatives-elect had died (including Speaker Nicholas Longworth). Special elections to fill the vacancies resulted in a net gain of 4 seats for the Democrats, giving them control of the House.

When the 107th Congress convened, the Senate was split at 50 members each for the Democrats and Republicans. Because Vice President Cheney was a Republican and could vote in the event of a tie vote, Republicans organized the chamber, but only after a "power-sharing agreement" was negotiated between the parties. Then, on June 6, 2001, Republican Sen. James Jeffords, VT, declared himself to be an independent who would caucus with the Democrats to organize the Senate. The power-sharing agreement remained partially in effect.

In January 1959, Alaska was declared a state, and, in August 1959, Hawaii was declared a state. In the House, the admission of Alaska and Hawaii to the Union was accommodated by a temporary increase in the number of House members, to 436 in the 86th Congress for the 1 seat allocated for Alaska, and 437 in the 87th Congress for the 1 seat allocated for Hawaii. The number was returned to 435 in the 88th Congress following the 1960 census and apportionment. In the 86th Congress, there were 98 senators to accommodate 2 Alaskan senators. In the 87th Congress, the Senate reached its current level of 100 Senators, reflecting the addition of the 2 Hawaiian senators.

The following table depicts party control at the start of a Congress. In Congresses where the numbers do not total 100 in the Senate or 435 in the House, there were vacancies at the start of the Congress. The numbers above 435 for the House in the 86th and 87th Congresses provided seats for Alaska and Hawaii, as described above.

Congress	Senate			House		
	Democrat	Republican	Other	Democrat	Republican	Other
80th Congress (1947–1949)	45	51		188	246	1
81st Congress (1949–1951)	54	42		263	171	1
82nd Congress (1951–1953)	48	47	1	234	199	2
83rd Congress (1953–1955)	46	48	2	213	221	1
84th Congress (1955–1957)	48	47	1	232	203	
85th Congress (1957–1959)	49	47		234	201	

Continued on page 219

Congress	Senate			House		
	Democrat	Republican	Other	Democrat	Republican	Other
86th Congress (1959–1961)	64	34		283	153	
87th Congress (1961–1963)	64	36		262	175	
88th Congress (1963–1965)	67	33		258	176	
89th Congress (1965–1967)	68	32		295	140	
90th Congress (1967–1969)	64	36		248	187	
91st Congress (1969–1971)	58	42		243	192	
92nd Congress (1971–1973)	54	44	2	255	180	
93rd Congress (1973–1975)	56	42	2	242	192	1
94th Congress (1975–1977)	60	37	2	291	144	1
95th Congress (1977–1979)	61	38	1	292	143	
96th Congress (1979–1981)	58	41	1	277	158	
97th Congress (1981–1983)	46	53	1	242	192	1
98th Congress (1983–1985)	46	54		269	166	
99th Congress (1985–1987)	47	53		253	182	
100th Congress (1987–1989)	55	45		258	177	
101st Congress (1989–1991)	55	45		260	175	
102nd Congress (1991–1993)	56	44		267	167	1
103rd Congress (1993–1995)	57	43		258	176	1
104th Congress (1995–1997)	48	52		204	230	1
105th Congress (1997–1999)	45	55		207	226	2
106th Congress (1999–2001)	45	55		211	223	1
107th Congress (2001–2003)	50	50		211	221	2
108th Congress (2003-2005)	48	51	1	205	229	1
109th Congress (2005-2007)	44	55	1	201	232	1
110th Congress (2007-2009)	49	49	2	233	202	

For the current party control of Congress, see TheCapitol.Net web page <*www.PartyNumbers.com*>.

7

leadership devises strategies for upsetting the plans of the majority, unless, of course, there is agreement on the legislation.

The basic function of the party leaders is to bring coherence and efficiency to a decentralized institution. As institutional leaders, they are responsible for knowing rules and procedures, and for organizing the committee system and chamber administrative machinery. The majority leadership has the added responsibility of scheduling measures for floor consideration. As leaders of their political parties in their chambers, the leaders meet with committee chairs and ranking minority members to discuss political strategies and legislative priorities, assess support and opposition to the leadership's initiatives, round up votes, and serve as congressional spokesmen for their parties' positions. *(See § 7.41, Party Control of Congress, 80th through 110th Congresses.)*

House Leadership

This section briefly describes the majority and minority party leadership in the House. *(See § 7.42, House Leadership Structure, 110th Congress.)*

Speaker of the House. The position of Speaker is established by the Constitution. The Speaker is the most senior officer of the House and third most senior official in the federal government. Institutionally, the Speaker presides over the House, refers measures to committee, makes rulings on points of order, has priority right of recognition on the floor, and sets the agenda. The Speaker appoints members to task forces, commissions, conference committees, some legislative committees, and select and special committees. The Speaker oversees the management of support functions. By tradition, the Speaker infrequently participates in floor debate and seldom votes.

The Speaker is elected by majority vote of the House. Candidates are nominated by their respective party caucus or conference. On rare occasions, such as at the beginning of the 109th Congress, other candidates, in addition to those nominated by the party caucus or conference, have had their names put in nomination. The Speaker does not have to be a member of Congress.

Majority Leader. The majority leader is the second most senior official in the House and the day-to-day manager of business on the floor. In concert with the other majority-party leadership, the majority leader builds and manages his or her party's consensus on legislation. The majority leader is elected by the party caucus or conference.

Majority Whip. The majority whip persuades members to support his or her party's position on votes, and also measures and rounds up support for party positions. Assisted by a network of assistant whips—including chief deputy whips, regional whips, and class whips—the majority whip is elected by his or her party caucus or conference. The term "whip" comes from British parliamentary practice, which adapted it from fox hunting. The "whipper in" is the term for the person responsible for keeping the fox hounds from leaving the pack. *(See § 7.43, The Parties' Whip Structures.)*

House Leadership Structure, 110th Congress

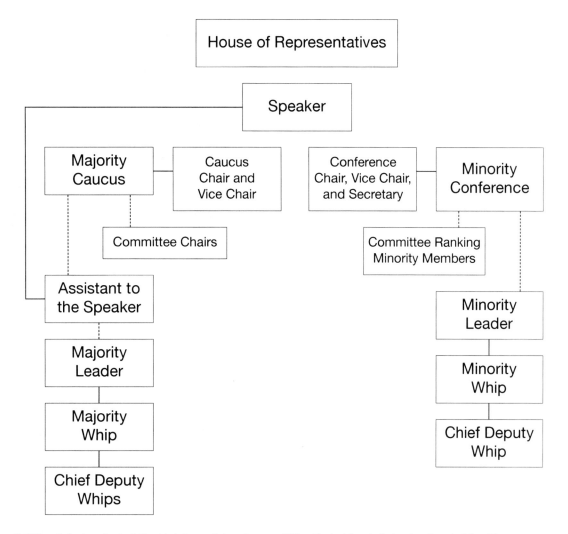

Solid lines indicate a direct relationship in terms of shared responsibilities. Dashed lines indicate a less formal relationship.
For the current House leadership, see TheCapitol.Net web page <*www.CongressLeaders.com*>.

Minority Leader. The minority leader is the senior official for his or her party, who works within the party to set an agenda, message, and strategy. He or she can appoint minority party members to task forces and commissions. The minority leader is elected by the party caucus or conference.

Assistant to the Speaker. A position unique within the House Democratic Caucus, the assistant to the Speaker works with other Democratic leaders on communication, message, and research. This position was created in the 106th Congress. The assistant to the Speaker is selected by the Speaker.

The Parties' Whip Structures

The parties in the House and Senate have an extensive array of whips assisting the elected majority and minority whips. The majority and minority whips appoint a number of deputy, assistant, or regional whips. Each party also elects zone whips, sometimes referred to as regional whips. Additional whips represent classes of members, such as freshmen members.

The titles associated with the various whip positions are not consistent between Congresses, between parties, or even within a party. Some members identify themselves as regional whips, when they might more accurately be called at-large whips, or vice versa. Party lists that identify whips elected or appointed by the party leadership may not consistently include whips selected by other groups. Different sources may identify different whip structures.

Because the whip organization is not yet complete for the 110th Congress, the table depicts the breadth of the whip structure.

Whip	House Democrats	House Republicans	Senate Democrats	Senate Republicans
Senior Chief Deputy Whip	1			
Chief Deputy Whip	6	1	1	1
Deputy Whip	12	17	3	7
Assistant Whip		49		
Regional Whip	24			
At-Large Whip	70			

Minority Whip. The minority whip persuades members to support his or her party's position on votes, and counts votes. To do the whip's job, he or she is assisted by a network of assistant whips, including regional whips and class whips. The minority whip is elected by his or her party caucus or conference.

Democratic Caucus. The caucus serves as the organizational vehicle for all House Democrats and is led by two officers elected by the caucus: chair and vice chair. The caucus hosts meetings and serves as the primary vehicle for communicating the party message to members.

Democratic Congressional Campaign Committee. Appointed by the Democratic leader, the chair and co-chairs oversee the political unit of House Democrats.

Republican Conference. The conference serves as the organizational vehicle for all House Republicans. It is led by three officers elected by the conference members: chair, vice chair, and secretary. The conference hosts meetings and serves as the primary vehicle for communicating the party message to members.

Republican Policy Committee. Elected by the Republican Conference, the chair assists party leaders in designing, developing, and executing policy ideas.

Republican Congressional Campaign Committee. Elected by the Republican Conference, the chair and executive committee oversee the political unit of House Republicans.

Senate Leadership

This section briefly identifies the majority and minority leadership in the Senate. *(See § 7.44, Senate Leadership Structure, 110th Congress.)*

President Pro Tempore. By tradition the longest serving member of the majority party, the president pro tempore is elected by the Senate to this constitutional but largely ceremonial position.

Majority Leader. The majority leader is the most senior Senate official, who manages the day-to-day business of the Senate floor. The majority leader is responsible for working with each committee on legislation and scheduling the sequence and manner of debate on legislation. The majority leader has priority recognition on the floor. The majority leader is elected by his or her party caucus or conference.

Assistant Majority Leader. The majority whip persuades members to support party positions on votes, and measures and rounds up support for party positions. The majority whip is elected by the party caucus or conference, and is assisted by an appointed chief deputy whip.

Minority Leader. The minority leader is the senior official for his or her party. The minority leader is elected by his or her party caucus or conference.

Assistant Floor Leader (Minority Whip). Elected by party members, the minority whip serves as the second-ranking leader for the minority. Assisted by a chief deputy whip, the minority whip counts votes and works to persuade members to support party positions.

Democratic Conference. The conference serves as the organization vehicle for Senate Democrats and is led by a chair, vice chair, and secretary elected by the conference.

Democratic Conference Vice Chair. The conference vice chair is the third-ranking leader of his or her party.

Democratic Conference Secretary. The conference secretary is the fourth-ranking leader elected by his or her party membership.

Democratic Policy Committee. The policymaking arm of the Senate Democrats, the Policy Committee works with the Democratic leader to develop policy proposals. The chair is appointed by the Democratic leader. The committee includes regional chairs.

Democratic Senatorial Campaign Committee. Appointed by the Democratic leader, the chair and vice chair oversee the political unit of Senate Democrats.

Democratic Steering and Outreach Committee. Appointed by the Democratic leader, the chair of the committee is responsible for building coalitions.

Senate Leadership Structure, 110th Congress

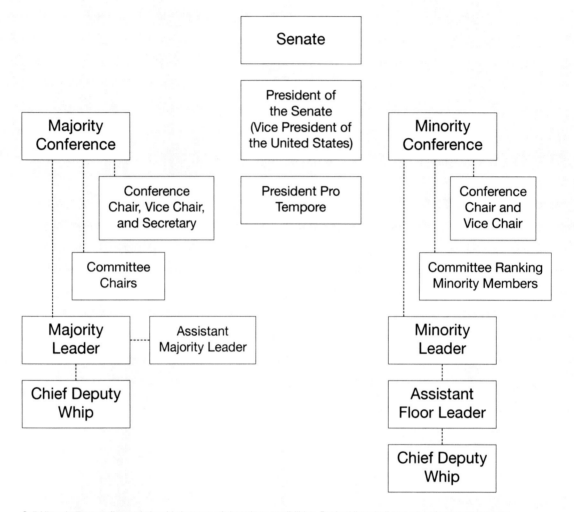

Solid lines indicate a direct relationship in terms of shared responsibilities. Dashed lines indicate a less formal relationship. For the current Senate leadership, see TheCapitol.Net web page <*www.CongressLeaders.com*>.

Democratic Committee on Committee Outreach. Appointed by the Democratic leader, the chair and vice chair are responsible for maintaining communication among committee leaders.

Rural Outreach. Appointed by the Democratic leader, the chair is responsible for rural, ex-urban, and suburban outreach.

Senate Republican Conference. The conference serves as the organizational vehicle for Senate Republicans and is led by a chair and vice chair elected by the conference. The conference hosts periodic meetings and is the primary vehicle for communicating party message.

Republican Policy Committee. The Policy Committee, and its elected chair, assists other Senate leaders in designing, developing, and executing policy ideas.

Republican Steering Committee. The steering committee, led by an appointed chair, is responsible for making committee assignments.

National Republican Senatorial Committee. The campaign committee serves as the political unit of Senate Republicans. It is led by a chair who is appointed by the Republican Conference.

§ 7.50 Committees and Subcommittees
Types of Committees

There are three types of committees. "Standing committees" are permanent entities with legislative authority identified in chamber rules. House Rule X and Senate Rule XXV list the jurisdiction of each committee. Referral is determined primarily by committee jurisdiction. *(See § 8.30, Referral of Legislation to Committee.)*

"Select committees" or "special committees" (the terms are interchangeable) are temporary panels created for a specified period of time and with a specific mandate. Most select committees do not have legislative authority, that is, the right to consider legislation. Select or special committees are created by simple resolution.

"Joint committees" are made up of members of both chambers. Joint committees are generally permanent panels with study or administrative authority.

Committee Sizes and Ratios

In both the House and Senate, the respective party leaders begin to negotiate individual committee sizes and ratios before the early organization meetings. They continue the discussions during the organization meetings. Occasionally, the negotiations continue until the beginning of the new Congress. Committee sizes are modified each Congress, but generally not by more than a few seats. Committee sizes are included in Senate rules, but not in House rules.

Ratios on House and Senate committees generally reflect party strength in the chamber. However, it is commonly acknowledged that House ratios are done in the aggregate (allocation of total number of committee seats), rather than on a committee-by-committee basis. This is done in part to attain a "working majority" on the more sought-after committees. Senate ratios also allow for a "working majority." However, ratios more closely approximate party strength in the chamber as a whole. *(See § 7.51, House and Joint Committee Ratios in the 110th Congress.)*

Subcommittees

Most committees form subcommittees to share specific tasks with the full committees. Subcommittees are responsible to—and work within the guidelines established by—their parent committees. House rules impose a limit of five subcommittees for most committees. Senate

House and Joint Committee Ratios
in the 110th Congress
(as of March 31, 2007)

Committee	Democrats	Republicans
Agriculture	25	21
Appropriations	37	29
Armed Services	34	28
Budget	22	17
Education and Labor	27	22
Energy and Commerce	31	26
Energy Independence and Global Warming, Select	9	6
Financial Services	39	33
Foreign Affairs	27	23
Homeland Security	19	15
House Administration	6	3
Intelligence, Permanent Select	12	9
Judiciary	23	17
Natural Resources	27	22
Oversight and Government Reform	23	18
Rules	9	4
Science and Technology	24	22
Small Business	18	15
Standards of Official Conduct	5	5
Transportation and Infrastructure	41	34
Veterans' Affairs	16	13
Ways and Means	24	17

Joint Committees

Committee	House Democrats	House Republicans	Senate Democrats	Senate Republicans
Economic	6	4	6	4
Library	3	2	3	2
Printing	3	2	3	2
Taxation	3	2	3	2

§ 7.52

Senate Committee Ratios in the 110th Congress

Committee	Democrats	Republicans
Agriculture, Nutrition, and Forestry	11	10
Appropriations	15	14
Armed Services[1]	13	12
Banking, Housing, and Urban Affairs	11	10
Budget[2]	12	11
Commerce, Science, and Transportation	12	11
Energy and Natural Resources[2]	12	11
Environment and Public Works[1,2]	10	9
Finance	11	10
Foreign Relations	11	10
Health, Education, Labor, and Pensions[2]	11	10
Homeland Security and Governmental Affairs[1]	9	8
Judiciary	10	9
Rules and Administration	10	9
Small Business and Entrepreneurship[1]	10	9
Veterans' Affairs[2]	8	7
Indian Affairs	8	7
Select Ethics	4	3
Select Intelligence	8	7
Special Aging	11	10

1. Sen. Joseph Lieberman, an Independent Democrat, receives his committee assignments from the Democrats and is counted as a Democrat for determining committee ratios. He serves on this committee.
2. Sen. Bernard Sanders, an independent, receives his committee assignments from the Democrats and is counted as a Democrat for determining committee ratios. He serves on this committee.

committees are not limited by Senate rule in the number of subcommittees they may create. The House Appropriations Committee has twelve subcommittees, and the Senate Appropriations Committee has twelve subcommittees. (*See § 9.82, New Appropriations Subcommittee Organization.*)

Some subcommittees have independent, autonomous staff; others do not, using instead

Member Press Release

For Immediate Release
January 5, 2005

CONTACT: Win Boerckel
202-225-4572

Congresswoman Moore Wins Seat on Powerful Financial Services Committee

WASHINGTON, DC -- Today, Congresswoman Gwen Moore (D-WI) won a seat on the prestigious House Committee on Financial Services when the Democratic Steering Committee nominated Moore, a freshman, to serve on this influential panel.

"It is an honor to have been selected for a position on the powerful Financial Services Committee," said Congresswoman Gwen Moore. "With jurisdiction over the entire financial services industry, including banking, credit, insurance, housing, and securities, as well as urban development, this assignment gives me great opportunities to fight for issues that are important to my constituents."

"In addition to the thousands of employees in Milwaukee's large financial and insurance sector, the desire to ensure affordable housing, better neighborhoods, and adequate access to credit for Milwaukee residents is a longtime passion of mine" said Moore.

Moore comes to the position with a wealth of experience in financial issues important to Wisconsin's working families. As a VISTA volunteer, Moore worked to spearhead the start-up of a community development credit union in Milwaukee. Before running for the state legislature, she worked as a housing officer for the Wisconsin Housing and Economic Development Authority (WHEDA). She served on WHEDA's Board of Directors for over a decade.

In the state legislature, she has been very active, creating a $50 million statewide venture capital program, serving on the Department of Financial Institutions' Task Force on Financial Competitiveness, and either chairing or serving on committees with jurisdiction over housing, economic development, urban infrastructure, and financial institutions.

The House Financial Services Committee is one of the few and much sought-after top Committees in the House of Representatives, a group that also includes the Committees on Ways and Means and Appropriations. The Committee's jurisdiction includes banks and banking, including deposit insurance and federal monetary policy, economic stabilization; financial aid to commerce and industry (other than transportation); insurance generally; international finance; international financial and monetary organizations; money and credit, including currency and the issuance of notes; valuation and revaluation of the dollar, public and private housing, securities and exchanges, and urban development.

--30--

§ 7.54

Example of a Senior Committee Member's Activities

7

§ 7.55

House Committee Chairs and Ranking Minority Members and Their Tenure

House Rule X, cl. (c)(2) addresses term limits for committee and subcommittee chairs. The rule does not address term limits for ranking minority members or term limits for members who accrue time as both chairs and ranking minority members. With the exception of the Committee on Rules, no member may serve as a chair of the same standing committee, or of one subcommittee of a standing committee, for more than three consecutive Congresses. Service for less than a full session of Congress does not count against a chair's term limit. Republican Conference rules go further than House rules. Conference rules limit Republican members to three consecutive terms as chair or ranking minority member of a standing, select, joint, or ad hoc committee or subcommittee beginning with the 104th Congress.

Committee	Chair	Year Became Chair	Year to Relinquish Chair	Ranking Minority Member	Year Became Ranking	Comments
Agriculture	Collin C. Peterson	2007	2013	Bob Goodlatte	2007	Rep. Goodlatte served four years as chair (2003-2007)
Appropriations	David R. Obey	2007	2013	Jerry Lewis	2007	Rep. Lewis served two years as chair (2005-2007)
Armed Services	Ike Skelton	2007	2013	Duncan Hunter	2007	Rep. Hunter announced he will not seek reelection to the 111th Congress; he served six years as chair (2001-2007)
Budget	John M. Spratt Jr.	2007	2013	Paul Ryan	2007	
Education and Labor	George Miller	2007	2013	Howard P. "Buck" McKeon	2007	Rep. McKeon served part of one year as chair (2006)
Energy and Commerce	John D. Dingell	2007	2013	Joe Barton	2007	Rep. Barton served two years as chair (2005-2007)
Financial Services	Barney Frank	2007	2013	Spencer Bachus	2007	
Foreign Affairs	Tom Lantos	2007	2013	Ileana Ros-Lehtinen	2007	
Homeland Security	Bennie G. Thompson	2007	2013	Peter T. King	2007	Rep. King served part of two years as chair (2005-2007)
House Administration	Vacancy*			Vernon J. Ehlers	2007	Rep. Ehlers served part of one year as chair (2006)
Judiciary	John Conyers Jr.	2007	2013	Lamar Smith	2007	

Continued on page 231

§ 7.55 *(continued)*

Committee	Chair	Year Became Chair	Year to Relinquish Chair	Ranking Minority Member	Year Became Ranking	Comments
Natural Resources	Nick J. Rahall II	2007	2013	Don Young	2007	Rep. Young served six years as chair of then-named Resources (1995-2001) and six years as chair of Transportation and Infrastructure (2001-2007)
Oversight and Government Reform	Henry A. Waxman	2007	2013	Tom Davis	2007	Rep. Davis served four years as chair (2003-2007)
Rules	Louise McIntosh Slaughter	2007		David Dreier	2007	House Rule X, cl. (c)(2) exempts the Rules Committee chair from term limits
Science and Technology	Bart Gordon	2007	2013	Ralph M. Hall	2007	
Small Business	Nydia M. Velázquez	2007	2013	Steve Chabot	2007	
Standards of Official Conduct	Stephanie Tubbs Jones			Doc Hastings		Rep. Hastings served two years as chair (2003-2007)
Transportation and Infrastructure	James L. Oberstar	2007	2013	John L. Mica	2007	
Veterans' Affairs	Bob Filner	2007	2013	Steve Buyer	2007	Rep. Buyer served two years as chair (2005-2007)
Ways and Means	Charles B. Rangel	2007	2013	Jim McCrery	2007	

*A permanent replacement for Chairwoman Juanita Millender-McDonald, who died April 22, 2007, had not been named at the time of publication.

full committee staff as needed. Some subcommittees have the authority to mark up legislation; others do not. Some subcommittees conduct only hearings.

Committee Leadership

A committee chair calls meetings and establishes the committee agenda. The chair arranges hearings, presides over hearings and markups, controls the selection of staff and expenditures from the committee budget, manages some or all of a measure reported from the committee on the floor for the majority party, and recommends conferees. The *ranking minority member* performs these functions for the minority-party members on a committee.

In the House, selection of committees' party leaders is determined by party rules. For the Democrats, nominations are drawn up by the Democratic Steering Committee and then elected by secret ballot by the entire Democratic Caucus. Republicans also rely on their Steer-

§ 7.56

House Committee Assignment
Request Form

COMMITTEE ASSIGNMENT REQUEST FORM
FOR INCOMING REPUBLICAN MEMBERS
108th Congress
(MUST BE RETURNED BY 12 NOON ON DECEMBER 2, 2002)

_____
Member's Name

_____
State & District

<u>108th Congress Committee Request</u>

1st Choice: _____

2nd Choice: _____

3rd Choice: _____

4th Choice: _____

5th Choice: _____

Comments: _____

_____

_____

Staff Contact & Phone Number: _____

RETURN TO: Republican Steering Committee
Speaker's Office, H-209, the Capitol
Washington, DC 20515

PLEASE RETURN BY 12 NOON ON DECEMBER 2, 2002

§ 7.57

Categories of Committees in the House of Representatives

Category	Democrats	Republicans
Exclusive	Appropriations	Appropriations
	Energy and Commerce (for service on the panel in the 104th and subsequent Congresses)	Energy and Commerce
	Financial Services (for service on the panel beginning in the 109th)	
	Rules	Rules
	Ways and Means	Ways and Means
Nonexclusive	Agriculture	Agriculture
	Armed Services	Armed Services
	Budget	Budget
	Education and Labor	Education and Labor
	Energy and Commerce (for service on the panel occurring in the 104th and earlier Congresses)	
	Financial Services (for service on the panel prior to the 109th Congress)	Financial Services
	Foreign Affairs	Foreign Affairs
	Homeland Security	Homeland Security
	House Administration	
	Judiciary	Judiciary
	Natural Resources	Natural Resources
	Oversight and Government Reform	Oversight and Government Reform
	Science and Technology	Science and Technology
	Small Business	Small Business
	Transportation and Infrastructure	Transportation and Infrastructure
	Veterans' Affairs	Veterans' Affairs
Exempt		House Administration
	Select Energy Independence and Global Warming	
	Select Intelligence	Select Intelligence
	Standards of Official Conduct	Standards of Official Conduct

7

Senate Committee Chairs and Ranking Minority Members and Their Tenure

Republican Conference rules address the issue of term limits for committee chairs and ranking minority members. Although the rule was agreed to in 1995, it was not made effective until 1997. A clarification to the rule was needed to say that senators could serve no more than six years as chair and six years as a ranking minority member of a single committee. If a senator has already served six years as chair of a committee, he or she could not become the ranking member. Time served as ranking member must come before, or interrupt, the six years of service as chair. With the change of party control of the Senate in 2001 as a result of the party switch to independent from Republican of former Sen. James Jeffords, the interpretation of the rule was addressed once again. In general, the 107th Congress was viewed by the Republican Conference as not counting against a senator's term limits. Because of the complexity of the Republican Conference rule, and its effect on all Republican senators, the exact language of the rule is provided here:

"B. Standing Committee Chair/Ranking Member Term Limits: (1) A Senator shall serve no more than six years, cumulatively, as Chairman of the same standing Committee. This limitation shall not preclude a Senator from serving for six years, cumulatively, as Chairman of other Committees, in series, if the Senator's seniority and election by Committee members provides the opportunity for such additional service. (2) Service as Ranking Member shall also be limited to six years, cumulatively, in the same pattern as described in (1) above. Time served as Ranking Member shall not be counted as time served as Chairman. Once a Senator has completed six years as Chairman of a committee, there will be no further opportunity for that Senator to serve as Ranking Member of that same committee if control of the Senate shifts and Republicans go into the minority. The opportunity for service as Ranking Member, outlined in (2) above, takes place either before or in interruption of the Senator's six year term as Chairman, not after."

Because the term limit is a Republican Conference rule, rather than a Senate rule, it does not apply to Democratic senators.

Committee	Chair	Ranking	Comments
Agriculture, Nutrition and Forestry	Tom Harkin	Saxby Chambliss	Sen. Chambliss served two years as chair (2005-2007)
Appropriations	Robert C. Byrd	Thad Cochran	Sen. Cochran served two years as chair (2005-2007)
Armed Services	Carl Levin	John McCain	
Banking, Housing, and Urban Affairs	Christopher J. Dodd	Richard C. Shelby	Sen. Shelby served four years as chair (2003-2007)
Budget	Kent Conrad	Judd Gregg	Sen. Gregg served two years as chair (2005-2007)
Commerce, Science, and Transportation	Daniel K. Inouye	Ted Stevens	Sen. Stevens served two years as chair (2005-2007)
Energy and Natural Resources	Jeff Bingaman	Pete V. Domenici	Sen. Domenici served four years as chair (2003-2007)

Continued on page 235

§ 7.58 (continued)

Committee	Chair	Ranking	Comments
Environment and Public Works	Barbara Boxer	James M. Inhofe	Sen. Inhofe served four years as chair (2003-2007)
Finance	Max Baucus	Charles E. Grassley	Sen. Grassley served six years as chair (2001-2007)
Foreign Relations	Joseph R. Biden Jr.	Richard G. Lugar	Sen. Lugar served four years as chair (2003-2007)
Health, Education, Labor, and Pensions	Edward M. Kennedy	Mike Enzi	Sen. Enzi served two years as chair (2005-2007)
Homeland Security and Governmental Affairs	Joseph I. Lieberman*	Susan M. Collins	Sen. Collins served four years as chair (2003-2007)
Judiciary	Patrick J. Leahy	Arlen Specter	Sen. Specter served two years as chair (2005-2007)
Rules and Administration	Dianne Feinstein	Robert F. Bennett	
Small Business and Entrepreneurship	John F. Kerry	Olympia J. Snowe	Sen. Snowe served four years as chair (2003-2007)
Veterans' Affairs	Daniel K. Akaka	Larry E. Craig	Sen. Craig served two years as chair (2005-2007)
Indian Affairs	Byron L. Dorgan	Craig Thomas	
Select Committee on Intelligence	John D. Rockefeller IV	Christopher S. Bond	Republican Conference rules on term limits affect only standing committees
Special Committee on Aging	Herb Kohl	Gordon Smith	Republican Conference rules on term limits affect only standing committees

* Independent Democrat

ing Committee to select committee leaders. The Republican Steering Committee is controlled by the party leader.

In the Senate, the Democratic Steering and Coordination Committee selects committee leaders generally based on seniority. The full Democratic Conference votes on the selection. For the Republicans, each committee selects its leader, subject to approval by the full Republican Conference.

In both the House and Senate, no member may chair more than one standing committee. In addition, Republican members in both chambers have imposed term limits on their committee and subcommittee leaders. Under the restrictions, committee or subcommittee leaders may not serve more than six years as leader. The House rule became effective in 1995. The

House rule also currently affects Democratic chairs. The Senate rule was agreed to in 1995 to become effective in 1997, but it was not fully implemented until 2005. *(See § 7.55, House Committee Chairs and Ranking Minority Members and Their Tenure, and § 7.58, Senate Committee Chairs and Ranking Minority Members and Their Tenure.)*

House and Senate rules also allow a full committee chair and ranking minority member to serve *ex officio* as a member of any of a committee's subcommittees. Some House committees allow ex officio members to vote; others do not. Senate rules prohibit ex officio members from voting.

House Committee and Subcommittee Assignment Process

Committee assignments often determine the character and course of a member's career. New members generally seek assignment to committees that address issues with which they are familiar, as well as issues important to their districts and states and key to their political ambitions. *(See § 7.53, Member Press Release, and § 7.54, Example of a Senior Committee Member's Activities.)* Committee assignments are also important to the party leaders who organize the chamber. Committee assignments shape the composition of the committees. In making assignments to committees, party leaders balance the wishes of the members against the sometimes differing political needs of the party. Both House rules and party rules (Democratic Caucus and Republican Conference) address the assignment process. *(See § 7.56, House Committee Assignment Request Form.)*

Numbers and Limitations on Committee Assignments. In general, no member may serve on more than two standing committees and four subcommittees of those committees, a total of six slots. As noted in § 7.57 *(Categories of Committees in the House of Representatives)*, both parties designate categories of committees and generally limit service to one exclusive committee, although a member can serve on the Budget or House Administration panels while on an exclusive committee. A Republican member of the Rules Committee can take a leave of absence from a standing committee to serve on Rules without losing seniority on the standing committee. Both parties allow service on two nonexclusive committees.

For Democrats and Republicans, service on the Standards of Official Conduct Committee is exempt from assignment limitations. Under House rules, service on this committee is limited to three Congresses during any five successive Congresses.

Service on the Budget Committee is limited to no more than four Congresses in any six successive Congresses for both Democrats and Republicans.

Party Organization Role. Both the Democrats and Republicans give their assignment function to steering committees, comprising the elected leadership, members elected from regions, and members appointed by the leadership. Representatives from specific classes are often also represented.

The steering committees vote by secret ballot to arrive at individual recommendations for assignments, and forward these recommendations to the respective party caucus or confer-

§ 7.59

Categories of Committees in the Senate

"A" Committees
Agriculture, Nutrition, and Forestry
Appropriations*
Armed Services*
Banking, Housing, and Urban Affairs
Commerce, Science, and Transportation
Energy and Natural Resources
Environment and Public Works
Finance*
Foreign Relations*
Health, Education, Labor, and Pensions
Homeland Security and Governmental Affairs
Judiciary
Select Intelligence

"B" Committees
Budget
Rules and Administration
Small Business and Entrepreneurship
Veterans' Affairs
Special Aging
Joint Economic

"C" Committees
Select Ethics
Indian Affairs
Joint Library**
Joint Printing**
Joint Taxation

* Categories are listed in Senate Rule XXV; however, Democratic and Republican party rules each designate four "A" committees as so-called "Super A" committees.
** The committee is not listed in Senate Rule XXV; it is treated as a "C" committee for assignment purposes.

ence. Although procedures exist to appeal steering committee recommendations, it is rare for the party to overturn a slate. Once ratified by the party, the House votes on each resolution comprising the committee lists for each party.

Subcommittee Assignment Process. Under House rules, members are generally limited to service on four subcommittees. Party rules and practice, however, govern the subcommittee assignment process. In Democratic Caucus rules, Democrats formally provide for a bidding process based on full committee seniority, whereby each member selects one choice before any member receives a second subcommittee assignment. Republicans leave the decision on subcommittee assignments to each individual committee leader. Many Republican committee leaders employ a bidding process similar to the one used by the Democrats.

Senate Committee and Subcommittee Assignment Process

Numbers and Limitations on Committee Assignments. Senate rules establish three categories of committees, popularly called "A," "B," and "C." *(See § 7.59, Categories of Committees in the Senate, for a list of the committees within each category.)* Each party also designates so-called "super A" committees. Senators are restricted to service on two "A" committees and one "B" committee. They are also restricted to service on one "Super A" committee. There are no restrictions on service on "C" committees. The limitations are often waived, and senators who serve on additional panels may be referred to as having "grandfather" rights on the additional committees.

Subcommittee Assignment Process. Neither Senate rules nor party rules discuss how subcommittee assignments are made. However, there are two prevalent practices. Under one practice, the full committee chair exercises discretion in selecting subcommittee members. Under the other common practice, senators choose assignments in a bidding process in order of seniority on the full committee, similar to the way the House members select subcommittee assignments.

There are limitations on subcommittee assignments. A senator may not serve on more than three subcommittees of each "A" committee (except Appropriations), and two subcommittees of a "B" committee. Because the full committee limitations are often waived, the subcommittee limitations are also often waived. There are no restrictions for service on "C" committees. The "C" committees, however, rarely create subcommittees.

§ 7.60 Informal Groups and Congressional Member Organizations (CMOs)

Informal groups, caucuses, congressional member organizations (CMOs)—the terms all relate to the same thing: they refer to ad hoc social or policy groups comprising a limited number of members of Congress from one or both houses. The groups are not recognized in chamber rules and are voluntary associations. Some have long lineages; others appear for just a few Congresses. They operate outside the formal committee structure and apart from the official party organizations. However, caucuses are an important link in the policy chain. These entities initiate policy actions, and their work touches on all aspects of the legislative arena.

Caucuses vary in membership, range of interest, issue focus, activity, and strategy. Some are formed to influence policy; some serve as information clearinghouses. Some represent constituency interests; others are aimed primarily at the orientation of new members. Some groups exist to develop member expertise on an issue; others exist to serve as liaison with outside organizations. Some groups are partisan; others are bipartisan. Some represent members of one chamber only; others are bicameral. Some meet frequently; some meet occasionally; some never meet. These groups represent the many policy and other concerns of the members of Congress.

Most groups have chairs, and many also have co-chairs. Groups that are made up mostly of House members often have steering or executive committees. Larger caucuses often organize their members into subgroups representing regional or ideological perspectives. Almost all groups rely on staff from their members' personal offices to do the work of the caucus.

Caucuses, CMOs, and informal groups can be categorized by type. They represent industry issues, national constituencies, regional concerns, state or district issues, personal interests, and party or political agendas. *(See § 7.61, Selected Caucuses and Informal Groups.)*

§ 7.61

Selected Caucuses and Informal Groups

Type of Caucus or Member Organization	Example	Comments
Industry issues	Congressional Mining Caucus	Bipartisan House members
	Congressional Steel Caucus	Bipartisan House members
	Congressional Travel and Tourism Caucus	Bipartisan House members
	Congressional Wireless Telecommunications Caucus	Bipartisan and bicameral
National constituency	Child Care Caucus	Bipartisan House members
	Congressional Black Caucus	Bipartisan and bicameral
	Congressional Caucus on Women's Issues	Bipartisan and bicameral
	Congressional Hispanic Caucus	Bipartisan and bicameral
	Federal Government Service Caucus	Bipartisan and bicameral
	Vietnam Era Veterans in Congress	Bipartisan and bicameral
Regional	Western Caucus	Bipartisan House members
	Western States Senate Coalition	Bipartisan Senate members
	Northeast-Midwest Coalition	Bipartisan and bicameral
	Western Water Caucus	Bipartisan and bicameral
State/district	Rural Health Care Coalition	Bipartisan House members
	Urban Caucus	Bipartisan House members
	Long Island Congressional Caucus	Bipartisan and bicameral
	Rural Health Caucus	Bipartisan Senate members
Personal interest	Congressional Arts Caucus	Bipartisan House members
	Missing and Exploited Children's Caucus	Bipartisan House members
	Sportsmen's Caucus	Bipartisan and bicameral
Party issues	Coalition (Blue Dogs)	"Conservative" House Democrats
	New Democrat Coalition	"Moderate" House Democrats
	Progressive Caucus	"Progressive" House Democrats
	Republican Study Committee	Social and economic conservative House Republicans
	Tuesday Group	"Moderate" House Republicans

7

CMOs are registered with the House Administration Committee as informal groups of members who "share official resources to carry out activities," according to regulations promulgated by the Committee on House Administration. These CMOs do not receive office space and cannot use the congressional frank. They are, however, officially recognized informal groups. CMOs are the successors to what were called *legislative service organizations* before the 104th Congress. A number of legislative service organizations restructured into CMOs. As of March 31, 2007, nearly one hundred informal groups were known to exist or were registered in the 110th Congress. Information on CMOs is available at the Committee on House Administration web site, *<http://cha.house.gov/index.php?option=com_content&task=view&id =45&Itemid=37>*. The Senate does not have a counterpart registration system for such informal groups.

Members of CMOs in the House and informal groups in the Senate are subject to rules and ethics codes of their respective chambers. The CMOs and informal groups may not hire staff or use official funds for such expenses as stationery. Members may list their membership in a CMO or informal group on their own stationery, and may use a portion of their own web sites for information on a CMO or informal group.

§ 7.70 Commissions and Boards

In addition to their other responsibilities, many members serve on commissions, boards, and other entities that Congress has created to oversee or study various governmental or quasi-governmental organizations, commemorations, or public policy issues. These organizations might also be used as decision-making bodies within or outside Congress. Appointment power might lie within Congress.

Members of Congress appoint individuals from their states and districts to the U.S. service academies. *(See § 3.112, Constituent Services and Courtesies.)* In addition, members serve on the boards of visitors to the academies. For example, the board of visitors of the U.S. Air Force Academy includes four senators and five representatives. Statute provides for the board and its composition. The senators include the chair of the Armed Services Committee or his or her designee and three senators appointed by the president pro tempore of the Senate or the vice president; two of these appointees must be members of the Appropriations Committee. Members also serve on entities such as the board of trustees of the John F. Kennedy Center for the Performing Arts and the board of regents of the Smithsonian Institution. The president pro tempore of the Senate and the Speaker of the House also name private citizens to serve on the Social Security Advisory Board.

Certain events are well worth commemorating in explaining to the American citizenry and the world what is the meaning of the United States of America. For example, Congress has established the Abraham Lincoln Bicentennial Commission. Its membership comprises two senators, one appointed by the majority leader and one by the minority leader; two representatives, one appointed by the Speaker and one by the minority leader; and six citizens, two each appointed by the Senate majority leader and Speaker and one each appointed by the Senate and House minority leaders.

Congress regularly uses a commission or similar form to provide itself with input on public policy issues outside of the normal process of committee hearings and other information channels or to monitor developments in policy areas where it has acted or has delegated authority to the executive. For example, because of grave concerns in the Senate over negotiations leading up to the Kyoto accords on global warming, the Senate passed a resolution giving expression to those concerns and creating an observer group of twelve senators appointed by the majority and minority leaders. In paving the way in law for China's membership in the World Trade Organization, Congress created the Congressional-Executive Commission on China, comprising nine senators appointed by the president pro tempore of the Senate, nine representatives appointed by the Speaker, and five executive officials appointed by the president (<*www.cecc.gov*>). Congress had similarly established a monitoring entity in agreeing to the treaty on Security and Cooperation in Europe, the Helsinki Commission (<*www.csce.gov*>).

Within Congress, decision making has been entrusted to entities such as the House Page Board (two members appointed by the Speaker and two by the minority leader), the House Office Building Commission (the Speaker and two representatives appointed by the Speaker), and the Senate Office Building Commission (nine senators appointed by the president pro tempore). Congressional influence on decision making extends beyond Capitol Hill with membership on entities such as the National Capital Planning Commission, which provides overall planning guidance for federal land and buildings in the national capital region; the chairs of the Senate Committee on Homeland Security and Governmental Affairs and the House Committee on Oversight and Government Reform, or their designees, serve as ex officio members.

Chapter Eight

Legislating in Congress:
Legislative Process

Analysis

8

8

§ 8.00 Introduction

If an idea or problem attracts the attention of policymakers, opinion leaders, and the public, it might begin to build political momentum. That momentum may lead members of Congress to introduce legislation, committees to hold hearings and markups, chamber leaders to schedule floor time, and the president to approve the resulting legislation. The legislative process is activated by policy proponents attempting to see a policy enacted into law. *(See § 8.01, Legislative Process Flowchart.)*

But, many problems can occur along the way. The framers of the Constitution devised a system that makes legislation difficult to pass—two very different chambers comprising members from fifty states must agree to the identical proposition by majority votes, and the president must then agree with Congress. Each member is concerned with different local, regional, political, personal, and other interests. The rules of the House and the Senate that build on the bare-bones constitutional system further add to the difficulty of making law by ensuring adequate consideration of proposals, allowing the airing of alternative points of view, and establishing procedural stages through which proposals must pass. In addition, each member of Congress is accountable in elections for his or her performance in office. This democratic cornerstone of the Constitution requires that members constantly weigh the sentiments of their constituencies against their own positions on legislation to determine how to cast their votes. *(See § 8.02, House Rules Citations; and § 8.03, Senate Rules Citations.)*

What follows is an analysis of the legislative process in Congress—a distillation and description of both major, well-known stages of the process and more nuanced points that play a critical role in members' ability to advance or impede legislative proposals. The explanations that supplement the text—definitions of specific terminology, examples, and resources—assist in understanding, monitoring, and participating appropriately and effectively in the policymaking process.

Additional, special legislative procedures applicable to budget legislation, the Senate's executive business, and other kinds of legislation and oversight are described in Chapters Nine and Ten. Congressional documents are described in Chapters Eleven and Twelve. Tracking of legislative action is described in § 14.50. A working example of the legislative process is the subject of Chapter Fifteen.

§ 8.01

Legislative Process Flowchart

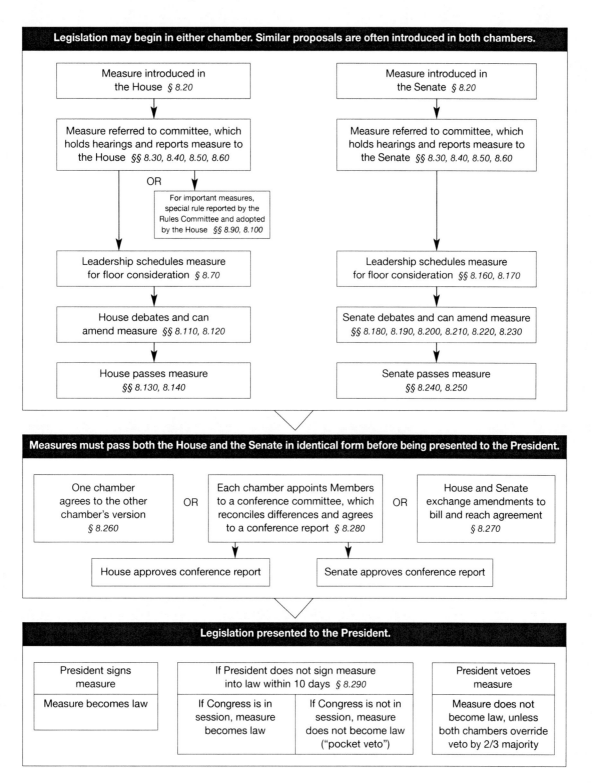

§ 8.02

House Rules Citations

House Rule Number	Subject Heading
I	The Speaker
II	Other Officers and Officials
III	The Members, Delegates, and the Resident Commissioner
IV	The Hall of the House
V	Broadcasting the House
VI	Official Reporters and News Media Galleries
VII	Records of the House
VIII	Response to Subpoenas
IX	Questions of Privilege
X	Organization of Committees
XI	Procedures of Committees and Unfinished Business
XII	Receipt and Referral of Measures and Matters
XIII	Calendars and Committee Reports
XIV	Order and Priority of Business
XV	Business in Order on Special Days
XVI	Motions and Amendments
XVII	Decorum and Debate
XVIII	The Committee of the Whole House on the State of the Union
XIX	Motions Following the Amendment Stage
XX	Voting and Quorum Calls
XXI	Restrictions on Certain Bills
XXII	House and Senate Relations
XXIII	Code of Official Conduct
XXIV	Limitations on the Use of Official Funds
XXV	Limitations on Outside Earned Income and Acceptance of Gifts
XXVI	Financial Disclosure
XXVII	Statutory Limit on the Public Debt
XXVIII	General Provisions

§ 8.03

Senate Rules Citations

Senate Rule Number	Subject Heading
I	Appointment of a Senator to the Chair
II	Presentation of Credentials and Questions of Privilege
III	Oaths
IV	Commencement of Daily Sessions
V	Suspension and Amendment of the Rules
VI	Quorum-Absent Senators May Be Sent For
VII	Morning Business
VIII	Order of Business
IX	Messages
X	Special Orders
XI	Papers-Withdrawal, Printing, Reading of, and Reference
XII	Voting Procedure
XIII	Reconsideration
XIV	Bills, Joint Resolutions, and Preambles Thereto
XV	Amendments and Motions
XVI	Appropriations and Amendments to General Appropriations Bills
XVII	Reference to Committees, Motions to Discharge, Reports of Committees, and Hearings Available
XVIII	Business Continued from Session to Session
XIX	Debate
XX	Questions of Order
XXI	Session with Closed Doors

Senate Rule Number	Subject Heading
XXII	Precedence of Motions
XXIII	Privilege of the Floor
XXIV	Appointment of Conferees
XXV	Standing Committees
XXVI	Committee Procedure
XXVII	Committee Staff
XXVIII	Conference Committees, Reports, Open Meetings
XXIX	Executive Sessions
XXX	Executive Session-Proceedings on Treaties
XXXI	Executive Session-Proceedings on Nominations
XXXII	The President Furnished with Copies of Records of Executive Sessions
XXXIII	Senate Chamber-Senate Wing of the Capitol
XXXIV	Public Financial Disclosure
XXXV	Gifts
XXXVI	Outside Earned Income
XXXVII	Conflict of Interest
XXXVIII	Prohibition of Unofficial Office Accounts
XXXIX	Foreign Travel
XL	Franking Privilege and Radio and Television Studios
XLI	Political Fund Activity, Definitions
XLII	Employment Practices
XLIII	Representation by Members

8

§ 8.04

Selected Procedures:
House and Senate Rules

Procedure	House Rule Citation	Senate Rule Citation
Amendment Process	XVI	XV
Appropriations Process	XXI	XVI
Committee Jurisdiction	X	XXV
Committee Procedure	XI, XIII	XXVI
Committee Referral	XII	XVII
Conference Committees	XXII	XXIV, XXVIII
Debate	XVII	XIX
Motions	XVI	XV
Order of Business	XIV	VIII
Outside Earned Income	XXVI	XXXVI
Voting	XX	XII

§ 8.10 Types of Measures

Legislation is the form in which policy ideas are translated into a procedural vehicle for consideration by a chamber. There are four types of legislative measures Congress may consider, in addition to the Senate's consideration of treaties and nominations. (*See § 8.11, Legislation Glossary.*)

Bills

A bill is the most commonly used form for legislation. A bill is prefixed with an *H.R.* in the House and with an *S.* in the Senate. A number assigned at the time of introduction signifies the order in which a bill was introduced during a Congress. A bill becomes law only if it is passed with identical language by both houses and signed by the president or passed over his veto. Under certain circumstances, a bill can become law without the president's signature. (*See § 8.290, Presidential Action on Enacted Measures.*) The bill form is used for authorization or reauthorization of federal policies, programs, and activities, among its many lawmaking purposes. (*See § 11.20, Legislation: Bills and Joint Resolutions, and § 9.80, Authorization and Appropriation Processes.*)

§ 8.11

Legislation Glossary

Act: Legislation that has passed both houses of Congress and been signed by the president or passed over his veto, thus becoming law. Also, parliamentary term for a measure that has been passed by one chamber and engrossed.

Bill: Measure that becomes law when passed in identical form by both houses and signed by the president or passed over his veto. Designated as *H.R.* or *S. (See also Joint Resolution.)*

Blue-Slip Resolution: House resolution ordering the return to the Senate of a Senate bill or amendment that the House believes violates the constitutional prerogative of the House to originate revenue measures.

By Request: A designation on a measure, which appears next to the sponsor's name, indicating that a member has introduced a measure on behalf of the president, an executive agency, or a private individual or organization.

Christmas-Tree Bill: Jargon for a bill containing many amendments unrelated to the bill's subjects; usually refers to Senate measures.

Clean Bill: A measure reported from a House committee that reflects the revised version of a measure considered in markup and repackaged into a new bill with a new number.

Commemorative Bill: Legislation designating a federal holiday or recognizing a particular issue, such as National Ice Cream Day or National Breast Cancer Awareness Month. Commemorative bills are currently disallowed in the House of Representatives.

Companion Bill: Identical or very similar bills introduced in both houses.

Concurrent Resolution: Used to express the sentiment of both houses on some matter without making law. Also used to carry out the administrative business of both houses. It does not require presidential approval or become law, but requires passage in identical form by both houses to take effect between them. Designated as *H. Con. Res.* or *S. Con. Res.*

Enacting Clause: Phrase at the beginning of a bill that gives it legal force when enacted: "Be it enacted by the Senate and House of Representatives of the United States of America in Congress assembled. . . ."

Engrossed Measure: Official copy of a measure as passed by one chamber, including the text as amended by floor action. Measure is certified by the clerk of the House or the secretary of the Senate.

Enrolled Measure: Final official copy of a measure as passed in identical form by both chambers and then printed on parchment. Measure is certified by the chamber of origin and signed by the Speaker of the House and the president pro tempore of the Senate before it is sent to the president.

Executive Document: A document, usually a treaty, sent by the president to the Senate for its consideration and approval.

Joint Resolution: Similar to a bill, though limited in scope (for example, to change a minor item in existing law). Becomes law when passed in identical form by both houses and signed by the president. It also is the form of legislation used to consider a constitutional amendment. A constitutional amendment requires a two-thirds vote in each house but does not require the president's signature. Designated as *H. J. Res.* or *S. J. Res. (See also Bill.)*

Continued on page 252

Law/Public Law/Private Law: Act of Congress signed by the president or passed over his veto.

Official Title: Statement of a measure's subject and purpose that appears above the enacting clause.

Omnibus Bill: A measure that combines the provisions of several disparate subjects into a single measure. Examples include *continuing resolutions* that might contain a number of the annual appropriations bills.

Original Bill: A measure drafted by a committee and introduced by its chair when the committee reports the measure back to its chamber. It is not referred back to the committee after introduction.

Popular Title: The informal, unofficial name or the short title by which a measure is known.

Preamble: Introductory language in a bill preceding the enacting clause. It describes the reasons for and intent of a measure. In a joint resolution, the language appears before the resolving clause. In a concurrent or simple resolution, it appears before the text.

Private Bill: A measure that generally deals with an individual matter, such as a claim against the government, an individual's immigration, or a land title. In the House, a private bill is considered via the Private Calendar on the first and third Tuesdays of each month.

Public Law: Act of Congress that has been signed by the president or passed over his veto. It is designated by the letters *P.L.* and numbers noting the Congress and the numerical sequence in which the measure was signed; for example, P.L. 107-111 was an act of Congress in the 107th Congress and was the 111th measure to become law during the 107th Congress.

Resolution/Simple Resolution: Sentiment of one chamber on an issue, or a measure to carry out the administrative or procedural business of one chamber. It does not become law. Designated as *H. Res.* or *S. Res.*

Resolution of Inquiry: A simple resolution calling on the president or the head of an executive agency to provide specific information or papers to one or both houses.

Resolving Clause: First section of a joint resolution that gives legal force to the measure when enacted: "Resolved by the Senate and House of Representatives of the United States of America in Congress assembled. . . ."

Rider: Term for an amendment unrelated to the subject matter of the measure to which it was attached. Usually associated with policy provisions attached to appropriations measures.

Slip Law: First official publication of a law, published in unbound single sheets or pamphlet form.

Star Print: A reprint of a measure, amendment, or committee report to correct errors in a previous printing. The first page carries a small black star. Rarely used today, with technology mitigating need.

A larger glossary is located at the back of the book.

Joint Resolution

A joint resolution is a legislative measure used for purposes other than general legislation. A joint resolution is designated *H. J. Res.* or *S. J. Res.* in the House and Senate respectively. Like a bill, it has the force of law when passed by both houses and signed by the president or passed over his veto. Joint resolutions are also used for proposing amendments to the Constitution, in which case a joint resolution passed in exactly the same form by a two-thirds vote in both chambers is submitted directly to the states rather than to the president. *(See § 11.20, Legislation: Bills and Joint Resolutions.)*

Concurrent Resolution

A concurrent resolution deals with the internal affairs of both chambers and requires approval by both houses but is not sent to the president. Therefore, it does not have the force of law. A concurrent resolution is designated *H. Con. Res.* or *S. Con. Res.* in the House and Senate respectively. Examples of concurrent resolutions are those providing for the adjournment of Congress or the congressional budget resolution. Nonbinding policy opinions of both chambers, such as "sense of the Congress," are traditionally in the form of concurrent resolutions. *(See § 11.30, Legislation: Simple and Concurrent Resolutions.)*

Resolution (Simple Resolution)

A simple resolution deals with the internal workings of only one chamber or with nonbinding public-policy statements. Designated *H. Res.* or *S. Res.* in the House and Senate respectively, a simple resolution does not require the concurrence of the other chamber or approval by the president. Special rules from the House Rules Committee, the creation of a select and special committee, and funding resolutions for individual committees are in the form of simple resolutions. *(See § 11.30, Legislation: Simple and Concurrent Resolutions.)*

§ 8.20 Drafting and Introducing Legislation
Sources of Legislation

Although legislation can be introduced only by members of Congress, ideas for legislation emanate from many sources. Members and their staffs may develop ideas based on promises made during election campaigns. The media also bring attention to issues that may need legislative solutions. Special-interest groups, and their lobbyists in Washington, often provide detailed ideas for legislation they want to see enacted. Constituents, either as individuals or groups, often suggest legislation to their own members of Congress. The executive branch is a key initiator of legislative proposals. The president in his State of the Union address to Congress outlines his priorities for the year, which may lead to legislation. Executive departments and agencies transmit drafts of legislation to Congress. Foreign governments often ask Congress to take up specific legislation, or seek ratification of certain treaties.

Drafting Legislation

Members and staff seek assistance in drafting legislation from the Office of Legislative Counsel in their respective chamber. The nonpartisan attorneys in these offices provide expert technical assistance in drafting bills, resolutions, and amendments. Legislative counsel are not only proficient in drafting but also knowledgeable about the substance of issues and the legislative process.

The Senate Committee on Rules and Administration has set drafting priorities for the Senate Office of Legislative Counsel. These priorities are measures in conference, measures pending on the floor, measures pending before a committee, and measures to be prepared for individual senators.

The House legislative counsel, as the senior attorney in the office, is appointed by the Speaker of the House. The Senate legislative counsel is appointed by the president pro tempore of the Senate. The staff attorneys are hired by the legislative counsel.

Introducing Legislation

The legislative process formally begins when a measure is introduced. Approximately 10,000 measures are introduced in each two-year Congress. Only a member can introduce legislation. There is no limit on the number of measures a member can introduce or on the issues such measures may address (with a few exceptions such as the House bar on commemorative legislation).

The Constitution stipulates that all revenue measures must originate in the House. House origination is the custom for appropriations bills as well. (When the Senate initiates a measure that the House believes affects revenues and sends it to the House, the measure is returned to the Senate by a so-called *blue-slip resolution*. The Senate may act on revenue measures before the House does, but it must wait for a House revenue measure to be sent to it before it can complete its legislative actions.) All other measures can originate in either the House or the Senate. Many pieces of legislation are introduced in both chambers as *companion bills*.

In the House, a measure is introduced by placing it in the *hopper*, a mahogany box that sits on the rostrum in the House chamber. Measures can be introduced only whenever the House is in session and sitting as the House. *(See § 8.110, Committee of the Whole: Debate.)* In the Senate, measures can technically be introduced only during the *morning business* portion of the *morning hour*. However, in practice they are introduced throughout the day. A senator need only hand a measure to a clerk at the desk in the chamber. In the Senate, a statement is often made on the floor or inserted in the *Congressional Record* when a measure is introduced.

On introduction, a measure is assigned a number by a bill clerk. The numbers are assigned sequentially throughout a Congress. Occasionally, a member will ask to reserve a specific number. For example, H.R. 2020 might be reserved for a measure affecting eye care, or S. 23 might be reserved to honor basketball star Michael Jordan. At the beginning of a new Con-

House Cosponsorship Form

U.S. House of Representatives

Congress: _____
Session: _____
Date: _____

Pursuant to clause 7 of Rule XII of the Rules of the House Representatives, the following sponsors are hereby added to:

H.R. _____   H.Con. Res. _____
H.J. Res._____   H.Res._____

1) _____   21) _____
2) _____   22) _____
3) _____   23) _____
4) _____   24) _____
5) _____   25) _____
6) _____   26) _____
7) _____   27) _____
8) _____   28) _____
9) _____   29) _____
10) _____   30) _____
11) _____   31) _____
12) _____   32) _____
13) _____   33) _____
14) _____   34) _____
15) _____   35) _____
16) _____   36) _____
17) _____   37) _____
18) _____   38) _____
19) _____   39) _____
20) _____   40) _____

Member Signature: _____

Sample "Dear Colleague" Letter

Congress of the United States
Washington, DC 20515

October 18, 1999

Oppose Unfunded Mandates
Cosponsor the Tiahrt Proposal to Require a 3/5 Majority Vote to Raise the Minimum Wage

Dear Colleague:

Clause 5(a) of rule XXI of the Rules of the House of Representatives provides in part . . . "A bill or joint resolution, amendment, or conference report carrying a Federal income tax rate increase may not be considered as passed or agreed to unless so determined by a vote of not less than three-fifths of the Members voting, a quorum being present. . ." Soon I will be introducing legislation which would add the same three-fifths voting requirement for bills, joint resolutions amendments or conference reports carrying a minimum wage increase, which is an unfunded mandate on small business owners as well as state and local governments.

Each time Congress mandates an increase in the starting wage, state and local governments along with small business owners are forced to make tough decisions about how to deal with this new unfunded mandate that has been imposed on them. This in turn becomes an unfunded mandate on all Americans. Consider the following examples from the restaurant industry in the aftermath of the most recent minimum wage increase:

- *Higher Prices* -- To cope with the increased labor costs, 42% of restaurant operators increased menu prices.

- *Job Elimination* -- As a result of the last increase, more than 146,000 jobs were cut from restaurant payrolls. In addition to existing jobs that were cut, restaurants had to delay expansions, resulting in the postponement of an additional 106,000 jobs.

- *Reduction in Employee Work Hours* -- Restaurants that did not eliminate jobs frequently scaled back on employee hours. More than 28% of operators reported reducing employee hours with the average reduction being 9 hours per week.

I hope you will join with me to support legislation that will make it harder for Congress to impose this unfunded mandate upon small business owners, state and local governments, and the American people. If you have any questions or would like to cosponsor this legislation, please contact me or Sarah Key of my staff at 5-6216.

Best regards,

gress, the first few bill numbers are often reserved for the majority-party leadership to signal their legislative priorities for Congress; the next few bill numbers might be reserved for the minority. Senators, by tradition, rarely introduce legislation until after the president delivers his State of the Union address.

Measures remain active between the two sessions of a Congress. If they are not enacted into law, they die with the adjournment of the Congress in which they were introduced. Treaties, however, which are considered only by the Senate, remain pending from one Congress until they are approved or formally withdrawn by the president, since the Senate is a *continuing body*.

House and Senate rules permit a member to introduce a measure at the request of the president, an executive agency, or a private individual although that member may be opposed to the legislation. The courtesy to introduce legislation on behalf of someone is granted because neither the president nor any person other than a member can introduce legislation. In such a case, "by request" appears on the measure following the name of the sponsor.

Cosponsorship

House and Senate measures may have numerous sponsors in addition to the member who proposes the legislation. It is common in both chambers for the key proponent of a measure to send a *Dear Colleague* letter (in print or electronically) to other members requesting their support for the legislation by cosponsoring its introduction. An original cosponsor signs on and is listed on the legislation when it is introduced. Cosponsors can be added throughout the legislative process until a measure is reported from a committee, or, in the Senate, at any time by unanimous consent. Names of cosponsors added after introduction appear in the *Congressional Record*, and in subsequent printings of a measure. A member can be removed as a cosponsor only by unanimous consent on the House or Senate floor. *(See § 8.21, House Cosponsorship Form; and § 8.22, Sample "Dear Colleague" Letter.)*

§ 8.30 Referral of Legislation to Committee

Once introduced in the House or Senate, or passed by one chamber and sent to the other, the vast majority of measures is referred to committee. Referral to committee occurs so that a committee can scrutinize the legislation by holding hearings and gauging sentiment for its enactment, and, if the committee proceeds to markup, may propose amendments to the parent chamber or write, introduce, and report a new measure.

To which committee(s) a measure is referred can have a significant impact on its fate. Referral of a measure is based on a committee's jurisdiction, which, in turn, is determined by a variety of factors. The principal factor in making a referral is Rule X in the House or Rule XXV in the Senate. Each rule lists the broad subject matter within the purview of each standing committee, although not all issues within a committee's jurisdiction are identified. In addition, these jurisdictional descriptions do not explicitly identify jurisdiction over particular

§ 8.31

Sample Jurisdictional Agreement

Ms. SLAUGHTER. Madam Speaker, I ask unanimous consent to insert in the RECORD a jurisdictional memorandum of understanding between the chairmen-designate from the Committee on Transportation and the Committee on Homeland Security.

The SPEAKER pro tempore. Is there objection to the request of the gentlewoman from New York?

There was no objection.

MEMORANDUM OF UNDERSTANDING BETWEEN THE COMMITTEE ON TRANSPORTATION AND INFRASTRUCTURE AND THE COMMITTEE ON HOMELAND SECURITY

January 4, 2007

On January 4, 2005, the U.S. House of Representatives adopted H. Res. 5, establishing the Rules of the House for the 109th Congress. Section 2(a) established the Committee on Homeland Security as a standing committee of the House of Representatives with specific legislative jurisdiction under House Rule X. A legislative history to accompany the changes to House Rule X was inserted in the Congressional Record on January 4, 2005.

The Committee on Transportation and Infrastructure and the Committee on Homeland Security (hereinafter "Committees") jointly agree to the January 4, 2005 legislative history as the authoritative source of legislative history of section 2(a) of H. Res. 5 with the following two clarifications.

First, with regard to the Federal Emergency Management Agency's, FEMA, emergency preparedness and response programs, the Committee on Homeland Security has jurisdiction over the Department of Homeland Security's responsibilities with regard to emergency preparedness and collective response only as they relate to terrorism. However, in light of the federal emergency management reforms that were enacted as title VI of Public Law 109-

295, a bill amending FEMA's all-hazards emergency preparedness programs that necessarily addresses FEMA's terrorism preparedness programs would be referred to the Committee on Transportation and Infrastructure; in addition, the Committee on Homeland Security would have a jurisdictional interest in such bill. Nothing in this Memorandum of Understanding affects the jurisdiction of the Committee on Transportation and Infrastructure of the Robert T. Stafford Disaster Relief and Emergency Assistance Act and the Federal Fire Prevention and Control Act of 1974.

Second, with regard to port security, the Committee on Homeland Security has jurisdiction over port security, and some Coast Guard responsibilities in that area fall within the jurisdiction of both Committees. A bill addressing the activities, programs, assets, and personnel of the Coast Guard as they relate to port security and non-port security missions would be referred to the Committee on Transportation and Infrastructure; in addition, the Committee on Homeland Security would have a jurisdictional interest in such bill.

This Memorandum of Understanding between the Committee on Transportation and Infrastructure and the Committee on Homeland Security provides further clarification to the January 4, 2005 legislative history of the jurisdiction of the Committees only with regard to these two specific issues. The Memorandum does not address any other issues and does not affect the jurisdiction of other committees.

JAMES L. OBERSTAR,
Chairman-designate, Committee on
Transportation & Infrastructure.
BENNIE G. THOMPSON,
Chairman-designate,
Committee on Homeland Security.

Announcement by Rules Committee Chair
Related to a Committee's Jurisdiction

RULES OF THE HOUSE

Ms. SLAUGHTER. Mr. Speaker, I offer a privileged resolution (H. Res. 5) and ask for its immediate consideration.

The Clerk read the resolution, as follows:

H. RES. 5

Resolved, That upon the adoption of this resolution it shall be in order to consider in the House the resolution

(H. Res. 6) adopting the Rules of the House of Representatives for the One Hundred Tenth Congress. The resolution shall be considered as read. The previous question shall be considered as ordered on the resolution to its adoption without intervening motion or demand for division of the question except as specified in sections 2 through 4 of this resolution.

****

Continued on page 259

January 4, 2007   CONGRESSIONAL RECORD—HOUSE

Renews the standing order approved during the 109th Congress that prohibits registered lobbyists from using the Members' exercise facilities.

Mr. Speaker, I consider it to be a great honor to have a chance to address our House on the first day of the 110th Congress. That is what serving as a Representative in this body is, an honor.

****

Today, the men and women of America have given us a very special gift. We have the ability to leave our mark on the future of our Nation. It is the only gift Members of Congress should ask for, and one we must cherish for the good of all. Let us begin.

Mr. Speaker, I would like to take this opportunity to reaffirm the jurisdiction of the Committee on Small Business as contained in House Rule X, clause 1(p). The Committee's jurisdiction includes the Small Business Administration and its programs, as well as small business matters related to the Regulatory Flexibility Act and the Paperwork Reduction Act. Its jurisdiction under House Rule X, clause 1(p) also includes other programs and initiatives that address small businesses outside of the confines of those Acts.

This reaffirmation of the jurisdiction of the Committee on Small Business will enable the House to ensure that it is properly considering the consequences of its actions related to small business.

Mr. Speaker, I reserve the balance of my time.

measures, executive-branch departments and agencies, or programs operated within those departments. Accordingly, the formal provisions of the rules are supplemented by an intricate series of precedents and informal agreements.

A referral decision is formally the responsibility of the Speaker for the House and the presiding officer for the Senate. In practice, however, the parliamentarian in each chamber advises these officials on an appropriate referral.

House of Representatives

In addition to House Rule X, precedents and agreements affect referral decisions. In general, these precedents dictate that once a measure has been referred to a given committee, the measure's subject matter remains the responsibility of that committee. The precedents further presume that amendments to laws that originated in a committee are within the purview of that committee as well.

Formal agreements, drafted between committees to stipulate their understanding of jurisdictional boundaries, also influence referral decisions. These agreements are usually in the form of an exchange of letters between committee chairs and are often entered in the *Congressional Record* during debate on a measure when it comes to the floor for consideration. The letters are also often kept in committees' so-called *jurisdiction files* and with the parliamentarian. *(See § 8.31, Sample Jurisdictional Agreement.)*

Several other factors may influence the referral of a measure. The committee assignment of the sponsor often serves as a signal that a bill should be referred to a committee on which

Sample of House Referral

I

110TH CONGRESS
1ST SESSION

H. R. 1064

To amend title 39, United States Code, to extend for 2 years the provisions under which the special postage stamp for breast cancer research is issued.

IN THE HOUSE OF REPRESENTATIVES

FEBRUARY 15, 2007

❶ Sponsor

❷ Original cosponsors

❸ Explanation of the referral

❶ Mr. BACA (for himself, Mr. MOORE of Kansas, Ms. McCOLLUM of Minnesota, Mr. VAN HOLLEN, Mr. FARR, Mrs. MALONEY of New York, Mr. FORTUÑO, Mr. MORAN of Virginia, Mr. McDERMOTT, Mr. CONYERS, Mr. CLEAVER, Mr. DINGELL, Mr. NEAL of Massachusetts, Mrs. McCARTHY
❷ of New York, Mr. ELLISON, Mr. BURTON of Indiana, Mrs. JONES of Ohio, Mr. AL GREEN of Texas, Mr. NADLER, Mr. STARK, Mr. SCOTT of Georgia, Ms. HOOLEY, Mrs. BOYDA of Kansas, Mr. MICHAUD, Mr. KLEIN of Florida, Mr. McINTYRE, Mr. KILDEE, Mr. GEORGE MILLER of California, Mr. SHAYS, Mr. GRIJALVA, Ms. ROYBAL-ALLARD, Mr. TERRY, Mr. BOSWELL, Mr. GENE GREEN of Texas, Mr. DENT, Mr. HINCHEY, Mr. HINOJOSA, Mr. CHANDLER, Mr. WEINER, Mr. SHIMKUS, Ms. WASSERMAN SCHULTZ, Mr. COOPER, Mr. HONDA, Mr. HOLT, Mr. ORTIZ, Mr. YOUNG of Alaska, Mr. HALL of Texas, Mrs. SCHMIDT, Mr. BERMAN, Mr. PRICE of North Carolina, Mr. DELAHUNT, Ms. KAPTUR, Ms. KIL-PATRICK, Mr. PATRICK J. MURPHY of Pennsylvania, Ms. HIRONO, Mr. ENGEL, Mr. ABERCROMBIE, Ms. BERKLEY, Mr. SHERMAN, Mr. KING of New York, and Mr. DOGGETT) introduced the following bill; which was
❸ referred to the Committee on Oversight and Government Reform, and in addition to the Committees on Energy and Commerce and Armed Services, for a period to be subsequently determined by the Speaker, in each case for consideration of such provisions as fall within the jurisdiction of the committee concerned

---

A BILL

To amend title 39, United States Code, to extend for 2 years the provisions under which the special postage stamp for breast cancer research is issued.

the sponsor serves. The timing of a measure's introduction can also influence its referral; for example, introduction following a series of issue hearings held by a committee could signal that the panel wants to legislate on the issue it recently studied.

Under House Rule X, the Speaker usually designates a "primary" committee to receive a referral. If other panels have jurisdictional responsibilities over some of the issues in the measure, they may receive a *sequential* referral. The language of a referral affecting more than one committee would be "to the Committee on XXXX, and in addition, to the Committee on YYYY." The primary panel is always named first. A referral can also designate specific titles or sections of a measure within each committee's responsibility. More common, however, is a referral for "issues within the jurisdiction of the committee." Referral without designation of a primary committee can be made under "exceptional circumstances." A sequential referral may be made after a measure's introduction or after the primary committee reports the measure.

The Speaker has authority to impose a time limit on committees receiving a referral. Sometimes the time limit is determined at the time of referral; sometimes a time limit is imposed after a measure has been referred. *(See § 8.32, Sample of House Referral.)*

Senate

Under Senate Rule XVII, measures are referred to committee based on "the subject matter which predominates" in the legislation, commonly referred to as *predominant jurisdiction.* The Senate generally refers a measure to a single committee based on this rule and the jurisdictions enumerated in Senate Rule XXV.

Predominant jurisdiction allows a measure to be guided to a specific committee, so that the referral predetermines its fate. Many senators, as well as lobbyists, understand that they can influence the legislative agenda by learning how creative drafting of a measure can possibly affect its referral. For example, is tobacco an agricultural issue within the purview of the Agriculture Committee, generally friendly to tobacco? Or, is tobacco a health risk, an issue within the predominant purview of a less friendly Health, Education, Labor, and Pensions Committee? Or, is the issue about tobacco advertising, and thus within the predominant purview of the Commerce, Science, and Transportation Committee? The drafting of a measure on tobacco is not simple if one wants a specific committee to obtain the referral.

The rule further allows a measure to be referred to more than one panel if an issue crosses jurisdictional boundaries or predominance is not clear-cut. Such *multiple referrals* are not common, in part because they are typically made by unanimous consent after negotiations among affected committee chairs. A joint motion made by the majority and minority leader for multiple referrals is also allowed under Senate Rule XVII, but it has never been used.

Finally, under Senate Rule XIV, the majority leader, his designee, or any senator may follow a set of procedures that allow a measure to be placed directly on the Senate's legislative calendar without referral to committee. Placement there, however, does not guarantee that floor action will ever be scheduled. *(See § 8.160, Senate Scheduling.)*

§ 8.40 Committee Hearings

Perhaps the most visible of all congressional actions is the committee hearing. As Woodrow Wilson wrote, "It is not far from the truth to say that Congress in session is Congress on public exhibition, whilst Congress in its committee rooms is Congress at work."

Types of Committee Hearings

Committees and their subcommittees hold hundreds of hearings each year. These hearings are nearly always one of four types.

Legislative Hearings. These hearings typically occur when there is a measure under consideration or when a committee is collecting information so it can draft legislation. Witnesses give their own or their organizations' views on a measure's provisions. They might also express views on competing proposals for legislation that a committee could develop with the input received in hearings and from other sources.

Investigative Hearings. These hearings are not directly connected with legislation, but are called to examine a subject in which a committee has an interest. These hearings are sometimes held when there is possible evidence of wrongdoing or criminal activity by specific individuals.

Oversight Hearings. These hearings are held to ensure that executive agencies are carrying out programs in the manner Congress intended.

Confirmation Hearings. These hearings are held to question presidential appointees when Senate confirmation is required and to investigate nominees' qualifications.

Rules That Govern Hearings

Each committee is required by its respective chamber's rules to adopt and publish rules of procedure. A committee's rules generally apply to its subcommittees, although some rules contain specific procedures for subcommittees. Many committee rules address hearings.

Notice and Scheduling. Under both House and Senate rules, the chair of a committee or subcommittee must publicly announce the date, place, and subject matter of a hearing at least one week in advance in the Daily Digest section of the *Congressional Record*, unless the chair and ranking member—or the committee by majority vote—determines that there is good cause to begin the hearing sooner. (*See § 8.41, Committee Hearings Schedule.*)

Senate committees may not hold a hearing after the Senate has been in session for two hours, or after 2:00 p.m. when the Senate is in session, whichever is earlier. This Senate rule is often waived by unanimous consent on the Senate floor or by agreement between the Senate majority and minority leaders. House hearings can be held at any time, except during a joint session or meeting of the House and Senate. (*See § 8.42, Keeping Up with House and Senate Committee Hearings.*)

Open Hearings. Hearings must be open to the public and the media unless the committee, in open session, decides by record vote to close a hearing. Hearings may be closed if dis-

Committee Hearings Schedule

<table>
<tr><td>HENRY A. WAXMAN, CALIFORNIA
CHAIRMAN</td><td>TOM DAVIS, VIRGINIA
RANKING MINORITY MEMBER</td></tr>
</table>

ONE HUNDRED TENTH CONGRESS

Congress of the United States
House of Representatives
COMMITTEE ON OVERSIGHT AND GOVERNMENT REFORM
2157 RAYBURN HOUSE OFFICE BUILDING
WASHINGTON, DC 20515–6143

Majority (202) 225–5051
Minority (202) 225–5074

REVISED

To: Members, Committee on Oversight and Government Reform

From: Henry A. Waxman, Chairman

Re: Committee Hearing Schedule

Date: April 12, 2007

Date	Time	Room	Committee
Mon. Apr. 16th			Nothing Scheduled
Tues. Apr. 17th	10:00 a.m.	2154 RHOB	Subcommittee on National Security and Foreign Affairs hearing on "Is This Any Way to Treat Our Troops – Part II: Follow-up on Corrective Measures Taken at Walter Reed and Other Medical Facilities Caring for Wounded Soldiers"
	10:00 a.m.	2247 RHOB	Subcommittee on Federal Workforce, Postal Service, and the District of Columbia hearing on "The U.S. Postal Service: 101"
Wed. Apr. 18th	**10:00 a.m.**	**2154 RHOB**	**Full Committee hearing with invited witness Secretary of State Condoleezza Rice, on "Unanswered Questions Regarding the Administration's Claims that Iraq Sought Uranium from Niger, White House treatment of Classified Information, the Appointment of Ambassador Jones as 'Special Coordinator' for Iraq, and Other Subjects."**
	2:00 p.m.	2154 RHOB	Subcommittee on Information Policy, Census, and National Archives hearing on "Ensuring Fairness and Accuracy in Elections Involving Electronic Voting Systems"
Thurs. Apr. 19th	10:00 a.m.	2154 RHOB	Subcommittee on Government Management, Organization, and Procurement legislative hearing on H.R. ___, the Contractor Tax Enforcement Act and H.R. ___, amends Title 31 of the United States Code by authorizing a pilot program for local governments to offset federal tax refunds to collect local tax debts
Fri. Apr. 20th			Nothing Scheduled

**If you are in need of special accommodations based on a disability, please contact the committee
at least 4 business days prior to the hearing (202) 225-5051
April 12, 2007

§ 8.42

Keeping Up with House and Senate Committee Hearings

See Chapters Eleven, Twelve, and Thirteen for descriptions of these and other sources.

Sources	Anticipating Hearings		During/After Hearings	
	Status	Substance	Status	Substance
Congressional Sources				
Congressional Record. See Daily Digest pages and advance Senate committee schedule. Also see announcements by committee chairs in House and Senate proceedings pages	x		x	
Committee web sites, available through the House <*www.house.gov*> and Senate <*www.senate.gov*> sites	x	x	x	x
Committee or committee members' press releases	x	x	x	x
For legislative hearings: the legislation itself (as introduced or committee draft); related documents such as draft administration legislation or a commission report		x		
For oversight hearings: relevant public law(s) and congressional documents from the law's legislative history		x		
For nomination hearings: press kits or other packets	x	x	x	x
Hearing transcripts, available from committee offices, some committee web sites, and eventually as printed congressional documents				x
Legislative Information System (Congress only)			x	x
THOMAS <*http://thomas.loc.gov*>	x		x	x
Non-Congressional Sources				
CongressDaily, from *National Journal* <*http://nationaljournal.com*>	x	x	x	x
CQ Today <*www.cq.com*>	x	x	x	x
CQ.com <*www.cq.com*>	x	x	x	x
C-SPAN (selectively) <*www.cspan.org*>				x
Prepared testimony, available from the witness's agency or organization				x
Trade press and daily newspapers	x	x	x	x
Relevant interest-group web sites	x	x	x	x
Other commercial database services	x	x	x	x
People *(Use these contacts after exhausting other resources.)*				
Committee professional staff (After hearings, what is the expected markup vehicle? When will markup begin?)		x	x	x
Documents clerks (What documents are available in advance or at the hearings? After hearings, are transcripts available?)		x		x
Committee and committee members' press assistants (What press releases or other press documents are available?)		x		x

cussion of the subject matter might endanger national security, compromise sensitive law-enforcement information, or violate a rule of the parent chamber. If testimony would defame, degrade, or incriminate a person, the testimony must be taken in closed session if a majority of committee members determines that the testimony might be problematic. Testimony taken in closed session can be released only by majority vote of the committee.

Quorums. Individual committees set their own quorum requirements to conduct a hearing. However, House rules require that not fewer than two members be present. Senate committees usually allow a single senator to be present to conduct a hearing. Individual House committee rules also set a quorum requirement for waiving a hearing notice, but House rules disallow the quorum from being less than one-third. Senate committees have no comparable rule. Finally, for House committees, a majority of members of a committee constitutes a quorum for authorizing a subpoena or closing a committee session.

Subpoena Power. Both House and Senate committees are authorized to issue subpoenas to witnesses and for documents. The rules of each committee delineate the procedures for issuing a subpoena. When a committee adopts its rules at the beginning of a Congress, it must decide how to issue subpoenas. A committee might determine that a subpoena can be issued under the signature of the chair or that the concurrence of the ranking minority member is required. Alternatively, it might choose to authorize a subpoena only by a majority vote of the committee.

Witnesses. Witnesses must be invited to appear before a committee or subcommittee. A formal letter of invitation is usually sent under the name of the chair or, sometimes, the chair and ranking minority member. Occasionally, a committee will ask for written witness testimony in lieu of an appearance before the committee. An organization or individual may also request an invitation to appear or to submit testimony for a hearing record. (See § 10.75, *Committee Investigations and Witness Protections.*)

House and Senate chamber rules, as well as individual committee rules, generally require a witness to file a specific number of copies of his or her prepared written statement in advance of an appearance. A nongovernmental witness appearing before a House committee is also required to comply with the so-called *truth in testimony* rule, which states that the witness should file a résumé and disclose the amount and source of any grant or contract money received from the federal government in the current or two preceding fiscal years. (See § 8.43, *Sample Truth in Testimony Form.*)

The minority party is entitled to one day of hearings to call its own witnesses if a majority of minority members so requests.

Conducting Hearings

Each committee determines if witnesses will appear individually or in a panel. In a panel format, committee members usually hold their questions until all panelists have made their presentations. A committee must also determine whether to swear in a witness.

§ 8.43

Sample Truth in Testimony Form

Committee on the Budget
Witness Disclosure Requirement – "Truth in Testimony"
Required by House Rule XI, Clause 2(g)

Your Name:		

	Yes	No
1. Will you be representing a federal, State, or local government entity? (If the answer is yes please contact the committee).	Yes	No

2. Please list any federal grants or contracts (including subgrants or subcontracts) which <u>you have received</u> since October 1, 2002:

	Yes	No
3. Will you be representing an entity other than a government entity?	Yes	No

4. Other than yourself, please list what entity or entities you will be representing:

5. Please list any offices or elected positions held and/or briefly describe your representational capacity with each of the entities you listed in response to question 4:

6. Please list any federal grants or contracts (including subgrants or subcontracts) received by the entities you listed in response to question 4 since October 1, 2002, including the source and amount of each grant or contract:

	Yes	No
7. Are there parent organizations, subsidiaries, or partnerships to the entities you disclosed in response to question number 4 that you will not be representing? If so, please list:	Yes	No

Signature: _____ Date: _____

Please attach this sheet to your written testimony.

§ 8.44

Celebrity Witnesses

As a means of generating publicity and public support for public-policy issues, committees have turned increasingly in recent years to "celebrity witnesses." Celebrity witnesses who have testified at hearings before House and Senate committees in recent years, and the issues on which they testified, include the following:

Environmental and Agricultural Issues
- Ted Danson—American Oceans Campaign
- Jessica Lange—Farm bill

Health Issues
- Michael J. Fox—Parkinson's disease research
- Mary Tyler Moore—Diabetes disease research
- Ben Vereen—Deafness research
- Sally Field—Osteoporosis
- Jack Klugman—Cancer research
- Diane Keaton—Cancer research
- Olivia Newton John—Cancer research
- Christopher Reeve—Spinal-cord injuries research
- Jason Alexander—Scleroderma research
- Shawn Colvin—Drug addiction
- Robert Guillaume—Drug addiction
- Katie Couric—Colon cancer research
- David Hyde Pierce—Alzheimer's disease research
- Elton John—HIV/AIDS
- Julia Roberts—Rett syndrome

International Issues
- Richard Gere—Tibet
- Sam Waterston—Immigration

Labor Issues
- Charlton Heston—Unemployment benefits
- Muhammad Ali—Regulation of boxing

Treatment of Animals
- Alec Baldwin—End to animal testing
- Kim Basinger—End to animal testing

Other
- Denyce Graves—Arts funding
- Muhammad Ali—Boxing reform
- Pearl Jam—TicketMaster dispute
- Martin Short—Foster parents
- Jack Nicklaus—Education
- Elmo—Music education
- Stephen Sondheim, Arthur Miller, Wendy Wasserstein—Playwrights' Licensing Antitrust Initiative Act
- Bobby McFerrin—Arts funding
- Edward James Olmos—Volunteer service programs
- Doris Roberts—Ageism in media
- Jose Canseco, Mark McGwire, Sammy Sosa, Curt Schilling, and Frank Thomas—Steroids abuse in Major League Baseball

Protocol and tradition dictate that members of Congress wishing to testify at hearings do so before other witnesses testify. Executive-branch officials and former members are also afforded consideration in the order in which they appear. A "celebrity witness" is likely to be placed to generate maximum media coverage. A witness generally summarizes his or her written testimony before a committee. *(See § 8.44, Celebrity Witnesses.)*

As a general practice, each House member is entitled to five minutes of questioning of each witness. However, the chair and ranking member can designate specific members or staff

§ 8.45

Field Hearing Announcement

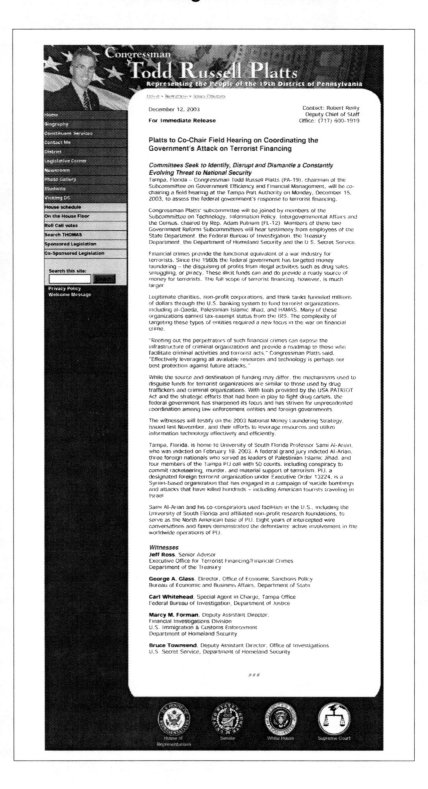

to pursue extended questioning of up to thirty minutes on behalf of their party's members. It is also possible for members to ask witnesses to respond to questions in writing after a hearing is concluded. Many Senate committees also have adopted committee rules limiting senators to five minutes for each witness.

An individual committee's rules spell out the order in which members are recognized to question witnesses. Many committees recognize members in order of their seniority on the committee. Several panels recognize members based on their "order of appearance" at a hearing, giving priority to those members who arrive early.

Most hearing rooms are equipped with small, color lights on the witness table. The green light is turned on when a member is recognized to speak or ask questions of a witness. The red light signifies a member's time has expired. An amber or orange light signifies that a member's time will soon expire. The committee chair or committee clerk controls the lights, but the lights are not always strictly monitored or even turned on. In many hearing rooms, digital clocks rather than lights have been installed on both the dais and the witness table.

Most committee hearings are held in Washington, DC. In recent years, however, committees have increased their use of *field hearings*. A field hearing is conducted the same way as a hearing in Washington, but is held in the home district or state of the member calling the hearing or in a locale relevant to the subject of the hearing. Field hearings allow local residents to attend or testify without coming to Washington *(see § 8.45, Field Hearing Announcement)*.

(For information on hearings transcripts and printed hearings, see § 12.10, Committee Documents.)

§ 8.50 Committee Markup

When hearings are completed, a committee may meet to *mark up* a measure. The connotation of a markup session is that the language of the original measure is analyzed line-by-line or section-by-section, and then *marked up*, that is, changed or amended. *(See § 8.51, Committee Markup and Reporting Glossary.)*

The rules of each chamber provide only general guidance to committees for conducting markups. The rules of the House and the Senate are the rules of their committees "so far as applicable." Each committee must also adopt written rules governing its procedures. House and Senate committee rules cannot be inconsistent with their chambers' rules. Committee markups follow committee rules made pursuant to these two guidelines. Subcommittees generally are covered by full committee rules. In recent years, several committees have conducted all markups at the full committee level after hearings were held at the subcommittee level. Both chambers require that markup sessions be open to the public unless a committee decides in open session by majority vote to close the markup.

Vehicle for Consideration and Amendment

A markup begins with the chair calling up a particular measure for consideration by the committee. The text the chair intends for the committee to consider is referred to as the *markup*

§ 8.51

Committee Markup and Reporting Glossary

Chairman's Mark/Staff Draft: Recommendation by chair of the measure to be considered in markup, usually drafted as a bill.

Clean Bill: New measure reported by a House committee, incorporating all changes made in markup. Measure, with new number, is introduced and referred to the committee, which then reports that measure.

Committee Report: Document accompanying measure reported from a committee, containing an explanation of the provisions of the measure, arguments for its approval, and certain other matters.

Cordon Rule: Senate rule that requires a committee report to show changes the reported measure would make in current law.

Mark: *See Vehicle.*

Minority, Supplemental, and Additional Views: Statements in a committee report, presenting individual or group opinions on the measure.

Ordered Reported: Committee's formal action of agreeing to report a measure to its chamber.

Original Bill: Bill drafted by a committee and introduced when the committee reports the measure to the chamber. Senate allows all committees to report original bills; House generally allows only the Appropriations Committee to do so.

Ramseyer Rule: House rule that requires a committee report to show changes the reported measure would make in current law.

Report/Reported: As a verb, formal submission of a measure to the chamber. As a noun, a committee document explaining the measure reported from committee. A report is designated *H. Rept.* in the House and *S. Rept.* in the Senate.

Vehicle/Legislative Vehicle: Term for legislative measure that is being considered.

A larger glossary is located at the back of the book.

---

vehicle, and the chair has several alternatives from which to choose. *(See § 8.52, Keeping Up with House and Senate Committee Markups.)*

Introduced Measure. Using an introduced measure as the vehicle is the easiest way to conduct a markup. The chair notifies committee members that the vehicle for the markup will be the introduced bill, identifying the bill number and, often, the original sponsor. At House markups, the measure is usually read for amendment by section. By unanimous consent, the measure can be open for amendment at any point or title by title. At Senate markups, measures are usually open to amendment at any point. In either case, each section

§ 8.52

Keeping Up with House and Senate Committee Markups[1]

See Chapters Eleven, Twelve, and Thirteen for descriptions of these and other sources.

Sources	Anticipating Markup		During/After Markup	
	Status	Substance	Status	Substance
Congressional Sources				
Congressional Record. See Daily Digest pages and advance Senate committee schedule. Also see announcements by committee chairs in House and Senate proceedings pages	x		x	
Committee and leadership web sites, available through the House *<www.house.gov>* and Senate *<www.senate.gov>* sites	x		x	
Committee or committee members' press releases	x	x	x	x
Committee markup vehicle		x		
Amendments printed or drafted by committee members (sometimes based on legislation previously referred to the committee)		x		x
Committee report and text of legislation as reported				x
Legislative Information System (Congress only)	x	x	x	x
THOMAS *<http://thomas.loc.gov>*	x	x	x	x
Non-Congressional Sources				
CQ Today <www.cq.com>	x	x	x	x
CQ.com *<www.cq.com>*	x	x	x	x
CQ Weekly (for major legislation) *<www.cq.com>*	x	x	x	x
CongressDaily, from *National Journal <http://nationaljournal.com>*	x	x	x	x
National Journal online service	x	x	x	x
National Journal (for major legislation) *<http://nationaljournal.com>*		x		x
Trade press and daily newspapers	x	x	x	x
Relevant interest-group web sites	x	x	x	x
Other commercial database services	x	x	x	x
People *(Use these contacts after exhausting other resources.)*				
Committee professional staff (What is expected to happen at markup? After markup, when is floor action expected?)		x	x	
Committee professional staff—*House only* (After markup, what type of rule will be sought? Is suspension of the rules an option?)			x	x
Committee clerks (When and where is markup scheduled? After markup, are amendment texts and recorded vote tallies available?)	x			x
Documents clerks (What documents are available?)		x		x
Committee and committee members' press assistants (What press releases or other press documents are available?)		x		x

1. Markups in a subcommittee do not usually result in formal documents. Information on substantive decisions must be gained from the media, subcommittee staff, and members who serve on the subcommittee or their personal staff.

can be amended in *two degrees*. (*See First-Degree Amendment and Second-Degree Amendment in § 8.121, Amendment Process Glossary.*)

Subcommittee Reported Version/Committee Print. Many measures considered by a full committee have already received subcommittee action. If a subcommittee reports its version of a text to the full committee, the product is often printed and referred to as a *committee print*. The committee print can then be used as the markup vehicle. An alternative is for a committee or subcommittee chair to offer the subcommittee reported version as an *amendment in the nature of a substitute* for the measure initially used as the markup vehicle. A third approach is for the subcommittee chair to introduce a new measure reflecting the subcommittee's changes to the earlier measure. This new measure could then be referred to the committee and used as the markup vehicle.

Staff Draft/Chairman's Mark. This option allows the committee to use as a vehicle a text that incorporates both changes made in subcommittee markup and additional changes negotiated afterward, yet before full committee markup. The product of these negotiations is incorporated into a *committee print*, often referred to as a *staff draft* or *chairman's mark*.

Amendment in the Nature of a Substitute. A chair sometimes prefers to offer an amendment in the nature of a substitute to the measure selected as the markup vehicle. This type of amendment, representing a full-text alternative, can be offered only at the outset of the amendment process, after the first section of the measure is read. (A full-text amendment can also be offered at the end of the markup process, but that practice is rare.)

Amendment Procedure

Committees do not actually amend measures during markup; instead, a committee votes on what amendments it wishes to recommend to its parent chamber. If a committee reports a measure with amendments, the parent chamber will ordinarily have to act on the amendments. How a panel conducts the amendment process in markup generally reflects procedures used in the chamber, possibly as modified by individual committee rules.

Reading the Measure. Bills must be *read* twice in committee. This second reading enables the amendment process to begin. Committees usually dispense with the first reading of a bill, either by unanimous consent or by a motion to dispense with the reading. A measure is not considered as read for a second time, for amendment, until a chair directs the clerk to read section one. A measure is usually read for amendment by section. By unanimous consent, a measure could be "considered as read and open for amendment at any point" or could be amended by title.

Recognition and Debate. In recognizing committee members to speak or offer amendments, the chair alternates between majority and minority members. The chair also gives preference to more senior members. When a member offers an amendment, the clerk reads the amendment and committee staff distribute copies of it. Reading of the amendment can be dispensed with by unanimous consent.

Before a sponsor speaks in support of an amendment, any committee member can either reserve or make a *point of order* against the amendment. A point of order must be reserved or made after the clerk reads but before the sponsor begins to speak. A point of order is a parliamentary device for questioning whether an amendment, measure, or motion is within the rules of a chamber or of a committee. If a point of order is sustained by a committee chair, the amendment cannot be offered. If the point of order is overruled, the amendment process can proceed. Although it is possible to appeal a chair's ruling—to question it—making a successful appeal is rare. (Although committee members and staff may seek advice from the parliamentarian before or during a markup, a parliamentarian is not present during a markup. Rather, a committee staff member is normally designated to be a committee's expert on chamber and committee rules.)

Amendments offered in House committee markups are considered under the five-minute rule; that is, any member may speak for up to five minutes. Additional time can be given by unanimous consent.

Amendments offered in Senate committee markups are generally not subject to debate limitations. Therefore, it is possible for opponents to filibuster an amendment. There is no Senate procedure for invoking cloture in a committee markup; however, several Senate committees have adopted committee rules to bring extended debate to an end.

An amendment may be agreed to or rejected by a voice, division, or roll-call vote. House committees may not use proxy voting; Senate committees may if a committee's rules authorize proxy voting. *(See § 8.131, House Voting Glossary.)*

Offering and Considering Amendments in House Markups. The most common method of conducting markups allows a member to offer an amendment to a section as it is read. When the last amendment to a section has been offered, the section is considered closed to further amendment, and the committee moves to the next section. By unanimous consent, amendments may be offered *en bloc*, that is, affecting more than one section of a measure.

Alternatively, the chair can open the bill to amendment at any point if unanimous consent is granted. This process enables members to offer amendments in an order convenient to the committee's members. Some committees use an amendment roster, a list agreed to in advance by all committee members, which provides the order in which amendments will be considered.

Another option is for the chair or another member, generally a senior majority member, to offer an amendment in the nature of a substitute. This is essentially a full-text alternative to the pending measure. This type of amendment can be offered only at the beginning or end of the markup process, and is itself open to amendment at any point (and may be made original text for the purpose of further amendment). An advantage of an amendment in the nature of a substitute is that a motion can be made after any debate on the amendment to cut off further debate and amendments. This motion is called the *previous question*.

An amendment must be read in full unless reading is dispensed with by unanimous consent. An amendment can be withdrawn if no action has occurred on it. Amendments are permitted only in *two degrees*, and they must be *germane*. *(See definitions in § 8.121, Amendment Process Glossary.)*

Ending the Amendment Process in House Markups. After the last section of the measure has been read, any committee member can move the previous question. A member can also move to *close debate* or *end debate* on amendments or to *limit debate* to a specified time. Unlike the previous question, closing or limiting debate does not preclude offering additional amendments, but it does mean that all subsequent amendments are decided without debate.

Offering and Considering Amendments in Senate Markups. A measure is usually open to amendment at any point in Senate committees. However, a committee can decide by unanimous consent to structure the amendment process. Otherwise, amendments are considered in whatever order senators offer them.

An amendment must be read in full unless reading is dispensed with by unanimous consent. An amendment can be withdrawn if no action has occurred on it. Germaneness of amendments is generally not required during markup; however, Senate rules prohibit the floor consideration of substantive committee amendments containing significant matter outside the jurisdiction of the reporting committee. Amendments are permitted in two degrees. *(See First-Degree Amendment, Second-Degree Amendment, and Germaneness at § 8.121, Amendment Process Glossary.)*

Reporting

At the end of the amendment process, a chair normally entertains a motion to report a measure favorably to its parent chamber. The motion is not a request for unanimous consent. In each chamber, a majority of the committee must be physically present in the committee when a measure is reported. Although Senate committees generally allow the use of proxies, proxy votes may not affect the outcome of the vote to report a measure from committee.

Once the motion to report is agreed to, a bill is *ordered reported*; it is not actually *reported* until the committee report is filed in the chamber. When a committee orders a measure reported, it is incumbent upon the chair to report it "promptly" and to take all steps necessary to secure its consideration by the House. Staff are usually granted authority to make "technical and conforming" changes to the measure reported.

Options for Reporting. A committee can report a measure without amendment. This means that the committee has made no changes to the text of the measure as introduced.

Second, a committee can report a measure "as amended" with an amendment or multiple amendments—so-called *cut and bite amendments*. Multiple amendments could be considered individually or adopted *en bloc* on the floor.

Third, a House committee can report a *clean bill*. That is a new bill incorporating the text of amendments adopted in markup. A committee member, often the chair, introduces the new measure in the House; it receives a new number and is referred to committee. By unanimous consent, a clean bill can be "deemed reported," thereby voiding the need for another committee meeting.

A Senate committee may report an *original bill* that embodies a text agreed to in markup. This new bill is given its own number when it is reported or called up or at another time after committee action has been completed. Reporting an original bill avoids separate floor votes on the changes adopted in markup.

Fourth, a committee can report an introduced measure with an amendment in the nature of a substitute. This is similar to reporting a clean bill, but it retains the original measure's number.

Which option a committee chooses may influence how the measure is considered on the floor of the respective chamber.

Options on How to Report. A committee can report a measure "favorably." This means that a majority of a committee is recommending that the full House or Senate consider and pass a measure. Alternatively, a committee can report "unfavorably" or "adversely." This often implies that the majority-party leadership believes that a majority of House members support a measure even though a majority of the committee does not. Third, a committee can report "without recommendation." This means that a committee believes a measure should receive floor consideration even though it could not find a majority to agree on what to report.

§ 8.60 Committee Reports

When a committee sends a measure to the floor by reporting it from the committee, the committee usually files a written report to accompany the measure. The report describes the purpose and intent of the legislation, and explains the committee's action on the measure, including votes taken in markup. The report indicates changes proposed to existing law, provides information on the measure's cost, and contains other information. Individual member statements can also be included in the report. A committee report provides a useful substantive and political explanation of a committee's intent.

Description and Requirements

The cover page of a committee report, usually formatted by the Office of Legislative Counsel, provides the title of the bill, the date the report was ordered printed, the name of the chair submitting the report, and a notation to the legislation it accompanies. There is a reference to the inclusion of a Congressional Budget Office (CBO) estimate and to any minority, supplemental, or additional views that were filed. The cover page also identifies committee action on the legislation and the number of the report itself. *(See § 8.61, Reading the Cover Page of a House Committee Report.)*

§ 8.61

Reading the Cover Page
of a House Committee Report

1 Committee reports, including those from conference committees, are numbered sequentially as the reports are filed by any committee with its parent chamber. "H. Rept." denotes a report from a House committee; "S. Rept." from a Senate committee. The numbers before the hyphen show the Congress; for example, "106" means 106th Congress. The numbers following the hyphen make up the unique, sequential number for the report.

2 If a measure is referred to more than one committee, each committee reporting the measure uses the same report number. But, each committee's report is printed separately and designated a "part" of the report. In this example, all reports were H. Rept. 106-74, but the Banking Committee reported "Part 1" and a supplement, "Part 2." The report from the Commerce Committee was then "Part 3." (Part designations may appear in Roman numerals.)

3 An identification of the measure, such as its "popular name" or "short title."

4 The reporting date and the calendar designation; in this case, the "Union Calendar."

5 The chair and committee reporting the measure.

6 The notation of minority, supplemental, or additional views, if one or more committee members requested their inclusion.

7 The measure that is being reported from the committee.

8 A brief description of the measure and the committee's recommendation to the parent chamber.

9 The report text begins, sometimes with a table of contents.

106TH CONGRESS *1st Session*	HOUSE OF REPRESENTATIVES	REPT. 106–74 Part 3

3 FINANCIAL SERVICES ACT OF 1999

---

4 JUNE 15, 1999.—Committed to the Committee of the Whole House on the State of the Union and ordered to be printed

---

5 Mr. BLILEY, from the Committee on Commerce,
submitted the following

R E P O R T

together with

6 ADDITIONAL VIEWS

7 [To accompany H.R. 10]

8 The Committee on Commerce, to whom was referred the bill (H.R. 10) to enhance competition in the financial services industry by providing a prudential framework for the affiliation of banks, securities firms, and other financial service providers, and for other purposes, having considered the same, report favorably thereon with an amendment and recommend that the bill as amended do pass.

CONTENTS

57–325

§ 8.62

House Committee Reports:
Required Contents

Requirement	Applies to
Statement of committee action on all record votes	Record vote to report measure of public character and on any amendment offered in committee
Statement of committee oversight findings and recommendations	Measure approved; all committees except Committees on Appropriations and Budget
Statement on new budget authority and related items	Measure (except continuing appropriations measure) providing new budget authority, new spending authority, new credit authority, or increase or decrease in revenues or tax expenditures
Statement of Congressional Budget Office (CBO) cost estimate and comparison, if submitted in timely fashion	Measure of public character; all committees except Committee on Appropriations
Statement of general performance goals and objectives, including outcome-related goals and objectives	Measure approved
Statement of constitutional authority of Congress to enact	Measure of public character
Supplemental, minority, or additional views, if submitted in writing and signed, and filed within two calendar days	Measure approved; all committees except Committee on Rules
Recital on cover of report to show inclusion of certain material	Reports that include CBO cost estimate and comparison, oversight findings, and supplemental, minority, or additional views
Changes in existing law ("Ramseyer rule")	Measure that amends or repeals existing law
Statement of committee cost estimate	Measure of public character; Committees on Appropriations, House Administration, Rules, and Standards of Official Conduct are exempt; requirement does not apply if CBO cost estimate is in report
Determination regarding new advisory committee	Legislation establishing or authorizing establishment of advisory committee
Applicability to legislative branch, or statement explaining why not applicable	Measure relating to terms and conditions of employment or access to public services or accommodations
Statement of federal mandates	Measure of public character
Macroeconomic analysis	Ways and Means Committee; requirement does not apply if analysis is inserted in *Congressional Record*

8

§ 8.63

Senate Committee Reports: Required Contents

Committee reports must include:

- Record of roll-call votes
- Cost estimate prepared by Congressional Budget Office
- Regulatory impact statement
- Changes in existing law, a requirement called the "Cordon rule"
- Minority, supplemental, or additional views, if requested

Committee reports usually include:

- Text of committee's proposed amendments, if any
- Discussion of policy issue addressed
- Summary of committee's deliberations
- Discussion of committee's conclusions and recommendations
- Section-by-section analysis of measure's provisions and proposed amendments

A committee report's sections then begin, generally in the following sequence. The initial section provides a brief description of the purpose of the legislation, a brief summary of the bill itself (referred to as a "section-by-section"), and a legislative history of the legislation, including a detailed explanation of the actions taken by the committee in hearings and markup. A House report must contain details on all votes taken in committee on each amendment offered and on the motion to report, including how each member voted on each item. A hearing summary is often included as well. A committee report then addresses the need for the legislation and the intent of the measure; this portion of a report is often cited in court decisions and by future Congresses.

A House report must include oversight findings and recommendations, CBO estimates, information on unfunded mandates (if appropriate), and a statement of authority. *(See § 8.62, House Committee Reports: Required Contents.)*

A Senate report must include cost estimates, a paperwork impact statement, a regulatory impact statement, and information on unfunded mandates (if appropriate). If a roll-call vote was ordered to report a measure, the report must also include the vote results. Finally, if appropriate, a statement explaining the extent to which the measure preempts any state, local, or tribal law must be provided. *(See § 8.63, Senate Committee Reports: Required Contents.)*

Ramseyer/Cordon. A comparative section in contrasting typefaces must be included in a committee report. It shows the text of a statute, or a part thereof, that is proposed to be amended or repealed. This section is usually prepared by the respective chamber's Office of Legislative Counsel. In House reports, this comparative section is eponymously called a "Ramseyer," and in Senate reports, a "Cordon." (These sections are named, respectively, for Representative Christian W. Ramseyer, R-IA, 1915–1933, and Senator Guy Cordon, R-OR, 1944–1955.)

Minority, Additional, and Supplemental Views. Views of individual committee members or groups of committee members are required to be included if a member or members request permission to include them. Minority views may be filed by committee members who are not minority-party members.

House Calendars

When a measure is reported from committee, it is placed on a calendar. These calendars are lists of pending measures. The calendars are not agendas, because measures are not assigned a day for consideration until the leadership determines when a measure will come up for consideration.

Union Calendar: All legislation dealing with raising, authorizing, or spending money.

House Calendar: Non-money measures, and measures dealing with internal House matters.

Private Calendar: Bills dealing with relief of a private individual or group of individuals.

Discharge Calendar (Calendar of Motions to Discharge Committees): All motions to take (discharge) a measure from a committee through the discharge procedure.

Individual Committee Requirements. Several House committees are required to include specific provisions in their committee reports. The Committee on Appropriations, for example, must provide a statement describing the effect of any provision of an appropriations bill that changes the application of a law, a list of appropriations for unauthorized expenditures, and a list of rescissions and transfers of unexpended balances.

In reports accompanying resolutions that change House rules, the Committee on Rules must include the text of the rule proposed to be changed and a comparative text showing the proposed change.

In reports on measures changing the Internal Revenue Code, the Committee on Ways and Means must include a tax complexity analysis prepared by the Joint Committee on Taxation. If the Ways and Means Committee reports legislation designated by the majority leader as major tax legislation, the report must include a *dynamic estimate* of the changes in federal revenues expected to result if the legislation is enacted.

(*For additional information on committee documents, see § 12.10, Committee Documents.*)

§ 8.70 House Floor: Scheduling and Privilege

Once a measure has been reported from committee, it goes on a calendar. The majority-party leadership is responsible for determining whether a measure should come off its respective calendar and when it should receive floor consideration. Working with the Rules Committee, the leadership also influences how a measure is considered. (*See § 8.71, House Calendars, and § 12.20, Floor Documents.*)

Decisions on how a measure comes to the floor are made within strictures in House rules that limit the kinds of measures that can go to the floor. The concept of *privilege* is used to categorize such procedures. *Privileged business* consists of those measures and matters that mem-

§ 8.72

Daily Starting Times in the House

Starting times are usually announced early in each session by the majority-party leadership.

January 4, 2007, through May 13, 2007:
- 2:00 p.m. on Monday (12:30 p.m. for morning hour)
- 12:00 noon on Tuesday (10:30 a.m. for morning hour)
- 10:00 a.m. on all other days

May 14, 2007, until the end of the first session:
- 12:00 noon on Monday (11:00 a.m. for morning hour)
- 10:00 a.m. on Tuesday, Wednesday, and Thursday (9:00 a.m. for morning hour)
- 9:00 a.m. on Friday

bers can bring up for consideration on the House floor and that are *privileged* to interrupt the regular order of business.

In the House, measures on certain calendars, or to be brought up for consideration subject to certain procedures, are privileged on certain days. These calendars and procedures are the Discharge and Private Calendars; District Day; Calendar Wednesday; and suspension of the rules. Business privileged on any day the House meets includes general appropriations bills; privileged reports from committees that have the right to report at any time, including special rules from the Rules Committee; and reported resolutions of inquiry. Amendments in disagreement and Senate amendments that do not require consideration in the Committee of the Whole are also privileged.

When the House is in session, it tends to follow meeting times announced by the majority-party leadership at the beginning of each session. *(See § 8.72, Daily Starting Times in the House.)*

(For information on House floor documents, see § 12.20.)

§ 8.80 House Floor: Methods of Consideration

There are numerous ways to bring a measure to the House floor for debate, possible amendment, and a vote on passage. A measure might come to the floor because of the calendar on which it was placed or because it is a certain day of the week or the month. Another measure might find its fate in the hands of the majority leadership, especially the Speaker of the House. One measure might come to the floor because it is noncontroversial, and another might make it there only after complex negotiations.

Unanimous Consent

Noncontroversial measures, which have been cleared by the respective party leaders, can come to the floor by unanimous consent. Once cleared, a member can ask permission to bring up the particular measure. A single objection by another member will stop the process. A member can, alternately, "reserve the right to object" in order to ask about the request, traditionally to check if the measure has been cleared by the minority party. Once the member seeking to bring up the measure responds, the member reserving the right to object withdraws the reservation, and the consent request is agreed to "without objection." This exchange, under the reservation, is all the discussion that occurs on a measure brought up by unanimous consent.

Suspension of the Rules

This procedure, for largely noncontroversial measures, accounts for more than half of all measures considered by the House. On Monday, Tuesday, and Wednesday of each week, and during the last six days of a session, the Speaker may recognize members to move to "suspend the rules and pass" a particular measure or conference report. Suspension measures can also be considered on other days by unanimous consent or pursuant to provisions of a special rule.

A measure traditionally will not be considered under the suspension procedure if it was controversial in committee. (The majority party's rules supplement House rules in guiding the leadership on legislative and other matters. However, party rules have no official status in House proceedings and cannot be a basis for a point of order.)

Debate on a motion to suspend the rules is limited to forty minutes, with twenty minutes controlled by a proponent and twenty minutes controlled by an opponent, regardless of party affiliation. In practice, a majority floor manager controls twenty minutes and a minority floor manager controls the other twenty minutes. Measures considered under this process are not subject to floor amendment, although the motion to suspend may incorporate an amendment. Because the motion would then be to "suspend the rules and pass the bill with an amendment," no separate vote is taken on the amendment. Points of order cannot be raised on a measure or conference report brought up under suspension of the rules.

To pass, a measure considered under the suspension procedure requires two-thirds of the members present and voting to vote for the motion. Unless a recorded vote is requested, however, a measure considered under this procedure can be passed by a voice vote.

Private Calendar

Bills on this calendar generally relate to individual immigration and claims matters and are placed there when reported by the Committee on the Judiciary or any committee considering a private bill. Measures on the Private Calendar can come to the floor on the first Tuesday of each month. At the discretion of the Speaker, private measures can also be considered on the third Tuesday of each month.

Each party usually appoints *official objectors* to review bills on the Private Calendar. If an official objector has a concern about a bill, there can be an objection to its consideration. More often, however, the bill is "passed over, without prejudice." It gives sponsors a chance to address concerns before the bill comes up under the next call of the Private Calendar.

Each bill is called up automatically in the order in which it was reported from committee and placed on the Private Calendar. A bill is considered under a special procedure, called "in the House as in the Committee of the Whole." Under this process, there is no general debate, but members may speak for five minutes. There is usually little debate and measures pass by voice vote.

Discharge Calendar

Any member may file a motion with the clerk of the House to discharge a committee from consideration of any measure that has been pending before the committee for thirty legislative days. A motion to discharge a special rule from the Committee on Rules can be filed if the special rule has been pending before that committee for seven legislative days. The Discharge Calendar is considered on the second and fourth Mondays of each month, although a measure eligible for discharge (by having 218 signatures on its discharge petition) must be on the Discharge Calendar for seven legislative days.

Discharge motions are considered in the House with twenty minutes of debate equally divided between a proponent and an opponent. The only intervening motion is a nondebatable motion to adjourn.

Special Rule

A measure not in order under the means discussed above generally comes to the floor under provisions of a *special rule*. A special rule sets the guidelines for a measure's consideration, including time for *general debate* and any limits on the *amendment process*. Most important and controversial legislation is considered under the terms of a special rule to enable the leadership to structure debate and amendments.

Rules are considered in the House under the *one-hour rule*, with time controlled by a majority floor manager. The majority floor manager customarily yields thirty minutes to the minority floor manager "for purposes of debate only." Accordingly, special rules can be amended only if the majority floor manager offers an amendment to the rule or yields time to another member to offer an amendment, or if the previous question on the rule is defeated. (The previous question is in the form of a motion ("I move the previous question"), which, if agreed to, cuts off further debate and the possibility of amendment.)

§ 8.90 Rules Committee and Special Rules

For most major legislation, it is the Rules Committee that determines if and how a measure will be considered on the floor. The Rules Committee is empowered to report *a special rule* in the form of a simple resolution (for example, H. Res. 123) to govern floor debate, the amendment process, and other procedures related to floor consideration of a measure. *(See § 8.91, Special Rules Glossary.)*

Requesting a Special Rule

When a committee reports a measure, the committee chair, usually by letter to the Rules Committee chair, requests that a Rules Committee hearing be scheduled on the measure. The

§ 8.91

Special Rules Glossary

Closed Rule: Permits general debate for a specified period of time but permits no floor amendments. Amendments reported by the reporting committee are allowed.

Modified Closed Rule: Permits general debate for a specified period of time, but limits amendments to those designated in the special rule or the Rules Committee report accompanying the special rule. May preclude amendments to particular portions of a bill.

Modified Open Rule: Permits general debate for a specified period of time, and allows any member to offer amendments consistent with House rules subject only to an overall time limit on the amendment process or a requirement that amendments be preprinted in the *Congressional Record*.

Open Rule: Permits general debate for a specified period of time and allows any member to offer an amendment that complies with the standing rules of the House.

Queen-of-the-Hill Rule: A special rule that permits votes on a series of amendments, usually complete substitutes for a measure, but directs that the amendment receiving the greatest number of votes is the winning amendment.

Rise and Report: Refers to the end of proceedings in the Committee of the Whole, which sends the measure it has been considering back to the House for final disposition.

Self-Executing Rule: If specified, the House's adoption of a special rule may also have the effect of amending or passing the underlying measure. Also called a "hereby" rule.

Structured Rule: Another term for a modified closed rule.

Waiver Rule: A special rule that waives points of order against a measure or an amendment.

A larger glossary is located at the back of the book.

8

letter often notes the type of rule requested, the amount of debate time needed, and whether any *waivers* of House rules are required. Individual members may also write to the Rules Committee requesting the opportunity to testify and make their cases for being allowed to offer amendments to the measure on the House floor. *(See § 8.92, Announcement on Amendments Prior to a Rules Committee Meeting.)*

Rules Committee Action

The Rules Committee hearing is typically scheduled after the majority leadership has decided to schedule floor time for a measure. The committee's hearing on this legislation resembles any other committee hearing, although only members of the House are witnesses. Following the hearing, the panel marks up a special rule, often drafted with the knowledge and input of the majority-party leadership.

§ 8.92

Announcement on Amendments Prior
to a Rules Committee Meeting

U.S. House of Representatives
★Committee on Rules

SPECIAL AMENDMENT PROCEDURES AND THE RULES COMMITTEE

REQUIRED FORM FOR SUBMITTING AMENDMENTS TO THE HOUSE COMMITTEE ON
RULES

Dear Colleague:

The Rules Committee has announced that it may meet next week to grant a rule which could limit
the amendment process for floor consideration of H.R. 27, the Job Training Improvement Act of
2005. The Committee on Education and the Workforce ordered the bill reported on February 17,
2005 and is expected to file its report with the House on Friday, February 25, 2005.

Any Member who wishes to offer an amendment should submit 55 copies of the amendment and
one copy of a brief explanation of the amendment to the Rules Committee in room H-312 of the
Capitol **by 12 noon Tuesday, March 1st**. The form used to submit amendments to the Rules
Committee is on the top of this page. Members should draft their amendments to the text of the
bill as reported by the Education and Workforce Committee, which will be available for their
review on the websites of both the Rules and Education and the Workforce Committees by Friday,
February 25, 2005.

Members should use the Office of Legislative Counsel to ensure that their amendments are drafted
in the most appropriate format. Members are also advised to check with the Office of the
Parliamentarian to be certain their amendments comply with the rules of the House. **If you have
any questions, please contact myself or Eileen Harley at x5-9191.**

Text of H.R. 27 -Job Training Improvement Act of 2005

Types of Special Rules

There are several types of rules the committee can craft. *(See § 8.93, Reading a Special Rule.)*
Under each type, *general debate* is permitted for a specified period of time. Under an *open rule*,
all *germane amendments* can be offered, provided they are offered in a timely manner, comply
with all House rules, and fit on the *amendment tree*. Under a *closed rule*, no amendments can
be offered to the bill. *(See § 8.120, Committee of the Whole: Amendment Process; and § 8.122,
Basic House Amendment Tree.)*

Modified rules fall into several categories. A *modified open rule* generally requires that amendments be preprinted in the *Congressional Record*, and the special rule may place an overall time limit on the amendment process. A *modified closed rule*, often called a *structured rule*, permits only specified amendments, which are listed in the Rules Committee report. A *queen-of-the-hill rule* allows a specified number of full-text substitutes to a measure, with the amendment receiving the most votes being the only amendment deemed adopted. The *king-of-the-hill rule* has not been used in recent years. Under this procedure, the last amendment to receive a majority vote was the amendment adopted.

A *waiver rule* provides for consideration of amendments or measures that might otherwise be subject to points of order.

A *self-executing* or *hereby rule* stipulates that, upon adoption of the rule, the House is deemed to have passed a measure, adopted an amendment, or taken some other action. A self-executing rule precludes a separate vote on the measure, amendment, or action.

A special rule might include more than one of these features. For example, any of these types of rules might include waiver provisions.

Providing for Floor Consideration

A special rule designates which measure is to be considered on the floor; for example, a committee-reported bill or a so-called leadership alternative. (Leadership alternatives appear regularly.) After the House has voted to approve the rule, the rule then allows the Speaker to declare the House resolved into the *Committee of the Whole House on the State of the Union (Committee of the Whole)* for the consideration of the measure. *(See §8.110, Committee of the Whole: Debate.)* The rule next generally waives the required *first reading* of a bill in full. Finally, the special rule states the amount of time available for discussion (called general debate), and further requires that debate be *germane*.

Structuring the Amendment Process

The special rule may address how the bill will be read for amendment; for example, by title, by section (which is the most common way), or open for amendment at any point. ("By section" is the default method for amending and would not typically be mentioned.) The rule also lays out the amendment process, although it does not state specifically that the rule is open, closed, or modified. The description of the amendment process in the rule enables one to classify and refer to the rule as open, closed, or modified. The rule may also allow the chair of the Committee of the Whole to postpone or cluster votes on amendments and reduce to five minutes the time for clustered votes after a fifteen-minute vote on the first amendment in a series.

Facilitating Final Passage

The special rule makes the motion for the Committee of the Whole to *rise and report* automatic upon completion of the amendment process, and further allows for a *separate vote* in the

Reading a Special Rule

H. Res. 289

[Report No. 106–317]

Original Text of the Resolution

Providing for consideration of the bill (H.R. 1655) to authorize appropriations for fiscal years 2000 and 2001 for the civilian energy and scientific research, development, and demonstration and related commercial application of energy technology programs, projects, and activities of the Department of Energy, and for other purposes.

❶ Authorizes the Speaker to transform ("resolve") the House into the Committee of the Whole House to consider the measure after adoption of the special rule.

❶ *Resolved,* That at any time after the adoption of this resolution the Speaker may, pursuant to clause 2(b) of rule XVIII, declare the House resolved into the Committee of the Whole House on the state of the Union for consideration of the bill (H.R. 1655) to authorize appropriations for fiscal years 2000 and 2001 for the civilian energy and scientific research, development, and demonstration and related commercial application of energy technology programs, projects, and activities of the Department of Energy, and for other purposes.

❷ Dispenses with the first reading of the bill. (Bills must be read three times before being passed.) Sets the amount of general debate time—one hour—and specifies which members control that time—in this instance, the chair and ranking minority member of the Committee on Science. Specifies that debate should be relevant to the bill.

❷ The first reading of the bill shall be dispensed with. General debate shall be confined to the bill and shall not exceed one hour equally divided and controlled by the chairman and ranking minority member of the Committee on Science.

❸ Sets reading for amendment one section at a time (or one paragraph at a time for appropriations bills), and provides that each member can speak for five minutes on each amendment. Because this special rule sets no limitations on amendments that can be offered, it is an open rule. Nonetheless, amendments still must comply with the House's standing rules, such as that on germaneness.

❸ After general debate the bill shall be considered for amendment under the five-minute rule.

Continued on page 287

❹ Identifies text to be open to amendment in the Committee of the Whole. A special rule can provide that a committee-reported substitute be considered as an original bill for the purpose of amendment. Allowing a full-text substitute to be considered as an original bill is usually done to permit second-degree amendments to be offered.

❺ Determines recognition order for offering amendments. Open rules customarily grant the chair of the Committee of the Whole discretion to give priority recognition to members who submitted their amendments for preprinting in the *Congressional Record*. Absent this provision, the chair would follow the custom of giving preferential recognition to members, based on seniority, who serve on the reporting committee, alternating between the parties.

❻ A special rule that allows amendments to be offered might allow the chair of the Committee of the Whole to postpone votes on amendments, as shown here. The chair may reduce to five minutes the time for electronic voting on a postponed question, provided that the voting time on the first in any series of questions is not less than fifteen minutes.

❼ Provides for transformation ("to rise") back to the House from the Committee of the Whole. This provision eliminates the need for a separate vote on a motion to rise and report.

❽ Enables separate votes to occur in the House on each amendment approved by the Committee of the Whole. House rules require the House to vote on each amendment approved by the Committee of the Whole.

❾ Expedites final passage. By automatically imposing the "previous question," intervening debate and the offering of motions is precluded. The only motion allowed is a motion to recommit.

❹ It shall be in order to consider as an original bill for purposes of amendment under the five-minute rule the amendment in the nature of a substitute recommended by the Committee on Science now printed in the bill. Each section of the committee amendment in the nature of a substitute shall be considered as read.

❺ During consideration of the bill for amendment, the Chairman of the Committee of the Whole may accord priority in recognition on the basis of whether the Member offering an amendment has caused it to be printed in the portion of the Congressional Record designated for that purpose in clause 8 of rule XVIII. Amendments so printed shall be considered as read.

❻ The Chairman of the Committee of the Whole may: (1) postpone until a time during further consideration in the Committee of the Whole a request for a recorded vote on any amendment; and (2) reduce to five minutes time for electronic voting on any postponed question that follows another electronic vote without intervening business, provided that the minimum time for electronic voting on the first in any series of questions shall be 15 minutes.

❼ At the conclusion of consideration of the bill for amendment the Committee shall rise and report the bill to the House with such amendments as may have been adopted.

❽ Any Members may demand a separate vote in the House on any amendment adopted in the Committee of the Whole to the bill or to the committee amendment in the nature of a substitute.

❾ The previous question shall be considered as ordered on the bill and amendments thereto to final passage without intervening motion except one motion to recommit with or without instructions.

8

House on any amendment agreed to in the Committee of the Whole. Finally, the rule allows a *motion to recommit* to be offered before a vote on *final passage*, which may be a *voice, division,* or *recorded vote*.

§ 8.100 Consideration of a Special Rule on the House Floor

When the House for parliamentary purposes is sitting as the House and has not resolved into the Committee of the Whole, House rules permit members, when recognized, to hold the floor for no more than one hour each. A special rule from the Rules Committee is privileged and is considered under this *hour rule*. *(See § 8.70, House Floor: Scheduling and Privilege.)* The *majority floor manager* for the Rules Committee, who calls up the simple resolution containing the special rule, customarily yields one half of this one hour to the control of a minority member of the committee, the *minority floor manager,* "for purposes of debate only."

When the House is meeting as the House, the Speaker or, more commonly, a Speaker pro tempore presides. The quorum in the House is a majority of the membership, or 218 representatives if there are no vacancies. *(See § 8.112, House versus Committee of the Whole.)*

Each floor manager then yields a portion of the time he or she controls to other members who wish to speak. The majority party has the right to close the debate—essentially to give the last speech. When all time has been consumed or yielded back, the majority floor manager "moves the previous question."

The *previous question* is a nondebatable motion that proposes to end debate on a measure, to preclude amendments, and to bring the House to a vote on a measure—in this case, the simple resolution containing the special rule. (A motion to adjourn, a motion to table, and a motion to recommit to committee are still in order.) The previous question requires a simple majority vote for adoption. After the previous question on a special rule is agreed to, there is a vote on adoption of the special rule.

There are three ways to offer amendments to a measure (such as a special rule) in the House sitting for parliamentary purposes as the House. First, a motion to recommit a measure can instruct a committee to report the measure back to the House with a specific amendment. The right to offer a motion to recommit is the prerogative of the minority party. Second, the majority floor manager can offer an amendment before the previous question is agreed to. In the case of a special rule, the majority party drafted the measure so that an amendment is rarely offered.

Third, an opponent of a measure can propose an amendment if he or she can gain control of the floor. To do this, the House would need to vote not to *order the previous question,* that is, to defeat it. Defeat of the previous question means that debate does not end, amendments are not precluded, and the resolution will not yet be voted on. If the previous question is defeated, a member, usually the minority floor manager, can proceed for one hour and offer an amendment to the special rule. At the end of the second hour, the minority floor manager would move the previous question on the measure and an amendment to it.

While neither the motion to recommit nor the defeat of the previous question routinely happen, the majority party occasionally mistakes majority sentiment. For example, when President Reagan's economic package was precluded from consideration in 1981 by the House by a special rule reported from the Rules Committee, the key vote was on ordering the previous question. A sufficient number of then-majority party Democrats joined Republicans to defeat the previous question and, subsequently, amend the special rule.

§ 8.110 Committee of the Whole: Debate

When the House is in session, it might be "sitting" in one of two ways for parliamentary purposes. For example, when the House considers and votes on a special rule, the House sits for parliamentary purposes as the House. The second way the House sits is as the *Committee of the Whole House on the State of the Union (Committee of the Whole)*, a parliamentary device created to expedite consideration of a measure.

The House "resolves" into the Committee of the Whole either by unanimous consent or by adoption of a special rule. The Committee of the Whole is a committee consisting of all members of the House. The Committee of the Whole meets in the House chamber, is presided over by a chair appointed by the Speaker of the House, and has a quorum requirement of 100 members. The mace, the symbol of the authority of the House, is removed from its pedestal when the Committee of the Whole is meeting. (*See § 8.111, The Mace.*) Measures from the Union Calendar are considered in the Committee of the Whole. (*See § 8.112, House versus Committee of the Whole.*)

General Debate

General debate is a period of time set aside for discussing a bill as a whole. During this period, no amendments or motions are in order.

The special rule specifies the amount of time available for general debate and how the time is allocated. (For those measures that are brought up by unanimous consent, but considered in the Committee of the Whole, the consent request specifies the time set aside for general debate.) The special rule typically provides one hour of general debate on a measure, with time usually divided equally between the control of the chair and ranking minority member of the committee of jurisdiction. These two members are referred to as the *floor managers* of the measure. (Once a special rule is adopted, the Rules Committee members' role as floor managers ends.)

The chair of the Committee of the Whole recognizes the majority floor manager to open the general debate. The majority floor manager reserves the balance of time after concluding

§ 8.111

The Mace

The mace is the symbol of authority of the House of Representatives. The following physical description of the mace appears with other information about the mace on the web site of the clerk of the House, at <http://clerk.house.gov/art_history/art_artifacts/ virtual_tours/splendid_hall/artifacts.html>:

> The mace is 46 inches high and consists of 13 thin ebony rods representing the original 13 states of the union. The rods are bound together by four crossing ribbons of silver, pinned together and held at the bottom and at the top by silver bands. The bands are decorated with floral borders and a repoussé design. The name "Wm. Adams/Manufacturer/New York/1841." is engraved in the cartouche, located in the front center of the bottom band. This shaft is topped by a silver globe 4-1/2 inches in diameter and engraved with the seven continents, the names of the oceans, lines of longitude, and the major lines of latitude. The Western Hemisphere faces the front. The globe is encircled with a silver rim marked with the degrees of latitude, on which is perched an engraved solid silver eagle with a wingspan of 15 inches. The total weight of the mace is 10 pounds.

an opening statement. The minority floor manager then does the same. Thereafter, the two managers yield specific periods of time to individual members to speak on the measure.

Recognition by the chair of the Committee of the Whole usually alternates between the parties, although one party may yield to several members in a row to keep the remaining general debate time fairly equal between the parties. When a member who has been yielded time addresses issues that the manager does not want addressed, the manager reclaims the balance of time. Throughout the debate, it is common for the floor managers to inquire of the chair how much time remains. The floor managers are usually accompanied by committee staff, who can respond privately to questions from their party's members. *(See § 8.113, Who Is Allowed on the House Floor?)*

When all time for general debate has been consumed or yielded back, general debate ends, and the amendment process begins. *(See § 8.114, Committee of the Whole and the House: Stages of Action.)*

§ 8.112

House versus Committee of the Whole

House	Committee of the Whole
Established by Constitution	Established by House for consideration of a specific measure
Mace raised	Mace lowered
Speaker presides	Chair of Committee of the Whole presides, appointed by Speaker
One-hour rule	Five-minute rule for amendments; special rule from Rules Committee dictates procedure, after adoption of rule by House
Quorum of 218	Quorum of 100
One-fifth of members (44 with minimum quorum) to trigger a recorded vote	25 members to trigger a recorded vote
Motion for previous question in order	Motion for previous question not in order; motion to limit or end debate may be offered
Motion to recommit in order	Motion to recommit not in order
Motion to reconsider in order	Motion to reconsider not in order
Routine business of House in order	Routine business of House not in order

8

§ 8.113

Who Is Allowed on the House Floor?

In addition to the representatives and pages, a variety of staff have permanent or temporary privileges to be on the floor of the House.

Standing next to or near the presiding officer are the parliamentarian, sergeant at arms, clerk of the House, and Speaker's page. At the desk immediately in front of the Speaker are seated the journal clerk, tally clerk, and reading clerk. At the desk below the clerks are the bill clerk, enrolling clerk, and daily digest clerk. Reporters of debate sit at a table below the rostrum. Staff members of committees and individual representatives are allowed on the floor by unanimous consent.

(See § 14.11, House Floor Plan.)

§ 8.114

Committee of the Whole and the House: Stages of Action

- House resolves into Committee of the Whole
- General debate
- Measure read or considered for amendment
- Amendments debated under five-minute rule
- Committee of the Whole rises and reports
- House votes on Committee of the Whole-approved amendments
- Opportunity for motion to recommit
- House votes on final passage

§ 8.120 Committee of the Whole: Amendment Process

Unless a special rule provides otherwise, a bill is usually read for amendment "by section." Bills can alternatively be read for amendment by title or be "open for amendment at any point." Reading a bill for amendment is referred to as the *second reading*.

When the first section of a measure is read, or *designated*, amendments recommended by the committee reporting the bill, called *committee amendments*, are first considered without being offered from the floor. A special rule often provides that committee amendments become part of the text of the measure for further amendment. (The text for purposes of debate or amendment is sometimes referred to as the *base text*.)

After committee amendments become part of the base text, individual members are then recognized to offer individual amendments. Priority recognition is given to members of the committee of jurisdiction, by seniority on the committee, with recognition usually alternating between the parties.

Amendments are debated under the *five-minute rule*, with the proponent and an opponent speaking first for up to five minutes each. Members may then make a motion to "strike the last word" or "strike the requisite number of words," that is, offer a pro forma amendment to gain five minutes to speak on an amendment. At the end of five minutes, the pro forma amendment is considered withdrawn. Time under the five-minute rule cannot be reserved, and a member may not speak more than once on an amendment. (See § 8.121, *Amendment Process Glossary*.)

If the special rule does not provide a cap on time for debating amendments, debate can be limited or ended by unanimous consent or by a motion to end or limit debate. (The previous question is not in order in the Committee of the Whole.) Such a motion may limit debate on a specific amendment, a section, or the entire measure. The motion can specify a specific time or a specific duration of minutes or hours for the consideration of amendments to continue. The motion may also designate how the remaining time is to be divided.

Amendment Tree

An amendment to the base text is called a *first-degree amendment*. Such an amendment can be further amended by either a *substitute amendment* (which is also a first-degree amendment) or a *perfecting amendment*—a second-degree amendment. The substitute is also subject to a perfecting amendment. These four amendments constitute what is referred to as the *amendment tree*. Once an amendment to a measure is pending, either a perfecting amendment or a substitute amendment can be offered first. (See § 8.122, *Basic House Amendment Tree*.)

If all four of these amendments are pending, the order of voting is as follows:
1. the perfecting amendment to the amendment to the bill (a second-degree amendment)
2. the perfecting amendment to the substitute (a second-degree amendment)
3. the substitute (considered a first-degree amendment)
4. the base amendment to the text

§ 8.121

Amendment Process Glossary

Amendment: Proposal of a member of Congress to alter the text of a measure.

Amendment in the Nature of a Substitute: Amendment that seeks to replace the entire text of the underlying measure. The adoption of such an amendment usually precludes any further amendment to that measure.

Amendment Tree: Diagram showing the number and types of amendments to a measure permitted by the chamber. It also shows the relationship among the amendments, their degree or type, the order in which they may be offered, and the order in which they are voted on.

"Bigger Bite" Amendment: Amendment that, although it amends previously amended language (not allowed under the rules), can be offered because it changes more of the measure than the original amendment.

Degrees of Amendment: Designation that indicates the relationship of an amendment to the text of a measure and of one amendment to another. Amendments are permitted only in two degrees.

En Bloc Amendment: Several amendments offered as a group, after obtaining unanimous consent.

First-Degree Amendment: Amendment offered to the text of a measure or a substitute offered to a first-degree amendment.

Five-Minute Rule: House rule that limits debate on an amendment offered in the Committee of the Whole to five minutes for its sponsor and five minutes for an opponent. In practice, the Committee of the Whole permits the offering of pro forma amendments, each debatable for five minutes.

Germaneness: Rule in the House requiring that debate and amendments pertain to the same subject as the bill or amendment under consideration. In the Senate, germaneness is not generally required.

Insert: Amendment to add new language to a measure or another amendment.

Perfecting Amendment: Amendment that alters—but does not substitute or replace—language in another amendment.

Point of Order: Objection to the current proceeding, measure, or amendment because the proposed action violates a rule of the chamber, written precedent, or rule-making statute.

Pro Forma Amendment: Motion whereby a House member secures five minutes to speak on an amendment under debate, without offering a substantive amendment. The member moves to "strike the last word" or "strike the requisite number of words." The motion requires no vote and is deemed automatically withdrawn at the expiration of the five minutes.

Second-Degree Amendment: Amendment to an amendment. It is also called a perfecting amendment.

Continued on page 294

8

§ 8.121 *(continued)*

Strike: Amendment to delete a portion of a measure or an amendment.

Strike and Insert: Amendment that replaces the text of a measure or an amendment.

Strike the Last Word/Strike the Requisite Number of Words: Also called a pro forma amendment. Means of obtaining time to speak on an amendment without offering a substantive change.

Substitute Amendment: Amendment that replaces the entire text of a pending amendment.

Unprinted Amendment: Senate amendment not printed in the *Congressional Record* before its offering. Unprinted amendments are numbered sequentially in the order of their submission during a Congress.

A larger glossary is located at the back of the book.

When an amendment has been disposed of, a branch of the amendment tree is open. An additional amendment may then be offered, provided that the new amendment does not propose to change what has already been amended. *(See § 8.123, Keeping Up with the House Floor: Scheduling and Proceedings.)*

Restrictions on Amendments

In general, an amendment must be in writing at the time it is offered. The amendment must be a first- or second-degree amendment. It is not in order to reoffer an identical amendment to an amendment that has already been acted upon.

An amendment may not amend text that has already been amended. In some circumstances, however, a bigger bite can be taken from the measure or amendment. A *bigger-bite amendment* substantively changes the unamended parts of the provision in which the previously amended language appears and is in order.

An amendment must be offered in a timely fashion—only at the time the Committee of the Whole is considering the section or title the amendment seeks to change. An amendment may not affect different parts of a bill unless unanimous consent is granted to offer the amendment *en bloc*.

Germaneness. In addition to the restrictions previously described, an amendment must be germane, or relevant, to the text it would amend. House Rule XVI, clause 7 is one of the most discussed rules of the House. Three tests of germaneness are noted in the rule. First, the amendment must relate to the subject matter under consideration. Second, the fundamental purpose of the amendment must be germane to the fundamental purpose of the bill or amendment. Third, the amendment should be within the jurisdiction of the committee reporting the

§ 8.122

Basic House Amendment Tree

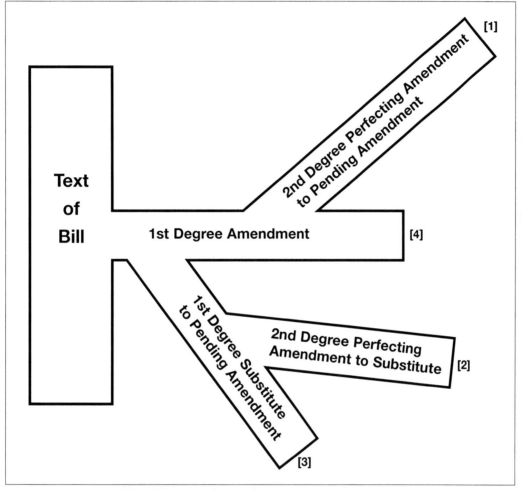

Text
of
Bill

1st Degree Amendment [4]

2nd Degree Perfecting Amendment to Pending Amendment [1]

2nd Degree Perfecting Amendment to Substitute [2]

1st Degree Substitute to Pending Amendment [3]

[Note: Bracketed numbers indicate voting order.]

bill. Hence, subject matter, fundamental purpose, and committee jurisdiction represent key tests of germaneness.

Beyond these tests, several principles also relate to germaneness. First, an individual proposition cannot be amended by another individual proposition. Second, a specific subject may not be amended by a general subject. Third, a general subject may be amended by a specific subject. These principles are difficult to interpret, and the Speaker or chair of the Committee of the Whole seeks the advice of the House parliamentarian if a ruling is required. If a point of order is raised that an amendment is not germane, and the point of order is sustained, the amendment cannot be considered. On the other hand, if the question of germaneness is

Keeping Up with the House Floor: Scheduling and Proceedings

See Chapters Eleven, Twelve, and Thirteen for descriptions of these and other sources.

Sources	Anticipating Scheduling		During/After Proceedings	
	Status	Substance	Status	Substance
Congressional Sources				
Congressional Record (for leadership announcement of legislative program; printed amendments; special rules; and House proceedings)	x	x	x	x
Reporting committee's, Rules Committee's and leadership web sites available through the House site, *<www.house.gov>*	x	x	x	x
Rules Committee announcement of deadline for providing it with proposed floor amendments, before reporting a special rule	x			
Rules Committee "special rule," for major legislation (Text different from that reported by committee *may* be made in order by special rule.)		x		
Amendments printed in Rules Committee's report on special rule or, if made in order by special rule, printed in *Congressional Record* or announced by members		x		
"Whip notices" from party leadership	x		x	
Committee report and text of legislation as reported		x		x
Text of legislation as passed ("engrossed measure")				x
Legislative Information System (Congress only)	x	x	x	x
THOMAS *<http://thomas.loc.gov>*	x	x	x	x
Non-Congressional Sources				
C-SPAN *<www.cspan.org>*			x	x
CQ Today *<www.cq.com>*	x	x	x	x
CQ.com *<www.cq.com>*	x	x	x	x
CQ Weekly (for major legislation) *<www.cq.com>*	x	x	x	x
CongressDaily, from *National Journal* *<http://nationaljournal.com>*	x	x	x	x
National Journal (for major legislation) *<http://nationaljournal.com>*		x		x
Trade press and daily newspapers	x	x	x	x
Relevant interest-group web sites	x	x	x	x
Other commercial database services	x	x	x	x
People *(Use these contacts after exhausting other resources.)*				
Reporting committee professional staff and leadership staff (When is floor action anticipated? What amendments, if any, are expected? What debate is anticipated? After the measure's passage, what is anticipated in dealing with the Senate?)	x	x	x	x
Chamber leaders, committee members, and interested members (What amendments or debate is anticipated? What happens next?)		x		x
Committee and interested members' press assistants (What press releases and other press documents are available?)		x		x

not raised, or if a special rule waives the point of order, it is possible for a nongermane but popular amendment to be agreed upon.

Over 2,000 pages of precedents in *Hinds and Cannon, Deschler's Precedents,* and the parliamentarian's annotations in the House *Rules Manual* address germaneness.

Ending the Amendment Process

In the Committee of the Whole, a member can move to *close debate* (end debate) on a pending amendment or to *limit debate* at a specified time. (After the last section of the bill has been read in the House sitting as the House, a member can move the previous question. This motion is not in order in the Committee of the Whole.) Unlike the previous question, closing or limiting debate does not preclude offering additional amendments. It means that all subsequent amendments are decided without debate.

At the conclusion of the amendment process, a member moves that the *committee rise and report*. The motion to rise and report in effect takes a measure from the Committee of the Whole back to the House for final disposition. A *motion to rise*, on the other hand, reports a measure back to the House temporarily. The adoption of a motion to rise indicates that the Committee of the Whole may reconvene at a later time to continue work on a measure.

Separate Vote on Amendments

Once the Committee of the Whole has risen and the House is again sitting as the House, any member may demand a separate vote on any amendment to the text of the measure under consideration agreed to in the Committee of the Whole.

§ 8.130 House Floor: Voting
Voting in the House

There are four types of votes: voice, division, yea and nay, and record votes. *Voice vote* means that members call out "yea" or "nay" when a question is put in the House. The Speaker determines the outcome of the vote by the volume of each response. On occasion, the Speaker can say "without objection," a variation on a voice vote meaning the question is adopted.

A *division vote* can be demanded by any member after a voice vote is taken. First the members in favor stand and are counted; then, those opposed stand and are counted. A division vote shows only vote totals and does not provide a record of how individual members voted. In recent times, there have been only a few division votes on the floor each year.

Under an automatic *yea and nay vote*, a member may "object on the ground that a quorum is not present and make a point of order that a quorum is not present." The actual vote then determines both the presence of a quorum and the outcome of the pending question.

A *record vote* is taken if one-fifth of a quorum, forty-four members, stand and support the request. Like a yea and nay vote, a record vote is taken by the electronic voting system. *(See § 8.131, House Voting Glossary.)*

House Voting Glossary

Agreed To: Usual parliamentary term for approval of motions, amendments, and simple and concurrent resolutions.

Cluster Voting: Allowance for sequential recorded votes on a series of measures or amendments that the House finished debating at an earlier time or on a previous date. The Speaker can reduce the minimum time for the second and subsequent votes in the series to five minutes each.

Division Vote: A vote in which a committee chair or the House presiding officer counts those in favor and those in opposition, with no record made of how each member votes. The chair or presiding officer can either ask for a show of hands or ask members to stand.

Electronic Vote: A vote in the House using the electronic voting machine. Members insert voting cards into one of the boxes located throughout the House chamber.

Proxy Vote: The committee practice of permitting a member to cast the vote of an absent colleague. Proxy voting is not permitted in House committees.

Quorum Call: A procedure for determining whether a quorum is present—218 in the House and 100 in the Committee of the Whole House on the State of the Union.

Roll-call (Record) Vote: A vote in which members are recorded by name for or against a measure.

Second: The number of members required to indicate support for an action, such as calling for a vote.

Teller Vote: A House procedure in which members cast votes by passing through the center aisle of the chamber to be counted; now used only when the electronic voting system breaks down.

Voice Vote: A method of voting where members who support a question call out "aye" in unison, after which those opposed answer "no" in unison. The chair decides which position prevails.

Yea and Nay: A vote in which members respond "aye" or "no" on a question when their names are called in alphabetical order.

A larger glossary is located at the back of the book.

Voting in the Committee of the Whole

Both voice votes and division votes are taken in the Committee of the Whole. To obtain a record vote, twenty-five members must support a member's request for a record vote. If fewer than one hundred members are present, which is the minimum number required for a quorum in the Committee of the Whole, a member may demand a record vote, and pending that make a point of order that a quorum is not present. The record vote would then be automatic.

Time for Voting

The minimum time for a record vote or quorum call is fifteen minutes in both the House and the Committee of the Whole. The Speaker has the authority to postpone and cluster certain votes and to reduce to five minutes votes after an initial fifteen-minute vote. The chair of the Committee of the Whole is usually granted the same authority in a special rule.

§ 8.140 House Floor: Motion to Recommit and Final Passage

After the third reading of a bill, but before the vote on final passage, a *motion to recommit* is in order. (The third reading is the required reading to a chamber of a measure by title only before the vote on passage.) The motion is traditionally the prerogative of a minority member to offer, providing the minority with one last opportunity to kill or amend a measure.

A member stands and says, "Mr. Speaker, I have a motion to recommit at the desk." The Speaker then asks if the member is opposed to the measure. That member signifies that he or she is opposed to the measure "in its current form."

There are two types of motions to recommit. Adoption of a motion to recommit *without instructions* kills a measure. If such a motion is offered, it is not debatable.

A motion to recommit *with instructions* attempts to amend a measure. The motion normally instructs that the measure be referred to the reporting committee and that the committee "report the bill back to the House forthwith with the following amendment. . . ." A motion to recommit with instructions is debatable for ten minutes, equally divided between the proponent and an opponent. The time is not controlled, meaning members may not yield or reserve time. At the request of the majority floor manager, the ten minutes can be extended to one hour, equally divided and controlled. If a motion to recommit with instructions is agreed to, the measure is immediately reported back to the House with the amendment, the amendment is voted on, and the House then votes on final passage of the bill.

The vote on final passage is then taken. (*See § 11.40, Versions of Legislation.*) When the results of the vote on final passage are announced, a pro forma *motion to reconsider* is made and *laid on the table*, that is, postponed indefinitely. There is rarely a vote on these motions. To table the motion to reconsider prevents a measure from being reconsidered at a later date. (*See § 8.141, Approval Terminology.*)

---

§ 8.141

Approval Terminology

Term	Used For
Adopted	Conference Reports
Agreed To	Amendments Simple Resolutions Concurrent Resolutions
Concur	Amendment of Other Chamber
Ordered	Engrossment Previous Question Third Reading Yeas and Nays
Passed	Bills Joint Resolutions
Sustained	Points of Order Rulings of Chair

8

§ 8.151

Comparison of Selected House and Senate Procedures

House	Senate
Four calendars (Union, House, Private, and Discharge)	Two calendars (Legislative and Executive)
Scheduling by Speaker and majority-party leadership, with limited consultation among members	Scheduling by majority-party leadership, with broad consultation among all senators
Role of Rules Committee and special rules to govern floor consideration	Unanimous consent and complex unanimous consent time agreements to govern floor consideration
Presiding officer has considerable discretion in recognition; rulings rarely challenged	Presiding officer has little discretion in recognition; rulings frequently challenged
Debate always restricted	Debate rarely restricted
Debate-ending motions by majority vote (218 representatives)	Cloture invoked by three-fifths vote (60 senators)
Germaneness of amendments generally required	Germaneness of amendments rarely required
Quorum calls permitted in connection with record votes	Quorum calls permitted almost any time and used for constructive delay
Adjourns at end of day	Recesses at end of many days

§ 8.150 House and Senate Compared

The Senate has an extensive framework of parliamentary procedure to guide its actions. Nevertheless, in practice, its procedures are more flexible than those of the House. While the House emphasizes its procedures, the Senate functions in a more ad hoc manner, adapting its procedures to accommodate individual senators. For example, scheduling and consideration of legislation can be accomplished in almost any manner the party leaders and individual senators can devise. *(See § 8.151, Comparison of Selected House and Senate Procedures.)*

§ 8.160 Senate Scheduling

The Senate sets its floor agenda to accommodate individual senators and to prepare for almost any contingency. Because of the privileges accorded individual senators, the Senate can rarely rely on its rules or customs to set the order of business. Because the rules have different influences at certain times, no Senate session day is truly typical. Scheduling the consideration of a measure can be accomplished in almost any manner the party leaders can arrange. Because the majority leader has priority recognition on the floor, it is that person's job to arrange the schedule.

Some measures can be raised for consideration, or even passage without debate, by *unan-*

Keeping Up with the Senate Floor: Scheduling and Proceedings

See Chapters Eleven, Twelve, and Thirteen for descriptions of these and other sources.

Sources	Anticipating Scheduling		During/After Proceedings	
	Status	Substance	Status	Substance
Congressional Sources				
Congressional Record (for leadership announcement of legislative program; printed amendments; time agreements; and Senate proceedings)	x	x	x	x
Reporting committee's and leadership web sites available through the Senate site, <*www.senate.gov*>	x	x	x	x
Amendments printed in the *Congressional Record,* announced by members or made in order by unanimous consent agreement(s)		x		
Time agreements (A text different from that reported by a committee *may* be made in order by the time agreement.)		x		
"Whip notices" from party leadership	x		x	
Text of legislation as originated in committee or reported by committee; possibly a House measure reported from a Senate committee or placed directly on the Senate Calendar		x		x
Committee report, if there is one		x		x
Text of legislation as passed ("engrossed measure")				x
Legislative Information System (Congress only)	x	x	x	x
THOMAS <*http://thomas.loc.gov*>	x	x	x	x
Non-Congressional Sources				
C-SPAN <*www.cspan.org*>			x	x
CQ Today <*www.cq.com*>	x	x	x	x
CQ.com <*www.cq.com*>	x	x	x	x
CQ Weekly (for major legislation) <*www.cq.com*>	x	x	x	x
CongressDaily, from *National Journal* <*http://nationaljournal.com*>	x	x	x	x
National Journal (for major legislation) <*http://nationaljournal.com*>		x		x
Trade press and daily newspapers	x	x	x	x
Relevant interest-group web sites	x	x	x	x
Other commercial database services	x	x	x	x
People *(Use these contacts after exhausting other resources.)*				
Senators' and reporting committee professional staff, and leadership staff (When is floor action anticipated? What amendments, if any, are expected? What is the status of holds or requests for consultation? After passage, what is anticipated in dealing with the House?)	x	x	x	x
Chamber and committee leaders, and interested members (What debate is anticipated? What happens next?)		x		x
Committee and interested members' press assistants (What press releases and other press documents are available?)		x		x

8

imous consent. However, a single objection can derail a unanimous consent request. Accordingly, the majority leader checks with all interested senators before bringing legislation to the floor by unanimous consent. Other measures are scheduled for consideration pursuant to a *unanimous consent time agreement.* A time agreement is negotiated among interested parties to avoid an objection to the unanimous consent request. Still other measures are brought up by a *motion to proceed to consider.* However, a motion to proceed in most instances is debatable. (*See § 8.161, Keeping Up with the Senate Floor: Scheduling and Proceedings.*)

§ 8.170 Legislative and Calendar Days; Morning Hour and Morning Business

How the Senate begins its session depends on how it ended its business the previous day.

Legislative and Calendar Days

A calendar day is recognized as each twenty-four-hour period. A *legislative day* begins when the Senate next meets after adjourning, rather than recessing, the previous daily session. Indeed, a legislative day can stretch over several calendar days or even weeks.

This practice enables the Senate to maintain flexibility. Because procedures are so strictly determined when a new legislative day is created, the Senate often recesses rather than adjourns at the end of the previous day's session. Recessing does not create a new legislative day. A legislative day continues until the Senate adjourns at the end of a daily session.

At the beginning of each day, whether a calendar day or legislative day, a period of *leader time* is set aside. During this time, the majority and minority leaders can be recognized by the presiding officer for ten minutes each to speak on whatever subjects they choose. They often discuss the legislative schedule for the day and the next several days.

Morning Hour and Morning Business

If it is a new legislative day, the Senate proceeds to *morning hour*, which constitutes the first two hours of a legislative day. Based on traditional Senate schedules, morning hour usually extends from 12:00 noon to 2:00 p.m. Within the morning hour, the Senate entertains *morning business.* The first hour is reserved for individual senators to deliver *morning hour speeches* on any subject. Each speech is usually limited to five minutes. By unanimous consent, morning business can be conducted throughout the day, and usually is.

After the completion of morning business, or at the end of the first hour, the other morning hour business occurs. It consists of messages from the president, messages from the House of Representatives, the presentation of petitions and memorials, reports of committees, and the introduction of bills and resolutions.

Because the Senate may remain in the same legislative day for several days, a morning business period is held almost every calendar day.

§8.180 Senate Calendars and Legislative and Executive Business before the Senate

The Senate has two calendars. The *Calendar of Business* contains all legislation, both bills and resolutions. The *Executive Calendar* is reserved for executive business, that is, business requiring the Senate to advise and consent on treaties and nominations. Both calendars are published every day the Senate is in session.

Calendar of Business

The *Calendar of Business* contains a list called "General Orders, under Rule VIII," which details all measures that committees have reported and any bills or joint resolutions that have been placed directly on the calendar without first being referred to committee. The order number reflects the chronological order in which a measure was placed on the calendar. Noted on the general order list are the following items:

- the measure's number
- the measure's sponsor
- the measure's title
- date the measure was placed on the calendar
- whether the measure was placed directly on the calendar without being referred to committee
- whether the measure is an original bill
- whether the measure was reported with or without amendment
- whether there is an accompanying report
- whether the report contains minority or additional views

Also included in the Calendar of Business are the following:

- a calendar that shows the days on which the Senate was in session and the anticipated recesses and nonlegislative periods
- a list of senators and the year in which each senator's term expires
- membership lists of Senate committees and Senate membership on joint committees
- a list of bills sent to conference, the names of House and Senate conferees on each bill, and the date either chamber acted on a conference report

The Calendar of Business also contains the text of unanimous consent time agreements and a list of "resolutions and motions over, under the rule." This is a list of simple and concurrent resolutions that have been placed directly on the calendar without first being referred to committee.

The back cover of the calendar shows the history of legislative action on appropriations bills during the current session of Congress.

Executive Calendar

The Executive Calendar has five sections:

- texts of any unanimous consent agreements, which have not been fully implemented, concerning executive business
- Senate executive resolutions that concern executive business (it is rare for there to be any resolutions listed)
- treaties that have been reported from committee, including each treaty's calendar number, document number, and subject, as well as information on how it was reported from the Foreign Relations Committee
- nominations that have been reported from committee, including each nomination's calendar number, the number of the presidential message transmitting the nomination, the name of the nominee and the office for which he or she has been nominated, and information on how the nomination was reported (a nomination listed for the first time appears under a heading of "new reports")
- routine nominations, such as those in the armed services and the Public Health Service

(For additional information on the calendars, see § 12.20, Floor Documents.)

§ 8.190 Holds, Clearance, and Unanimous Consent

By custom, the majority leader of the Senate, or that person's designee, has the right to set the agenda on the floor. The majority leader decides the order in which bills on the calendar should come to the floor for action, and negotiates with other senators to agree to take up measures the majority leader wishes to consider.

Custom, however, also allows a senator to place a *hold* on the consideration of any legislative or executive business. A hold is a notice that a senator intends to object to any unanimous consent request made on the floor to bring up a matter for consideration by the Senate. Current policy regarding holds, which has not been consistently followed, dictates that a senator placing a hold should notify the sponsor of the legislation (if legislation is the object of the hold) and the committee of jurisdiction that he or she is concerned about the measure. A written notice should also be provided to the senator's respective party leader and placed in the *Congressional Record*. Before the 106th Congress, holds could be placed anonymously.

In addition, to learn whether there may be objection to bringing up a measure or executive matter if no hold has been placed, or to identify controversy associated with a measure, the party leadership attempts to obtain *clearance* to have a measure considered. To obtain clearance, the party leaders ask individual senators to file *requests to be consulted* with the party leaders. A request signifies that a senator wants to participate in any negotiations regarding when and how a measure or executive matter might be considered on the Senate floor. Further, quorum calls conducted throughout the day—a form of constructive delay—

allow the leadership time to conduct negotiations. A hotline telephone, provided to all Senate offices, is often used to obtain clearance. Once all requests have been considered and addressed, the majority leader may choose to call up a measure or executive matter on the floor.

Through these negotiations, the majority leader can determine how best to bring a measure or executive matter to the floor. For most noncontroversial items, the majority leader, or that person's designee, asks "unanimous consent to proceed to the consideration" of a measure or executive matter. By bringing a measure or executive matter to the floor by *unanimous consent*, debate and amendment options are usually unlimited, although a further unanimous consent request could be made to set debate and amendment limitations. A *complex unanimous consent agreement*, also called a *time agreement*, generally limits debate and amendments.

Finally, there is also a class of routine unanimous consent requests that allows senators to obtain floor privileges for selected staff and to "proceed as if in morning business" throughout the day. *(See § 8.191, Who Is Allowed on the Senate Floor?)* Unanimous consent is also obtained to allow the Senate to go into *executive session* to consider business on the Executive Calendar.

§ 8.191

Who Is Allowed on the Senate Floor?

In addition to senators, a variety of staff have permanent or temporary privileges to be on the floor of the Senate.

At the desk immediately in front of the presiding officer are seated the parliamentarian, legislative clerk, journal clerk, and, often, the executive clerk and bill clerk. Reporters of debates sit at a table below the rostrum. Seats near the rostrum are reserved for the secretary and assistant secretary of the Senate and the sergeant at arms. Majority- and minority-party secretaries and other staff members who have floor privileges may be seen on the floor. Pages sit on either side of the presiding officer's desk. Staff members of individual senators are allowed on the floor by unanimous consent.

(See § 14.21, Senate Floor Plan.)

§ 8.200 Time Agreements and Motions to Proceed on the Senate Floor

There are three typical ways to bring a measure to the Senate floor for consideration. *Unanimous consent*, often referred to as a *simple unanimous consent agreement*, implies agreement among all senators, as a single objection can stop its implementation. A *complex unanimous consent agreement*, referred to as a time agreement, and a *motion to proceed to consideration*, called a motion to proceed, are the other options available to the majority leader to bring up a measure for consideration.

Time Agreements

The Senate conducts much of its work by agreeing to unanimous consent requests. *Simple unanimous consent requests* cover noncontroversial and routine matters. Complex unanimous

§ 8.201

Example of a Senate Unanimous Consent Time Agreement

S. 343 (ORDER NO. 118)

2. – *Ordered,* That prior to the Senate recessing for Independence Day, debate only be in order on S. 343, with the exception of the withdrawal of the committee amendments, and the offering of a substitute amendment by the Majority Leader.

Ordered further, That at 1:00 p.m. on Monday, July 10, 1995, the Senate resume consideration of S. 343, the Regulatory Reform bill, and that the Senator from Michigan (Mr. Abraham) be recognized to offer an amendment to the Dole substitute relative to small business; that no second degree amendments be in order; and that a vote occur on, or in relation to, the Abraham amendment at 5:00 p.m., Monday, July 10, 1995.

Ordered further, That at 3:00 p.m. on Monday, July 10, 1995, the Abraham amendment be laid aside, and the Senator from Georgia (Mr. Nunn) be recognized to offer a Nunn/Coverdell amendment, relative to the Regulatory Flexibility Act; that no second degree amendments be in order; and that a vote occur on, or in relation to, the Nunn/Coverdell amendment immediately following the vote on the Abraham amendment. (June 28, 1995.) (June 29, 1995.)

S. 343 (ORDER NO. 118)

2. – *Ordered,* That during the pendency of S. 343, a bill to reform the regulatory process, and for other purposes, no amendments regarding the USDA's HACCP rule, proposed on February 3, 1995, be in order. (July 12, 1995.)

Ordered further, That during the pendency of S. 343, no amendments regarding mammography be in order. (July 13, 1995.)

consent requests, often called *time agreements*, establish another procedure under which measures are considered on the floor. Without a time agreement, a measure could be debated for as long as senators spoke on the floor, and amendments, whether germane or not, could be offered without restriction. Time agreements are intended to expedite consideration and establish predictability by imposing restrictions on the time available and limiting the amendments that could be offered. *(See § 8.201, Example of a Senate Unanimous Consent Time Agreement.)*

After consultation and negotiation with other senators, which can take days or weeks or months on highly contentious matters, the majority leader obtains a time agreement that satisfies all concerned senators and that meets the policy objectives of the majority party. The majority leader then asks on the Senate floor that a measure be considered "under the following time agreement."

A time agreement can cover consideration of an entire measure or consideration for just

---

§ 8.202

Comparing a House Special Rule and a Senate Time Agreement

House Special Rule	Senate Time Agreement
Called up as a simple resolution	Called up by unanimous consent
Requires majority vote for passage	Agreed to by unanimous consent
Specifies time for general debate	Specifies time for debating amendments
Permits or prohibits amendments	Generally restricts only the offering of nongermane amendments
Does not specify date for vote on passage of measure	Generally sets date for vote on final passage
Effect is often to waive House rules	Effect is often to waive Senate rules

---

one day. It can cover time allocation for all amendments or debate on a particular amendment. It can limit debate on the measure itself or on part of the measure. A time agreement can limit senators to offering only germane amendments, or it can contain a negotiated list of nongermane amendments. It can also restrict the offering of amendments to pending amendments. (*See § 8.202, Comparing a House Special Rule and a Senate Time Agreement.*)

The Senate often begins consideration of a measure by unanimous consent without a time agreement but then adopts piecemeal agreements. A time agreement can be changed by agreeing to a subsequent unanimous consent agreement.

Time agreements are printed in the *Congressional Record* and the daily Calendar of Business.

Motions to Proceed

Because of the difficulty of negotiating a time agreement, which can be stopped by a single objection, any senator as an alternative can attempt to call up a measure by making a "motion to proceed to consideration," usually referred to as a *motion to proceed*. Although any senator may offer a motion to proceed, by custom the Senate reserves the right to the majority leader or that person's designee. A motion to proceed is generally debatable, and there is no limit on the duration of the debate under Senate rules. Debate on the motion to proceed can be ended by unanimous consent or by invoking cloture. (*See § 8.230, Cloture in Senate Floor Proceedings.*) A motion to proceed, however, needs only a majority vote for passage. (The motion to proceed is not debatable under certain circumstances, such as during a new legislative day.)

§ 8.211

Longest Senate Filibusters

- Strom Thurmond, 1957
  24 hours, 18 minutes on civil rights bill

- Wayne Morse, 1953
  22 hours, 26 minutes on Tidelands oil bill

- William Proxmire, 1961
  19 hours, 6 minutes (held floor for 25 hours, 36 minutes, but yielded for 6 hours and 30 minutes to other senators to debate foreign aid bills) on confirmation of Lawrence O'Connor for post at Federal Power Commission

- Robert LaFollette, Sr., 1908
  18 hours, 23 minutes on Aldrich-Vreeland currency bill

- William Proxmire, 1981
  16 hours, 12 minutes on bill raising public debt limit

- Huey Long, 1935
  15 hours, 30 minutes on extension of National Industrial Recovery Act

- Alfonse D'Amato, 1992
  15 hours, 14 minutes on tax bill

- Robert C. Byrd, 1964
  14 hours, 13 minutes on civil rights bill

§ 8.210 Consideration and Debate on the Senate Floor
Presiding Officer and Recognition to Speak

The presiding officer of the Senate is the vice president of the United States. However, the vice president rarely presides over daily sessions of the Senate. He presides only when a close vote is anticipated and when his vote may be needed to break a tie vote, the only occasion under the Constitution when he is allowed to cast a vote in the Senate.

The president pro tempore, the most senior majority-party senator, generally opens a day's session. Yet, the president pro tempore does not preside throughout the day. The president pro tempore designates other majority-party senators to preside, usually in one-hour or two-hour blocks of time. Junior majority-party senators preside often early in their careers, providing them opportunities to learn Senate procedures. In fact, a *golden gavel award* is granted to the first senator in each Congress to preside for one hundred hours.

The main authority of the presiding officer is to recognize members to speak. Priority recognition is almost always granted to the majority and minority leaders if they are seeking recognition, and then to the floor managers of pending legislation. In the absence of any of these senators, the presiding officer must recognize the first senator on his or her feet seeking recognition. The presiding officer is addressed as "Mr. (Madam) President."

Filibusters

When a senator is recognized to speak on a pending measure, few limitations are placed on him or her. Debate is generally unlimited on all pending measures. A senator may yield to another senator for a question, but the senator still controls the floor. One of the most visible of Senate characteristics is the right of an individual senator to maintain the floor, that is, to speak for an extended period of time. Continuing, extended debate is referred to as a *filibuster*. The image of James Stewart in the film, *Mr. Smith Goes to Washington*, presents an exaggerated picture of one senator tying up the work of the Senate. *(See § 8.211, Longest Senate Filibusters.)*

A contemporary approach to filibusters is the so-called "tag-team filibuster." A senator speaks for a period and then yields to another senator. When several senators participate in extended debate, it takes some time for the Senate to realize a filibuster is being conducted. Therefore, even the threat of a filibuster carries weight as the Senate attempts to schedule and consider legislation.

Debate is limited only when the Senate:

1. invokes cloture *(see § 8.230, Cloture in Senate Floor Proceedings)*,
2. limits debate by unanimous consent or operates under a unanimous consent time agreement,
3. considers a motion to table, or
4. considers a measure governed by a rule-making statute. (Examples of rule-making statutes with built-in debate limitations include the Congressional Budget Act of 1974, and the 1974 Trade Act, which allows so-called *fast-track* procedures.)

Senate rules prohibit a senator from speaking more than twice on the same subject on the same legislative day. Because each amendment is considered a different subject, the so-called two-speech rule is not a practical limit on debate.

§ 8.220 Senate Amendment Procedure

Amendments to a measure in the Senate can be offered at practically any time during consideration of the measure, can be debated for an unlimited amount of time, and, in most situations, can deal with any subject, even if it is unrelated to the measure being amended.

When a measure is being considered on the floor of the Senate, committee amendments are considered first. The Senate often agrees by unanimous consent to committee amendments as a package, called *en bloc amendments*. By unanimous consent, the Senate might then provide that the measure, as amended by the committee amendments, be "considered as an original bill for the purpose of further amendment." This facilitates further amending on the floor by not taking up a branch on the *amendment tree. (See one amendment tree in § 8.122, Basic House Amendment Tree.)*

Amendments can be either printed or unprinted. *Printed amendments* are provided in advance of floor consideration of a measure and are printed in the *Congressional Record*. Although a sponsor usually calls up his or her own amendment, any senator can call up a printed amendment. *Unprinted amendments* are not available in advance and may be drafted on the floor while a measure is being considered.

Senate amendments do not usually need to be *germane*, that is, relevant to the measure. Nongermane amendments are often referred to as *riders*. Measures that contain numerous nongermane amendments have been called *Christmas-tree bills*. Germaneness, however, is necessary for general appropriations bills, bills on which cloture has been invoked, concurrent budget resolutions, and measures regulated by unanimous consent time agreements.

8

An amendment can also be classified as either *first degree* or *second degree*. A first-degree amendment would change the text of the measure under consideration; a second-degree amendment proposes to change the text of the first-degree amendment.

Both *perfecting amendments* and *substitute amendments* can be offered. Perfecting amendments change or modify language. Substitute amendments add new language as an alternative to the existing text. Perfecting amendments are considered second-degree amendments, and are always voted on before substitute amendments.

Separate *amendment trees* are possible based on the effect of the initial amendment offered. One tree is designed for *motions to strike and insert*, another for *insert*, and a third to *strike*. This complexity is rare in the Senate. Unanimous consent is more likely to be reached so that one amendment can be temporarily set aside to consider a different amendment.

A *motion to table* is frequently offered to avoid voting directly on an amendment. To "table" means to kill a provision. Any senator can make a nondebatable motion to table. Often, a senator announces that he or she intends to offer a motion to table an amendment but does not do so until debate has occurred on the amendment. By agreeing to a motion to table, the Senate does not vote directly on an amendment, and thereby avoids having to vote against it.

§ 8.230 Cloture in Senate Floor Proceedings

A filibuster can be ended by negotiation among senators or by *invoking cloture*. Cloture is the only procedure by which the Senate can vote to set an end to debate without also rejecting the measure under consideration.

Invoking Cloture

Senate Rule XXII describes several stages to invoke cloture. To begin the process, at least sixteen senators sign a *cloture motion*, often referred to as a *cloture petition*. The motion is presented on the Senate floor, where the clerk reads it. The motion needs to "mature" or "ripen" before it can be considered. To do this, it lies over until the second calendar day on which the Senate is in session. For example, if a petition is filed on Monday, it ripens on Wednesday.

On the day the motion is ready for consideration, Senate rules require a vote on cloture one hour after the Senate convenes and after a quorum call establishes the presence of a quorum. However, the Senate can waive the quorum call or change the time by unanimous consent, and often does so. When the vote occurs, it generally requires three-fifths of the senators chosen and sworn; that is, sixty votes if there are no vacancies. (However, to invoke cloture on a motion to amend Senate rules, a two-thirds vote, or sixty-seven senators, is required.)

There are no limits to the number of cloture petitions that can be filed on any measure or amendment. Often, senators file petitions every day so that a vote occurs almost daily with the expectation that cloture will eventually be invoked. (*See § 8.231, Steps to Invoke Cloture.*)

§8.231

Steps to Invoke Cloture

- Must be filed on a pending question
- At least sixteen senators must sign a cloture motion (also called "cloture petition")
- Amendments must be filed before the vote
- Vote on a motion occurs two days of session later
- Live quorum call precedes the vote and occurs one hour after the Senate convenes
- Vote immediately follows the quorum call
- Roll-call vote is automatic
- Affirmative vote by three-fifths of the senators chosen and sworn is required, except on a rules change, which requires two-thirds of the senators present

§8.232

Senate Procedures under Cloture

- Thirty-hour cap on post-cloture consideration
- One hour maximum for debate for each senator
- Amendments must have been submitted before the vote on the cloture motion
- Presiding officer may count for a quorum rather than conduct a quorum call
- No nongermane amendments
- No dilatory motions
- Points of order and appeals not debatable

8

Limitations Following Cloture

If cloture is invoked, certain limitations on how the Senate considers a measure are put into place. Generally, this period, often referred to as *post-cloture consideration*, operates under procedures different from normal Senate process. (*See* § 8.232, *Senate Procedures under Cloture.*)

Time Cap. The most important effect of invoking cloture is the cap of thirty hours of time for the Senate to continue consideration of a measure. The filibuster—one senator's or a group of senators' unfettered control of the floor—is over. Time for recorded votes, quorum calls, and points of order count in the cap, as does all debate time. Within the cap, each senator is guaranteed at least ten minutes to speak. No senator can speak for more than one hour, although time can be yielded to other senators.

Amendments. Once cloture is invoked, all amendments to be considered must have been submitted in writing during the time the Senate was in session before invoking cloture. First-degree amendments must be filed by 1:00 p.m. on the day the cloture motion is filed, and second-degree amendments must be filed at least one hour before a cloture vote begins. In addition, unlike normal amendment procedures, no amendment is in order unless it is germane to the matter on which cloture was invoked.

Presiding Officer. The presiding officer has the authority to count to determine the presence of a quorum. The presiding officer may also make rulings without a point of order being raised. Finally, the presiding officer may rule out of order certain motions or quorum calls if he or she deems them dilatory. In contrast to regular procedures, no senator can suggest the absence of a quorum once cloture is invoked.

§ 8.240 Senate Floor: Motion to Reconsider and Final Passage

After passage of an amendment, measure, or motion, a senator *moves to reconsider the vote.* Approving this motion to reconsider allows the Senate an opportunity to review its decision and, essentially, revote. Therefore, once a proposition has been agreed to, a senator immediately moves to reconsider the vote, and another senator immediately moves to table the motion to reconsider. The motion to table effectively kills the motion to reconsider and makes the original vote final. Approval of the motion to table also blocks any future attempts to reverse the vote.

Only a senator who voted on the prevailing side or who did not vote at all on a proposition can offer a motion to reconsider. The motion is usually offered by the majority floor manager. The motion to table is made immediately after the motion to reconsider and is generally made by the minority floor manager. Usually, the motion to table is then routinely disposed of: "Without objection, the motion to table is agreed to."

The motion to reconsider can be made on the same day or within the next two days in which the Senate is in session.

When action is completed, a measure is ready for *engrossment and third reading.* Third reading is usually by title only. The measure is then ready for a vote on final passage.

§ 8.250 Voting in the Senate

Voting in the Senate is by *voice, division,* or *roll call.* On a voice vote, the presiding officer normally announces which side seems to have won based on how loudly they voted. More typically, the presiding officer states that "without objection the item is agreed to." This is a variation of a voice vote.

Division votes, often called standing votes, are rarely employed. If used, any senator may demand a division vote. Those senators in favor stand and the chair counts. Those opposed then stand and are counted. A division vote does not provide a record of how each senator voted.

Roll-call votes are known as *yea and nay votes* in the Senate. There is not an electronic voting device as there is in the House. Any senator can seek the yeas and nays. The presiding officer asks if there is a sufficient second. A sufficient second is one-fifth of a quorum—a minimum of eleven senators—which is an easy threshold to reach. Often, a senator receives support for the yeas and nays well in advance of the time the vote actually occurs. Thus, it is possible for debate on a proposition to be held and a request made for a vote. Yet, the vote does

§ 8.261

Reconciling Differences Glossary

Amendments between the Houses: Basic method for reconciling differences between two chambers' versions of a measure by passing the measure back and forth between them until both have agreed to identical language.

Amendments in Disagreement: Provisions in dispute between the two chambers.

Amendments in Technical Disagreement: Amendments agreed to in a conference but not included in the conference report because they may violate the rules of one of the houses and would open the conference report to a point of order.

Concur: Agree to amendment of the other house, either as is or with an amendment.

Conference Committee: Temporary joint committee of representatives and senators created to resolve differences between the chambers on a measure.

Conference Report: Document containing the conference committee's agreements and signed by a majority of conferees from each chamber.

Conferees: The representatives and senators from each chamber who serve on a conference committee; also referred to as managers.

Custody of the Papers: Custody of the engrossed measure and other documents that the two houses produce as they try to reconcile differences in their versions of a measure. *(See Papers.)*

Disagree: To reject an amendment of the other chamber.

Insist: Motion by one house to reiterate its previous position during amendments between the houses.

Instruct Conferees: Formal action by one chamber urging its conferees to uphold a particular position in conference.

Joint Explanatory Statement of Managers: Portion of the conference report providing the history, explanation, and intent of the conferees.

Managers: Representatives and senators serving on a conference committee; also called conferees.

Papers: Documents—including the engrossed measure, the amendments, the messages transmitting them, and the conference report—that are passed back and forth between the chambers.

Recede: Motion by one chamber to withdraw from its previous position during amendments between the houses.

Recede and Concur: Motion to withdraw from a position and agree with the other chamber's position.

Recede and Concur with an Amendment: Motion to withdraw from a position and agree, but with a further amendment.

Scope of Differences: Limits within which a conference committee is permitted to resolve the chambers' disagreement.

Stage of Disagreement: Stage when one house formally disagrees with an amendment proposed by the other house, and insists on its amendment. A measure generally cannot go to conference until this stage is reached.

A larger glossary is located at the back of the book.

§ 8.262

Keeping Up with Reconciling House-Senate Differences

See Chapters Eleven, Twelve, and Thirteen for descriptions of these and other sources.

Sources	Anticipating Conference Procedures		During/After Conference Procedures	
	Status	Substance	Status	Substance
Congressional Sources				
Congressional Record (for the appointment of full and partial conferees)	x			
Congressional Record (for leadership announcement of legislative program; text of conference report and joint explanatory statement; and House and Senate proceedings, including motions to instruct conferees)	x		x	x
Congressional Record Daily Digest (for scheduling of full conference meetings, appointment of additional full or partial conferees, or replacement of a conferee)	x		x	
Reporting committee's and leadership web sites available through the House *<www.house.gov>* and Senate *<www.senate.gov>* web sites	x	x	x	x
Announcements from the conference committee chair and from other House or Senate committee chairs serving on the conference	x	x	x	x
House and Senate engrossed measures		x		
For conference, possibly side-by-side analysis		x		
Depending on procedure used: measure passed in identical form by both chambers, amendments between the houses, or conference report and joint explanatory statement				x
Special rule from Rules Committee (House only)				x
Completion of House and Senate action on the same measure, text of the enrolled measure				x
"Whip notices" from party leadership (conference report on floor)			x	
Legislative Information System (Congress only)	x	x	x	x
THOMAS *<http://thomas.loc.gov>*	x	x	x	x
Non-Congressional Sources				
C-SPAN (floor proceedings) *<www.cspan.org>*		x		x
CQ Today *<www.cq.com>*	x	x	x	x
CQ.com *<www.cq.com>*	x	x	x	x
CQ Weekly (for major legislation) *<www.cq.com>*	x	x	x	x
CongressDaily, from *National Journal* *<http://nationaljournal.com>*	x	x	x	x
National Journal (for major legislation) *<http://nationaljournal.com>*		x		x
Trade press and daily newspapers	x	x	x	x
Other commercial database services	x	x	x	x

Continued on page 315

People *(Use these contacts after exhausting other resources.)*				
Professional staff of reporting committees, leadership staff, and interested members:				
• Will differences between the houses be reconciled with amendments between the houses or a conference?	x			
• Under what circumstances might a conference be necessary, even if a process of amendments between the houses is tried?	x			
• How might conference proceed? Which issues will be delegated to staff and which will the conferees handle? In what order might conference proceed?	x	x		
• For floor action between the houses or on a conference report, when will action occur?			x	
• During floor proceedings, what debate is anticipated?			x	x
• For floor action between the houses or on a conference report, what outcome is anticipated?			x	x
• What is anticipated on presidential action?				x
Chamber and committee leaders, and interested members (What are your expectations for a conference? After conference, how might specific sections be interpreted?)		x		x
Leadership, committee, and interested members' press assistants (What press releases and other press documents are available?)		x		x

not occur until after debate has concluded, which may be minutes or hours after the request for the vote was made. A fifteen-minute period is the time allocated for yea and nay votes, although votes are often kept open beyond this time to accommodate senators trying to reach the floor. *(See § 11.40, Versions of Legislation.)*

§ 8.260 Reconciling Differences between House-Passed and Senate-Passed Legislation

Legislation must pass both chambers in identical form before it can be sent to the president for signature or veto. Differences between the two versions can be worked out either by *amendments between the houses* or by convening a *conference committee*. *(See § 8.261, Reconciling Differences Glossary.)*

After a measure has been passed by one house, an *engrossed version* is transmitted to the other chamber. When a measure is received in the second chamber, it is either ordered "held at the desk" or referred to the appropriate committee.

When the second chamber considers and passes the measure in identical form to that passed by the first chamber, the measure can be sent to the president without further consideration in either chamber.

If the second chamber, the recipient chamber, considers and passes the measure with changes, it returns it to the chamber of origin. The originating chamber has several options. It can accept the second chamber's amendment, it can accept the second chamber's amendment with a further amendment, or it can disagree to the other chamber's amendment and request a conference.

The second chamber can also request a conference immediately rather than returning the measure to the first chamber with an amendment. A chamber must possess the *papers* to request a conference. The papers are the *engrossed measure* (measure as passed by the first chamber), *engrossed amendments* (measure as passed by the second chamber), and *messages of transmittal* between the chambers. (See § 8.262, *Keeping Up with Reconciling House-Senate Differences.*)

§ 8.270 Amendments between the Houses

The House and Senate must approve identical versions of a measure before it can be sent to the president. This process begins with one house notifying the second house that it has passed a measure and transmitting to the second chamber the measure as passed (the *engrossed measure*). If the second house passes the measure with changes, the two houses can opt to either offer *amendments between the houses* or convene a conference committee to resolve differences.

When one chamber sends a measure, it is *messaged* to the other chamber. At this stage, several actions are possible. The second chamber can ultimately approve, or *concur*, in the first chamber's version. If that happens, the measure is cleared and sent to the president.

Or, the second chamber can ultimately pass the measure with one or more amendments, that is, *to concur with a further amendment*. If that happens, the measure is returned to the originating chamber with "an amendment to the measure."

The first chamber may accept the amendment. If that occurs, the amended measure is cleared and sent to the president. Alternatively, the first chamber may propose a further amendment.

This first option of resolving differences between the two houses—the process of amendments between the houses—allows two degrees of amendments. The amendment of the second chamber is considered text that is subject to amendment. Each chamber has one opportunity to propose an amendment to the amendment of the other chamber. The process is often conducted by informal negotiations between the members and staff of the committees of jurisdiction in the two houses. An extended exchange of amendments is rare.

At any point in the process, either house may choose not to act on the version sent by the other house. It may insist on its own position, and formally disagree with the version sent by the other house. If a chamber insists on its own position, it reaches a *stage of disagreement*. This allows the houses to proceed to the second option of resolving differences by convening a conference committee. *(See § 8.280, Conference Committees.)*

Amendments between the houses is an attempt to reconcile differences in lieu of a conference committee, or even after a conference if items are reported in *true disagreement* or *technical disagreement*. The process of amendments between the houses is most often used when a measure is not controversial, there are few differences between the two chambers' versions of a measure, or it is late in a session and there is insufficient time or will to convene a conference.

House Consideration of Senate Amendments

Assume a fictitious bill, H.R. 1111, is messaged to the Senate and then returned from the Senate with an amendment. Several scenarios are then possible. The House floor manager could ask unanimous consent to "concur" in the Senate amendment. If that option is selected, the house bill as amended by the Senate amendment is the version sent to the president. Alternatively, the House floor manager could ask unanimous consent to concur in the Senate amendment with a further amendment. If unanimous consent is granted, the House bill with the "House amendment to the Senate amendment to the House bill" is returned to the Senate. If objection is heard to either scenario, or is even anticipated, the House manager could seek to bring up the Senate amendment under suspension of the rules or under the terms of a special rule.

Senate Consideration of House Amendments

Assume a fictitious bill, S. 2222, is messaged to the House, which returns it to the Senate with a "House amendment to the Senate bill." The Senate can accept the House amendment by unanimous consent, that is, concur in the House amendment. The measure is then sent to the president. Alternatively, the Senate can concur in the House amendment with a further amendment.

Senate rules provide that a motion to proceed to consider a House amendment to a Senate measure is not debatable. However, if the Senate agrees to concur in the House amendment or to concur with a further Senate amendment to the House amendment, then the amendment itself is debatable. Therefore, the Senate normally disposes of House amendments by unanimous consent or agrees to proceed to conference.

§ 8.280 Conference Committees

Either chamber can request a conference once both houses have passed versions of a measure treating the same subject and using the same bill or resolution number but containing substantive differences. Generally, the chamber that first approved the legislation disagrees to the amendments made by the other chamber and requests that a conference be convened. Sometimes, however, the second chamber requests a conference immediately after it passes legisla-

Size of Conference Committees

The conference committee delegation on the 1981 Budget Reconciliation Act had 280 conferees—208 representatives and 72 senators. This is believed to be the largest conference committee ever assembled.

The smallest conference committee would have 6 members, 3 from the House and 3 from the Senate. That was the practice in early Congresses.

tion, making the assumption that the other chamber will not accept its version.

A conference cannot be held until both chambers formally agree to convene one. The House generally requests a conference by unanimous consent, by motion, or by adoption of a special rule. The Senate usually agrees to a conference by unanimous consent or by motion.

Selection of Conferees

Although House rules grant the Speaker the right to appoint conferees, the Speaker usually does so after consultation with the chair(s) of the committee(s) of jurisdiction. The Senate presiding officer appoints Senate conferees, although the presiding officer, too, draws selections from recommendations of the chair of the committee of jurisdiction and party leaders. Conferees are also referred to as *managers*.

Although seniority on a committee of jurisdiction plays a role in selecting conferees, junior committee members are also appointed to conference committees. A member not on the committee of jurisdiction may be appointed if he or she had an important amendment included in the chamber's version of the measure or in the other chamber's version. In some instances, especially when a measure was considered by multiple committees, representatives or senators can be appointed as *limited-purpose conferees*. Precedents in both chambers indicate that conferees are supposed to support their chamber's legislation in conference.

The number of conferees can range from three to every member of a chamber. Generally, the size of a chamber delegation reflects the complexity of a measure. Moreover, the size of one chamber's delegation does not necessarily affect the size of the other chamber's delegation. Decisions are made by majority vote of *each delegation*, never by a majority vote of all the conferees. Each chamber appoints a majority of conferees to its delegation from the majority party. *(See § 8.281, Size of Conference Committees.)*

Instructing Conferees

Because a conference committee is a negotiating forum, there are few rules imposed on conferees. However, there are two circumstances under which House conferees may be given direction: first, before conferees are named, and second, when conferees have been appointed for twenty calendar days and ten legislative days and have not yet filed a report.

By custom, recognition to offer a *motion to instruct conferees*—a motion before the conferees are named—is a prerogative of the minority party. The motion is debatable for one hour. Only one motion to instruct conferees before their being named is in order.

For a motion to instruct conferees who have been appointed but not yet reported, any

§8.282		
Authority of Conferees		
Provision in First Chamber's Measure	**Provision in Second Chamber's Measure**	**Contents Permitted in Conference Report**
No provision	No provision	No provision
Provision A	Provision A	Provision A
Provision A	No provision	Provision A or current law or a compromise position between Provision A and current law
Provision A	Provision B	Between Provision A and Provision B

member, regardless of party, can be recognized to make a motion to instruct, and numerous motions to instruct can be offered.

Motions to instruct House conferees are not binding but express the sentiment of the House on a particular issue in either the House or Senate version of a measure sent to conference.

Motions to instruct in the Senate are rarely made. If made, a motion to instruct is both debatable and amendable, and, as in the House, must be offered before conferees are named. Unlike the House, however, a motion to instruct is not available after conferees have been appointed but the conference committee has not yet reported.

Authority of Conferees

Conferees are expected to meet to reconcile differences between the competing versions of a bill. As such, they are generally limited to matters in disagreement between the versions. They cannot delete provisions that exist in both measures or add provisions not in either measure. However, when the second chamber has adopted a full-text substitute, the latitude in such matters has proven to be quite wide. In appropriations measures, it is often easier to determine the *scope* of differences between House and Senate versions because specific dollar amounts can often be used to determine scope. (See § 8.282, *Authority of Conferees*.)

Conference Committee Deliberations

Conference committees are bargaining sessions. As such, they are characterized by inter-chamber negotiations and trade-offs as each chamber's conferees try to fashion a compromise that will pass their chamber while upholding the basic position their chamber brought into conference.

There are no formal rules in conference. Staff negotiations are customary, often leaving only the most contentious issues to the members themselves. Decisions on how managers work through these issues are determined by the conferees themselves. All conferees may meet together to consider the two chambers' full alternatives. Conferees might agree to consider a measure in conference title by title and to close a title after it has been considered and reconciled. Conferees sometimes create subgroups or subconferences to consider specific issues in the measure in conference.

There is one restriction placed on House managers. The House in the 110th Congress agreed to new chamber rules that House conferees should "endeavor to ensure" that conference meetings occur only if notice is provided and House managers are given the opportunity to attend.

Conference chairs are determined informally; however, when committees conference regularly, the chair normally rotates between the chambers.

When agreement is reached, a majority of each chamber's conference delegation must agree to the *conference report*. No vote is taken seeking a majority of all conferees. The agreement is formally indicated by signing the report. *(See § 8.283, Conference Signature Sheet.)*

Conference Report and Joint Explanatory Statement

The conference report and joint explanatory statement are two distinct documents. The conference report contains a formal statement of the procedural actions the conferees took and the formal legislative language the conferees propose. The joint explanatory statement is a more readable document. It identifies the major matters in disagreement, and then summarizes each chamber's position and the conferees' recommendations. The joint explanatory statement also often contains an explanation of the conferees' intent. Two copies of each document must be signed by a majority of the House conferees and a majority of the Senate conferees.

The documents are printed in the House portion of the *Congressional Record,* and are also printed together as a single House committee report. Although Senate rules require printing as a Senate document as well, the Senate usually waives this requirement.

Consideration of Conference Report

The chamber that agrees to a request for a conference is normally the chamber that considers the conference report first. That chamber can agree to, or disagree with, a conference report, or it can agree to a motion to recommit a conference report to conference. However, after one chamber has acted on a conference report, its conferees are discharged, and the second chamber may only accept or reject the conference report.

Consideration on House Floor. House rules provide that a conference report cannot be called up for consideration until the third calendar day (excluding Saturday, Sunday, or holidays, unless the House is in session) after the conference documents have been filed. Furthermore, copies of the conference report and joint explanatory statement must be available at least two hours before the chamber begins consideration. Both requirements can be waived

§ 8.283

Conference Signature Sheet

S. 2845	
Managers on the part of the HOUSE	Managers on the part of the SENATE
Mr. HOEKSTRA *[signature]*	
Mr. DREIER *[signature]*	
Mr. HYDE *[signature]*	
Mr. HUNTER *[signature]*	
Mr. SENSENBRENNER	

S. 2845—Continued	
Managers on the part of the HOUSE	Managers on the part of the SENATE
Ms. HARMAN *[signature]*	
Mr. MENENDEZ *[signature]*	
Mr. SKELTON *[signature]*	

Managers on the part of the House	Managers on the part of the Senate
Peter Hoekstra, Chair	Susan M. Collins *[signature]*
Jane Harman	Joseph I. Lieberman *[signature]*
David Dreier	Trent Lott *[signature]*
Robert Menendez	Carl Levin
Henry J. Hyde	Richard J. Durbin *[signature]*
Ike Skelton	Mike DeWine *[signature]*
Duncan Hunter	Pat Roberts *[signature]*
James F. Sensenbrenner, Jr.	John D. Rockefeller, IV *[signature]*
	George V. Voinovich *[signature]*
	John E. Sununu *[signature]*
	Bob Graham *[signature]*
	Frank Lautenberg *[signature]*
	Norm Coleman *[signature]*

by unanimous consent or by adoption of a special rule from the Rules Committee containing a waiver of the requirements.

Conference reports are privileged and can be brought up when available. They are considered under the one-hour rule. Occasionally, conference reports are brought to the floor by a special rule or under suspension of the rules.

Consideration on Senate Floor. When available, a conference report can be called up. A conference report is debatable under normal Senate rules and procedures. A motion to proceed to consider a conference report, however, is not debatable. A conference report can also be considered under the provisions of a time agreement.

§ 8.290 Presidential Action on Enacted Measures

When a measure has been approved by both chambers, the original papers are provided to the *enrolling clerk* of the chamber that originated the legislation. The enrolling clerk prepares an *enrolled version* of the measure—essentially, the measure printed on parchment. (In infrequent circumstances, Congress may submit to the president a *hand-enrolled measure*, one in draft form and not printed on parchment.) This enrolled measure is then certified by the clerk of the House or the secretary of the Senate, depending on the house in which the measure originated, and signed—first by the Speaker of the House and then by the president pro tempore of the Senate.

The enrolled measure is subsequently sent to the White House, although transmittal can occur any time from a few hours to several weeks after an enrolling clerk has been provided with the original papers. At the White House, the Office of the Executive Clerk logs the receipt of the enrolled measure. *(Information on the status of presidential receipt and action on measures is available from the Executive Clerk's Office, 202-456-2226.)*

Within ten days, not counting Sundays, the president must act on the legislation. Counting begins at midnight of the day he receives the enrolled measure. If the president wishes to approve the measure, he signs it, dates it, and writes "Approved" on it, although the Constitution requires only his signature.

Signing ceremonies for major pieces of legislation are often held on the White House lawn, in the Rose Garden, or in a place related to or signified by the legislation. Presidential pens are given to selected people at the ceremony, with the president using several pens to sign and date the document—essentially one pen for each letter or number, to accommodate all those wanting a pen used to sign the measure.

Contemporary presidents have often issued *signing statements* when they signed a measure into law. These statements are often congratulatory toward Congress and the president for having enacted a new law that the president believes will benefit the American people. However, they have in the last three decades become an additional source of information on the president's attitude toward a new law, perhaps expanding on views expressed in statements of administration policy issued during floor and conference consideration of legislation. *(See § 10.20, Congress and the Executive: Legislation.)* Although a president will not have vetoed a measure passed by Congress, he might nonetheless have reservations about provisions in the measure. He may then use a signing statement to explain his reservations and indicate how he will deal with them. A president might indicate that he will seek new legislation from Congress to overcome perceived problems, that implementation of certain provisions will occur pursuant to a certain interpretation of those provisions, or that certain provisions will be carried out consistent with the president's perceived constitutional prerogatives.

A signing statement does not amend or nullify a provision of a law—only Congress and the president together may do that. It may show how the president will use his constitutional duty to execute a law. If the president's interpretation offends Congress, Congress through

§ 8.291

Vetoes and Veto Overrides: Presidential Clout
(as of May 1, 2007)

Of the 1,448 vetoes exercised by President Washington through President Bush, only 104 were overridden by Congress. Of the 36 vetoes exercised by President Clinton, only 2 were overridden. In addition, presidents, including President Clinton, pocket vetoed another 1,066 measures enacted by Congress, for which Congress had no recourse.

The record for contemporary presidents follows:

President	Regular Vetoes	Regular Vetoes Overridden	Pocket Vetoes
Carter (1977–1981)	13	2	18
Reagan (1981–1989)	39	9	39
Bush, G.H.W. (1989–1993)	29	1	15
Clinton (1993–2001)	36	2	1
Bush, G.W. (2001–)	2	0	0

Through the end of his term, President Clinton vetoed 36 measures and returned the vetoed measures to Congress. No override attempt was made on 23 of his vetoes. On seven occasions, the House voted first and sustained his veto. On three occasions, the House overrode a veto only to have the Senate sustain the veto twice and not attempt an override the third time. On one occasion, the Senate voted first and sustained President Clinton's veto. On the two remaining occasions, the House voted to override the president's veto, and the Senate followed suit. The House failed to override either of President Bush's vetoes.

8

oversight, appropriations, or new legislation may seek to redirect the president. If the president's interpretation is challenged in court, courts have generally looked to the law and its textual development in Congress in their decision making. *(See § 10.73, Legislative History.)*

If the president does not want to approve the legislation, he may *veto* it. He does this by returning the measure without his signature, but including his objections in writing, called a *veto message*. If Congress, or one chamber of Congress, takes no action on a veto, the measure dies. Neither chamber must take action.

Alternately, Congress can attempt to override a veto and enact the bill "the objections of the president to the contrary notwithstanding." A two-thirds vote of those present and voting is required in each chamber to override a veto. The vote must be by roll call. Once the first chamber successfully overrides a veto, the measure is sent to the second house. The second house does not have to attempt a veto override. However, if a veto override in the second house is attempted and is successful, the measure becomes law. Procedures in each chamber allow debate and motions to table, postpone action, or refer a veto message to committee.

Under the Constitution, a measure may become law without the president's signature if the president does not sign it within ten days, not counting Sundays, provided Congress is in session. Why might a president choose this course of action? President George H. W. Bush allowed two measures to become law without his signature. In both cases he cited his agreement with the legislation's goals, but he also in both cases expressed his belief that the laws would be found to be unconstitutional violations of First Amendment rights in any court challenges. The two measures that became law were the Children's Television Act of 1990 (P.L. 101-385) and the Flag Protection Act of 1989 (P.L. 101-131).

If Congress is not in session, a measure not signed does not become law. Such measures are considered to be *pocket vetoed.* Current understanding of the pocket veto allows the practice after Congress has adjourned *sine die.* Pocket vetoes at other times have been challenged in both Congress and the courts. (*See § 8.291, Vetoes and Veto Overrides: Presidential Clout.*)

§ 8.300 Publication of Public Laws

Once the president has signed a measure into law, the president has not signed it within the constitutional ten days, or Congress has passed it over his veto, the measure is transmitted to the National Archives and Records Administration (NARA) and within NARA to the Office of the Federal Register (OFR). At OFR, the measure is assigned a sequential public-law number, such as P.L. 107-8, which would indicate that the law was enacted in the 107th Congress and that it was the eighth public law of that Congress. (*Public-law numbers are announced in the Congressional Record, Federal Register, and other print and electronic resources, including the NARA web site at <www.archives.gov/federal-register/laws/current.html>; they are also available by phone at 202-741-6043.*)

The law is first published in *slip form,* essentially a pamphlet form similar to that of other congressional documents, and is referred to as a *slip law. (Slip laws are available from the House Legislative Resource Center, the Senate Document Room, the Government Printing Office, and other print and electronic resources.)*

OFR also assigns each new public law a *Statutes at Large* page citation. Each new public law is added sequentially to the Statutes at Large. Once a slip law is out-of-print, it is easy to find provisions of a specific public law by using its statutory cite.

Finally, the House's Office of Law Revision Counsel organizes the parts of a new public law in the *U.S. Code.* Unlike the organization scheme of the Statutes at Large—sequential—the U.S. Code organizes all laws by subject matter, and the user can readily understand what is current law. Other print and electronic resources also provide U.S. Code reporting. (*Additional information and samples of the Statutes at Large and U.S. Code are found in § 11.50, Laws and Their Implementation by the Executive.*)

Chapter Nine

Legislating in Congress:
Federal Budget Process

Contributing Author
Bill Heniff Jr.

with update by
Robert Keith

9

Analysis

9

§ 9.00 Introduction: Congress's "Power of the Purse"

Congress is distinguished from nearly every other legislature around the world by the high degree of control it exercises over fashioning the government's budgetary policies. This power, referred to as "the power of the purse," ensures Congress's primary role in setting revenue and borrowing policies for the federal government and in determining how these resources are spent.

The congressional power of the purse derives from two key provisions in the Constitution. *(See § 9.01, Congress's Constitutional "Power of the Purse.")* Article I, Section 8, Clause 1 declares in part that Congress shall have the power to originate (that is, "to lay and collect") revenues of various types, including taxes and duties, among other things. Section 8, Clause 2 declares that the power to borrow funds "on the credit of the United States" belongs to Congress. In addition to its powers regarding revenues and borrowing, Congress exerts control over the expenditure of funds. Article I, Section 9, Clause 7 declares in part that funds can be withdrawn from the Treasury only pursuant to laws that make appropriations.

Under the Constitution, revenue measures must originate in the House of Representatives. Beyond this requirement, however, the Constitution does not prescribe how the House and Senate should organize themselves, or the procedures they should use, to conduct budgeting. Over the years, however, both chambers have developed an extensive set of rules (some set forth in statute) and precedents that lay out complicated, multiple processes for making budgetary decisions. The House and Senate have also created an intricate committee system to support these processes. *(See § 9.02, Federal Budgeting Concepts and Terminology.)*

As American society has grown and become ever more complex, and as the role of the federal government in the national economy has steadily expanded, Congress has also increasingly shared power over budgetary matters with the president and the executive branch. It has refashioned the president's role in budgeting. Congress has given the president a formal leadership role in the development of the budget and has defined the tools at his disposal in executing it. The president is a coequal with Congress and also exercises considerable influence over key budget decisions.

§ 9.01

Congress's Constitutional "Power of the Purse"

Revenues and Borrowing

The Congress shall have the Power

[1] To lay and collect Taxes, Duties, Imposts, and Excises . . .

[2] To borrow Money on the credit of the United States . . .

(Art. I, sec. 8.)

Spending

No Money shall be drawn from the Treasury, but in Consequence of Appropriations made by Law . . .

(Art. I, sec. 9, cl. 7.)

9

§ 9.02

Federal Budgeting Concepts and Terminology

Federal budgeting involves a complex web of legislative and executive procedures, categories of budgetary legislation, and types of financial transactions. Some concepts and terms fundamental to understanding federal budgeting include those that follow.

Revenues

Income received by the federal government is referred to as *revenues* or *receipts*. (Congress tends to use the former term and the executive branch tends to use the latter.) Revenues are raised from several different sources. In recent decades, revenues have stemmed mainly from individual income taxes, social insurance taxes, corporate income taxes, and excise taxes. Revenues also are raised by tariffs, fees, fines, gifts and bequests, and other means.

A *tax expenditure* is revenue forgone due to an exemption, deduction, or other exception to an underlying tax law. A tax expenditure represents a means of pursuing federal policy that is an alternative to a spending program. For example, home ownership is encouraged by allowing deductions from individual income taxes for mortgage interest paid during the year; the same goal could be promoted on the spending side of the budget by issuing grants or loans for home ownership to individuals.

Spending

When Congress enacts legislation providing legal authority for an agency to spend money, it provides *budget authority*. The most well-known type of legislation that provides budget authority is an annual appropriations act. Budget authority authorizes agencies to enter into *obligations*. An obligation is any type of action that creates a financial liability on the part of the federal government, such as entering into a contract, submitting a purchase order for goods, or employing personnel. When the obligation is liquidated, an outlay ensues. *Outlays* represent the actual payment of obligations, and usually take the form of electronic fund transfers, the issuance of checks, or the disbursement of cash. The stages of spending involving the enactment of budget authority and the incurring of obligations and outlays are referred to informally as the "spending pipeline."

The rate at which funds are spent (that is, converted from budget authority into outlays) is known as the *spendout rate*. Spendout rates vary from account to account, and from program to program within accounts. An account that involves personnel-intensive activities may have a high spendout rate, obligating and expending 90 percent or more of its budget authority during the fiscal year. Conversely, an account that involves the procurement of major weapons systems may have a low spendout rate, with only 5 or 10 percent of its budget authority being disbursed, or converted to outlays in the first year.

Congress exercises direct control over the enactment of budget authority, but its influence over obligations—and, to a greater degree, outlays—is indirect. Ultimately, federal agencies determine the outlay levels for a particular year through thousands of discrete actions.

Some income to the federal government is not treated as revenue. Rather, it is offset against spending. *Offsetting collections and receipts* arise from fees collected by the federal government for its business-type operations, from the sale of assets, and from other sources. Most such receipts are offsets against the outlays of the agencies that collect the money, but in the case of offshore oil leases and certain other activities, the revenues are deducted from the total outlays of the federal government.

Continued on page 329

Surplus and Deficit

The relationship between spending and revenues is reflected in the surplus or deficit figure. A *surplus* is an excess of revenues over outlays, while a *deficit* is an excess of outlays over revenues. Congress controls the enactment of legislation providing budget authority and raising revenues, but not the occurrence of outlays. Because of this, Congress's efforts to control the level of the surplus or the deficit are less effective over the short run compared with the long run.

Baseline Budgeting

Congress and the president employ baseline budgeting as a tool to analyze the context in which budget policy choices are made and to assess the impact of particular proposals. In the simplest terms, a *baseline* is a set of projections of future spending and revenues, and the resulting surplus or deficit, based upon assumptions about the state of the economy and the continuation of current policies without change. Overall revenue and spending levels usually increase from year to year under the baseline because of demographic trends, workload changes, and other factors.

The Office of Management and Budget develops a budget baseline, referred to as the *current services estimates*, to support the president's budget, while the Congressional Budget Office develops its own baseline, referred to as *baseline budget projections,* to aid the congressional budget process. Although, for the most part, the two agencies share a common approach to constructing budget baselines, differences in aggregate projections and estimates for particular accounts and programs are inevitable. Sometimes the differences may be significant enough to complicate the process of resolving policy differences.

The national economy can exert a significant influence on the federal budget. If projections about economic growth, unemployment levels, inflation, and other economic factors prove to be significantly inaccurate, projected budgetary levels may change by tens of billions of dollars during the course of a year. For this reason, the economic assumptions that underlie the budget baseline are crucially important. Congress and the president usually require that economic assumptions be revised only once or twice a year, to avoid complicating the decisionmaking process.

Statutory Limit on the Debt

When the federal government needs to borrow funds, it issues debt to the public. In addition, the federal government is compelled to incur debt because of requirements that trust fund surpluses be invested in federal securities. As a consequence, the federal government owes debt to the public and to itself. As a general matter, the amount of money that the federal government is able to borrow is constrained by a limit in statute. As long as the federal government incurs annual deficits and trust funds incur annual surpluses, Congress and the president from time to time must enact legislation to raise the statutory limit on the debt.

Federal Funds and Trust Funds

The budget consists of two main groups of funds: *federal funds* and *trust funds.* Federal funds—which comprise mainly the general fund—largely derive from the general exercise

Continued on page 330

of the taxing power and general borrowing. For the most part, they are not earmarked by law to any specific program or agency. One component of federal funds, called *special funds*, is earmarked according to source and purpose. The use of federal funds is determined largely by annual appropriations acts.

Trust funds are established, under the terms of statutes that designate them as trust funds, to account for funds earmarked by specific sources and purposes. The Social Security trust funds (the Old-Age and Survivors Insurance Fund and the Disability Insurance Fund) are the largest of the trust funds; revenues are collected under a Social Security payroll tax and are used to pay for Social Security benefits and related purposes. The use of trust funds is controlled primarily by entitlement laws and other substantive legislation.

The total budget includes both the federal funds and the trust funds. The merging together of federal funds and trust funds into a single budget sometimes is referred to as the "unified budget approach."

On-Budget and Off-Budget Entities

On-budget entities are federal agencies and programs that are fully reflected in the totals of the president's budget and the congressional budget resolution. *Off-budget entities*, on the other hand, specifically are excluded by law from these totals. The revenues and spending of the Social Security trust funds, as well as the financial transactions of the Postal Service Fund, are at present the only off-budget entities. These transactions are shown separately in the budget. Thus, the budget reports two deficit or surplus amounts—one excluding the Social Security trust funds and the Postal Service Fund and the other including these entities.

Further, off-budget entities are excluded from the budget enforcement procedures applicable to federal programs generally. Congress has established special procedures for the consideration of measures affecting Social Security revenues and spending.

§ 9.10 Key Budget Process Laws

Many different statutes lay the foundation for the modern budget process used by the federal government, but three laws are key: the Budget and Accounting Act of 1921, the Congressional Budget and Impoundment Control Act of 1974, and the Balanced Budget and Emergency Deficit Control Act of 1985. Each of these laws has been amended on numerous occasions.

The 1974 Congressional Budget Act and the 1985 Balanced Budget Act contain provisions that set forth congressional, as well as executive, budget procedures. The provisions dealing with congressional procedure were enacted as an exercise of Congress's *rule-making authority*, and effectively serve as rules of the House and Senate. As such, either chamber may modify the provisions that affect its operations without the concurrence of the other chamber and without the enactment of a law.

Budget and Accounting Act of 1921

The Budget and Accounting Act of 1921 *(P.L. 13, 67th Congress; 42 Stat. 20–27)* required for the first time that the president submit to Congress each year a *budget* for the entire federal government. The president is free to submit the budget in the form and detail he deems appropriate, but certain information is required. In addition, the estimates of the legislative and judicial branches must be incorporated in his budget without change. *(See § 9.40, Presidential Budget Process.)*

The 1921 Budget and Accounting Act also established the Bureau of the Budget, now called the Office of Management and Budget (OMB) and headed by a director subject to Senate confirmation, to assist the president in formulating the budget, in presenting it to Congress, and in monitoring the execution of the enacted budget by agencies. In addition, the 1921 act established the General Accounting Office, recently renamed the Government Accountability Office, a congressional agency, headed by the *comptroller general*, to audit and evaluate federal programs. *(See § 5.130, Legislative-Branch Support Agencies.)*

Congressional Budget and Impoundment Control Act of 1974

The 1974 Congressional Budget and Impoundment Control Act *(P.L. 93-344; 88 Stat. 297–339)* requires the House and Senate each year to adopt a *concurrent resolution on the budget*, which serves as a guide for the subsequent consideration of spending, revenue, and debt-limit legislation. *(See § 9.50, Congressional Budget Process.)* The 1974 act created the House and Senate Budget Committees to develop the budget resolution and monitor compliance with its policies, and the Congressional Budget Office to serve as an independent, nonpartisan agency to gather, develop, and analyze budgetary information for Congress. *(See § 5.130, Legislative-Branch Support Agencies.)* New procedures were established for congressional review of *impoundments* by the president; the comptroller general was given an oversight role in this process. *(See § 9.150, Impoundment: Deferrals and Rescissions.)*

Balanced Budget and Emergency Deficit Control Act of 1985

To strengthen control over spending and *deficit* levels, and to promote more efficient legislative action on budgetary issues, Congress and the president enacted the Balanced Budget and Emergency Deficit Control Act of 1985 *(P.L. 99-177, title II; 99 Stat. 1038–1101)*. At the time, the measure was commonly known as the Gramm-Rudman-Hollings Act, after its three primary sponsors in the Senate (then-Senators Phil Gramm, R-TX, Warren Rudman, R-NH, and Ernest Hollings, D-SC).

The 1985 Balanced Budget Act sought to drive the deficit downward, from nearly $200 billion in fiscal year (FY) 1986 to zero in FY1991. *Sequestration*, a process largely involving across-the-board spending cuts made toward the beginning of a fiscal year, was established as

§ 9.11

Budget Enforcement Act Procedures

Between 1990 and 2002, Congress and the president were constrained by *statutory* limits on discretionary spending and a pay-as-you-go (PAYGO) requirement on new direct spending and revenue legislation. These mechanisms supplemented the enforcement procedures associated with the annual budget resolution under the 1974 Congressional Budget Act. However, while the budget resolution is enforced by points of order while legislation is considered on the floor of each chamber, the discretionary-spending limits and PAYGO requirement were enforced by a sequestration process after legislative action for a session of Congress ended. Under the sequestration process, if legislative action was determined to violate the budget constraints, the president was required to issue a sequestration order canceling budgetary resources, on a largely across-the-board basis, in non-exempt programs in the category in which the violation occurred.

Initially, these budget enforcement controls applied to FY1991–1995. In 1993, they were modified and extended through FY1998. Finally, the controls were extended again in 1997 to apply to legislation enacted through FY2002 (and, in the case of PAYGO, to the effects of such legislation through FY2006). In each case, the controls were designed to enforce multi-year budget agreements between Congress and the president. Without any legislative action by Congress and the president to extend them, the discretionary spending limits expired on September 30, 2002 (the end of FY2002), and PAYGO effectively was terminated in December of that year by the enactment of P.L. 107-312. *(See § 9.50, Congressional Budget Process, Points of Order.)*

Since 2002, some members of Congress, as well as President George W. Bush, have proposed restoring and modifying these budget enforcement procedures.

the means of enforcing deficit targets. The sequestration process was designed to trigger automatically, based on a report issued by the comptroller general.

The 1985 act was revised in 1987 to meet a constitutional challenge and to modify the timetable for achieving a balanced budget *(P.L. 100-119, 101 Stat. 754)*. The Supreme Court, in *Bowsher v. Synar*, 478 U.S. 714 (1986), ruled that the comptroller general, as a legislative-branch official, could not be involved in the execution of laws. Accordingly, the authority to trigger a sequester (based upon conditions carefully set forth in law) was placed in the hands of the OMB director. Also, the target for bringing the budget into balance was shifted to FY1993.

The Budget Enforcement Act of 1990 *(P.L. 101-508, title III; 104 Stat. 1388–628)* fundamentally revised the process under the 1985 act. The deficit targets were effectively replaced by two new mechanisms: statutory limits on *discretionary spending* and a *pay-as-you-go* requirement aimed at keeping the projected effect of *revenue* and *direct-spending* legislation enacted during a session deficit-neutral. Sequestration was retained as the means of enforcing the new mechanisms. Congress and the president enacted several measures since 1990 that have extended the discretionary-spending limits and the pay-as-you-go requirement. *(See § 9.30,*

Budget Enforcement Framework.) The most recent of these extensions was the Budget Enforcement Act of 1997 (*P.L. 105-33, title X; 111 Stat. 677–712*), which extended these budget control mechanisms through 2002. At that time, they were allowed to expire or effectively were terminated. As the 110th Congress began, Congress and the president had not extended them further. (*See § 9.11, Budget Enforcement Act Procedures.*)

§ 9.20 The Budget Cycle

Federal budgeting is a cyclical activity that begins with the formulation of the president's annual budget and concludes with the audit and review of expenditures. The process spreads over a multiyear period. The first stage is the formulation of the president's budget and its presentation to Congress. The next stage is congressional action on the budget resolution and subsequent spending, revenue, and debt-limit legislation. The third stage is implementation of the budget by executive agencies. The final stage is *audit* and *review*. While the basic steps continue from year to year, particular procedures often vary in accord with the style of the president, the economic and political considerations under which the budget is prepared and implemented, and other factors.

Budget decisions are made on the basis of the *fiscal year*. Originally, the fiscal year used by the federal government coincided with the calendar year. In the 1840s, the fiscal year was changed to a July 1 through June 30 cycle. Finally, the 1974 Congressional Budget Act pushed back the start of the fiscal year by three months, to October 1, to give Congress more time to finish legislative action during a session. Under current procedures, for example, fiscal year 2008 began on October 1, 2007, and ended on September 30, 2008; during the 2007 session, Congress considered regular appropriations and other budgetary legislation for fiscal year 2008, as well as supplemental appropriations for fiscal year 2007.

The activities related to a single fiscal year usually stretch over a period of at least two-and-a-half calendar years. As the budget is being considered, federal agencies must deal with three different fiscal years at the same time: implementing the budget for the current fiscal year; seeking funds from Congress for the next fiscal year; and planning for the fiscal year after that.

§ 9.30 Budget Enforcement Framework

Congress considers budgetary legislation within the framework of budget enforcement procedures established under the 1974 Congressional Budget Act, which are intended generally to uphold the policies underlying the annual budget resolution. Enforcement relies principally on the reconciliation process and, while legislation is under consideration, on points of order to prevent the passage of legislation that would violate established policies (both are discussed in more detail later in this chapter). The House and Senate Budget Committees have primary responsibility for enforcement.

In addition to provisions in the 1974 act, the House and Senate also incorporate enforcement provisions into annual budget resolutions and their standing rules. PAYGO procedures affecting the consideration of direct spending and revenue legislation, for example, were established by the Senate in 1993 as a provision in an annual budget resolution (and modified by subsequent budget resolutions), and by the House in 2007 as an amendment to House Rule XXI.

The availability of information is crucial to the effective operation of enforcement procedures. The Budget Committees rely on *cost estimates* on legislation prepared by the Congressional Budget Office (with assistance from the Joint Committee on Taxation in the case of revenue measures) and integrates them into a *scorekeeping system*, which shows the impact of budgetary legislation compared to budget resolution levels.

As indicated previously, until late 2002, Congress and the president also were constrained by enforcement procedures established under the 1985 Balanced Budget Act (but modified substantially in 1990 and later years). The constraints took the form of (1) discretionary-spending limits and (2) a pay-as-you-go (PAYGO) requirement. PAYGO required that legislation affecting spending for *entitlements* and other *mandatory programs*, as well as revenues, be deficit-neutral. Violations of these constraints were remedied, using *sequestration* procedures, after legislative action for the session ceased. The president, assisted by the Office of Management and Budget (OMB), had the chief enforcement responsibilities under these procedures.

§ 9.40 Presidential Budget Process

The president's budget, officially referred to as the *Budget of the United States Government*, is required by law to be submitted to Congress early in the legislative session, no later than the first Monday in February. The budget consists of estimates of spending, revenues, borrowing, and debt; policy and legislative recommendations; detailed estimates of the financial operations of federal agencies and programs; data on the actual and projected performance of the economy; and other information supporting the president's recommendations.

Before the deadline for submission of the budget was changed in 1990, presidents usually had to submit their budgets in January. In years in which a new president was inaugurated (which occurs on January 20), the outgoing president usually submitted a budget before the inauguration. Later in the session, the new president submitted revisions to this budget that reflected his priorities and initiatives. In the two transition years since 1990, however, the incoming president rather than the outgoing president has submitted the budget (President Bill Clinton in 1993 for FY1994, and President George W. Bush in 2001 for FY2002).

The president's budget is only a request to Congress; Congress is not required to adopt or even consider the president's recommendations. Nevertheless, the power to formulate and submit a budget is a vital tool in the president's direction of the executive branch and of national policy. The president's proposals often influence congressional revenue and spending

§ 9.41

Typical Executive Budget Process Timetable

Calendar Year Prior to the Year in Which Fiscal Year Begins

Date	Activities
April–June	Agencies begin development of budget requests. The president, with the assistance of OMB, reviews and makes policy decisions for the budget that will begin October 1 of the following year.
July–August	OMB issues policy directions to agencies, providing guidance for agencies' formal budget requests.
Early fall	Agencies submit initial budget requests to OMB.
November–December	OMB and the president review and make decisions on agencies' requests, referred to as OMB "passback." Agencies may appeal these decisions to the OMB director, and in some cases directly to the president.

Calendar Year in Which Fiscal Year Begins

Date	Activities
By first Monday in February	President submits budget to Congress.
February–September	Congressional phase. Agencies interact with Congress, justifying and explaining president's budget.
By July 15	President submits mid-session review to Congress.
October 1	Fiscal year begins.
October–September (the fiscal year)	OMB apportions enacted funds to agencies. Agencies incur obligations, and the Treasury makes payments to liquidate obligations, resulting in outlays.

decisions, though the extent of the influence varies from year to year and depends more on political and fiscal conditions than on the legal status of the budget.

The Constitution does not provide for a budget, nor does it require the president to make recommendations concerning the revenues and spending of the federal government. Until 1921, the federal government operated without a comprehensive presidential budget process. As stated previously, the Budget and Accounting Act of 1921 provided for an executive budget process, requiring the president to prepare and submit a budget to Congress each year (beginning with FY1923). Although it has been amended many times, this statute provides the legal basis for the presidential budget, prescribes much of its content, and defines the roles of the president and the agencies in the process.

§ 9.42

Office of Management and Budget Publications

The Office of Management and Budget (OMB) coordinates preparation of the president's budget, plays a leading role in its defense in Congress, and oversees implementation of the spending bills passed by Congress. OMB policies take many forms. The following types of publications contain instructions and guidelines to other federal entities from OMB:

- **Circulars**, expected to have a continuing effect of generally two years or more.

- **Bulletins**, containing guidance of a more transitory nature that would normally expire after one or two years.

- **Regulations** and **Paperwork**, daily reports that list regulations and paperwork under OMB review.

- **Financial Management** policies and **Grants Management** circulars and related documents.

- **Federal Register** submissions, including copies of proposed and final rules.

For information on OMB policies and publications, check the OMB web site (*<www.whitehouse.gov/omb>*) and the Federal Register *(at GPO Access,* *<www.gpoaccess.gov/fr/index.html>).*

Formulation and Content of the President's Budget

Preparation of the president's budget typically begins in the spring (or earlier) each year, at least nine months before the budget is submitted to Congress, about seventeen months before the start of the fiscal year to which it pertains, and about twenty-nine months before the close of that fiscal year. *(See § 9.41, Typical Executive Budget Process Timetable.)* The early stages of budget preparation occur in federal agencies. When they begin work on the budget for a fiscal year, agencies already are implementing the budget for the fiscal year in progress and awaiting final appropriations actions and other legislative decisions for the fiscal year after that. The long lead times and the fact that appropriations have not yet been made for the next year mean that the budget is prepared with a great deal of uncertainty about economic conditions, presidential policies, and congressional actions.

As agencies formulate their budgets, they maintain continuing contact with the Office of Management and Budget (OMB) budget examiners assigned to them. These contacts provide agencies with guidance in preparing their budgets and also enable them to alert OMB to any needs or problems that may loom ahead. *(See § 9.42, Office of Management and Budget Publications.)* Agency requests are submitted to OMB in late summer or early fall, and are reviewed by OMB staff in consultation with the president and his aides. The 1921 Budget and Accounting Act bars agencies from submitting their budget requests directly to Congress.

§9.43

Volumes Containing and Explaining the President's Annual Budget

The principal volumes currently part of the president's annual budget submission include the following:

- **Budget** (officially the *Budget of the United States Government*)—includes the president's budget message, presentations on the president's major budgetary initiatives organized by department and major agencies (or, in some years, by budget function), discussions of management initiatives and performance data, and summary tables.

- **Appendix**—sets forth detailed information for accounts within each department and agency, including funding levels, program descriptions, proposed appropriations language, and object classification and employment data.

- **Analytical Perspectives**—contains analyses and information on specific aspects of the budget or budget-related areas, such as budget and performance integration, economic assumptions, and current services estimates; crosscutting programs, such as research and development, federal investment, and aid to state and local governments; and budget process reform proposals.

- **Historical Tables**—provides data, covering an extended time period, on receipts, budget authority, outlays, deficits and surpluses, federal debt, and other matters.

Within a few days of the submission of the budget, the president also transmits an annual ***Economic Report of the President*** to Congress, which includes the report of the Council of Economic Advisers.

The president is required by law to update his submissions, and he does this in a far briefer, more summary fashion in his ***Midsession Review***, which is due by July 15.

Online access to the president's budget documents is available in several places, including the Office of Management and Budget web site, <*www.whitehouse.gov/omb*>, and GPO Access, <*http://www.access.gpo.gov/usbudget*>.

Moreover, OMB regulations provide for confidentiality in all budget requests and recommendations before the transmittal of the president's budget to Congress. However, it is not uncommon for budget recommendations for some programs to become public while the budget is still being formulated.

The format and content of the budget are partly determined by law, but the 1921 act authorizes the president to set forth the budget "in such form and detail" as he may determine. Over the years, there has been an increase in the types of information and explanatory material presented in the budget documents.

In most years, the budget is submitted as a multivolume set consisting of a main document setting forth the president's message to Congress and an analysis and justification of his major

§ 9.44

Program and Financing Schedule in President's Budget Appendix

1 Each account is identified by an 11-digit code. The first two digits indicate the agency; the next four digits are the account numbers; the seventh digit is the type of request (regular or supplemental); the eighth digit is the type of fund; and the last three digits specify the budget function. *(See § 9.52; the category 999 indicates that an account involves more than one function.)*

2 The schedule covers three fiscal years: the past year (2006); the current year (2007); and the upcoming year, also referred to as the budget year (2008). The last column contains the president's most recent request.

3 Agency obligations are classified by program activity. If applicable, the obligations are arranged by operating and capital investment.

4 New budget authority may be derived from several sources. In this example, the total new budget authority for FY2008 is expected to be derived not only from new discretionary appropriations, but also from offsetting collections (spending authority resulting from business-type activities).

5 Outlays may be derived from several sources as well. In this example, outlays for the Salaries and Expenses account of the Federal Bureau of Investigation result from new discretionary authority and balances from previous years.

Source: Office of Management and Budget, *Budget of the United States Government, Fiscal Year 2008, Appendix* (Washington: GPO, 2007), pp. 659–660.

Federal Bureau of Investigation Salaries and Expenses
Program and Financing *(in millions of dollars)*

1 Identification code 15-0200-0-1-999	**2** 2006 actual	2007 est.	2008 est.
3 Obligations by program activity:			
Intelligence	1,053	1,055	1,073
Counterterrorism/Counterintelligence	2,055	2,056	2,313
Criminal Enterprises and Federal Crimes	1,897	1,898	1,905
Criminal Justice Services	263	264	432
Total operating expenses	5,268	5,273	5,723
Intelligence	79	79	125
Counterterrorism/Counterintelligence	155	155	245
Criminal Enterprises and Federal Crimes	143	143	226
Criminal Justice Services	20	20	31
Total capital investment	397	397	627
Total	5,665	5,670	6,350
Reimbursable program	753	760	760
Total new obligations	6,418	6,430	7,110
4 New budget authority (gross), detail:			
Discretionary:			
Appropriation	5,859	5,670	6,350
Appropriation permanently reduced	-98	…	…
Transferred to other accounts	-7	-7	…
Transferred from other accounts	4	…	…
Appropriation (total discretionary)	5,758	5,663	6,350
Spending authority from offsetting collections:			
Offsetting collections (cash)	536	770	760
Change in uncollected customer payments from Federal sources (unexpired)	315	…	…
Spending authority from offsetting collections (total discretionary)	851	770	760
Mandatory:			
Transferred from other accounts	…	139	…
Total new budget authority (gross)	6,609	6,572	7,110
5 Outlays (gross), detail:			
Outlays from new discretionary authority	5,163	5,367	5,927
Outlays from discretionary balances	1,192	965	1,122
Outlays from new mandatory authority	…	111	…
Outlays from mandatory balances	…	…	42
Total outlays (gross)	6,355	6,443	7,091

proposals (the *Budget*). Supplementary documents contain account and program-level details, historical information, and special budgetary analyses, among other things. *(See § 9.43, Volumes Containing and Explaining the President's Annual Budget.)*

During the congressional phase of the federal budget process, the *Appendix* volume in particular is a useful source of detailed financial information on individual programs and *appropriations accounts*. It provides for each annually appropriated account: (1) the text of the current appropriation and proposed changes; (2) a program and financing schedule; (3) a narrative statement of programs and performance; (4) an object classification schedule; and (5) an employment summary. Among other financial information, the program and financing schedule shows obligations for specific programs (distinguishing between operating expenses and capital investments, where appropriate), budgetary resources available for obligation, and sources of new budget authority for each of the previous, current, and upcoming fiscal years. *(See § 9.44, Program and Financing Schedule in President's Budget Appendix.)* New budget authority available to an agency for obligation may come from several sources, not just an annual appropriation. Other typical sources include *permanent appropriations*, *transferred appropriations*, and *offsetting collections*.

Much of the budget is an estimate of requirements under existing law rather than a request for congressional action. (More than half the budget authority in the budget becomes available without congressional action.) The president is required to submit a budget update—reflecting changed economic conditions, congressional actions, and other factors—referred to as the *Midsession Review*, by July 15 each year. The president may revise his recommendations anytime during the year.

Executive Interaction with Congress

OMB officials and other presidential advisors appear before congressional committees to discuss overall policy and economic issues, but they generally leave formal discussions of specific programs to the affected agencies. Agencies thus bear the principal responsibility for defending the president's program recommendations at congressional hearings and in other interactions and communications with Congress.

Agencies are supposed to justify the president's recommendations, not their own. OMB maintains an elaborate legislative clearance process to ensure that agency *budget justifications*, testimony, and other submissions are consistent with presidential policy.

Increasingly in recent years, the president and his chief budgetary aides have engaged in extensive negotiations with Congress over major budgetary legislation. These negotiations sometimes have occurred as formal budget "summits" and at other times as less visible, behind-the-scenes activities.

One tool used by the president to signal his position on legislation in order to influence congressional action is a *Statement of Administration Policy* (SAP). These statements are issued at several different stages of legislative activity and are maintained on the OMB web site. In a

SAP, the president may indicate his concurrence with congressional action on a measure, identify provisions in the measure with which he disagrees, and even signal his intent to veto the measure if it is not adjusted according to his wishes. At the conclusion of the legislative process, presidents sometimes issue *signing statements* on legislation that is being signed into law, often using a statement to register objections to particular provisions in the law. *(See § 10.20, Congress and the Executive: Legislation, and § 8.290, Presidential Action on Enacted Measures.)*

§ 9.50 Congressional Budget Process

The Congressional Budget and Impoundment Control Act of 1974 established the congressional budget process as the means by which Congress coordinates the various budget-related actions taken by it during the course of the year, such as the consideration of appropriations and revenue measures. The process is structured around an *annual concurrent resolution on the budget* (H. Con. Res. ___ or S. Con. Res. ___) that sets aggregate budget policies and functional priorities for at least the next five fiscal years. (The budget resolution and appropriations processes described in the following sections take place each year.)

Because a concurrent resolution is not a bill or joint resolution, it is not submitted to the president to be signed or vetoed. The budget resolution cannot have statutory effect; no money can be raised or spent pursuant to it. However, as a concurrent resolution, it requires House and Senate agreement to the same text to have maximum effect or utility to Congress. The main purpose of the budget resolution is to establish the framework within which Congress considers separate revenue, spending, and other budget-related legislation in a year. Revenue and spending amounts set in the budget resolution establish the basis for the enforcement of congressional budget policies through points of order. The budget resolution also initiates the reconciliation process for conforming existing revenue and spending laws to congressional budget policies. *(For another explanation of the congressional budget process and other budget information, see the Senate Budget Committee's web site at <www.budget.senate.gov>, and the House Budget Committee's web site at <www.budget.house.gov>.)*

Formulation and Content of the Budget Resolution

The congressional budget process begins upon the presentation of the president's budget in January or February. *(See § 9.51, Congressional Budget Process Timetable and § 9.53, Congressional Budget Process Flowchart.)* The timetable set forth in the 1974 Congressional Budget Act calls for the final adoption of the budget resolution by April 15, well before the beginning of the new fiscal year on October 1. Although the House and Senate often pass the budget resolution separately before April 15, they often do not reach final agreement on it until after the deadline—sometimes not at all. *(See § 9.52, Completion Dates of Budget Resolutions.)* The 1974 act bars consideration of revenue, spending, and debt-limit measures for the upcoming fiscal year until the budget resolution for that year has been adopted. However, certain excep-

§9.51

Congressional Budget
Process Timetable[1]

Deadline	Action
First Monday in February	President submits budget to Congress[2]
February 15	Congressional Budget Office submits report on economic and budget outlook to Budget Committees
Six weeks after president's budget is submitted	House and Senate committees submit reports on views and estimates to respective Budget Committees
April 1	Senate Budget Committee reports budget resolution
April 15	Congress completes action on budget resolution
May 15	House usually begins action on annual appropriations bills
June 10	House Appropriations Committee reports last regular appropriations bill
June 30	House completes action on regular appropriations bills and any required reconciliation legislation
July 15	President submits midsession review of his budget to Congress
October 1	Fiscal year begins[3]

1. While this timetable is set forth in statute, the deadlines generally are regarded as hortatory and Congress and the president sometimes do not meet them.
2. At any time after the president submits the budget for the upcoming fiscal year, he may submit revisions to the budget, referred to as budget amendments, as well as request supplemental appropriations for the current fiscal year.
3. One or more continuing resolutions may be needed until Congress and the president complete action on all pending appropriations bills.

tions are provided, such as the exception that allows the House to consider the regular appropriations bills after May 15, even if the budget resolution has not yet been adopted.

The 1974 Congressional Budget Act requires the budget resolution, for each fiscal year covered, to set forth budget aggregates and spending levels for each *functional category* of the budget. *(See § 9.54, Functional Categories in a Congressional Budget Resolution.)* The aggregates included in the budget resolution are as follows:

- total revenues (and the amount by which the total is to be changed by legislative action)
- total new budget authority and outlays
- the deficit or surplus
- the debt limit

§ 9.52

Completion Dates of Budget Resolutions

The timetable in the 1974 Congressional Budget Act provides for the House and Senate to reach agreement on the budget resolution by April 15, but this deadline is not always met. During the 30-plus years that the congressional budget process has been in effect, the House and Senate did not reach final agreement four times (all shown here). Completion dates for the past 10 years are as follows:

Fiscal Year	Date
1998	June 5, 1997
1999	Not Completed
2000	April 15, 1999
2001	April 13, 2000
2002	May 10, 2001
2003	Not Completed
2004	April 11, 2003
2005	Not Completed
2006	April 28, 2005
2007	Not Completed

For each of the functional categories, the budget resolution must indicate for each fiscal year the amounts of new budget authority and outlays. All figures in the budget resolution must be arithmetically consistent.

Aggregate amounts in the budget resolution do not reflect the revenues or spending of the Social Security trust funds, although these amounts are set forth separately in the budget resolution for purposes of Senate enforcement procedures.

The budget resolution does not allocate funds among specific programs or accounts, but the major program assumptions underlying the functional amounts are often discussed in the reports accompanying each resolution and during floor debate. Some recent reports have contained detailed information on the program levels assumed in the resolution. These assumptions are not binding on the affected committees. Finally, the 1974 act allows certain additional matters to be included in the budget resolution. The most important optional feature of a budget resolution is *reconciliation* directives. (See § 9.110, *Reconciliation Legislation.*)

House and Senate Budget Committee Action. The House and Senate Budget Committees are responsible for marking up and reporting the budget resolution. (See § 9.55, *Membership on the House and Senate Budget Committees.*) In the course of developing the budget resolution, the Budget Committees hold hearings, receive *views and estimates* reports from other committees, and obtain information from the Congressional Budget Office (CBO). These views and estimates reports of House and Senate committees provide the Budget Committees with information on the preferences and legislative plans of congressional committees regarding budgetary matters within their jurisdiction. (Views and estimates are available from issuing committees and the Budget Committees; they can also often be found on committee web sites.)

CBO assists the Budget Committees in developing the budget resolution by issuing, early each year, a report on the economic and budget outlook, which includes *baseline budget projections*. The baseline projections presented in the report are supported by more detailed projections for accounts and programs; CBO usually revises the baseline projections once more (in March) before the Budget Committees mark up the budget resolution. In addition, CBO issues a report analyzing the president's budgetary proposals in light of CBO's own economic and technical assumptions.

The extent to which the Budget Committees (and the House and Senate) consider particular programs when they act on the budget resolution varies from year to year. Specific program decisions are supposed to be left to the Appropriations Committees and other committees of jurisdiction, but there is a strong likelihood that major issues are discussed in markup, in the Budget Committees' reports, and during floor consideration of the budget resolution. Although any programmatic assumptions generated in this process are not binding on the committees of jurisdiction, they often influence the final outcome. *(For news, information, tables, and graphs related to congressional action on the budget resolution and budgetary legislation, see, for example, the Budget Bulletin online at the Senate Budget Committee's web site at <www. senate.gov/~budget/republican/NewBB.htm>.)*

Floor Consideration. A budget resolution is marked up and reported from a Budget Committee in the same fashion as most other measures are considered in other committees. Both the House and Senate Budget Committees write reports to accompany the budget resolutions they report (although, in recent years, the Senate Budget Committee has issued a committee print in lieu of a report). Either the House or Senate committee may report first, and either the House or Senate may consider a budget resolution first. Because of the need to adopt a budget resolution to allow orderly and timely consideration of budgetary legislation, action in the two committees and in the two chambers can occur simultaneously and within a short period of time.

Floor consideration of the budget resolution is guided by House and Senate rules and practices. In the House, the Rules Committee usually reports a *special rule* (a simple House resolution), which, once agreed to by the House, establishes the terms and conditions under which the budget resolution is considered by the House. This special rule typically sets aside a period for general debate, and specifies which amendments may be considered and the sequence in which they are to be offered and voted on. It has been the practice in recent years to allow consideration of a limited number of amendments (as substitutes for the entire resolution) that present different policy choices. In the Senate, the amendment process is less structured, relying on agreements reached by the leadership through a consultative process. The amendments offered in the Senate may entail major policy choices or may be focused on a single issue.

The House and Senate normally pass budget resolutions with differences that are significant enough to warrant the convening of a conference. Conferees, typically drawn from the two Budget Committees, reconcile differences and prepare a conference report, which must be adopted in both houses. Among other Senate rules, Senate debate on budget resolutions and corresponding conference reports is limited.

Achievement of the policies set forth in the annual budget resolution depends on the legislative actions taken by Congress (and the president's approval or disapproval of those actions), the performance of the economy, and technical considerations. Many of the factors that determine whether budgetary goals will be met are beyond the direct control of Congress.

9

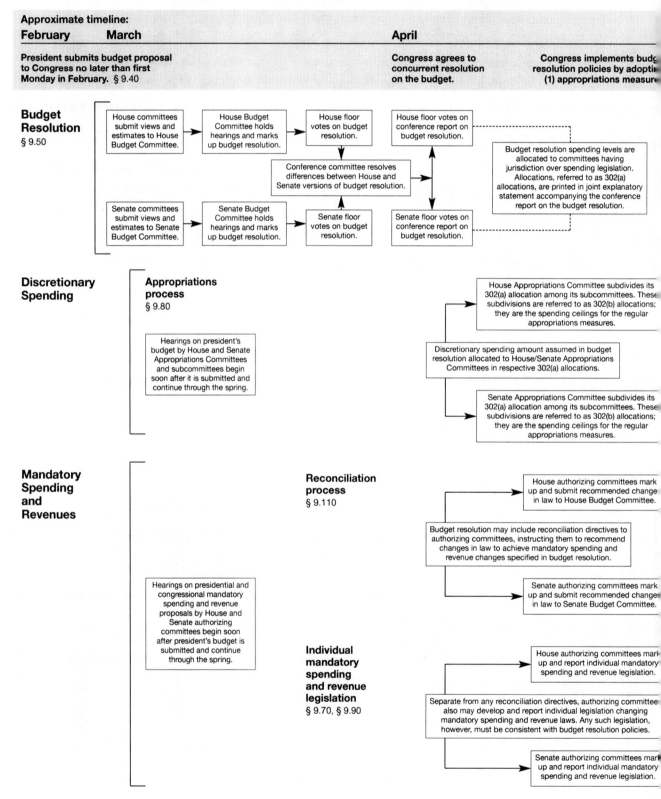

§ 9.53

Congressional Budget Process Flowchart

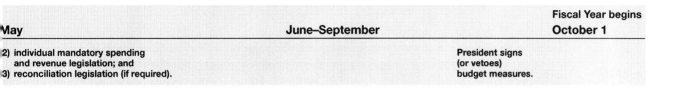

May	June–September	Fiscal Year begins October 1

2) individual mandatory spending
   and revenue legislation; and
3) reconciliation legislation (if required).

President signs
(or vetoes)
budget measures.

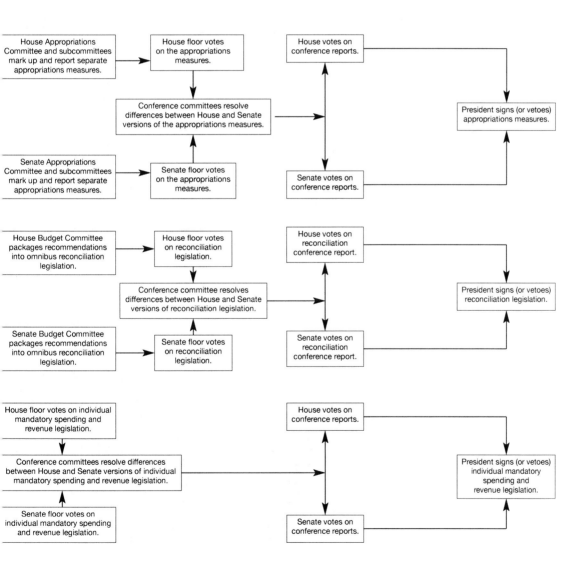

9

§ 9.54

Functional Categories in a Congressional Budget Resolution

A budget resolution shows proposed aggregate spending levels for the functional categories of the budget. These functional categories group programs by broad purposes without regard to the agencies that administer them; a function is further divided into subfunctions. Budget account identification numbers include the three-digit code related to a function.

- National Defense (050)
- International Affairs (150)
- General Science, Space, and Technology (250)
- Energy (270)
- Natural Resources and Environment (300)
- Agriculture (350)
- Commerce and Housing Credit (370)
- Transportation (400)
- Community and Regional Development (450)
- Education, Training, Employment, and Social Services (500)
- Health (550)
- Medicare (570)
- Income Security (600)
- Social Security (650)
- Veterans' Benefits and Services (700)
- Administration of Justice (750)
- General Government (800)
- Net Interest (900)
- Allowances (920)
- Undistributed Offsetting Receipts (950)

If economic conditions—growth, employment levels, inflation, and so forth—vary significantly from projected levels, so too will actual levels of revenue and spending. Similarly, actual levels may differ substantially if the technical factors upon which estimates are based, such as the rate at which agencies spend their discretionary funds or participants become eligible for entitlement programs, prove faulty.

Budget Resolution Enforcement

Once a budget resolution is agreed to, Congress's regular tools for enforcing it are overall spending ceilings and revenue floors, and committee allocations and subdivisions of spending. (In addition, in recent years the Senate enforced discretionary-spending limits in the budget resolution, which paralleled the adjustable discretionary-spending limits established in statute and enforced by the sequestration process.) For enforcement procedures to work, Congress must have access to complete and up-to-date budgetary information so that it can relate individual measures to overall budget policies and determine whether adoption of a particular measure would be consistent with those policies, as explained below. Substantive and procedural *points of order* are designed to obtain congressional compliance with budget rules. A point of order may bar House or Senate consideration of legislation that violates the spending ceilings and revenue floors in the budget resolution, committee subdivisions of spending, or congressional budget procedures.

In years Congress is late in agreeing to, or does not agree to, a budget resolution, the House and Senate independently may agree to a "deeming resolution" for the purpose of enforcing certain budget levels. A deeming resolution, sometimes in the form of a simple resolution, specifies certain budget levels normally contained in the budget resolution, including aggregate spending and revenue levels, spending allocations to House and Senate committees, spending allocations to the Appropriations Committees only, or a combination of these. In some cases, an entire budget resolution, adopted earlier by one chamber, may be deemed to have been passed. Under a deeming resolution, the enforcement procedures related to the Congressional Budget Act, as discussed below, have the force and effect as if a budget resolution had been adopted by Congress.

Allocations of Spending to Committees. The key to enforcing budget policy is to relate the budgetary impact of individual pieces of legislation to overall budget policy. Because Congress operates through its committee system, an essential step in linking particular measures to the budget is to allocate the spending amounts set forth in the budget resolution among House and Senate committees.

Section 302(a) of the 1974 act provides for allocations to committees to be made in the statement of managers accompanying the conference report on the budget resolution. A *section 302(a) allocation* is made to each committee that has jurisdiction over spending. The Appropriations Committees receive allocations for one year, while the legislative committees receive allocations both for the budget year and the full period covered by the budget resolution—at least five fiscal years.

The committee allocations do not take into account jurisdiction over discretionary authorizations funded in annual appropriations acts. The amounts of new budget authority and outlays allocated to all committees in the House or Senate may not exceed the aggregate amounts of budget authority and outlays set forth in the budget resolution. Although these allocations are made by the Budget Committees, they are not the unilateral preferences of these committees. They are based on assumptions and understandings developed in the course of formulating the budget resolution.

After the allocations are made under section 302(a), the House and Senate Appropria-

---

§ 9.55

Membership on the House and Senate Budget Committees

The House Budget Committee, unlike other House standing committees (except the House Committee on Standards of Official Conduct), is composed of a rotating membership. House rules limit a member's service on the committee to four Congresses in a period of six successive Congresses. In addition, House rules require five members from the Appropriations Committee, five members from the Ways and Means Committee, one member from the Rules Committee, one member designated by the elected majority party leadership, and one member designated by the elected minority party leadership to serve on the committee.

In contrast, membership on the Senate Budget Committee is permanent; Senate rules do not limit the duration of a senator's service on the committee.

tions Committees subdivide the amounts they receive among their subcommittees, as required by section 302(b). The subcommittees' *section 302(b) allocations or subdivisions* may not exceed the total amount allocated to the committees. Each Appropriations Committee reports its subdivisions to its respective chamber; the appropriations bills may not be considered until such a report has been filed.

Scorekeeping and Cost Estimates. *Scorekeeping* is the process of measuring the budgetary effects of pending and enacted legislation and assessing its impact on a budget plan—in this case, the budget resolution. In the congressional budget process, scorekeeping serves several broad purposes. First, it informs members of Congress and the public about the budgetary consequences of congressional actions. When a budgetary measure is under consideration, scorekeeping information lets members know whether adopting the amendment or passing the bill at hand would breach the budget. Further, such information enables members to judge what must be done in upcoming legislative action to achieve the year's budgetary goals. Finally, scorekeeping is designed to assist Congress in enforcing its budget plans. In this regard, scorekeeping is used largely to determine whether points of order under the 1974 act may be sustained against legislation violating budget resolution levels.

The principal scorekeepers for Congress are the House and Senate Budget Committees, which provide the presiding officers of the respective chambers with the estimates needed to determine if legislation violates the aggregate levels in the budget resolution or the committee subdivisions of spending. The Budget Committees make summary scoring reports available periodically, usually geared to the pace of legislative activity. CBO assists Congress in these activities by preparing *cost estimates* of legislation, which are included in committee reports, and scoring reports for the Budget Committees.

Cost estimates prepared by CBO show how a measure would affect spending or revenues over at least five fiscal years. While most cost estimates are provided in the committee report to accompany a measure, they may be provided at any stage of the legislative process, subject to available resources of CBO. For revenue legislation, CBO is required to use estimates made by the Joint Committee on Taxation (JCT). *(See § 9.92, Revenue Estimates.)* CBO and JCT cost estimates are available on their respective web sites at <www.cbo.gov> and <www.house.gov/jct>.

Points of Order. The 1974 Congressional Budget Act provides for both substantive and procedural points of order to block violations of budget resolution policies and congressional budget procedures.

One element of substantive enforcement is based on section 311 of the act. This section bars Congress from considering legislation that would cause total revenues to fall below the level set in the budget resolution. It also forbids total new budget authority or total outlays to exceed the budgeted level. In the House (but not the Senate), section 311 does not apply to spending legislation if the committee reporting the measure has stayed within its allocation of new discretionary budget authority. Accordingly, the House may take up any spending measure that is within the appropriate committee allocations, even if it would cause total spending to be exceeded. Legislation that would cause functional allocations in the budget resolution to be exceeded is not prohibited in either chamber.

Section 302(f) of the 1974 act bars the House and Senate from considering any spending measure that would cause the relevant committee's spending allocations to be exceeded. In the House, the point of order applies only to violations of allocations of new discretionary budget authority. Further, the point of order also applies to suballocations of spending made by the Appropriations Committees.

In addition to points of order to enforce compliance with the budget resolution and the allocations and subdivisions made pursuant to it, the 1974 act contains points of order to ensure compliance with its procedures. Perhaps the most important of these is section 303, which bars consideration of any revenue, spending, entitlement, or debt-limit measure before adoption of the budget resolution. However, the rules of the House permit it to consider regular appropriations bills after May 15, even if the budget resolution has not yet been adopted.

When the House or Senate considers a revenue or a spending measure, the chair of the respective Budget Committee sometimes makes a statement advising the chamber concerning whether the measure violates any of these points of order. If no point of order is made, or if the point of order is waived, the House or Senate may consider a measure despite any violations of the 1974 act. The House may waive points of order by adopting a special rule. The Senate may waive points of order by unanimous consent or by motion under section 904 of the act. The Senate requires a three-fifths vote of the membership to waive certain provisions of the act.

As mentioned previously, the House and Senate may include additional points of order for budget enforcement purposes as provisions in budget resolutions or as part of their standing rules. The Senate established a "pay-as-you-go" (PAYGO) point of order in 1993 as part of the FY1994 budget resolution and has amended it several times over the years (it currently is in effect though the end of FY2008). (See § 9.11, *Budget Enforcement Act Procedures*.) The Senate PAYGO rule generally requires direct spending and revenue legislation to be deficit-neutral over a 10-year period. Specifically, it prohibits the consideration of direct spending or revenue legislation that would increase or cause an on-budget deficit in any one of three time periods: the first year, the first five years, and the second five years, covered by the most recently adopted budget resolution. Under the current rule, however, any direct spending and revenue legislation assumed in the most recently agreed-to budget resolution is exempt from the deficit-neutrality requirement. The Senate PAYGO rule also requires a three-fifths vote to waive.

In 2007, at the beginning of the 110th Congress, the House added a PAYGO requirement to its standing rules (as Clause 10 of Rule XXI). The House's PAYGO rule provides a point of order against the consideration of any direct spending or revenue measure that would increase the deficit or reduce the surplus during either a six-year period (covering the current

§ 9.61

Budgeting for Direct and Guaranteed Loans

The Federal Credit Reform Act of 1990 made fundamental changes in the budgetary treatment of direct loans and guaranteed loans. Among its many provisions, the law required that budget authority and outlays be budgeted for the estimated subsidy cost of direct and guaranteed loans. This cost is defined in the 1990 law as the "estimated long-term cost to the Government of a direct loan or a loan guarantee, calculated on a net present value basis, excluding administrative costs. . . ." Under this law, Congress appropriates budget authority or provides indefinite authority equal to the subsidy cost. This budget authority is placed in a program account, from which funds are disbursed to a financing account.

year, the budget year, and the four following fiscal years) or an 11-year period (the previously cited period and the ensuing five fiscal years). The Senate has proposed (in the FY2008 budget resolution, on which action still was pending as of this writing) a modification in its PAYGO rule that would, among other things, extend it through FY2017 and eliminate the exception for direct spending increases and revenue reductions assumed in the budget resolution.

§ 9.60 Spending, Revenue, and Debt-Limit Legislation

Congress implements the policies of the budget resolution through the enactment of spending (§§ 9.70, 9.80), revenue (§ 9.90), and debt-limit (§ 9.100) legislation. In many of the years since 1980, Congress has employed the reconciliation process (§ 9.110) to enact budget changes through legislation considered under expedited procedures. Reconciliation legislation can include revenue changes, changes in direct spending (but not usually changes in discretionary spending), and adjustments to the debt limit. Special procedures also apply to federal credit programs. (See § 9.61, Budgeting for Direct and Guaranteed Loans.)

For information on how Congress processes legislation, including budgetary legislation, see Chapter Eight, Legislating in Congress: Legislative Process.

§ 9.70 Spending Legislation

The spending policies of the budget resolution generally are implemented through two different types of spending legislation. Policies involving *discretionary spending* are implemented in the context of *annual appropriations acts*, whereas policies affecting *direct* or *mandatory spending* (which, for the most part, involves *entitlement* programs) are carried out in substantive legislation. (See § 9.71, Differences between Discretionary and Direct Spending.)

All discretionary spending is under the jurisdiction of the House and Senate Appropriations Committees. Direct spending is under the jurisdiction of the various legislative committees of the House and Senate; the House Ways and Means Committee and the Senate Finance Committee have the largest shares of direct-spending jurisdiction. (Some entitlement programs, such as Medicaid, are funded in annual appropriations acts, but such spending is not considered to be discretionary.) The enforcement procedures under the con-

Differences between Discretionary and Direct Spending

Feature	Discretionary Spending	Direct Spending
Budgetary impact of authorizing legislation	No direct impact; authorizes an appropriation	Direct impact; provides budgetary resources
Committees that process budgetary legislation	Appropriations Committees	Authorizing committees; technically, Appropriations Committees for *appropriated entitlements*
Frequency of decision making	Annual	Periodic
Means of enforcing budget resolution	Committee allocations and suballocations and points of order	Committee allocations and points of order and the reconciliation process
Basis of computing budget impact	Current year's spending and president's request	Baseline budget projections
Impact of economic changes	Indirect	Direct, often automatic

gressional budget process, mentioned in § 9.50, apply equally to discretionary and direct spending.

In past years, many of the most significant changes in direct-spending programs, from a budgetary standpoint, have been made in the reconciliation process. *(See § 9.110, Reconciliation Legislation.)* The greatest number of spending decisions in any year occurs in the annual appropriations process.

§ 9.80 Authorization and Appropriation Processes

The Constitution requires appropriations laws. To complement this power, Congress has created a system of spending legislation that includes authorization laws and annual appropriations acts. Authorizations are separate from appropriations and are intended to precede them in enactment.

Authorization Measures

An *authorization act* is a law that (1) establishes a program or agency and the terms and conditions under which it operates, and (2) authorizes the enactment of *appropriations* for that program or agency. *Authorizing legislation*, which is used to make authorization law, is one type of legislation that Congress commonly considers. Authorizing legislation may originate in either the House or the Senate, and may be considered any time during the year. It can prescribe what an agency must do—or proscribe what it may not do—in the performance of its assigned responsibilities. It can give the agency a broad grant of authority and discretion, or define parameters, decision making, and decisions in great detail. In an authorization bill, Congress by its own rules can include nearly any type of provision other than appropriations or revenue provisions.

Unless an authorization measure contains direct spending, which itself enables an agency to enter into obligations, authorizing legislation does not have budgetary impact. It authorizes discretionary spending, for which funding is provided in annual appropriations acts.

House rules do not expressly require authorizations. Instead, they bar *unauthorized appropriations*. The House may waive the rule against unauthorized appropriations by adopting a special rule before taking up an appropriations bill. The House rule barring unauthorized appropriations applies only against *general appropriations measures*. Under House precedents, a *continuing appropriations measure* is not considered to be a general appropriations bill, and it may thus fund unauthorized programs.

Senate rules also bar unauthorized appropriations, although many exceptions are allowed. Accordingly, the House rule is stricter than the Senate rule.

House rules also prohibit the inclusion of appropriations in authorizing legislation. Senate rules do not contain this prohibition.

House rules bar *legislation in an appropriations bill*, but a special rule from the Rules Committee can waive this requirement. *(See § 8.90, Rules Committee and Special Rules.)* Legislation in appropriations is also prohibited by Senate rules.

Permanent versus Temporary Authorizations. An authorization is presumed to be permanent unless the authorizing law limits its duration. *Permanent authorizations* (such as for Individuals with Disabilities Education Act programs) do not have any time limit and continue in effect until they are changed by Congress. An agency having a permanent authorization need only obtain appropriations to continue in operations. *Annual authorizations* (such as for the Department of Defense) are for a single year and, usually, for a fixed amount of money. These authorizations need to be renewed each year. *Multiyear authorizations* (such as for Federal Aviation Administration programs) are typically in effect for several years and must be renewed when they expire. New authorizations of programs or activities with annual or multiyear authority are often referred to as *reauthorizations*.

Permanent authorizations rarely specify amounts of money. Temporary authorizations usually do.

An authorization of appropriations in a specific amount is intended to serve as a very general guideline for the Appropriations Committees in drafting appropriations measures and for Congress in approving them. However, one regularly finds large differences between enacted authorized and appropriated amounts. A member or group of members advocating "full funding" of a program is often in favor of an appropriation matching an authorization. Moreover,

Congress does not need to make an appropriation for an authorization in law if it chooses not to fund an activity.

An authorization of appropriations for a specific amount is also intended to serve as a ceiling on the amount that the Appropriations Committees might include or that Congress might approve in an appropriations measure for the authorized program or activity. But, it occasionally happens that enacted appropriated amounts exceed authorized amounts.

Annual Appropriations Measures

An appropriations act is a law passed by Congress that provides federal agencies with authority to incur *obligations* and make payments out of the Treasury for the purposes specified. As noted in § 9.00, the power to appropriate is a congressional power. Funds in the Treasury may not be spent in the absence of an appropriation. This prohibition includes any spending in excess of an appropriation. Spending may also occur only in accordance with the purposes and conditions Congress established in making an appropriation.

The Constitution does not require annual appropriations, but since the First Congress the practice has been to make most appropriations for a single fiscal year. Appropriations must be used (obligated) in the fiscal year for which they are provided, unless the law provides that they are available for a longer period of time. All provisions in an appropriations act, such as *limitations* on the use of funds, expire at the end of the fiscal year, unless the language of the act extends their period of effectiveness. (*See § 9.81, Limitations, Earmarks, and General Provisions.*)

The president requests annual appropriations in his budget submitted each year. In support of the president's appropriations requests, agencies submit *justification* materials to the House and Senate Appropriations Committees. These materials provide considerably more detail than is contained in the president's budget and are used in support of agency testimony during appropriations subcommittee hearings on the president's budget.

Congress passes three main types of appropriations measures. *Regular appropriations acts* provide budget authority to agencies for the next fiscal year. *Supplemental appropriations acts* provide additional budget authority during the current fiscal year when the regular appropriation is insufficient. Supplemental appropriations also finance activities not provided for in regular appropriations. *Continuing appropriations acts*, often referred to as *continuing resolutions* (after the form of legislation in which they are usually considered, the joint resolution [H.J. Res ___]), provide stopgap (or full-year) funding for agencies that have not received regular appropriations. For purposes of House and Senate rules, all regular and supplemental appropriations measures covering two or more agencies or purposes are considered *general appropriations measures*.

The number of regular appropriations acts was fixed for several decades at 13, but realignment of the Appropriations subcommittees in the 109th and 110th Congresses reduced that number; at present, there are 12 regular appropriations acts. (*See § 9.82, New Appropriations Subcommittee Organization.*) In some years, Congress merges two or more of the regular appro-

Limitations, Earmarks, and General Provisions

In addition to appropriating specific dollar amounts, appropriations and their accompanying reports contain numerous other provisions that affect how federal departments and agencies spend appropriations. The principal categories of these provisions include the following:

- **Limitation**—language in legislation or in legislative documents that restricts the availability of an appropriation by limiting its use or amount.

- **Earmark**—a set-aside within an appropriation for a specific purpose that might be included either in legislation or in legislative documents.

- **Directive**—an instruction, probably in a legislative document, to an agency concerning the manner in which an appropriation is to be administered.

- **General Provision**—policy guidance on spending included in an appropriations measure; it may affect some or all appropriation accounts in the measure or even have government-wide application; it may also be one-time or permanent.

Appropriations measures might also contain legislative provisions that are included in appropriations measures despite House and Senate rules discouraging the practice.

priations bills into an *omnibus measure*. In a typical session, Congress also acts on at least one supplemental appropriations measure. Because of recurring delays in the appropriations process, Congress also typically passes one or more continuing appropriations each year. The scope and duration of these measures depend on the status of the regular appropriations bills and the degree of budgetary conflict between Congress and the president. Funding levels for activities under a continuing appropriations act usually are restrictive and keyed to formulas, such as the lower of the current rate or the president's budget request, or the lower of the House-passed or Senate-passed amount.

In the House. By precedent, appropriations originate in the House of Representatives. In the House, appropriations measures are originated by the Appropriations Committee (when it marks up or reports the measures) rather than being introduced by an individual member.

Before the full Appropriations Committee acts on a measure, the measure is considered in the relevant subcommittee. The House subcommittees typically hold extensive hearings on appropriations requests shortly after the president's budget is submitted. In marking up their appropriations bills, the various subcommittees are guided by the allocations made to them under section 302 of the 1974 Congressional Budget Act.

The subcommittees are generally quite influential. It is common for the full Appropriations Committee to mark up and report an appropriations measure prepared for it by a subcommittee without making substantive changes. The subcommittees also draft the committee

§ 9.82

New Appropriations
Subcommittee Organization

For several decades, Congress considered thirteen regular appropriations acts developed by thirteen parallel subcommittees; each regular appropriations act was developed by the relevant House and Senate Appropriations subcommittee. Realignment of the Appropriations subcommittees in the 109th Congress reduced the number to ten in the House and twelve in the Senate, resulting in subcommittees (and regular appropriations acts) that in some cases were no longer parallel. Further realignment in the 110th Congress resulted in twelve subcommittees in each committee and restored parallelism between them. In some cases, subcommittee jurisdictions were not the same in the 110th Congress as they had been before realignment occurred. The current Appropriations subcommittees are as follows:

- Agriculture, Rural Development, Food and Drug Administration, and Related Agencies
- Commerce, Justice, Science, and Related Agencies
- Defense
- Energy and Water Development
- Financial Services and General Government
- Homeland Security
- Interior, Environment, and Related Agencies
- Labor, Health and Human Services, Education, and Related Agencies
- Legislative Branch
- Military Construction, Veterans Affairs, and Related Agencies
- State, Foreign Operations, and Related Programs
- Transportation, and Housing and Urban Development, and Related Agencies

reports that accompany appropriations measures to the floor. Although the Appropriations Committee might begin reporting bills in early May, the House may not consider a regular appropriations measure before May 15.

Because general appropriations measures are privileged and thus have direct access to the House floor for consideration, they can be brought to the floor without first obtaining a special rule from the Rules Committee. Nonetheless, most appropriations bills come to the floor under a rule waiving one or more standing rules, such as the rule against unauthorized appropriations. *(See § 9.83, Sequence of Appropriations Measures through Congress.)* During June, July, August, September, and, regularly, October, the House often spends many of its days in session processing appropriations measures reported from the House Appropriations Committee or from the conference committees that are normally convened on each of the regular appropriations measures, supplemental appropriations measures, and continuing resolutions. *(See Chapter Eight, Legislating in Congress: Legislative Process.)*

§ 9.83

Sequence of Appropriations Measures through Congress

House

Subcommittee hearings

Subcommittee markup (no measure number is assigned yet)

Full committee markup and report (measure is introduced and number is assigned)

House floor action

Senate

Subcommittee hearings

Subcommittee markup (either a House-passed measure or an unnumbered Senate measure)

Full committee markup and report (either a House-passed measure or a Senate measure is introduced and number is assigned)

Senate floor action (if a Senate measure is considered, it is held at the stage of final passage so that the Senate can amend and pass the House measure, fulfilling the tradition that the House originates appropriations measures)

House-Senate Conference
(on a House-numbered measure)

House agrees to conference report
(and any amendments in disagreement)

Senate agrees to conference report
(and any amendments in disagreement)

Enrolled Measure Sent to President

In the Senate. Subcommittees of the Senate Appropriations Committee also begin their hearings on appropriations requests shortly after the president's budget is submitted. They are also guided by section 302 allocations. Hearings in Senate appropriations subcommittees may not be as extensive as those held by the counterpart subcommittees of the House Appropriations Committee. Subcommittee markup and reporting to the full Appropriations Committee is followed by full committee markup and reporting.

Up until the latter part of the 1990s, the Senate usually would consider appropriations measures after they had been passed by the House. When the Senate changed a House-passed appropriations measure, it did so by inserting amendments numbered consecutively through the measure.

Under current practice, the Senate sometimes considers a Senate-numbered measure up to the stage of final passage, routinely using complex unanimous consent agreements to frame floor consideration. When the House-passed measure is received in the Senate, it is amended with the text that the Senate has already agreed to (as a single amendment) and then passed by the Senate. This practice allows the Senate to consider appropriations measures without having to wait for the House to adopt its version, facilitating the timely consideration and completion of the regular appropriations measures.

Like the House, the Senate often spends many of its days in session in June, July, August, September, and, regularly, October, engaged in processing appropriations measures reported from the Senate Appropriations Committee or from the conference committees that are normally convened on each of the regular appropriations measures, supplemental appropriations measures, and continuing resolutions.

Conference. As appropriations measures pass both the House and Senate, conference committees are appointed to resolve differences. As is the case on most major pieces of legislation, conference is a critical stage in the legislative process for key policy decisions and many details. Conference reports must pass the House and Senate before an enrolled measure is transmitted to the president for signature or veto. *(See Chapter Eight, Legislating in Congress: Legislative Process.)*

Additional Congressional Controls in Appropriations Acts

The basic unit of an appropriation is an *account*. A single unnumbered paragraph in an appropriations act comprises one account. All provisions of that paragraph pertain to that account and to no other, unless the text expressly gives them broader scope. Any provision limiting the use of funds enacted in that paragraph is a restriction on that account alone.

Over the years, appropriations have been consolidated into a relatively small number of accounts. It is typical for a federal agency to have a single account for all its expenses of operation and additional accounts for other purposes, such as construction. Accordingly, most appropriation accounts encompass a number of activities or projects. An appropriation sometimes *earmarks* specific amounts to particular activities within the account, but the more common practice is to provide detailed information on the amounts intended for each activity in other sources, principally the committee reports accompanying the measures.

Over the years, the House and Senate Appropriations Committees have developed procedures for considering earmark requests from members of their respective chambers. In most cases, the appropriations subcommittees require members to submit written requests for program or project funding in the regular appropriations bills by a certain deadline, often in March or April of each year. Some subcommittees provide request forms, including electronic forms posted on the House Intranet, or questionnaires to facilitate an orderly process for the consideration of member requests. *(See § 9.84, Examples of Appropriations Subcommittees' Requirements for Member Requests.)*

At the start of the 110th Congress, in 2007, the House amended its rules to regulate the inclusion of earmarks in annual appropriations acts, as well as in other spending measures, and the inclusion of limited tax benefits and limited tariff benefits in revenue legislation. The House rules require the distribution of a list of all earmarks, limited tax benefits, or limited tariff benefits in legislation (and accompanying committee reports) before the legislation may be considered, as well as the identification in each case of the members requesting them. Fur-

§ 9.84

Examples of Appropriations Subcommittees' Requirements for Member Requests

JERRY LEWIS, CALIFORNIA, Chairman
C. W. BILL YOUNG, FLORIDA
RALPH REGULA, OHIO
HAROLD ROGERS, KENTUCKY
FRANK R. WOLF, VIRGINIA
JIM KOLBE, ARIZONA
JAMES T. WALSH, NEW YORK
CHARLES H. TAYLOR, NORTH CAROLINA
DAVID L. HOBSON, OHIO
ERNEST J. ISTOOK, JR., OKLAHOMA
HENRY BONILLA, TEXAS
JOE KNOLLENBERG, MICHIGAN
JACK KINGSTON, GEORGIA
RODNEY P. FRELINGHUYSEN, NEW JERSEY
ROGER F. WICKER, MISSISSIPPI
RANDY "DUKE" CUNNINGHAM, CALIFORNIA
TODD TIAHRT, KANSAS
ZACH WAMP, TENNESSEE
TOM LATHAM, IOWA
ANNE M. NORTHUP, KENTUCKY
ROBERT B. ADERHOLT, ALABAMA
JO ANN EMERSON, MISSOURI
KAY GRANGER, TEXAS
JOHN E. PETERSON, PENNSYLVANIA
VIRGIL H. GOODE, JR., VIRGINIA
JOHN T. DOOLITTLE, CALIFORNIA
RAY LaHOOD, ILLINOIS
JOHN E. SWEENEY, NEW YORK
DON SHERWOOD, PENNSYLVANIA
DAVE WELDON, FLORIDA
MICHAEL K. SIMPSON, IDAHO
JOHN ABNEY CULBERSON, TEXAS
MARK STEVEN KIRK, ILLINOIS
ANDER CRENSHAW, FLORIDA
DENNIS R. REHBERG, MONTANA
JOHN R. CARTER, TEXAS
RODNEY ALEXANDER, LOUISIANA

DAVID R. OBEY, WISCONSIN
JOHN P. MURTHA, PENNSYLVANIA
NORMAN D. DICKS, WASHINGTON
MARTIN OLAV SABO, MINNESOTA
STENY H. HOYER, MARYLAND
ALAN B. MOLLOHAN, WEST VIRGINIA
MARCY KAPTUR, OHIO
PETER J. VISCLOSKY, INDIANA
NITA M. LOWEY, NEW YORK
JOSE E. SERRANO, NEW YORK
ROSA L. DeLAURO, CONNECTICUT
JAMES P. MORAN, VIRGINIA
JOHN W. OLVER, MASSACHUSETTS
ED PASTOR, ARIZONA
DAVID E. PRICE, NORTH CAROLINA
CHET EDWARDS, TEXAS
ROBERT E. "BUD" CRAMER, JR., ALABAMA
PATRICK J. KENNEDY, RHODE ISLAND
JAMES E. CLYBURN, SOUTH CAROLINA
MAURICE D. HINCHEY, NEW YORK
LUCILLE ROYBAL-ALLARD, CALIFORNIA
SAM FARR, CALIFORNIA
JESSE L. JACKSON, JR., ILLINOIS
CAROLYN C. KILPATRICK, MICHIGAN
ALLEN BOYD, FLORIDA
CHAKA FATTAH, PENNSYLVANIA
STEVEN R. ROTHMAN, NEW JERSEY
SANFORD D. BISHOP, JR., GEORGIA
MARION BERRY, ARKANSAS

CLERK AND STAFF DIRECTOR
FRANK M. CUSHING

TELEPHONE:
(202) 225-2771

Congress of the United States
House of Representatives
Committee on Appropriations
Washington, DC 20515–6015

February 22, 2005

Dear Colleague:

It is an honor and a privilege for us to serve as the Chairman and Ranking Minority Member of the Subcommittee on Agriculture, Rural Development, Food and Drug Administration and Related Agencies in the 1st session of the 109th Congress.

As we begin to develop the fiscal year 2006 Agriculture Appropriations bill, we would seek input from both member offices and outside parties interested in expressing their views on matters under the Subcommittee's purview. The Subcommittee will collect member requests via an electronic form posted on the House Intranet. We will collect this information in order to evaluate the need and/or merits of particular projects and programs. The due date is **April 8, 2005.**

As all of you are well aware, the Appropriations Committee faces a tight discretionary allocation in fiscal year 2006. As a result, we cannot guarantee that a particular project or program will be funded, either in part or in full. If your office is requesting funding for specific projects, it is especially important that your office assign a priority number to each project for which you are requesting funding. Each member office should prioritize their projects amongst the total number of requests (i.e., a member's office cannot have a number one priority for projects under the Agricultural Research Service and then another number one priority under the Natural Resources Conservation Service.) The Subcommittee will only accept requests for project funding or bill / report language from a Member's office. A signed letter MUST accompany the electronic submission from the Member of Congress to the Subcommittee Chairman that briefly mentions EACH of the items submitted electronically. No electronic file submissions will be considered without delivery of a signed letter that references each submission. Your office may access the electronic request form at the following link: http://onlinecao.house.gov/appropriations/AGApprops.asp .

If you or an outside party are interested in providing written testimony for the record in connection with our fiscal year 2006 budget hearings, please provide three copies to the Subcommittee at 2362A Rayburn House Office Building no later than **April 8, 2005.** Testimony is limited to not more than five single-spaced, letter-size pages, typed on only one side of each page. Although maps, pictures, graphs, letters, petitions and the like may be submitted for the information of the Subcommittee, it is not feasible to include them in the printed hearing record.

Of course, all testimony will be thoroughly reviewed by the Subcommittee. The Subcommittee will also review and consider all information received by Members at any time, whether or not submitted for publication in the formal hearing record.

We hope that this process will help expedite our hearing schedule and result in fewer disruptions and inconveniences for Members. If you have any questions or require further information, please contact the Subcommittee staff at (202) 225-2638.

Sincerely,

Henry Bonilla
Chairman
Subcommittee on Agriculture, Rural
Development, Food and Drug
Administration and Related Agencies

Rosa DeLauro
Ranking Minority Member
Subcommittee on Agriculture, Rural
Development, Food and Drug
Administration and Related Agencies

Continued on page 359

**LABOR, HHS, EDUCATION AND RELATED AGENCIES SUBCOMMITTEE
FY06 PROJECT QUESTIONNAIRE SHEET**

Due to the large number of requests received by the Subcommittee, please assemble your request letter as follows:
- **If the answers to a project questionnaire exceed one page please staple the pages together.**
- **Please provide (3) copies of each completed project questionnaire.**
- **Please clip this set of three copies together.**
- **If you are requesting funding for multiple projects, please collate questionnaires – e.g. three copies of the questionnaire for your project #1 clipped together, followed by three copies of the questionnaire for project #2 clipped together, etc.**

1. Name of Member of Congress.

2. Congressional Staff contact, phone number, and email address.

3. Priority ranking: Due to the funding constraints, please assign a priority number to each project for which you are requesting funding.

4. Name and address of the project grant recipient, and name, telephone number (and e-mail address, if available) of a contact person at the recipient organization. If the potential recipient is a school, please provide the name and location of the school district in which the school is located. Also, if the project is to be carried out in a location that is different from the grantee address, please provide that city and State.

5. Provide a brief description of the activity or project for which funding is requested. **The only construction funding available is for health-related activities.** If the request is for health-related construction, please identify the activity(s) that will be carried out in the health facility.

6. Funding details:
    a. Total project cost (i.e., including all funding sources and all years):
    b. Amount you are requesting for this project in fiscal year 2006 (your FY 2006 request should not exceed the amount that will be used in one year):
    c. **Break down/budget** of the amount you are requesting for this project in fiscal year 2006. (For example, salary $40,000; computer $3,000 etc.)
    d. What other funding sources are contributing to this project? What amount does each of these funding sources contribute?
    e. Has the potential recipient received funding for this project from any Federal agency currently or in the past five years? If yes, include information on the amount of funds, the years received, and the name of the Federal agency and program providing the funding.

7. Describe the organization's main activities, and whether it is a public, private non-profit, or private for-profit entity.

8. What is the national significance of the project, and what specific federal responsibility does the funding of this project or activity further? For example, what measurable improvements in health status, educational achievement, or similar outcomes will result from this project?

9

ther, the rules require that the members requesting such items identify the intended beneficiaries and purposes and certify that they (or their spouses) have no financial interest in them. The Senate also passed legislation in 2007 imposing similar requirements, but as of this writing the legislation still was pending. As an interim step, the Senate Appropriations Committee incorporated the requirements into its rules for the development and reporting of appropriations acts.

In addition to the substantive limitations and other provisions associated with each account, each appropriations act has *general provisions* that apply to all the accounts in a title or in the whole act. These general provisions appear as numbered sections, usually at the end of the title or act.

In a typical appropriations act, most funding is provided as *one-year appropriations* (i.e., the funds are available for obligation during the single fiscal year and lapse after the year has expired). The account language usually does not indicate the period that funds are available; instead, a general provision indicates that all funding provided in the act is available for one year unless otherwise indicated. Congress also makes *no-year appropriations* by specifying that the funds shall remain available until expended. No-year funds are carried over to future years, even if they have not been obligated. Congress sometimes makes *multiyear appropriations*, which provide for funds to be available for two or more fiscal years. *Permanent appropriations*, such as those to pay interest on the national debt or to pay the salaries of members of Congress, remain available without additional action by Congress.

Appropriations measures also contain other types of provisions that serve specialized purposes, such as provisions that liquidate (pay off) obligations made pursuant to certain *contract authority* and that *reappropriate* funds provided in previous years. These provisions also *transfer* funds from one account to another; *rescind* funds (or release *deferred* funds); and set ceilings on the amount of obligations that can be made under permanent appropriations, on the amount of direct or guaranteed loans that can be made, or on the amount of administrative expenses that can be incurred during the fiscal year. In addition to providing funds, appropriations acts often contain substantive limitations on government agencies.

Detailed information on how funds are to be spent, along with other directives or guidance, is provided in the committee and conference reports accompanying the various appropriations measures. Agencies ordinarily abide by this *report language* in spending the funds appropriated by Congress.

The appropriations reports do not comment on every item of expenditure. Report language is most likely when the Appropriations Committee prefers to spend more or less on a particular item than the president has requested or when the committee wants to earmark funds for a particular project or activity. When a particular item is mentioned by the committee, there is a strong expectation that the agency will adhere to the instructions. *(See § 10.73, Legislative History.)*

§ 9.91

Tax Expenditures

In enacting revenue legislation, Congress often establishes or alters tax expenditures. As defined in the 1974 Congressional Budget Act, "tax expenditures" include revenue losses due to deductions, exemptions, credits, and other exceptions to the basic tax structure. Tax expenditures are a means by which Congress pursues public policy objectives and, frequently, can be regarded as alternatives to other policy instruments such as grants and loans. The Joint Committee on Taxation estimates the revenue effects of legislation changing tax expenditures, and also publishes five-year projections of these provisions as an annual committee print. Every two years, the Senate Budget Committee issues a compendium of tax expenditures (prepared by the Congressional Research Service); the current volume is titled, *Tax Expenditures: Compendium of Background Material on Individual Provisions* (S. Prt. 109-072, December 2006). An example of a well-known tax expenditure is the mortgage-interest deduction available to home owners.

§ 9.90 Revenue Legislation

The Constitution requires that all revenue measures originate in the House of Representatives. The Senate, however, may amend a House-originated revenue measure. If the Senate adopts an original Senate measure carrying a revenue provision, the House usually enforces its constitutional prerogative over originating revenue measures by adopting a simple resolution stating that the Senate measure infringes upon the privileges of the House and returning the measure to the Senate, a process referred to as "blue-slipping." The term "blue-slipping" refers to the blue paper on which the resolution is printed.

In the House, revenue legislation is under the jurisdiction of the Ways and Means Committee; in the Senate, jurisdiction is held by the Finance Committee. House rules bar other committees from reporting revenue legislation. Sometimes, however, another committee will report legislation levying user fees on a class that benefits from a particular service or program or that is being regulated by a federal agency. In many of these cases, the user-fee legislation in the House is referred subsequently to the Ways and Means Committee.

Most revenues derive from existing provisions of the tax code or Social Security law, which continue in effect from year to year unless changed by Congress. This tax structure can be expected to produce increasing amounts of revenue in future years as the economy expands and incomes rise. Nevertheless, Congress usually makes some changes in the tax laws each year, either to raise or lower revenues or to redistribute the tax burden. *(See § 9.91, Tax Expenditures.)*

Congress typically acts on revenue legislation pursuant to proposals in the president's budget. An early step in congressional work on revenue legislation is publication by the Congressional Budget Office (CBO) of its own estimates of the revenue impact of the president's

§ 9.92

Revenue Estimates

The Joint Committee on Taxation (JCT) prepares estimates of proposed revenue legislation for Congress. Generally, the estimates measure the effects of revenue proposals on the revenue projections under existing law. In recent years, some members of Congress have questioned whether or not the estimates of revenue proposals currently provided by the JCT (referred to as "static" by some) adequately take into account macroeconomic effects and incorporate such effects into revenue estimates (referred to as "dynamic estimates").

House standing rules require a "macroeconomic impact analysis" of most revenue measures reported by the Committee on Ways and Means, unless the JCT determines that such an analysis is "not calculable."

The House rule defines a "macroeconomic impact analysis" as:

(i) an estimate prepared by the Joint Committee on Internal Revenue [sic] Taxation of the changes in economic output, employment, capital stock, and tax revenues expected to result from enactment of the proposal; and

(ii) a statement from the Joint Committee on Internal Revenue [sic] Taxation identifying the critical assumptions and the source data underlying that estimate.

Neither the House rule nor the Congressional Budget Act (CBA) requires that such estimates be used for budget enforcement purposes. However, neither the rule nor the CBA precludes the use of such estimates for that purpose.

budget proposals, developed with assistance from the Joint Committee on Taxation. The congressional estimates often differ significantly from those presented in the president's budget. *(See § 9.92, Revenue Estimates.)*

The revenue totals in the budget resolution establish the framework for subsequent action on revenue measures. The budget resolution contains only revenue totals and total recommended changes. It does not allocate these totals among revenue sources, or specify which provisions of the tax code are to be changed.

The House and Senate periodically consider major revenue measures, under their regular legislative procedures. However, as has been the case with direct-spending programs, many of the most significant changes in revenue policy in recent years have been made in the context of the reconciliation process. *(See § 9.110, Reconciliation Legislation.)* Although revenue changes in the past sometimes were incorporated along with spending changes (and sometimes debt-limit increases) into omnibus budget reconciliation measures, under recent practices revenue reconciliation legislation is considered on a separate track (for example, the Tax Increase Prevention and Reconciliation Act of 2005 *(P.L. 109-222; 120 Stat. 345))*.

§ 9.100 Debt-Limit Legislation

When the revenues collected by the federal government are not sufficient to cover its expenditures, it must finance the shortfall through borrowing. In addition, the federal government is compelled to incur debt because of requirements that trust fund surpluses be invested in federal securities. Federal borrowing is subject to a public-debt limit established by statute. As long as the federal government incurs annual deficits and trust funds incur annual surpluses, the public-debt limit must be increased periodically. The frequency of congressional action to raise the debt limit has ranged in the past from several times in one year to once in several years.

Legislation to raise the public-debt limit falls under the jurisdiction of the House Ways and Means Committee and the Senate Finance Committee. Congress may develop debt-limit legislation in any of three ways: (1) under regular legislative procedures; (2) as part of reconciliation legislation; or (3) in the House, under Rule XXVII (referred to as the "Gephardt rule" after its author, former Representative Richard Gephardt, D-MO). House Rule XXVII requires that the House Clerk automatically engross and transmit to the Senate, upon the adoption of the budget resolution, a joint resolution changing the public debt limit to the level specified in the budget resolution. This automatic engrossing process was added to the House rules in 1979, remained in the House rules until it was removed at the beginning of the 107th Congress, and was restored at the beginning of the 108th Congress. The Senate has no comparable procedure and may consider this joint resolution under the regular legislative process. With fewer constraints on the consideration of such measures than the House, the Senate may add nongermane provisions to debt-limit legislation. For example, the 1985 Balanced Budget Act (Gramm-Rudman-Hollings) was an amendment to a debt-limit bill.

§ 9.110 Reconciliation Legislation

Beginning in 1980, Congress has used *reconciliation legislation* to implement many of its most significant budget policies. Section 310 of the 1974 Congressional Budget Act sets forth a special procedure for the development and consideration of reconciliation legislation. Reconciliation legislation is used by Congress to bring existing revenue and spending law into conformity with the policies in a budget resolution. Reconciliation is an optional process, but Congress has used it more years than not since 1980.

The reconciliation process has two stages—the adoption of *reconciliation directives* in the budget resolution and the enactment of reconciliation legislation that implements changes in revenue or spending laws. Although reconciliation has been used for some time, specific procedures tend to vary from year to year.

Reconciliation is used to change the amount of revenues, budget authority, or outlays generated by existing law. In a few instances, reconciliation has been used to adjust the public-debt limit. On the spending side, the process focuses on entitlement laws; it may not be used, however, to impel changes in Social Security law. Reconciliation sometimes has been applied to discretionary authorizations, which are funded in annual appropriations acts, but this is not the usual practice.

Reconciliation Directives

Reconciliation begins with a directive in a budget resolution instructing one or more designated committees to recommend legislation changing existing law. These directives have three components: (1) they name the committee or committees directed to recommend legislation; (2) they specify the amounts of changes in revenues or outlays that are to be achieved by changes in existing law, but do not indicate how these changes are to be made, which laws are to be altered, or the programs to be affected; and (3) they usually set a deadline by which the designated committee or committees must recommend the changes in law. The directives typically cover the same fiscal years covered by the budget resolution. The dollar amounts are computed with reference to the Congressional Budget Office *baseline*. Thus, a change represents the amount by which revenues or spending would decrease or increase from baseline levels as a result of changes made in existing law.

Although the instructions do not mention the programs to be changed, they are based on assumptions concerning the savings or deficit reduction (or, in some cases, increases) that would result from particular changes in revenue provisions or spending programs. These program assumptions are sometimes printed in the reports on the budget resolution. Even when the assumptions are not published, committees and members usually have a good idea of the specific program changes contemplated by the reconciliation directives.

A committee has discretion to decide the legislative changes to be recommended. It is not bound by the program changes recommended or assumed by the Budget Committees in the reports accompanying the budget resolution. However, a committee is expected to recommend legislation estimated to produce the dollar changes delineated in its reconciliation directives.

When a budget resolution containing a reconciliation directive has been approved by Congress, the instruction has the status of an order by the House and Senate to designated committees to recommend legislation, usually by a date certain.

Development and Consideration of Reconciliation Measures

When more than one committee in the House and Senate is subject to reconciliation directives, the proposed legislative changes are consolidated by the Budget Committees into an omnibus bill. The 1974 Congressional Budget Act does not permit the Budget Committees to revise substantively the legislation recommended by the committees of jurisdiction. This restriction pertains even when the Budget Committees estimate that the proposed legislation will fall short of the dollar changes called for in the instructions. Sometimes, the Budget Committees—working with the leadership—develop alternatives to the committee recommendations. These alternatives may be offered as floor amendments to achieve greater compliance with the reconciliation directives.

The 1974 act requires that amendments offered to reconciliation legislation in either the House or the Senate be deficit-neutral. To meet this requirement, an amendment reducing revenues or increasing spending must offset these deficit increases by equivalent revenue increases or spending cuts. In addition, nongermane amendments may not be offered in either chamber.

During the first several years of experience with reconciliation, the legislation contained many provisions that were extraneous to the purpose of the reconciliation measures, such as reducing the deficit. The reconciliation submissions of committees included such things as provisions that had no budgetary effect, that had a budgetary effect merely incidental to a significant policy change, or that violated another committee's jurisdiction. In 1985, the Senate adopted a rule (commonly referred to as the *Byrd rule*, after Senator Robert C. Byrd, D-WV) on a temporary basis as a means of curbing these practices. The Byrd rule has been extended and modified several times over the years. In 1990, the Byrd rule was incorporated into the 1974 Congressional Budget Act as section 313 and made permanent. The Senate, nonetheless, may waive the Byrd rule by unanimous consent or by a waiver motion requiring a three-fifths vote of the membership. Although the House has no rule comparable to the Senate's Byrd rule, it may use other devices to control the inclusion of extraneous matter in reconciliation legislation. In particular, the House has used *special rules* to make in order amendments to strike extraneous matter. *(See § 8.90, Rules Committee and Special Rules.)*

Senate debate on reconciliation legislation is limited to twenty hours. The Senate may continue to consider amendments, motions, and appeals after that time, but no additional debate is allowed. The House is not restricted by the 1974 act in debate on reconciliation legislation, but it typically adopts a special rule limiting general debate, amendments, and other floor procedures.

§ 9.120 Implementation of the Budget by Executive Agencies

Federal agencies implement the various spending and revenue measures enacted into law through thousands of discrete actions. While the submission of the president's budget proposals and the subsequent consideration of them by Congress in the legislative process usually garner considerable attention in the media, less scrutiny is often paid to what actually happens to funds after congressional action is finished. Three categories of executive agency actions are of particular interest to Congress: apportionment (§ 9.130), transfer and reprogramming (§ 9.140), and impoundment (§ 9.150).

§ 9.130 Apportionment

After budget authority is enacted into law, one of the first steps in making the funds available for spending by agencies is *apportionment*. Apportionment procedures are set forth in the Antideficiency Act *(31 U.S.C. §§ 1341–1342, 1512–1519)*, which evolved from legislation first enacted in the 1870s. Under these procedures, the Office of Management and Budget (OMB) determines how increments of budget authority will be advanced to each agency on an account-by-account basis. For a typical account, OMB apportions one-fourth of the available budget authority at the beginning of each fiscal quarter. A violation of the Antideficiency Act may occur when an agency obligates more funds than were apportioned to it; the comptroller general is tasked by Congress with monitoring such violations.

§ 9.140 Transfer and Reprogramming

After spending measures have been enacted into law, agencies sometimes shift funds from one purpose to another. A *transfer* involves the shifting of funds from one account to another, while a *reprogramming* involves shifting funds from one program to another within the same account. In either case, Congress is involved in these adjustments, although in varying degrees.

Permanent law, in Title 31 (Money and Finance) of the U.S. Code, requires that agencies spend funds only according to the purposes specified in law. For this reason, the transfer of funds from one account to another requires the enactment of a law. In some cases, Congress anticipates the need to transfer funds and may grant a department or agency head transfer authority, subject to limitations. If Congress anticipates this need, it can include a provision in the law providing the funds. In other instances, Congress might enact legislation providing for specified transfers.

Unlike transfers, reprogrammings do not shift funds from one account to another and therefore do not require the enactment of a law. The Appropriations Committees exert control over reprogrammings by establishing specific rules that agencies must follow when pursuing such actions. In recent years, these rules have been included as provisions in annual appropriations acts. The rules set forth restrictions such as requiring prior committee notification and approval for reprogrammings beyond a certain dollar threshold and barring reprogrammings from terminating any program.

§ 9.150 Impoundment: Deferrals and Rescissions

Although an appropriation limits the amounts that can be spent, it also establishes the expectation that the available funds will be used to carry out authorized activities. Hence, when an agency fails to use all or part of an appropriation, it deviates from the intentions of Congress. The Impoundment Control Act of 1974 *(P.L. 93-344, title X; 88 Stat. 332–339)*, enacted as part of the Congressional Budget and Impoundment Control Act of 1974, prescribes rules and procedures for instances in which available funds are *impounded. (See § 9.10, Key Budget Process Laws.)*

An impoundment is an action or inaction by the president or a federal agency that delays or withholds the obligation or expenditure of budget authority provided in law. The 1974 Impoundment Control Act divides impoundments into two categories and establishes distinct procedures for each. A *deferral* delays the use of funds; a *rescission* is a presidential request that Congress rescind (cancel) an appropriation or other form of budget authority. Deferral and rescission are exclusive and comprehensive categories. An impoundment is either a rescission or a deferral—it cannot be both or something else.

To propose a rescission, the president must submit a message to Congress specifying the amount to be rescinded, the accounts and programs involved, the estimated fiscal and program effects, and the reasons for the rescission. Multiple rescissions can be grouped in a single message. After the message has been submitted to it, Congress has forty-five days of "continuous session" (usually a larger number of calendar days) during which it can pass a rescission bill. Congress may rescind all, part, or none of the amount proposed by the president.

If Congress does not approve a rescission in legislation by the expiration of this period, the president must make the funds available for obligation and expenditure. If the president fails to release funds at the expiration of the forty-five-day period for proposed rescissions, the comptroller general may bring suit to compel their release. This has been a rare occurrence, however.

To defer funds, the president submits a message to Congress setting forth the amount, the affected account and program, the reasons for the deferral, the estimated fiscal and program effects, and the period of time during which the funds are to be deferred. The president may not propose a deferral for a period of time beyond the end of the fiscal year, and he may not propose a deferral that would cause the funds to lapse or otherwise prevent an agency from spending appropriated funds prudently. In accounts where unobligated funds remain available beyond the fiscal year, the president may defer the funds again in the next fiscal year.

At present, the president may defer only for the reasons set forth in the Antideficiency Act, including to provide for contingencies, to achieve savings made possible by or through changes in requirements or greater efficiency of operations, and as specifically provided by law. He may not defer funds for policy reasons (for example, to curtail overall federal spending or because he is opposed to a particular program).

The comptroller general, head of the Government Accountability Office (GAO), reviews all proposed rescissions and deferrals and advises Congress of their legality and possible budgetary and program effects. The comptroller general also notifies Congress of any rescission or deferral not reported by the president. The comptroller general may also reclassify an improperly classified impoundment. In all cases, a notification to Congress by the comptroller general has the same legal effect as an impoundment message of the president. The president's impoundment messages, as well as the comptroller general's reports, are printed as House documents (H. Doc. ___). The GAO also issues its reports separately.

The 1974 Impoundment Control Act provided for special types of legislation—rescission bills and deferral resolutions—for Congress to use in exercising its impoundment control powers. However, pursuant to court decisions that held the *legislative veto* to be unconstitutional, Congress may not use deferral resolutions to disapprove a deferral. Further, Congress has been reluctant to use rescission bills regularly. Congress, instead, usually acts on impoundment matters within the framework of the annual appropriations measures.

During the first six years of his administration, President George W. Bush did not propose any rescissions under the Impoundment Control Act. Instead he proposed the "cancellation" of funds; under this approach, he did not have to submit a report on his proposed cancellations to Congress, but neither could he withhold spending the funds while the proposals were pending. Congress responded to the proposed cancellations by enacting many of them—amounting to billions of dollars—into law.

Line Item Veto

During the 104th Congress, the Line Item Veto Act *(P.L. 104-130; 110 Stat. 1200)* was enacted as an amendment to the 1974 Impoundment Control Act. President Clinton applied the line-item veto to several measures in 1997, but the Supreme Court ruled the Line Item Veto Act unconstitutional in June 1998 and the earlier line-item vetoes were nullified. (*Clinton v. City of New York*, 524 U.S. 417 (1998).) The authority granted to the president under the Line Item Veto Act, which differed markedly from the veto authority available to most chief executives at the state level, was intended to reverse the presumption underlying the process for the consideration of rescissions under the 1974 Impoundment Control Act. Under the Line Item Veto Act, presidential proposals would take effect unless overturned by legislative action. The act authorized the president to identify at enactment individual items in legislation that he proposed should not go into effect. The identification was based not just upon the statutory language, but on the entire legislative history and documentation. The president had to notify Congress promptly of his proposals and provide supporting information. Congress had to respond within a limited period of time by enacting a law if it wanted to disapprove the president's proposals. Otherwise, the president's proposals would take effect.

§ 9.160

Budget Process Glossary

Account: Control and reporting unit for budgeting and accounting.

Appropriated Entitlement: An entitlement for which budget authority is provided in annual appropriations acts.

Appropriation: Provision of law providing budget authority that permits federal agencies to incur obligations and make payments out of the Treasury.

Authorization: Provision in law that establishes or continues a program or agency and authorizes appropriations for it.

Baseline: Projection of future revenues, budget authority, outlays, and other budget amounts under assumed economic conditions and participation rates without a change in current policy.

Borrowing Authority: Spending authority that permits a federal agency to incur obligations and to make payments for specified purposes out of funds borrowed from the Treasury or the public.

Budget Authority: Authority in law to enter into obligations that normally result in outlays.

Budget Resolution: Concurrent resolution incorporating an agreement by the House and Senate on an overall budget plan; may contain reconciliation instructions.

Byrd Rule: A Congressional Budget Act rule (Section 313), named after its author, Senator Robert C. Byrd (D-WV), that prohibits extraneous matter in a reconciliation measure considered in the Senate. Under the rule, extraneous matter includes, among other things specified in the act, any provision that has no direct budgetary effect or that increases the deficit (or reduces the surplus) in a fiscal year beyond those covered in the reconciliation measure.

Continuing Appropriations Act: An appropriations act that provides stop-gap (or full-year) funding for agencies that have not received regular appropriations. (Also referred to as a continuing resolution.)

Cost Estimate: An estimate of the impact of legislation on revenues, spending, or both, generally as reported by a House or Senate committee or a conference committee; the 1974 Congressional Budget Act requires the Congressional Budget Office to prepare cost estimates on all public bills.

Credit Authority: Authority to incur direct loan obligations or make loan guarantee commitments.

Deferral: Action or inaction that temporarily withholds, delays, or effectively precludes the obligation or expenditure of budget authority.

Direct Spending: Spending controlled outside of annual appropriations acts, and specifically including the Food Stamp program; also referred to as mandatory spending.

Discretionary Spending: Spending provided in, and controlled by, annual appropriations acts.

Continued on page 370

Earmark: For expenditures, an amount set aside within an appropriation account for a specified purpose.

Entitlement Authority: Law that obligates the federal government to make payments to eligible persons, businesses, or governments.

Fiscal Year: The period from October 1 through September 30; fiscal year 2008 began October 1, 2007, and ended September 30, 2008.

Impoundment: Action or inaction by an executive official that delays or precludes the obligation or expenditure of budget authority.

Mandatory Spending: *See Direct Spending.*

Obligation: A binding agreement that requires payment.

Outlays: Payments to liquidate obligations.

PAYGO (Pay-As-You-Go): Process by which direct spending increases or revenue decreases must be offset so that the deficit is not increased or the surplus reduced. A statutory PAYGO requirement was in effect from 1991 through 2002; the House and Senate each have their own PAYGO rules.

Reconciliation: Process by which Congress changes existing laws to conform revenue and spending levels to the levels set in a budget resolution.

Regular Appropriations Act: An appropriations act that provides budget authority for the next fiscal year.

Reprogramming: Shifting funds from one program to another in the same appropriations account.

Rescission: Cancellation of budget authority previously provided by Congress.

Revenues: Income from individual and corporate income taxes, social insurance taxes, excise taxes, fees, tariffs, and other sources collected under the sovereign powers of the federal government.

Scorekeeping: Process for tracking and reporting on the status of congressional budgetary actions affecting budget authority, outlays, revenues, and the surplus or deficit.

Supplemental Appropriations Act: An appropriations act that provides additional budget authority during the current year when the regular appropriation is insufficient.

Tax Expenditure: Loss of revenue attributable to an exemption, deduction, preference, or other exclusion under federal tax law.

Transfer: Shift of budgetary resources from one appropriation account to another, as authorized by law.

Views and Estimates: Annual report of each House and Senate committee on budgetary matters within its jurisdiction.

Chapter Ten

Legislating in Congress:
Special Procedures and Considerations

Contributing Authors

Eugene Boyd

(Congress and Federalism)

Henry B. Hogue

(Congress and the Executive)

Analysis

10

§10.00 Introduction: Separation of Powers, Checks and Balances, and Federalism

The three branches of the federal government are intertwined by the Constitution and by experience and practice. The executive and the judiciary have explicit and inherent powers under the Constitution. Congress has the authority to legislate not only in areas enumerated in Article I of the Constitution but also to "make all Laws which shall be necessary and proper for carrying into Execution the foregoing Powers, and all other Powers vested by this Constitution in the Government of the United States, or in any Department or Officer thereof." *(Art. I, sec. 8, cl. 18.)* The *Necessary and Proper Clause* of the Constitution, also called the *Elastic Clause*, provides Congress with powers beyond those enumerated in Article I. It gives Congress authority to legislate on many of the grants of power to the executive and to the judiciary.

When the Constitution was drafted and ratified, the thirteen original states and the people in them gave certain powers to the national government. After considerable debate, they decided that foreign policy, a common defense, interstate commerce, and other governmental powers were more effectively handled through a constitutionally empowered national government. The states continued as a separate level of government, exercising a separate set of sovereign powers within their physical territories. The federal system, however, is not static. The challenges and advances of the last century and this one—world wars, foreign totalitarian states, religious and ethnic fanaticism, the Great Depression, economic globalization, rights of citizens, and advances in transportation and communications—seemed to favor an expansive and dominant national government.

Separation of Powers and Checks and Balances

The framers of the Constitution differentiated among the three branches of the national or federal government, but they also provided a system of *checks and balances* intended to make the three branches work together and remain in an equilibrium.

The declarative statements introducing the first three articles of the Constitution are the foundation for separation of powers:

- "All legislative Powers herein granted shall be vested in a Congress of the United States. . . ." *(Art. I, sec. 1.)*
- "The executive Power shall be vested in a President of the United States of America." *(Art. II, sec. 1, cl. 1.)*
- "The judicial Power of the United States, shall be vested in one supreme Court, and in such inferior Courts as the Congress may from time to time ordain and establish." *(Art. III, sec. 1.)*

The Constitution then spells out the authority of each of the branches in the three respective articles.

However, the framers interlocked the exercise of the three great governmental powers by assigning roles in each branch that affect or limit power in the other two branches. Perhaps the most important of these to Congress and government affairs professionals alike is the president's role in the legislative process. Article I, Section 7 provides for the presentation of every measure passed by Congress to the president. If the president signs a measure, it becomes law. Article I also provides for his veto, but, lest the president be arbitrary or autocratic, it also limits his time to weigh approval or veto to ten days (Sundays excepted) and allows Congress, by a two-thirds vote in each chamber, to override a veto.

The president is specifically given the power to make treaties and appoint judges, ambassadors, and designated officers of the federal government. The president's power is limited by the need to obtain a two-thirds vote in the Senate consenting to the ratification of a treaty, and the need to obtain a majority vote in the Senate consenting to those of his appointments designated in law as subject to Senate confirmation.

Other provisions of the Constitution—such as Article II, Section 1, and Article III, Section 1—explicitly constrain another branch. These two sections, respectively, provide for compensation to the president and judges, but the president's salary cannot be increased or decreased during his tenure and judges' salaries cannot be decreased during their service.

The framers also provided checks and balances within the legislative branch. To make law, a measure must pass both houses in identical form before presentation to the president. Revenue measures must originate in the House, but the Senate may amend them. The House has sole power to impeach, and the Senate has sole power to try an impeachment. And, neither house may adjourn for more than three days without the consent of the other house.

Still other constitutional checks and balances have arisen from experience under the Constitution. For example, the power of the judiciary to declare acts of Congress unconstitutional is nowhere explicitly stated in the Constitution. However, in *Marbury v. Madison*, 5 U.S. 137 (1803), the Supreme Court established its authority in interpreting the Constitution.

Federalism

In the American system of government, sovereignty is shared between the national and state governments. Through the exercise of its powers, the national government can affect all people in all states, the District of Columbia, and U.S. territories and possessions. Each state government—through the exercise of its powers—can affect all people within the state's physical territory.

The national government is a government of enumerated powers. It is important to note that the grant of power to the legislative branch quoted above says, "All legislative Powers *herein granted. . . ." (Art. I, sec. 1; emphasis added.)* The phrase reemphasizes the concept of enumerated powers. The Bill of Rights also includes the Tenth Amendment, which provides as follows: "The powers not delegated to the United States by the Constitution, nor prohibited by it to the States, are reserved to the States respectively, or to the people."

The Constitution contains both grants of authority to, and restrictions on, the national government concerning its power over the states. For example, Article IV, Section 4 empowers the national government: "The United States shall guarantee to every State in this Union a Republican Form of Government. . . ." On the other hand, Article IV, Section 3 strictly circumscribes its authority: ". . . but no new State shall be formed or erected within the Jurisdiction of any other State. . . ." States, in turn, are directed to treat each other and each other's citizens without discrimination. For example, the Fourteenth Amendment provides as follows:

> Section 1. All persons born or naturalized in the United States, and subject to the jurisdiction thereof, are citizens of the United States and of the State wherein they reside. No State shall make or enforce any law which shall abridge the privileges or immunities of citizens of the United States; nor shall any State deprive any person of life, liberty, or property, without due process of law; nor deny to any person within its jurisdiction the equal protection of the laws.

States are also prohibited from taking certain governmental action, either unequivocally or in the absence of congressional consent. For example, in the former case, Article I, Section 10, Clause 1 states in part: "No State shall enter into any Treaty, Alliance, or Confederation. . . ." In the latter instance, Article I, Section 10, Clause 3 provides in part: "No state shall, without the consent of Congress . . . enter into any Agreement or Compact with another State. . . ."

Finally, the sovereignty of the states is recognized and protected in the manner by which the Constitution can be amended. Either the legislatures of three-fourths of the states or conventions in three-fourths of the states must ratify a constitutional amendment for it to become effective.

This chapter describes or illustrates some of the ways in which Congress exercises its powers vis-à-vis the executive and judicial branches and the states.

§10.10 Congress and the Executive

Within the constitutional framework, Congress and the executive continuously devise and revise formal and informal means of making their relationship work. Over time, Congress has given the executive branch authority and responsibilities that are executive (administering the law), legislative (for example, rulemaking), and judicial (through adjudication). Congress uses its constitutional authority, including the Necessary and Proper, or Elastic, Clause (*art. I, sec. 8, cl.18: "To make all Laws which shall be necessary and proper . . ."*), to pass laws establishing federal government agencies and programs. In addition to program-specific laws, Congress passes laws dictating government-wide procedures. One way that Congress attempts to ensure that the vast array of federal programs is carried out with due consideration for democratic, constitutional values and a minimum of waste, fraud, and abuse is by passing general management laws, such as the Administrative Procedure Act (*5 U.S.C. § 551 et seq. and § 701 et seq.*), that specify the processes that each agency must follow when carrying out its responsibilities. In addition to its legislative powers, Congress has the power to influence the executive through appropriations, appointments advice and consent, and oversight and investigation. It requires reports from the executive, conducts hearings, monitors the *Federal Register,* and pursues its checks on executive power in dozens of other ways. Congressional use of these powers and methods for checking the executive varies; some Congresses assert their constitutional prerogatives more than other Congresses.

§ 10.20 Congress and the Executive: Legislation

The president and his administration are key sources of legislative proposals. The president might have an economic program that he wants enacted soon after his election, as both Presidents Clinton and George W. Bush did. Or, he might request *fast-track* authority to facilitate his negotiation of trade agreements. The president might request legislation on any subject. Department and agency officials, too, regularly seek changes in law in accordance with administration policy, and participate fully in congressional deliberations over new *authorization* measures and *reauthorization* measures.

The president is likely to make key portions of his legislative program known in his annual State of the Union address and his annual budget request. He sends other messages on legislation to Congress, and submits draft legislation or outlines of legislation that he would like to see enacted. The president might also endorse legislation that has been introduced in Congress, and work for its adoption. And his liaison office and affected departments and agencies work together to ensure that legislation moving in Congress is acceptable to the president. *(See § 10.21, Letter Opposing Legislation (from the General Counsel of the U.S. Department of Commerce).)* The administration also tries to develop common legislative interests with the president's party's leadership in each chamber and, if possible, with the leadership of the other party, especially if the other party is in the majority in a chamber. *(See § 3.33, White House Legislative Affairs.)*

Congress also delegates to the president authority to recommend specific actions to Congress. For example, under the Arms Export Control Act *(22 U.S.C. § 2751 et seq.)*, the president must notify Congress of major weapons sales, which Congress might then disapprove by a joint resolution subject to presidential signature or veto. Congress has set a high hurdle for itself—a two-thirds vote in each house if it and the president disagree. However, the president usually consults or negotiates with Congress so that Congress does not respond broadly to curtail his discretion in managing foreign relations generally or arms sales specifically.

Congressional committees and chamber leadership may seek the input of the administration on legislation. During the course of congressional deliberations, administration officials testify at hearings, attend markups, and remain active throughout floor and conference proceedings to provide information to members. Committees solicit written agency comments on

10

§ 10.21

Letter Opposing Legislation
(from the General Counsel of the
U.S. Department of Commerce)

GENERAL COUNSEL OF THE
UNITED STATES DEPARTMENT OF COMMERCE
Washington, D.C. 20230

March 9, 2005

The Honorable Ted Stevens
Chairman, Committee on Commerce,
 Science, and Transportation
United States Senate
Washington, DC 20510-6125

Dear Mr. Chairman:

In anticipation of the mark-up by the Committee on Commerce, Science, and Transportation
of S. 268, the "Training for Realtime Writers Act of 2005," we would like to express the
Administration's opposition to establishing a grant program within the National
Telecommunications and Information Administration (NTIA) for eligible entities to promote
training and job placement for realtime writers.

We understand that this program was designed to meet the requirements for closed-captioning of
video programming as set forth in section 723 of the Communications Act of 1934 and the rules
prescribed thereunder. NTIA does not have the subject-matter expertise necessary to administer
the program envisioned in S. 268. Moreover, the President's FY 2006 Budget does not provide
for the funding authorized under the bill. Accordingly, the Administration opposes enactment of
S. 268.

Thank you for the opportunity to provide these views to you. The Office of Management and
Budget has advised that there is no objection to the submission of these views from the
standpoint of the Administration's program.

Sincerely,

Jane T. Dana
Acting General Counsel

cc: The Honorable Daniel K. Inouye
        Co-Chairman

introduced legislation, usually at the time of hearings or markup. Both chambers' rules require these comments to be included in committee reports on legislation. *(See § 5.170, Congressional Liaison Offices.)* The Office of Management and Budget (OMB) coordinates the administration position, and might also coordinate one or more *Statements of Administration Policy (SAPs)* on active legislation, which represent the coordinated views of the president and agencies affected by—or interested in—a piece of legislation covered by the SAP. *(See OMB Circular No. A-19, Legislative Coordination and Clearance, <www.whitehouse.gov/omb/circulars/ a019/a019.html>, which continues to express policy guidance, and the OMB director's memorandum on legislative coordination and clearance on the OMB web site at <www.whitehouse.gov/omb/ memoranda/m01-12.html>.)*

In its guidance to executive branch departments and agencies, OMB has identified the purposes of its legislative coordination and clearance function to be to assist the president in developing a position on legislation, to make the administration's position known to the agencies and to Congress, to ensure that all agencies affected by or interested in specific legislation have had the opportunity to consider and provide their views on the legislation, and to assist the president in decision making related to bill signature or veto. Therefore, an agency wishing to submit draft legislation to Congress, or to comment or testify on legislation, first submits its legislation or testimony to OMB. OMB in turn circulates the document to affected and interested agencies and to appropriate staff within the Executive Office of the President. OMB also coordinates the reconciliation of differing views, and discussion or negotiation can occur during the clearance process. OMB subsequently advises an agency that the administration has "no objection" to the legislation or testimony, or that the legislation or testimony is "in accord with the president's program." The meaning of the latter designation is that the legislation or testimony implements a presidential proposal, or advances the president's program or policies, and deserves the president's support. *(See § 10.22, Presidential Letter.)* Agencies convey this advice to Congress with their legislation or testimony. Legislation or testimony that conflicts with the administration's program, however, may not be submitted to Congress. *(See also § 5.180, Office of Management and Budget.)*

OMB prepares SAPs, again in consultation with agencies affected by or interested in the specific legislation and with appropriate officials in the Executive Office of the President. SAPs tend to be prepared in anticipation of or during floor debate. OMB's Legislative Affairs Office transmits SAPs to Congress. *(See examples of SAPs at § 15.08 and § 15.13.)*

OMB also coordinates the preparation of a memorandum to the president on measures that have been enrolled and will be sent to the president for his signature or veto. OMB circulates the enrolled measure to affected or interested agencies, and they are expected to submit their analysis and recommendation of the legislation within 48 hours. An agency that recommends a signing statement or a veto is also responsible for drafting an appropriate statement for the president's consideration. *(See § 8.291, Vetoes and Veto Overrides: Presidential Clout.)*

The Lobbying with Appropriated Moneys Act *(18 U.S.C. § 1913)* and other statutes related to agencies and programs generally prohibit the use of appropriated funds to lobby Congress. However, the prohibitions, at the very least, do not restrict the responsiveness of executive departments and agencies to congressional requests for information on legislation, including appropriations.

§ 10.22

Presidential Letter

THE WHITE HOUSE

WASHINGTON

May 3, 2007

Dear Madam Speaker:

I am concerned that this year the Congress may consider legislation that could substantially change Federal policies and laws on abortion, and allow taxpayer dollars to be used for the destruction of human life. I am writing to make sure that there is no misunderstanding of my views on these important issues.

Our Nation was founded on the belief that every human being has rights, dignity, and matchless value. Every child should be welcomed into life and protected in law. The advancement of science and medicine need not conflict with the ethical imperative to cherish and protect every life. In fact, advances in science have made it possible to see life developing at earlier stages and underscore Americans' obligation to protect helpless and innocent life from destruction, whether it is in the womb or elsewhere. These issues are deeply emotional and are made even more complicated when the American taxpayer is asked to fund efforts that end human life.

As you know, current law prohibits Federal funding for abortion, both domestically and internationally, except in cases of rape, incest, or where the life of the mother is endangered. Recent legislative practice has ensured that taxpayer funds do not underwrite organizations that perform or promote abortion as a method of family planning. Current U.S. law protects human embryos. The standing pattern is that appropriate conscience protections must be in place for health care entities, and that taxpayer dollars may not be used in coercive or involuntary family planning programs.

I urge that these and other existing, important protections be respected and continued. I believe it is the most basic duty of Government to guard the innocent. With that in mind, I will veto any legislation that weakens current Federal policies and laws on abortion, or that encourages the destruction of human life at any stage.

Sincerely,

The Honorable Nancy Pelosi
Speaker of the
    House of Representatives
Washington, D.C. 20515

The president also uses his authority to approve or veto measures as part of his leverage with Congress. The president can effectively use the threat of a veto to influence the outcome of legislation. Should a measure with which he disagrees pass, he can veto the legislation to drive home his strong position. As demonstrated by the table in § 8.291 *(Vetoes and Veto Overrides: Presidential Clout)*, presidents normally prevail on vetoes.

(See also § 3.30, Executive-Branch Pressure; and, in § 11.50, Laws and Their Implementation by the Executive, the subsection, Executive Orders, Proclamations, and Other Presidential Directives.)

§ 10.30 Congress and the Executive: Ratification of Treaties, and Foreign Policy

The president can negotiate treaties with foreign nations and, subject to the advice and consent of the Senate, ratify them. Under the Constitution *(art. II, sec. 2, cl. 2)*, ratification of a treaty requires consent of two-thirds of senators present and voting. The Senate has developed special procedures applicable to treaties. The House and Senate together have also developed other special procedures, including so-called fast-track procedures, applicable to some trade agreements, arms sales, and other foreign policy activities. *(See § 10.150, Congress and Foreign Policy: Treaties and International Agreements; § 10.151, Fast-Track Procedures; and § 10.160, Congress and Foreign Policy: Legislation, Appropriations, and Nominations.)*

Congress has developed a number of other formal and informal means to control, guide, or influence the president in his conduct of foreign policy. While only Congress can declare war, it has rarely done so. Today, commitments of American troops to armed conflict may be debated in Congress in the context of the War Powers Resolution *(50 U.S.C. § 1541 et seq.)*. The roles of Congress and the president in authorizing the use of U.S. troops in international conflict appear to be in flux. *(See § 10.140, Congress and Foreign Policy: Declaring War and Committing Troops.)*

Through legislation, appropriations, and Senate advice and consent on nominations and treaties, Congress can dictate or influence the foreign policy of the United States and its management by the president. Hearings, fact-finding missions overseas, and other activities assist Congress in being informed and having sources of information independent of the president or the executive branch. *(See § 10.170, Congress and Foreign Policy: Nonbinding Actions.)*

Although Congress has these constitutionally based tools for influencing foreign policy, its level of control vis-à-vis the president has varied over time.

§ 10.40 Congress and the Executive: Rulemaking

Together with taxing and spending, regulation is one of the fundamental ways the federal government implements public policy. Rulemaking is the process by which regulations are put in place. Given the complex and constantly changing modern world, among other factors, Congress does not necessarily enact legislation that is sufficiently detailed to cover every eventuality related to a given area of legislative policy. Therefore, Congress often delegates authority to further refine legislative policy through the assignment of rulemaking authority to executive departments and agencies, as well as to independent regulatory agencies. For example, a statute may contain standards for achieving the statute's purposes and assign responsibility for its administration to a specific governmental entity. The statute might authorize and perhaps guide the promulgation of regulations, or rules, implementing the law by, for example, listing considerations to be included in developing the regulations and mandating a time frame within which regulations are to be issued. Rulemaking authority is sometimes referred to as *quasi-legislative authority* because it can be seen as an extension of Congress's legislative function.

In addition to enacting laws assigning specific rulemaking authority to various governmental entities, Congress has established government-wide rulemaking requirements that guide the rulemaking process more generally. For example, the Federal Register Act (*44 U.S.C. § 1501 et seq.*), enacted in 1935, created a uniform system for notifying the public of agency rulemaking activity that includes publication of documents in the *Federal Register* and codification of rules in the *Code of Federal Regulations*. The Administrative Procedure Act of 1946 (*5 U.S.C. § 551 et seq. and § 701 et seq.*) established general procedures for rulemaking, including, for example, requirements that a notice of proposed rulemaking be published in the *Federal Register* and that interested persons have the opportunity to comment.

In granting rulemaking authority through numerous laws to various federal entities, Congress still maintains vigilance over the rulemaking process and specific rulemaking initiatives. (*See §10.41, Congressional Review of Agency Rulemaking.*) Occasionally, Congress acts to increase the importance of certain considerations in the development of regulations, as it did with the enactment of the National Environmental Policy Act of 1969 (*83 Stat. 852*), regarding rules' environmental impact; the Regulatory Flexibility Act of 1980 (*5 U.S.C. § 601 et seq.*) and the Small Business Regulatory Enforcement Fairness Act of 1996 (*110 Stat. 857*), regarding rules' impact on "small entities"; the Unfunded Mandates Act of 1995 (*see § 10.202*), regarding rules' unfunded requirements of state, local, or tribal governments, or the private sector; and the Data Quality Act of 2001 (*114 Stat. 2763A-153*), regarding standards for the quality and use of information underlying rules.

In 1980, Congress passed the Paperwork Reduction Act (*44 U.S.C. § 3501 et seq.*), which it also amended in 1986 and 1995. Among other things, this law was intended to decrease the paperwork burden imposed on individuals and entities by federal regulations. It established the Office of Information and Regulatory Affairs (OIRA) within the Office of Management and Budget (OMB), which is part of the Executive Office of the President. In February 1981, newly elected President Reagan issued Executive Order 12291, which, among other things, gave OMB, and, in turn, OIRA, responsibility for acting as a gatekeeper for new federal regulations. Under the order, all federal agencies except independent regulatory agencies were required to weigh the costs of a potential rule against its benefits; prepare a regulatory impact analysis for each rule that might impose costs of $100 million or more on the U.S. economy;

§ 10.41

Congressional Review of Agency Rulemaking

When the Supreme Court struck down a form of legislative veto in *INS* v. *Chadha (see § 10.51)*, Congress still had other means at its disposal for responding to regulations, such as including changes in authorization or appropriations bills, or using oversight hearings. However, with the extensive number of laws through which it had granted rulemaking authority to a large number of governmental entities, Congress sought a flexible mechanism to increase its oversight of regulations.

As part of the Small Business Regulatory Enforcement Fairness Act of 1996 *(110 Stat. 857)*, Congress enacted the Congressional Review Act, which provided for congressional review of agency rulemaking *(5 U.S.C. § 801 et seq.)*. Among the law's provisions, Congress established a process whereby federal agencies must submit all of their rules to both houses of Congress and the Government Accountability Office (GAO) before the rules can become effective. For each rule that OMB considers "major" (for example, the rule will have $100 million effect on the U.S. economy), GAO must prepare a report describing the issuing agency's compliance with various rulemaking requirements (for example, cost-benefit estimates under Executive Order 12866). (*For copies of these reports and other information, see the GAO web site at <www.gao.gov/decisions/majrule/ majrule.htm>*.) Major rules cannot take effect until sixty days after the rule is submitted to GAO and Congress or published in the *Federal Register*, whichever is later.

The Congressional Review Act provides specific procedures under which Congress can, by joint resolution, disapprove an agency rule. It provides, for example, for expedited procedures in the Senate, but not in the House. Using these procedures, Congress has at least sixty legislative days in which to pass a joint resolution of disapproval. Such a resolution, like any joint resolution, would require passage in both houses and presidential approval. While there are conditions under which a rule might be implemented before Congress acts, if a joint resolution of disapproval is subsequently enacted into law, the rule "shall be treated as though such rule had never taken effect." Once a rule has been disapproved in this manner, "it may not be reissued in substantially the same form, and a new rule that is substantially the same as such a rule may not be issued," unless such a rule is subsequently specifically authorized by law.

As a joint resolution, the measure is subject to possible veto by the president,which is subject to a possible veto override by Congress. The Congressional Review Act was successfully used to overturn a rule on only one occasion between 1996 and the end of 2006. In early 2001, the Republican-led Congress passed, and newly inaugurated President George W. Bush signed, a joint resolution of disapproval nullifying an ergonomics standards rule that had been promulgated by the Occupational Safety and Health Administration (OSHA) during the administration of President Clinton. Although overturning a rule requires overcoming a high political threshold, members of Congress may use the procedures put in place by the law in an effort to draw attention to, and influence the outcome of, specific rulemaking processes. Nearly forty joint resolutions of disapproval have been introduced since the law was enacted.

10

and submit drafts of proposed and final rules to OMB prior to publication in the *Federal Register*. This executive order was controversial because it unilaterally increased the president's ability to shape public policy through increased control at OMB over the rulemaking process. Executive Order 12866, issued by President Clinton in October 1993, replaced Executive Order 12291. It limited OMB review to "significant" rules from non-independent regulatory agencies, and established certain transparency requirements, while retaining OMB's role in the rulemaking process. In January 2007, President Bush issued Executive Order 13422, which appeared to strengthen the president's control over rulemaking. Among its changes, the Bush executive order seemed to increase the importance of identifying a "market failure" in justifying a new regulation, extended coverage of OIRA's review to agencies' guidance documents, and appeared to increase administration control over decisions to undertake and guide rulemaking.

Congress and its members cannot intervene with impunity in regulatory proceedings outside of the legislative process or the formal procedures Congress has enacted. While House and Senate ethics rules recognize the right of members to assist their constituents in matters before executive-branch departments and agencies, criminal laws and ethics rules set parameters on that assistance. (*For sources of information on congressional ethics, see § 4.30, Congressional Ethics.*)

§ 10.50 Congress and the Executive: Appropriations

One of Congress's most effective means of exercising control over the executive is through the appropriations process. The Constitution provides that "No Money shall be drawn from the Treasury, but in Consequence of Appropriations made by Law. . . ." (*Art. I, sec. 9, cl. 7.*) By setting the level of funding or denying funding for federal programs, and by attaching strings to funding, Congress ensures its role in establishing the priorities and policies of the executive branch. (*See Chapter Nine, Legislating in Congress: Federal Budget Process.*)

Congress can employ *limitations* in appropriations measures. A limitation restricts spending, such as by prohibiting the use of funds for a specific purpose or setting a ceiling on the amount that might be spent on an activity within an account, or by restricting the management and uses of funds in some other way. Congress might also *earmark* funds, often doing so in reports or other documents rather than in an appropriations measure itself. However, recent guidance from OMB to department and agency heads sought to limit the implementation of earmarks to those contained in statute. (*See OMB memorandum, To provide guidance to Departments and Agencies about obligating FY 2007 funds under a full-year Continuing Resolution (CR) with no Congressional earmarks, at <www.whitehouse.gov/omb/memoranda/fy2007/m07-10.pdf>.*) An earmark may direct spending to a specific recipient or to a specific project. (*See § 9.81, Limitations, Earmarks, and General Provisions.*)

Congress also may include *reprogramming* or *transfer* authority in appropriations measures. (*See § 9.140, Transfer and Reprogramming.*) Reprogramming authority allows a department or

§ 10.51

Legislative Veto

The practice of giving Congress a "veto" over executive actions is long-standing. With broad grants of discretion to the executive, Congress often found it useful to include a *one-house* or *two-house legislative veto* as part of a grant of authority and discretion. In that way, the executive could shape an outcome to its liking. Congress would then have an opportunity to review the policy decision, and, if unhappy with it, adopt a simple resolution of disapproval in one house or a concurrent resolution of disapproval in both houses.

This type of legislative veto, however, was struck down by the Supreme Court in *INS v. Chadha*, 462 U.S. 919 (1983). Congress exercised a one-house veto regarding a specific type of decision of the attorney general under the Immigration and Nationality Act *(8 U.S.C. § 1101 et seq.)*. The Court said that the legislative veto violated the Constitution's principle of bicameralism and the Presentment Clause, which states: "Every Bill which shall have passed the House of Representatives and the Senate, shall, before it become a Law, be presented to the President of the United States." *(Art. I, sec. 7, cl. 2.)*

Congress has responded with procedures in various forms that are constitutional, such as joint resolutions of approval or disapproval. A joint resolution requires the president's signature or an override of his veto to take effect. It has also continued to use the legislative veto formally and informally at the committee level to ensure oversight of the executive branch's exercise of discretion. Many of these legislative vetoes involve the House and Senate Appropriations Committees, and are included in appropriations measures or accompanying documents, such as committee or conference committee reports.

agency to shift funds within a spending account, while transfer authority allows a department or agency to shift funds from one account to another. In both cases, Congress usually places limitations on such authority, often requiring the department or agency to notify the Appropriations Committees within a certain period of time before any shifting of funds may occur. In some cases, the reprogramming or transfer authority is contingent on the approval of the Appropriations Committees, a form of the legislative veto still used. *(See § 10.51, Legislative Veto.)*

As explained in § 9.150 *(Impoundment: Deferrals and Rescissions)*, the president may also recommend deferrals and rescissions of budget authority in accordance with provisions of the Congressional Budget and Impoundment Control Act. *(88 Stat. 297; 2 U.S.C. § 601 et seq.)*

§ 10.60 Congress and the Executive: Management

Congress places controls on the executive branch not only through its appropriations authority but also by making laws for managing the executive branch. Personnel systems (including personnel benefits), procurement systems, financial management, and other areas of management of the executive branch are covered in laws enacted by Congress. Management of the regulatory process, aspects of which are described in § 10.40 *(Congress and the Executive: Rule-*

§ 10.61

Program Performance
Information Resources

Over the years, Congress and the president have established performance measurement requirements to assist them in assessing the effectiveness of government programs. In particular, various initiatives have sought to establish a connection between program budget levels and performance. Two such initiatives, and sources of information on program performance, are the Government Performance and Results Act *(P.L. 103-62; 107 Stat. 285)* and the Program Assessment and Rating Tool.

In 1993, Congress passed, and President Clinton signed, the Government Performance and Results Act (generally known by its acronym GPRA or the Results Act). GPRA applies to most executive-branch departments and agencies with budgets exceeding $20 million annually, or approximately seventy-five organizations. It requires those entities to have six-year strategic plans, annual performance plans, and annual reports on program performance, all of which are to be submitted to Congress. Strategic plans, matching mission to results and resources, are to be updated at least once every three years. In developing strategic plans, departments and agencies are to consult their "stakeholders," including Congress. The annual performance plans, based on those strategic plans, are to inform the appropriations process, among other purposes. They contain performance goals, performance indicators, and other information. The Office of Management and Budget (OMB) is also required to prepare annual government-wide performance plans. Budget requests are expected to support performance plans. The annual performance reports measure performance against goals. Discrepancies between actual performance and goals are to be explained, and proposals for corrective action—including legislative changes—are to be included, among other types of information.

As a result of later statutes and administrative directives, the processes used to implement GPRA goals have been altered. For example, agency annual financial reports are now combined with the annual performance reports, and performance plans must articulate the strategies and training that will be needed to meet goals and objectives.

Beginning in 2001, the Bush administration focused on "Budget and Performance Integration" as one of five major management initiatives. Among other things, the initiative spawned the development of the Program Assessment Rating Tool (PART). PART is a set of questionnaires that attempt to evaluate a program's purpose and design, strategic planning, program management, and program results. OMB created and administers PART, and PART results for many programs have been included in the president's budget proposal since FY2004. Unlike GPRA and other management-related laws that have been established by Congress, PART is an executive-branch initiative and is not statutory.

Implementation of such performance measurement initiatives in the federal government faces many challenges, however. Programs often have multiple constituencies and objectives. Furthermore, objective, apolitical performance measures may be difficult to develop, particularly for programs with complex, long-term goals. Even if accurate performance measures and reports are developed, it is unclear whether or not Congress would use them in the budgeting and appropriations processes. These processes are often driven by the need to make difficult choices between competing priorities and policy goals among multiple constituencies through the political decision-making process. Nevertheless, the program performance information produced by GPRA and PART are additional resources available to Congress in evaluating, reforming, and budgeting for the various programs of the federal government.

making), is another example of the legal imposition of standards for the executive branch to follow in its operations.

Congress can apply a management law to all parts of the executive branch. Through another law, Congress may also exempt an agency from specific management laws, or even exempt a category of agencies from specific laws. Congress might also impose different or additional management standards on an agency or a category of agencies.

Recent administrations have developed federal government management initiatives, such as President Clinton's National Performance Review (NPR) and President George W. Bush's President's Management Agenda (PMA). Administration officials have sought to implement changes under these initiatives through a combination of the president's existing management authority and legislative proposals. The role of the president as day-to-day "manager-in-chief" of the federal bureaucracy provides him with a prominent vantage point from which to promote and implement particular reforms. Although Congress might not adopt an administration's plan in its entirety, some members and committees might elect to incorporate elements into their own legislative agenda. Statutory changes are usually necessary in order for a president's management initiatives to take hold and have an impact on the federal government that outlasts the administration.

In addition to providing standards of management and accountability, Congress might also wish to ensure the flow of information to itself to aid in the development of legislation or appropriations, as it did when it enacted the Government Performance and Results Act. *(P.L. 103-62; 107 Stat. 285.) (See § 10.61, Program Performance Information Resources.)*

§ 10.70 Congress and the Executive: Oversight and Investigation

Congressional oversight and investigation are key components of the system of checks and balances between the branches of the federal government, as well as a means of making determinations about the need for additional lawmaking. With oversight, Congress—through its standing and specially authorized committees—reviews the implementation of public policy. Through investigations, these committees use powers granted them by their parent chambers to probe governmental and private activities for potential misconduct or mismanagement, and to compel the appearance and testimony of witnesses and the provision of documents. Although Congress often conducts oversight and investigatory activities itself, other governmental actors, such as the Government Accountability Office (GAO) and inspectors general (IGs) in departments and agencies, are regularly called upon by Congress to assist with these functions. As one of many elements of congressional-executive relations, oversight and investigations are part of a largely seamless web where one element overlaps with another. Congress sometimes conducts oversight hearings as distinct activities, but the review of agencies and programs also pervades routine congressional activities, such as the appropriations and confirmation processes. *(See § 10.71, Examples of Oversight Letters.)*

§ 10.71

Examples of Oversight Letters

HENRY A. WAXMAN, CALIFORNIA
EDWARD J. MARKEY, MASSACHUSETTS
RICK BOUCHER, VIRGINIA
EDOLPHUS TOWNS, NEW YORK
FRANK PALLONE, JR., NEW JERSEY
BART GORDON, TENNESSEE
BOBBY L. RUSH, ILLINOIS
ANNA G. ESHOO, CALIFORNIA
BART STUPAK, MICHIGAN
ELIOT L. ENGEL, NEW YORK
ALBERT R. WYNN, MARYLAND
GENE GREEN, TEXAS
DIANA DeGETTE, COLORADO
VICE CHAIRMAN
LOIS CAPPS, CALIFORNIA
MIKE DOYLE, PENNSYLVANIA
JANE HARMAN, CALIFORNIA
TOM ALLEN, MAINE
JAN SCHAKOWSKY, ILLINOIS
HILDA L. SOLIS, CALIFORNIA
CHARLES A. GONZALEZ, TEXAS
JAY INSLEE, WASHINGTON
TAMMY BALDWIN, WISCONSIN
MIKE ROSS, ARKANSAS
DARLENE HOOLEY, OREGON
ANTHONY D. WEINER, NEW YORK
JIM MATHESON, UTAH
G.K. BUTTERFIELD, NORTH CAROLINA
CHARLIE MELANCON, LOUISIANA
JOHN BARROW, GEORGIA
BARON P. HILL, INDIANA

JOE BARTON, TEXAS
RANKING MEMBER
RALPH M. HALL, TEXAS
J. DENNIS HASTERT, ILLINOIS
FRED UPTON, MICHIGAN
CLIFF STEARNS, FLORIDA
NATHAN DEAL, GEORGIA
ED WHITFIELD, KENTUCKY
BARBARA CUBIN, WYOMING
JOHN SHIMKUS, ILLINOIS
HEATHER WILSON, NEW MEXICO
JOHN B. SHADEGG, ARIZONA
CHARLES W. "CHIP" PICKERING, MISSISSIPPI
VITO FOSSELLA, NEW YORK
STEVE BUYER, INDIANA
GEORGE RADANOVICH, CALIFORNIA
JOSEPH R. PITTS, PENNSYLVANIA
MARY BONO, CALIFORNIA
GREG WALDEN, OREGON
LEE TERRY, NEBRASKA
MIKE FERGUSON, NEW JERSEY
MIKE ROGERS, MICHIGAN
SUE MYRICK, NORTH CAROLINA
JOHN SULLIVAN, OKLAHOMA
TIM MURPHY, PENNSYLVANIA
MICHAEL C. BURGESS, TEXAS
MARSHA BLACKBURN, TENNESSEE

ONE HUNDRED TENTH CONGRESS

U.S. House of Representatives
Committee on Energy and Commerce
Washington, DC 20515–6115

JOHN D. DINGELL, MICHIGAN
CHAIRMAN

April 3, 2007

DENNIS B. FITZGIBBONS, CHIEF OF STAFF
GREGG A. ROTHSCHILD, CHIEF COUNSEL

The Honorable Samuel W. Bodman
Secretary
U.S. Department of Energy
1000 Independence Avenue, SW
Washington, D.C. 20585

Dear Mr. Secretary:

Pursuant to Rules X and XI of the Rules of the House of Representatives, the Committee on Energy and Commerce and the Subcommittee on Oversight and Investigations are requesting the following documents related to the Department's A-76 competitive sourcing evaluation for the Radiological and Environmental Sciences Laboratory (RESL) located in Idaho Falls, Idaho:

1) Competitive Sourcing Feasibility Review for the RESL, May 17, 2006; and
2) Market Research Analysis Related to RESL (Second Round), March 15, 2007.

The Committee is evaluating whether the reference laboratory functions carried out by RESL are inherently governmental, or, if not inherently governmental, should nonetheless be performed by the Government. We are also evaluating whether there are qualified firms who would not have any potential conflicts of interest in running this reference radio chemical lab.

We understand the office of Nuclear Energy currently operates RESL in support of activities carried out, in part, by the Office of Health Safety and Security.

Please arrange for the production of these documents by no later than the close of business, Tuesday, April 10, 2007. If you have any questions, please have your staff contact Richard Miller with the Committee on Energy and Commerce staff at (202) 226-2424.

Sincerely,

John D. Dingell
Chairman

Bart Stupak
Chairman
Subcommittee on Oversight and Investigations

cc: The Honorable Joe Barton, Ranking Member
Committee on Energy and Commerce

The Honorable Ed Whitfield, Ranking Member
Subcommittee on Oversight and Investigations

HENRY A. WAXMAN, CALIFORNIA
EDWARD J. MARKEY, MASSACHUSETTS
RICK BOUCHER, VIRGINIA
EDOLPHUS TOWNS, NEW YORK
FRANK PALLONE, JR., NEW JERSEY
BART GORDON, TENNESSEE
BOBBY L. RUSH, ILLINOIS
ANNA G. ESHOO, CALIFORNIA
BART STUPAK, MICHIGAN
ELIOT L. ENGEL, NEW YORK
ALBERT R. WYNN, MARYLAND
GENE GREEN, TEXAS
DIANA DeGETTE, COLORADO
VICE CHAIRMAN
LOIS CAPPS, CALIFORNIA
MIKE DOYLE, PENNSYLVANIA
JANE HARMAN, CALIFORNIA
TOM ALLEN, MAINE
JAN SCHAKOWSKY, ILLINOIS
HILDA L. SOLIS, CALIFORNIA
CHARLES A. GONZALEZ, TEXAS
JAY INSLEE, WASHINGTON
TAMMY BALDWIN, WISCONSIN
MIKE ROSS, ARKANSAS
DARLENE HOOLEY, OREGON
ANTHONY D. WEINER, NEW YORK
JIM MATHESON, UTAH
G.K. BUTTERFIELD, NORTH CAROLINA
CHARLIE MELANCON, LOUISIANA
JOHN BARROW, GEORGIA
BARON P. HILL, INDIANA

DENNIS B. FITZGIBBONS, CHIEF OF STAFF
GREGG A. ROTHSCHILD, CHIEF COUNSEL

JOE BARTON, TEXAS
RANKING MEMBER
RALPH M. HALL, TEXAS
J. DENNIS HASTERT, ILLINOIS
FRED UPTON, MICHIGAN
CLIFF STEARNS, MICHIGAN
NATHAN DEAL, GEORGIA
ED WHITFIELD, KENTUCKY
BARBARA CUBIN, WYOMING
JOHN SHIMKUS, ILLINOIS
HEATHER WILSON, NEW MEXICO
JOHN B. SHADEGG, ARIZONA
CHARLES W. "CHIP" PICKERING, MISSISSIPPI
VITO FOSSELLA, NEW YORK
STEVE BUYER, INDIANA
GEORGE RADANOVICH, CALIFORNIA
JOSEPH R. PITTS, PENNSYLVANIA
MARY BONO, CALIFORNIA
GREG WALDEN, OREGON
LEE TERRY, NEBRASKA
MIKE FERGUSON, NEW JERSEY
MIKE ROGERS, MICHIGAN
SUE MYRICK, NORTH CAROLINA
JOHN SULLIVAN, OKLAHOMA
TIM MURPHY, PENNSYLVANIA
MICHAEL C. BURGESS, TEXAS
MARSHA BLACKBURN, TENNESSEE

ONE HUNDRED TENTH CONGRESS

U.S. House of Representatives
Committee on Energy and Commerce
Washington, DC 20515-6115

JOHN D. DINGELL, MICHIGAN
CHAIRMAN

April 12, 2007

The Honorable Kevin J. Martin
Chairman
Federal Communications Commission
445 12th Street, S.W.
Washington, D.C. 20554

Dear Chairman Martin:

The Committee on Energy and Commerce and its Subcommittee on Oversight and Investigations plan to reopen an investigation into the Universal Service Fund (USF), and have requested the assistance of the U.S. Government Accountability Office in reviewing the Federal Communications Commission's corrective actions to remove waste, fraud, and abuse in the USF programs.

Given that universal service spending has risen appreciably over the past few years – with the overwhelming majority of that growth being attributable to the USF's High Cost program – it is imperative that the Committee examine whether the High Cost program has programmatic flaws and whether the program has sufficient accountability measures in place to protect the public interest.

Accordingly, pursuant to Rules X and XI of the U.S. House of Representatives, we are writing to advise the Commission that the Committee is conducting an official inquiry into the High Cost program. Your cooperation in this investigation is requested and will be greatly appreciated.

If you have any questions relating to this investigation, please contact us or have your staff contact Steven Rangel with the Committee Majority staff at (202) 226-2424 or Peter Spencer with the Committee Minority staff at (202) 225-3641.

Sincerely,

John D. Dingell
Chairman

Joe Barton
Ranking Member

Bart Stupak
Chairman
Subcommittee on Oversight and Investigations

Ed Whitfield
Ranking Member
Subcommittee on Oversight and Investigations

Executive Privilege

The phrase "executive privilege" is a shorthand reference to the "qualified privilege" of the executive to decline to respond to a request for information—documents or testimony or both—from either of the other two branches of the federal government. A unanimous circuit court opinion in 1997 distinguished between two different kinds of executive privilege—presidential communications privilege and deliberative process privilege—with different legal bases and different thresholds of need required to compel disclosure.

Presidential communications privilege is based in "the constitutional separation of powers principles and the President's unique constitutional role." (*In re Sealed Case*, 121 F.3d 729 at 745 (D.C. Cir. 1997).) This privilege allows the president to protect from disclosure the details of decision making and deliberations with close advisers. Presidential communications are considered to be "presumptively privileged," but the privilege is not absolute; it may be overcome by an adequate showing of need. The court indicated that "the privilege should apply only to communications authored or solicited and received by those members of an immediate White House adviser's staff who have broad and significant responsibility for investigating and formulating the advice to be given the President on the particular matter to which the communications relate." The privilege protects such communications where they involve government operations that require the president's direct decision making. The *In re Sealed Case* court limited the claim of such privilege to those advisers in close decisional proximity to the president. The court specified that "the privilege should not extend to staff outside the White House in executive branch agencies." Presidential claims of executive privilege are unusual, and they are normally made by the president or at his direction. Such claims usually lead to negotiations between the White House and Congress.

Deliberative process privilege is a common law privilege and applies to executive officials generally. The threshold of need for overcoming this claim of privilege is lower than for overcoming a claim of presidential communications privilege. If a claim is made by a department or agency that does not involve the president and his assertion of the claim, the practice is for a requesting congressional committee to make a case-by-case evaluation of the claim. The department or agency and Congress normally negotiate over the requested material, and a congressional committee might begin drafting a congressional contempt citation to add leverage to its request. If negotiations between Congress and the executive fail, the parent chamber can adopt a contempt citation and even seek relief in the courts. Alternatively, Congress may use other constitutional powers, such as its appropriations authority or the Senate's confirmation power, as leverage in obtaining the needed information.

Congress's authority to conduct oversight and investigation is implied from its enumerated powers in the Constitution and the Necessary and Proper Clause. This authority is viewed as essential to Congress's lawmaking role. The 1946 and 1970 Legislative Reorganization Acts (*60 Stat. 812 and 84 Stat. 1140, respectively*) directed congressional committees to conduct continuous oversight, and other statutes—such as the Whistleblowers Protection Act of 1978 (*103 Stat. 16*), the Inspectors General Act of 1978 (*92 Stat. 1101*), and the Chief Financial Officers Act of 1990 (*104 Stat. 2838*)—added to committees' capacity to do so. (*See § 10.72, Executive Privilege.*)

§ 10.73

Legislative History

It is impossible to quantify the impact of legislative history on the executive and the judiciary; it is difficult even to define legislative history. In its narrowest sense, legislative history means changes in the text of measures on their way to enactment. Presumably, examining changes to words, sentences, paragraphs, or more allows one to refine an understanding of what Congress meant in enacting a statute. Somewhat more broadly, legislative history includes documents, such as committee and conference reports, that explain congressional intentions in making changes. Even more broadly, legislative history encompasses other congressional documents as well as debate on the House and Senate floors. Some might even argue that a "Dear Colleague" letter signed by the chair and ranking minority member of the committee of jurisdiction, statements of administration policy, a presidential signing message, and other materials are also part of a measure's legislative history.

Executive departments and agencies, which interact with Congress repeatedly on appropriations, authorizations, proposed regulations, liaison activities, and other matters, pay consistently closer attention to the range of legislative history materials than do the courts. Executive departments and agencies seek to understand legislative intent through these materials and to resolve conflicting views expressed in the House and Senate or between a committee report and floor statements. Indeed, committee and conference reports, materials annexed to them, and even committee correspondence and other documents can contain essential information for an agency that is attempting to carry out a law. For example, public-works projects authorized by legislation might be listed in the joint explanatory statement to a conference report on the measure.

Agency practices differ in the manner in which they use legislative history materials. Some give them great deference; others de-emphasize their role in administering programs and writing regulations. Administration policy also strongly influences the regard given legislative history. Nonetheless, an agency might find it risky to ignore instructive language in reports of the Appropriations Committees or legislative committees with which the agency interacts regularly on its programs.

The courts begin with a principle called the *plain-meaning rule* in analyzing a statute. A court will generally look to the plain meaning of a statute's words, and seek any needed guidance within the statute as a whole. A court still might decide to look outside a statute and at the deliberations of Congress at any time, and for any number of reasons—such as to clarify ambiguous language, confirm an interpretation, or learn more about legislative purpose. A court might look first to the textual changes that Congress made during its consideration of a measure at the different stages of the legislative process. It might also seek background information on the purposes of the legislation. Courts, in general, proceed warily if they go further and seek enlightenment from congressional documents or proceedings on the meaning of a word, phrase, or provision of a statute.

A court's attention to varying statutory interpretations regularly arises from opposing counsel's arguments. The court, then, might elect to examine the legislative history as it deems appropriate. However, in appellate rulings and other forums, the judiciary continues to debate the appropriate role of legislative history in interpreting statutes.

10

§ 10.74

Hearings May Affect Public or Private Practices

Early in the 110th Congress, the Senate Banking, Housing, and Urban Affairs Committee and the Permanent Investigations Subcommittee of the Senate Homeland Security and Governmental Affairs Committee conducted well-publicized hearings on business practices in the credit card industry that some senators and some consumer advocates considered to be unfair or unethical. Shortly after the hearings, individual companies announced changes in their business practices. Presumably the publicity of the hearings and an industry desire to try to head off prescriptive regulatory legislation played a part in fostering the changes.

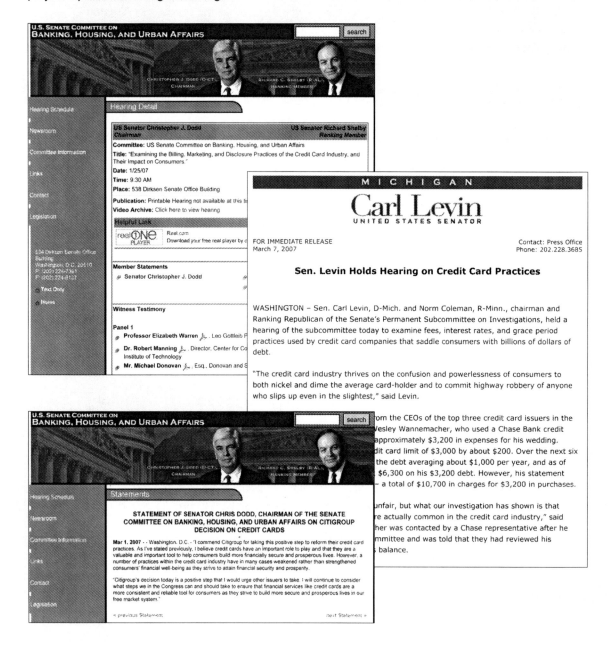

Congressional oversight and investigation can serve a number of purposes. Oversight might be undertaken to determine whether or not the executive is administering federal programs and policies as Congress intended. With the broad discretion that laws often grant executive departments and agencies, congressional committees' oversight ensures that Congress is informed of the manner in which the executive is interpreting and carrying out laws. Committees might also use oversight to influence the direction of rulemaking that implements a law. In addition, oversight is an important means of establishing and measuring accountability in the administration of federal programs and policies. Oversight also helps both the executive and Congress to establish priorities within and between federal activities. (See § 10.73, *Legislative History*.)

With its power to investigate, Congress can publicly expose debasement of government and the rule of law. It can investigate private organizations, economic activities, or any other area where it might legislate.

Although oversight and investigation findings might lead Congress to modify existing law or enact new laws, these activities often lead to changes by other means. They might lead to changes in procedures in governmental or private entities, for example, or additional rulemaking by executive departments and agencies with authority and jurisdiction in the area under investigation. (See § 10.74, *Hearings May Affect Public or Private Practices*.) Either or both chambers of Congress may elect to modify their own rules and procedures as a result of the findings of an investigation. Under some circumstances, investigation might lead to prosecution by the executive for violations of criminal laws. In such situations, congressional committees are mindful of the potential impact on prosecutions of providing witness protections during investigative activities. (See § 10.75, *Committee Investigations and Witness Protections*.)

Congress has many oversight and investigation tools and methods at its disposal, some of which are described briefly here. One frequently used oversight tool is a statutorily required report to Congress from an executive agency. Reports might be required for any number of purposes, such as to detail results of a department's or agency's study of a public policy problem or to inform Congress about a government-wide management concern. Another way Congress might use a report requirement is to monitor the administration of a federal program, particularly at its outset or when significant changes have been made. As suggested above, another frequently used tool of oversight is a committee hearing. Such hearings are carefully planned by members and senior committee staff, and often are used to review governmental activity in a particular policy area and to assess the need for administrative or legislative change.

As previously noted, members of Congress often use appropriations and confirmation hearings as opportunities to pose oversight-oriented questions. In the latter case, Senate committees with jurisdiction over a nomination often use confirmation hearings to conduct an examination of the administration of the department or agency in which the office is located. They sometimes extract commitments from the nominee to look into certain issues, report

Committee Investigations and Witness Protections

When a congressional committee (or subcommittee) conducts an investigation, there is no doubt about Congress's power to investigate. But a number of questions or issues often appear as the committee attempts to obtain the specific information it believes it needs.

One set of issues surrounds the committee's authority and conduct. What is the authority in chamber rules or specially adopted resolutions enabling the committee to conduct the investigation? What do the committee's rules of procedure, published in the *Congressional Record*, provide? What are quorum requirements for taking testimony? Are those requirements different for sworn testimony? The committee must also follow procedures in chamber and committee rules for issuing subpoenas, or procedures established in an authorizing resolution. Enforcement through one of the forms of contempt proceedings available to the House and Senate is undertaken only after committee and chamber approval.

Other questions that involve committee conduct include decisions on using staff depositions, taking testimony in open or executive session, and allowing broadcast or photographing of a witness testifying. For example, while the rules of both chambers favor open meetings, in some instances a House rule requires a closed meeting if a majority of the committee agrees on the defamatory or incriminating effect of the testimony. Even when a committee has authority in various aspects of conducting an investigation, it still must consider the strategic and tactical implications of exercising that authority.

At hearings, witnesses are allowed to be accompanied by counsel to advise them on their constitutional rights, but it is generally understood that counsel may not "coach" witnesses. Chamber and committee rules and other factors come into play if a chair believes counsel's behavior is interfering with the committee's hearing.

Yet another set of questions involves the protections afforded witnesses by the freedoms of the Bill of Rights, a matter that can involve the judiciary if Congress or a witness resorts to the courts to validate an assertion of congressional powers or witness rights. The Fifth Amendment freedom against self-incrimination is recognized. The Fourth Amendment requirement of probable cause (for congressional subpoenas) and freedom from unreasonable searches and seizures also seems to be recognized. An assertion of rights under the First Amendment, however, has resulted in weighing committee and witness interests both in committees and, subsequently, in the courts. The courts look especially closely at a committee's authority and legislative purpose in such cases. Congressional committees do not, however, pay the deference to common-law privileges (such as attorney-client) that is given in a court.

If a witness invokes a Fifth Amendment privilege against testifying, a committee might still compel testimony with a two-thirds vote of the committee in favor of seeking a court order to grant immunity and direct the witness to testify. The immunity granted protects the witness from use of the testimony in a criminal prosecution. A grant of immunity might then jeopardize criminal prosecution, the prosecutor bearing the burden of showing that the case is not based on or derived from the immunized testimony. The appellate court decisions that reversed the convictions of Oliver North and John Poindexter in the Iran-Contra scandal made the burden in future prosecutions even more difficult to overcome. *(See § 10.77, Seeking to Compel Testimony.)*

back to the committee on certain matters, or effect some change. Individual senators might also place a hold on one or more nominations to exert leverage on the administration for production of information or for a commitment to examine a policy.

Tools available to Congress during investigations include subpoenas, contempt power, grants of immunity, and staff interviews and depositions. *(See § 10.76, Example of Subpoena to Executive Branch Official.)* House and Senate rules authorize standing committees and sub-committees to compel individuals to appear and testify in hearings or to require the provision of documents to Congress. Either chamber could also by resolution delegate that power, or additional powers, to special or select committees. If an individual fails to provide testimony or documents as required, provisions in statute allow the full House or Senate to cite a witness for criminal contempt and refer the matter to the U.S. attorney; the Senate also has recourse to a civil contempt proceeding against witnesses other than executive-branch officials. In the past, the threat of a congressional subpoena or contempt citation has often led to negotiated or full compliance on the part of the targeted individual or office.

The House can also adopt a simple resolution—a *resolution of inquiry*—requesting information or documents from the president or directing a department or agency head to supply such information. Such a resolution is used to obtain factual information, not to request opinions or investigations.

Congressional committees often use staff interviews to collect information as part of an investigation. This staff work provides tighter focus to the questioning and witness list for investigative hearings. On some occasions, House and Senate resolutions have provided specific authority to a committee for staff members to take sworn depositions. Special committee procedures have usually been established under these circumstances. Among other things, depositions, which are conducted in private, might lead to more efficient use of hearing time, facilitate more candid responses from witnesses than they would provide in a hearing, and allow further investigation of witness allegations prior to the airing of those allegations at a public hearing. Under certain circumstances, a committee might seek a court order to grant partial or full immunity to a witness as a means of obtaining testimony. (See § 10.75, *Committee Investigations and Witness Protections.*)

Within Congress, the rules of both chambers support their committees' active oversight. Some of these rules have already been discussed. In addition to these, House rules give the Oversight and Government Reform Committee wide latitude in conducting oversight. Senate rules do the same for the Homeland Security and Governmental Affairs Committee. Each committee may conduct oversight government-wide and on intergovernmental programs and activities, and each is given a special responsibility to study GAO reports and recommend action to Congress based on those reports. In addition to general provisions encouraging oversight, House and Senate rules give specific committees "special" or "comprehensive" authority to conduct oversight in certain policy areas, although a particular policy area might fall within the legislative jurisdiction of several committees.

In the House, each standing committee is directed to provide the Oversight and Government Reform Committee and House Administration Committee with an oversight plan for the new Congress by February 15 of the first session of a Congress. The Oversight and Government Reform Committee consolidates these reports and issues an oversight agenda by March 31. House committees are to include oversight findings in their reports on legislation. Each House committee must file an activities report, including oversight activities, for the previous Congress by January 2 of each odd-numbered year.

The House and Senate may also establish temporary committees to conduct oversight. The Senate, for example, created the Special Committee on the Year 2000 Technology Problem to monitor the preparedness of computer systems in the executive branch and various economic sectors to recognize the year 2000. The House and Senate have also acted jointly in the past, such as when both chambers established committees to investigate the Iran-Contra affair, and the committees then worked together. The Speaker may also be authorized by resolution to appoint ad hoc oversight committees.

In addition to the oversight and investigation activities Congress undertakes itself, Congress often calls on certain government organizations to provide support in carrying out these functions. Prominent among these organizations is GAO, which Congress created, in part, to address oversight needs. Generally, at the behest of a congressional committee or pursuant to authority granted to it by statute, GAO undertakes audits and evaluations of federal programs and activities, and reports its findings to Congress. GAO's professional staff has the investigatory experience and authority to ensure that Congress is well-informed on the implementation of laws and options for their improvement. (*See § 5.130, Legislative-Branch Support Agencies.*)

IGs, established statutorily in nearly sixty departments and agencies, also provide support to Congress's oversight and investigation functions. These offices are required, among other things, to report the findings of their audits and investigations semiannually to their respective department or agency heads. These administrative leaders must then forward the reports with their comments to Congress within thirty days. Shorter reporting times apply in some situations, and Congress itself can request information directly from an IG.

From time to time, Congress has also established temporary commissions to investigate particular events or issues. Such commissions have varied in their mandates, authorities, and profiles. The 9/11 Commission, for example, was established by law (*P.L. 107-306; 116 Stat. 2408*), and was populated by experienced and knowledgeable individuals who demonstrated a determination to reach consensus and see the commission's recommendations implemented. The commission had the power to hold hearings and collect evidence, and was granted subpoena power.

§ 10.76

Example of Subpoena to Executive Branch Official

SUBPOENA

BY AUTHORITY OF THE HOUSE OF REPRESENTATIVES OF THE
CONGRESS OF THE UNITED STATES OF AMERICA

To The Honorable Alberto R. Gonzales, United States Attorney General

You are hereby commanded to be and appear before the Committee on the Judiciary
Subcommittee on Commercial and Administrative Law
of the House of Representatives of the United States at the place, date and time specified below.

☐ **to testify** touching matters of inquiry committed to said committee or subcommittee; and you are not to depart without leave of said committee or subcommittee.

> Place of testimony: _____
>
> Date: _____   Time: _____

☑ **to produce the things identified on the attached schedule** touching matters of inquiry committed to said committee or subcommittee; and you are not to depart without leave of said committee or subcommittee.

> Place of production: 2138 Rayburn House Office Building, Washington, D.C. 20515
>
> Date: April 16, 2007   Time: 2:00 p.m.

To Any authorized staff member of the House Committee on the Judiciary
_____ to se

Witness my hand and the seal of the House of Representatives
at the city of Washington, this 10th day of April

Attest _____   _____
Clerk   Chairman or

**SCHEDULE OF
DOCUMENT REQUESTS
SUBPOENA TO THE ATTORNEY GENERAL
APRIL 10, 2007**

Documents requested

1. Complete and unredacted versions, including complete paper and electronic versions, of any and all documents created by or sent to anyone at the Department, referring or otherwise relating in any way to the termination of former U.S. Attorneys David Iglesias, H.E. Cummins, John McKay, Carol Lam, Daniel Bogden, Paul Charlton, Kevin Ryan, or Margaret Chiara (hereinafter "the terminated U.S. Attorneys"), or any of them, or to the consideration or selection of their possible replacements, or any of them.

nd unredacted versions, including complete paper and electronic
f any and all documents referring to or otherwise relating in any way to
cation between anyone at the Department and any Member of Congress
any of the terminated U.S. Attorneys occurring in advance of the
involved.

nd unredacted versions, including complete paper and electronic
any and all documents that anyone at the Department submitted to, or
otherwise relate in any way to a communication that anyone at the
had with, any of the terminated U.S. Attorneys during his or her tenure
ncerning any failure in performance, including any failure to comply
ment priorities and directives.

nd unredacted versions, including complete paper and electronic
any and all documents previously requested in writing by the
tee that the Department has withheld, in whole or in part, from
on any basis or for any reason, including, but not limited to, those
'generated within the Executive Branch for the purpose of responding
essional (and media) inquiries about the resignations." as described in
ent's March 19, 2007 letter.

om paragraphs 1-4 is the paper version of any document previously
complete, unredacted paper form by the Department to the
ee on March 13, 19, 20, 23, or 28, 2007.

JOHN CONYERS, JR., Michigan
CHAIRMAN

LAMAR S. SMITH, Texas
RANKING MINORITY MEMBER

**U.S. House of Representatives
Committee on the Judiciary
Washington, DC 20515–6216
One Hundred Tenth Congress**

April 10, 2007

The Honorable Alberto R. Gonzales
Attorney General of the United States
U.S. Department of Justice
950 Pennsylvania Ave., NW
Washington, DC 20530

Dear Mr. Attorney General:

Attached is a subpoena for documents and electronic information that we previously requested from the Department in connection with its investigation into the circumstances surrounding the recent termination of several United States Attorneys and related matters, which the Department has furnished to us thus far only in redacted form, or has told the Subcommittee it was withholding. The subpoena is being issued pursuant to authority granted by the House Judiciary Subcommittee on Commercial and Administrative Law on March 21, 2007.

I appreciate your cooperation in voluntarily supplying a number of documents in response to the Subcommittee's request. As we have written and told you and your staff on a number of occasions, however, and reiterated most recently in our letters of March 22, March 28, and April 2, 2007, the incomplete response we have received thus far falls far short of what is needed for the Subcommittee and Committee to effectively exercise their oversight responsibilities in ascertaining the truth behind the very serious concerns that have been raised regarding this matter.

10

397

§ 10.77

Seeking to Compel Testimony

For Immediate Release   4/25/2007

House Judiciary Committee Approves Immunity Order, Authorizes Subpoena for Former DoJ Official Monica Goodling

For Immediate Release   Contact: Jonathan Godfrey(202) 226-6888
April 25, 2007   Melanie Roussell(202) 226-5543

Washington, DC)- Today, the House Judiciary Committee authorized a subpoena and voted in support of seeking a judicial order of immunity to compel testimony for former Justice Department-White House Liaison Monica Goodling. The immunity order required a two-thirds vote of the Committee - 32 Members voted in support, six voted against and two were not present. Chairman John Conyers, Jr. (D-MI) made the following opening remarks at the hearing:

> We will first turn to the two items remaining on our agenda from last week, involving Monica Goodling and our continuing investigation into the circumstances surrounding the terminations of U.S. Attorneys, the representations that have been made to Congress regarding those circumstances, and related matters.

> There are two resolutions – one to direct the House General Counsel to apply for a court order that would permit the Committee to give Ms. Goodling use immunity for testimony and related information she provides under compulsion to us, and the other to authorize the issuance of a subpoena for Ms. Goodling. Pursuant to notice, I call up first the resolution regarding use immunity.

> We had a good discussion of this matter last week, when we decided, at the request of our Ranking Minority Member, Mr. Smith, to postpone voting on the resolutions to permit us all to gain a little more familiarity and comfort with the immunity procedure and to speak informally with the Department of Justice. We have done that this week, and based on that meeting, I believe it is prudent that we proceed with the process of considering immunity for Ms. Goodling.

> Allow me to briefly recount how we have come to this point.
> The matters we have been examining go to the very heart of the public's ability to rely on the integrity of our legal system, and we have been working diligently to get to the truth. We have encountered some obstacles, and we are working to overcome them. We have been working closely with our Minority in all of these efforts, and we appreciate their support.

> We have a subpoena pending with the Justice Department for e-mails and related information, which the Department has thus far only partially complied with, but we continue to be in discussions with the Department regarding their compliance. We have requested interviews with a number of current and former high-level Department officials, and those interviews are being scheduled and conducted.

> We have asked the White House for information, and for interviews with selected current and former White House officials who appear, based on information we have obtained thus far, to be significantly involved in the decisionmaking. As of yet, the White House has not been forthcoming, but we continue to hope and expect that we will reach an accommodation with them.

> It is against this backdrop that we consider Monica Goodling, who recently resigned from her position as senior counsel to the Attorney General. Among her duties in that position was serving as the Justice Department's principal liaison with the White House.

> She was apparently involved in crucial discussions over a two-year period with senior White House aides, and with other senior Justice officials, in which the termination list was developed, refined, and finalized. She was also in the small group of senior Justice lawyers who prepared Deputy Attorney General Paul McNulty and his Principal Associate, William Moschella, for congressional testimony that we believe inaccurately portrayed the surrounding circumstances.

> So Ms. Goodling appears to be a key witness for us, as to any possible undue or improper interference, and as to any internal discussions as to how forthcoming to be to Congress. But she has notified the Committee that she would invoke her Fifth Amendment privilege against self-incrimination were she called to testify. And I don't think at this point that all of her potential grounds for invoking the privilege can be dismissed out of hand.

> Under these circumstances, it would appear that the Committee has exhausted all reasonable efforts to obtain Ms. Goodling's critical information short of providing her with limited use immunity under the applicable statute, 18 U.S.C. 6005.

> Taking this step will compel her to testify, under penalty of contempt, but under the protection that information she provides to us under compulsion could not be used against her for any prosecution, as long as the information is truthful.

Continued on page 399

§ 10.77 (continued)

U.S. Department of Justice

Office of the Inspector General

May 7, 2007

The Honorable John Conyers, Jr.
Chairman
Committee on the Judiciary
U.S. House of Representatives
Washington, D.C. 20515-6216

Dear Mr. Chairman:

 This is in response to your letter of April 27, 2007, in which you provided notice to the Attorney General that the House of Representatives Committee on the Judiciary (Committee) has authorized an application to a United States District Court for an order that would grant use immunity to former Department of Justice (Department) employee Monica Goodling in exchange for her testimony before the Committee.

 As you know, the Attorney General and Deputy Attorney General have recused themselves from this matter. Therefore, because the Office of the Inspector General (OIG) and the Office of Professional Responsibility (OPR) are conducting a joint investigation of the removal of United States Attorneys and related issues, and after consultation with the Solicitor General in his capacity as Acting Attorney General in this matter, we are responding on behalf of the Department pursuant to 18 U.S.C. § 6005.

 As we previously discussed with Committee staff in response to their questions, the OIG/OPR joint investigation is in its early stages, and we intend to take the investigation wherever it leads. As in any investigation that potentially could involve evidence of criminal conduct, we would prefer that any potential subject not be granted immunity at this stage of the investigation.

 However, we understand the Committee's interest in obtaining Ms. Goodling's testimony. Therefore, after balancing the significant congressional and public interest against the impact of the Committee's actions on our ongoing investigation, we will not raise an objection or seek a deferral pursuant to the provisions of 18 U.S.C. § 6005.

 Please contact us if you have additional questions about this matter.

Sincerely,

Glenn A. Fine
Inspector General

H. Marshall Jarrett
Counsel, Office of
 Professional Responsibility

cc: The Honorable Lamar Smith
Ranking Member
Committee on the Judiciary
U.S. House of Representatives

The Honorable Linda T. Sanchez
Chairwoman, Subcommittee on Commercial and Administrative Law
Committee on the Judiciary
U.S. House of Representatives

The Honorable Chris Cannon
Ranking Member, Subcommittee on Commercial and Administrative Law
Committee on the Judiciary
U.S. House of Representatives

The Honorable Paul D. Clement
Solicitor General
U.S. Department of Justice

Continued on page 400

UNITED STATES DISTRICT COURT
FOR THE DISTRICT OF COLUMBIA

COMMITTEE ON THE JUDICIARY)
)
United States House of Representatives)   Misc. No. 07-198
Washington, D.C. 20515)
)
            Applicant.)
)

FILED

MAY 1 1 2007

NANCY MAYER WHITTINGTON, CLERK
U.S. DISTRICT COURT

ORDER

UPON CONSIDERATION of the Application of the Committee on the Judiciary of the

U.S. House of Representatives ("the Committee") for an Order Immunizing the Testimony of,

and Other Information Provided by, Monica Goodling, and the Memorandum of Points and

Authorities in Support thereof, and having determined that the requirements of 18 U.S.C. § 6005

have been satisfied, it is by the Court this 11ᵗʰ day of May, 2007 ORDERED

That Monica Goodling may not refuse to testify, and may not refuse to provide other

information, when compelled to do so at proceedings before or ancillary to the Committee

(including its subcommittees) on the basis of her constitutional privilege against self-

incrimination, and it is FURTHER ORDERED

That no testimony or other information compelled under this Order (or any information

directly or indirectly derived from such testimony or other information) may be used against

Monica Goodling in any criminal proceeding, except prosecutions for perjury, giving a false

statement, or otherwise failing to comply with this Order.

Thomas F. Hogan
Chief U.S. District Judge

§10.80 Congress and the Executive: Appointments

The Senate and the president share the power to appoint the leadership of the executive branch of the federal government and all federal judges. The legal framework for the appointment of the top officers of the United States is established by provisions in the Constitution and in law. The Constitution states:

> [The President] shall nominate, and by and with the Advice and Consent of the Senate, shall appoint Ambassadors, other public Ministers and Consuls, Judges of the supreme Court, and all other Officers of the United States, whose Appointments are not herein otherwise provided for, and which shall be established by Law: but the Congress may by Law vest the Appointment of such inferior Officers, as they think proper, in the President alone, in the Courts of Law, or in the Heads of Departments. *(Art. II, sec. 2, cl. 2.)*

Over time, this clause has been interpreted to provide that certain officers, including those specifically named and all agency heads, must be appointed with the advice and consent of the Senate. In the case of most inferior officers, the Constitution gives Congress discretion to establish whether or not Senate approval of an appointment will be required. If Congress elects not to involve the Senate, it may delegate the appointment authority to the president alone, a court, or an agency official.

Appointments to more than 1,300 civilian executive and legislative branch positions require Senate confirmation at present. These include the leaders of departments (such as secretaries, deputy secretaries, under secretaries, and general counsels), independent agencies (such as administrators and deputy administrators), and boards and commissions (such as commissioners). Presidential appointments of federal judges, U.S. attorneys, and U.S. marshals are also subject to the advice and consent of the Senate.

The president and agency heads are authorized to make appointments to several thousand other full- and part-time positions throughout the executive branch without the involvement of the Senate. These positions, some of which have significant policymaking authority, include advisers, senior-level managers, confidential assistants, and advisory committee members. At the end of each presidential election year, the Senate Committee on Homeland Security and Governmental Affairs and the House Committee on Oversight and Government Reform alternate in publishing a book-length committee print of politically appointed positions entitled *Policy and Supporting Positions*, more popularly known as the "Plum Book," named for its serendipitous cover color the first time it was published. *(See the Government Printing Office web site at <www.gpoaccess.gov/plumbook>.)* This cadre of political appointees has grown in recent decades, and political layers have been added at departments and agencies that are intended to increase presidential control over policymaking.

Political appointments are less influential in most independent regulatory boards and commissions, which are structured to be more independent of the president than other parts

Confirmation Procedure

Appointments subject to Senate confirmation include most senior government officials and federal judges. Most commissions and promotions of officers in the armed forces, Public Health Service, National Oceanic and Atmospheric Administration, and Foreign Service are also subject to the advice and consent of the Senate.

The president transmits nominations for such appointments to the Senate by message, it is read, and the Senate executive clerk assigns a consecutive number to each message as it is received. Nominations are then referred to the committee with jurisdiction over the agency in which the positions exist. In some cases, a nomination may be referred to more than one committee.

Committees adopt procedures for the consideration of nominations, consistent with Senate rules, and may include those procedures in committee rules. Committees often begin their consideration of a nomination by gathering information about a nominee. About half of civilian nominations, including senior-level executive branch officials and most federal judges, are also subject to a committee hearing. The nominee and others testify. A nominee is often introduced at a hearing by one or both senators from his or her home state. Committees generally do not hold hearings on routine nominations such as military promotions.

During consideration of executive branch nominations, many committees exact a commitment from the nominee to testify before committees of Congress. This commitment is intended to strengthen congressional oversight capacity.

A committee has several options regarding the disposition of a nomination. It is not required to act on a nomination at all. If a committee elects to report a nomination, it can report it favorably, unfavorably, or without recommendation. In some cases, a reported nomination will be accompanied by a written report. The Senate may discharge a committee from further consideration of a nomination at any time, but this step is normally taken by unanimous consent.

Nominations are typically reported to the full Senate by the committee chair, who informs the legislative clerk at the desk. The legislative clerk, in turn, notifies the executive clerk, who assigns the nomination, or, in some cases, the list of nominations, a number and places it on the Senate's executive calendar. *(See § 8.180, Senate Calendars and Legislative and Executive Business before the Senate.)*

When the full Senate considers a nomination it does so in executive, rather than legislative, session. Procedures in executive session are similar to those in legislative session, although floor consideration cannot begin, except by unanimous consent, until a nomination has been on the calendar for one day. In most cases, a nomination is subject to the clearance process and then confirmed by unanimous consent. *(See § 8.190, Holds, Clearance, and Unanimous Consent.)* The Senate sometimes resolves nominations conflicts by crafting unanimous consent agreements providing for limited debate or by bundling a group of nominations that are of interest to a wide group of senators. Nominations that come up frequently are called up en bloc and usually approved without objection.

The Senate rarely votes to reject a nomination; unsuccessful nominations usually die from inaction. Occasionally, a nomination may be sent back to a committee for further consideration. Nominations that have not been acted upon by adjournment *sine die* are returned to the president. Senate rules provide that nominations pending when the Senate adjourns or recesses for more than thirty days are also returned to the president, but the Senate may waive this rule by unanimous consent.

If a nominee is confirmed, the secretary of the Senate attests to a "resolution of confirmation," which is sent to the White House. Of course, the president may withdraw a nomination at any time, thereby ending the process.

of the executive branch. For example, rather than serving at the pleasure of the president, as do most presidential appointees, members of these bodies generally have fixed terms and often have some form of protection from removal. Statutes creating such entities may also require that seats must be allocated between members of different party affiliation.

Vacancies and Recess Appointments

The Constitution provides the president with the power to make limited-term appointments during Senate recesses to positions that otherwise would require the Senate's advice and consent. Article II, Section 2, Clause 3 states that "[t]he President shall have Power to fill up all Vacancies that may happen during the Recess of the Senate, by granting Commissions which shall expire at the End of their next Session." Presidents have sometimes used this power to circumvent the Senate confirmation process, especially in cases of controversial nominations. In response, Congress has attempted to constrain the president's power through a statute that prohibits payment from the Treasury to recess appointees unless certain nomination guidelines are followed (5 U.S.C. § 5503). In addition, a general provision included in the Financial Services (formerly Treasury) appropriations bill has prohibited payment from the Treasury to recess appointees whose nominations have been rejected by the Senate. *(See, for example, P.L. 108-447, Division H, Section 609.)* Nonetheless, recess appointments can be a source of congressional-executive tension. The president's authority to make a recess appointment to a judgeship on the Court of Appeals for the Eleventh Circuit, for example, was challenged in court, with an amicus brief filed by a senator. The Eleventh Circuit upheld the president's authority in this case. (*Evans et al. v. Stephens et al.*, 387 F.3d 1220 (11th Cir. 2004), *cert. denied*, 544 U.S. 942 (2005)).

Although Congress has tried to limit the president's recess appointment power, it has also acknowledged the need to maintain leadership in the federal bureaucracy during the appointment process by enacting the Federal Vacancies Reform Act of 1998 (5 U.S.C. §§ 3345-3349d), which allows for three kinds of limited-term appointments to most advice and consent positions in executive branch departments and agencies. In the event of a vacancy, (1) the first assistant to such position may automatically take over; (2) the president may direct another officer from any agency who holds an advice and consent position to take over the tasks of the vacant office; or (3) the president may select any officer or upper-level employee who has been at the agency where the vacancy exists for more than ninety days of the preceding year.

§ 10.90 Congress and the Executive: Presidential Election and Succession

Under Article II and the Twelfth, Twentieth, and Twenty-fifth Amendments to the Constitution, Congress has critical roles to play in the selection of the president and vice president during the quadrennial election process and in the event of a vacancy between elections.

Article II, Section 1, as modified by the Twelfth Amendment, established Congress's role in the electoral college system. Under these constitutional provisions and federal law, Congress, in joint session on January 6 (or another date set by Congress) following a presidential election, receives and counts electoral votes, and the election of the president and vice president is announced. Congress is empowered to resolve objections regarding the electoral votes at that time. *(See § 10.91, Electoral College.)*

In order to be elected president or vice president by the electoral college, a candidate must receive a majority, and not merely a plurality, of the electoral votes (currently 270 of 538). The Twelfth Amendment, as modified by the Twentieth Amendment, established a system for the *contingent election* of the president and vice president in the event that no candidate attains this threshold. In the case of the president, the House of Representatives chooses the president from among the three candidates with the largest numbers of electoral votes; each state delegation casts a single vote. A majority of states is needed for election. Although an amendment to the Constitution provided electors for the District of Columbia, it did not provide the District with a role in a contingent election. In the event that no vice presidential candidate receives a majority of electoral votes, the Senate chooses between the two candidates with the largest numbers of electoral votes; each senator has one vote, and a majority of votes is needed for election.

The Twelfth Amendment was proposed by Congress in 1803 in response to difficulties encountered during the presidential election of 1800-1801. After ratification by the states, the Twelfth Amendment went into effect in 1804. There have been two contingent elections under its provisions. The president was elected by the House of Representatives in 1825, and the vice president was elected by the Senate in 1837. The Twelfth Amendment mandates some of the specific procedures that must be used during a contingent election. Other procedures were developed by the House and Senate during the respective contingent elections, but those procedures could be altered in the event of another contingent election.

The Twentieth Amendment provided that the vice president serve as acting president until the House is able to choose a president, should the House be unable to reach a decision by inauguration day, January 20. (The Twentieth Amendment provided that a president's and vice president's terms of office end at 12:00 noon on January 20 following a presidential election.) This amendment also allows Congress to establish by law who serves as acting president in the event that neither a president nor a vice president is qualified by January 20. In the Presidential Succession Act of 1947 *(61 Stat. 380; 3 U.S.C. § 19)*, Congress addressed this matter, naming first the Speaker of the House, alternatively the president pro tempore of the Senate, and then the Cabinet secretaries in the order in which their departments were created (beginning with the secretary of state). To serve, an individual would need to meet the constitutional qualifications required for any president—a natural-born citizen, a resident of the United States for at least fourteen years, at least 35 years old, and not disqualified by previous service as president.

Article II, Section 1, Clause 6 of the Constitution originally provided for presidential succession in the event of "the Removal of the President from Office, or of his Death, Resigna-

§ *10.91*

Electoral College

The Constitution provided for *electors* in choosing the president and vice president; the states' electors by long practice are collectively called the *electoral college*. The Constitution in Article II, Section 1, Clause 2, states as follows:

> Each State shall appoint, in such Manner as the Legislature thereof may direct, a Number of Electors, equal to the whole Number of Senators and Representatives to which the State may be entitled in the Congress: but no Senator or Representative, or Person holding an Office of Trust or Profit under the United States, shall be appointed an Elector.

When a voter on election day casts a ballot for president and vice president, he or she is voting *indirectly* for a presidential and vice presidential ticket and *directly* for a slate of electors. Under authority granted in Article II, Section 1, Clause 3 of the Constitution to set the time of choosing electors, Congress set election day as the Tuesday after the first Monday in November.

There are currently 538 electors. In addition to each state's constitutional allocation based on two senators and its number of representatives—ranging for the 2004 and 2008 elections from a minimum of three electors to California's fifty-five—the District of Columbia also has three electors pursuant to the Twenty-third Amendment to the Constitution. To be elected president and vice president, the Twelfth Amendment requires candidates to obtain a majority in the electoral college, or, currently, 270 votes.

Electors for a presidential and vice presidential ticket in a state are chosen in accordance with law made by a state's legislature. While state laws vary on the selection of electors, slates of nominees for electors are partisan, usually reflecting choices of state party conventions or state party central committees; electors are expected to support their party's candidates for president and vice president. State law also governs contests involving presidential electors, and, pursuant to federal law, a state's resolution of contests is conclusive when it occurs at least six days before the electoral college meets. As soon as practicable after the election, or after the resolution of any contests, each state's governor sends a certificate of ascertainment of the electors appointed to the archivist of the United States and six duplicate-originals to the state's electors.

In locations designated by state law, electors representing each state's winning slate meet in their states on the first Monday after the second Wednesday in December (following the 2008 general election, it will be December 15), and cast separate ballots for their party's presidential and vice presidential candidates. All but two states (Maine and Nebraska) award electoral votes on a winner-take-all basis for the presidential and vice presidential ticket—technically, the ticket's slate of electors—that receives the greatest number of votes state-wide. Maine and Nebraska award two electoral votes on the basis of statewide results and the balance of their electoral votes (two for Maine and three for Nebraska) on the basis of congressional district results. A state constitutional amendment in Colorado to change the awarding of electors to a proportional allocation was defeated by voters in the 2004 general election, but other states are continuing to review changes to how they award electoral votes. Although electors can, and occasionally have, cast ballots for individuals other than the winning ticket's candidates, electors are expected to vote for their party's candidates. Some states have laws that attempt to enforce that expectation.

Records of each state's electors' balloting are transmitted to the vice president of the United States in his role as president of the Senate, to the archivist of the United States, to the state's secretary of state, and to the federal district court of the district in which the electors met.

Continued on page 406

On January 6 following the election, unless Congress has changed the law to designate another day, the House and Senate assemble at 1:00 p.m. in the House chamber for the counting of the electoral votes. The vice president of the United States presides, although the Senate president pro tempore may preside if the vice president declines or the vice president's office is vacant. The certificates and ballots of each state's electors are opened, proceeding in the alphabetical order of the states. The vice president reads a state's certificate and ballot, and calls for objections. He then presents the ballot to the four tellers–two from each chamber–who were previously selected by their respective chambers. When all the certificates and ballots are opened, read, and counted, the tellers present the results to the vice president. If one of the candidates for each of the offices receives a majority of the electoral votes (currently 270 of 538), the vice president announces the election of the president and vice president. *(For subsequent procedure in the absence of this outcome, see the discussion of contingent election in § 10.90, Congress and the Executive: Presidential Election and Succession.)*

An objection to a state's electoral votes must be in writing and signed by one representative and one senator. If there is a valid objection, the joint session is recessed at that point, the Senate withdraws to its chamber, and the two houses consider the objection. In these sessions, members may speak just once and for no more than five minutes. At the end of two hours, the chambers vote and then reconvene their joint session. Unless both chambers vote to uphold the objection, it fails. If both houses agree to the objection, the vote or votes objected to are not counted. This procedure was followed in 2005 after an objection by Rep. Stephanie Tubbs Jones, D-OH, and Sen. Barbara Boxer, D-CA, to the Ohio ballot. Neither chamber upheld the objection. The principal reasons there might be an objection are that a vote was not "regularly given" by an elector, for example, a "faithless" elector voting for someone other than the winners in his or her state, or that an elector was not lawfully certified, or both. Federal law *(3 U.S.C. § 1 et seq.)* provides guidance on resolving instances when there might be more than one list of electors.

(For specific information on electoral college procedures and the reasons therefore, see the web site of the National Archives and Records Administration at <www.archives.gov/federal-register/electoral-college>. Electoral college procedures and the role of Congress are codified at 3 U.S.C. § 1 et seq.)

Allocation of Electoral Votes for the 2004 and 2008 Presidential and Vice Presidential Elections

Alabama - 9	Idaho - 4	Missouri - 11	Pennsylvania - 21
Alaska - 3	Illinois - 21	Montana - 3	Rhode Island - 4
Arizona - 10	Indiana - 11	Nebraska - 5	South Carolina - 8
Arkansas - 6	Iowa - 7	Nevada - 5	South Dakota - 3
California - 55	Kansas - 6	New Hampshire - 4	Tennessee - 11
Colorado - 9	Kentucky - 8	New Jersey - 15	Texas - 34
Connecticut - 7	Louisiana - 9	New Mexico - 5	Utah - 5
Delaware - 3	Maine - 4	New York - 31	Vermont - 3
District of	Maryland - 10	North Carolina - 15	Virginia - 13
Columbia - 3	Massachusetts - 12	North Dakota - 3	Washington - 11
Florida - 27	Michigan - 17	Ohio - 20	West Virginia - 5
Georgia - 15	Minnesota - 10	Oklahoma - 7	Wisconsin - 10
Hawaii - 4	Mississippi - 6	Oregon - 7	Wyoming - 3

Presidential and
Vice Presidential Succession

In three different places, the Constitution *(art. II, sec. 1, cl. 5)* and amendments to it *(the Twentieth and Twenty-fifth Amendments)* provide for presidential and vice presidential succession, and authorize Congress to enact laws to carry out the constitutional provisions. The Twenty-fifth Amendment restated the original constitutional provision that the vice president becomes president if the president died, resigned, or was removed from office. (Nine vice presidents have succeeded to the presidency on the death or resignation of the president.)

The Twenty-fifth Amendment also authorized the president to nominate a vice president if a vacancy occurred in that office. (The vice presidency has been vacant on eighteen occasions.) The nomination must be confirmed by a majority vote in both the House and Senate. This provision of the Twenty-fifth Amendment has been used twice—President Richard M. Nixon nominated Gerald R. Ford to be vice president after the resignation of Vice President Spiro T. Agnew, and, after Ford succeeded Nixon as president, then-President Ford nominated Nelson A. Rockefeller to the vice presidency. The House and Senate Judiciary Committees conducted investigations of the nominees' fitness, held hearings on the nominations, and reported the nominations. The full House and Senate then debated and voted on the nominations.

In 1947, following the 1945 death in office of President Franklin D. Roosevelt, Congress enacted the Presidential Succession Act. *(62 Stat. 677; 3 U.S.C. § 19.)* Under this act, if vacancies exist in both the presidency and vice presidency, the Speaker of the House succeeds to the presidency if he qualifies (for example, being a naturalized citizen would be a disqualification). If the speakership is vacant or the Speaker is disqualified, then the president pro tempore succeeds to the presidency. If the office of president pro tempore is vacant or its occupant is disqualified, succession moves to the Cabinet, with the order based on the dates on which the departments were created. With ratification of the Twenty-fifth Amendment, however, the likelihood of invoking the Presidential Succession Act was substantially reduced.

The Twenty-fifth Amendment also provided for the event of presidential disability. Under certain circumstances, Congress might be called upon to decide whether a president is unable perform the duties of his office. Congress would be required to assemble within forty-eight hours if it is not in session. A determination of presidential disability would need to be made within twenty-one days of assembling and would require a two-thirds vote in each house.

10

tion, or Inability to discharge the Powers and Duties of the said Office." The Twenty-fifth Amendment, ratified in 1967, superseded this provision. It established a role for Congress in confirming a president's nomination to fill a vice presidential vacancy. The amendment also provided a role in determining, under certain circumstances, whether a president was "unable to discharge the powers and duties of his office." *(See § 10.92, Presidential and Vice Presidential Succession.)*

§ 10.100 Congress and the Executive: Impeachment

One or the most profound powers bestowed on Congress is the power to remove from office the president, federal judges, and other "civil Officers of the United States." Removal requires action by both houses of Congress. The Constitution empowers the House to impeach, or bring charges against, an official in Article I, Section 2, Clause 5, which states, "The House of Representatives . . . shall have the sole Power of Impeachment." After an official has been impeached, the trial is conducted in the Senate, as provided by Article I, Section 3, Clause 6:

> The Senate shall have the sole Power to try all Impeachments. When sitting for that Purpose, they shall be on Oath or Affirmation. When the President of the United States is tried, the Chief Justice shall preside: And no Person shall be convicted without the Concurrence of two thirds of the Members present.

The scope of the judgments resulting from such trials is defined in the next clause:

> Judgment in Cases of Impeachment shall not extend further than to removal from Office, and disqualification to hold and enjoy any Office of honor, Trust or Profit under the United States: but the Party convicted shall nevertheless be liable and subject to Indictment, Trial, Judgment and Punishment, according to the Law.

Although the House has initiated impeachment proceedings more than sixty times since the Constitution was adopted, it has voted to impeach only seventeen times. Seven of these impeachments, all federal judges, led to Senate convictions. Three of these convictions have occurred since 1985. Seven of the seventeen impeachments led to Senate acquittals, and the remaining three resulted in resignations.

Impeachment proceedings have been initiated against nine presidents. In two cases, those of Presidents Andrew Johnson and Bill Clinton, the House voted to impeach, and the president was acquitted in the Senate. In 1974, President Nixon resigned the presidency after the House Judiciary Committee voted for articles of impeachment, but before the full House acted. Since World War II, four other presidents–Truman, Reagan, George H.W. Bush, and George W. Bush–have been the subject of proposed articles of impeachment.

The Constitution sets a high standard for removal in Article II, Section 4, which provides that "The President, Vice President, and all civil Officers of the United States, shall be removed from Office on Impeachment for, and Conviction of, Treason, Bribery, or other high Crimes and Misdemeanors."

Three other standards and restrictions related to impeachment also exist in the Constitution. Article III, Section 1 states as follows: "The Judges, both of the supreme and inferior Courts, shall hold their Offices during good Behaviour. . . ." Article III, Section 2, Clause 3 exempts cases of impeachment from jury trial. And, in Article II, Section 2, Clause 1, the president is disallowed from granting pardons in cases of impeachment.

Impeachment Process

A summary of the principal steps in the impeachment process follows. The impeachment process might begin with a resolution introduced by one or more members of the House or through a referral from an outside entity, such as the Judicial Conference of the United States or an independent counsel. After authorization by the House, an examination or investigation into charges is undertaken, normally by the Judiciary Committee. The committee, by majority vote, may report a resolution and articles of impeachment. It then writes a committee report, which might contain minority, additional, and supplemental views of committee members.

The House considers impeachment resolutions under the one-hour rule or pursuant to a special rule reported from the Rules Committee and agreed to by the House. A majority vote, usually on each article of impeachment, is necessary. The House has voted to impeach on only seventeen occasions; it has voted articles of impeachment on just two presidents, Andrew Johnson and Bill Clinton.

If it adopts one or more articles of impeachment, the House appoints *managers* (generally members of the Judiciary Committee) to argue the case for impeachment in the Senate, and notifies the Senate of its action. The Senate informs the House when it is ready to receive the managers, who then appear *before the bar* of the Senate and *exhibit* the articles of impeachment. The Senate then summons the impeached official, and any pleadings are resolved before the trial begins.

The Senate proceeds under its *Rules of Procedure and Practice in the Senate When Sitting on Impeachment Trials*, a part of the *Senate Manual* (S. Doc. 107-1), as modified by subsequent action of the Senate. The Senate can subpoena witnesses and documents, and may delegate the receipt of testimony and evidence to a committee created for this purpose.

In a presidential impeachment trial, the chief justice of the Supreme Court presides. In all other trials in the Senate, an individual senator serves as the presiding officer, who rules on objections and questions and who may present such matters to the Senate for its decision. The House managers make their opening statements, followed by the impeached official's counsel. Evidence is presented, and witnesses may be called, examined, and cross-examined. Senators may submit questions in writing. Final arguments are presented by each side, but the House managers open and close these last presentations.

The Senate may deliberate in open or closed session. It then may choose to vote on any or all of the articles of impeachment; the Senate might also choose to adjourn an impeachment trial *sine die*. Concurrence of two-thirds of those present is necessary for conviction and removal from office. After adoption of one or more articles of impeachment, the Senate might also, by majority vote, disqualify the convicted official from again holding a federal office.

Under Article II, Section 2, Clause 1, the president may "grant Reprieves and Pardons for Offences against the United States," but this power cannot be used in "Cases of Impeachment." (*A one-page history of impeachment proceedings, from Congressional Directory, 2005-2006 (Washington: Government Printing Office, 2005), p. 545, follows.*)

10

IMPEACHMENT PROCEEDINGS

The provisions of the United States Constitution which apply specifically to impeachments are as follows: Article I, section 2, clause 5; Article I, section 3, clauses 6 and 7; Article II, section 2, clause 1; Article II, section 4; and Article III, section 2, clause 3.

For the officials listed below, the date of impeachment by the House of Representatives is followed by the dates of the Senate trial, with the result of each listed at the end of the entry.

WILLIAM BLOUNT, a Senator of the United States from Tennessee; impeached July 7, 1797; tried Monday, December 17, 1798, to Monday, January 14, 1799; charges dismissed for want of jurisdiction.

JOHN PICKERING, judge of the United States district court for the district of New Hampshire; impeached March 2, 1803; tried Thursday, March 3, 1803, to Monday, March 12, 1804; removed from office.

SAMUEL CHASE, Associate Justice of the Supreme Court of the United States; impeached March 12, 1804; tried Friday, November 30, 1804, to Friday, March 1, 1805; acquitted.

JAMES H. PECK, judge of the United States district court for the district of Missouri; impeached April 24, 1830; tried Monday, April 26, 1830, to Monday, January 31, 1831; acquitted.

WEST H. HUMPHREYS, judge of the United States district court for the middle, eastern, and western districts of Tennessee; impeached May 6, 1862; tried Wednesday, May 7, 1862, to Thursday, June 26, 1862; removed from office and disqualified from future office.

ANDREW JOHNSON, President of the United States; impeached February 24, 1868; tried Tuesday, February 25, 1868, to Tuesday, May 26, 1868; acquitted.

WILLIAM W. BELKNAP, Secretary of War; impeached March 2, 1876; tried Friday, March 3, 1876, to Tuesday, August 1, 1876; acquitted.

CHARLES SWAYNE, judge of the United States district court for the northern district of Florida; impeached December 13, 1904; tried Wednesday, December 14, 1904, to Monday, February 27, 1905; acquitted.

ROBERT W. ARCHBALD, associate judge, United States Commerce Court; impeached July 11, 1912; tried Saturday, July 13, 1912, to Monday, January 13, 1913; removed from office and disqualified from future office.

GEORGE W. ENGLISH, judge of the United States district court for the eastern district of Illinois; impeached April 1, 1926; tried Friday, April 23, 1926, to Monday, December 13, 1926; resigned office Thursday, November 4, 1926; Court of Impeachment adjourned to December 13, 1926, when, on request of House managers, the proceedings were dismissed.

HAROLD LOUDERBACK, judge of the United States district court for the northern district of California; impeached February 24, 1933; tried Monday, May 15, 1933, to Wednesday, May 24, 1933; acquitted.

HALSTED L. RITTER, judge of the United States district court for the southern district of Florida; impeached March 2, 1936; tried Monday, April 6, 1936, to Friday, April 17, 1936; removed from office.

HARRY E. CLAIBORNE, judge of the United States district court of Nevada; impeached July 22, 1986; tried Tuesday, October 7, 1986, to Thursday, October 9, 1986; removed from office.

ALCEE L. HASTINGS, judge of the United States district court for the southern district of Florida; impeached August 3, 1988; tried Wednesday, October 18, 1989, to Friday, October 20, 1989; removed from office.

WALTER L. NIXON, judge of the United States district court for the southern district of Mississippi; impeached May 10, 1989; tried Wednesday, November 1, 1989, to Friday, November 3, 1989; removed from office.

WILLIAM JEFFERSON CLINTON, President of the United States; impeached December 19, 1998; tried Thursday, January 7, 1999, to Friday, February 12, 1999; acquitted.

Mark H. Delahay, judge for the U.S. district court for Kansas, resigned in 1873 after his impeachment but before his Senate trial began.

§ 10.110 Congress and the Courts

Congress and the courts do not have the myriad daily interactions that are part and parcel of congressional-executive relations. But, the courts depend on Congress to legislate their organization, and on the Senate to confirm judicial appointees. Congress appropriates money for judicial salaries, personnel, operations, and facilities. The legislative decisions of Congress can have a large impact on the courts' workloads. Congress creates new rights or benefits for citizens and residents, with judicial remedies for disputes; creates or changes regulatory schemes, with rights of appeal to the courts; enacts new criminal laws, which must be prosecuted in the courts; and so on. Congress can also remove judges through impeachment by the House and conviction by the Senate. *(See § 10.100, Congress and the Executive: Impeachment.)*

§ 10.120 Congress and the Courts: Exercising Congressional Powers

There are a number of means by which Congress can exercise checks and balances vis-à-vis the courts. This section does not list exhaustively the extent of Congress's power and influence over the judicial branch, but summarizes some key aspects of that power and influence.

In matters related to the administration of the courts, the Senate confirms presidential nominations to the courts. *(See § 10.121, Nominations to Federal Courts.)* Congress, as a whole, enacts appropriations to operate the courts and, within the constraints of the Constitution, establishes judicial compensation. It creates law courts inferior to the Supreme Court and creates special courts, such as the United States Court of International Trade. Congress long ago created the system of district and circuit courts, but it occasionally legislates additional districts or circuits, as it did in 1980 when it split the former Fifth Judicial Circuit to create a new Fifth Judicial Circuit and a new Eleventh Judicial Circuit. *(94 Stat. 1994.)* Congress decides the number of judgeships that should exist for any court, and appropriates money for new courthouses.

In matters involving judicial power, Congress passes laws under which cases are brought in the federal courts by the executive, other governmental bodies, and private entities and cit-

Nominations to Federal Courts

Because appointments to federal district and circuit courts, and to the Supreme Court, are essentially lifetime appointments, the Senate often plays a more active (and sometimes contrarian) role in these appointments than when it considers presidential nominations to executive positions. Frequently, senators perceive the stakes in judicial appointments to be very high. That is especially the case with Supreme Court appointments, as indicated by the fact that, over the past 200 years, nearly one in five presidential nominations to the Supreme Court has been rejected or withdrawn.

In making judicial nominations, a president is generally expected to consult the senators from a potential nominee's home state, particularly if a senator is of the same party as the president. The president might also consult more widely, such as with members of the Senate Judiciary Committee or the Senate leadership, or at least with members of those two groups from his own party. And senators, other public officials, and other citizens regularly forward the names of prospective judges to the president and his staff.

Once a judicial nomination is received by the Senate, it is referred to the Judiciary Committee. The committee chair sends a blue-colored form (a "blue slip") to the senators from a state where the president has nominated a circuit or district judge (or a U.S. marshal or U.S. attorney). The senators may use the blue slips to indicate their approval or disapproval of the nominee. The committee reviews any investigation that was conducted by the Federal Bureau of Investigation at the request of the White House. The committee also examines a far-reaching questionnaire that it requires of nominees, the research of its staff, and information supplied by outside groups. *(See § 10.122, Gathering Information on a Judicial Nominee.)* A Supreme Court nominee typically makes a "courtesy call" on members of the committee, and often on other senators as well.

In contemporary practice, the Judiciary Committee will then schedule hearings. A district judge nomination supported by both of a state's senators and with no controversy attached to the nominee might be handled in a hearing covering several judges or several items of committee business. A nomination to the Supreme Court will undoubtedly be subject to at least several days of hearings, with an opportunity to testify afforded to the nominee and an opportunity to ask questions at length afforded to committee members. The nominee may be followed by numerous witnesses providing a range of views on the nominee or on factors for the committee and Senate to weigh in considering the nomination.

The final step is for the committee to vote to report the nomination to the full Senate, which it may do favorably, unfavorably, or without recommendation. The committee reports Supreme Court nominees, unless withdrawn, in one of these ways to give the Senate the opportunity to consider such an important nomination.

Nominations to lesser courts are sometimes tied up in committee or, once reported, in scheduling of floor time. A nomination might be in trouble because of concerns about the nominee's views or character, or because of political factors independent of the nominee. In presidential election years, the Senate may be loathe to oblige a sitting president by confirming a large number of nominees to the federal courts. *(See § 8.190, Holds, Clearance, and Unanimous Consent.)*

Once scheduled for floor time, a judicial nomination proceeds in the same manner as other presidential nominations. The process is described in § 10.81 *(Confirmation Procedure).* In the 108th and 109th Congresses, there was discussion in the Senate of possibly having a mechanism to allow a majority vote to shut off debate on judicial nominations rather than to have to invoke cloture, which requires sixty votes.

Gathering Information on a Judicial Nominee

As a nominee to be an associate justice of the U.S. Supreme Court, Samuel A. Alito Jr., a judge on the U.S. Court of Appeals for the Third Circuit, received a twelve-page questionnaire, the first page of which is shown here. In addition to making so-called courtesy calls on many senators, Judge Alito received letters from members of the Senate Judiciary Committee informing him of senators' interests that might be the bases for questions at his confirmation hearing. The first pages of letters from the then-chair and ranking minority member of the committee are shown here.

UNITED STATES SENATE
COMMITTEE ON THE JUDICIARY

NOMINEE FOR THE SUPREME COURT OF THE UNITED STATES

GENERAL (PUBLIC)

1. **Name**: Full name (include any former names used).

2. **Position**: State the position for which you have been nominated.

3. **Address**: List current office address. If state of residence differs from your place of employment, please list the state where you currently reside.

4. **Birthplace**: State date and place of birth.

5. **Marital Status**: (include maiden name of wife, or husband's name). List spouse's occupation, employer's name and business address(es). Please, also indicate the number of dependent children.

6. **Education**: List in reverse chronological order, with most recent first, each college, law school, and any other institutions of higher education attended and indicate for each the dates of attendance, whether a degree was received, and the date each degree was received.

7. **Employment Record**: List in reverse chronological order, listing most recent first, all governmental agencies, business or professional corporations, companies, firms, or other enterprises, partnerships, institutions and organizations, non-profit or otherwise, with which you have been affiliated as an officer, director, partner, proprietor, elected official or employee since graduation from college, whether or not you received payment for your services. Include the name and address of the employer and job title or job description, or the name and address of the institution or organization and your title and responsibilities, where appropriate.

8. **Military Service and Draft Status**: Identify any service in the U.S. Military, including dates of service, branch of service, rank or rate, serial number and type of discharge received. Please list, by approximate date, Selective Service classifications you have held, and state briefly the reasons for any classification other than I-A.

9. **Honors and Awards**: List any scholarships, fellowships, honorary degrees, academic or professional honors or awards, honorary society memberships, military awards, and any other special recognition for outstanding service or achievement you have received.

10. **Bar Associations**: List all bar associations or legal or judicial-related committees, selection panels or conferences of which you are or have been a member, and give the titles and dates of any offices which you have held in such groups. Also, if any such

Continued on page 414

ARLEN SPECTER, PENNSYLVANIA, CHAIRMAN

ORRIN G. HATCH, UTAH
CHARLES E. GRASSLEY, IOWA
JON KYL, ARIZONA
MIKE DeWINE, OHIO
JEFF SESSIONS, ALABAMA
LINDSEY O. GRAHAM, SOUTH CAROLINA
JOHN CORNYN, TEXAS
SAM BROWNBACK, KANSAS
TOM COBURN, OKLAHOMA

PATRICK J. LEAHY, VERMONT
EDWARD M. KENNEDY, MASSACHUSETTS
JOSEPH R. BIDEN, JR., DELAWARE
HERBERT KOHL, WISCONSIN
DIANNE FEINSTEIN, CALIFORNIA
RUSSELL D. FEINGOLD, WISCONSIN
CHARLES E. SCHUMER, NEW YORK
RICHARD J. DURBIN, ILLINOIS

MICHAEL O'NEILL, *Chief Counsel and Staff Director*
BRUCE A. COHEN, *Democratic Chief Counsel and Staff Director*

United States Senate

COMMITTEE ON THE JUDICIARY

WASHINGTON, DC 20510–6275

November 30, 2005

Honorable Samuel A. Alito, Jr.
c/o The Department of Justice
Washington, DC

Dear Judge Alito:

I write to give you advance notice of some of the issues I intend to ask at your confirmation hearing. In addition to identifying topics, I think it is helpful to outline the background for the questions to save time at the hearing.

Affirmative action is an area of law that has undergone many major changes in the last 25 years. During the late 1970s and early 1980s, when the Supreme Court first began grappling with affirmative action programs, it appeared to have considerable difficulty elucidating clear standards as to determining the constitutionality of such programs. The decisions in Regents of University of California v. Bakke in 1978, Fullilove v. Klutznick in 1980, and Wygant v. Jackson Board of Education in 1986, failed to develop a clear test.

In 1989, in City of Richmond v. Croson, a majority of the Court held that state and local government affirmative action programs are subject to strict scrutiny and thus struck down a Richmond, Virginia affirmative action program that set aside construction contracts for minority-owned businesses. Only a year later, however, the court upheld a federal affirmative action program, applying a lower standard of review in Metro Broadcasting v. FCC.

In 1995, the Court again considered a federal affirmative action program in Adarand v. Pena. In that case, the Court reviewed the Department of Transportation's policy of awarding extra compensation to contractors who hired minority-owned subcontractors. Overruling Metro Broadcasting, decided just five years earlier, the Court concluded that federal affirmative action programs, like state and local affirmative action programs, must be subject to strict scrutiny.

Most recently, the Court considered two higher education affirmative action programs. In Grutter v. Bollinger and Gratz v. Bollinger, the Court rendered a split verdict on the University of Michigan's undergraduate and law school admissions policies. It held that the law school's admission policy was constitutional because it was narrowly tailored and considered race only "a 'plus' factor in the context of individualized consideration of each and every applicant." It did not award "mechanical, predetermined diversity 'bonuses' based on race or ethnicity." In contrast, Michigan's undergraduate admission policy was struck down because it "automatically distribute[d] 20 points, one one-fifth of the points needed to guarantee admission, to every single 'underrepresented minority' applicant solely because of race." The Court held that such rigid policy was "not narrowly tailored to achieve the interest in educational diversity."

Continued on page 415

§ 10.122 (continued)

United States Senate
COMMITTEE ON THE JUDICIARY
WASHINGTON, DC 20510-6275

December 19, 2005

The Honorable Samuel A. Alito
United States Circuit Judge for the Third Circuit
357 U.S. Post Office and Courthouse
Federal Square and Walnut Street
Newark, NJ 07101

Dear Judge Alito:

I was glad that we had a chance to meet last month, if only briefly, and look forward to hearing from you at the upcoming hearings. I expect to ask you a number of questions about the role of the courts and judges in our democratic government. I write to you now, in advance of the hearing, so that you will have an opportunity to reflect on these issues and provide fully responsive answers at the hearings.

Last week, we celebrated the 214th anniversary of the adoption of the Bill of Rights to the Constitution. The Framers also embedded protections into the structure of our democracy. The checks and balances among our three branches of government provide fundamental safeguards for the rights of all Americans by ensuring that when one branch overreaches, it can be constrained by the others. Americans rely on this governmental structure to maintain the critical stability and balance necessary to preserve our freedoms and liberty.

At your nomination hearing next month I plan to ask you about your views on the President's power as Commander in Chief under our Constitution and the scope of congressional power in the time of war. There have been times throughout our history when the separation of powers has been tested by Presidents claiming unfettered power. Recent revelations that the President authorized domestic eavesdropping without following the statute that requires approval of the Foreign Intelligence Surveillance Court is but one of several areas where the Court's role as a check on overreaching by the Executive may soon prove crucial. The Supreme Court's role in resolving disputes between the two political branches of federal government involving the withdrawal of troops, and the methods of interrogation, are two other examples of issues that I will want to discuss with you.

Just as with any Federal judge, I view a Supreme Court Justice's willingness to serve as a check on executive power as among the most important issues to consider in a nomination process. It is ironic that after years of issuing decisions that were strongly supportive of executive claims of authority, especially in cases involving so-called "enemy combatants," the Fourth Circuit is now questioning the Bush Administration's switch in its position on whether Jose Padilla can be tried as a civilian in federal criminal court. These issues were also raised in the case of Hamdi v. Rumsfeld, in which Justice O'Connor wrote that our Constitution does not afford the President a blank check, even

10

415

§ 10.123

Congressional Response to Court Decisions

Congress, the president, and the courts regularly find themselves at odds over court decisions. But, if Congress has strong feelings about a matter decided by the courts, it might respond with legislation. In 1991, for instance, it enacted a civil rights bill in response to Supreme Court rulings between 1986 and 1991 that had restricted the application of civil rights laws and the remedies available under them in employment discrimination cases. In this example, the three branches spoke to each other through the formal procedures of their constitutional roles, and the two political branches—Congress and the executive—ultimately made a policy decision answering questions raised by the Supreme Court's rulings.

Beginning in 1986, the Supreme Court made a series of rulings on employment discrimination, principally under Title VII of the Civil Rights Act of 1964, which prohibits employment discrimination, and under a post-Civil War law *(42 U.S.C. § 1981)*, which prohibits racial discrimination in the making and enforcing of contracts. In the nine rulings subsequently addressed through legislation by Congress, the thrust of the Court's decisions was to make it harder for employees to allege, prove, and obtain relief for employment discrimination.

For example, pursuant to an earlier Supreme Court decision on Title VII (*Griggs v. Duke Power Co.,* 401 U.S. 424 (1971)), employees were able to offer statistical evidence to show the discriminatory effect of an employer's personnel practices. They did not have to prove an intention to discriminate. The courts, in handling cases after that decision, required employers to carry the burden of proof in defending their personnel practices. In 1989, the Court returned to the matter of burden of proof in employment discrimination cases under Title VII. It ruled in *Wards Cove Packing Co. Inc. v. Atonio*, 490 U.S. 642 (1989), that proving discrimination caused by a specific employment practice was a burden carried by plaintiffs and that statistical evidence of the impact of employment practices was insufficient to establish discrimination.

Decisions such as *Wards Cove* alarmed civil rights organizations and a number of members of Congress. In 1990, companion measures were introduced in the House and Senate to deal with the effects of six of the rulings, among the measures' other provisions. An administration bill that dealt with just two of the decisions was also introduced in both chambers. Proponents and opponents of the competing legislation attempted to reach a compromise at various stages of the legislative process, but failed. The administration and those members of Congress opposed to the measures backed by the civil rights organizations were successful at painting those measures with the politically charged moniker of "quota" bills, arguing that employers would adopt quotas for hiring and promotion to avoid lawsuits. Proponents of the measures backed by the civil rights organizations questioned the administration's commitment to enactment of any civil rights measure.

Neither the House nor the Senate mustered veto-proof majorities by the time they voted on the conference report, despite some of the concessions made by civil rights organizations and included in the legislation in an attempt to build wider political support. President George H.W. Bush vetoed the bill *(S. 2104; Oct. 22, 1990)*, noting in his veto message a number of areas of agreement between himself and the majority in Congress, but arguing that the effect of the measure would be to create "powerful incentives for employers to adopt hiring and promotion quotas." The Senate took up the veto, and the override attempt failed by a single vote to obtain the two-thirds vote needed to override. *(66 to 34; Oct. 24, 1990.)* The political branches had not yet found a new equilibrium in employment antidiscrimination policy.

Continued on page 417

When the 102nd Congress convened in 1991, the House Democratic leadership reserved H.R. 1 for a new civil rights bill, giving it prominence and visibility. An administration bill was also introduced in both houses. In the fall of 1991, against the backdrop of the confirmation fight over Clarence Thomas's appointment to the Supreme Court and other political factors, senators and the administration reached compromise on a new bill. The Senate adopted the new measure by a vote of 93 to 5. *(S. 1745; Oct. 30, 1991.)* During Senate consideration of the new bill, senators were very cognizant of how the courts would interpret the measure once it was enacted into law. Because of the number of points on which the bill was not specific, the discretion in interpretation became part of the compromise. Interestingly, the Senate agreed to an amendment attempting to limit the courts' consideration of legislative history surrounding the measure's provisions to a short memo inserted in the *Congressional Record*.

The House followed the Senate in adopting the new measure *(381 to 38; Nov. 7, 1991)*, and President Bush signed it *(P.L. 102-166)*. The bill that became law addressed policy issues in nine different Supreme Court rulings on employment discrimination, and provided new but limited monetary damages under Title VII. Its language, however, left questions to be resolved by the courts in cases brought before them. The language also allowed the Bush and subsequent administrations leeway in choosing whether and how to participate in those cases.

The political process of making a law does not necessarily result in a law that answers explicitly the variety of cases that might arise under it. As in the situation described above, Congress and the president felt compelled to respond to policy issues raised by the Supreme Court's decisions on discrimination in employment, but the answer eluded them and was ultimately found only in enacting a law with new provisions open to differing interpretations. It might be expected that a future Congress and a future president will find it desirable to address court decisions made under these changes to the employment antidiscrimination laws, again offering new policy direction to the courts.

10

izens. Among many possible categories of lawmaking, these laws might include initiatives in federal regulation within Congress's enumerated powers, such as changes in immigration and naturalization laws. Congress might federalize what have traditionally been areas of state law, such as new criminal statutes dealing with violent crimes or activities with a potential for violence. Congress might pass laws that respond to court decisions that run counter to majority sentiment in Congress on public-policy issues. *(See § 10.123, Congressional Response to Court Decisions.)*

Congress can also in its lawmaking determine the process by which a matter might be brought in the federal courts. For example, appeals from agency adjudicatory decisions are normally taken to a U.S. appeals court. Congress can also say in law which court might hear a matter first, whether administrative remedies must be exhausted before a lawsuit may be filed, what the threshold considerations are for determining that the federal courts are the appropriate judicial forum, and what remedies are available to prevailing litigants. In language included in committee and conference reports and in colloquies on the floor, members are conscious of the potential impact of legislative history on some court decisions. *(See § 10.73, Legislative History.)*

Congress is empowered by the Constitution to impeach and try judges, which it has done as recently as 1989. The Constitution also empowers Congress to make exceptions to the Supreme Court's appellate jurisdiction and to regulate that jurisdiction. (A related, more common exercise of congressional power involving congressional concern about actual or potential judicial decisions is to amend the underlying law on which a decision might be based, for example, amending an environmental law to eliminate a basis for litigation.) Congress might also propose constitutional amendments to the states.

Members of Congress themselves might be litigants or *amici* (filing an *amicus*, or friend of the court, brief) in some cases. Finally, the House general counsel and the Senate legal counsel monitor court cases with a view toward the institutional prerogatives and interests of Congress. Members receiving subpoenas for their appearances or for documents notify the chamber by letter. The letter is usually printed in the *Congressional Record*.

§10.130 Congress and Foreign Policy

Foreign policy is a power shared by Congress and the executive. The president represents the United States in foreign relations, as head of state and head of government, and as the commander in chief. Beyond that, the framers of the Constitution gave both Congress and the president powers in foreign commerce and foreign policy, including what is now broadly called national security. Congress exerts extensive control over foreign policy and national security, particularly through the appropriations process. The president regularly resorts to his explicit and inherent constitutional powers to take action in foreign and national security policy, including an initial commitment of American troops, but he regularly acts within the framework of policies or grants of authority that exist in law. Either Congress or the executive might initiate a change in foreign policy within its constitutional powers. These actions put the other branch in the position of reacting. Congress and the executive might also work jointly, in either consultative or lawmaking roles.

§10.140 Congress and Foreign Policy: Declaring War and Committing Troops

Despite the number of times that American troops have been committed both to large-scale, long-lasting wars and to hostilities or hostile situations of limited duration, Congress has declared war in only five conflicts: the War of 1812, the Mexican-American War, the Spanish-American War, World War I, and World War II. Congress is empowered by Article 1, Section 8, Clause 11 of the Constitution "To declare War . . ." but presidents have rarely asked for declarations of war and Congress has rarely found it necessary to do so. Congress is also empowered in Section 8 "To raise and support Armies . . ." *(cl. 12)* and "To provide and maintain a Navy . . ." *(cl. 13)*.

To declare war, Congress passes a joint resolution naming one or more foreign nations. The joint resolution may originate in either house. Normal congressional procedures would apply to the joint resolution. These include normal procedures such as suspension of the rules and a special rule from the Rules Committee in the House, and unanimous consent in the Senate, for waiving procedures that might delay a vote on the joint resolution.

However, for any number of reasons, Congress might instead support a war, limited hostilities, or the potential for hostilities in another way. Congress might choose to "authorize" military action, as it did in 1991 in the instance of the Persian Gulf War *(105 Stat. 3)*. It might pass a concurrent resolution, not binding on the president, dealing with some aspect of a foreign crisis, as it did with the Kosovo crisis in March 1999 *(H. Con. Res. 42 and S. Con. Res. 21)*. In response to the terrorist attacks of September 11, 2001, Congress passed a joint resolution authorizing the president to use "all necessary and appropriate force" against nations, organizations, or individuals he determined to be responsible *(S.J. Res. 23, P.L. 107-40)*. Congress again employed a joint resolution in 2002 to authorize the use of military force in Iraq *(H.J. Res. 114; P.L. 107–243)*. Congress also has often supported military action through spending authorization and appropriation measures.

War Powers Resolution

To balance the president's responsibility as commander in chief for actions to defend the United States with Congress's powers in foreign policy, Congress, in 1973, enacted over President Nixon's veto the War Powers Resolution *(87 Stat. 555; 50 U.S.C. § 1541 et seq)*. The history of the War Powers Resolution has exposed flaws or problems in dealing with situations that arise abroad and with presidential decisions on military actions. Presidents since the enactment of the War Powers Resolution have found it to infringe unconstitutionally on their power as commander in chief, and have interpreted its provisions to favor presidential power and discretion. Yet, whenever troops are committed or may be committed, the War Powers Resolution is now the legal framework invoked and debated by the president and Congress.

The interbranch tensions of the War Powers Resolution begin with its policy statements. These statements assert that, as commander in chief, the president may commit troops to hostilities or imminent hostilities only if there is a declaration of war, a congressional authorization, or an attack on the United States, its territories or possessions, or its armed forces. The War Powers Resolution also requires consultation between Congress and the president before troops are committed. However, presidents have generally chosen to inform Congress rather than consult it, and to do so at varying times in the course of committing troops.

The heart of the War Powers Resolution deals with presidential commitment of troops into "hostilities" or "imminent hostilities." In these circumstances, it requires the president to report to Congress within forty-eight hours after the introduction of troops. A report must explain the reasons for committing troops, the authority under which the president took the action, and an estimate of the scale and duration of the commitment. The president must withdraw the troops within sixty days unless Congress has authorized or extended the commitment by law, or is unable to meet because of an attack on the United States. The president may certify the need for a presence for an additional thirty days to ensure the safe withdrawal of troops.

The War Powers Resolution created expedited, or fast-track, procedures for introducing a joint resolution or bill declaring war or authorizing troop commitments. The procedures apply to committee, floor, and conference proceedings, and operate to bring Congress to a decision by the time the sixty-day period is complete.

The War Powers Resolution also enabled Congress to order the withdrawal of troops by concurrent resolution, a legislative veto presumably invalidated by the Supreme Court's subsequent, unrelated decision in *INS v. Chadha*, 462 U.S. 919 (1983). To rectify this situation, Congress enacted a procedure—independent of the War Powers Resolution—to use a joint resolution, which would then require presidential approval or a congressional veto override to take effect *(97 Stat. 1062; 50 U.S.C. § 1546a.)*.

Among other provisions, the War Powers Resolution also requires reports on troop commitments in situations other than hostilities or imminent hostilities, and includes U.S. troops accompanying foreign military forces in hostilities as an introduction of U.S. armed forces.

The War Powers Resolution was enacted amidst the extraordinary environment of the Vietnam War, Watergate, and congressional actions that led eventually to the House Judiciary Committee's adoption of an impeachment resolution against President Nixon. Nonetheless, it seems to have provided a needed framework for the two branches to debate the commitment of American troops. Except in one instance, presidents have not reported hostilities under the section of the law that would set the sixty-day clock running. However, they have not overtly ignored the War Powers Resolution, and have informed Congress about military engagements consistent with their interpretations of the law. Congress, for its part, has responded differently in different circumstances. For example, it took the initiative in legislation to set the date on which the War Powers Resolution was triggered in 1983 when U.S. Marines were participating in a multinational force in Lebanon.

§10.150 Congress and Foreign Policy: Treaties and International Agreements

Article II, Section 2, Clause 2 of the Constitution says of the president: "He shall have Power, by and with the Advice and Consent of the Senate, to make Treaties, provided two thirds of the Senators present concur. . . ." In accordance with Article VI, a ratified treaty, like the Constitution and laws enacted by Congress, is the supreme law of the land.

In foreign affairs, the president often acts under a grant of authority from Congress to negotiate *international* or *executive agreements* with foreign nations. For example, Congress might grant negotiating authority to the president pursuant to its constitutional power to regulate foreign commerce. Like a treaty, an agreement is a binding arrangement between the United States and another nation or other nations. Unlike a treaty, it is not submitted to the Senate for its advice and consent. An agreement may, however, be subject to a *joint resolution of approval* or *disapproval* by the House and Senate, pursuant to the statute under which the president acted, or, to take effect, it might require *implementing legislation.*

Some trade agreements serve as examples of the process of congressional delegation of specific negotiating authority to the president, and subsequent congressional action on an agreement negotiated by the president pursuant to that grant of authority. For example, Congress granted the president specific *trade negotiating authority* (also now being called *trade promotion authority*) for the "Uruguay Round" of multilateral trade negotiations in 1988 *(102 Stat. 1121; 19 U.S.C. § 2901).* The breadth of the president's authority was spelled out. The president was then to submit implementing legislation to Congress, which would include, among other provisions, changes to existing laws to bring them into conformity with the agreement. To give the president and other nations assurance that Congress would enact what the president negotiated, Congress agreed to consider the agreement under *fast-track procedures*—if the agreement was entered by April 15, 1994. The president submitted the agreement and implementing bill in time, and Congress enacted the bill *(108 Stat. 4809; 19 U.S.C. § 3501). (See § 10.151, Fast-Track Procedures.)*

Congress acted in 2002 to give the president trade promotion authority for an agreement to be entered into by June 1, 2005, or, through possible extension, June 1, 2007.

Presidents also claim inherent powers of their own to enter into agreements. Congress, in an attempt to protect its prerogatives and keep the executive in check, has enacted statutes requiring these agreements to be reported to Congress.

While international agreements might be considered in Congress by regular legislative procedures or by fast-track procedures, treaties—along with nominations—form the *executive business* of the Senate. The Senate has developed special procedures for its handling and consideration of treaties.

Treaty Procedure in the Senate

Consideration of a treaty by the Senate is a type of legislative action that possesses similarities to and differences from regular legislative action.

A treaty may not be ratified for the United States and, pursuant to the treaty's terms, become effective for the nation unless the president obtains the *advice and consent* of the Senate. That consent is given only by a two-thirds favorable vote of senators present and voting. (The House has no constitutional role in the advice and consent process.)

The Senate might have an informal role before the conclusion of treaty negotiations. Individual senators might serve as observers at the negotiations, or the negotiators might hold

§ 10.151

Fast-Track Procedures

Fast-track procedures are unique legislative procedures Congress adopts to expedite timely action on a specifically defined type of measure. Fast-track procedures are, therefore, also referred to as *expedited procedures.* The congressional budget resolution and reconciliation bills, resolutions authorizing the use of the armed forces under the War Powers Act, certain foreign military sales, military base closings, and measures to implement international trade agreements are examples of issues considered under fast-track procedures. There is not one form of fast-track procedure; each fast-track procedure is particular to specific legislation or a specific form of legislation.

The *House Rules and Manual* has a section called *Congressional Disapproval Provisions* that contains the complete texts of laws with expedited procedures. These disapproval statutes, applicable in both chambers, are referenced in the rules of each chamber.

Fast-track procedures are in force to limit the opportunity for delay or inaction in either the House or Senate or both. Accordingly, procedures generally require introduction of a measure after Congress receives a presidential message on an expedited procedure issue, and generally require the committee receiving a referral to report on the measure in a specified period of time. If the committee fails to act, an *automatic discharge* of the committee becomes effective, thereby removing the measure from the committee. Most fast-track procedures provide *privilege* to the measure for prompt floor action. They also generally impose time limits on debate on the floor and preclude floor amendments.

Examples of laws in which fast-track procedures exist include the Arms Export Control Act *(22 U.S.C. §§ 2776(b), 2776(c), 2776(d), and 2753)* and the 1974 Trade Act *(19 U.S.C. §§ 2191, 2253, 2432, and 2437).*

periodic briefings for individual senators, leaders, and committees. The Senate's formal role, however, begins with a presidential message—the president's submission of a letter of transmittal and the accompanying treaty documents to the Senate. The treaty documents comprise the text of the treaty, a letter submitted to the president by the secretary of state (usually analyzing the treaty), other documents deemed integral parts of the treaty, and informational documents. The president asks for favorable consideration of the treaty.

Upon receipt, the set of documents is numbered by the executive clerk. Treaty documents are numbered sequentially through a Congress, in a numbering sequence separate from other Senate documents, using the Congress and a sequential number, for example, Treaty Doc. 106-1, where "106" refers to the 106th Congress. Also, upon receipt of the treaty documents, the majority leader may ask unanimous consent on the Senate floor to remove the *injunction of secrecy* concerning the treaty, which today is usually a pro forma step, treaties having been made public before submission to the Senate by the president.

All treaties are referred to the Foreign Relations Committee. (This referral, however, does not preclude other committees with jurisdiction over the subject matter of the treaty from holding their own hearings or even presenting their views or recommendations to the Foreign Relations Committee.) The committee usually holds hearings, taking testimony from administration officials who participated in treaty negotiations and from others—experts, advocates, and opponents. The committee can choose *not* to act on a treaty. If it takes action and chooses to report the treaty to the full Senate, it may report it favorably, unfavorably, or without recommendation. If the Foreign Relations Committee reports a treaty, it also generally submits a written report, referred to as an *executive report*. (Executive reports are assigned numbers that run sequentially through a Congress.)

The Foreign Relations Committee also reports a proposed resolution of ratification that may include committee-recommended conditions. Two conditions seem to have become standard in contemporary resolutions. The first is informally called the Byrd-Biden condition, after Sens. Robert Byrd, D-WV, and Joseph Biden, D-DE. In essence, the condition says that the Senate may rely on the presentations made by the president and his representatives in developing a shared understanding of a treaty. The second condition, based on concerns most recently raised by former Sen. Jesse Helms, R-NC, notes the supremacy of the U.S. Constitution.

The reported treaty is placed on the Senate's *executive calendar*. To consider a treaty, the Senate must go into *executive session*. (If the Senate is considering legislative business, it is in *legislative session*; treaties and nominations are considered in executive session.) The majority leader typically asks unanimous consent that the Senate go into executive session. If unanimous consent is not granted (that is, there is an objection to the unanimous consent request), the majority leader can move that the Senate go into executive session. The motion is not debatable, but it could trigger the first test vote of Senate sentiment on the treaty.

The Senate considers a treaty just as it considers a bill. A treaty is both debatable and amendable (proposed changes to the treaty's text, which the Senate subsequently incorporates into its resolution of ratification). When debate and action on amendments are completed, the Senate considers a *resolution of ratification,* which is the actual document on which the Senate gives *advice and consent.* The Senate does not consider further amendments to the treaty. The resolution of ratification is a simple resolution. The Senate can offer, debate, and amend reservations, declarations, understandings, provisos, or statements in connection with the resolution:

- *Reservations* are "specific qualifications or stipulations which change U.S. obligations without necessarily changing treaty language."
- *Understandings* are "interpretive statements that clarify or elaborate the provisions of the treaty but do not alter its language."
- *Declarations* are "statements of the Senate's position, opinion or intentions on matters relating to issues raised by the treaty, but not to its specific provisions."
- *Provisos or statements* do not affect or explain the treaty, but express concern about issues of U.S. law or procedure.

Each of these matters requires a majority vote for adoption. Filibuster and the invoking of cloture are possible, as usual. Approval of a resolution of ratification requires a two-thirds vote of those present and voting, a quorum being present, under the Constitution. Occasionally, several treaties (usually noncontroversial) might be voted on en bloc individually or by division. Upon approval of a resolution of ratification, it is transmitted by the executive clerk to the White House. A president does not have to ratify a treaty after Senate approval. If the president concludes that any condition attached by the Senate alters obligations under the treaty, he must notify the other treaty parties.

It is important to remember that, unlike bills, a treaty does not die at the end of a Congress. A treaty remains pending before the Senate until it is either agreed to by the Senate or withdrawn by the president. However, floor proceedings on a treaty that remain uncompleted at the *sine die* adjournment of a Congress terminate, and the treaty is returned to the calendar and then to the Foreign Relations Committee. A treaty might also require implementing legislation, which would be in the form of a bill or joint resolution passed in the same form by the House and Senate and submitted to the president for his signature or veto.

The outright rejection of a treaty is rare. Upon rejection, the treaty would be returned to the executive calendar and, at adjournment, to the Foreign Relations Committee. The Senate could adopt a resolution informing the president of its action and return the treaty to him, but the Senate would need to adopt such a resolution.

§ 10.160 Congress and Foreign Policy: Legislation, Appropriations, and Nominations

Nearly every year, Congress has at its disposal a number of possible legislative vehicles for reaching its own foreign policy decisions. These bills might include authorization bills for foreign relations and foreign aid, the Department of Defense (DOD), and the intelligence agencies. They also include annual appropriations bills for foreign operations, the State Department, military construction, and DOD. In the course of a year, Congress might also enact other measures that concern or include foreign policy, such as those dealing with trade, international organizations, or supplemental or continuing appropriations resolutions. Despite House and Senate rules generally intended to prevent the addition of legislative provisions to appropriations measures, foreign policy legislative provisions can end up in those measures. *(For a description of the legislative process, see Chapter Eight, Legislating in Congress: Legislative Process; and § 10.151, Fast-Track Procedures. See also Chapter Nine, Legislating in Congress: Federal Budget Process.)*

In one of these legislative vehicles or another measure, Congress might enact a program or an extensive set of policies, such as the program to assist Russia in dismantling nuclear weapons *(107 Stat. 1777; 22 U.S.C. § 5951 et seq.)* or the set of policies to guide U.S. diplomacy on other nations' restrictions on religious liberty *(112 Stat. 2787; 22 U.S.C. § 6401 et seq.)* or to prohibit import into or export from the United States of "conflict diamonds" *(117 Stat. 631; 19 U.S.C. § 3901 et seq.)*. The president and appropriate executive agencies then carry out these programs.

Congress often conditions U.S. assistance to foreign nations on their observing specified norms of behavior, such as the various aid and arms export laws aimed at curbing nuclear proliferation. It might also prohibit or cut off assistance in one or more forms until behavior changes, as occurs with the various laws that restrict trade and aid to nations that violate U.S. antiterrorism or human rights policies. For example, concerns over Syria's role in Lebanon were not new in the 109th and 110th Congresses. In 2003, Congress passed and the president signed the Syria Accountability and Lebanese Sovereignty Restoration Act *(117 Stat. 2482)*, imposing trade restrictions and other penalties.

In the foreign policy area, Congress regularly requires the president to report to it, and to wait to act until Congress has had time to approve or disapprove a proposed policy or action. For example, U.S. trade law requires the president to request permission annually to waive freedom-of-emigration provisions. Until Congress voted for *normal trade relations* (NTR, formerly called *most favored nation*) with China, the president's waiver request and congressional action on it made China eligible for NTR status. Once the request was made, Congress had sixty days to adopt a joint resolution disapproving the president's request for waiver authority. Otherwise, the waiver authority was automatically renewed.

Treaties and international agreements can also impose requirements on the United States that require lawmaking. For example, following congressional agreement to legislation implementing agreements reached under the "Uruguay Round" of multilateral trade negotiations *(P.L. 103-465)*, the World Trade Organization (WTO) was formed as the new structure for member nations to discuss trade issues, negotiate trade agreements, and settle trade disputes. The United States lost a challenge in the WTO to U.S. tax provisions benefiting U.S. exporters, called the Foreign Sales Corporation (FSC). Congress responded in 2000 by repealing the FSC provisions and creating a new export benefit excluding certain "extraterritorial income" (ETI) from corporate gross income *(P.L. 106-519)*. The United States lost a challenge in the WTO to these new tax law provisions, and Congress responded in 2004 with new changes to corporate tax law *(P.L. 108-357; 118 Stat. 1418)* that were intended to comply with WTO rules.

The House or Senate or both often adopt simple or concurrent resolutions *(sense of the House, sense of the Senate, or sense of the Congress resolutions)* expressing their attitudes on foreign policy issues. Resolutions garnering numerous cosponsors, even if never considered on the floor of the House or Senate, can be important to the administration. In support of an administration policy, a resolution might strengthen the position of the president and his representatives in negotiating with other nations or within a multilateral entity. That appeared to be the case with resolutions introduced early in the 109th Congress to oppose European moves to end the arms embargo against China imposed in 1989 after the Chinese army's assault on demonstrators in Tiananmen Square; the resolutions generally reinforced the Bush administration's position.

A resolution opposing an administration policy might be an early warning, and cause the administration to change course, lest Congress legislate a policy. In the 110th Congress, the House passed a concurrent resolution expressing opposition to the president's so-called troop surge in Iraq *(H. Con. Res. 63, agreed to in the House February 16, 2007)*. This resolution was the opening salvo in legislative attempts to force a change in the president's goals and conduct of the war in Iraq. *Sense of* language is regularly included in legislation as a means of bringing a concern to the administration's attention. It may invite compromise with Congress, but without making law.

In legislating on foreign policy, Congress can tie the hands of the president, or, alternately, may allow him to make an independent determination of what course of action is in the best interests of the United States. Congress may require the president merely to report to it, which leaves him considerable discretion, or may direct the president or other executive officials in some way, narrowing his discretion. Congress sometimes acquiesces to a presidential initiative by taking no action. However, the stronger the sentiment in Congress on a foreign policy matter, the more tightly the president's discretion is likely to be circumscribed. So, for example, Congress cut off any funds after September 30, 1994, to maintain U.S. military personnel in Somalia *(P.L. 103–335)*.

Congressional influence over foreign policy might be at its strongest in the annual appropriations bills and other appropriations measures. Congress can choose to fund a presidential budget request, not fund it, increase or decrease it, condition or limit funding attached to a request, or fund one or more items that are different from the president's requests. The president is unlikely to win on every budget request and policy matter in a wide-ranging appropriations bill. For example, congressional-presidential disagreement on paying U.S. "arrearages" to the United Nations, and on U.S. policy on international population and family planning assistance, delayed adoption of the foreign operations appropriations legislation in 1999. The president eventually accepted conditions on appropriations *(P.L. 106-113)*.

Each year, through the appropriations process, Congress also makes decisions on defense spending. The House, Senate, and president may each have different views, for example, on the effectiveness or need or procurement rate for different weapons systems. Weapons systems are also often positioned by their proponents in policy debates as vital for employment in various states and congressional districts, in addition to being promoted for their contributions to national security. The annual defense appropriations bill can also be a vehicle for foreign policy debates. In the 110th Congress, Congress and the president fought over defense funding regarding the president's goals and conduct of the war in Iraq. *(See also Chapter Nine, Legislating in Congress: Federal Budget Process.)*

The Senate also holds great influence over foreign policy with its constitutional role in confirming presidential nominations to foreign policy posts. The Senate confirms nominations for U.S. ambassadors, U.S. representatives to international organizations, and senior-level staff in the State Department, Defense Department, Central Intelligence Agency, and other government agencies. The confirmation of a nomination cannot be taken for granted, and may occur after the Senate and the president arrive at an understanding concerning a foreign policy issue.

The Senate Foreign Relations Committee, Armed Services Committee, and other Senate committees with jurisdiction over nominations to foreign and national security policy and military posts regularly use nominations to inquire more broadly about foreign policy, in an attempt to influence the nominees or the administration. Nominations to foreign policy posts are handled in the same way as other nominations to executive positions. *(See § 10.80, Congress and the Executive: Appointments.)* However, they regularly become a vehicle that the Senate can use to extract information from the executive branch, cause a reexamination of a policy, or trigger some other course of action. *(See § 8.190, Holds, Clearance, and Unanimous Consent.)*

§ 10.170 Congress and Foreign Policy: Nonbinding Actions

A number of committees have jurisdiction over aspects of foreign policy, including national defense policy. The House Foreign Affairs and Senate Foreign Relations Committees are obvious players, and the jurisdiction of the House Ways and Means and Senate Finance Committees over foreign trade is well-known. The House and Senate Armed Services Committees are key committees in national security policy.

Additional committees handle important components of foreign policy. The House Financial Services Committee and the Senate Foreign Relations and Banking, Housing, and Urban Affairs Committees have jurisdiction over international economics and finance. The two Agriculture Committees may assert jurisdiction over international agricultural and food policy. Each chamber has a Select Committee on Intelligence with jurisdiction over the Central Intelligence Agency, the National Security Agency, and other intelligence agencies. Other legislative committees have jurisdictions that are directly or indirectly related to foreign policy; for example, the two Judiciary Committees handle immigration, antiterrorism, and crime legislation; the House Energy and Commerce Committee and Senate Energy and Natural Resources Committee handle energy legislation; and the House Homeland Security Committee and the Senate Homeland Security and Governmental Affairs Committee have jurisdiction over the Department of Homeland Security.

The two Appropriations Committees have several subcommittees that each have jurisdiction over appropriations bills that fund portions of the foreign policy and national defense policy budgets. These subcommittees include those handling foreign operations; the Departments of Commerce, Defense, Justice, and State; agriculture; and military construction. In addition, the House Oversight and Government Reform and the Senate Homeland Security and Governmental Affairs Committees have authority to conduct oversight government-wide.

The import of this list is that numerous committees can claim jurisdiction over aspects of foreign policy, and thereby legislate, conduct oversight, monitor rulemaking, and attempt to influence the administration's conduct of foreign policy. Perhaps one indication of "globalization" is seen in the work of congressional committees, where the distinction between domestic and foreign or international issues is becoming blurred. *(See also § 10.160, Congress and Foreign Policy: Legislation, Appropriations, and Nominations.)*

Legislative and oversight hearings by these committees allow Congress to inform itself about an administration's conduct of foreign policy. Hearings identify possible courses for legislative action, and, in some instances, raise public awareness. Committees also conduct investigations, perhaps drawing on the resources of the Government Accountability Office and other entities, to evaluate the efficacy and efficiency of foreign policy agencies and programs. Committees might also sponsor fact-finding travel to countries or regions to obtain first-hand information on foreign policy issues. (These missions are popularly called *CODELS* (congressional delegations). The importance of this travel is sometimes dismissed as a *junket*, connoting pleasure rather than work and waste rather than results.)

Committees review reports made to Congress on matters within their jurisdiction, consult the president or executive officials on foreign policy matters as required by law or informally, and might organize other means of nonlegislative influence on the administration, such as preparing a letter signed by key members of Congress expressing perspectives on a foreign policy issue. For example, eight members of the House Ways and Means Committee (including the chair, ranking minority member, and trade subcommittee chair) sent a letter March 6, 2001, to then-Treasury Secretary Paul O'Neill, challenging the U.S. Customs Service's interpretation of a provision of the African Growth and Opportunity Act *(P.L. 106–200, title I; 114 Stat. 251, 252)*. This letter followed another bipartisan committee letter in fall 2000 and, after the convening of the 107th Congress, questioning of Secretary O'Neill at a committee hearing early in 2001. In 2004 and 2005, members objected in letters to then-Treasury Secretary John Snow and by other means to a change in interpretation of the Trade Sanctions Reform and Export Enhancement Act of 2000 *(114 Stat. 1549A–67)*, which they perceived would reduce U.S. agricultural exports to Cuba. The administration eased its interpretation of the trade law, but legislative efforts for additional changes continued.

Committee members might also serve as observers at key international meetings or negotiations, such as the congressional observers who attended the World Trade Organization meeting in Seattle in December 1999. In this regard, the views of committee members are important in anticipating and dealing with policy problems that could arise between Congress and the executive. Members of Congress might also serve as intermediaries in international problems. For example, in 2004, a delegation of members of the then-named House International Relations Committee, some of whom were also members of a caucus, the U.S.-Venezuelan Interparliamentary forum, traveled to Venezuela to discuss the presidential recall vote with President Hugo Chavez. *(See also § 10.171, Letter to Foreign Leader.)*

Congress might also formalize its observation of U.S. participation in international agree-

§ 10.171

Letter to Foreign Leader

Congress of the United States
Washington, DC 20515

President Vicente Fox
United Mexican States
Residencia Oficial de Los Pinos
Puerta #5, Casa Anexa P.B.
Col. San Miguel Chapultepec
11850 Mexico, D.F.

June 25, 2004

Dear President Fox:

We are writing in regards to your public announcement to U.S. Senator Norm Coleman last week that Ms. Cynthia Kiecker, a Minnesota resident, would not be prosecuted and would be released pending the victim's family's agreement not to pursue a civil case.

We join Senator Coleman in expressing our deep concern about the revelation from the U.S. Department of State that your statement was inaccurate, and that the Mexican government now intends to move forward and prosecute this case without regard to the very serious due process and human rights concerns involved. We are especially disturbed about the news from Mexico that charges against Mexican law enforcement authorities relative to the due process and human rights violations have been dropped. Clearly, you can understand our concerns regarding this inconsistent and disappointing decision by the Mexican government.

Since taking office in 2000, you have repeatedly expressed your commitment to improving human rights in Mexico. We know you are making efforts to address the intolerable murders of over 300 women in the border town of Ciudad Juárez, Chihuahua. Therefore, we sincerely hope that Mexico will stand by the commitment you made to Senator Coleman.

We look forward to your prompt reply to this most urgent matter.

Sincerely,

10

429

ments. For example, Congress, in 1976, created the Commission on Security and Cooperation in Europe *(90 Stat. 661; 22 U.S.C. § 3001 et seq.)* to monitor and encourage compliance with the Helsinki Final Act. The Final Act established the Organization for Security and Cooperation in Europe to enhance European security and cooperation in numerous fields, including humanitarian endeavors. *(See the congressional commission's web site, <www.csce.gov>.)* Members of Congress also participate in international organizations and exchanges, such as the Interparliamentary Union, and regularly host foreign officials visiting Washington, DC.

Congress also expresses its approval or support for other nations and specific foreign leaders or dignitaries by inviting them to address a joint meeting of Congress. *(See § 7.24, Joint Meetings and Joint Sessions.)*

§10.180 Congress and Federalism

Since the adoption of the U.S. Constitution, creating a federal system of governance, the relationship between the federal government and the states and their political subunits, the localities, has been marked by a history spotted with conflict, cooperation, and indifference. During the more than 225-year history of the republic, two questions have generated considerable debate among observers of American federalism. What is the nature of the federal union of states? And what powers, privileges, duties, and responsibilities does the Constitution grant to the national government, including Congress, and reserve to the states and the people? The Supreme Court, often the final arbiter of conflicts within the federal system, has sometimes seemed to change its views in its decisions on issues of federalism. It has recently identified limits to congressional authority over the states and over the exercise of national powers within the federal structure, after decades of upholding congressional initiatives.

A tremendous expansion in federal grants to state and local governments began in the 1960s, accelerated in the 1970s, contracted in the 1980s, and grew again in the 1990s. By the end of FY2006, federal assistance to state and local governments comprised just over 16 percent of total federal outlays. This recent increase in growth was largely concentrated in two areas—welfare assistance payments under the Temporary Assistance to Needy Families (TANF) program and Medicaid. By FY2006 these two programs represented over 45 percent of the $434 billion in projected grant outlays to state and local governments, including aid to individuals. The prospects for growth in grants-in-aid to state and local governments during the remainder of the first decade of the new millennium seem unlikely, due in large part to budget deficits and military, counterterrorism, and foreign aid needs. The most recent evidence suggests that a decline in federal assistance to states and localities was well underway. In FY2003, outlays for state and local assistance represented 18 percent of federal outlays and, in constant dollars, exceeded outlays for FY2006. Increasingly, Congress has also opted to abandon categorical grants in favor of block grants, tax incentives, and regulatory relief as the preferred methods of providing federal assistance to the states and localities.

Increasing federal involvement and preemption in areas that have traditionally been the domain of state and local governments has further enlivened the debate over the proper role of the federal government in elementary and secondary education, in fighting crime, in welfare, and in other areas where states and localities have traditionally been the providers. Greater awareness of terrorism as a threat to national security requiring coordination of federal authority and the involvement of all levels of government has further blurred the lines of responsibility and, in some respects, shifted costs to state and local governments. Since the terrorist attacks of September 11, 2001, every state has established an office of homeland security or assembled a task force to develop and direct a state's homeland security efforts. According to the National Conference of State Legislatures, the nearly $1.2 billion that Congress made available in 2003 for homeland security was far less than the $20 billion estimated to be needed to reimburse state and local government for the cost of equipping state and local emergency workers.

Congress and the states and localities relate in other ways as well. For instance, Congress, in the second half of the twentieth century and the first years of the new century in particular, has played a leading role in expanding the right to vote and protecting its exercise. Congress continued this involvement with passage of the Help America Vote Act of 2002, which allocated grant funds to states to finance improvements in vote-counting technology, and established election administration standards for states and units of local government with responsibility for the administration of federal elections.

In addition, in amending the Constitution, Congress and the states are partners. Under the Constitution, three-fourths of the states must ratify a constitutional amendment approved by Congress for the amendment to take effect.

§10.190 Congress and Federalism: Exercising Congressional Powers

In the American system of government, national laws on a subject may fully or partially preempt state laws, or national and state laws on a subject may operate concurrently. The basis for preemption is the Supremacy Clause contained in Article VI, Clause 2 of the Constitution:

> This Constitution, and the Laws of the United States which shall be made in Pursuance thereof; and all Treaties made, or which shall be made, under the Authority of the United States, shall be the supreme Law of the Land; and the Judges in every State shall be bound thereby, any Thing in the Constitution or Laws of any State to the Contrary notwithstanding.

Congress might make law based in enumerated powers and other powers vested in the national government, or "necessary and proper" to carry out constitutional powers (*art.I, sec. 8, cl.*

18). In doing so, Congress might well act on a subject on which states have also enacted laws. Congress, the executive, the states, and the judiciary all have roles in determining the relationship of federal and state laws on a subject.

In making national law that overlaps with state law, Congress might expressly state a preemption in a statute, or the preemption might be implied from the construction and provisions of a statute. Within the context of implied preemption three subgroups might be identified:

- Instances where there is conflict between the federal statute and state and local laws. However, under certain circumstances the federal and state law may operate concurrently when the federal statute sets a minimum standard for compliance and the state statute exceeds it.
- Instances where state law impedes or interferes with the federal government's ability to achieve a national objective. Under such a scenario a state legislature might act to amend the state law to be compatible with the federal law or risk partial or complete preemption of the state law. Alternately, the state could raise a constitutional challenge to the preemption.
- Instances where federal law occupies the field, such as foreign policy or arms control.

In rulemaking to carry out a federal law, a federal agency might develop regulations that raise the same issues as a statute in terms of preemption or the concurrent exercise of federal and state laws. Either the courts or Congress might be the final arbiter of the operation of a statute that preempts state law. Courts might interpret or even find such a statute unconstitutional. Congress might clarify its intent or change a statute's operation through amendment.

It should be noted that the answer on preemption might not be straightforward, as fifty states and the District of Columbia can have fifty-one different laws. Unless Congress fully preempts state laws, some might continue without change while others might require at least some change to operate concurrently.

Unless Congress expressly preempts state laws, as was the case of the Internet Tax Nondiscrimination Act *(118 Stat. 2615)*, which exempted the nascent e-commerce industry from state and local sales taxes, courts weigh federal and state interests and congressional intent. They do not assume federal preemption. Considerations might include the pervasiveness of a federal statute and conflict between federal and state laws. In the words of the late Justice Hugo Black, the courts' function in considering the validity of state laws in light of federal laws and treaties on the same subject is to determine whether state law "stands as an obstacle to the accomplishment and execution of the full purposes and objectives of Congress." (*Hines v. Davidowitz*, 312 U.S. 52, 67 (1941).)

Restraints on Congress

In recent years, the Supreme Court has ruled in several cases on possible restraints on Congress's exercise of its powers within the federal system. In one set of cases, the Court seems to have warned Congress about directing the actions of state legislatures and state executive officials. In another set, the Court seems to have warned Congress about the limits of its powers in the federal system.

The question in the first issue is the extent to which Congress may regulate state conduct and activity. In *New York v. United States*, 505 U.S. 144 (1992), the Supreme Court found that the Tenth Amendment constrained Congress in the exercise of an enumerated power. Congress had directed states to dispose of waste generated in their borders. It then required states that failed to do so to take title to the wastes, take possession of them, and assume liability for them. *(99 Stat. 1842.)* The Supreme Court found that the law breached state sovereignty. The federal structure of government under the Constitution, the Court said, disallowed Congress from compelling the states to enact and enforce a federal regulatory program.

Subsequently, in *Printz v. United States*, 521 U.S. 898 (1997), the Court struck down a provision of a federal statute: the part of the Brady Handgun Violence Protection Act *(107 Stat. 1536)* that required state and local law enforcement officers to conduct background checks on individuals wishing to purchase handguns. The Court followed the same reasoning as in *New York*, finding an unconstitutional violation of state sovereignty in directing state officials to administer a federal regulatory program.

The second issue involving restraints on Congress's exercise of power in the federal system concerns the scope of its powers. Some of these cases have limited congressional authority under the Commerce Clause *(Art. I, sec. 8, cl. 3)*. In *United States v. Lopez*, 514 U.S. 549 (1995), the Supreme Court struck down a criminal conviction under the Gun-Free School Zones Act *(104 Stat. 4844)*. It found that Congress had exceeded its authority under the Commerce Clause, the first such ruling of the Court in nearly sixty years. The Court said that Congress may regulate channels of commerce, instrumentalities of commerce, and activities (presumably largely economic activities) that affect commerce, including only intrastate activities that substantially affect commerce. As enacted, the Gun-Free Zones Act failed to meet these criteria.

The Court more recently narrowed the Corps of Engineers' jurisdiction over intrastate waters under the Clean Water Act. While seeking to avoid constitutional and federalism issues, the Court noted that the grant of authority to Congress under the Commerce Clause is not "unlimited." *Solid Waste Agency of Northern Cook County v. U.S. Army Corps of Engineers*, 531 U.S. 159 (2001).

In *Gonzales v. Raich*, 545 U.S. 1 (2005), the Supreme Court held that the Commerce Clause empowered Congress to prohibit local cultivation and use of marijuana permitted under California's Compassionate Use Act. The Court stated that case law established Congress's power under the Commerce Clause to regulate local activities that have a substantial effect on interstate commerce, and that Congress had a rational basis for regulating local cultivation and use of marijuana to ensure the success of the federal Controlled Substance Act *(84 Stat. 1242)*.

10

In another case, *Kimel v. Florida Board of Regents*, 528 U.S. 62 (2000), the Supreme Court noted that the Age Discrimination in Employment Act of 1967 *(29 U.S.C. § 623)* was a constitutional exercise of congressional power under the Commerce Clause. However, in abrogating the states' Eleventh Amendment immunity from federal lawsuits, the Court found that Congress failed to identify unconstitutional conduct or to develop a record showing unconstitutional discrimination on the basis of age by state and local governments against their employees. The Court again invoked the Eleventh Amendment in *Board of Trustees of the University of Alabama v. Garrett*, 531 U.S. 356 (2001), to disallow state employees to recover money damages under the Americans with Disabilities Act.

§ 10.200 Congress and Federalism: Financial Support for State and Local Governments

The financial relationship between the federal government and state and local governments is a critical and far-reaching one. Federal financial assistance to states, local governments, and Indian tribes includes grants, loans, loan guarantees, and tax subsidies and is intended to assist these entities to address national objectives articulated in federal legislation. States maintain offices in Washington, DC, that monitor federal aid legislation and other federal activities. States and localities also belong to associations, such as the National Conference of State Legislatures and the Council of State Governments, and hire lobbyists to advocate their interests. *(See § 10.201, States' Washington Offices and State and Local Governments' National Organizations.)*

Federal grants to states and localities cover the range of government-sponsored or -supported services and objectives. Grants include health services, such as the State Children's Health Insurance Program; training of displaced workers; transportation, such as highways, mass-transit, and airports; and empowerment zones and enterprise zones, as part of the federal government's support for community development. Federal grants to state and local governments in FY2006 totaled $434 billion, accounting for just over 16 percent of total federal outlays. In FY2003, federal grants represented over 31 percent of total state and local expenditures.

Federal grants awarded to state and local governments include programs that provide payments to individuals, such as Medicaid. In FY2006 such payments accounted for 63 percent of grants to states and localities, which in turn represented about 10 percent of total federal outlays. Programs such as Medicaid are also classified as direct, or mandatory, spending. In such a case, the authorizing law provides the spending authority. For FY2006, outlays for federal grants in the form of payments to individuals were estimated at $273 billion. *(See § 9.30, Budget Enforcement Framework.)*

Grants for infrastructure, education, community development, and other purposes are discretionary and are funded through the appropriations process. Outlays for these federal grants were estimated at $161 billion in FY2006.

Loans and loan guarantees include programs such as low-interest loans to localities to assist them in meeting the requirements of the Safe Drinking Water Act. *Tax subsidies* include such *tax expenditures* as the exclusion of interest on state and local securities from federal taxation and employment tax credits awarded to qualifying businesses that hire and train disadvantaged individuals in distressed neighborhoods.

Many of these programs are described in detail in the *Catalog of Federal Domestic Assistance*, maintained by the General Services Administration. The catalog exists to assist users—state and local governments, other governmental authorities, not-for-profit entities, individuals, and others—in identifying programs that meet their objectives or needs. It provides essential information on each program, such as a précis of application procedures. As described in the catalog's introduction, "assistance" includes "grants, loans, loan guarantees, scholarships, mortgage loans, insurance, and other types of financial assistance, including cooperative agreements; property, technical assistance, counseling, statistical, and other expert information; and service activities of regulatory agencies." The catalog is updated semiannually, in June and December. It is available online at *<www.cfda.gov>*. Another source is the relatively new federal web site, Grants.gov at *<www.grants.gov>*.

Congress usually attaches conditions to its spending programs, and its authority to do so is well established. Congress creates federal spending programs for purposes stated in law, and it wants to ensure that federal funds are spent for those purposes. In addition, Congress might attach other conditions in law to spending under a program, to ensure the integrity of the program's management, to guide decision making, to ensure public participation in decision making, to establish priorities, or for myriad other reasons.

Congress might also attach conditions to a program in order to achieve a national purpose. For example, in order to encourage states to raise the drinking age to twenty-one, Congress conditioned a state's receipt of its full allocation of federal highway funds on its adopting an age twenty-one drinking law. Congress might also attach financial participation—matching funds—requirements or even "maintenance-of-effort" requirements to a program. The former is in part intended to promote better program administration, since the state or local government also has funds at stake. The latter is to prevent a government from replacing its own funds with federal funds, leaving the activity no better off than it was before federal dollars became available.

While Congress may attach conditions to federal spending, it has established a restraint on itself in doing so. After many years of complaints from states and localities about conditions that imposed costly duties on state and local governments, Congress enacted the Unfunded Mandates Reform Act of 1995. The law, among other provisions, forces committees reporting legislation to obtain from the Congressional Budget Office information on *unfunded mandates* in the legislation. This information may affect procedures in floor consideration of the measure, and ensures that the House and Senate know the cost implications of the proposed legislation to state and local governments. *(See § 10.202, Unfunded Mandates.)*

10

States' Washington Offices and State and Local Governments' National Organizations

Many states and some local governments maintain a presence in Washington, DC, to work with Congress and the executive branch to promote state-federal relations. The Hall of the States, 444 North Capitol Street, NW, houses most, but not all, of these state and territorial offices.

- **Alaska**, Hall of the States, Suite 336
- **American Samoa,** 1101 Vermont Ave., NW, Suite 403
- **Arizona,** Hall of the States, Suite 428
- **Arkansas,** 400 N. Capitol Street, NW, Suite 365
- **California,** Hall of the States, Suite 134
- **Connecticut**, Hall of the States, Suite 317
- **Delaware**, Hall of the States, Suite 230
- **Florida**, Hall of the States, Suite 349
- **Georgia**, 400 N. Capitol Street, NW, Suite 376
- **Illinois,** Hall of the States, Suite 400
- **Indiana,** 1455 Pennsylvania Ave., NW, Suite 1140
- **Iowa**, 400 N. Capitol Street, NW, Suite 359
- **Kansas,** 500 New Jersey Ave., NW, Suite 400
- **Kentucky,** Hall of the States, Suite 224
- **Louisiana**, Hall of the States, Suite 372
- **Maryland**, Hall of the States, Suite 311
- **Massachusetts**, Hall of the States, Suite 208

- **Michigan**, Hall of the States, Suite 411
- **Minnesota**, 400 N. Capitol Street, NW, Suite 380
- **Nevada**, Hall of the States, Suite 209
- **New Jersey**, Hall of the States, Suite 201
- **New Mexico**, Hall of the States, Suite 400
- **New York**, Hall of the States, Suite 301
- **North Carolina**, Hall of the States, Suite 332
- **North Dakota**, Hall of the States, Suite 224
- **Ohio**, Hall of the States, Suite 546
- **Oregon**, Hall of the States, Suite 400
- **Pennsylvania**, 600 New Hampshire Ave., NW
- **Puerto Rico,** 1100 17th Street, NW, Suite 800
- **South Carolina**, Hall of the States, Suite 203
- **Texas**, 122 C Street, NW, Suite 200
- **Vermont**, 412 First Street, SE
- **Virgin Islands**, Hall of the States, Suite 305
- **Virginia**, Hall of the States, Suite 214
- **Washington**, Hall of the States, Suite 411
- **Wisconsin**, Hall of the States, Suite 613

There are numerous organizations and lobbying firms representing the interests of state and local governments. Some organizations also serve as professional organizations for specific state or local officials. Seven of the most prominent are:

- **National Governors Association (NGA)** *<www.nga.org>*: Bipartisan organization representing the views and policy positions of the nation's governors on issues affecting state and federal relations. NGA also provides a forum for the sharing of ideas and information between states.

- **National Conference of State Legislatures** *<www.ncsl.org>*: Bipartisan organization representing the legislators and staffs of the nation's fifty states, its commonwealths and territories. Serving as an advocate for the interests of states before Congress and federal agencies is part of its core mission. In addition, NCSL provides research, technical assistance, and opportunities for policymakers to exchange ideas across a broad range of issues of interest to affected states.

Continued on page 437

- **Council of State Governments** *<www.csg.org>*: Led by governors and state legislators, CSG helps states increase efficiency through sharing information and leadership training. Its Washington office monitors federal developments.

- **National Association of State Budget Officers** *<www.nasbo.org>*: Professional membership organization for state finance officers. The major functions of the organization consist of research, policy development, education, training, and technical assistance. NASBO is an affiliate of the National Governors Association.

- **U.S. Conference of Mayors** *<www.usmayors.org>*: Nonpartisan organization representing the views, priorities, and policy positions of the more than 1,000 U.S. cities with a population of 30,000 or more. The Conference of Mayors' mission includes promoting effective national urban/suburban policies; improving intergovernmental relations, and providing a forum for the sharing of ideas and information.

- **National League of Cities** *<www.nlc.org>:* Represents the interests of forty-nine municipal leagues that include over 18,000 cities, towns, and villages. NLC has nearly 1,600 dues-paying communities. The NLC's stated mission is to strengthen and promote cities as centers for opportunity, leadership, and governance. Advocacy before the national government is among its core activities. The NLC also provides programs and services aimed at strengthening local leaders' abilities to serve their communities.

- **National Association of Counties** *<www.naco.org>:* Nonpartisan national organization that represents county governments. It serves as a national advocate for counties and as a liaison with other levels of government. In addition, NACO provides its member communities with an extensive line of services, including legislative, research, technical, and public affairs assistance, as well as enterprise services.

- **International City/County Managers Association** *<www.icma.org>:* Represents the interests of professional administrators of city, county, and regional governmental entities. It provides an array of services, including technical and management assistance, training, and information resources to its members and the local government community.

These organizations, and a number of other associations representing the views of specific disciplines, such as civil engineers, public works directors, or local housing and community development officials, are involved in policy analysis, congressional testimony, and advocacy on issues and policies that affect intergovernmental relations.

Grant Programs

Grant programs are a common form of financial support to states and localities. Some of the features of a debate in Congress over providing financial support to state and localities might include a policy decision on what to fund, the level of funding, whether to use a categorical or block grant, and the formula (if any) to be used to allocate the funds between eligible governmental units.

§ 10.202

Unfunded Mandates

Congress enacted the *Unfunded Mandates Reform Act* (*109 Stat. 48*) in 1995 to give itself information to identify an unfunded mandate in a bill or joint resolution and a mechanism for explicitly deciding whether to consider a piece of legislation containing an unfunded mandate. An *unfunded mandate* in legislation is a duty that the legislation, if enacted, would impose on state, local, or tribal governments, or the private sector without also providing funds to cover the cost of compliance with the mandate.

A mandate in legislation would be considered *to be funded* in one of two ways. First, the legislation could automatically provide the funding needed to cover the costs of the mandate. Alternately, the legislation could authorize appropriations to cover the costs of compliance. An authorization of appropriations, however, also needs to meet additional criteria for a mandate to be considered funded. It must (1) provide that the mandate would be curtailed or eliminated if insufficient or no appropriations were provided; or, alternately, (2) ensure that Congress would vote to continue the mandate as an unfunded mandate. Only if the legislation made funding automatic or if it authorized appropriations as required would a mandate be considered to be funded.

Under the Unfunded Mandates Reform Act (UMRA), Congress created several exceptions to the law for some types of legislation, including antidiscrimination laws, emergency assistance, treaty obligations, and Social Security. It also exempted appropriations measures, but not legislative provisions in appropriations measures that created unfunded mandates. Finally, the law exempted from its operation any unfunded mandate that failed to meet a threshold: for an intergovernmental mandate, $50 million in any year of its first five years in effect, and, for a private-sector mandate, $100 million in any year of its first five years.

Committee Requirements

UMRA set requirements for committees and the Congressional Budget Office (CBO) to study and report on the impact and magnitude of proposed federal mandates. A committee must send CBO a copy of any measure ordered reported that contains a federal mandate, and CBO must prepare a report of estimated mandate costs for the committee. The committee must include this report in its report on the measure or submit it for publication in the *Congressional Record*. (Additional requirements in UMRA govern the CBO report and the committee's response to it.) Early in a year, committees must also identify issues they will address that year, which will have costs for the private sector and state, local, and tribal governments. This information is to be included in the *views and estimates reports* that committees provide to the House and Senate Budget Committees. *(See § 9.50, Congressional Budget Process.)*

Points of Order on the House and Senate Floors

UMRA is implemented in the House and Senate through points of order against legislation containing an unfunded mandate. When an authorization measure is brought up for consideration, a member may make a point of order against its consideration. The point of order would be that the measure contains an unfunded mandate exceeding $50 million for an intergovernmental mandate. A point of order can also be raised if a CBO estimate was not published in either the committee report or the *Congressional Record*.

Normally, a point of order in the House is resolved by a ruling of the presiding officer, but UMRA requires the full House to vote on whether to consider a measure despite a point of order. If a special rule reported from the Rules Committee waives a point of order against consideration of a measure containing an unfunded mandate, the special rule itself is subject to a point of order. Debate on the

Continued on page 439

point of order is limited to twenty minutes, divided between the member raising the point of order and an opponent. In the Senate, if the point of order against consideration is sustained, the measure cannot be considered. The Senate by majority vote can also waive any point of order. In ruling, the Senate presiding officer consults with the Committee on Homeland Security and Governmental Affairs. Points of order in each chamber can also be raised against the consideration of an amendment, conference report, or motion that contains an unfunded mandate exceeding the threshold amount. There is no requirement that amendments have a CBO estimate. Conferees, however, must request a cost estimate of CBO on a conference report, and CBO must attempt to respond.

What to Fund? Congress often grapples with the proper federal role in an area of governmental services. For example, in education, states and localities employ teachers, build schools, set promotion and graduation standards for students, and so on. What is the federal role in the education of American schoolchildren? How should the federal government be involved? To what degree should it provide financial support? Among the spending possibilities related to education—schools, teachers, books, special classes, computers, and so on—which should be given financial support? What should be the objectives of the grant—national standards, a lifeline to those most in need, equalization of resources nationally, or other objectives?

The vehicle for policy decisions on a program of aid to state and local governments is normally an *authorization bill*. The measure might be referred to as a reauthorization bill once a program has been created. An authorization bill is often within the jurisdiction of one legislative committee in each chamber. For example, federal aid programs to support education are within the jurisdiction of the House Committee on Education and Labor and the Senate Committee on Health, Education, Labor, and Pensions. (*See § 9.80, Authorization and Appropriation Processes.*)

Categorical or Block Grant? Some federal legislation in the 1990s provided financial assistance to states and localities in the form of *block grants*. In some instances, such as welfare reform in 1996, Congress combined or superseded related, existing *categorical grants* for specific purposes into one or more block grants. A categorical grant provides spending targeted to a specific purpose. In contrast, a block grant provides wider discretion to state and local governments in identifying problems and designing programs that meet the goals of the block grant. In either case, Congress defines some set of eligible activities—in a broad area with wide discretion for a block grant or very specific for a categorical grant.

According to some estimates, about 90 percent of all federal grants are categorical grants with 33 percent of such grants awarded by formula. There are approximately twenty federal block grants, all allocated by formula. In addition to block grants authorized by statute, at

10

least one agency, EPA, allows states to consolidate any combination of seventeen environmental grants into a single Performance Partnership Grant. Recipients of EPA categorical grants may use these block-granted funds for activities that are within the aggregated eligible activities of any of the seventeen grants for which they are eligible.

A recent development in the federal grant system is performance-based grants aimed at rewarding program recipients for improvements measured against a set of criteria. Two examples are the Personal Responsibility and Work Opportunity Reconciliation Act of 1996 (PRWORA) *(110 Stat. 2105)*, which authorized the Temporary Assistance to Needy Families (TANF) program, and the No Child Left Behind Act. As part of the TANF program, PRWORA authorized funding for annual performance achievement bonuses, called the high-performance bonus, to states for significant improvements in moving TANF recipients into jobs or reducing the number of out-of-wedlock births and the number of abortions, or increasing the percentage of children living in families with married parents. Under the No Child Left Behind Act *(115 Stat. 1425)*, states and local schools that make significant progress in closing the disadvantaged student achievement gap may receive performance bonuses while states that fail to show adequate yearly progress for their disadvantaged students are subject to losing a portion of their administrative funds.

Waivers of federal grant requirements are also an important element of the federal grant matrix, allowing states to experiment with the delivery of assistance. Section 1115 of the Social Security Act is a prime example of the use of waivers. The waiver provision allows a state to restructure its Medicaid program with the aim of fostering innovation and expanding services. Waivers were also an important element in Congress's response to speeding hurricane recovery in 2005.

What Formula Factors to Use? When Congress debates legislation for a grant program that uses a formula to distribute federal funds, it can sometimes seem like a rerun of the constitutional convention, but at a programmatic level: large-population states versus small population states; states with certain population characteristics versus states with different population characteristics; states with certain physical or man-made resources versus states with different resources. What formula factors should Congress use to distribute federal funds associated with a program? Congress as a political institution—"who gets what"—is on display when Congress debates funding formulas. Congress can target grants to certain groups or activities depending on its formula and other considerations.

Because each program has a different purpose—educating children, building highways, providing services to special population groups, and so on—the criteria to be used differ. An education program might use the numbers of school-age children, children within some measure of poverty, or schoolchildren with special learning needs. A highway program might use miles of existing highways, state population, or a needs survey. Members of Congress are on the lookout for combinations of factors that most favor their states, sometimes making it difficult to find a formula that appeals to a majority of members in each chamber.

As an alternative to a formula, Congress might create a project grant program. This kind of program is likely to require an extensive application by potential recipients, create a competitive award process, and place discretion with the agency administering the program. Some programs might also combine a formula and project grant format. For example, a program might allocate federal funds to states based on a formula; money within the states then could be allocated to local governments on a project basis.

Finally, Congress frequently *earmarks* spending for particular projects or even entities. For example, the FY2005 appropriations act for the Department of Housing and Urban Development (P.L. 108-447) included $262 million in grant assistance earmarked for more than 1,000 projects identified in the conference report accompanying the Consolidated Appropriations Act for FY2005. *(See § 9.81, Limitations, Earmarks, and General Provisions.)*

Level of Funding. Funding for a discretionary grant program is normally a two-step process. An authorization bill is first considered. It typically contains several related programs. An authorization bill normally provides recommended authorizations of appropriations for each of these programs for one, two, or more years. For example, one of the principal authorization bills for federal education programs is the Elementary and Secondary Education Act (ESEA), which has largely been transformed into the No Child Left Behind Act (NCLB) (P.L. 107-110). Its historic reauthorization schedule is five years. Typically, the first decision on spending is a recommendation made in the authorization bill, with the actual funding included in an appropriations measure. It is not without precedent that funding recommendations included in an authorization measure may not match the amount provided in an appropriations measure.

An authorization for a discretionary grant program, once passed by both houses and signed into law by the president, does not make budgetary resources available for spending. Each year, the president submits a budget to Congress with recommended levels of spending for federal programs. The House and Senate Appropriations Committees then develop *appropriations bills*. In the example of ESEA/NCLB, funds for its programs are included in the Departments of Labor, Health and Human Services, and Education (Labor-HHS-Education) appropriations bill. Once Congress passes and the president signs the Labor-HHS-Education appropriations bill, budget authority is available for obligation. The second decision on spending, then, is made in an appropriations bill, and that decision makes funds available. *(See § 9.80, Authorization and Appropriation Processes.)*

§ 10.210 Congress and Federalism: Amending the Constitution

One of the ways in which federalism is most clearly expressed in the Constitution is in the process for its amendment. Nine of the thirteen original states were required to ratify the Constitution to establish it. Amendments must be ratified by three-fourths of the states (thirty-eight states today) to take effect.

The Constitution provides two methods for proposing amendments and two methods for ratifying amendments. Article V reads as follows:

> The Congress, whenever two thirds of both Houses shall deem it necessary, shall propose Amendments to this Constitution, or, on the Application of the Legislatures of two thirds of the several States, shall call a Convention for proposing Amendments, which, in either Case, shall be valid to all Intents and Purposes, as Part of this Constitution, when ratified by the Legislatures of three fourths of the several States, or by Conventions in three fourths thereof, as the one or the other Mode of Ratification may be proposed by the Congress. . . ."

All amendments to the Constitution that have been adopted have been proposed by Congress. All but the Twenty-First Amendment, which repealed the Eighteenth Amendment (Prohibition), were ratified by state legislatures. The Twenty-First Amendment was ratified by the convention method.

Any member of Congress may propose a constitutional amendment by introducing a joint resolution. A joint resolution may be introduced in the House (H. J. Res.) or Senate (S. J. Res.), or companion joint resolutions might be introduced by likeminded members in each chamber. Joint resolutions proposing to amend the Constitution are within the jurisdiction of the House and Senate Judiciary Committees, to which these resolutions are referred.

If the committees choose to act, they would most likely follow normal legislative procedures—hearings at the subcommittee or full committee level or both, possibly subcommittee markup, full committee markup, and reporting. Floor consideration of a joint resolution proposing to amend the Constitution would also likely happen under a set of procedures that the House or Senate normally crafts to consider important legislation.

The Constitution, however, requires supermajority votes in the full House and Senate—a two-thirds vote in each chamber. This provision has been interpreted as two-thirds present and voting, a quorum being present; it is not two-thirds of the membership. Like other legislation, each chamber must agree to exactly the same proposed amendment before it can be submitted to the states. A conference committee might be needed to reconcile differences in joint resolutions approved in the House and Senate. A two-thirds vote of those voting in each chamber would be needed to adopt the conference report on the joint resolution.

The president does not have a formal role in the amendment process. He might exhort Congress to submit a constitutional amendment to the states on some subject, lending his political support to a movement to amend the Constitution, or he might oppose an amendment. But a proposed amendment does not need the president's review or approval before being submitted to the states.

Once Congress has completed its role in proposing an amendment, the joint resolution is transmitted to the archivist of the United States, who is the head of the National Archives and Records Administration (NARA). The archivist has delegated ministerial functions related to the amendment process to the Office of the Federal Register (OFR) within NARA. OFR adds legislative history notes to the joint resolution, and publishes it in slip-law format. OFR also prepares official and informational documents for the archivist to submit to the states.

The archivist notifies each state governor with a letter and the documents prepared by OFR. Assuming the joint resolution provides for ratification by three-fourths of the states' legislatures, the governors submit the proposed amendment to the legislatures.

State legislatures have adopted different procedures for ratification. For example, some require a supermajority vote. (States also adopted or had in effect differing provisions for the state conventions that ratified the Twenty-First Amendment, repealing the Eighteenth Amendment.) Legislatures must ratify the exact amendment proposed by Congress, and must include a clear statement of ratification in the legislative act they use to express ratification. They may not amend the proposed amendment or attach conditions to ratification. The question of whether ratification by a legislature can subsequently be rescinded is not settled. Because the Constitution requires ratification by state legislatures, governors are not required to approve or sign ratification legislation, although they might lend support or express opposition during legislative debate over the amendment.

States send ratification documents to the archivist, where OFR examines them for legal sufficiency. OFR retains the documents until the amendment is ratified or fails ratification. Once ratification documents are received from the constitutionally required three-fourths of the states, the archivist issues a proclamation certifying ratification. The certification is published in the Federal Register and the Statutes at Large.

Twenty-seven amendments to the Constitution have been ratified. Seven other amendments submitted to the states have failed ratification.

Additional Considerations

In the twentieth century, Congress began the practice of setting a time limit for states to ratify a proposed amendment. Seven years has been the time limit used, although amendments that have been ratified have usually achieved ratification within one or two years.

Like other legislation, members might introduce the same constitutional amendments in one Congress after another, making their opinions known and working to change the Constitution. Even if an amendment is submitted to the states and fails ratification within the prescribed time period, members might introduce a new joint resolution with the same or similar language in another Congress and work for its adoption and submission to the states.

Congress has also extended a time limit once, when it adopted, by majority vote, a joint resolution to extend by just under three years the seven-year limit for considering the Equal Rights Amendment. Congress also acted by passing concurrent resolutions to recognize the archivist's decision to certify ratification of the Twenty-Seventh Amendment (congressional pay) after it had taken over 200 years to obtain ratification by three-fourths of the states.

10

While two-thirds of the states have not petitioned for an amending convention, applications by a sufficient number of states have prompted congressional action in the past. For example, two-thirds of the states, less one, petitioned Congress in the late nineteenth and early twentieth centuries for a convention to propose an amendment providing for the direct election of senators. Congress responded in 1912 by submitting such an amendment to the states, which was ratified as the Seventeenth Amendment. Not every such movement in the states has been successful, however. For example, Congress failed to adopt a joint resolution on a balanced budget amendment despite applications from nearly two-thirds of the states.

Constitutional scholars have always been concerned about the process of states petitioning for an amending convention. In addition to issues such as the time frame in which applications are made to Congress and the effect of rescinding an application, another procedural issue is the subject for which the application is made, that is, how similar do the applications have to be? Another great concern and subject of debate among other issues involving amending conventions is whether an amending convention could be confined to one or more specified subjects or whether it could recommend additional amendments. Both limited and unlimited conventions have scholarly support.

§ 10.220 Congress and Federalism: Extending the Franchise

A major theme in Congress's involvement with elections is extending and enhancing the exercise of the franchise. The Constitution gave Congress certain powers over elections (*art. I, sec. 4, cl. 1*), and congressional enforcement powers were included in amendments subsequently ratified that enhanced the right to vote.

Many extensions in the exercise of the franchise have taken place through constitutional amendments, which were submitted to the states and ratified. In the Fifteenth Amendment (1870) to the Constitution, the right to vote was guaranteed without reference to "race, color, or previous condition of servitude." The Seventeenth Amendment (1913) provided for the direct popular election of senators, who to that point were elected by state legislatures. In the Nineteenth Amendment (1920), the right to vote was guaranteed without reference to sex. In the Twenty-Third Amendment (1961), the District of Columbia was provided presidential electors. The Twenty-Fourth Amendment (1964) barred the poll or other tax in denying or abridging the right to vote. And the Twenty-Sixth Amendment (1971) extended the right to vote to citizens who had reached the age of eighteen.

In addition, Congress has used its legislative powers to enhance the exercise of the franchise. Four statutes of broad impact representative of congressional concerns include the Voting Rights Act (*42 U.S.C. § 1971 et seq.*), as amended; the National Voter Registration Act (*42 U.S.C. § 1973gg–gg-10*); the Uniformed and Overseas Absentee Voting Act (*42 U.S.C. § 1973 ff–ff-6*); and the Help America Vote Act (*P.L. 107-252; 116 Stat. 1666*).

Originally enacted in 1965, the Voting Rights Act has been renewed by Congress on four occasions. While Congress initially wished to address the disenfranchisement of African-American citizens in Southern states, the original act and its extensions have also covered other parts of the citizenry subject or potentially subject to disenfranchisement. Over the course of its history, the act and amendments to it have ended literacy tests and curtailed English-language literacy requirements, required bilingual election materials and assistance in certain circumstances, enabled challenges to election laws that denied or abridged voting rights, required Justice Department "preclearance" of changes in election and related laws in counties and states with discriminatory voting practices, allowed federal workers to register voters and watch polls, and prevented disenfranchisement in presidential elections through registration requirements that exceeded thirty days. The Voting Rights Act authorized citizens and the federal government to sue to address discriminatory voting practices and procedures, and proscribed any jurisdiction in the United States from enacting an election law to "deny or abridge" voting rights on the basis of race, color, or language-group membership.

Some provisions of the Voting Rights Act are temporarily authorized, and Congress must pass legislation to continue these provisions in force. Congress extended the 2007 expiration with a bill signed into law by President George W. Bush to 2032 (*P.L. 109-246*). The new law reinvigorated preclearance requirements, which Congress found had been limited contrary to congressional intent by Supreme Court decisions.

Congress also began to address issues of accessibility for disabled persons through an amendment to the Voting Rights Act in 1982 (*P.L. 97-205*). A provision in this law allowed a disabled person to have assistance from another person chosen by the voter. Congress followed up in 1984 with the Voting Accessibility for the Elderly and Handicapped Act (*P.L. 98-435*), requiring accessibility in polling places and registration facilities and availability of registration and voting aids for handicapped and elderly individuals. Additional requirements were included in the Help America Vote Act, which is described below.

The National Voter Registration Act of 1993, also called the "motor voter law," addressed the issue of states' voter registration practices, which Congress perceived as an impediment to voting participation. The principal national standards that Congress set in the law included the following: (1) allowing an application for a driver's license or renewal also to serve as a voter registration application; (2) allowing mail-in voter registration; (3) mandating other public offices (including public-assistance offices) to serve as voter registration sites; and (4) circumscribing procedures for dropping a voter from a voter registry.

The Uniformed and Overseas Citizens Absentee Voting Act allows military personnel, their dependents, and overseas voters who no longer maintain a residence in the United States to register and vote absentee in federal elections. Overseas voters register in the jurisdiction of their last residence, and registrations must be honored for applications received at least thirty days before an election. Under the law, the U.S. Postal Service carries voting materials free of charge.

In response to the breakdowns in election administration in the 2000 general election, Congress responded with the Help America Vote Act. It authorized several grants programs to states, establishing, however, requirements and standards for voting systems and election administration. It created the Election Assistance Administration to implement the grant programs and other provisions of the law and to test and certify voting systems. This entity was also authorized to issue voluntary guidelines for voting systems, replacing authority previously vested in the Federal Election Commission. Grants may be used to eliminate punch-card and lever voting machines, improve election administration, and make polling places accessible. The largest grant program at least partially funded state plans for activities such as procuring statewide voter registration systems. The law required the use of provisional ballots, and mandated disability access and other changes at polling places. The law also amended the military and overseas voting law to overcome problems that were identified in the 2000 election.

Other powers of Congress also bear on its legislating in the area of elections. For example, Congress has established the Tuesday after the first Monday in November as the day for electing federal officials. The Constitution provides for a decennial census, which is to be used, among other purposes, to apportion seats in the House of Representatives. Through law and appropriations, Congress has implemented these constitutional provisions. *(See § 2.13, Reapportionment and Redistricting.)* As described earlier in this section, Congress has submitted constitutional amendments to the states, which have been ratified, and enacted laws dealing with the election of the president and vice president of the United States. These laws include implementation of the constitutional provisions dealing with presidential electors. *(See § 10.90, Congress and the Executive: Presidential Election and Succession, and § 10.91, Electoral College.)*

On five occasions in the 1970s, Congress enacted campaign-finance laws applicable to the election of federal officials. It has regularly debated changes to those laws since then, and in 2002 passed the Bipartisan Campaign Reform Act. Highlights of these laws applicable to congressional candidates are discussed in § 2.20 *(Election Laws)*.

Congressional Documents:

Overview, Legislation, and Laws

11

Analysis

11

§11.00 Introduction

This chapter guides the reader to many types and sources of congressional documents, and to other governmental and private sources of legislative and related research information. These resources are highly useful in monitoring Congress and researching its activities.

Types of Documents

The first critical step is to understand the principal forms of documents that Congress has developed, and the types of information or purposes for which they are used.

Bills and Resolutions. All legislation by which Congress intends to make law is in the form of a *bill (H.R. or S.)* or *joint resolution (H.J. Res. or S.J. Res.)*. A joint resolution is also the form generally used by Congress to propose amendments to the Constitution. *(See § 11.20, Legislation: Bills and Joint Resolutions.)*

There are two other types of legislation. *Simple resolutions (H. Res. or S. Res.)* are used in a single chamber to express its opinion on some matter or to administer the chamber. *Concurrent resolutions (H. Con. Res. or S. Con. Res.)* are used by the two chambers together to express congressional opinion on some matter without making law, which by the Constitution must include the president, or to deal with joint administrative matters. *(See § 11.30, Legislation: Simple and Concurrent Resolutions.)*

Prints. A *print* is a flexible document format used by committees—hence the phrase *committee print*. It might contain almost anything that is of interest to a committee—draft legislation, a committee calendar, a report of a study, the printed transcript of hearings, a compilation of laws in a topical area, and so on. *(See § 12.10, Committee Documents.)*

Reports. *Reports* are also associated with committees, including conference committees. A committee might file a report when it forwards a matter to its parent chamber—such as the results of an investigation, legislation, and, in the Senate, executive business (that is, treaties and nominations). House reports are designated *H. Rept.* and Senate reports, *S. Rept.*; executive reports in the Senate are designated *Exec. Rept.* A two-part number, divided by a hyphen, follows the designation; the first number is the Congress in which the report was issued, the second is a unique number identifying the specific report. *(See § 8.60, Committee Reports, and § 12.10, Committee Documents.)*

It is important to remember that the report of a conference committee contains the text of legislation agreed to by the conferees. The House and Senate vote on a conference report. The explanation of a conference agreement appears in a joint explanatory statement, akin to House and Senate committees' reports on legislation.

Documents. A print is a document produced by a committee. The House and Senate use *documents*, designated *H. Doc.* in the House and *S. Doc.* in the Senate, for similar purposes. The designation is followed by a number. Documents might be used for matters of interest to the whole House or whole Senate, such as the *Senate Manual* and the *Constitution, Jefferson's Manual, and Rules of the House of Representatives of the United States*; veto messages;

11

administrative documents; and special publications for informing the public, such as *How Our Laws Are Made* or *Our American Government* (available for distribution to constituents by congressional offices). *(The specific documents mentioned here are described in §§ 12.40, 12.50, and 12.60.)*

Congressional Record and Journals. The *Congressional Record* is published each day the House or Senate is in session. It contains a transcript of floor debate and proceedings for that day and a record of other legislative business, such as floor and committee schedules. The official records of floor proceedings are the *Journal of the U.S. House of Representatives* and *Journal of the United States Senate*; the text of debates is not included in the *Journals*. The Senate also maintains the *Journal of Executive Proceedings of the Senate*. *(For detailed descriptions of these documents, see § 12.20, Floor Documents. For information on the Senate's executive business, see § 10.80, Congress and the Executive: Appointments; and § 10.150, Congress and Foreign Policy: Treaties and International Agreements.)*

There are other, special congressional documents not covered by these forms, such as the *Calendars of the United States House of Representatives and History of Legislation*, which are described in Chapter Twelve. *(For a complete description of the Congressional Record and the Calendars, see § 12.20, Floor Documents.)*

Congress is also making congressional documents and a vast array of other information available through its World Wide Web sites: THOMAS, the web-based legislative status and information system (*<http://thomas.loc.gov>*) made available through the Library of Congress to the public by the direction of Congress; and the Legislative Information System, a system internal to Congress and legislative-branch agencies and somewhat similar to THOMAS. Few congressional documents before those of the 104th Congress have been available until recently on congressional or other web sites. However, providers, including the Library of Congress, are digitizing historical collections. Over time, information in electronic form, such as hearings transcripts, might eventually replace one or more types of printed congressional documents. Information available in electronic form is also examined below. *(See § 11.10, Finding and Obtaining Congressional Documents.)*

§ 11.10 Finding and Obtaining Congressional Documents

The growth of the World Wide Web has made it easy, convenient, and inexpensive to find and obtain contemporary congressional documents—legislation, committee reports, the *Congressional Record*, and so on. It also matters little whether one is monitoring Congress in Washington, DC, or from any one of the fifty states, the U.S. territories, or foreign countries. The following sources should answer many needs for contemporary congressional documents.

THOMAS

(See § 11.11; <http://thomas.loc.gov>)

The place to begin any research on the current Congress—texts of legislation, reports, legislative status, access to committee and member information, and so on—is THOMAS. In conjunction with the House and Senate, the Library of Congress operates this web service to make congressional information and documents easily available to everyone. Some users need more value-added information than THOMAS supplies, but THOMAS's quick, easy access to current status information, texts of documents, schedules, and links to complementary web resources makes it a site to visit daily. At the very least, the potential user should set aside thirty to sixty minutes to explore the site and get to know it before an emergency need for information arises. *(Additional information on the Library of Congress appears at § 5.130, Legislative-Branch Support Agencies; and § 13.10, Legislative-Branch Agencies and Offices.)*

GPO Access

(See § 11.12; accessible through THOMAS, <http://thomas.loc.gov>
or directly at <www.gpoaccess.gov>.)

For the texts of current congressional documents, including the *Congressional Record*, THOMAS provides links to GPO Access, the web site of the U.S. Government Printing Office (GPO). However, it is worthwhile to explore this site directly to find out what other congressional and governmental documents are available. For example, many government affairs professionals use the *Federal Register* as frequently as they use the *Congressional Record*, and it is available through GPO Access. *(Additional information on GPO appears at § 5.140, Government Printing Office.)*

Congressional Web Sites

(See §§ 11.13 and 11.14; accessible through THOMAS, <http://thomas.loc.gov>
or directly at the House and Senate web sites, <www.house.gov> and <www.senate.gov>.)

One of the best developments beginning in the mid-1990s for everyone who monitors Congress has been the growth in the content and currency of committee, leadership, and member web sites. The information available at these sites complements that available from THOMAS and GPO Access. If THOMAS and GPO Access are the first and second stops on a daily check of congressional information and documents, Congress's own sites are indispensable third and fourth stops.

Sites for Committee, Scheduling, and Member Information

Committee Information. While committees still vary in the content and currency of their sites, the most useful committee sites provide—at no charge—an array of information not likely to be found elsewhere. Many committees, for example, put the following on their

THOMAS Web Site

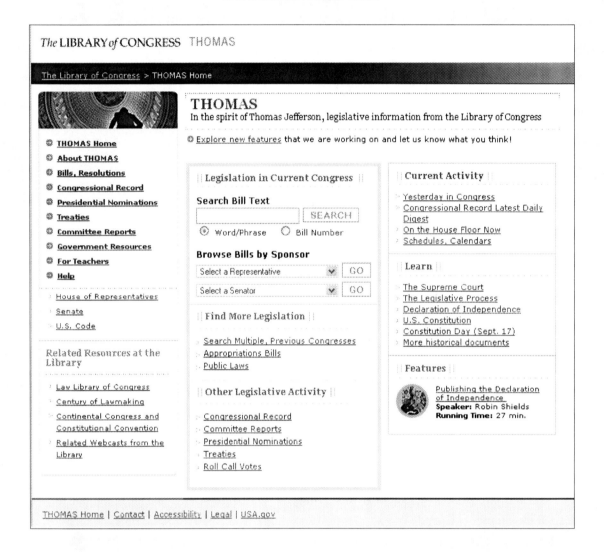

web sites: scheduling information, witness testimony, hearings transcripts, lists of measures referred to the committee, lists of committee publications, committee rules, rosters of committee and subcommittee members and staff, and other electronic versions of documents, including noncongressional ones, of interest to members and the public. The sites might also link to THOMAS and GPO Access and to other web sites with related or supplementary information.

Committee offices also continue to serve as distributors of certain kinds of information, such as printed committee hearings and *committee prints*. A committee might have a *documents* or *publications clerk*, or someone designated to handle those responsibilities. If one regu-

§ 11.12

GPO Access Web Site

larly follows the work of a specific committee, it is important to learn how the committee handles its publications.

Scheduling Information. While congressional leaders and party caucuses or conferences also still vary in the content and currency of their web sites, the most useful leadership sites are an aid in obtaining long-term and immediate scheduling information, descriptions of the party leadership's legislative priorities, overviews of House-wide or Senate-wide legislative

§ 11.13

House of Representatives Web Site

activity, party talking points on important issues, and other information. The *whip notices*, which are frequently updated, are particularly useful in monitoring floor schedules.

Web access to House and Senate floor schedules (and long-range planning calendars) is available through THOMAS and, among other places, at the following web sites:

- House web site: *<www.house.gov/house/floor/thisweek.htm>*
- House Democratic whip: *<http://majoritywhip.house.gov>*
- House Republican whip: *<http://republicanwhip.house.gov/index.asp>*
- Senate web site: *<www.senate.gov/pagelayout/legislative/d_three_sections_ with_teasers/calendars.htm>*
- Senate majority leader: *<http://reid.senate.gov>*

§ 11.14

Senate Web Site

Recorded Congressional Information

Some congressional and related information is regularly updated on telephone recordings.

House of Representatives Floor Schedule Information:
Democratic Recording (advance schedule), 202-225-1600

Democratic Recording (current proceedings), 202-225-7400

Republican Recording (advance schedule), 202-225-2020

Republican Recording (current proceedings), 202-225-7430

Senate Floor Schedule Information:
Democratic Recording, 202-224-8541
Republican Recording, 202-224-8601

Government Printing Office:
New Congressional Publications, 202-512-1809

White House Executive Clerk:
Status of Bills Received, 202-456-2226

Office of the Federal Register:
New Public Law Numbers, 202-741-6043

- Senate Democrats: <*http://democrats.senate.gov*>
- Senate Republicans: <*http://republican.senate.gov/public/index.cfm? FuseAction=Home.MonthlyView*>

(See also § 11.15, Recorded Congressional Information.)

Member Information. Individual members publish a variety of information on their web sites. A number of members have sites that have been recognized, at least informally, as well-designed and content-rich. Press releases, position statements, home-district or home-state schedules of appearances, staff rosters and photos, and continuously running polls are just a portion of the information individual members might make available. One is well-advised to take a careful look at a member's web site before paying a call on the member or a staffer in his or her office. And research on a bill or resolution as it makes its way through the legislative process must include monitoring the web sites of members of the committee of jurisdiction, as well as the sites of the sponsor and cosponsors of the measure.

House and Senate Document Rooms

The House and Senate maintain "document rooms" to distribute—to both members and the public—print copies of current legislation, committee reports, calendars, *slip laws*, and a limited number of other congressional documents, such as those with an identifier of H. Doc. or S. Doc. (Printed committee hearings, however, are available from the authoring committees or GPO, and most committee prints are available only from the authoring committee.) While GPO Access has generally replaced the congressional document rooms and federally designated depository libraries as the source of congressional documents for many individuals, the document rooms continue to be a convenient and free source of printed documents. However, the document rooms quickly run out of sought-after items.

The House document room is a function of the Legislative Resource Center (LRC), a unit within the Office of the Clerk of the House of Representatives. One may visit or write the LRC at B-106 Cannon House Office Building, Washington, DC 20515-6612, and one may fax document orders to the LRC at 202-226-4362. Information on the LRC is available at the clerk's web site (*<http://clerk.house.gov/about/offices_lrc.html>*) or by calling 202-226-5200.

One may visit or write the Senate document room at B-04 Hart Senate Office Building, Washington, DC 20510. One may also fax a document order to the Senate document room at 202-228-2815. Information on the availability of a document can be obtained by calling the Senate document room at 202-224-7701. Additional information on document services is available at *<www.senate.gov/legislative/common/generic/Doc_Room.htm>*.

Federal Depository Libraries

(Information on the depository library program and on depository libraries in the District of Columbia and each state can be found at the GPO Access web site, <www.gpoaccess.gov/libraries.html>.)

Within the Washington metropolitan area or anywhere in the country, one is likely to be close to a federal depository library—there are nearly 1,300 of them around the country. Depository libraries are usually units of public, college, or other libraries, and, as a condition of being a depository library, they are open to all users.

Depository libraries offer an array of congressional and other "core documents of U.S. democracy," as GPO describes the basic collection. The depository libraries provide the public with access to collections of congressional and other federal documents, reference librarians who know the collections, and, often, other useful tools in researching Congress, such as the *CQ Weekly* and Congressional Quarterly annual almanacs.

§11.20 Legislation:
Bills and Joint Resolutions

Legislation and amendments are the lifeblood of congressional lawmaking. Several thousand bills and resolutions are introduced in the House and Senate in the two-year duration of a Congress. Thousands of amendments are considered in subcommittees and full committees, on the House and Senate floors, and in conference committees.

At the beginning of a Congress, hundreds of measures are introduced within the first few days of the first session. Members do this because they want to continue to push legislation that did not make it through the legislative process in the last Congress, or they want to fulfill a campaign promise. They might also want to be on record early with a position on certain matters, or they might have spent some time since the election developing new initiatives on which they want to get an early and quick start. At the end of a Congress, when it adjourns *sine die*, all legislation that has made it only to an interim step dies. If a piece of legislation has not been approved in identical form by both the House and Senate, its proponents must introduce it anew in the next Congress and pursue it along the same path of referral to committee, committee consideration, and so on.

The assistance of the House and Senate Offices of Legislative Counsel are integral to members in drafting many of the measures and amendments proposed.

Designation and Numbering

As mentioned in the introduction to this chapter, all legislation by which Congress intends to make law is in the form of a bill or joint resolution—designated *H.R.* and *H. J. Res.*, respectively, in the House, and *S.* and *S. J. Res.*, respectively, in the Senate. A unique number follows the designation. The House and Senate maintain separate series of numbers for their bills and joint resolutions, and assign the numbers in the sequential order in which measures are introduced. For example, H.R. 1 is followed by H.R. 2, and S. J. Res. 1 is followed by S. J. Res. 2. Once both houses of Congress agree to a bill or joint resolution in identical form, the measure is sent to the president for his signature or veto.

The designations *H.R.* and *H. Res.*, and *S.* and *S. Res.*, are often confused. *H.R.* stands for House of Representatives and signifies a bill. *H. Res.* stands for House Resolution and is the form of legislation used within the House for internal matters. *S.* stands for Senate and signifies a bill. *S. Res.* stands for Senate Resolution and is the form of legislation used within the Senate for internal matters. *(See § 11.30, Legislation: Simple and Concurrent Resolutions.)*

Bills

Most legislation is in the form of a bill (introduced as *H.R.* or *S.*), and nearly all bills on introduction are referred to the committee with legislative jurisdiction over the subject of the bill. For example, a House bill to establish or change a housing program—most likely an *authorization bill*—would probably be referred on introduction to the House Financial Services Committee, and a comparable Senate bill to the Senate Banking, Housing, and Urban Affairs Committee. Some of the uses of a bill include the following:

- authorization bills
- appropriation bills
- tax bills
- amendments to existing federal laws
- private bills

Some practices involving bills are important to remember. Under the Constitution, all tax bills must originate in the House. This does not mean that the Senate cannot consider tax legislation before passage by the House, but it must wait until a House-passed tax measure is sent to it before it procedurally completes its work. By custom, appropriations bills also originate in the House. Again, the Senate might begin its consideration of an appropriations bill before it has received a House-passed measure, but it may not procedurally complete its work until it receives the House bill. Therefore, tax and appropriations bills agreed to by Congress and sent to the president are designated *H.R.* (or, in the case of most continuing appropriation measures, *H. J. Res.*). *(See § 9.80, Authorization and Appropriation Processes, and § 9.90, Revenue Legislation.)*

Bills might be introduced in either or both chambers, and might carry an *H.R.* or an *S.* designation, with the exception of tax and appropriations measures, as the two houses attempt to reach agreement on legislation that both houses have passed.

The House Appropriations Committee usually drafts appropriations bills in its subcommittees. Appropriations bills are not introduced as the president transmits a budget to Congress. Rather, each of the subcommittees of the Appropriations Committee holds hearings and drafts a bill as the committee works through the appropriations matters within its jurisdiction. Once subcommittee and committee markups are completed on a draft appropriations bill, the resulting bill is introduced. Like any other bill, it is then assigned the next sequential number; for example, H.R. 1905 was the legislative-branch appropriations bill for fiscal year 2000. The Appropriations Committee develops supplemental and continuing appropriations measures in the same manner.

The Senate Appropriations Committee normally proceeds in a similar fashion. If, however, the House passes an appropriations bill before the Senate Appropriations Committee reports a *companion bill*, the Senate committee has the option of marking up the House-passed bill.

Senate committees are authorized to *originate* measures, and a committee might develop legislation that receives a number after the committee reports it. House committees sometimes work from legislative drafts and then introduce a *clean bill*. Upon introduction, where a bill number is assigned, the bill is referred to the committee, and the committee immediately reports it. *(See § 8.50, Committee Markup.)*

The numbers of the first bills introduced in a new Congress are often reserved for the legislative priorities of the two parties. For example, S. 1 through S. 10 might be reserved for the Senate majority party's legislative priorities and S. 11 through S. 20 for the minority party's legislative priorities.

As a Congress proceeds, a sponsor might find that he or she can time the introduction of a measure to obtain a number that relates to the subject matter of the measure, for example, H.R. 1040 or S. 1040 for amendments to the tax code. Or, a member can reserve a specific number for the same reason. A member might also wish to retain a bill number from the former Congress in the new Congress to make it easier for proponents to publicize and build momentum over the course of more than one Congress.

Joint Resolutions

Some of the uses of a joint resolution include the following:
- continuing appropriations resolution
- declaration of war
- approval or disapproval of a presidential action or recommendation (pursuant to procedures under the War Powers Act, for example)
- narrow or very specific purpose, such as establishing a national holiday

As one might conclude from this list, joint resolutions generally serve a narrower or more specific purpose than bills. There are no procedural differences in how they are treated in the legislative process. Indeed, Congress might occasionally opt to use a bill form in instances in which it could use the form of a joint resolution.

The term *continuing resolution* refers to a joint resolution that Congress uses to provide itself with additional time to pass appropriations bills. If Congress has not completed its work on one or more appropriations bills by the time the new fiscal year begins on October 1, it adopts a joint resolution to "continue" the availability of funding at a specific level for a specific time. The president, of course, must sign such a joint resolution for it to become law and take effect. *(See § 9.80, Authorization and Appropriation Processes.)*

Constitutional Amendments in the Form of Joint Resolution. A joint resolution is also the form generally used by Congress to propose amendments to the Constitution. In this case, however, Congress is not making law and does not send the joint resolution to the president for his signature or veto. Rather, once there is a two-thirds vote on passage in each chamber on an identical joint resolution proposing to amend the Constitution, the measure is transmitted to the archivist of the United States, who is the head of the National Archives and Records Administration (NARA), to begin the ratification process by the states. *(See § 10.210, Congress and Federalism: Amending the Constitution.)*

§ 11.30 Legislation:
Simple and Concurrent Resolutions

Simple Resolutions

There are two other types of legislation besides bills and joint resolutions. Simple resolutions are used in a single chamber to express its opinion on some matter or to administer the chamber. Simple resolutions are designated *H. Res.* in the House and *S. Res.* in the Senate. A unique number follows the designation, using a separate series and sequential numbering, just as is done for bills and joint resolutions. Some of the uses of a simple resolution include the following:
- additions or changes to chamber rules
- administration of the chamber, such as resolution of election contests
- election of chamber officers

- election of committee members
- sense of the House (or Senate) on some matter (commending an athlete on an achievement, for example)
- in the House, special rules from the Rules Committee

Special rules from the House Rules Committee, discussed in § 8.90 (*Rules Committee and Special Rules*), are perhaps the most frequent manner in which the House simple resolution is used. Nearly all significant legislation comes to the House floor under a special rule. After the Rules Committee reports a special rule in the form of a simple resolution and the House adopts it, the special rule governs debate and amendment of the underlying legislation.

Concurrent Resolutions

Concurrent resolutions are used by the two chambers together to express congressional opinion on some matter without making law, which by the Constitution must include the president, or to deal with joint administrative matters. Concurrent resolutions are designated *H. Con. Res.* in the House and *S. Con. Res.* in the Senate, with a number following the designation, using a separate series and sequential numbering just as is done for bills and joint resolutions. Some of the uses of a concurrent resolution include the following:

- congressional budget resolution
- adjournment of Congress
- corrections of enrolled measures
- creation of joint committees
- providing for a joint meeting or session of Congress
- sense of Congress on some matter (expressing sympathy over the loss of life in another nation due to a natural disaster, for example)

The important aspect of concurrent resolutions is that they must be passed in identical form by both the House and Senate to have effect between them. The chambers might even convene a conference committee to resolve differences over a very important matter that is contained in a concurrent resolution, such as a proposed joint committee or a congressional budget resolution. (*See* § 9.50, *Congressional Budget Process.*)

§11.40 Versions of Legislation

As a measure makes its way through the legislative process, first in one house and then the other, it changes. To do their work, members of Congress must have the number and text of the latest version of a measure. The House or Senate must have the changes that one of its committees recommended in a measure that was introduced and marked up in committee. Both the House and Senate must have exactly what the full House agreed to and what the full Senate agreed to, and so on. As a measure makes its way through the legislative process, it is reprinted to reflect changes at each major stage of the process; sometimes, additional printings are made because of the complexity of the legislation or the particular procedures being employed. A case study in Chapter Fifteen illustrates the explanation that follows here.

Following are common versions of a measure that is first considered in the House:

- as introduced
- as reported from committee
- as passed by the House (the *engrossed* measure; a bill or joint resolution is now labeled *An Act* rather than *A Bill* or *A Resolution*)
- as received by the Senate
- as reported from a Senate committee
- as passed by the Senate (the Senate *engrossed amendment*)
- as reported from a conference committee
- as *enrolled* (the version sent to the president)
- as *public law*

Following are common versions of a measure that is first considered in the Senate:

- as introduced
- as reported from committee
- as passed by the Senate (the *engrossed measure*; a bill or joint resolution is now labeled *An Act* rather than *A Bill* or *A Resolution*)
- as received by the House
- as reported from a House committee
- as passed by the House (the House *engrossed amendment*)
- as reported from a conference committee
- as *enrolled* (the version sent to the president)
- as *public law*

Certain procedural variations occur regularly. For example, House and Senate committees might report bills on the same subject—the House committee reporting a House bill and the Senate committee reporting a Senate bill—and the House might consider the House bill and the Senate, the Senate bill. One must track both bills until both the House and Senate have acted. The second chamber to act would probably take the first step toward agreement between the chambers by "striking everything after the enacting clause" in the first chamber's bill, and inserting the text of the second chamber's bill. This action results in one bill number with a House-passed text and a Senate-passed text. This process is explained in § 8.260 (*Reconciling Differences between House-Passed and Senate-Passed Legislation*).

The versions of a bill might look like this if the House acted first and the Senate second:

- House bill as introduced
- as reported from committee
- as passed by the House (the *engrossed bill*, now *An Act*)
- as received by the Senate
- Senate bill as introduced

- Senate bill as reported from a Senate committee
- as passed by the Senate (the Senate *engrossed amendment*, which uses the House bill number but contains the Senate-passed amendment, or a *public print*, which uses the House bill number but incorporates the Senate-passed text)
- as reported from a conference committee
- as *enrolled*
- as *public law*

It should be relatively apparent from the first one or two pages of a measure what the version is:

- An *introduced version* is labeled *A Bill* or *A Resolution* and shows the measure number, date of introduction, sponsor and cosponsors, and committee or committees to which the measure was referred.
- The *reported version* will still be labeled *A Bill* or *A Resolution*, but it will bear a calendar number, a report number (and part numbers if more than one committee reported the measure), any additional cosponsors, the action of the committee or committees to which the measure was referred (for example, "Reported from the Committee on the Judiciary with an amendment"), and the proposed committee amendment(s) in italicized type. If two or more committees report amendments to a measure, each committee's amendments are printed in a different typeface in the body of the measure.
- The first page of an *engrossed version* is simple in contrast—it contains just the measure number and the designation *An Act* rather than *A Bill* or *A Resolution*.
- The *received version* has the same number and the designation *An Act*, but has the name of the second chamber: "In the Senate of the United States" for House-passed bills and "In the House of Representatives" for Senate-passed bills. It also shows how the second chamber is handling the measure, either by placing it directly on a calendar, in which case there is a calendar number, or by referring it to committee, in which case the referral is noted.
- The second chamber's *engrossed version* appears as an amendment or amendments to the first chamber's measure. (A *public print* might also be printed, incorporating the second chamber's—almost always the Senate's—amendment into the text of the measure.)
- A *conference version* (that is, the conference report) looks on the first page more like a committee report on a measure, but then contains the proposed final text of the measure to be agreed to by the full House and Senate.
- An *enrolled version* prominently features the Congress and session, uses a formal typeface for the Congress and *An Act*, and shows the measure number in small type in the upper left corner of the first page.

11

- The *public law* still says *An Act* and shows the public-law number, statutory citation, and date of the president's signing. It also contains margin notes, including the measure number.

One other point to remember about versions of legislation is that more or fewer versions are possible than the examples provided here. In addition, both the House and the Senate leadership may develop different versions of legislation than those reported from committee, and may use those versions for floor consideration.

In the House, the Rules Committee might report a special rule to provide a text reflecting majority leadership desires concerning the floor vehicle. A special rule might also deal with conflicting amendments from several committees acting on a measure. In the Senate, the leadership might negotiate changes to the floor text to deal with individual senators' concerns and to facilitate Senate consideration and passage. These changes or understandings could be reflected in a unanimous consent agreement.

If the House adopts the special rule or the Senate majority leader is able to negotiate a unanimous consent agreement, the text considered on the floor might be different from that reported from committee. The text considered on the floor might not be separately printed as a bill or resolution before passage by the respective chamber.

§ 11.50 Laws and Their Implementation by the Executive

This section describes the publication of laws and key executive documents produced once the president signs a measure into law, or when Congress passes a measure over the president's veto. These documents are available in federal depository libraries, in addition to the sources included with each document's description.

Public Laws

As explained in § 8.290 (*Presidential Action on Enacted Measures*), a measure must be presented to the president for his consideration and signature to become law. When the president receives an *enrolled measure* from Congress, he has ten days (Sundays excepted) to sign or veto it if Congress is in session. (If Congress has adjourned *sine die*, he need not take any action if his intent is to prevent a measure from becoming law; he exercises a *pocket veto*.) The ten days start to run at midnight of the day on which the Office of the Executive Clerk acknowledges receipt of a measure, whether the president is at the White House or traveling inside or outside the United States. The Office of the Executive Clerk manages the official paperwork. The status of legislation at the White House can be obtained from the executive clerk's office by calling 202-456-2226.

Congress might send the president a measure quickly after final congressional action, such as when a continuing appropriations measure is needed to provide temporary funding to government agencies. Or, at the end of a session, when Congress clears numerous pieces of

Excerpt from a Public Law

Shown in §§ 11.51, 11.52, and 11.53 is how a provision of law appears in a public law (also popularly called a *slip law* after the pamphlet form in which it is published), the Statutes at Large, and the U.S. Code. P.L. 104-4, the Unfunded Mandates Act, was signed into law by President Clinton on March 22, 1995. It had been passed earlier by Congress as S. 1.

This first example shows an excerpt from the public law, section 201.

TITLE II—REGULATORY ACCOUNTABILITY AND REFORM

SEC. 201. REGULATORY PROCESS.

Each agency shall, unless otherwise prohibited by law, assess the effects of Federal regulatory actions on State, local, and tribal governments, and the private sector (other than to the extent that such regulations incorporate requirements specifically set forth in law).

---

legislation for the president's consideration, legislation might continue to be transmitted to the president for several weeks after adjournment.

A bill or resolution of a "public character," in the phrasing of House and Senate rules, that the president has signed into law, or that Congress has passed over his veto, is transmitted to the National Archives and Records Administration (NARA) and within it to the Office of the Federal Register (OFR). At OFR, the measure is assigned a sequential *public-law number*, such as P.L. 106-8, which would indicate that it was enacted in the 106th Congress and that it was the eighth public law of that Congress. (This form for numbering public laws began in the 85th Congress (1957–1958); the Congress designation was then added, for example, P.L. 85-100, rather than P.L. 100.) OFR also assigns a statutory citation *(see Statutes at Large, below)*, and its editors add margin notes, citations, and a summary legislative history. *(See § 11.51, Excerpt from a Public Law.)*

Public-law numbers also appear in the *Congressional Record, Federal Register*, and other print and electronic resources, including the NARA web site at, <*www.archives.gov/federal-register/laws*>. They are also available by phone at 202-741-6043.

Publication occurs first in *slip form*, essentially a pamphlet form similar to that of other congressional documents. *Slip laws* are available from the resources listed in § 11.10 *(Finding and Obtaining Congressional Documents)* and from other print and electronic resources. In addition, convenient resources for retrospective research of public laws include the Congres-

11

Excerpt from the Statutes at Large

An excerpt from P.L. 104-4 is shown in § 11.51. When the National Archives and Records Administration (NARA) received the document signed by the president, it assigned the public-law number and also pages in the U.S. Statutes at Large. The excerpt here shows section 201 in the Statutes at Large; its statutory citation is 109 Stat. 64. The margin notes also show where section 201 appears in the U.S. Code.

---

109 STAT. 64   PUBLIC LAW 104-4—MAR. 22, 1995

(1) as an exercise of the rulemaking power of the Senate and the House of Representatives, respectively, and as such they shall be considered as part of the rules of such House, respectively, and such rules shall supersede other rules only to the extent that they are inconsistent therewith; and

(2) with full recognition of the constitutional right of either House to change such rules (so far as relating to such House) at any time, in the same manner, and to the same extent as in the case of any other rule of each House.

2 USC 1516.   **SEC. 109. AUTHORIZATION OF APPROPRIATIONS.**

There are authorized to be appropriated to the Congressional Budget Office $4,500,000 for each of the fiscal years 1996, 1997, 1998, 1999, 2000, 2001, and 2002 to carry out the provisions of this title.

2 USC 1511 note.   **SEC. 110. EFFECTIVE DATE.**

This title shall take effect on January 1, 1996 or on the date 90 days after appropriations are made available as authorized under section 109, whichever is earlier and shall apply to legislation considered on and after such date.

TITLE II—REGULATORY ACCOUNTABILITY AND REFORM

2 USC 1531.   **SEC. 201. REGULATORY PROCESS.**

Each agency shall, unless otherwise prohibited by law, assess the effects of Federal regulatory actions on State, local, and tribal governments, and the private sector (other than to the extent that such regulations incorporate requirements specifically set forth in law).

2 USC 1532.   **SEC. 202. STATEMENTS TO ACCOMPANY SIGNIFICANT REGULATORY ACTIONS.**

(a) IN GENERAL.—Unless otherwise prohibited by law, before promulgating any general notice of proposed rulemaking that is likely to result in promulgation of any rule that includes any Federal mandate that may result in the expenditure by State, local, and tribal governments, in the aggregate, or by the private sector, of $100,000,000 or more (adjusted annually for inflation) in any 1 year, and before promulgating any final rule for which a general notice of proposed rulemaking was published, the agency shall prepare a written statement containing—

(1) an identification of the provision of Federal law under which the rule is being promulgated;

(2) a qualitative and quantitative assessment of the anticipated costs and benefits of the Federal mandate, including the costs and benefits to State, local, and tribal governments or the private sector, as well as the effect of the Federal mandate on health, safety, and the natural environment and such an assessment shall include—

(A) an analysis of the extent to which such costs to State, local, and tribal governments may be paid with Federal financial assistance (or otherwise paid for by the Federal Government); and

---

§ 11.53

Excerpt from the U.S. Code

An excerpt from the Statutes at Large, in which public laws are placed chronologically, is shown in § 11.52. The Statutes at Large are a convenient place to find all the provisions of a specific public law. However, many times, if not most of the time, one is seeking the current law on a specific subject. The U.S. Code, therefore, places each provision of a public law in the appropriate place in the appropriate subject title. In the example used here, section 201 of P.L. 104-4, which also appeared at 109 Stat. 64, is codified at 2 U.S.C. § 1531. Notes following section 1531 show the public law and statutory origins of the provision, and provide other useful information.

> **SUBCHAPTER II—REGULATORY ACCOUNTABILITY AND REFORM**
>
> **§ 1531. Regulatory process**
>
> Each agency shall, unless otherwise prohibited by law, assess the effects of Federal regulatory actions on State, local, and tribal governments, and the private sector (other than to the extent that such regulations incorporate requirements specifically set forth in law).
>
> (Pub. L. 104-4, title II, § 201, Mar. 22, 1995, 109 Stat. 64.)
>
> **EFFECTIVE DATE**
>
> Section 209 of title II of Pub. L. 104-4 provided that: "This title [enacting this subchapter] and the amendments made by this title shall take effect on the date of the enactment of this Act [Mar. 22, 1995]."
>
> **REGULATORY PLANNING AND REVIEW**
>
> For provisions stating regulatory philosophy and principles and setting forth regulatory organization, procedures, and guidelines for centralized review of new and existing regulations to make the regulatory process more efficient, see Ex. Ord. No. 12866, Sept. 30, 1993, 58 F.R. 51735, set out as a note under section 601 of Title 5, Government Organization and Employees.

sional Information Service (a part of LEXIS-NEXIS) and Thomson West's U.S. Code Congressional and Administrative News. *(See § 11.51, Excerpt from a Public Law.)*

The process of presidential signature or veto, possible congressional consideration of a veto, and processing by OFR is the same for bills of a "private character"—a phrase that appears in House and Senate rules—as it is for public bills and resolutions. The same numbering scheme is also used, so that one finds a Private Law 106-8 as well as a Public Law (P.L.) 106-8.

Statutes at Large

OFR provides a *statutory citation* for public laws. It also does this for constitutional amendments, private laws, concurrent resolutions adopted in the same form by both houses of Congress, approved executive reorganization plans, and presidential proclamations. The statutory citation refers to the *Statutes at Large. (See § 11.52, Excerpt from the Statutes at Large.)*

The Statutes at Large are hardbound books in which each public law appears sequentially in the order it was signed by the president and assigned a public-law number. Constitutional amendments, private laws, concurrent resolutions, and presidential proclamations appear in separate sections after public laws. There are also popular name and subject indices.

One or more volumes are published annually and are available through the Government Printing Office (GPO). The volumes published for each year have a single volume number associated with them. For example, the 105th Congress, first session, coincides with Volume 111, Parts 1, 2, and 3 of the Statutes at Large. Continuing the example, P.L. 105-1 appears in Volume 111 on page 3, Part 1; its statutory citation is 111 Stat. 3.

The Statutes at Large are important for several reasons. Congress by law *(2 U.S.C. § 285b)* has provided that the Statutes at Large are "legal evidence of laws, concurrent resolutions . . . proclamations by the President and proposed or ratified amendments to the Constitution of the United States therein contained, in all the courts of the United States. . . ." This provision of law states that the Statutes at Large are *positive law*; that is, recognized as the determinative text of law by governmental authority. Also, bills and joint resolutions may need to be drafted to amend statutes, as explained below *(see U.S. Code)*.

The Statutes at Large are found in federal depository libraries, law libraries, and other special libraries.

U.S. Code

Following the assignment of a public-law number and statutory citation, and the publication of a slip law, the House of Representatives' Office of Law Revision Counsel, working largely under the auspices of the Speaker of the House, organizes those public laws that are "general and permanent" into the *United States Code*, popularly referred to as the *U.S. Code* or just the *Code. (See § 11.53.)* Unlike the sequential organization scheme of the Statutes at Large, all laws in the U.S. Code are organized by subject matter. The user can readily understand what is current law by checking the Code; all cumulative changes in federal law are reflected in the Code.

The U.S. Code is divided into fifty subject *titles*, and each title is divided into *sections*. Sections in a title might be grouped as *subtitles, chapters, subchapters, parts, subparts,* or *divisions.* Some titles also have *appendices.*

Those titles enacted into positive law by Congress are legal evidence of the law contained in those titles *(1 U.S.C. § 204)*. In legislative drafting, amendments to existing law are drafted to positive law, which explains why some legislation amends statutes while other legislation amends the U.S. Code.

The subjects covered by the fifty titles of the U.S. Code, with positive law titles so far enacted indicated by an asterisk (*), are as follows:

* 1. General Provisions
2. The Congress
* 3. The President
* 4. Flag and Seal, Seat of Government, and the States
* 5. Government Organization and Employees
6. Surety Bonds (repealed by the enactment of Title 31)
7. Agriculture

8. Aliens and Nationality

* 9. Arbitration

* 10. Armed Forces; and Appendix

* 11. Bankruptcy; and Appendix

12. Banks and Banking

* 13. Census

* 14. Coast Guard

15. Commerce and Trade

16. Conservation

* 17. Copyrights

* 18. Crimes and Criminal Procedure; and Appendix

19. Customs Duties

20. Education

21. Food and Drugs

22. Foreign Relations and Intercourse

* 23. Highways

24. Hospitals and Asylums

25. Indians

26. Internal Revenue Code; and Appendix

27. Intoxicating Liquors

* 28. Judiciary and Judicial Procedure; and Appendix

29. Labor

30. Mineral Lands and Mining

* 31. Money and Finance

* 32. National Guard

33. Navigation and Navigable Waters

34. Navy (eliminated by the enactment of Title 10)

* 35. Patents

* 36. Patriotic Societies and Observations

* 37. Pay and Allowances of the Uniformed Services

* 38. Veterans' Benefits; and Appendix

* 39. Postal Service

* 40. Public Buildings, Property, and Works; and Appendix

41. Public Contracts

42. The Public Health and Welfare

43. Public Lands

* 44. Public Printing and Documents

45. Railroads

* 46. Shipping; and Appendix

47. Telegraphs, Telephones, and Radiotelegraphs

48. Territories and Insular Possessions

* 49. Transportation

50. War and National Defense; and Appendix

A citation to the U.S. Code might look like this: 5 U.S.C. § 1101, indicating Title 5 and section 1101.

The full U.S. Code is printed once every six years by GPO. The current edition is the 2000 edition. Annual *supplements* bring the Code up-to-date, but the publishing process is slow and use of supplements is cumbersome. *Classification tables* assist the user in identifying which sections of the Code have been amended and where recently enacted laws appear.

The Code, supplements, and classification tables are available online through the web site of the Office of the Law Revision Counsel, <*http://uscode.house.gov*>. An easier-to-use interface and updating feature is available through Cornell University's Legal Information Institute, <*www.law.cornell.edu/uscode*>.

Thomson West's *United States Code Annotated*, LEXIS Law Publishing's *United States Code Service*, other print services, and online services such as WESTLAW and LEXIS provide more current, cumulative versions of the U.S. Code than the Office of the Law Revision Counsel provides. They also add research aids that enhance the usability and utility of their products.

Federal Register

In the course of its lawmaking, Congress often delegates *quasi-legislative authority* to executive departments and agencies so that they might effectively implement laws and carry out the broader policy determinations that Congress itself made. Departments and agencies engage in *rulemaking* in exercising this authority. Congress also often empowers departments and agencies with *quasi-judicial authority* to make *adjudications*. To guide the overall use of this authority, Congress enacted the Administrative Procedure Act (APA) *(5 U.S.C. § 551 et seq. and 5 U.S.C. § 701 et seq.)* and the Federal Register Act *(44 U.S.C. § 1501 et seq.)*, so that there is a prescribed process for rulemaking and adjudications and for public notification.

Rulemaking is the term used in APA to describe the process of drafting, making available for public comment, and issuing rules and regulations. Adjudication under APA might involve a range of activities—a dispute involving a regulation between the federal government and an entity (such as a citizen, an organization, or another governmental unit), the issuance or renewal of a license that an agency has been empowered to grant, or permission to undertake an activity regulated by an agency.

Rulemaking, adjudications, and other activities of the executive branch in carrying out laws enacted by Congress, and actions of the president acting pursuant to statute or on the basis of his constitutional authority, must appear in the *Federal Register* and can be monitored or tracked there. The *Federal Register* contains federal agency regulations, proposed rules and notices, and executive orders and other presidential documents.

A citation to the *Federal Register* might look like this: 64 Fed. Reg. 34109, indicating volume 64 and page 34109. For convenience, the date of the *Federal Register* in which a cited page appears is often also provided. The *Federal Register* is indexed monthly.

The *Federal Register* is published every business day. It is available in print from GPO, and online through GPO Access, <*www.gpoaccess.gov/fr/index.html*>. The *Federal Register* is also available in electronic formats from a number of sources.

The publisher of the *Federal Register*, the Office of the Federal Register (OFR) within the National Archives and Records Administration (NARA), provides other services as well in carrying out its mission under the Federal Register Act. Because OFR must make documents available one day before publication in the *Federal Register*, it publishes a *List of Federal Register Documents on Public Inspection* on its web site at <*www.archives.gov/federal-register/public-*

inspection>. The documents themselves are available for public inspection at OFR's office, 800 North Capitol St., Suite 700, Washington, DC; 202-523-5240.

Twice a year, usually in April and October, OFR also publishes the *Unified Agenda*, also called the semiannual regulatory agenda, which lists rules and proposed rules that federal agencies expect to issue in the following six months. This document is also available in print from GPO and online through GPO Access.

Code of Federal Regulations

Just as the U.S. Code provides a subject arrangement of general and permanent federal laws, the *Code of Federal Regulations* (CFR) contains a subject arrangement of general and permanent rules and regulations published in the *Federal Register* and promulgated by federal executive departments and agencies. (Title 3 of the CFR cumulates executive orders, proclamations, and other presidential administrative orders.) Its fifty titles each cover a subject area; the CFR and U.S. Code titles, however, do not correspond to each other. Most CFR titles are further subdivided into *chapters* (usually coinciding with an agency), *parts*, and *sections*, and there also exist *subchapters* and *subparts*. (A full set of the CFR encompasses approximately 200 volumes.)

A citation to the CFR might look like this: 20 C.F.R. 404.1576, indicating Title 20, part 404, and section 1576.

Unlike the U.S. Code, revision of each CFR title occurs annually on a schedule approximately as follows:

- Titles 1–16, as of January 1
- Titles 17–27, as of April 1
- Titles 28–41, as of July 1
- Titles 42–50, as of October 1

To assist the user between revisions, there is the *List of CFR Sections Affected* (LSA), which shows amendments published in the *Federal Register* and not yet incorporated into the appropriate, revised CFR title. The LSA is published quarterly and cumulates amendments to a title until that title is next revised.

The CFR's publisher is OFR, within NARA. Print editions are available from GPO.

The CFR, LSA, and an unofficial Electronic CFR are available online through GPO Access, *<www.gpoaccess.gov/cfr>*. Other online providers include WESTLAW and LEXIS.

Executive Orders, Proclamations, and Other Presidential Directives

How the executive branch implements a law or administers a program or activity pursuant to statutory authority can be critically affected by administrative decisions of the president, who is responsible for the execution of the laws, the management of the executive branch of the federal government, and other executive functions. In the course of the president's discharge of his responsibilities, he often finds it useful to issue *presidential directives*, which are manifested in several forms. The following description covers some of the principal, current forms of presidential directives.

Executive orders, made pursuant to statutory authority or in the exercise of the president's constitutional authority, direct officials of the executive branch in the discharge of their responsibilities. Executive orders deal with executive-branch activities ranging from foreign policy to the existence of various federal offices and agencies to the coordination of various federal domestic programs and activities.

Executive orders are numbered sequentially, and a citation might look like this: E.O. 12833 (or Exec. Order No. 12833), which was the last executive order of President George H.W. Bush, and E.O. 12834 (or Exec. Order No. 12834), which was the first executive order of President Clinton.

The president also uses *proclamations* in exercising his responsibilities. These also might be made pursuant to statutory authority or the president's constitutional authority. A few of them contain policy statements, such as findings or determinations made pursuant to U.S. trade laws. Most often, a proclamation is a public exhortation, such as the traditional Thanksgiving and Mother's Day proclamations. Proclamations are numbered sequentially, so that a citation might look like this: Proclamation 7028 or Proc. 7028.

A third form of presidential directive has been designated as an *administrative order*. It is a catchall for some directives not designated as executive orders or proclamations.

A fourth principal type of presidential directive deals with national security. The forms and designations of these directives have changed often in the post-World War II era. Most are secret when issued and remain so for many years. In recent presidencies, two types of these directives have dealt with national security studies and national security policy. President Clinton used *presidential review directives* for national security studies; the equivalents were *national security study memoranda* under President Reagan and *national security reviews* under President George H.W. Bush. President Clinton used *presidential decision directives* for national security policy statements; the equivalents were *national security decision directives* under President Reagan and *national security directives* under President George H.W. Bush. President George W. Bush seems to be using one format instead of two, which is called a *national security presidential directive*.

OFR, within NARA, publishes executive orders and proclamations. OFR maintains a list of executive orders and proclamations from the Truman administration through today at the NARA web site, *<www.archives.gov/federal-register/executive-orders>*. The list also shows which executive orders have been revoked or amended, but it does not include their full text. (Regulations governing executive orders and proclamations are the subject of E.O. 11030, as amended.)

Almost all executive orders and proclamations must be published in the *Federal Register* upon their issuance to have legal effect. They are available online through GPO Access,

<www.gpoaccess.gov/executive.html>. Executive orders and proclamations are cumulated in Title 3 of CFR. (Administrative orders also appear in the *Federal Register* and in Title 3 of CFR.) If an executive order or proclamation is made pursuant to statutory authority, it often appears in the appropriate place in the U.S. Code.

Executive orders and proclamations also are provided through other print and electronic resources, such as the U.S. Code Congressional and Administrative News. Current presidential documents are also available through the White House web site, *<www.white house.gov/news/orders>* and *<www.whitehouse.gov/news/proclamations>*.

Weekly Compilation of Presidential Documents

One of the most complete pictures of presidential and White House activities can be obtained through the *Weekly Compilation of Presidential Documents*. This is not a legal publication, but a convenient reference or compilation and digest of most presidential documents and activities. Published every Monday, it contains the full text of presidential statements, messages, executive orders and proclamations, and materials released by the president's Office of the Press Secretary and issued in the previous week. It digests various White House announcements, nominations submitted to the Senate, and presidential action on measures enacted by Congress. There are quarterly, semiannual, and annual indexes.

The Weekly Compilation of Presidential Documents is available in print from GPO and online through GPO Access, *<www.gpoaccess.gov/wcomp/index.html>*. Current presidential documents are also available through the White House web site, *<www.whitehouse.gov/news>*. It is a good idea to check both GPO Access and the White House web site when looking for the full text of a presidential document.

Public Papers of the Presidents

Public Papers of the President is a series published semiannually, which since 1977 has contained most items appearing in the *Weekly Compilation of Presidential Documents*, plus additional material. It is a convenient means of conducting retrospective research on presidential activities (beginning with President Hoover, but omitting President Franklin Roosevelt), and finding full texts of presidential documents in one place.

Printed volumes of the Public Papers of the President are available from GPO. NARA is in the process of putting the Public Papers online. In early 2007, the Public Papers of President George H.W. Bush (for part of 1991 and for 1992 only), President Clinton, and President George W. Bush (for 2001, 2002, and part of 2003 only) were online, *<www.gpoaccess.gov/pub papers/index.html>*. Check the NARA web site for additional information, *<www.archives. gov/federal-register/publications/presidential-papers.html>*.

Chapter Twelve

Congressional Documents:

Committee, Chamber, Party, and Administrative Publications

12

Analysis

12

§12.00 Introduction

The House and Senate produce a number of official publications related to the legislative and administrative functions of their chambers. These publications include ones dealing with rules and procedures, anticipated and past legislative activities, committee matters, and chamber proceedings.

This chapter identifies and describes official committee, chamber, party, and administrative publications.

§12.10 Committee Documents

House and Senate committees prepare a variety of documents in the process of doing their work. In the conduct of their legislative function, committees publish hearings, drafts of legislation, reports accompanying legislation, reports summarizing their legislative activities over a single Congress, and committee calendars. Within their investigative and oversight roles, they prepare committee prints and reports. Committees also prepare administrative documents on their internal affairs.

Committee Calendars

A committee calendar provides a comprehensive record of a committee's actions during one Congress. All committees *except* the following prepare calendars: the House and Senate Appropriations Committees, the House Administration Committee, the House Committee on Standards of Official Conduct, and the Senate Select Ethics Committee. Many committees publish a calendar at the end of each session; all publish a final calendar at the end of a Congress. Final calendars are cumulative, superseding any interim calendars prepared during a Congress. Some committees post their calendars on their web sites.

Each committee calendar presents similar information, although formats vary. Some present information in a summary fashion; others present detailed information on most or all aspects of a committee's work. Some committees present information arranged by subcommittee; some prepare it by topic; some arrange it chronologically. Some committees prepare entries in several ways within a calendar, such as by subcommittee, by topic, and in chronological order. All committee calendars provide committee and subcommittee membership lists. *(See § 12.11, Excerpt from a House Committee Calendar.)*

Committee Histories

Numerous committees have prepared histories of their panels and published them as official committee documents. Some histories are simple overviews listing former members and briefly describing selected legislation considered by a committee. Other histories have several hundred detailed pages. Some committees prepare histories at the time of historic milestones, such as anniversaries of their organization for fifty, one hundred, or two hundred years. Some

12

§ 12.11

Excerpt from a House Committee Calendar

UNITED STATES HOUSE OF REPRESENTATIVES
LEGISLATIVE CALENDAR

COMMITTEE ON
AGRICULTURE

ONE HUNDRED FIFTH CONGRESS

FIRST SESSION   CONVENED JANUARY 7, 1997
       ADJOURNED NOVEMBER 13, 1997
SECOND SESSION   CONVENED JANUARY 27, 1998
       ADJOURNED NOVEMBER 13, 1998
       CONVENED DECEMBER 17, 1998
       ADJOURNED DECEMBER 19, 1998

Copies of Bills, Reports, Public Laws and House Documents listed herein may be obtained, so
as they remain available, from the Superintendent of Documents, Document Room,
U.S. House of Representatives, Washington, D.C. 20515

For sale by the U.S. Government Printing Office
Superintendent of Documents, Congressional Sales Office, Washington, DC 20402
ISBN 0-16-058353-5

CONTENTS

Number of bills and resolutions referred to this Committee during 105th Congress—215

panels prepared histories at the time of the 1989 bicentennial of Congress. Most committee histories have not been updated since their original publication.

Many of these histories are available from the respective House or Senate committee. Some committees provide excerpts on their web sites. Some histories are available from the Government Printing Office (GPO) and depository libraries.

House Committee Histories. The following is a list of published House committee histories:

- *Committee on Agriculture, 150th Anniversary*, printed as H. Doc. 91-350
- *180 Years of Service: A Brief History of the Committee on Interstate and Foreign Commerce*, committee print from the 94th Congress
- *History of the Committee on the Judiciary*, printed as H. Doc. 109-153
- *Historical Information of the Committee on Resources and Its Predecessor Committees, 1807–2002*, printed as Comm. Print No. 107–H
- *A History of the Committee on Rules, 1789–1981*, committee print from the 97th Congress
- *Toward the Endless Frontier: History of the Committee on Science and Technology, 1959–1979*, committee print from the 96th Congress
- *History and Accomplishments of the Permanent Select Committee on Small Business, 77th to 92nd Congress*, printed as H. Doc. 93-197
- *History of House Committees Considering Veterans' Legislation*, committee print from the 101st Congress
- *The Committee on Ways and Means: A Bicentennial History, 1789–1989*, committee print from the 101st Congress

Senate Committee Histories. The following is a list of published Senate committee histories:

- *United States Senate Committee on Agriculture, Nutrition, and Forestry, 1825–1998*, printed as S. Doc. 105-24
- *United States Senate Committee on Appropriations*, printed as S. Doc. 107-13
- *Committee on Banking and Currency, United States Senate: 50th Anniversary, 1913–1963*, printed as S. Doc. 88-15
- *Committee on the Budget, 1974–2006*, printed as S. Doc. 109-24
- *Brief History of the Senate Committee on Commerce, Science, and Transportation and Its Activities Since 1947*, printed as S. Doc. 95-93
- *History of the Committee on Energy and Natural Resources, 1816–1988, United States Senate*, printed as S. Doc. 100-46
- *History of the Committee on Environment and Public Works, United States Senate*, printed as S. Doc. 100-45
- *History of the Committee on Finance*, printed as S. Doc. 97-5
- *Committee on Foreign Relations, Millennium Edition, 1816–2000*, printed as S. Doc. 105-28
- *Committee on Government Operations, United States Senate, 50th Anniversary, 1921–1971*, printed as S. Doc. 92-31
- *History of the Committee on the Judiciary, 1816–1981*, printed as S. Doc. 97-18
- *History of the Committee on Labor and Human Resources, United States Senate, 1869–1979*, printed as S. Doc. 96-71
- *History of the Committee on Rules and Administration*, printed as S. Doc. 96-27

12

§ 12.12

Example of a Committee Print

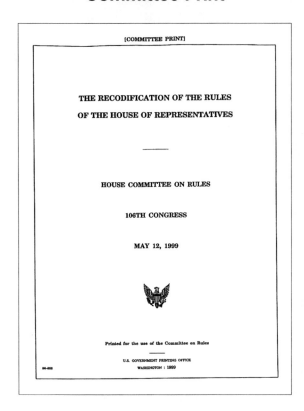

[COMMITTEE PRINT]

THE RECODIFICATION OF THE RULES
OF THE HOUSE OF REPRESENTATIVES

———

HOUSE COMMITTEE ON RULES

106TH CONGRESS

MAY 12, 1999

Printed for the use of the Committee on Rules
———
U.S. GOVERNMENT PRINTING OFFICE
WASHINGTON : 1999

Committee Prints

Committee prints represent a catchall form of publication and are often used to provide information not directly related to legislative activity. Following are examples of documents usually designated as committee prints: committee and subcommittee membership lists, committee rules, staff studies (including those prepared by the Congressional Research Service), and compilations of laws within a committee's jurisdiction or closely related to its jurisdiction. Draft legislation to be considered in markup is also often prepared as a committee print. (*See § 12.12, Example of a Committee Print.*)

Some prints are numbered; others are not. The decision to number a print and the numbering system used is left to each committee. Committee prints are available from the respective committee; some are available from the GPO Access web site, at <*www.gpoaccess. gov/cprints*>.

Committee Rules

In every Congress, the House Committee on Rules and the Senate Committee on Rules and Administration issue documents that compile the rules of procedure for all committees in their respective chamber. Although committee rules appear in the *Congressional Record*, and are also usually printed by each committee as a committee print and appear on the committee's web site, the House and Senate compilations are useful because all the rules appear in a single publication.

The House compilation for the 109th Congress was published as a committee print by the Committee on Rules. The Senate compilation for the 109th Congress was published as S. Doc. 109-8, prepared by the Committee on Rules and Administration. The documents can be obtained from the issuing committee. The 110th Congress committee rules compilations were expected to be published in late 2007. More detailed information on rules and precedent publications can be found below in §§ 12.40, 12.50, and 12.60.

Hearings

Witnesses present oral and written testimony at hearings, and are questioned by committee members and, occasionally, by committee staff. Statistical data, correspondence, written answers to questions, and other information can also be submitted by committee members and witnesses for inclusion in the hearing record. Hearings might be broadcast or webcast.

Stenographers are always present at committee and subcommittee hearings. They record transcripts of all the proceedings. The transcripts are then edited by committee staff. Hearing records are generally published by committees, but they are often not available until months after a hearing or series of hearings is held. However, committees maintain transcripts of hearings in the committee offices. The transcripts are usually available for inspection, often the day following a hearing.

Many committees put witness testimony on their web sites soon after a hearing. Many committees are posting transcripts as well, and some make audio or video recordings available online. Although most witnesses provide written testimony to a committee, printed copies may be difficult to obtain before a hearing transcript is printed (unless one attends the hearing). However, for executive-branch witnesses, the respective agency web site, or the Office of Management and Budget web site, often provides the full text of agency witnesses' testimony. If a witness is representing a private organization, testimony may be posted on that organization's web site.

House committees use House stenographers. Transcripts may be purchased when committees grant sale permission. Availability and cost information may be obtained from the Office of Official Reporters, at 202-225-2627.

Senate committees make use of reporting services to transcribe their hearings. Copies may be purchased directly from reporting services, when committees grant sale permission. Individual committees can provide information on the reporting services.

If printed, hearings are available from the respective committee. However, they are generally printed in limited quantities. Printed hearings are also often available online at GPO Access, at <*www.gpoaccess.gov/chearings/index.html*>. (*Congressional Information Service is a source for nearly all committee documents. Information can be found at the Lexis-Nexis web site,* <*www.lexisnexis.com/academic*>.)

House Committee Oversight Plans

House committees are required to prepare oversight plans and provide them to the Committee on House Administration and the Committee on Oversight and Government Reform. The Committee on Oversight and Government Reform then compiles all the submissions into one publication. The oversight plans provide useful information about issues that a committee intends to study during a Congress. The compilation of 109th Congress oversight plans was published as H. Rept. 109-29. The 110th Congress compilation was expected in late summer. (*House committees' oversight plans are usually available on the committees' own web sites and on THOMAS,* <*http://thomas.loc.gov*>.)

12

§ 12.13

Example of a House Legislative Activity Report

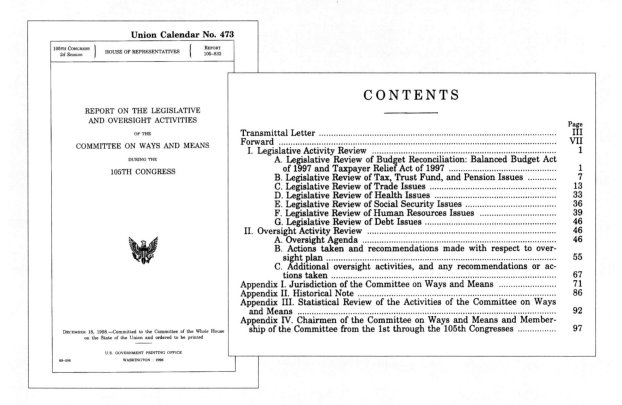

Reports

There are several types of committee reports: those that accompany legislation, those that result from oversight or investigative activity, those from conference committees, and those reflecting the activities of committees over the course of a Congress. *(See § 8.60, Committee Reports, for an extensive discussion of committee reports on legislation and their required contents; and § 8.280, Conference Committees, for a discussion of conference reports and joint explanatory statements.)*

An activity report published at the conclusion of a Congress provides a narrative description of a committee's actions over the course of a Congress. These reports usually include summaries of legislation referred to or acted on by the committee, hearings held by the committee and its subcommittees, oversight activities, and the titles of documents issued by the committee. *(See § 12.13, Example of a House Legislative Activity Report.)* Senate committee activity reports include information on nominations and treaties referred and considered.

All reports are designated *H. Rept.* or *S. Rept.* to show whether they are House or Senate committee reports. They are numbered sequentially in the order they are filed with a committee's parent chamber. For example, H. Rept. 107-123 was prepared by a House committee in the 107th Congress and was the 123rd report filed by a committee with the House. If two committees filed legislative reports on the same legislation, they would carry the same report number and be designated Part I and Part II.

§12.20 Floor Documents

The House and Senate each publish documents related to rules and procedures, anticipated legislation, and chamber proceedings.

Calendars of the United States House of Representatives and History of Legislation ("House Calendar")

The *Calendars of the United States House of Representatives and History of Legislation*, more commonly (if confusingly) referred to as the *House Calendar*, contains a history of each House and Senate measure once it has been reported from committee, otherwise placed on a House or Senate calendar, or acted on by the House or Senate, and compiles all the calendars published by the House: the House Calendar, Private Calendar, Discharge Calendar, and Union Calendar. A list of motions to discharge committees that have received 218 signatures and are awaiting floor action is included. Also provided is a list of public and private laws, cross-referenced to their corresponding measure numbers. Additional sections contain other useful information. A chart depicting the status of appropriations, tax, and other key budget legislation is displayed on the back page of the House Calendar.

The Monday version of the House Calendar contains information on measures that have completed the conference committee process, an alphabetical index of the short titles of pending measures, and a subject index of House and Senate measures listed in the House Calendar. *(See § 12.21, Calendars of the United States House of Representatives and History of Legislation.)*

A final calendar is published at the end of each Congress; it contains a list of measures that became law, measures vetoed by the president, and statistical workload data comparing the present Congress with prior Congresses.

The calendar is distributed to House offices each day the House is in session. *(Available online at GPO Access, <www.gpoaccess.gov/calendars/house/index.html>.)*

Calendar of Business ("Senate Calendar")

The *Calendar of Business*, more commonly referred to as the *Senate Calendar*, the *Legislative Calendar*, or the *Calendar of General Orders*, contains a list called "General Orders, under Rule VIII," which records all measures that have been reported and any bills or joint resolutions that have been placed directly on the calendar without first being referred to committee. The order number reflects the chronological order in which a measure has been placed on the calendar. *(See § 12.22, Senate Calendar of Business.)*

12

§ 12.21

Calendars of the United States House of Representatives and History of Legislation

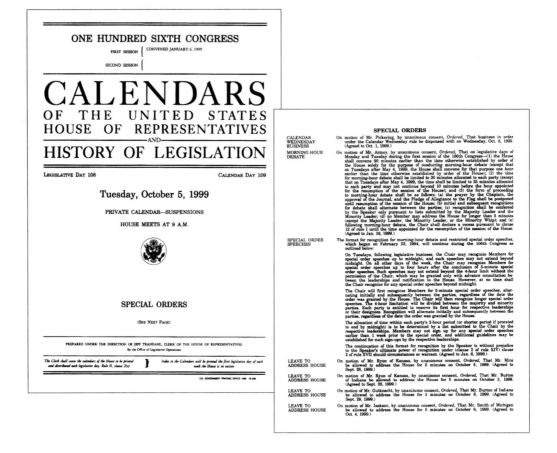

Included in the Senate Calendar on the general order list are the measure's number, sponsor, and title. Information on when the measure was placed on the calendar and how it was placed there is also included.

One of the most useful parts of the Senate Calendar appears on the inside front cover. The texts of operative or pending unanimous consent agreements are reprinted here. (*See § 8.200, Time Agreements and Motions to Proceed on the Senate Floor.*)

The Senate Calendar shows the days the Senate was in session, and contains a list of senators and the year in which each senator's term expires, membership lists on Senate and joint committees, and a list of bills sent to conference, with the names of the conferees.

The Senate Calendar is distributed to all Senate offices each day the Senate is in session. (*Available online at GPO Access, <www. gpoaccess.gov/calendars/senate/index.html>.*)

§ 12.22

Senate Calendar of Business

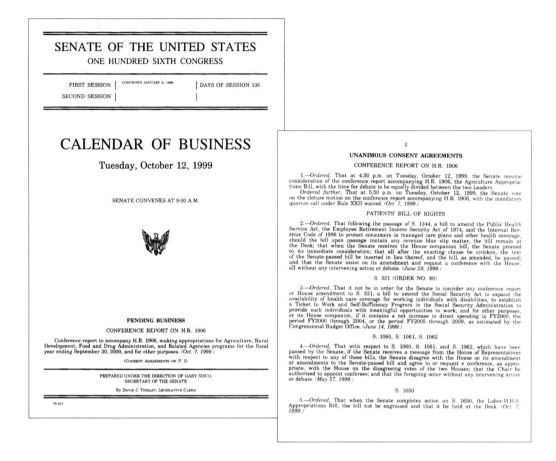

Executive Calendar

The *Executive Calendar* is used to track the Senate's executive business, such as nominations and treaties. It lists treaties, nominations, and executive resolutions that have been reported by a committee or placed on the calendar. Unanimous consent agreements on treaties or nominations are also carried in the Executive Calendar. *(See § 12.23, Senate Executive Calendar.)*

The Executive Calendar is distributed to all Senate offices each day the Senate is in session. *(Available online on the Senate web site, <www.senate.gov/pagelayout/legislative/one_item_ and_teasers/exec_calendar_page.htm>.)*

Congressional Record

The *Congressional Record* is a substantially verbatim account of daily proceedings of the House and Senate. It consists of five principal parts: House floor proceedings, Senate floor proceed-

§ 12.23

Senate Executive Calendar

SENATE OF THE UNITED STATES
ONE HUNDRED SIXTH CONGRESS

FIRST SESSION { CONVENED JANUARY 6, 1999

SECOND SESSION {

EXECUTIVE CALENDAR

Tuesday, October 12, 1999

Unanimous Consent Agreements

Ordered, That amendments to the Comprehensive Nuclear Test-Ban Treaty must be filed at the desk by 9:45 a.m. on Tuesday, October 12, 1999.

(October 7, 1999)

Ordered, That the debate on the Comprehensive Nuclear Test-Ban Treaty resume at 9:00 a.m. on Tuesday, October 12, 1999.

PREPARED UNDER THE DIRECTION OF GARY SISCO, SECRETARY OF THE SENATE

By Michelle Haynes, Executive Clerk

ings, Extensions of Remarks, Daily Digest, and time and agenda for the next meeting of the House and Senate.

Floor proceedings appear first. On alternate days, the Senate and then the House proceedings appear first. House pages are preceded by an *H* and Senate pages are preceded by an *S*. The pages are numbered consecutively from the previous day's House and Senate pages. Both sections are generally arranged chronologically for the day. Both sections contain floor debate, the text of amendments, and vote tallies. The numbers and official titles of measures introduced are provided in both sections. Amendments submitted for printing and the addition and withdrawal of cosponsors follow the lists of new measures introduced. Floor schedule announcements appear in both sections. Nearly all conference reports are printed in the House section. *(See § 14.10, How to Follow Floor Proceedings in the House, and § 14.20, How to Follow Floor Proceedings in the Senate.)*

The next section of the *Congressional Record*, called Extensions of Remarks, has pages that are preceded by an *E*. Pages are numbered consecutively from the previous day, and contain statements by members (usually House members) on a wide range of topics. Members receive permission on the floor to insert statements into this section.

The Daily Digest appears at the end of the *Congressional Record*, and its pages, consecutive from the previous day's Daily Digest, are preceded by a *D*. The Daily Digest is the key to each *Congressional Record* and the place to begin a review. The first section of the Daily Digest is labeled *Senate* and the second, *House.* House and Senate floor proceedings are summarized in the appropriate part of the Daily Digest. Also listed are the sequential numbers of measures introduced that day in each chamber, treaties and nominations received by the Senate, presidential and executive communications received in each chamber, and conferees appointed in each chamber. Individual statements by members are not indexed in the Daily Digest.

In the House and Senate sections of the Daily Digest is a summary of each chamber's committee and subcommittee activities that day. Committees are listed alphabetically, with subcommittees listed under their parent committee. Joint and conference committees and new public-law numbers are also listed. The next day's committee schedules follow the public laws. In the last issue of a week's *Congressional Record*, the next week's floor and committee schedules are printed.

The time and agenda for the next meeting of the House and Senate are listed on the back page of the *Congressional Record*. An index, by House member, of Extensions of Remarks for the day also appears on the back page.

In the course of a week, preceding the Daily Digest, are House and Senate membership lists, each member's office number, and committee rosters. The advance (long-range) Senate committee schedule also appears in these pages. Periodically, the *Congressional Record* prints committees' foreign travel reports and lobby registrations filed with the clerk of the House and the secretary of the Senate. Soon after the end of a month, a *Résumé of Congressional Activity* (summary statistics on the work of the Congress) is printed. (*See § 7.23, Résumé of Congressional Activity, 109th Congress.*)

A noncumulative, biweekly index of the *Congressional Record* is published, about a month after the period covered. The index is organized alphabetically by subject, and under each member's name is a list of measures introduced by that member. A history of bills and resolutions is organized by number at the end of each index.

Permanent bound volumes of the *Congressional Record* are published, but publication lags by several years. In addition, the bound volumes are repaginated sequentially and without the chamber letter designation. A cumulative subject and name index and a history of all measures introduced or acted upon appears in one bound index volume, and a reprint of the Daily Digests of a session and a cumulative index to them appear in a second bound index volume.

Publication of the *Congressional Record* began in 1873. Predecessor publications were the *Annals of Congress (The Debate and Proceedings in the Congress of the United States),* which was published from 1789 to 1824; the *Register of Debates,* which was published from 1824 to 1837; and the *Congressional Globe,* which was published from 1833 to 1873. These documents, plus the *Congressional Record* for 1873–1877 are available online from the Library of Congress, at *<http://memory.loc.gov/ammem/amlaw/lwcr.html>*.

12

The *Congressional Record* is provided to each congressional office. *(Available online at GPO Access, <www.gpoaccess.gov/crecord/index.html>, or through THOMAS, <http://thomas.loc.gov>.)*

House Journal and Senate Journal

The *Journal of the House of Representatives of the United States* is the official record of the House, and the *Journal of the Senate of the United States of America* is the official record of the Senate. A journal for each chamber is required by Article I of the Constitution. The Journals are published on a periodic basis, but at least annually, and they chronicle actions such as bills introduced, amendments offered and agreed to, and votes. The Journals also provide a narrative account of legislative proceedings and contain an alphabetical index. At the beginning of each day, each chamber approves its Journal of the preceding day.

The Government Printing Office (GPO) provides copies of the House and Senate Journals to each office, as well as to the Library of Congress and all depository libraries. However, the Journals' contents derive from the *Congressional Record*, so the Journals are of limited practical use. *(The House Journal from 1991 to 1999 is available online at GPO Access, <www.access.gpo.gov/hjournal/index.html>.)*

Journal of the Executive Proceedings of the Senate

The *Executive Journal* records the Senate's actions on nominations and treaties—its executive business. Produced by the Senate executive clerk, the Executive Journal is not available for general distribution, although GPO distributes copies to select depository libraries.

§ 12.30 Congressional Rules and Precedents

Rules and procedures can be complicated and cumbersome. Precedents further affect our understanding of the legislative process. The next two sections (§ 12.40 and § 12.50) describe the official rules publications that provide definitive information on how the House and Senate operate. The third section (§ 12.60) provides a compilation of congressional resources that describe House and Senate procedures in an explanatory format.

§ 12.40 Official Rules Publications of the House
House Rules and Manual

The *Constitution, Jefferson's Manual, and Rules of the House of Representatives of the United States*, referred to as the *House Rules and Manual*, governs the House comprehensively. Recodified for the first time in over one hundred years at the beginning of the 106th Congress, the rules themselves describe the selection, powers, and duties of the Speaker and House officials, enumerate the jurisdictions of committees, establish procedures for the House and the Committee of the Whole, prescribe the conduct of representatives, and regulate the House in other ways. Extensive parliamentarian's annotations accompany each rule.

Jefferson's Manual, originally drafted by Thomas Jefferson as president of the Senate while serving as vice president of the United States, supplements House rules to the extent it does not conflict with the rules. The *House Rules and Manual* also contains the Constitution, a list of rules changes from previous Congresses, selections from relevant statutes (such as the Congressional Budget Act), and other provisions governing the House.

The *House Rules and Manual* is generally printed once during each Congress to reflect rules changes adopted at the convening of a Congress and to update the parliamentarian's notes. The edition for each Congress bears a document number from the preceding Congress, because the House typically authorizes the next edition during the preceding Congress. The 110th Congress *House Rules and Manual* was H. Doc. 109-157. *Jefferson's Manual* has also been printed separately as S. Doc. 103-8. (*The 109th Congress House Rules and Manual is available online at GPO Access, <www.gpoaccess.gov/hrm/index.html>. The House Rules Clerk's Print (see next entry) of House rules for the 110th Congress is available on the House Rules Committee web site, <www.rules.house.gov/ruleprec/110th.pdf>.*)

House Rules Clerk's Print

For each Congress, early in the first session, the clerk of the House issues an unnumbered print containing the rules of the House. This so-called "Clerk's Print" incorporates any rules changes adopted on opening day, and is the first document available containing House rules. No annotations to the rules are included. (*Available online at the House Rules Committee web site, <www.rules.house.gov/ruleprec/110th.pdf>.*)

House Practice: A Guide to the Rules, Precedents, and Procedures of the House

This volume, commonly referred to as *House Practice*, was compiled by Parliamentarian Emeritus of the House William Holmes Brown, and updated by the House parliamentarian to be current through the 107th Congress. *House Practice* summarizes the most common procedures used by the House and explains their usage in lay language. An update was expected in late 2007.

The book is organized alphabetically by topic and cites other parliamentary reference sources. It is thoroughly indexed. (*Available online at GPO Access, <www.gpoaccess.gov/hpractice/index.html.*)

Procedure in the House of Representatives (Deschler's)

This single-volume document, referred to as *Deschler's Procedure* (after former House Parliamentarian Lewis Deschler), presents selected precedents from 1959 through 1980. A 1985 supplement covers 1981 through 1984, and a 1987 supplement covers precedents created from 1981 through 1986. *House Practice*, described above, was designed to replace *Deschler's Procedure.*

This document is arranged around topics of procedure, with each chapter divided into broad subtopics. As such, a knowledge of procedure is helpful in navigating the publication.

Deschler's Procedure is out of print. Copies are available for reference at the House Legislative Resource Center, B-106 Cannon House Office Building.

Deschler-Brown Precedents of the U.S. House of Representatives

This multivolume series contains precedents from 1936 to the recent past. Additional volumes are being prepared by the office of the parliamentarian. The first nine volumes are called *Deschler's Precedents of the U.S. House of Representatives*; the volumes thereafter, numbered 10 to 16 as of 2007, are referred to as *Deschler-Brown Precedents*, to acknowledge the work of former Parliamentarian William Holmes Brown. Additional volumes are anticipated by 2008.

The books are organized by topical chapter parallel to those in *Deschler's Procedure*. For many of the topics, the full text of discussion creating or interpreting precedent on the House floor is provided, as well as the page citation from the *Congressional Record*.

Some of these volumes are out of print. Copies are available for reference at the House Legislative Resource Center, B-106 Cannon House Office Building. (*Available online at GPO Access, <www.gpoaccess.gov/precedents/deschler/index.html>.*)

Hinds' and Cannon's Precedents of the U.S. House of Representatives

This multivolume series provides an historical overview of House precedents during the period 1789 to 1936. Volumes 1 through 5 are known as *Hinds' Precedents* and volumes 6 through 11 are known as *Cannon's Precedents*. (Collectively, they are referred to as *Hinds' and Cannon's Precedents*.) Asher C. Hinds was a Republican representative from Maine from 1911 to 1917, and Clarence Cannon was a Democratic representative from Missouri from 1923 to 1964 and a parliamentarian of the House from 1915 to 1920.

These volumes are out of print. Copies are available for reference at the House Legislative Resource Center, B-106 Cannon House Office Building. (*Available online at GPO Access, <www.gpoaccess.gov/precedents/hinds/index.html>, and <www.gpoaccess.gov/precedents/cannon/index.html>.*)

Cannon's Procedure in the House of Representatives

This document is largely of historical interest, as much of it is no longer relevant to contemporary practice.

Cannon's Procedure, published in 1963, is a one-volume summary of the major precedents presented in *Hinds' and Cannon's Precedents*, with a few additional precedents from 1936 to 1963. The document also contains examples of floor dialogue or specific parliamentary actions.

This volume is out of print. Copies are available for reference at the House Legislative Resource Center, B-106 Cannon House Office Building.

§12.50 Official Rules Publications of the Senate
Senate Manual

The Senate is the chamber of individual members' rights, and the relative brevity of its rules compared with those of the House of Representatives reflects this fact. The *Senate Manual* contains the Senate's rules, the *standing orders* that function like rules, and additional rules and precedents covering specific activities such as conferences and impeachment trials. Unlike the House, the Senate does not organize itself by adopting rules at the beginning of each new Congress. Since a quorum of the Senate is always serving (only one-third of the Senate is up for election every two years), the Senate views itself as a "continuing body." The Senate adopts standing orders and temporary resolutions to modify the operation of its rules for the duration of a Congress or for a longer period. In addition, Senate precedents guide the Senate and provide an evolving interpretation by the Senate of the operation of its rules.

The *Senate Manual* also contains are excerpts from laws affecting the Senate and the texts of four historical documents—the Declaration of Independence, the Articles of Confederation, the Ordinance of 1787 (the Northwest Ordinance), and the Constitution. Extensive historical tables on the Senate, the executive, the Supreme Court, elections, and the states form a unique, convenient reference in themselves. The *Senate Manual* is generally printed once during each Congress. The most recent *Senate Manual* is S. Doc. 107-1. *(Available online through GPO Access at <www.gpoaccess.gov/smanual/index.html>.)*

Standing Rules of the Senate

The *Standing Rules of the Senate* is a document, issued by the Senate Committee on Rules and Administration, that contains only the standing rules. It was last issued in the 106th Congress as S. Doc. 106-15. Footnotes in this document show changes from 1979, when the most recent extensive revision of the standing rules was made, to 1999. *(Available online at <http://rules.senate.gov/senaterules>.)*

Senate Procedure (Riddick's)

Published in 1992, this single volume presents significant Senate precedents established from 1883 to 1992. Prepared by Floyd Riddick, a former Senate parliamentarian, and updated by Alan Frumin, the current parliamentarian, the document is organized around topics presented in alphabetical order. For each topic there is a review of the general principles governing a procedure, the text of the relevant standing rule, and, where appropriate, citations to the *Congressional Record* or other official publication pages. An extensive index is one of the document's useful features.

All Senate offices were provided with copies of this document. It is otherwise out of print but is available in library collections. *(Available online at <www.gpoaccess.gov/riddick/index.html>.)*

12

Impeachment

A number of Senate documents on Senate impeachment procedure, including relevant *Congressional Record* pages, have been cumulated on GPO Access. Two of the most important documents appearing there are S. Doc. 99-33, *Procedure and Guidelines for Impeachment Trials in the U.S. Senate,* and S. Doc. 106-2, *Impeachment of President William Jefferson Clinton, Constitutional Provisions; Rules of Procedure and Practice in the Senate When Sitting on Impeachment Trials; Articles of Impeachment Against President William Jefferson Clinton; President Clinton's Answer; and Replication of the House of Representatives. (Available at GPO Access at <www.gpo access.gov/serialset/cdocuments/106cat2.html>.)*

§ 12.60 Other Congressional Sources of Information on Rules and Procedures
Enactment of a Law

This publication, prepared by the Senate parliamentarian, describes a typical day in the Senate, explaining in lay terms Senate procedure, both in committee and on the floor. Descriptions of the functions of Senate officials are also provided. *(Available online at THOMAS, <http://thomas.loc.gov/home/enactment/enactlawtoc.html>.)*

How Our Laws Are Made

Prepared by the House parliamentarian, this document is intended for the non-specialist and explains the legislative process, from the drafting of legislation to final approval and presidential action. It presents information on both House and Senate procedure, although it focuses primarily on the House. Sample documents that accompany each stage of the process are presented in the back of the publication.

A printed edition exists as H. Doc. 108-93. *(Available online at THOMAS, <http://thomas. loc.gov/home/lawsmade.toc.html>.)*

Our American Government

Prepared by the Congressional Research Service under the auspices of the House Administration Committee, this document uses a question-and-answer format to explain the three branches of the national government and the electoral process. It contains other useful information, such as a table of party control of the two houses of Congress and a glossary of legislative terminology. It is available in print as H. Doc. 106-216. *(Available online at GPO Access with Miscellaneous House Publications at <http://frwebgate.access.gpo.gov/cgi-bin/getdoc. cgi?dbname=106_cong_documents&docid=f:hd216.pdf>.)*

§ 12.61

Byrd and Dole
Historical Documents

Historical Almanac of the United States Senate

During the 100th Congress, Senator Bob Dole delivered a series of *Bicentennial Minutes*, short speeches made on the Senate floor. These speeches addressed both substantive and anecdotal aspects of Senate history. Every day the Senate was in session, from January 6, 1987, until the adjournment in 1988, Senator Dole spoke on a discrete topic, delivering speeches on approximately 300 different subjects.

From the first entry in the volume, cited as *June 7, 1787, Method of Senatorial Election Decided*, to the last, cited as *April 6, 1989, Senate Celebrates Its 200th Anniversary*, the volume provides a wealth of information on people and events in the Senate's history.

These bicentennial minutes were compiled under the auspices of the Commission on the Bicentennial of the Senate and published as S. Doc. 100-35. The volume is available from the Government Printing Office.

Senate, 1789–1989

This four-volume history of aspects of the Senate, prepared by Senator Robert Byrd, is commonly referred to as the Byrd books. Volumes I and II are subtitled *Addresses on the History of the United States Senate*. Volume I takes a chronological approach to the Senate's history; Volume II takes a topical approach. Volume III contains *Classic Speeches, 1830–1993,* and Volume IV contains *Historical Statistics, 1789–1992*. Taken together, the Byrd history is rich in historical detail and the flavor and evolution of the life of the nation and the Senate over a 200-year period.

Compiled under the auspices of the Commission on the Bicentennial of the Senate, the volumes were published as S. Doc. 100-20. They are available from the Government Printing Office.

200 Notable Days:
Senate Stories, 1987 to 2002

A complementary volume to the Dole and Byrd Senate histories is this book by Senate Historian Richard A. Baker. For over a decade, Baker has researched and written vignettes from the Senate's history; these glimpses of the Senate have been called "historical minutes." This volume collects 200 of these essays. As noted on the Senate's web site: "Read collectively, these stories reveal a larger picture about the uniqueness of the Senate as an institution, providing readers with a more complete image of the modern Senate, and advancing Dr. Baker's belief that to understand today's Senate, one must explore this institution's rich history." *200 Notable Days* was prepared by the Senate historian under the direction of the secretary of the Senate. Available online, at *<www.gpoaccess.gov/congress/senate/notabledays/index.html>*, and for purchase in print from the Government Printing Office.

12

Constitution of the United States

Congress has authorized the printing of the Constitution of the United States in several formats. *The Constitution of the United States of America as Amended, Unratified Amendments, Analytical Index* (H. Doc. 108-95) is very useful because the analytical index quickly guides the reader to any phrase in the Constitution. *The Constitution of the United States and the Declaration of Independence* is available in print as S. Doc. 109-17.

U.S. Constitution, Analysis and Interpretation, 2002 Edition (S. Doc.108-17), and 2004 Supplement (S. Doc. 108-19), is a massive text maintained by the Congressional Research Service, that provides analysis of each clause of the Constitution. The analysis includes examinations of Supreme Court cases and footnotes to case law, scholarly commentary, historical documents, and other sources. *(All of these documents are available online at GPO Access at <www.gpoaccess.gov/constitution>.)*

Floor Procedures in the
U.S. House of Representatives

Commonly referred to as the *Floor Manual* or the *Republican Floor Manual* (because it was originally prepared by Republican members in the early 1980s), this short document describes the daily order of business in the House and provides references to applicable House rules. Sample language is also provided for selected actions. It is written in "user-friendly" English. An abridged dictionary of parliamentary terms is provided. *(Available online at the House Rules Committee web site, <www.rules.house.gov/archives/floor_man.htm>, or in print from the House Committee on Rules.)*

Legislative Manual

Several committees have issued their own legislative manuals. The manuals provide, from the perspective of each committee, an explanation of the legislative process with a sample of the legislative documents generated at each stage of the process. Each document can be obtained from the issuing committee.

Treaties and Other International Agreements:
The Role of the United States Senate

Treaties and Other International Agreements: The Role of the United States Senate (S. Prt. 106-71) provides information about the steps involved in making treaties and executive agreements. It covers in detail the procedures that govern Senate consideration of treaties and other international agreements. It is available from the Senate Committee on Foreign Relations. *(Available online at <www.access.gpo.gov/congress/senate/senate11cp106.html>.)*

§12.70 Party Publications

Each party in each chamber generates a series of documents generally issued only to each party's members, although several are made available to the public. Some of these publications address party perspectives on legislative issues; others address upcoming floor schedules. Some documents are provided in paper form only, some are sent by email to subscribers, and some are placed on party web sites.

Rules of Party Caucus/Conference

Each party in each chamber adopts rules governing the work of its caucus or conference. These rules are usually adopted by the party members at the early organization meetings held after the election but before the swearing in of the new Congress. *(See § 7.30, Early Organization Meetings.)* The rules cover such topics as the selection of party leaders and the organization of the party leadership, the committee assignment process, and the work of the party organization. Majority-party rules also often affect selected floor procedures. Copies of party rules are generally available only to a caucus's or conference's members.

Whip Advisories and Whip Notices

Each party in each chamber provides to its members *whip notices, whip alerts, legislative alerts*, or *whip advisories*. Prepared by the party whip, each notice provides information on the anticipated schedule for the day, week, or longer period.

A daily whip notice is distributed before the daily convening of a chamber and usually states the time the chamber convenes, the legislation that is scheduled, how the legislation is expected to be considered on the floor, and, if available, the time the chamber will finish its business that day.

A weekly whip notice is traditionally provided at the conclusion of a week's work and addresses the agenda for the following week. (The paper copies of weekly whip notices distributed to member offices are accompanied by copies of the measures scheduled for floor action and committee reports on those measures.) Oftentimes, a monthly calendar is prepared so members may anticipate the days on which votes are scheduled and periods when the chamber will not be in session.

The House Democratic whip's notices are available online at *<http://majoritywhip.gov>*. The House Republican whip's notices are available online at *<http://republicanwhip.house.gov>*.

The Senate floor schedule is available at *<http://senate.gov>*.

Legislative Issue Documents

Each party in each chamber prepares a variety of documents—with varying degrees of depth—that address the substantive issues associated with upcoming legislation. These documents can be found at chamber leaders' and party organizations' web sites:

12

House Democrats:
- *Speaker,* <http://speaker.house.gov>
- *Majority Leader,* <http://majorityleader.gov>
- *Majority Whip,* <http://majoritywhip.gov>
- *Democratic Caucus,* <www.dems.gov>

House Republicans:
- *Minority Leader,* <http://republicanleader.house.gov>
- *Minority Whip,* <http://republicanwhip.house.gov>
- *Republican Conference,* <http://gop.gov>
- *Republican Policy Committee,* <http://policy.house.gov>

Senate Democrats:
- *Majority Leader,* <http://reid.senate.gov>
- *Assistant Majority Leader,* <http://durbin.senate.gov>
- *Democratic Conference,* <http://democrats.senate.gov>
- *Democratic Policy Committee,* <http://democrats.senate.gov/dpc>

Senate Republicans:
- *Minority Leader,* <http://mcconnell.senate.gov>
- *Assistant Minority Leader,* <http://lott.senate.gov>
- *Republican Conference,* <http://src.senate.gov/public>
- *Republican Policy Committee,* <http://rpc.senate.gov>

Cloakroom Recordings

Each party in each chamber operates cloakroom recordings for members. Each cloakroom has one telephone line that provides recorded information about the upcoming schedule. A second taped message details the results of votes, ongoing proceedings, summaries of recent actions, and the times of adjournment and convening of the next session. Each of the four cloakrooms operates a *hot line* that automatically notifies members through pagers whenever a major floor action is imminent or, when the bells ring for a vote, the subject of that vote. Members can also call cloakroom staff to ask about pending and anticipated action in the chamber.

The public can obtain the same taped information that is provided to members by calling the following numbers:
- *House Democratic Cloakroom: 202-225-1600 for advance schedule and 202-225-7400 for current proceedings*
- *House Republican Cloakroom: 202-225-2020 for advance schedule and 202-225-7430 for current proceedings*
- *Senate Democratic Cloakroom: 202-224-8541*
- *Senate Republican Cloakroom: 202-224-8601*

§12.80 Administrative Documents

In addition to the manuals of rules and precedents and the procedural documents prepared by Congress, numerous other publications are integral to understanding Congress. Prepared by the historian's office or the administrative personnel in each chamber, these documents address not the rules but the management of Congress and information about members who have served. (*See § 12.81, Selected Congressional Documents about Members of Congress.*)

Audit of the Financial Statements for the Year Ended December 31, 2005

Prepared by the House inspector general, this volume provides the results of the 2005 audit of the House (*Report No. 06-HOC-08*), mandated by the House Administration Committee. (*Available online along with other inspector general reports at the House inspector general's web site,* <www.house.gov/IG>.)

Statement of Disbursements of the House and Report of the Secretary of the Senate

The quarterly *Statement of Disbursements of the House* and the semiannual *Report of the Secretary of the Senate* provide data on staff salaries and committee expenses during the reporting period. In addition, *Expenditure Authorizations for Senate Committees*, a committee print prepared by the Senate Committee on Rules and Administration, describes existing staffing and budgeting regulations, and provides historical data on committee staffs and budgets. (The Statement of Disbursements of the House was formerly prepared by the clerk of the House, called the *Report of the Clerk of the House*, and commonly referred to as the *Clerk's Report*.)

The most recent *Statement of Disbursements of the House*, H. Doc. 110-9, covered the period April to June 2006. The most recent *Report of the Secretary of the Senate*, S. Doc. 109-014, covered the period April 1, 2006, to September 30, 2006.

Elections, Expulsion and Censure Cases, 1793–1990, United States Senate

Prepared by the Senate Historical Office under the direction of the secretary of the Senate, this compilation summarizes all ethics cases considered by the Senate from 1793 to 1990. Printed as S. Doc. 103-33, it is for sale by the Government Printing Office (GPO).

Ethics Manuals of the House and Senate

The House Committee on Standards of Official Conduct and the Senate Ethics Committee publish ethics manuals for their members. The House *Ethics Manual for Members, Officers, and Employees of the U.S. House of Representatives* details the Code of Official Conduct and addresses general ethics standards for members and staff. The Senate *Ethics Manual* addresses the Senate Code of Conduct and provides a compilation of interpretive rulings issued by the

12

§ 12.81

Selected Congressional Documents about Members of Congress

Biographical Directory of the United States Congress

This directory provides individual biographies of everyone who ever served in Congress. It is updated online through the 110th Congress. The online version is available at *<http://bioguide.congress.gov/ biosearch/biosearch.asp.>. (See also § 13.20, Directories.)*

Black Americans in Congress, 1870–1989

Prepared by the Office of the House Historian under the direction of the Commission on the Bicentenary of the U.S. House of Representatives, this volume provides biographical essays on the lives of African-American representatives who served in the House and Senate from 1870 to 1989. The document was printed as H. Doc. 101-117.

The Cannon Centenary Conference: The Changing Nature of the Speakership

This volume contains the 2003 presentations made and papers written to commemorate the centenary of the speakership of Joseph Gurney Cannon, R-IL, perhaps the most powerful Speaker the House has ever known. The presentations examined the modern speakerships of Thomas P. O'Neill Jr., D-MA; James C. Wright Jr., D-TX; Thomas S. Foley, D-WA; and Newt Gingrich, R-GA. Speaker O'Neill is deceased, but Speakers Wright, Foley, Gingrich, and then-sitting Speaker J. Dennis Hastert, R-IL, participated in the proceedings. The proceedings were printed as H. Doc. 108-204.

Guide to the Research Collections of Former Members of the U.S. House of Representatives, 1789–1987

This guide presents a listing of archival repositories housing the papers of former members, related collections, and oral history interviews. It was printed as H. Doc. 100-171. Entries in this volume are appended to the appropriate representatives' biographies contained in the *Biographical Directory of the United States Congress*, listed above.

Guide to the Research Collections of Former Senators, 1789–1995

This guide presents a listing of archival repositories housing the papers of former senators, related collections, and oral history interviews. The collections of 1,658 of the 1,726 senators who served before January 3, 1995, are included, although the document does contain an entry for all 1,726 senators. Printed as S. Doc. 103-35 and prepared under the direction of the secretary of the Senate by the Senate Historical Office, the guide is available for sale by the Government Printing Office. Entries in this volume are appended to the appropriate senators' biographies contained in the *Biographical Directory of the United States Congress*, listed above.

Hispanic Americans in Congress, 1822–1995

Prepared under the direction of the Joint Committee on Printing and the Hispanic Division of the Library of Congress, this volume provides biographical essays on the lives of Hispanic members who served in the House and Senate from 1822 to 1995. The document was printed as H. Doc. 325. *(Available online at <www.loc.gov/rr/hispanic/congress>.)*

Continued on page 499

§ *12.81 (continued)*

History of the United States Senate Republican Policy Committee, 1947–1997

Prepared by the Senate Historical Office, this compilation provides a narrative history of the Republican Policy Committee. Appendices identify senators who served as Policy Committee chairs and those who served as Republican leaders. Also identified are staff directors of the Policy Committee. It was printed as S. Doc. 105-5 and is available online at GPO Access, *<www.access. gpo.gov/congress/senate/repub_ policy>*.

Senators of the United States, A Historical Bibliography, 1789–1995

This volume is a compilation of works by and about senators from 1789 to 1995. It presents information on approximately 1,164 senators. Prepared by the Senate Historical Office under the direction of the secretary of the Senate, the volume was printed as S. Doc. 103-34. Entries in this volume are appended to the appropriate senators' biographies contained in the *Biographical Directory of the United States Congress*, listed above.

Vice Presidents of the United States, 1789–1993

This volume presents short biographical essays on vice presidents who served from 1789 to 1993. It was printed as S. Doc. 104-26. *(Available online at <www.senate.gov/artandhistory/history/common/ briefing/Vice_President.htm>.)*

Women in Congress, 1917–2006

Prepared by the Office of History and Preservation under the direction of the clerk of the House, this volume provides biographical essays on the lives of the 230 women representatives and senators who served during the period covered in the study. The document was printed as H. Doc. 108-233. *(A version of this publication is available online at <http://womenincongress.house.gov>.)*

Senate Ethics Committee. *(The House Ethics Manual is available online at <www.house.gov/ ethics>. The Senate Ethics Manual is printed as S. Pub. 106-001, and is available online at the Senate Ethics Committee's web site at <http://ethics.senate.gov>.)*

Financial Disclosure Forms

Members of Congress and senior government officials are required to file financial disclosure forms. The statements members submit are compiled by their respective chambers and printed as House and Senate documents. The 2003 House compilation was printed in three volumes as H. Doc. 108-205. The House disclosure forms are on optical disk and available for inspection at the Legislative Resource Center, B-106 Cannon House Office Building. An individual requesting access to the records must complete a form providing his or her name, address, and occupation, before reviewing the compilation. Senate financial disclosure forms are available in the Senate Public Records Office, SH-232 Hart Senate Office Building.

12

Guide to the Records of the United States House of Representatives at the National Archives, 1789–1989, Bicentennial Edition

This reference work identifies the records of the House and its committees from 1789 to 1989, which are now located at the National Archives. Prepared by the House historian and updated by the clerk of the House, it was originally printed as H. Doc. 100-245. *(An online version is available at <http://archives.gov/legislative/finding-aids>.)*

Guide to the Records of the United States Senate at the National Archives, 1789–1989, Bicentennial Edition

This reference work, located at the National Archives, identifies the records of the Senate and its committees from 1789 to 1989. It was printed as S. Doc. 100-42 *(<http://archives.gov/legislative/finding-aids>).*

House Smart: House Reference Guide to Information and Services

Prepared by the chief administrative officer (CAO) of the House, *House Smart* is a summary of services provided to member offices. Each entry has a brief summary of the service provided; the location, phone and fax numbers, and hours of operation of the House offices that provide the service; and, when available, a web site that offers additional information. *House Smart* is provided to each member's office, and a limited number of additional copies are available for public distribution from the CAO, by calling 202-225-6900.

Members' Congressional Handbook: Regulations Governing the Members' Representational Allowance of the U.S. House of Representatives

This publication, prepared by the Committee on House Administration, provides nuts-and-bolts information about the official expenses that may be incurred to support a member's legislative and representational duties. It details the regulations promulgated by the House Administration Committee in the administration of members' accounts. *New Member Fact Sheets*, adapted from the handbook, provide one-page overviews of some of the information; these are given to incoming freshmen representatives at early organization meetings. *(An extensive publication is provided to member offices; a summary version is available from the Committee on House Administration web site, <http://cha.house.gov>.)*

Committees' Congressional Handbook:
Regulations Governing the Expenditure of
Committee Funds of the U. S. House of Representatives

A counterpart publication to the *Members' Congressional Handbook*, prepared by the Committee on House Administration, guides committees in the administration of their accounts. *(Online version available from the Committee on House Administration web site, <http://cha.house. gov>.)*

Regulations on the Use of the Congressional
Frank by Members of the House of Representatives

This document, prepared by the House Commission on Congressional Mailing Standards, identifies rules pertaining to the use of the *congressional frank*. A June 1998 version is available from the Committee on House Administration. *(Available online from the Committee on House Administration web site, <http://cha.house.gov>.)*

U.S. Senate Handbook, 2006

Prepared by the Senate Committee on Rules and Administration, the *U.S. Senate Handbook* summarizes federal law, Senate rules, and Senate practices regarding the administration, financial management, information management, constituent services, and legislative activity of Senate offices. Written by Senate staff with responsibilities for these activities, the handbook is a good resource for an overview of the work in a Senate office. *(Available from the Committee on Rules and Administration. The Senate Handbook is available online, but only to Senate offices.)*

12

Chapter Thirteen

Legislative Research:
Private and Government Information Providers

Contributing Author
Peggy Garvin

Analysis

13

§13.00 Introduction

Chapters Eleven and Twelve identified the congressional documents created in the course of the legislative process, and the chamber, party, and administrative documents closely related to the legislative process. This chapter guides the reader to other, complementary information sources for researching Congress, policy, and legislative topics.

The following sections identify a selection of publishers and products—databases, directories, magazines, news wires, and search engines—commonly relied on in offices and libraries all around Washington. This selection can be used as a guide for setting up the information system one needs, whether it be for one's office shelf, a small library, or an organized set of bookmarks or favorites on one's web browser.

The Washington Information Scene

The information needs of official Washington have always supported private publishing companies. The first versions of what became the *Congressional Record* were privately published. As government grew in the twentieth century, newsletter services appeared on the scene to digest and report the latest legislative and regulatory developments and to analyze them for businesses and investors. When commercial database services came into business in the 1970s, government information was some of the first to appear online. Now, with the ubiquity of the Internet, information about and recycled from the government is available for free or for fee from some of the same traditional print publishers as always, and from a sea of new sources.

The federal government itself is a major player in the Washington information scene. The government publishes legal material, research, statistics, and records of its own activities. Originally set up to handle congressional printing, the Government Printing Office (GPO) has long been the printer and distribution channel for documents from all branches of government, making documents available throughout the United States via a system of federal depository libraries. GPO's web site, GPO Access, also distributes documents online, and GPO reports that the overwhelming majority of government documents distributed to federal depository libraries are now available in electronic format. The web has made each government agency its own de facto publisher and distributor. Adding to the dynamics of this scene, private publishers readily take both printed and electronic government information, which is for the most part not copyright-protected, and reformat it to sell to those who need some value added to the government's version.

Nonprofit organizations, policy institutes, and academia also play a special role in the Washington information scene. These organizations generally fill niche information needs with their ideas, advocacy, and scholarship. Not bound to reach a large audience as some of the government and private publishers are, this sector can often provide more depth on a given topic. These organizations are usually free to provide much more in the way of editorial opinion and persuasive analysis. And almost all of these organizations can be counted on to

13

have a web site and to make some, if not many, of their writings available online. The latest development on this information scene is the emergence of serious news and political blogs published by individual citizens, policy groups, traditional media outlets, and even individual politicians or political candidates.

Making the Most of Online Information

Knowing how to use the tools is as important as knowing what they are. Gathering and filtering news and information is no less of a task than it has always been, but the shift to online services and information technology has put the spotlight on some specific skills. One can make the most of online information by following a few tips:

- Know how to search. Many researchers are comfortable typing in a word or two in a search box and seeing what comes up. This is rarely the fastest or most effective approach to finding what one needs. *(See § 13.40 for specific tips.)*
- Know what you are searching. Is it a database of all committee reports, or just selected ones? Does the database have information from the past year, or from the past two weeks? Too often, assumptions are made that "everything" has been searched when, in fact, the database does not include everything.
- Evaluate information for accuracy, quality, and currency. Be an information skeptic. The proliferation of new information sources makes this particularly important, and even the best of tested sources can make mistakes with specific details. This tip applies to all information, of course, not just online sources.
- Be selective. Information overload occurs when one spends too much time managing information that is duplicative or of marginal value. Choose information sources that provide the scope, format, or indexing you need.
- Have some awareness of copyright law. Digital formats make copying and mass distribution easy, but private publishers still value their copyright. Most premium online services will make it clear to their customers what is and is not allowed.

Of course, not all information is online. Getting certain information still requires a personal visit to a library or records center and, as has been said elsewhere in the *Deskbook*, personal contacts can provide some of the most valuable information.

Information Sources

The information sources described in this chapter fill some needs not met by the legislative documents discussed earlier. They may make the legislative documents easier to use. They explain the "why" behind the documents. They anticipate future actions or compile information from the past. They report on the institution of Congress and on processes outside of official floor and committee action. These resources will be of use to one when researching a new issue, keeping abreast of legislative developments, following popular and editorial opinion on a topic, researching the people and institutions involved, or simply tracking down facts and phone numbers. Those people and phone numbers are important. Despite the value of written or otherwise recorded information, people are still some of the most important information resources in official Washington.

§13.10 Legislative-Branch Agencies and Offices

A number of agencies and offices within the legislative branch assist Congress in its lawmaking, representational, and administrative roles. Some, like the Congressional Research Service, work exclusively for Congress. Others, such as the Government Accountability Office, make many of their work products available directly to the public, although the release of some work might be delayed to give a committee or members a first chance to read or release it. Following is a selection of some of the most important legislative branch agencies and offices, and highlights of their publicly available information.

Architect of the Capitol

(<www.aoc.gov>)

Rich in historical information, the Architect of the Capitol (AOC) web site is also a good source for updates on the ongoing Capitol Visitor Center construction project. Additional content includes Capitol tour information and a map of the U.S. Capitol complex.

(For more information on the AOC, see § 5.121.)

(For more information on Capitol Hill congressional buildings, see § 6.20.)

Clerk of the House

(<http://clerk.house.gov>)

The clerk's multifaceted legislative and quasi-legislative responsibilities within the House make this office very important. The clerk's office manages the House voting system and posts roll-call floor votes on its web site. The online list of roll-call votes is a simple reverse chronological listing, with links to the party breakdown and individual yeas and nays. The clerk's office also publishes the "House Calendar" and the official member and committee directories, and posts these documents on its web site. *(For more information on the House Calendar, see § 12.20.)*

The clerk's office administers the House public disclosure system for lobbyist registration and members' financial activities. It posts the blank lobbyist forms online, but researchers must visit the Legislative Resource Center in B-106 of the Cannon House Office Building to view the lobbyist and member filings. These include financial disclosure, candidates' campaign reports, materials approved for mass mailing under the congressional franking privilege, members' and staffers' foreign travel reports, members' and staffers' gift and travel filings, and legal expense fund disclosures. (For campaign finance reports, the clerk's web site refers researchers to the web site for the Federal Election Commission; see their entry in the Information Sources section below.) It is important to note that the Senate does make lobbyist filings available online at <*http://sopr.senate.gov*>. Often researchers will check the Senate filings to find information about a House lobbyist since lobbyists will commonly register with both chambers. See the secretary of the Senate listing below for more information.

The clerk's site also provides such useful information as the current party alignment count and current House vacancies, current committee assignments, downloadable mailing labels for members of the House, congressional election results, and data on previous Congresses.

(For additional information on the Clerk of the House, see § 5.110, Administrative Offices of the House.)

Congressional Budget Office

(<www.cbo.gov>)

The Congressional Budget Office (CBO) is known for its budget analyses, budget projections, and economic forecasts; these reports are available on its web site. The congressional budget committees use CBO's projections to develop their annual budget resolutions, and assumptions about the budget and economy factor into other CBO analyses.

While CBO is most concerned with the overall budget picture, its cost estimate documents provide detail on specific pieces of legislation. For most bills reported by a committee, CBO is required to produce a cost estimate and report on how the bill would affect federal spending and revenues in the future. These cost estimates feed into CBO's scorekeeping system, which continually monitors the total budgetary effect of those bills. The cost estimates are available on the CBO web site, and can provide additional insight into a bill.

To stay on top of CBO activity, one may wish to use their web site to sign up for the New-Document Notification email alert service.

(For additional information on CBO, see § 5.130, Legislative Branch Support Agencies.)

Congressional Research Service

(Use <www.loc.gov/crsinfo> for general information and CRS employment news.)
(For information on the availability of CRS reports, see the article "CRS Reports"
by Stephen Young at <www.llrx.com/features/crsreports.htm> and the
Open CRS web site at <www.opencrs.com>.)

The Congressional Research Service (CRS) is the component of the Library of Congress that works strictly for Congress, providing nonpartisan policy analysis. A full collection of CRS reports is not publicly available on CRS or congressional web sites. The public can obtain CRS reports through their representatives in Congress, or can use one of the free or pay services (described in the "CRS Reports" article cited above) that have sprung up to meet the demand for these reports.

CRS also contributes summaries of legislation and additional information to the THOMAS legislative database (<*http://thomas.loc.gov*>).

Government Accountability Office

(<www.gao.gov>)

Among its statutory duties, the Government Accountability Office (GAO) is best known publicly for its performance of independent audits and evaluations of government agencies, programs, and other activities. Its reports and its officials' testimony and briefings, often undertaken at the request of a committee chair or ranking minority member, are influential in the legislative process and the conduct of oversight. Testimony and completed reports (unless classified) are quickly made available to the public in print and through GAO's web site, although GAO may delay release of a report for up to thirty days if a congressional requester asks for a delay.

The comptroller general, the head of GAO, is also assigned statutory duties to render decisions and opinions in specific areas of federal law. For example, under the Congressional Review Act *(5 U.S.C. § 801 et seq.)*, the comptroller general reports to the committees of jurisdiction of both houses of Congress on major rules proposed by federal agencies. Decisions and opinions of the comptroller general are available through GAO's web site.

Lists and finding aids on the web site assist in identifying useful reports and other GAO documents. GAO also provides notices of newly released reports and testimony via email or RSS feed.

(For additional information on GAO, see § 5.130, Legislative-Branch Support Agencies.)

Government Printing Office

(<www.gpo.gov>)

(The GPO Access <www.gpoaccess.gov> web site provides access to government information.)
(Go to <www.gpoaccess.gov/legislative.html> for direct access to congressional documents.)
The Government Printing Office (GPO), in Title 44 of the U.S. Code, is charged with printing, binding, and electronic information dissemination for Congress, as well as for the president and federal agencies. GPO prints the *Congressional Record* and the *Federal Register* and makes both publications available online.

The GPO Access web site is the primary host for online versions of congressional documents. It includes the *Congressional Record*, from 1994 forward; all versions of legislation, from the 103rd Congress (1993-1994) forward; and public and private laws, from the 104th Congress (1995-1996) forward. The Library of Congress THOMAS web service *(<http://thomas.loc.gov>)* links to GPO Access for the full text of legislation and public laws in PDF format.

Many publishers and commercial online services buy content like the *Congressional Record* or the *Federal Register* from GPO to index and reformat for their systems. Because GPO is the source, GPO will often have the information online first; however, other services often have more powerful searching and more convenient features than what GPO offers.

GPO distributes copies of government documents to over 1,000 federal depository libraries across the United States. Located within public, university, and other libraries, these depository collections allow local, public access to current and historical documents that may not be available on the Internet and to several online databases that are not freely available. The depository libraries are staffed with librarians experienced in using these resources. GPO also maintains an online bookstore for purchasing congressional and other government documents.

Law Library of Congress

(<www.loc.gov/law>)
(For the Law Library's guide to U.S. legislative sources,
see <www.loc.gov/law/guide/uscong.html>.)
(Historical congressional documents are available at the Law Library's
A Century of Lawmaking site, <http://memory.loc.gov/ammem/amlaw>.)

The collection of the Law Library of Congress includes both domestic and foreign legal materials. A user of the Law Library's public reading room on the second floor of the Library of Congress Madison Building (*see Library of Congress, in this section*) will find the full range of congressional materials, and federal and state statutory and administrative materials, court decisions, legal research treatises and aids, and Supreme Court records and briefs.

The Law Library web site includes a *Guide to Law Online* (*<www.loc.gov/law/guide>*) to help researchers find state, national, and international materials on the Internet. A web page titled "Compilations and Other Law-Related Congressional Committee Prints" (*<www.loc.gov/law/guide/compilations.html>*) links to publications such as the House Ways and Means Committee's *Overview and Compilation of U.S. Trade Statutes.*

The Library of Congress has digitized many historical congressional documents. The Law Library's site links to the project *A Century of Lawmaking for a New Nation: U.S. Congressional Documents and Debates, 1774-1875,* an excellent resource for 18th and 19th century laws and documents.

Members of Congress draw on the Law Library for its foreign legal expertise. Public users of the reading room and web site will also find assistance in this area.

Library of Congress

(<www.loc.gov>) *(All sites below are available through the library's home page.)*
(To search the library's catalog, <http://catalog.loc.gov>.)
(To identify Internet newspaper, periodical, and government resources,
<www.lcweb.loc.gov/rr/news/othint.html>.)
(To identify Internet resources on the legislative branch of the
federal government, <http://thomas.loc.gov/links>.)
(To identify Internet resources on the executive branch of the
federal government, <www.loc.gov/rr/news/fedgov.html>.)
(To identify Internet resources on the judicial branch of the
federal government, <www.loc.gov/law/guide/usjudic.html>.)

The Library of Congress web site reflects the size and complexity of the library itself. However, there are easily accessible resources on the site that a legislative affairs specialist may want in his or her set of bookmarks or favorites. Using the site can be an end in itself, or good preparation before actually visiting the library.

Aside from its link to the THOMAS legislative database, much of the topical information on the site is provided on pages hosted by the library's specialized reading rooms or research centers. In addition to the key resources listed above, researchers can find selected Internet resources in the fields of science, business, genealogy, and general reference.

Other material on the reading room sites will help one understand the nature of the library's collections and services before one visits. Personal visits can be time consuming; research at the library is most justified when the material one needs cannot be found elsewhere. Library users must first obtain a library identification card, available in LM-140 Madison Library of Congress Building, 101 Independence Avenue, SE. *(Information on this procedure and the privileges a card provides are explained on the web site, at <www.loc.gov/rr/security/readerreg.html>.)* In addition to the Law Library *(see separate entry, above)*, the government affairs professional might have most need for the materials available through the Newspaper and Current Periodicals Reading Room: current and retrospective newspapers; current periodicals; foreign government and international organization documents; and current serial publications of U.S. federal, state, and local governments, including a federal depository library collection.

The Library of Congress collections span many topics and formats, and are especially strong in American history and foreign language materials. The library does not focus on clinical medicine, handled by the National Library of Medicine, or on agricultural sciences, handled by the National Agricultural Library.

Office of the Law Revision Counsel

(<http://uscode.house.gov>)

The Office of the Law Revision Counsel, an office within the House, prepares and publishes the *United States Code*, which is a "consolidation and codification by subject matter of the general and permanent laws of the United States." This office maintains the U.S. Code, including classification tables for recently enacted laws, online. GPO Access also carries the Code online at *<www.gpoaccess.gov/uscode/index.html>*, and GPO sells the Code in printed, bound volumes.

While the Law Revision Counsel is the official source of the Code, commercial publishers offer print and online versions with annotations and other features that make it easier to use and a much more powerful legal research tool. A free version is also maintained by Cornell University's Legal Information Institute and is available online at *<www.law.cornell.edu/uscode>*.

(For a more complete explanation of the U.S. Code, see § 11.50, Laws and Their Implementation by the Executive.)

13

Secretary of the Senate

(See <www.senate.gov/artandhistory/history/common/briefing/secretary_senate.htm>
for information about the office and its functions.)

(See <www.senate.gov/pagelayout/legislative/one_item_and_teasers/opr.htm>
for the public records information the office maintains.)

The secretary of the Senate has responsibilities in the areas of legislation and public records, and in the financial and administrative realms. The parliamentarian, bill clerks, reporters of debates, Disbursing Office, Security Office, Public Records Office, curator, Senate Historical Office, library, documents, and other functions all fall under the Office of the Secretary of the Senate. More information on the office is provided in the Art and History section of the Senate web site, under People.

Information on public records available through the Secretary of the Senate Office is given at the web address cited above. The office provides both lobby disclosure forms and scanned copies of the filings for 1998 forward. The scanned filings are also available directly at <http://sopr.senate.gov>. Researchers must go to the Office of Public Records in SH-232 Hart Building to view members' financial disclosure records, candidates' campaign reports, materials registered for mass mailing under the congressional franking privilege, members' and staffers' travel reports, and other public documents filed with the secretary. (For more Senate campaign finance information, see the web site for the Federal Election Commission listed in the Information Sources section below.)

(For additional information on the secretary of the Senate, see § 5.120, Administrative Offices of the Senate.)

§ 13.20 Directories

The following congressionally and commercially published directories are available in either print or electronic format. This list is by no means exhaustive. Additional publishers of print and online directories and other information products are listed in the next section, § 13.30.

Almanac of American Politics

(Available by purchase from <http://nationaljournal.com/about/almanac>.)

The *Almanac of American Politics* is published by National Journal every two years, and online updates are available for those who have purchased the book. It profiles members of Congress and the states and districts they represent. Purchasers of the book can access an online edition on the National Journal web site.

Biographical Directory of the United States Congress, 1774–Present

(<http://bioguide.congress.gov/biosearch/biosearch.asp>)

Both the House and Senate web sites link to this comprehensive collection of congressional biographies covering the Continental Congress forward. Each entry provides a brief biography, dates of congressional service and party affiliation, and information on related manuscripts collections or books. The *Biographical Directory* can be searched by name, state, party, year/Congress, or office held.

The directory is also available in a print edition, *Biographical Directory of the United States Congress, 1774-2005* (Washington, DC: Government Printing Office).

Congressional Directory

(Updated online at <www.gpoaccess.gov/cdirectory/index.html>.)

The Government Printing Office publishes a new edition of the official *Congressional Directory* every other year, for each new Congress. Unfortunately, it is often not available until well after the start of the congressional term. This directory, however, has so much valuable reference material beyond the congressional roster that each edition is worth having and keeping.

The first third of the *Congressional Directory* is dedicated to presenting biographies, office locations, and phone numbers for the members of each state's delegation. For House members, the entries include the zip codes and counties covered by their districts. This is followed by a table of congressional terms of service for the sitting senators and representatives. Other sections cover congressional committees (including committee assignments listed by member name), officers, boards, and commissions. The other major section of the book is a directory of executive and judicial branch offices, including regional offices and phone numbers. A set of basic congressional district maps at the back of the book is preceded by a listing of members of the House and Senate media galleries.

For those with an interest in congressional history and trivia, the *Congressional Directory* also includes a statistical section with lists covering the First Congress forward: dates for all sessions; joint sessions, joint meetings, and inaugurations; number of representatives per state after each decennial apportionment; times the Senate has sat as a Court of Impeachment; and presidents and vice presidents and the Congresses coincident with their terms.

Congressional Pictorial Directory

(<www.gpoaccess.gov/pictorial/index.html>)

At the beginning of each Congress, GPO publishes a pictorial directory of the new Congress. It is pocket-sized and inexpensive. However, members of Congress do not always choose current photographs of themselves to appear in it, and this directory lacks the enhanced information of privately published directories.

Congressional Staff Directory

(Available from <http://csd.cq.com/scripts/index.cfm> by subscription.)

The *Congressional Staff Directory* is updated three times a year in print, and daily on its web version. This is the "granddaddy" of the major commercially published guides to members of Congress and congressional staff. It includes substantial biographical information for members as well as for key personal and legislative-branch staff. Each member and committee entry provides a directory of the staff serving them. The directory has maps and data on each state and congressional district.

Congressional Yellow Book

(Available from <www.leadershipdirectories.com> by subscription.)

The *Congressional Yellow Book* is available in print, updated quarterly, from Leadership Directories Inc. It provides the standard member and committee directory information, and puts an emphasis on identifying staff and their key issue responsibilities. It includes helpful information on caucuses and member organizations, congressional leadership, and congressional agencies. The publisher has also launched a related web-based directory called *Congressional Leadership Directory Online* with additional information on Members and staff and features such as daily updates and formatted downloads. The *Congressional Yellow Book* is also available online, updated daily, as part of a much larger database called *Leadership Libraries*.

Politics in America

(Available from CQ Press Online Bookstore, <www.cqpress.com>.)

Published every two years, *Politics in America* provides detailed profiles of members and of the state or district they represent. These profiles include demographic, business, and election information. An online edition available from CQ Press includes the four most recent editions of the book. (CQ.com, described in the Information Sources section below, also carries the current version of the member profiles from *Politics in America*.)

The United States Government Manual

(Available online at <www.gpoaccess.gov/gmanual>.)

The *United States Government Manual* is an annual, official, government-wide directory. The manual identifies the statutory authority and describes principal units and functions for each legislative, executive, or judicial office. It also has sections on quasi-official agencies, selected multilateral and bilateral organizations, and federal boards, commissions, and committees. For those tracking policy and law back through any period of time, the *Government Manual* has a section documenting federal executive agencies terminated, transferred, or changed in name since March 4, 1933. The *Government Manual* also features organization charts for Congress, the judiciary, the White House, and each federal department or independent agency.

The *Government Manual* is compiled by the Office of the Federal Register within the National Archives and Records Administration. It is printed, sold, and made available online by the Government Printing Office.

U.S. Congressional Bibliographies

(<www.lib.ncsu.edu/congbibs>)

This specialized resource is provided for free by the North Carolina State University Library. The web site indexes congressional committee meetings from 1983 to the present. It can be useful in finding witness names and tracking all meetings information.

United States House of Representatives Telephone Directory
United States Senate Telephone Directory

(Use the online GPO Bookstore <http://bookstore.gpo.gov> to locate current edition information.)

When these congressional telephone directories appear in print from the Government Printing Office, they are a recommended supplement to any commercial directory of Congress. They include staff listings and also provide good coverage of congressional administrative offices. The telephone directories are distributed to congressional offices and are available for purchase through GPO's U.S. Government Online Bookstore. The directories are updated several times in the course of a Congress.

Washington Information Directory

(Available for purchase from <www.cqpress.com>.)

This annual directory takes a subject approach to its listings. Congressional committees, federal agencies, and private organizations are arranged by the issue they cover, such as energy or health. Each entry contains address, telephone numbers, contact names, and a description of the office's role or expertise in the subject matter. The *Washington Information Directory* is published by Congressional Quarterly.

§13.30 Information Sources: A Selective List

A core group of public and private information providers, most of them located in the Washington, DC, area, publish and broadcast much of the information that government affairs professionals use every day. Rather than list the books, databases, programs, or other products they supply, we have listed the publishers themselves. Many are continually changing their product lines, or offer different levels of services for different types of audiences. Reflecting the dynamism the Internet has brought to the Washington information scene, this list includes selected web sites produced by individuals and other nontraditional publishers.

This list is not comprehensive and does not constitute recommendation of one source over any other. Selected products by each publisher or source are described; complete offerings can be obtained from the sources themselves. Please keep in mind that product offerings can change over time. Contact the publishers or their web site for the most current information.

Bernan

(<www.bernan.com>)

Phone: 301-459-2255 or 800-274-4447

Bernan publishes *The Almanac of the Unelected*, which profiles key committee staff, and *The United States Government Internet Manual*, a directory of government web sites and documents on the Internet. Bernan also distributes official documents from U.S. and international government agencies.

Bureau of National Affairs (BNA)

(<www.bna.com>)

Phone: 800-372-1033

BNA is known for its series of newsletters, available in print and on the web. Its emphasis is on legal and government news of interest to private industry. BNA's core newsletter, *Daily Report for Executives*, reports on key developments from Congress, federal regulatory agencies, and the White House. BNA also publishes *United States Law Week*, a news service reporting Supreme Court developments as well as significant legal cases and relevant legislative and regulatory actions nationwide.

C-SPAN

(<www.c-span.org>)

Phone: 202-737-3220

On cable television, only C-SPAN provides live coverage of all sessions of the House (C-SPAN) and Senate (C-SPAN2). C-SPAN3 airs live events, such as news briefings, along with American history features and other C-SPAN programs. C-SPAN programming also covers a selection of congressional committee meetings. C-SPAN's radio station is available at 90.1 FM in the Washington, DC, area. C-SPAN Alert, a free email service, can be set up to send one program schedules each weekday.

C-SPAN can also deliver video and radio through broadband Internet connections, making it easier to monitor Congress throughout the day. Its Capitol Hearings service, at *<www. capitolhearings.org>*, offers live streaming audio of all Senate hearings. Indexed and archived C-SPAN broadcasts are available through the video section of the C-SPAN Store (*<www. c-spanstore.org/shop>*). In 2007, C-SPAN clarified its copyright policy to state that, for broadcasts of House and Senate floor proceedings, C-SPAN "does not hold a copyright in that video coverage. That government-produced video is in the public domain which means that it belongs to the American people and may be used without restrictions of any kind" (*<www. cspan.org/about/copyright.asp>*). Other C-SPAN content is subject to copyright restrictions.

Campaigns & Elections Magazine

(<www.campaignline.com>)

Phone: 703-778-4028

Founded in 1980, this monthly magazine covers the business of politics. The print and full online editions are available only by paid subscription. Free online content includes lists of political events and blogs, and special sections on the politics of New Hampshire, Ohio, and South Carolina.

Capitol Advantage

(<www.capitoladvantage.com>)

Phone: 703-289-4670 or 800-659-8708

Capitol Advantage provides a number of services to assist organizations with their advocacy efforts. They publish the booklet *Congress At Your Fingertips*, a directory that can be customized with an organization's logo if ordered in bulk. The company's CapWiz service supplies an array of interactive public affairs content that other web and media services can lease for use in their own products. Congress.org—their free, public web site—has directories of national and local elected officials and news media contacts.

Carroll Publishing

(<www.carrollpub.com>)

Phone: 301-263-9800 or 800-336-4240

Carroll is known for its series of government executive and staff directories, including the *Federal Directory*, *Federal Regional Directory*, and directories covering state, municipal, and county levels of government. They are available in print and on the web.

Census Bureau

(<www.census.gov>)

Phone: 301-763-4636

The Department of Commerce Census Bureau traces its authority to the U.S. Constitution, which calls for a decennial enumeration of the population in order that "Representatives shall be apportioned among the several States according to their respective numbers" *(amend. XIV, sec. 2)*. Few other government agencies collect or report data by congressional district. The web site's section called *Fast Facts for Congress* (*<http://fastfacts.census.gov>*) links directly to data by congressional district, congressional district maps, and other demographic news and data of interest to Congress.

Aside from its well-known Census of Population and Housing, the bureau also reports data on the economy and specific industries; federal, state, and local government finances; federal expenditures and obligations to state and local governments; and foreign trade.

13

Center for Responsive Politics

(<www.opensecrets.org>)

Phone: 202-857-0044

The Center for Responsive Politics is a private, nonprofit organization interested in the influence of campaign contributions on politics and policy. Its Open Secrets web site offers a user-friendly interface to data from the Federal Elections Committee so that researchers can easily track who is giving and who is getting.

Columbia Books

(<www.columbiabooks.com>)

Phone: 202-464-1662

Columbia Books publishes a series of directories useful for identifying national "movers and shakers." Its lobbyist directory, *Washington Representatives*, is published twice a year. *Washington Representatives* is available in print and on the web through subscription to *Lobbyists.info*. The *National Trade and Professional Associations of the United States* directory is also available in print and online *(<www.columbiabooks.com/servlet/Detail?no=16>)*.

Congressional Management Foundation

(<www.cmfweb.org>)

Phone: 202-546-0100

The Congressional Management Foundation (CMF) is a nonprofit, nonpartisan organization specializing in congressional office management. In addition to training and consulting services, CMF publishes books such as *Setting Course: A Congressional Management Guide* and *Frontline Management: A Guide for Congressional District/State Offices*, and a series of reports on managing communications.

Congressional Quarterly

(<www.cq.com>)

Phone: 202-419-8500 or 800-432-2250

One company has always focused fully on Congress, and this is it. The *CQ Weekly* magazine, *CQ Today*, *House Action Reports*, *Politics In America* directory, and books such as *Guide to Congress* and *Congressional Staff Directory* make Congressional Quarterly an indispensable component of monitoring Congress (*see Directories, above*). Their subscription-based web services—including *CQ.com*, *CQ Budget Tracker*, and *PoliticalMoneyLine*—provide the tools and information for tracking legislative activity and campaign finance.

Federal Election Commission

(<www.fec.gov>)

Phone: 202-694-1100 or 800-424-9530

The Federal Election Commission (FEC) is the regulatory agency for campaign finance. Through its publications, web site, and public records office, the FEC offers access to campaign finance reports from candidates, reports from parties and PACs, and compilations and analyses of campaign finance data. The FEC also provides guidance on campaign finance regulations.

Federal News Service

(<www.fnsg.com>)

Phone: 202-347-1400 or 800-211-4020

Federal News Service got its start transcribing selected congressional hearings and speeches by government officials. These and other transcription services are available by subscription or upon request. Additional information services, such as online news clips, are also offered by subscription.

Gale

(<www.gale.cengage.com>)

Phone: 1-800-877-4253

Thomson Gale publishes the standard library reference *Encyclopedia of Associations* and its online version, *Associations Unlimited*.

GalleryWatch.com

(<www.gallerywatch.com>)

Phone: 202-248-5300

GalleryWatch.com combines searchable legislative and budget/appropriations databases with tracking and notification services. Subscribers can be notified of bill, committee, and floor actions via email or pager. GalleryWatch.com also partners with Penny Hill Press (*<www.pennyhill.com>*) to provide subscription access to reports from the Congressional Research Service. GalleryWatch.com is owned by Roll Call.

GovTrack.us

(<www.govtrack.us>)

GovTrack.us provides an alternative interface to legislative information and congressional documents made available through official government sites such as THOMAS (*<http://thomas.loc.gov>*) and GPO Access (*<www.gpoaccess.gov>*). The web site is nonpartisan and free of charge.

Hudson's Directory

(<http://hudsonsdirectory.com>)
Phone: 781-647-3200

Hudson's Washington News Media Contacts Directory has long been an important tool in identifying news organizations, the trade press, and reporters. Listings include news services and syndicates, specialized newsletters, radio and TV stations, columnists, freelance writers, and the reporters representing U.S. national and local papers and foreign news services in Washington. The directory is updated throughout the year. *Hudson's* is owned by the small publisher Penn Hill Publications.

KnowWho

(<www.knowwho.com>)
Phone: 703-619-1544

KnowWho provides such data services as email contact files for state and federal officials and electronic files mapping legislative districts to zip codes.

Law Librarians' Society of Washington, DC

(<www.llsdc.org>)

A nonprofit and nonpartisan professional association, the Law Librarians Society of Washington, DC (LLSDC) provides free web access to useful content developed by its members. Resources include the Legislative Source Book, a compilation of legislative research guides, and a listing of newly released congressional documents from GPO.

Leadership Directories

(<www.leadershipdirectories.com>)
Phone: 202-347-7757

Leadership Directories publishes a series of government staff directories in print and online. Its *Congressional Yellow Book* (*see Directories, above*), *News Media Yellow Book*, and directories for the executive branch are Washington standards.

LegiStorm

(<www.legistorm.com>)
Phone: 202-360-4172

The LegiStorm web site presents congressional staff pay information culled from Secretary of the Senate and House Chief Administrative Officer reports. LegiStorm is the name of both the product and publisher.

LexisNexis

(<www.lexisnexis.com>)
Phone: 800-227-4908

In business since 1966 (albeit under a different name), LexisNexis is one of the giants in online legal, news, and business research. The company has expanded its business by acquiring new content as well as by packaging that content differently for different audiences. The mix of products available to one may vary according to whether one is subscribing for a business, a college, an individual, or a government agency. LexisNexis carries congressional content (such as the searchable text of the *Congressional Record*) that is available on a number of commercial services. It is currently unique in its ownership of content created by the former Congressional Information Service (CIS) company: indexing and summaries of congressional documents from 1789 to present. LexisNexis is also digitizing the historic *United States Congressional Serial Set* of bound House and Senate reports and documents. The LexisNexis Congressional online service is this publisher's primary stand-alone congressional information database, but different product options are available; LexisNexis representatives can explain what is available for specific customers.

National Archives and Records Administration

(<www.archives.gov>)
(For the Office of the Federal Register, <www.archives.gov/federal-register>)
(For records of Congress, <www.archives.gov/records_of_congress>)
Phone: 202-357-5400 or 866-272-6272

Not just a repository for historical documents, the National Archives includes the very current Office of the Federal Register (OFR). In the OFR web site section called "Hot Off the Press," researchers can find today's *Federal Register*, notices and rules scheduled to be published in upcoming issues of the *Federal Register*, and links to copies of recent public laws and executive orders.

The Archives also houses the Center for Legislative Archives, located in its downtown building at Pennsylvania Avenue and Seventh Street, NW. The center holds historic congressional documents, particularly those of House and Senate committees.

National Journal Group

(<http://nationaljournal.com>)
Phone: 202-739-8400

The weekly *National Journal* magazine is an essential read for government affairs professionals in Washington, DC. Other Washington standards published by the National Journal Group include *CongressDaily*, the daily campaign newsletter *The Hotline*, the monthly *Government Executive*, *The Capital Source* directory, and the biennial *Almanac of American Politics* volume. Their online package for the academic library market is called Policy Central. The National

Journal Group has also launched several free online services: *The Gate* blog and *Policy Council*, a database of position papers and related content submitted voluntarily by think tanks, trade associations, corporations, and others.

Office of Management and Budget

(<www.whitehouse.gov/omb>)
Phone: 202-395-3080

The Office of Management and Budget develops the president's annual budget submission to Congress. It also influences government management, information, and regulatory policies. OMB's web site is the place to turn for the administration's budget documents and policies for agency management. OMB also issues on behalf of the president and his administration Statements of Administration Policy (SAPs) on specific pieces of legislation, and posts these to the web site.

OMB has initiated several innovative information projects. The agency published a list of appropriations earmarks in 2007 *(<http://earmarks.omb.gov>)* and plans to launch, in 2008, a federal spending database *(<www.federalspending.gov>)* tracking federal grants, awards, contracts, and other assistance.

OpenCongress.org

(<www.opencongress.org>)

Sponsored by the nonprofit group Sunlight Foundation, OpenCongress provides an alternative interface to official legislative information along with editorial features such as a blog.

Politico

(<www.politico.com>)
Phone: (866) 504-4251

Launched in January 2007, *Politico* is the newest Capitol Hill newspaper. The paper's content is available for free at the Politico.com web site. A print edition is published Tuesdays through Thursdays when Congress is in session. Printed copies are distributed for free at selected locations on Capitol Hill and elsewhere in Washington, DC; print subscriptions are available for a fee. *Politico* is published by Capitol News Company LLC.

PR Newswire

(<www.prnewswire.com>)
Phone: 888-776-0942

Through its U.S. Newswire brand, PR Newswire distributes press releases from government agencies, congressional offices, advocacy groups, public relations firms, and others involved in the public policy arena. Selected U.S. Newswire items are posted to the publisher's blog, News Unfiltered *(<http://newsunfiltered.com>)*, which also offers an RSS feed of U.S. Newswire items.

Readex

(<www.readex.com>)

Phone: 800-762-8182

Like LexisNexis *(see above)*, Readex is digitizing the historic *United States Congressional Serial Set* of bound House and Senate reports and documents.

Roll Call

(<www.rollcall.com>)

Phone: 202-824-6800

Roll Call and *The Hill (see below)* are two indispensable newspapers that specifically cover Capitol Hill. *Roll Call* is published Monday through Thursday when Congress is in session, and only on Mondays when it is not. The web site contains some updates between printed issues, but users will need a subscription to view most of the online articles.

Roll Call acquired the online legislative information service GalleryWatch.com *(<www.gallerywatch.com>)* in 2006. GalleryWatch.com combines searchable legislative, budget, and appropriations databases with tracking and notification services. GalleryWatch.com also partners with Penny Hill Press *(<www.pennyhill.com>)* to provide subscription access to reports from the Congressional Research Service.

Roll Call and GalleryWatch launched a new CongressNow *(<www.congressnow.com>)* legislative news service in 2007. The service is free for members of Congress and their staff members, but requires a paid subscription for all other users.

TheCapitol.Net

(<www.thecapitol.net>)

Phone: 703-739-3790

TheCapitol.Net specializes in professional development seminars on the legislative process, the budget process, and strategies for working effectively with Congress. The company also publishes books for public affairs professions, including *Congressional Deskbook*, *Legislative Drafter's Deskbook: A Practical Guide*, and *Real World Research Skills: An Introduction to Factual, International, Judicial, Legislative, and Regulatory Research*.

The Hill

(<www.thehill.com>)

Phone: 202-628-8500

The Hill and *Roll Call (see above)* are two indispensable newspapers that specifically cover Capitol Hill. *The Hill* is published on Tuesdays, Wednesdays, Thursdays, and Fridays when Congress is in session, and on Wednesdays when Congress is not in session. *The Hill* also makes many of its recent articles available on its web site.

13

Thomson West

(<http://west.thomson.com>)
Phone: 800-344-5008

Founded in 1872 as West Publishing, West Group is today a major publisher of legal information in print and online. Essential products of West Group include the Westlaw online service, the *United States Code Annotated* and the *United States Code Congressional and Administrative News.*

U.S. Congress Votes Database

(<http://projects.washingtonpost.com/congress>)

This site presents the results for congressional roll call votes from 1991 to present. The site also offers RSS feeds for the votes of each member of Congress and for the results of recent congressional votes. The database is maintained by *The Washington Post.*

White House

(<www.whitehouse.gov>)
(Go to <www.whitehouse.gov/news> for press briefings, speeches, and other documents.)
Phone: 202-456-1414

Aside from providing basic directory, educational, and historical information, the White House web site serves a major role in communicating administration policy. The news section cited above includes White House press releases, press briefings, presidential speeches, presidential proclamations, executive orders, and the weekly presidential radio address. Users can subscribe to RSS feeds for news releases, press briefing transcripts, and other information.

William S. Hein & Co.

(<www.wshein.com>)
Phone: 716-882-2600 or 800-828-7571

Through its commercial online service, HeinOnline (*<http://heinonline.org>*), Hein & Co. provides digitized materials such as the *United States Statutes at Large* and a library of federal legislative histories.

§ 13.40 Web Search Tips

Searching for a known entity, perhaps a particular organization or book one has been trying to find, is a relatively easy task. Once you have found it, you know that your search is done. Trying to find the best information on a topic, looking for that needle in a haystack, or—worst of all—trying to prove that some information does not exist, can be much more difficult. If one's organization has expert searchers on staff, use their services. If you are searching on your own, the following tips may help.

§ 13.41

Search Engine Tips

Use more than one search engine.

Different search engines will find different results. To learn about the variety of search engines available, see the Internet Public Library's Search Engine page at *<www.ipl.org/div/subject/browse/ref72.00.00>*.

Try a few variations on your first search.

Slight variations will almost always bring up different results.

- Vary your search by trying synonyms or alternate forms of a name. Searches on "british cars," "british motorcars," and "british autos" will all find different results.

- Vary your search by adding a related word or words that will make it more specific. Example: make a search on "social security" more specific by adding the word "reform" or the phrase "policy debate."

- Learn from the results of your first search. The first search should always give one a sample of what's out there, and provide ideas about different words or strategies to use in the next search.

Learn some advanced search techniques.

One technique that can help give you more precise results is to use the minus sign to specify that a word not appear in your results. For example, if one is interested in bats—the animals, and not baseball bats—try the search: bats –baseball.

Do not hesitate to try the optional advanced search page some search engines offer. These often make it easier for one to get relevant results. They can make it easier to limit results to just those in the English language or just those with, for example, a .gov or .edu extension. Many search engines simplify matters by letting one select search boxes with labels such as "without the words" or "find exact phrase," so that you do not need to memorize commands like the minus sign example above.

General Search Engines

The general-purpose search engine, handy as it is, is not the most appropriate tool for specialized legislative research. Having said that, there are times when any professional will want to do a quick search in Yahoo! or Google. Some of the same tips that will help one with general search engines will also help one with searching the more specialized databases. Because we now spend a good deal of our time searching for information online, this section has been developed to help one do it well.

A general-purpose search engine can be the appropriate tool when one wants to quickly find the web site of a known organization. It can help when a word, phrase, or topic is so unfamiliar to you that you do not know where to begin your research. And it can help when you are doing anything akin to competitive intelligence research, tracking down news and relationships that might not pop up in databases of a more focused scope.

The major caveat to keep in mind is that no single search engine indexes everything on

13

§ 13.42

Additional Search Tips

- Searching is an interactive process. Review your initial search results and see if there are words you should add or drop.

- One-word searches will seldom find the information you need, unless that word is very rare and has no other meanings. A search on "hearing" will find many items that "congressional hearing" will not.

- Depending on your search results, see if you need a more specific or general term. Perhaps "heart attack" is too popular a term for your database, or perhaps "myocardial infarction" is too technical.

- Last, but not least, check your spelling.

the web. A web search is never exhaustive or complete. Even if a search engine has included a particular web site, it may have indexed only a small portion of the information on that web site. The newest information, changes, or additions made within the past day to week will likely not be found by a general-purpose search engine. Some sites do not allow search engines to index their web pages, so one will not find them at all using a search engine. There can be significant differences between what one search engine finds and what another finds, so you should not rely on just one. And, finally, not everything is on the web for search engines to find. In fact, it is often the most valuable information that one will not find on the public web; the information may be proprietary, closely guarded, or otherwise too valuable to give away.

Specialized Search Engines

In addition to the popular search engines, there are also free, specialized search engines that dig deeper and can bring more focused results. Here are a few:

- USA.gov, at <*www.usa.gov*>, has a search box that will find web sites from U.S. federal or state governments. Go directly to <*http://usasearch.gov*> for the main search page and the helpful advanced search options.
- DTIC Search, at <*www.dtic.mil/dtic/search/dod_search.html*>, searches multiple Defense Department web sites. It is provided by the Defense Technical Information Center.
- BlawgSearch, at <*http://blawgsearch.justia.com*>, searches law-oriented blogs. It is owned by Justia.com.

Guides to Web Resources

The country is full of librarians, educators, and private companies all spending time reviewing, selecting, and updating links to quality web sites covering any number of topics. Often it is more effective to use these existing resources rather than to reinvent the wheel with one's own bookmarks or favorites or take a shot in the dark with a general search engine. Here are a few:

- FedStats, at <*www.fedstats.gov*>, is a time-saving gateway to federal government statistical reports published on the web. An interagency effort, it covers statistics on agriculture, demographics, economics, transportation, and more.
- Refdesk.com, at <*www.refdesk.com*>, has been on the web for ten years and has grown tremendously to include multiple levels of links to dictionaries, statistics, and other reference resources.

§ 13.43

Email Alert and News Services

Email alert and news services are announcements sent out via email to a list of interested subscribers. They are one-way communications, as opposed to interactive email discussion forums. They can be useful for those areas in which it is essential for one to keep informed. The advantage is that one does not need to remember to check a web site or news service; news is emailed to you automatically. They can be less helpful if they generate a high volume of email that is of marginal use to you.

The official U.S. government web portal, USA.gov at <www.usa.gov>, maintains a page of links to government email newsletters and similar online services at <www.usa.gov/Topics/Reference_Shelf/News.shtml>.

The following list of email alert services is selective. These are free services, for which one can easily subscribe or unsubscribe using the web. Service names and web addresses are provided.

- Advocacy Tipsheet, tips on communicating with officials and one's constituency, <www.advocacyguru.com/tipsheet.htm>

- C-SPAN Alert, program schedules, <www.c-span.org/watch/cspanalert.asp?code=Watch>

- Congressional Budget Office (CBO) New-Document Notification List, <www.cbo.gov/pubs_index.cfm>

- GAO Email Alerts, notification of new reports from the Government Accountability Office, <www.gao.gov/subscribe>

- GPOLISTERV, several alert services, including daily Federal Register table of contents, <http://listserv.access.gpo.gov>

- National Archive's PUBLAWS-L, notification of new public laws, <www.archives.gov/federal-register/laws/updates.html>

- White House Email Updates, <www.whitehouse.gov/email>

- The Virtual Chase, at <www.virtualchase.com> maintains several specialized web research guides including the Company Information Guide (<www.virtualchase.com/topics/company_information_index.shtml>) and a legal research section (<www.virtualchase.com/topics/legal_research_index.shtml>).
- University of Michigan Documents Center, at <www.lib.umich.edu/govdocs>, links to numerous U.S. and international government sites, government statistics, and government information in the news.

Database Searching

Moving from a simple or simplistic general search engine to a more complex and specialized database service like the government's THOMAS or the Thomson West's Westlaw service can seem like a big leap. And it often should. These databases can be much more sensitive to requiring the correct use of commands. Searchers must review the basics of these systems before proceeding. If it is a database one will use often, check to see if any online tutorials or in-person training classes are provided.

Of the databases one might use frequently, THOMAS and GPO Access may be some of the most difficult. In each case, you will be using the same system to search many different types of databases, from the full text of the *Congressional Record* to much briefer documents. You will benefit from reading the search tips at each of these sites. For GPO Access, putting phrases in quotes and using the AND connector between words you want to have appear in your results will help tremendously. For THOMAS, you may not wish to rely entirely on the word or subject search. If you know other things about a bill, such as the sponsor's name or the type of legislation, use those to help narrow your search.

§ 13.50 Media, Policy, and Opinion on the Web

Primary congressional information sources—such as the *Congressional Record*, C-SPAN broadcasts of floor debate, or committee reports—allow one to learn what Congress is saying and doing. Media, policy, and opinion resources allow one to learn what is being said about what Congress is saying and doing.

The sections below list selected Internet sites and journals that are of particular interest to the government affairs professional and other followers of Congress.

Online Media

Washington is a news town. While one should be following key legislative interests so closely that one does not need to rely exclusively on news reporters, there are always other developments to follow. The web changes every day, but online news sites are some of the most dynamically evolving services around. Web users can watch C-SPAN on their computer screen or monitor radio news through streaming audio. Blogs (web sites in the form of a daily journal) have become popular for disseminating political news and opinion. While many blogs are short-lived or deal in rumors, others are valuable news sources. The blog beSpacific.com (<*www.bespacific.com*>), for example, reports on government and law technology issues, and the SCOTUSblog (<*www.scotusblog.com*>) delivers news about the U.S. Supreme Court. Blogs and existing official web sites are also using a standard called RSS to distribute regular news updates independent of email accounts and on handheld, mobile devices. The State Department (<*www.state.gov/issuesandpress*>) was among the first agencies to provide news via RSS. The White House (<*www.whitehouse.gov/rss*>) and some congressional web sites also provide RSS feeds. To see if a news source one uses provides RSS news feeds, look for an orange icon which may be labeled "RSS" or "XML." Most sites provide information on how to use the service.

§13.51

Selected Media Web Sites

This is a selective list. There are many excellent news sources on the web.

Print Newspapers Online

- Washington Post, <*www.washingtonpost.com*>
- Washington Times, <*www.washingtontimes.com*>
- Christian Science Monitor, <*www.csmonitor.com*>
- Los Angeles Times, <*www.latimes.com*>
- New York Times, <*www.nytimes.com*>
- Wall Street Journal, <*www.wsj.com*>

Hill Newspapers

- Politico, <*www.politico.com*>
- Roll Call, <*www.rollcall.com*>
- The Hill, <*www.thehill.com*>

Legal Affairs

- Legal Times, <*www.law.com/dc*>
- National Law Journal, <*www.nlj.com*>

Television

- ABC News, <*www.abcnews.go.com*>
- BBC News, <*http://news.bbc.co.uk*>
- C-SPAN, <*www.c-span.org*>
- CBS News, <*www.cbsnews.com*>
- CNN, <*www.cnn.com*>
- FOX News, <*www.foxnews.com*>
- NBC News, <*www.msnbc.msn.com*>
- NewsHour with Jim Lehrer, <*www.pbs.org/newshour*>

Radio

- C-SPAN Radio, <*www.c-span.org*>
- FederalNewsRadio.com, <*http://federalnewsradio.com*>
- National Public Radio, <*http://news.npr.org*>
- WTOP, <*www.wtopnews.com*>

On the Wires

- Associated Press, <*www.ap.org*>
- Bloomberg, <*www.bloomberg.com/news*>
- Reuters, <*www.reuters.com*>
- US Newswire, <*www.prnewswire.com/publicinterest*>
- UPI, <*http://about.upi.com*>
- Voice of America News, <*www.voanews.com*>

Magazines

- CQ Weekly, <*www.cq.com*>
- Governing, <*www.governing.com*>
- Economist, <*www.economist.com*>
- National Journal, <*http://nationaljournal.com*>
- Newsweek, <*www.newsweek.com*>
- Time, <*www.time.com*>
- US News and World Report, <*www.usnews.com*>

Other

- National Press Club, <*http://npc.press.org*>

Important traditional news sources are listed in §13.51. In addition to these, here are a few web sites that aggregate news from many sources:

- Google News, at <*http://news.google.com*>, and Yahoo! News, at <*http://news.yahoo.com*>, include browsing and word searching of multiple news sources and are updated throughout the day.

13

Selected Policy Institutes
and Think Tanks

The organizations listed below cover a wide range of public policy areas. Additional policy institutes and think tanks can be identified by topic in publications such as Congressional Quarterly's *Washington Information Directory*, an annual publication. Also, see § 5.190 for a listing of organizations that focus on congressional operations and issues of a representative democracy.

- American Enterprise Institute for Public Policy Research, *<www.aei.org>*
- Aspen Institute, *<www.aspeninstitute.org>*
- Brookings Institution, *<www.brookings.org>*
- Carl Albert Congressional Research & Studies Center, *<www.ou.edu/special/albertctr/cachome.html>*
- Carnegie Endowment for International Peace, *<www.carnegieendowment.org>*
- Cato Institute, *<www.cato.org>*
- Center for American Progress, *<www.americanprogress.org>*
- Center for Congressional and Presidential Studies, *<http://spa.american.edu/ccps>*
- Center for National Policy, *<www.cnponline.org>*
- Center for Strategic and International Studies, *<www.csis.org>*
- Center on Budget and Policy Priorities, *<www.cbpp.org>*
- Center on Congress, *<http://congress.indiana.edu>*
- Council on Foreign Relations, *<www.cfr.org>*
- Dirksen Congressional Center, *<www.dirksencongressionalcenter.org>*
- Heritage Foundation, *<www.heritage.org>*
- Hoover Institution, *<www.hoover.org>*
- Institute for International Economics, *<www.iie.com>*
- Institute for Policy Studies, *<www.ips-dc.org>*
- James A. Baker III Institute for Public Policy, *<http://bakerinstitute.org>*
- Joint Center for Political and Economic Studies, *<www.jointcenter.org>*
- National Bureau for Economic Research, *<www.nber.org>*
- National Center for Policy Analysis, *<www.ncpa.org>*
- Progressive Policy Institute, *<www.ppionline.org>*
- Public Forum Institute, *<www.publicforuminstitute.org>*
- Rand Corporation, *<www.rand.org>*
- Urban Institute, *<www.urban.org>*
- Woodrow Wilson International Center for Scholars, *<www.wilsoncenter.org>*

- World-newspapers.com, at *<www.world-newspapers.com>*, is a well-organized directory linking to web sites for newspapers by country.
- Memeorandum, at *<www.memeorandum.com>*, calls itself the "Political Web, page A1." Memeorandum links to blogs from both traditional newspapers and independent bloggers.

Policy: Analysis and Opinion

Policy institutes, think tanks, special interest organizations, government "watchdogs," academia, and industry associations all have roles in the Washington information scene. Some organizations do not follow a particular ideology, but, rather, seek to foster debate from multiple viewpoints, or take a strict nonpartisan stance. Others promote a point of view, advocate for a group or industry, or seek to appeal to a particular constituency. While these sources require more skepticism and diligence on the part of those who use their information, they do bring a depth to issues that may not be covered well in the general news. These organizations are also an excellent source for finding the experts and opinion leaders on a given topic. The web sites for policy organizations typically provide access to their policy papers and reports, journals, seminar and event schedules, videos of past seminars, blogs and online forums, and publications catalogs, among other resources.

The following feature boxes list a selection of policy institutes and journals of opinion.

In addition to these, here are a few resources for finding policy and advocacy organizations.

- ASAE Gateway to Associations, at *<www.asaecenter.org/Directories/AssociationSearch.cfm>*, is an online database of over 6,000 associations, searchable by name, topic, and location.

§ 13.53

Selected Journals of Opinion

Policy institutes, private publishers, and academia publish a variety of journals of opinion and policy. These journals are all available in printed form.

- The American, *<www.american.com>*
- The American Prospect, *<www.prospect.org>*
- The American Spectator, *<www.spectator.org>*
- City Journal, *<www.city-journal.org>*
- Commentary, *<www.commentarymagazine.com>*
- Congressional Digest, *<www.congressionaldigestcorp.com/pcp/pubs/cd>*
- Focus, *<www.jointcenter.org/publications_recent_publications/focus_magazine>*
- Foreign Affairs, *<www.foreignaffairs.org>*
- Foreign Policy, *<www.foreignpolicy.com>*
- Human Events, *<www.humanevents.com>*
- The Nation, *<www.thenation.com>*
- National Review, *<www.nationalreview.com>*
- The New Republic, *<www.tnr.com>*
- Policy Review, *<www.hoover.org/publications/policyreview>*
- The Progressive, *<www.progressive.org>*
- Reason Magazine, *<www.reason.com>*
- Regulation, *<www.cato.org/pubs/regulation>*
- The Washington Monthly, *<www.washingtonmonthly.com>*
- The Weekly Standard, *<www.weeklystandard.com>*

13

§ 13.54

Selected Academic Journals

The following journals present scholarly articles on Congress, government, and politics. Most are available only by subscription. Some provide the current issue or selected articles online for free.

- American Journal of Political Science
  <www.ajps.org>
  Midwest Political Science Association. Quarterly.

- American Political Science Review
  <www.apsanet.org/section_327.cfm>
  American Political Science Association. Quarterly.

- Harvard Journal on Legislation
  <www.law.harvard.edu/students/orgs/jol>
  Harvard Law School. Semiannual.

- Journal of Law & Politics
  <www.student.virginia.edu/~jalopy>
  University of Virginia School of Law. Quarterly.

- Journal of Legislation
  <http://law.nd.edu/jleg>
  University of Notre Dame Law School. Semiannual.

- The Journal of Politics
  <www.journalofpolitics.org>
  Southern Political Science Association. Quarterly.

- Legislative Studies Quarterly
  <www.uiowa.edu/~lsq>
  University of Iowa Comparative Legislative Research Center. Quarterly.

- Perspectives on Politics
  <www.apsanet.org/section_328.cfm>
  American Political Science Association. Quarterly.

- Political Science Quarterly
  <www.psqonline.org>
  Academy of Political Science. Quarterly.

- PS: Political Science & Politics
  <www.apsanet.org/section_223.cfm>
  American Political Science Association. Quarterly.

- The Capital Source, at *<http://nationaljournal.com/about/capitalsource>*, is an annual directory published by National Journal. It supplements government listings with sections covering trade associations, law and lobbying firms, interest groups, and think tanks. *(See § 13.20 for other relevant directories in print.)*
- University of Michigan Documents Center links to many private and academic policy institutes at *<www.lib.umich.edu/govdocs/psthink.html>*.

§ 13.60 For Further Reading: Books by and about Congress
Selected Books by Members of the 110th Congress

The following bibliography lists a selection of books by members of the 110th Congress. The selection includes only books published since 1991 and only the most current book or books written by a member. To find additional books by members of Congress, or those published after March 2007, use the Library of Congress online catalog (*<http://catalog.loc.gov>*) or other online sources, or ask for assistance at your local library. Check your local bookstore or local library for availability.

Representatives

Abercrombie, Neil, and Richard Hoyt. *Blood of Patriots.* New York: Forge, 1996.

Baird, Brian. *The Internship, Practicum, and Field Placement Handbook: A Guide for the Helping Professions.* 4th ed. Upper Saddle River, NJ: Pearson Education, 2005.

Clyburn, James, with Jennifer Revels. *Uncommon Courage: The Story of Briggs v. Elliott, South Carolina's Unsung Civil Rights Battle.* Spartanburg, SC: Palmetto Conservation Foundation/PCF Press, 2004.

Emanuel, Rahm and Bruce Reed. *The Plan: Big Ideas for America.* New York: Public Affairs, 2006.

Faleomavaega, Eni F.H. *U.S. Samoa/Pacific Relations: An Islander's Perspective.* Carson, CA: Kin Publications, 1995.

Frank, Barney. *Speaking Frankly: What's Wrong with the Democrats and How to Fix It.* New York: Times Books/Random House, 1992.

Granger, Kay. *What's Right about America: Celebrating Our Nation's Values.* Los Angeles: World Ahead Publishing Inc., 2005.

Hastert, J. Dennis. *Speaker: Lessons from Forty Years in Coaching and Politics.* Washington, DC: Regnery, 2004.

Jackson, Jesse L. Jr., Jesse L. Jackson Sr., and Bruce Shapiro. *Legal Lynching: The Death Penalty and America's Future.* New York: Anchor Books, 2003.

Johnson, Sam, and Jan Winebrenner. *Captive Warriors: A Vietnam POW's Story.* College Station, TX: Texas A&M University Press, 1992.

Kaptur, Marcy. *Women of Congress: A Twentieth-Century Odyssey.* Washington, DC: Congressional Quarterly, 1996.

King, Peter T. *Vale of Tears: A Novel.* Lanham, MD: Taylor Trade, 2003.

Kucinich, Dennis J. *A Prayer for America.* New York: Thunder's Mouth Press/Nation Books, 2003.

Lewis, John, with Michael D'Orso. *Walking with the Wind: A Memoir of the Movement.* San Diego: Harcourt Brace, 1999.

Lipinski, Daniel. *Congressional Communication: Content & Consequences.* Ann Arbor, MI: University of Michigan Press, 2004.

Murphy, Tim and Loriann Hoff Oberlin. *Overcoming Passive-Aggression: How to Stop Hidden Anger from Spoiling Your Relationships, Career and Happiness.* New York: Marlow & Co., 2005.

Murtha, John P., with John Plashal. *From Vietnam to 9/11: On the Front Lines of National Security.* University Park, PA: Pennsylvania State University Press, 2005.

Price, David E. *The Congressional Experience.* 3rd ed. Boulder, CO: Westview Press, 2004.

13

Rangel, Charles B. *And I Haven't Had a Bad Day Since: From the Streets of Harlem to the Halls of Congress.* New York: Thomas Dunne Books/St. Martin's Press, 2007.

Tancredo, Thomas G. *In Mortal Danger: The Battle for America's Border and Security.* Nashville, TN: WND Books, 2006.

Weldon, Dave, and William Proctor. *Moongate: A Novel.* Nashville, TN: T. Nelson, 2002.

Senators

Alexander, Lamar. *Lamar Alexander's Little Plaid Book.* Nashville: Rutledge Hill Press, 1998.

Bayh, Evan. *From Father to Son: A Private Life in the Public Eye.* Indianapolis, IN: Guild Press/Emmis Books, 2003.

Boxer, Barbara. *Strangers in the Senate: Politics and the New Revolution of Women in America.* Washington, DC: National Press Books, 1994.

Brown, Sherrod. *Congress from the Inside: Observations from the Majority and the Minority.* 3rd ed. Kent, OH: Kent State University Press, 2004.

Brownback, Sam, and James B. Wadley. *Kansas Agricultural Law.* 2nd ed. Topeka, KS: Lone Tree Publishing Co., 1994.

Byrd, Robert C. *Robert C. Byrd: Child of the Appalachian Coalfields.* Morgantown, WV: West Virginia University Press, 2005.

Byrd, Robert C. *Losing America: Confronting a Reckless and Arrogant Presidency.* New York: W.W. Norton, 2004.

Clinton, Hillary Rodham. *Living History.* New York: Simon & Schuster, 2003.

Coburn, Tom. *Breach of Trust: How Washington Turns Outsiders into Insiders.* Nashville, TN: WND Books, 2003.

Dole, Elizabeth. *Hearts Touched with Fire: My 500 Favorite Inspirational Quotations.* New York: Avalon Publishing Group, 2004.

Domenici, Pete, with Blythe J. Lyons and Julian J. Steyn. *A Brighter Tomorrow: Fulfilling the Promise of Nuclear Energy.* Lanham, MD: Rowman & Littlefield; distributed by National Book Network, 2004.

Dorgan, Byron. *Take This Job and Ship It: How Corporate Greed and Braindead Politics Are Selling Out America.* New York: St. Martin's Press, 2006.

Hatch, Orrin. *Square Peg: Confessions of a Citizen Senator.* New York: Basic Books, 2002.

Hutchison, Kay Bailey. *American Heroines: The Spirited Women Who Shaped Our Country.* New York: William Morrow, 2004.

Kennedy, Edward. *America Back on Track.* New York: Viking, 2006.

Kennedy, Edward. *My Senator and Me: A Dog's Eye View of Washington, D.C.* New York: Scholastic Press, 2006.

Kerry, John. *This Moment on Earth: Today's New Environmentalists and Their Vision for the Future.* New York: Public Affairs, 2007.

Lieberman, Joseph, with Hadassah Lieberman and Sarah Crichton. *An Amazing Adventure: Joe and Hadassah's Personal Notes on the 2000 Campaign.* New York: Simon & Schuster, 2003.

Lott, Trent. *Herding Cats: A Life in Politics.* New York: Regan Books, 2005.

Lugar, Richard. *Letters to the Next President.* 2nd ed. Bloomington, IN: Authorhouse, 2004.

McCain, John, with Mark Salter. *Character Is Destiny: Inspiring Stories Every Young Person Should Know and Every Adult Should Remember.* New York: Random House, 2005.

Mikulski, Barbara, et al. *Nine and Counting: Women in the Senate.* New York: William Morrow, 2000.

Obama, Barack. *The Audacity of Hope: Thoughts on Reclaiming the American Dream.* New York: Crown Publishers, 2006.

Reid, Harry. *Searchlight: The Camp That Didn't Fail.* Reno, NV: University of Nevada Press, 1998.

Sanders, Bernard, with Huck Gutman. *Outsider in the House.* New York: Verso, 1997.

Schumer, Charles. *Positively American: Winning Back the Middle-Class Majority One Family at a Time.* Emmaus, PA: Rodale Books, 2007.

Smith, Gordon. *Remembering Garrett: One Family's Battle with a Child's Depression.* New York: Carroll and Graf, 2006.

Specter, Arlen. *Passion for Truth: From Finding JFK's Single Bullet to Questioning Anita Hill to Impeaching Clinton.* New York: William Morrow, 2000.

Webb, Jim. *Born Fighting: How the Scots-Irish Shaped America.* New York: Broadway Books, 2004.

Selected Books About Congress*

Bacon, Donald D., Roger H. Davidson, and Morton Keller, eds. *The Encyclopedia of the United States Congress.* 4 vols. New York: Simon & Schuster, 1995.

Baker, Richard Allan. *The Senate of the United States: A Bicentennial History.* Malabar, FL: Robert E. Krieger Publishing Co., 1988.

Baker, Ross K. *House and Senate.* 3rd ed. New York: W.W. Norton, 2001.

Baran, Jan Witold. *The Election Law Primer for Corporations.* 4th ed. Chicago: American Bar Association, 2004.

13

* Additional books about Congress appear in § 6.15 (*Resources on the Capitol*) and § 4.21 (*Resources on Lobbying*). Book-type documents published by Congress appear in Chapters 11 and 12, which describe congressional documents. Additional publishers are listed earlier in this chapter.

Bendavid, Naftali. *The Thumpin': How Rahm Emanuel and the Democrats Learned To Be Ruthless and Ended the Republican Revolution.* New York: Doubleday, 2007.

Binder, Sarah A. *Stalemate: Causes and Consequences of Legislative Gridlock.* Washington, DC: The Brookings Institution, 2003.

Binder, Sarah A. and Paul J. Quirk, eds. *The Legislative Branch.* New York: Oxford University Press, 2005.

Birnbaum, Jeffrey H., and Alan S. Murray. *Showdown at Gucci Gulch.* New York: Random House, 1987.

Campbell, Colton C., and Nicol Rae, ed. *The Contentious Senate: Partisanship, Ideology, and the Myth of Cool Judgment.* Lanham, MD: Rowman & Littlefield, 2001.

Cigler, Allan J. and Burdett A. Loomis. *Interest Group Politics.* 7th ed. Washington, DC: CQ Press, 2007.

Cole, John, and Jane Aiken, ed. *Encyclopedia of the Library of Congress: For Congress, The Nation and the World.* Washington, DC: Library of Congress; Lanham, MD: Bernan Press, 2004.

Congress A to Z. 4th ed. Washington, DC: CQ Press, 2003.

Congress and the Nation XI, 2001-2005. Washington, DC: Congressional Quarterly Inc., 2006. (Predecessor volumes coincide with four-year presidential terms, beginning in 1965; a single volume covers the period 1945-1964.)

Congressional Management Foundation. *Setting Course.* 10th ed. Washington, DC: Congressional Management Foundation, 2006.

Congressional Quarterly's American Congressional Dictionary. 3rd ed. Washington, DC: CQ Press, 2001.

Congressional Quarterly's Guide to Congress. 6th ed. 2 vols. Washington, DC: CQ Press, 2007.

Corrado, Anthony, Thomas E. Mann, Daniel R. Ortiz, and Trevor Potter. *The New Campaign Finance Sourcebook.* Washington, DC: Brookings Institution Press, 2005.

Davidson, Roger H., and Walter J. Oleszek. *Congress and Its Members.* 11th ed. Washington, DC: CQ Press, 2007.

Dodd, Lawrence C., and Bruce I. Oppenheimer, ed. *Congress Reconsidered.* 8th ed. Washington, DC: CQ Press, 2005.

Dorsey, Tobias A. *Legislative Drafter's Deskbook: A Practical Guide.* Alexandria, VA: TheCapitol.Net, 2006.

Ehrenhalt, Alan. *The United States of Ambition: Politicians, Power, and the Pursuit of Office.* New York: Times Books, 1991.

Eilperin, Juliet. *Fight Club Politics: How Partisanship Is Poisoning the House of Representatives.* Lanham, MD: Rowman & Littlefield, 2006.

Elving, Ronald D. *Conflict and Compromise: How Congress Makes the Law.* New York: Simon & Schuster, 1995.

Fenno, Richard F. *Home Style: House Members in Their Districts.* Reprint. New York: Longman, 2003.

Fisher, Louis. *Congressional Abdication on War and Spending.* College Station, TX: Texas A&M University Press, 2000.

Fisher, Louis. *Constitutional Conflicts Between Congress and the President.* 5th ed., rev. Lawrence, KS: University Press of Kansas, 2007.

Fisher, Louis, *The Politics of Shared Power.* 4th ed. College Station, TX: Texas A&M University Press, 1998.

Frey, Lou, Jr., and Michael T. Hayes, ed. *Inside the House: Former Members Reveal How Congress Works.* Lanham, MD: University Press of America, 2001.

Garvin, Peggy. *Real World Research Skills: An Introduction to Factual, International, Judicial, Legislative, and Regulatory Research.* Alexandria, VA: TheCapitol.Net, 2006.

Garvin, Peggy, ed. *The United States Government Internet Manual.* Lanham, MD: Bernan Press, 2005.

Gill, LaVerne McCain. *African American Women in Congress: Forming and Transforming History.* New Brunswick, NJ: Rutgers University Press, 1997.

Gold, Martin B. *Senate Procedure and Practice.* Lanham, MD: Rowman & Littlefield, 2004.

Hager, George, and Eric Pianin. *Balancing Act: Washington's Troubled Path to a Balanced Budget.* New York: Vantage Books, 1998.

Hamilton, Lee. *How Congress Works and Why You Should Care.* Bloomington, IN: Indiana University Press, 2004.

Herrnson, Paul S. *Congressional Elections: Campaigning at Home and in Washington.* 4th ed. Washington, DC: CQ Press, 2004.

Herrnson, Paul S. *The Financiers of Congressional Elections.* New York: Columbia University Press, 2004.

Jacobson, Gary C. *The Politics of Congressional Elections.* 6th ed. New York: Pearson Longman, 2004.

Johnson, Dennis W. *Congress Online: Bridging the Gap between Citizens and Their Representatives.* New York: Routledge, 2004.

Loomis, Burdett, ed. *Esteemed Colleagues: Civility and Deliberation in the U.S. Senate.* Washington, DC: Brookings Institution Press, 2001.

Mann, Thomas E. and Norman J. Ornstein. *The Broken Branch: How Congress Is Failing America and How to Get It Back on Track.* New York: Oxford University Press, 2006.

13

Mayer, Kenneth R. *With the Stroke of a Pen: Executive Orders and Presidential Power.* Princeton, NJ: Princeton University Press, 2001.

Mayhew, David R. *America's Congress: Actions in the Public Sphere, James Madison through Newt Gingrich.* New Haven, CT: Yale University Press, 2002.

Mayhew, David R. *Divided We Govern: Party Control, Lawmaking, and Investigations, 1946-2002.* 2nd ed. New Haven, CT: Yale University Press, 2005.

McGillivray, Alice, Rhodes Cook, and Richard Scammon. *America Votes 27, 2005-2006: Election Returns by State.* Washington, DC: CQ Press, 2007. (Predecessor volumes were published every two years covering elections beginning with the 1965-1966 election cycle.)

Oleszek, Walter J. *Congressional Procedures and the Policy Process.* 7th ed. Washington, DC: CQ Press, 2007.

Ornstein, Norman J., Thomas E. Mann, and Michael J. Malbin. *Vital Statistics on Congress, 2005-2006.* Washington, DC: National Journal, 2007.

Palazzolo, Daniel J. *Done Deal? The Politics of the 1997 Budget Agreement.* Chatham, NJ: Chatham House, 1999.

Polsby, Nelson W. *How Congress Evolves: Social Bases of Institutional Change.* New York: Oxford University Press, 2004.

Redman, Eric. *The Dance of Legislation.* Rev. ed. Seattle, WA: University of Washington Press, 2000.

Remini, Robert V. *The House: The History of the House of Representatives.* New York: HarperCollins, 2006.

Ritchie, Donald A. *The Young Oxford Companion to the Congress of the United States.* New York: Oxford University Press, 1993.

Ritchie, Donald A. *Reporting from Washington: The History of the Washington Press Corps.* New York: Oxford University Press, 2005.

Rosenbloom, David H. *Building a Legislative-Centered Public Administration: Congress and the Administrative State, 1946-1999.* Tuscaloosa, AL: University of Alabama Press, 2000.

Rozell, Mark J., and Clyde Wilcox. *Interest Groups in American Campaigns: The New Face of Electioneering.* 2nd ed. Washington, DC: CQ Press, 2005.

Schick, Allen. *The Federal Budget: Politics, Policy, Process.* 3rd ed. Washington, DC: Brookings Institution Press, 2007.

Setting Course: A Congressional Management Guide. 10th ed. Washington, DC: Congressional Management Foundation, 2006.

Silbey, Joel H., ed. *Encyclopedia of the American Legislative System.* 3 vols. New York: Charles Scribner's Sons, 1994.

Sinclair, Barbara. *Party Wars: Polarization and the Politics of National Policymaking.* Norman, OK: University of Oklahoma Press, 2006.

Sinclair, Barbara. *Unorthodox Lawmaking: New Legislative Processes in the U.S. Congress.* 3rd ed. Washington, DC: CQ Press, 2007.

Smith, Steven S., Jason M. Roberts, and Ryan J. Vander Wielen. *The American Congress.* New York: Cambridge University Press, 2006.

Stathis, Stephen W. *Landmark Legislation 1789-2002.* Washington, DC: CQ Press, 2003.

Strokoff, Sandra L. and Lawrence E. Filson. *Legislative Drafter's Desk Reference.* 2nd ed. Washington, DC: CQ Press, 2007.

Thurber, James A., ed. *The Battle for Congress: Consultants, Candidates, and Voters.* Washington, DC: Brookings Institution Press, 2001.

Thurber, James A. *Rivals for Power: Presidential-Congressional Relations.* 3rd ed. Lanham, MD: Rowman & Littlefield, 2006.

Thurber, James A., and Colton C. Campbell, ed. *Congress and the Internet.* Upper Saddle River, NJ: Prentice Hall, 2003.

Vance, Stephanie D. *Government by the People: How to Communicate with Congress.* Washington, DC: AdVanced Consulting, 1999.

Wawro, Gregory J. and Eric Schickler, *Filibuster: Obstruction and Lawmaking in the U.S. Senate.* Princeton, NJ: Princeton University Press, 2006.

Wilson, Woodrow. *Congressional Government: A Study in American Politics.* New Brunswick, NJ: Transaction Publishers, 2002. (Originally published in 1885.)

Wolfensberger, Donald R. *Congress and the People: Deliberative Democracy on Trial.* Washington, DC: Woodrow Wilson Center Press, 2000.

Zelizer, Julian E. *On Capitol Hill: The Struggle to Reform Congress and Its Consequences, 1948–2000.* New York: Cambridge University Press, 2006.

13

Chapter Fourteen

Legislative Research:

How to Monitor and Research Congress

Analysis

14

§ 14.00 Introduction

This chapter provides advice on how to follow floor proceedings on the House and Senate floors, by describing what to look for when watching C-SPAN. It also describes how to research or monitor committees and members, by offering lists of information one may need and where that information may be found.

§ 14.10 How to Follow Floor Proceedings in the House

Proceedings in the House are carried on C-SPAN I, the Cable Satellite Public Affairs Network. For those who need more than a professional interest as a motivating factor for tuning in, watching the House has often been compared to the best soap opera that television has to offer. *(See also Chapter Eight, Legislating in Congress: Legislative Process, especially sections on House floor proceedings, beginning at § 8.70, House Floor: Scheduling and Privilege.)*

For those watching outside the Capitol complex, classical music is played while a vote is in progress; for those inside the Capitol complex, there is no sound during a vote. (Inside the Capitol complex, House proceedings are carried on House channels as well as on C-SPAN I.)

In the course of a day, the Senate or the president might transmit a message to the House of Representatives. In that case, a House clerk walks down the center aisle and bows to the Speaker. The House clerk announces a *message from the Senate/president* and bows again. An accompanying Senate or executive branch clerk bows and reads the message. The message is handed to the House clerk and taken to the desk (also referred to as the rostrum or dais). Business on the message does not necessarily occur then or even soon thereafter. *(For information on tracking the status of action, see § 8.123, Keeping Up with the House Floor: Scheduling and Proceedings.)*

Steps in the Proceedings

Who Is on the Floor. When the president delivers his annual State of the Union message, he is in the House chamber. There are enough seats to accommodate the entire House membership, all one hundred senators, the president's Cabinet, the justices of the Supreme Court, the joint chiefs of staff, and the diplomatic corps. There are, in fact, more than 700 seats on the floor of the House.

When the House uses the chamber for its own proceedings, House members do not have assigned seats. Facing the presiding officer's dais, by tradition, Democrats sit to the left of the center aisle, and Republicans to the right. Two lecterns are stationed in the *well*, the open area between the dais and the seats. Four tables, called *party tables* or *committee tables*, are situated among the seats near the front of the chamber. Members may speak only from the well or from one of the party or committee tables. *(See § 8.113, Who Is Allowed on the House Floor?, and § 14.11, House Floor Plan.)*

At the opening of a session, a staffer in white gloves places the *mace*—the parliamentary

14

House Floor Plan

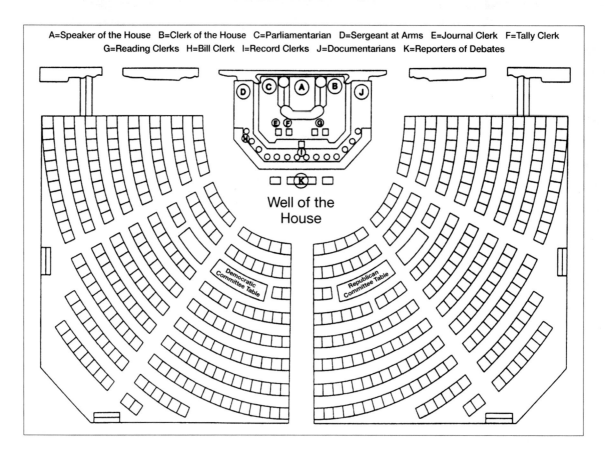

A=Speaker of the House   B=Clerk of the House   C=Parliamentarian   D=Sergeant at Arms   E=Journal Clerk   F=Tally Clerk
G=Reading Clerks   H=Bill Clerk   I=Record Clerks   J=Documentarians   K=Reporters of Debates

Well of the House

Democratic Committee Table

Republican Committee Table

symbol of authority of the House—on a pedestal to the Speaker's right. *Pages*, dressed in navy blue suits and wearing name tags, also are seen around the presiding officer's dais.

Call to Order. The Speaker of the House—the presiding officer—calls the House to order and taps the gavel. The time to convene is set at the end of the previous House session, although there is some regularity of meeting times throughout the year. *(See § 8.72, Daily Starting Times in the House.)* If the Speaker is not presiding that day, another majority member calls the House to order, and a clerk reads a letter from the Speaker designating that member to preside over the House and serve as *Speaker pro tempore* for the day. One may call the Democratic or Republican cloakroom tape to learn the time the House is scheduled to convene and the day's program. *(Democratic cloakroom tape: 202-225-1600; Republican cloakroom tape: 202-225-2020.)* The *Congressional Record* for the previous session also identifies the time.

Opening Prayer. The House chaplain or a guest chaplain delivers a brief opening prayer.

Approval of the Journal. The chair announces that he or she has approved the Journal of the previous day's session. (The *Journal of the House of Representatives of the United States* is

View of the Speaker's Dais and Well of the House

The Speaker or Speaker pro tempore sits on the uppermost level of the dais, and the mace is on the pedestal to the Speaker's right if the House is meeting as the House. If the House is meeting as the Committee of the Whole House on the State of the Union, the chairman of the Committee of the Whole occupies this level, and the mace is placed on a lower pedestal. If Congress is conducting a joint session or meeting, the vice president is seated on this level with the Speaker, a second chair having been added. *(See § 8.110, Committee of the Whole: Debate, and § 8.111, The Mace.)*

One might also see one of the parliamentarians to the Speaker's or chairman's right, advising on parliamentary statements or rulings, and a time clerk is on the presiding officer's left.

The reading clerk as well as several other clerks occupy the middle level. The reading clerk is regularly directed by the Speaker or the chairman of the Committee of the Whole to read measures or amendments or provide other information to the membership, which he or she does from the lectern on this level.

Members may speak from the well of the House, using the Democratic lectern on the Speaker's right or the Republican lectern on the Speaker's left. The official reporters of debate use the table and chairs.

Illustration by Marilyn Gates-Davis. Copyright ©2005 by TheCapitol.Net

14

View of the Speaker's Dais, Floor of the House, and Galleries

While the view of the Speaker's dais in § 14.12 identifies some of the occupants of the dais, this illustration gives a better indication of the size of the dais. On the lowest level of the dais nearest to the viewer are seats occupied by the bill clerk, who is responsible for the "hopper" in which House members place bills and resolutions for introduction.

This illustration also shows in the lower right one of the four committee or party tables from which members may address the House, in addition to the lecterns they may use in the well of the House. Each party has two tables on its side of the center aisle of the House.

The door to the Speaker's left and another out of view to the Speaker's right provide access to the Speaker's Lobby. (The party cloakrooms are in the back of the chamber, out of view in this illustration.)

Immediately above the Speaker's dais is the press gallery. In the walls above the press gallery are the display panels where members' names and votes appear when a vote is taken by electronic device. One of the voting stations is shown at the bottom center-left of the illustration.

Also on the gallery level, to the Speaker's left, one can also see some of the seats that are used for specific guests such as family members and for other visitors and tourists. Visitor seating surrounds the House chamber on the gallery level.

Illustration by Marilyn Gates-Davis. Copyright ©2005 by TheCapitol.Net

the official record of the House and is different from the *Congressional Record (see § 12.20, Floor Documents*).) A member can *demand a vote on the Speaker's approval of the Journal.* This could require a record vote. It can be taken at that time or postponed to a time later in the day. Voting on the Journal provides a count of members who are present for proceedings that day, but it is rarely an indication of a member's support for the Journal itself.

Pledge of Allegiance. A member is called upon to lead the House and those in the gallery in the Pledge of Allegiance.

One-Minute Speeches. At the beginning of most days, some members are seated in the front row of the chamber. This alignment indicates these members' desire to make *one-minute speeches.* These speeches are made in the well of the House. One-minute speeches are allowed when the Speaker recognizes members to *address the House for one minute [and revise and extend his or her remarks].* The Speaker is authorized to announce a limitation on the number of members recognized on a day for one-minute speeches, and can even announce that no "one minutes" will be allowed or that they will be postponed to later in the day. One-minute speeches can be on any subject, and often are not on legislative issues. A one-minute speech might concern a congressional district issue, such as congratulations for an individual constituent or a winning sports team.

Morning Hour Speeches. On Mondays and Tuesdays the House convenes early to allow members to make five-minute speeches on any subject. No legislative business is conducted during this time. *(See § 8.72, Daily Starting Times in the House.)*

Legislative Business. What happens next is often determined by what day of the week it is. For example, bills under *suspension of the rules* are in order on Mondays, Tuesdays, and Wednesdays. *(See § 8.80, House Floor: Methods of Consideration.)* Other legislation may come to the floor under the provisions of a *special rule* reported from the Rules Committee. Each of these two procedures have time limitations associated with them. For suspension of the rules, forty minutes of debate time is allotted, with twenty minutes to the majority party and twenty minutes to the minority party. When debating a special rule, one hour of debate is provided. Proceedings in the House sitting as the House are often referred to as proceedings under the *one-hour rule. (See § 8.90, Rules Committee and Special Rules.)* At the end of an hour of debate on a special rule, a majority-party member will *move the previous question.* This motion enables the House to end debate on the special rule and proceed to a vote on it. Once the rule is agreed to, the House can consider the underlying legislation. *(See § 8.100, Consideration of a Special Rule on the House Floor.)*

Committee of the Whole. When a special rule is agreed to, the House *resolves into the Committee of the Whole House on the State of the Union,* referred to as the Committee of the Whole, to consider the measure referred to in the special rule. The mace is lowered from its pedestal, and the Speaker appoints a member to preside in his stead as *chairman of the Committee of the Whole. (See § 8.111, The Mace.)*

All members serve on this fictitious but procedurally significant committee, and nothing

14

physically changes except that the mace is lowered and the Speaker does not preside. However, measures in the Committee of the Whole are not considered under a one-hour rule but under what is called the *five-minute rule*, allowing a proponent, an opponent, and other members on each side five minutes each to speak on an amendment.

The provisions of the special rule dictate what happens in the Committee of the Whole. There is usually a set period for *general debate* to discuss the legislation. Members then offer amendments pursuant to the special rule, either substantive or so-called *pro forma* amendments. These latter amendments can be identified when a member moves to *strike the last word* or *strike the requisite number of words*. Each pro forma amendment enables the member to speak for five minutes. Pro forma amendments are not voted on. *(See § 8.110, Committee of the Whole: Debate; and § 8.120, Committee of the Whole: Amendment Process.)*

Votes on amendments can occur throughout the proceedings. Votes are taken almost always by voice or by *electronic device*, that is, by electronic voting device. To cast their votes electronically, members insert cards into readers located on the backs of the seats throughout the chamber. Television viewers cannot see large panels behind the rostrum that contain the names of all members and a record of how each voted—yea, nay, or present. Viewers see a running tally of vote totals, broken down by party. *Record votes* are left open for a minimum of fifteen minutes. *(See § 8.130, House Floor: Voting.)*

Committee of the Whole Rises. After consideration of amendments in the Committee of the Whole, the committee *rises and reports* the measure back to the House. The mace is replaced on its pedestal, and the Speaker or Speaker pro tempore assumes the chair. Final action is taken on the measure. A *separate vote* may be requested on any amendment agreed to in the Committee of the Whole. A *motion to recommit* can be offered by the minority party. Upon disposition of this motion to recommit, a vote occurs on *final passage*, and a motion to reconsider is normally laid on the table. *(See § 8.140, House Floor: Motion to Recommit and Final Passage.)*

Special Orders. At the end of legislative business on most days, the House allows members to address the House for as little as five or as long as sixty minutes on any subject they wish. The chamber is usually nearly empty during these *special order speeches*.

End of the Day. When the last special order is concluded, a member *moves that the House adjourn*. The gavel comes down, and the House adjourns for the day.

§ 14.20 How to Follow Floor Proceedings in the Senate

Proceedings in the Senate are carried on C-SPAN II, the Cable Satellite Public Affairs Network. While cable television affords one the opportunity to see important debates, listen to votes as they occur, and monitor the Senate efficiently without leaving the office, it can nonetheless be frustrating to try to view the Senate in session. *(See also Chapter Eight, Legislating in Congress: Legislative Process, especially sections on Senate floor proceedings beginning at § 8.160, Senate Scheduling.)*

Oftentimes, for much of the day there is nothing to watch but a sign across the screen saying *quorum call*, a constructive delay of the proceedings. For those watching outside the Capitol complex, classical music is played while a quorum call is in progress; for those inside the Capitol complex, there is no sound. (Inside the Capitol complex, Senate proceedings are carried on a Senate channel as well as on C-SPAN II.) Quorum calls can last a few seconds, or they can last several hours. And, they can happen repeatedly throughout the day. No senator answers when his or her name is called. Therefore, any attempt to describe a typical day must start by saying the day will likely be interrupted by repeated quorum calls.

In the course of a day, the House of Representatives or the president might transmit a message to the Senate. In that case, a Senate clerk walks down the center aisle and bows to the presiding officer. The Senate clerk announces a *message from the House* or *president* and bows again. An accompanying House or executive branch clerk bows and reads the message. The message is handed to the Senate clerk and taken to the desk (also referred to as the rostrum or dais). Business on the message does not necessarily occur then or even soon thereafter. Again, this is another kind of interruption that can occur throughout the day. *(For information on tracking the status of action, see § 8.161, Keeping Up with the Senate Floor: Scheduling and Proceedings.)*

Steps in the Proceedings

Who Is on the Floor. Senators have assigned desks on the floor of the Senate. Facing the presiding officer's dais, Democrats are seated to the left and Republicans to the right. Seniority (that is, length of service) generally determines desk location, with more senior members often having desks closer to the rostrum. However, senators can choose not to move to a closer desk; for example, Senator Kennedy's desk is in the back row—a desk used by both his brothers.

Certain desks are designated for specific senators. For example, since 1974, the senior senator from New Hampshire has always occupied the desk previously used by Daniel Webster, who represented Massachusetts in the Senate but was born in New Hampshire. Since 1995, the senior senator from Mississippi is assigned the desk formerly occupied by Jefferson Davis.

A so-called "candy desk," filled with sweets, exists on an aisle in the last row on the Republican side of the chamber. The desk is usually assigned to a junior senator. It is currently occupied by Senator Craig Thomas.

Floor managers (senators controlling a discussion) stand or sit at the desks closest to the front of the chamber. *(See § 14.21, Senate Floor Plan.)*

Several people other than senators can be seen on the floor. A committee or personal staffer might be seated on a low chair or stool directly behind a senator who is speaking. Desks in the well are for the party secretaries. For senators with desks in the back row, staff sit on couches against the wall. *Pages*, dressed in navy blue suits and wearing name tags, also are seen either around the presiding officer's dais or walking throughout the chamber. *(See § 8.191, Who Is Allowed on the Senate Floor?)*

14

Call to Order. The first order of business is the call to order of the Senate. The time to reconvene is set at the end of the previous Senate session. One may call the Democratic or Republican cloakroom tape to learn the time the Senate is scheduled to convene and the day's program, to the extent it is known. *(Democratic cloakroom tape: 202-224-8541; Republican cloakroom tape: 202-224-8601.)* The *Congressional Record* for the previous session also identifies the time.

The presiding officer taps the gavel, and calls the Senate to order. The constitutional presiding officer, the vice president, rarely presides. The president pro tempore—the majority senator with the longest service—normally opens proceedings in the Senate. The president pro tempore does not preside throughout the day. For one- or two-hour blocks of time, other senators assume the chair. Junior senators traditionally preside more than senior senators.

Opening Prayer. The Senate chaplain or a guest chaplain delivers a brief morning prayer.

Pledge of Allegiance. A senator is called upon to lead the Senate and those in the gallery in the Pledge of Allegiance.

Leader Time. The majority and minority leaders can make brief remarks at the beginning of the session. They each often use this time to address the business of the day.

Morning Business. The period of time when bills are introduced and routine matters are handled is called "morning business." Morning business usually is conducted throughout the day by gaining unanimous consent to *speak as if in morning business.* As such, morning business can be conducted at any time of day or night. *(See § 8.170, Legislative and Calendar Days; Morning Hour and Morning Business.)*

Legislative or Executive Business. Whether considering legislation (legislative business) or a nomination or treaty (executive business), this activity represents the heart of the Senate's work. How that business is conducted is often difficult to determine in advance. If a measure or executive matter is brought up under a *unanimous consent time agreement,* some order can be foreseen simply by obtaining the text of the agreement.

If no agreement is reached, the legislative measure or executive matter can be brought up under a *motion to proceed to consideration.* Under most circumstances, the motion to proceed is debatable. Most often, a measure or executive matter is brought up by unanimous consent. Under either of these procedures, the measure or executive matter itself is debatable. Thus, absent an agreement, the Senate might quickly dispose of the pending business or be caught in a *filibuster. (See § 8.200, Time Agreements and Motions to Proceed on the Senate Floor.)*

Watching a filibuster can be interesting (if a senator addresses at great length a policy issue) or frustrating (if a senator reads a phone book or sings). Filibusters may be conducted by a single senator, or by several senators yielding to each other, a so-called *tag-team filibuster.* If a filibuster is being conducted, a *cloture petition* can be filed by sixteen senators, asking in effect to stop the filibuster. A vote on the petition occurs two days after it is filed. It takes sixty votes to *invoke cloture,* that is, to stop debate. And, even invoking cloture may not stop the

Senate Floor Plan

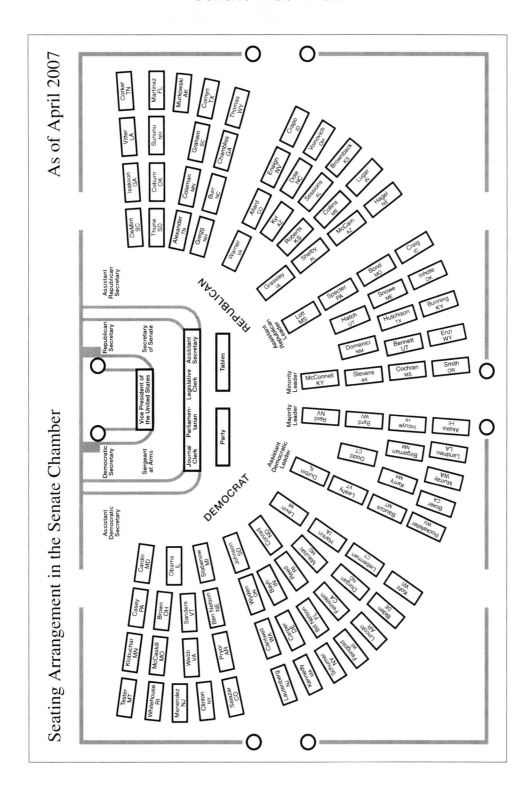

Seating Arrangement in the Senate Chamber

As of April 2007

§ 14.22

View of the Senate Rostrum, or Presiding Officer's Dais

The presiding officer of the Senate—the vice president, the president pro tempore, or a designee of the president pro tempore—alone occupies the upper of the two levels of the Senate rostrum.

On the lower level of the rostrum, the journal clerk sits. That person reads bills and amendments and other information as directed by the presiding officer. The journal clerk also calls the roll on votes and quorum calls. The parliamentarian also sits on this level and advises the presiding officer on parliamentary statements and rulings.

The two tables in front of the rostrum are controlled by the parties, the one to the presiding officer's right by the Democrats and the one to the presiding officer's left by the Republicans.

In the foreground, the aisle desk on the presiding officer's right is occupied by the Democratic leader of the Senate and may be used by the Democratic floor manager of legislative or executive business being considered by the Senate. The aisle desk on the presiding officer's left is occupied by the Republican leader of the Senate and may be used by the Republican floor manager of legislative or executive business.

Doors to the presiding officer's left and right lead to the Senate Lobby. Immediately above the presiding officer and outside of this view is the press gallery. Visitor galleries surround the Senate chamber on the same level as the press gallery.

Illustration by Marilyn Gates-Davis. Copyright ©2005 by TheCapitol.Net

debate immediately. A period of thirty hours is set aside for *post-cloture consideration. (See § 8.230, Cloture in Senate Floor Proceedings.)*

Watching a measure being considered on the Senate floor also entails watching *amendments* being offered. This too can be frustrating, as the Senate in many circumstances does not require amendments to be *germane* or *relevant* to the measure being considered. So, an education bill can be amended by an amendment addressing abortion, or a trade bill can have an amendment dealing with student loans. *(See § 8.220, Senate Amendment Procedure.)*

Voting. Throughout consideration of a legislative measure or executive matter, the Senate can take votes. Any member may request a *roll-call* vote on an amendment or the measure itself. The vote, however, will not occur until all debate has finished on a proposition. Often a senator will move to *table* an amendment. In essence, if approved, a motion to table kills the amendment. A senator will usually announce in advance that he or she intends to offer a motion to table the proposition, allowing debate to continue. When a vote occurs either on a motion to table or on an amendment or the measure, the clerk calls the roll. A clock is exhibited on the television screen showing fifteen minutes allotted for the vote. Many votes are held open beyond the fifteen minutes, to enable senators to get to the floor at their convenience. As each member arrives, a clerk announces the senator's name and, after the senator responds, the clerk states how the senator wishes to be recorded. Often, a member will merely put a thumb up or down to indicate voting preference. At tables in front of the dais, senators can read the text of what is being voted on and see the tally of how each senator has voted. *(See § 8.250, Voting in the Senate.)*

End of the Day. When all business for a day has been completed, the majority leader (or a designee) comes to the floor to announce that no further voting or business is expected for that day. The majority leader may also announce the anticipated schedule for the next session. The Senate at that point either recesses or adjourns, or allows other senators to speak *as if in morning business.* When all senators who wish to speak are finished, a senator will yield the floor. The presiding officer will announce that the Senate is *in recess* or has *adjourned* until the next scheduled session. *(See § 8.170, Legislative and Calendar Days; Morning Hour and Morning Business.)*

§14.30 How to Research Committees

The previous thirteen chapters of this book provide the reader with an understanding of how Congress works and the resources available for monitoring activities in Congress. This section lists the components that might be included in a committee profile, and describes where to research the policy, politics, and procedures of House and Senate committees. What the reader should know about a committee, and where to go to obtain the information, is the intent of this section. *(See also Chapter Eight, Legislating in Congress: Legislative Process, especially sections beginning at § 8.30, Referral of Legislation to Committee, and § 12.10, Committee Documents.)*

14

There are numerous sources of many of these components. Public-record sources are cited where appropriate. Commercial sources are cited where public-record sources are lacking or have great limitations. One can find many of both kinds of resources listed in Chapters Twelve and Thirteen.

Information is provided roughly in "chronological" order, from the appointment of a committee's members, to the organization of a committee, to the processing of legislation, and the conduct of oversight.

Components and Sources for a Committee Profile

Information Needed	Where to Obtain It	Comments
Names of committees and members assigned to a committee; committee seniority	*Congressional Record* (adoption of simple resolution on the floor); THOMAS; committee web site; clerk of the House web site; Senate web site	Committee assignments are made at early organization meetings in November or December after an election. If they are not finished at that time, they are completed early after the swearing in of a new Congress. Be alert to changes made throughout a Congress, recorded in the *Congressional Record*.
Names and number of subcommittees created and subcommittee membership	Committee press releases; committee web site	Subcommittees are created soon after committee assignment resolutions are adopted in the chamber, although selections may begin at early organization meetings. Be alert to changes made throughout a Congress.
Names of committee and subcommittee chairs and ranking members	Committee press releases; committee web site	Committee leaders are selected at early organization meetings in November or December after an election or soon after the next Congress convenes. Committee and subcommittee chairs set their panels' agendas. Be alert to changes made throughout a Congress. House and Senate chairs are now "term limited," although there are exceptions or "waivers."

Components and Sources for a Committee Profile

Information Needed	Where to Obtain It	Comments
Committee size and ratio	Committee web site	Ratios are often indicators of the ability to obtain a majority vote, and of the possible impact of a single majority member voting with the minority party.
Committee and subcommittee staff	House and Senate telephone directories; *Congressional Staff Directory*; *Congressional Yellow Book*; *Roll Call*	Titles and issue responsibilities for staffers are available in commercial resources. Be alert to changes made throughout a Congress.
Committee jurisdiction	House Rule X, *House Rules and Manual*; Senate Rule XXV, *Senate Manual*	Bills are referred based principally on a committee's jurisdiction.
Measures referred to a committee	THOMAS; *Congressional Record*; committee web site	A substantial number of measures are introduced on the first day, but measures can be introduced any day a chamber is in session.
Cosponsorship of a measure	THOMAS; *Congressional Record*	Several committees decide, in part, whether to consider measures based on the number of a measure's cosponsors.
Committee rules	*Congressional Record*; THOMAS; House Rules Committee and Senate Rules and Administration Committee compilations of committee rules; committee web site	Committees must publish rules in the *Congressional Record*; committee rules provide a sense of how a committee will operate (for example, power of chair versus majority rule and chair-ranking minority member relationship).
Committee funding request	House Administration Committee and Senate Rules and Administration Committee; *Congressional Record*	Funding requests are accompanied by summary information on how the funds are to be used and, often, the issues anticipated to be considered; they also provide information on consultants that committees may employ.
Committee expenditures	Statement of Disbursements of the House; Report of the Secretary of the Senate	These resources include salaries of staff, travel expenditures, and all items on which a committee spends money.

14

Components and Sources for a Committee Profile

Information Needed	Where to Obtain It	Comments
Committee travel reports	*Congressional Record*	These reports explain which members and staff traveled where, and for how long.
Committee oversight plans	Committee web site; Committee on Oversight and Government Reform's oversight plans compilation	House committees file oversight plans with the House Oversight and Government Reform Committee and the House Administration Committee. They provide useful advance information of each committee's agenda for a Congress.
Committee views and estimates	Committee web site; Committees on the Budget	Committees in both chambers file "views and estimates" with their chamber's Budget Committee early each Congress on likely agenda items that have budgetary impact.
Committee activity summary from prior Congress	Committee calendar; committee activity report	These resources provide summaries of consideration of issues in the prior Congress.
Committee press releases	Committee web site	Provide notification of agenda issues, possible timing for consideration, and summaries of committee meetings.
Committee hearings schedule	*Congressional Record* (Daily Digest); THOMAS	Rules of each chamber generally require advance notice for hearings.
Witness lists	*Congressional Record*; committee web site; Office of Management and Budget web site	Who is to testify can signal the approach a committee is taking to an issue.
Witnesses' testimony	Committee web site; Office of Management and Budget web site; organization web sites	These resources indicate the positions taken by the administration and advocacy groups.
Hearing transcript or printed hearing record	Committee offices; committee web site	A document may not be printed for months.
Committee markup schedule	*Congressional Record* (Daily Digest)	Markups do not necessarily follow quickly after hearings.

Components and Sources for a Committee Profile

Information Needed	Where to Obtain It	Comments
Legislative vehicle to be used in markup	Committee offices	Chamber rules require notification before markup.
Amendments offered in markup	Committee offices	If an amendment is defeated, it may be offered again on the floor; if adopted by a close vote, it may be voted on again on the floor.
Votes taken in committee	Committee report; committee office	The votes help in preparation for floor consideration, depending on the closeness of the vote.
Markup transcript	Committee offices	This offers the only source on markup outcome available until the report is printed.
Committee-reported measure	Committee offices, until report is printed; committee web site; THOMAS	A committee may change the number of a measure under consideration, as well as the text. *(See § 11.40, Versions of Legislation.)*
Committee report accompanying legislation	Printed as H. Rept. or S. Rept.; GPO Access; THOMAS	*(See § 8.60, Committee Reports.)*

§ 14.40 How to Research Members

The previous section identifies the components one might include in a committee profile. To interact effectively with members and staff and to understand members' positions and pressures, it is important to understand their roles in Congress. It is necessary to know who the players are, both as representatives of a district or state and as legislators. It is important to know what members do to advance a specific legislative agenda and how they interact with each other.

Some information is basic, but critical. Directories at the end of this book provide a listing of members of the 110th Congress, along with their office addresses and phone numbers. Identified in § 13.51 are the key resources available to follow the members as they represent their constituents and legislate in committee and on the floor.

The information provided below is a starting point and is not intended to be a comprehensive list of everything one should know or of all resources available to learn about members. Some readers may want to maintain a full library; others, for budgetary reasons, might be more selective.

14

Components and Sources for a Member Profile

Information Needed	Where to Obtain It	Comments
List of members and their party affiliations	*Congressional Directory; Congressional Record;* House and Senate web sites; THOMAS (LC web links: House Clerk and Senate Directory)	Be alert to changes throughout a Congress.
Address, phone and fax numbers, email address	*Congressional Staff Directory; Congressional Yellow Book;* House and Senate telephone directories; House and Senate web sites; THOMAS (LC web links: House Clerk and Senate Directory)	Information is provided for both Washington and district/state offices.
Biography	*Biographical Directory of the U.S. Congress; Congressional Directory; Almanac of American Politics; Politics in America*	Private sources describe prior legislative service; work experience may provide clues to a member's policy interests.
Election statistics	*Congressional Directory; CQ Weekly* and *Almanac; National Journal*	The margin of victory may influence a legislative agenda.
District/state demographics	*Almanac of American Politics; Politics in America*	These sources contain data on district demographics and other statistics. Knowledge of a state or district is integral to understanding a member's positions.
Seniority in chamber	*Congressional Directory*	Seniority may indicate influence.
Staff	*Congressional Directory;* House and Senate telephone directories; *Congressional Staff Directory; Congressional Yellow Book*	These sources explain the responsibilities of staff, and the distribution of staff between Washington and district/state offices.
Committee and subcommittee assignments	*Congressional Directory; Congressional Staff Directory; Congressional Yellow Book;* House and Senate web sites; THOMAS (LC web links: House Committees and Senate Committees)	Assignments generally (but not always) reflect a member's interests and issue influence; they may also affect fund-raising ability.

Components and Sources for a Member Profile

Information Needed	Where to Obtain It	Comments
Informal group membership	House Administration Committee web site	This source has information on membership in congressional member organizations, members' sponsorship of staff organizations, and regulations governing their creation.
Measures introduced	*Congressional Record*; THOMAS; individual member's web site	Measures introduced reveal legislative priorities; a substantial number of measures are introduced on the first day, but measures can be introduced any day a chamber is in session.
Measures cosponsored	*Congressional Record*; THOMAS; individual member's web site	Cosponsorship reveals legislative priorities and relations with other members.
One-minute speeches made on House floor; Senate speeches in morning business	*Congressional Record*	Speaker announces number of one-minute speeches allowed for a specific day; generally speeches are about district/state matters, yet also cover legislative matters.
Press releases	Individual member's web site	This source reveals the issues and other matters a member considers important, and his or her spin on them.
Statements made at hearings and questions asked of witnesses	Hearing transcript	This information is available in committee offices, sometimes on committee web sites, and, ultimately, in printed hearings (if they are printed).
Amendments offered in committee	Committee report	Amendments may be reoffered, or the issue discussed again, on the floor.
Amendments offered on the floor	*Congressional Record*	An amendment may be offered in one chamber and not the other.
Extensions of remarks	*Congressional Record*	These are generally statements by House members about district/state matters, yet also about legislative matters.

14

Components and Sources for a Member Profile

Information Needed	Where to Obtain It	Comments
Financial disclosure form	Compiled in Financial Disclosure Statement, printed as House or Senate document	This provides information on trips taken; also reported on travel forms available in House Legislative Resource Center and Senate Office of Public Records.
Federal Election Commission reports	FEC web site; House Legislative Resource Center and Senate Office of Public Records	The reports show contributions to campaigns, as well as political action committee information.
Voting record in committee	Committee report	What position was taken in committee? Why might a position change on a floor vote?
Voting record on floor	*Congressional Record*; House clerk's web site; Senate web site	This is the most visible and objective statement of a member's views.
Conference committee appointment	*Congressional Record*; THOMAS	What views and positions and alliances does the member take into conference?
Party support voting record	*CQ Weekly and Almanac*	Is the member a good soldier, a maverick, or somewhere in between?
Presidential support voting record	*CQ Weekly and Almanac*	Is the member "persuadable" to back the president on some votes?
Interest group voting record	Interest group publications; *Almanac of American Politics*; *Politics in America*	Who are a member's supporters and opponents?

§ 14.50 Checklist of Jobs to Undertake in the Office: Tracking Legislative Action

This section provides a selective list of information needed to track legislative activity. Many congressional offices and outside organizations prepare a "table" on each issue or measure they are tracking to identify key players and actions. Spreadsheet or flowchart software can assist with this task. A checklist such as the following guides the government affairs professional in planning strategy and identifying legislative actions that may require an activity or response at a specific time.

Tracking Legislative Action Checklist

Tracking a Measure: Introduction and Referral

- **Key Documents**

  Measure as introduced

  Sponsor statements and press releases

- **Key Actions and Events**

  Timing of introduction

  Sponsor

  Cosponsors

  Committee(s) and subcommittee(s) of referral

Tracking a Measure: Committee Action, Hearings, and Markup

- **Key Players**

  Members of committee and subcommittee

  Key committee staff

  Key subcommittee staff

  Key committee and subcommittee members and their positions on measure

  Party leadership position on measure

  Outside groups, both proponents and opponents

  Administration position on measure

- **Key Documents**

  Committee rules

  Committee hearing schedule

  Witness testimony

  Hearing transcript

  Agency views

  Congressional Budget Office estimate

  Vehicle for markup consideration

  Amendments offered in markup

  Vehicle reported (for example, clean bill or original bill)

  Committee report

  Additional, supplemental, and minority views, if filed

- **Key Actions and Events**

  Witnesses scheduled

  Hearings held

  Markup schedule

  Markup

  Disposition of amendments

  Votes in markup on each amendment

  Vote to report measure

14

Tracking a Measure: Floor Action

• Key Players
Leadership, which schedules measure
House Rules Committee
Floor managers
Amendment sponsors

• Key Documents
House and Senate calendars
Floor schedule/whip notices
Special rule or unanimous consent time agreement, if appropriate
Amendments prefiled
Measure made in order
Measure as passed (engrossed)

• Key Actions and Events
Rules Committee meeting (House)
Unanimous consent agreement announced (Senate)
Whip notices
Debate and amendment
Final passage

Tracking a Measure: Reconciling Differences

• Key Players
House and Senate conferees
Staff members working with conferees

• Key Documents
House-passed and Senate-passed versions of measure
Side-by-side comparison of measures
Conference report
Joint explanatory statement

• Key Actions and Events
Conference meetings
Amendments offered in conference
Votes in conference
Procedures to be followed in conference

Outside the Formal Legislative Process
Proponents and opponents of measure
Lobbying activity on measure
Campaign contributions to sponsors and key opponents of measure
Press coverage of issue, local and national
Polls taken on issue, local and national
Administration activity

Chapter Fifteen

Putting It All Together:

A Working Example

Analysis

§15.00 Key Legislative Documents Depicting the History of Financial Services Modernization Legislation in the 106th Congress

Throughout this book, we have presented the legislative process by describing its often eso-teric procedures and the documents that are generated at each stage. In this section, our goal is to bring life to the process by describing the progression of a representative piece of legisla-tion—financial services modernization—as it moved through various procedural stages in 1999, the first session of the 106th Congress. It is representative in that more or fewer steps or documents might occur as Congress considers another piece of legislation.

On each following page, the reader will find cover pages and selections from the principal, formal documents generated during the consideration of the financial services legislation. The reader will also find on each of these pages an explanation of the purpose of the repre-sentative document in the legislative process and the information that can be gleaned from it. As mentioned throughout this book, many of the documents generated in the legislative process are available from THOMAS, GPO Access, and the House and Senate web sites.

Recall that comprehensive legislation is rarely introduced, considered, and enacted with-in one session of Congress. It is the product of years of hearings, negotiation, and political tim-ing. For example, the hearings that were held by the House Banking and Financial Services Committee in February 1999, and by the House Commerce Committee's Subcommittee on Finance and Hazardous Materials in April 1999, were the last in a series of hearings on the financial services industry and its regulation by the federal and state governments that had begun years before.

Therefore, to get a full appreciation of the history of this particular legislation, it would be useful to go back at least several Congresses, read the hearings, examine the earlier legislation introduced and perhaps considered, and review statements and any debate that appeared in the *Congressional Record*. There is always a history to a legislative issue, and many members of Congress have participated in at least part of that history before one Congress is able to align policy, politics, and procedure to enact legislation that the president signs into law.

In the 107th Congress, the Banking and Financial Services Committee was renamed the Financial Services Committee, and the Commerce Committee was renamed the Energy and Commerce Committee. In addition, the Financial Services Committee was given jurisdiction over the "business of insurance" and "securities and exchanges," jurisdictional authority that had generally resided in the Commerce Committee. An important cause of the name change and jurisdictional realignment was the enactment of the financial services modernization leg-islation.

A January 30, 2001, memorandum of understanding that was printed in the *Congressional Record* supplemented the jurisdictional changes to explain certain aspects of insurance and securities issues that would remain in the Energy and Commerce Committee. In the 109th Congress, the Speaker announced that the memorandum of understanding would be modi-

15

fied by deleting a paragraph. The announcement was printed in the *Congressional Record* on January 4, 2005. The paragraph deleted read:

> While it is agreed that the jurisdiction of the Committee on Financial Services over securities and exchanges includes anti-fraud authorities under the securities laws, the Committee on Energy and Commerce will retain jurisdiction only over the issue of setting accounting standards by the Financial Accounting Standards Board.

It is important to know as well that financial services reform as an issue has been considered, in various forms, almost from the time that the Glass-Steagall Act of 1933, the New Deal foundation of twentieth-century financial services regulation, was originally enacted. Major financial services legislation—covering banking, insurance, securities, and related financial services—was subsequently enacted in 1934, 1940, 1945, 1956, 1974, 1977, 1978, 1989, 1991, and 1994. Other major laws preceded Glass-Steagall and numerous other changes were reflected in amendments and minor legislation over the years. Likewise, oversight continues, and changes to the financial services modernization law can be tucked into new legislation on related subjects or be considered in separate legislation. The government affairs professional, scholar, or anyone working in a subject area needs to develop a good knowledge of the legislative and regulatory history of that subject area.

§ 15.01 Bill as Introduced in the House

H.R. 10 was introduced by Mr. Leach, chair of the House Committee on Banking and Financial Services, on January 6, 1999, the first day of the 106th Congress. Upon introduction there were eleven original cosponsors. The measure was referred to the Committee on Banking and Financial Services (*primary committee*), and in addition to the Committee on Commerce for consideration of provisions within its jurisdiction. Those provisions were not spelled out in the referral language. The Speaker was granted authority to impose time limitations on the referral.

H.R. 10 is designated as *A Bill* at this stage of the process. The *official title* is the language immediately following the bill designation. The *enacting clause*, "*Be it enacted by the Senate and House of Representatives of the United States of America in Congress assembled,*" provides force of law to the measure, if enacted. Section 1(a) identifies the *short (popular) title*; a short title is how most people refer to a measure as it makes its way through the legislative process. (*See § 15.01a.*)

§15.01a

Bill as Introduced
in the House

① Measure number

106TH CONGRESS
1ST SESSION **① H. R. 10**

To enhance competition in the financial services industry by providing a prudential framework for the affiliation of banks, securities firms, and other financial service providers, and for other purposes.

IN THE HOUSE OF REPRESENTATIVES

JANUARY 6, 1999

② Sponsor and original cosponsors

③ Primary committee referral and sequential referral

② Mr. LEACH (for himself, Mr. MCCOLLUM, Mrs. ROUKEMA, Mr. BAKER, Mr. LAZIO, Mr. BACHUS, Mr. CASTLE, Mr. KING, Mr. NEY, Mr. COOK, Mr. LATOURETTE, and Mrs. KELLY) introduced the following bill; which was ③ referred to the Committee on Banking and Financial Services, and in addition to the Committee on Commerce, for a period to be subsequently determined by the Speaker, in each case for consideration of such provisions as fall within the jurisdiction of the committee concerned

A BILL

④ Official title

④ To enhance competition in the financial services industry by providing a prudential framework for the affiliation of banks, securities firms, and other financial service providers, and for other purposes.

⑤ Enacting clause

⑤ 1   *Be it enacted by the Senate and House of Representa-*

2 *tives of the United States of America in Congress assembled,*

2

1 **SECTION 1. SHORT TITLE; PURPOSES; TABLE OF CON-**

2   **TENTS.**

⑥ Short (popular) title

⑥ 3   (a) SHORT TITLE.—This Act may be cited as the

4 ''Financial Services Act of 1999''.

15

§ 15.02 Bill as Reported

The Committee on Banking and Financial Services reported H.R. 10 from committee to the House on March 23, 1999, by a vote of 51 to 8. The vote to report followed two markup sessions held on March 10 and 11. The language on the cover of the reported measure following the phrase "March 23, 1999" indicates that the committee reported a full-text substitute to H.R. 10, *an amendment in the nature of a substitute. (See § 15.02a, notes 3, 4.)*

The accompanying committee report was H. Rept. 106-74, the 74th House report filed in the 106th Congress. It was filed in three parts. When more than one committee reports a measure, the report number remains the same for all committees. Each committee version is identified as Part I, Part II, and so forth. (Arabic numbers are gaining popularity for numbering parts, but Roman numerals are traditional.) For H.R. 10, the Banking Committee filed both Parts I and II *(see explanation at § 15.04)*. The measure was placed on the *Union Calendar* and was the 105th measure placed on the calendar. *(See § 15.02a, note 1.)*

H.R. 10 was *sequentially* referred to the Committee on Commerce until May 14, 1999. On May 13, the Commerce Committee received an extension until June 11, and, on June 11, it received another extension until June 15. On June 15, the Committee on Commerce reported H.R. 10 from committee to the House with *an amendment in the nature of a substitute.* Within the document (the bill as reported by the two committees), the Commerce Committee amendment followed the Banking Committee amendment. The Banking Committee amendment was printed in italicized type, and the Commerce Committee amendment, in boldface Roman type. *(Compare excerpts at notes 9 and 10 in § 15.02a.)*

On June 15, Mr. Maloney, a member of the Banking and Financial Services Committee, was also added as a cosponsor on the legislation. Members can be added as cosponsors until the measure is reported by all committees that received a referral. *(See § 15.02a, note 6.)*

§ 15.02a

Bill as Reported

1 Calendar number

2 Committee report in three parts

3 Reported from primary committee

4 Form in which amendment was reported (amendment in the nature of a substitute)

5 Sequential referral

6 Additional cosponsor

IB

1 **Union Calendar No. 105**

106TH CONGRESS
1ST SESSION

H. R. 10

2 **[Report No. 106–74, Parts I, II, and III]**

To enhance competition in the financial services industry by providing a prudential framework for the affiliation of banks, securities firms, and other financial service providers, and for other purposes.

IN THE HOUSE OF REPRESENTATIVES

JANUARY 6, 1999

Mr. LEACH (for himself, Mr. MCCOLLUM, Mrs. ROUKEMA, Mr. BAKER, Mr. LAZIO, Mr. BACHUS, Mr. CASTLE, Mr. KING, Mr. NEY, Mr. COOK, Mr. LATOURETTE, and Mrs. KELLY) introduced the following bill; which was referred to the Committee on Banking and Financial Services, and in addition to the Committee on Commerce, for a period to be subsequently determined by the Speaker, in each case for consideration of such provisions as fall within the jurisdiction of the committee concerned

MARCH 23, 1999

3 Reported from the Committee on Banking and Financial Services with an amendment

4 [Strike out all after the enacting clause and insert the part printed in italic]

MARCH 23, 1999

5 Referral to the Committee on Commerce extended for a period ending not later than May 14, 1999

MAY 13, 1999

Referral to the Committee on Commerce extended for a period ending not later than June 11, 1999

JUNE 11, 1999

Referral to the Committee on Commerce extended for a period ending not later than June 15, 1999

JUNE 15, 1999

6 Additional sponsor: Mr. MALONEY of Connecticut

15

Continued on page 570

Bill as Reported

7 Reported from Commerce Committee

8 Form in which amendment was reported (amendment in the nature of a substitute)

9 Banking Committee amendment

2

JUNE 15, 1999

7 Reported from the Committee on Commerce with an amendment, committed to the Committee of the Whole House on the State of the Union, and ordered to be printed

8 [Strike out all after the enacting clause and insert the part printed in boldface roman]

[For text of introduced bill, see copy of bill as introduced on January 6, 1999]

A BILL

To enhance competition in the financial services industry by providing a prudential framework for the affiliation of banks, securities firms, and other financial service providers, and for other purposes.

1   *Be it enacted by the Senate and House of Representa-*

2 *tives of the United States of America in Congress assembled,*

9 3 ***SECTION 1. SHORT TITLE; PURPOSES; TABLE OF CON-***

4   ***TENTS.***

5   *(a) SHORT TITLE.—This Act may be cited as the "Fi-*

6 *nancial Services Act of 1999".*

7   *(b) PURPOSES.—The purposes of this Act are as fol-*

8 *lows:*

9   *(1) To enhance competition in the financial serv-*

10   *ices industry, in order to foster innovation and effi-*

11   *ciency.*

12   *(2) To ensure the continued safety and soundness*

13   *of depository institutions.*

Continued on page 571

Bill as Reported

375

1   *of a Federal savings association to a national bank*

2   *or a State bank after the date of the enactment of the*

3   *Financial Services Act of 1999 may retain the term*

4   *'Federal' in the name of such institution if such de-*

5   *pository institution remains an insured depository*

6   *institution.*

7   *"(2) DEFINITIONS.—For purposes of this sub-*

8   *section, the terms 'depository institution', 'insured de-*

9   *pository institution', 'national bank', and 'State*

10 *bank' have the same meanings as in section 3 of the*

11 *Federal Deposit Insurance Act.".*

 12 SECTION 1. SHORT TITLE; PURPOSES; TABLE OF CON-

13   TENTS.

14   (a) SHORT TITLE.—This Act may be cited as

15 the "Financial Services Act of 1999".

16   (b) PURPOSES.—The purposes of this Act

17 are as follows:

18   (1) To enhance competition in the fi-

19 nancial services industry, in order to fos-

20 ter innovation and efficiency.

21   (2) To ensure the continued safety

22 and soundness of depository institutions.

23   (3) To provide necessary and appro-

24 priate protections for investors and en-

⑩ Commerce
Committee
amendment

15

§ 15.03 Banking and Financial Services Committee Report

Both the Banking Committee and the Commerce Committee reported H.R. 10. Part 1 of H. Rept. 106-74 was filed in the House by the primary committee, the Committee on Banking and Financial Services. When that panel reported H.R. 10 on March 23, 1999, the committee chose to retain H.R. 10 as the legislative vehicle and to report an *amendment in the nature of a substitute*. The committee could have chosen to introduce the amended language as a new, or *clean bill*.

Supplemental, additional, and dissenting views were also filed. They are included in the body of the report. Minority committee members usually request the inclusion of supplemental, additional, and dissenting views in a committee report. Although the request is traditionally made by minority-party members, all committee members are entitled to file such views. To be included, supplemental, additional, and dissenting views must be filed within two days of a committee vote to report. The cover page of the report must indicate when such views are included.

§ 15.03a

Banking and Financial Services
Committee Report

1 Committee report and part number

106TH CONGRESS
1st Session } HOUSE OF REPRESENTATIVES { **1** REPT. 106–74
Part 1

FINANCIAL SERVICES ACT OF 1999

MARCH 23, 1999.—Ordered to be printed

2 Reporting committee

2 Mr. LEACH, from the Committee on Banking and Financial Services, submitted the following

REPORT

together with

3 Other views

3 SUPPLEMENTAL, ADDITIONAL AND

DISSENTING VIEWS

[To accompany H.R. 10]

The Committee on Banking and Financial Services, to whom was referred the bill (H.R. 10) to enhance competition in the financial services industry by providing a prudential framework for the affiliation of banks, securities firms, and other financial service providers, and for other purposes, having considered the same, report favorably thereon with an amendment and recommend that the bill as amended do pass.

The amendment is as follows:

4 Banking Committee amendment

4 Strike out all after the enacting clause and insert in lieu thereof the following:

SECTION 1. SHORT TITLE; PURPOSES; TABLE OF CONTENTS.

(a) SHORT TITLE.—This Act may be cited as the "Financial Services Act of 1999".

(b) PURPOSES.—The purposes of this Act are as follows:

★69–006

§ 15.04 Banking and Financial Services Committee Supplementary Report

The Committee on Banking and Financial Services filed in the House a supplementary report containing a cost estimate from the Congressional Budget Office. According to House rules, such an estimate must be included in a committee report. The committee filed a supplementary report to comply with this requirement. The supplementary report also contains an errata correction to Part 1 of the report. The report retains the same number, but is designated Part 2.

§ 15.04a

Banking and Financial Services Committee
Supplementary Report

❶ Committee report and part number

❷ Reporting committee

❸ Supplementary report

❹ Purpose of supplementary report

106TH CONGRESS ⎫
1st Session ⎬ HOUSE OF REPRESENTATIVES ❶ REPT. 106–74
⎭ Part 2

FINANCIAL SERVICES ACT OF 1999

JUNE 10, 1999.—Ordered to be printed

---

❷ Mr. LEACH, from the Committee on Banking and Financial
Services, submitted the following

❸ SUPPLEMENTARY REPORT

[To accompany H.R. 10]

❹ This supplemental report shows the cost estimate of the Congressional Budget Office with respect to the bill (H.R. 10), as reported, which was not included in part 1 of the report submitted by the Committee on Banking and Financial Services on March 23, 1999 (H. Rept. 106–74, pt. 1).

This supplemental report is submitted in accordance with clause 3(a)(2) of rule XIII of the Rules of the House of Representatives.

This supplemental report also contains an errata correction to page 2 of part 1 of the report.

U.S CONGRESS,
CONGRESSIONAL BUDGET OFFICE,
Washington, DC, June 10, 1999.

Hon. JAMES A. LEACH,
*Chairman, Committee on Banking and Financial Services, House of
Representatives, Washington, DC.*

DEAR MR. CHAIRMAN: The Congressional Budget Office has prepared the enclosed costs estimate and mandate statements for H.R. 10, the Financial Services Act of 1999. One enclosure includes the estimate of federal costs and the estimate of the impact of the legislation on state, local, and tribal governments. The estimated impact of mandates on the private sector is discussed in a separate enclosure.

If you wish further details on these estimates, we will be pleased to provide them. The CBO staff contacts are Robert S. Seiler (for costs to the Federal Home Loan Banks); Mary Maginniss (for other federal costs); Carolyn Lynch (for federal revenues); Susan Seig (for

57–234

15

§ 15.05 Commerce Committee Report

Here is the report filed in the House by the House Committee on Commerce, which received a sequential referral of H.R. 10. The report was filed by Mr. Bliley, the chair of the Committee on Commerce, on June 15, 1999, the day the measure was reported with an *amendment in the nature of a substitute*. The report is designated Part 3 of H. Rept. 106-74. Additional views were also filed and included in the body of the report.

§ 15.05a

Commerce Committee Report

① Committee report and part number

② Reporting committee

③ Additional views

106TH CONGRESS } HOUSE OF REPRESENTATIVES { **①** REPT. 106–74
1st Session   Part 3

FINANCIAL SERVICES ACT OF 1999

JUNE 15, 1999.—Committed to the Committee of the Whole House on the State of the Union and ordered to be printed

② Mr. BLILEY, from the Committee on Commerce, submitted the following

R E P O R T

together with

③ ADDITIONAL VIEWS

[To accompany H.R. 10]

The Committee on Commerce, to whom was referred the bill (H.R. 10) to enhance competition in the financial services industry by providing a prudential framework for the affiliation of banks, securities firms, and other financial service providers, and for other purposes, having considered the same, report favorably thereon with an amendment and recommend that the bill as amended do pass.

CONTENTS

57–325

Continued on page 578

15

§ 15.05a (continued)

Commerce Committee Report

4 Commerce
Committee
amendment

2

AMENDMENT

4 The amendment is as follows:

Strike out all after the enacting clause and insert in lieu thereof the following:

SECTION 1. SHORT TITLE; PURPOSES; TABLE OF CONTENTS.

(a) SHORT TITLE.—This Act may be cited as the "Financial Services Act of 1999".

(b) PURPOSES.—The purposes of this Act are as follows:

(1) To enhance competition in the financial services industry, in order to foster innovation and efficiency.

(2) To ensure the continued safety and soundness of depository institutions.

(3) To provide necessary and appropriate protections for investors and ensure fair and honest markets in the delivery of financial services.

(4) To avoid duplicative, potentially conflicting, and overly burdensome regulatory requirements through the creation of a regulatory framework for financial holding companies that respects the divergent requirements of each of the component businesses of the holding company, and that is based upon principles of strong functional regulation and enhanced regulatory coordination.

(5) To reduce and, to the maximum extent practicable, to eliminate the legal barriers preventing affiliation among depository institutions, securities firms, insurance companies, and other financial service providers and to provide a prudential framework for achieving that result.

(6) To enhance the availability of financial services to citizens of all economic circumstances and in all geographic areas.

(7) To enhance the competitiveness of United States financial service providers internationally.

(8) To ensure compliance by depository institutions with the provisions of the Community Reinvestment Act of 1977 and enhance the ability of depository institutions to meet the capital and credit needs of all citizens and communities, including underserved communities and populations.

(c) TABLE OF CONTENTS.—The table of contents for this Act is as follows:

§ 15.06 Special Rule from the Rules Committee

On June 30, 1999, the House Rules Committee reported from committee to the House H. Res. 235, a *special rule* providing for consideration of H.R. 10. The special rule was placed on the *House Calendar* as the 81st item. The special rule was reported by Mr. Sessions, a Rules Committee majority member, who was selected to manage the special rule on the floor. The special rule was accompanied by H. Rept. 106-214.

A special rule itself is considered in the House under the *one-hour rule*. Mr. Sessions yielded half of his one hour to a minority member of the Rules Committee *for purposes of debate only*. The two floor managers then parceled out short blocks of time to their colleagues to speak on the rule.

The special rule on H.R. 10 provided ninety minutes of general debate time on the bill, equally divided and controlled by the chairs and ranking minority members of the two committees that reported the legislation, Banking and Financial Services, and Commerce. The special rule also provided for consideration of a new version of H.R. 10, included in the Rules Committee report (H. Rept. 106-214) and cited as "Rules Committee Print dated June 24, 1999." The special rule referred to the Rules Committee report for a list of amendments made in order and the time allocated for each amendment.

§ *15.06a*

Special Rule from the Rules Committee

IV

① Calendar number

② Resolution number

③ Committee report number

④ Majority manager of special rule

⑤ Special rule for the consideration of H.R. 10

---

① **House Calendar No. 81**

106TH CONGRESS
1ST SESSION **②** **H. RES. 235**

③ **[Report No. 106–214]**

Providing for consideration of the bill (H.R. 10) to enhance competition in the financial services industry by providing a prudential framework for the affiliation of banks, securities firms, and other financial service providers, and for other purposes.

IN THE HOUSE OF REPRESENTATIVES

JUNE 30, 1999

④ Mr. SESSIONS, from the Committee on Rules, reported the following resolution; which was referred to the House Calendar and ordered to be printed

---

RESOLUTION

⑤ Providing for consideration of the bill (H.R. 10) to enhance competition in the financial services industry by providing a prudential framework for the affiliation of banks, securities firms, and other financial service providers, and for other purposes.

1   *Resolved,* That at any time after the adoption of this

2 resolution the Speaker may, pursuant to clause 2(b) of

3 rule XVIII, declare the House resolved into the Committee

4 of the Whole House on the state of the Union for consider-

5 ation of the bill (H.R. 10) to enhance competition in the

Continued on page 582

15

Special Rule from the Rules Committee

2

⑥ General debate

⑦ Alternate version
of H.R. 10

⑧ Amendment
process

⑥ 1 financial services industry by providing a prudential

2 framework for the affiliation of banks, securities firms,

3 and other financial service providers, and for other pur-

4 poses. The first reading of the bill shall be dispensed with.

5 All points of order against consideration of the bill are

⑥ 6 waived. General debate shall be confined to the bill and

7 shall not exceed 90 minutes, with 45 minutes equally di-

8 vided and controlled by the chairman and ranking minor-

9 ity member of the Committee on Banking and Financial

10 Services and 45 minutes equally divided and controlled by

11 the chairman and ranking minority member of the Com-

12 mittee on Commerce. After general debate the bill shall

13 be considered for amendment under the five-minute rule.

⑦ 14 In lieu of the amendments now printed in the bill, it shall

15 be in order to consider as an original bill for the purpose

16 of amendment under the five-minute rule an amendment

17 in the nature of a substitute consisting of the text of the

⑧ 18 Rules Committee Print dated June 24, 1999. That

19 amendment in the nature of a substitute shall be consid-

20 ered as read. All points of order against that amendment

21 in the nature of a substitute are waived. No amendment

22 to that amendment in the nature of a substitute shall be

23 in order except those printed in the report of the Com-

24 mittee on Rules accompanying this resolution. Each

25 amendment may be offered only in the order printed in

Continued on page 583

Special Rule from the Rules Committee

3

1 the report, may be offered only by a Member designated

2 in the report, shall be considered as read, shall be debat-

3 able for the time specified in the report equally divided

4 and controlled by the proponent and an opponent, shall

5 not be subject to amendment, and shall not be subject to

6 a demand for division of the question in the House or in

7 the Committee of the Whole. All points of order against

8 the amendments printed in the report are waived. The

9 Cluster voting   **9**   9 Chairman of the Committee of the Whole may: (1) post-

10 pone until a time during further consideration in the Com-

11 mittee of the Whole a request for a recorded vote on any

12 amendment; and (2) reduce to five minutes the minimum

13 time for electronic voting on any postponed question that

14 follows another electronic vote without intervening busi-

15 ness, provided that the minimum time for electronic voting

16 on the first in any series of questions shall be 15 minutes.

10 House action   **10**   17 At the conclusion of consideration of the bill for amend-

18 ment the Committee shall rise and report the bill to the

19 House with such amendments as may have been adopted.

20 Any Member may demand a separate vote in the House

21 on any amendment adopted in the Committee of the Whole

22 to the bill or to the amendment in the nature of a sub-

23 stitute made in order as original text. The previous ques-

24 tion shall be considered as ordered on the bill and amend-

25 ments thereto to final passage without intervening motion

1 except one motion to recommit with or without instruc-

2 tions.

15

§ 15.07 Rules Committee Report

Accompanying H. Res. 235 was H. Rept. 106-214, a report from the Committee on Rules. The special rule was reported from the Rules Committee by a recorded vote of 9 to 3, and the report filed in the House June 30, 1999, by Mr. Sessions. The report summarized the provisions of the special rule, provided information on all votes taken in the Rules Committee, and, most importantly, designated which amendments would be allowed to be offered on the floor and how much time would be allocated for each amendment. Eleven amendments were made in order under the special rule. Each amendment's sponsor was identified, the amendment was summarized, and the amount of time allocated for each amendment was noted. The full text of each amendment was also included in the Rules Committee report.

§15.07a

Rules Committee
Report

1 Committee report number

2 Purpose of special rule

3 Provisions of special rule

106TH CONGRESS *1st Session*	HOUSE OF REPRESENTATIVES	**1** REPORT 106–214

2 PROVIDING FOR THE CONSIDERATION OF H.R. 10,
FINANCIAL SERVICES ACT OF 1999

JUNE 30, 1999.—Referred to the House Calendar and ordered to be printed

---

Mr. SESSIONS, from the Committee on Rules,
submitted the following

REPORT

[To accompany H. Res. 235]

The Committee on Rules, having had under consideration House Resolution 235, by a record vote of 9 to 3, report the same to the House with the recommendation that the resolution be adopted.

3 SUMMARY OF PROVISIONS OF RESOLUTION

The resolution provides for the consideration of H.R. 10, the "Financial Services Act of 1999," under a structured rule. The rule provides 90 minutes of general debate: 45 minutes divided equally between the chairman and ranking minority member of the Committee on Commerce.

The rule waives all points of order against consideration of the bill. The rule makes in order the amendment in the nature of a substitute consisting of the text of the Rules Committee Print dated June 24, 1999, as original text for the purpose of amendment. The rule waives all points of order against the amendment in the nature a substitute.

The rule provides that no amendment to the amendment in the nature of a substitute shall be in order except those printed in this report, which may be offered in the order printed in this report, may be offered only by a Member designated in this report, shall be considered as read, shall be debatable for the time specified in this report equally divided and controlled by the proponent and an opponent, shall not be subject to amendment, and shall not be subject to a demand for a division of the question. The rule waives all points of order against the amendments printed in this report.

The rule allows the chairman of the Committee of the Whole to postpone recorded votes and reduce voting time to five minutes on any postponed question, provided voting time on the first in any se-

69–008

15

§ 15.08 Statement of Administration Policy (House)

On July 1, 1999, the Office of Management and Budget issued a Statement of Administration Policy on H.R. 10, the House bill. The statement announced the president's support for the legislation and opposition to selected amendments to be offered to it.

§ 15.08a

Statement of Administration Policy (House)

EXECUTIVE OFFICE OF THE PRESIDENT
OFFICE OF MANAGEMENT AND BUDGET
WASHINGTON, D.C. 20503

STATEMENT OF ADMINISTRATION POLICY
(THIS STATEMENT HAS BEEN COORDINATED BY OMB WITH THE CONCERNED AGENCIES.)

July 1, 1999
(House)

H.R. 10 - Financial Services Act of 1999
(Leach (R) IA and 12 co-sponsors)

The Administration supports H.R. 10, the Financial Services Act of 1999. The Administration has been a strong proponent of financial modernization legislation that would best serve the interests of consumers, business, and communities, while protecting the safety and soundness of the financial system. H.R. 10 would:

- allow affiliations among banks, securities firms, and insurance companies, thereby increasing the competitiveness of the U.S. financial services sector and giving consumers greater choice and lower prices;

- preserve the relevance of the Community Reinvestment Act by requiring that banks have and maintain a satisfactory CRA record as a condition for their affiliates or subsidiaries engaging in new financial activities;

- uphold a bipartisan compromise allowing financial services firms to conduct financial activities in the structure -- subsidiaries or affiliates of banks -- that best serves their customers, in a way that is best for safety and soundness;

- generally provide for the continued separation of banking and commerce.

The President has stated the importance of adopting protections to ensure the privacy of consumers' financial records. The amendment to be considered by the House would improve the bill by including new privacy protections, although it does not address all of the issues involved. The Administration will continue to pursue additional protections.

The Administration strongly opposes the medical privacy provisions of the bill. Unfortunately, those provisions would preempt important existing protections and do not reflect the extensive legislative work that has already been done on this complex issue. The Administration thus urges striking the medical privacy provisions and will pursue medical privacy in other fora.

The Administration strongly opposes the Barr-Paul-Campbell Amendment, which would seriously erode our ability to fight financial criminals and the drug cartels. The amendment would effectively eliminate suspicious activity reporting by financial institutions -- one of our

Continued on page 587

§ *15.08a (continued)*

Statement of Administration Policy (House)

most important tools in fighting money laundering and fraud. The amendment would mark a significant retreat in our fight against narcotraffickers. The Administration strongly opposes the bill's Federal Home Loan Bank System provisions, particularly a provision that would allow each Home Loan Bank to cut its capital requirement in half and thereby effectively increase the System's taxpayer subsidy without any commensurate return in public benefits. In addition, the Administration believes that the System must focus more on lending to community banks and less on arbitrage activities and short-term lending that do not advance its public purpose. The Administration opposes granting the Federal Housing Finance Board independent litigating authority, which would be inconsistent with the Attorney General's authority to coordinate and conduct litigation on behalf of the United States.

The Administration strongly objects to the refusal to allow House consideration of Representative Lee's anti-redlining amendment, which would help deter violations of the Fair Housing Act. The Administration strongly supports the amendment.

The Administration is concerned that the bill would unduly restrict banks' authority to sell insurance, thereby diminishing competition and reducing choice for consumers.

Because of its commitment to maintaining a separation of banking and commerce, the Administration continues to favor a clear prohibition on existing unitary thrift holding companies selling their subsidiary thrifts to non-financial firms. Allowing such sales could lead to substantial non-financial ownership of insured depository institutions.

The Administration opposes section 154 because it could be seen as undermining principles of normal trade relations and national treatment, which could weaken efforts to negotiate further market access liberalization and expose U.S. firms to additional restrictions abroad.

15

§15.09 Legislation as Passed the House

Pursuant to the provisions of the special rule that had been adopted, the legislation was considered in the Committee of the Whole. Of the eleven amendments made in order under H. Res. 235 (the special rule), five were agreed to by voice vote, four were agreed to by recorded vote, and two failed by recorded vote. The measure passed the House on a 343-to-86 vote.

The measure was now designated as *An Act*, which is how the reader knows that the legislation has passed one chamber. This document is also now referred to as the *House engrossed bill*.

---

§ 15.09a

Legislation as
Passed the House

> 106TH CONGRESS
> 1ST SESSION
> # H. R. 10
>
> ---
>
> ## ❶ AN ACT
>
> To enhance competition in the financial services industry by providing a prudential framework for the affiliation of banks, securities firms, and other financial service providers, and for other purposes.
>
> 1   *Be it enacted by the Senate and House of Representa-*
> 2   *tives of the United States of America in Congress assembled,*

❶ No longer *A Bill* but *An Act* (engrossed measure)

Continued on page 589

Legislation as
Passed the House

2

1 SECTION 1. SHORT TITLE; PURPOSES; TABLE OF CON-

2   TENTS.

3   (a) SHORT TITLE.—This Act may be cited as the

4 "Financial Services Act of 1999".

5   (b) PURPOSES.—The purposes of this Act are as fol-

6 lows:

7   (1) To enhance competition in the financial

8   services industry, in order to foster innovation and

9   efficiency.

10   (2) To ensure the continued safety and sound-

11   ness of depository institutions.

12   (3) To provide necessary and appropriate pro-

13   tections for investors and ensure fair and honest

14   markets in the delivery of financial services.

15   (4) To avoid duplicative, potentially conflicting,

16   and overly burdensome regulatory requirements

17   through the creation of a regulatory framework for

18   financial holding companies that respects the diver-

19   gent requirements of each of the component busi-

20   nesses of the holding company, and that is based

21   upon principles of strong functional regulation and

22   enhanced regulatory coordination.

23   (5) To reduce and, to the maximum extent

24   practicable, to eliminate the legal barriers preventing

25   affiliation among depository institutions, securities

26   firms, insurance companies, and other financial serv-

•HR 10 EH

15

§ 15.10 Legislation as Received in the Senate

H.R. 10 was received by the Senate on July 12, 1999. It was not referred to a Senate committee, although that could have happened. It was *placed directly on the calendar*, in part because a companion Senate measure had already been considered by a Senate committee.

---

§ 15.10a

Legislation as Received in the Senate

❶ Calendar number

❷ House-passed measure received by Senate

II

❶ Calendar No. 204

106TH CONGRESS
1ST SESSION

H. R. 10

---

❷ IN THE SENATE OF THE UNITED STATES

JULY 12, 1999
Received; read twice and placed on the Calendar

AN ACT

To enhance competition in the financial services industry by providing a prudential framework for the affiliation of banks, securities firms, and other financial service providers, and for other purposes.

1   *Be it enacted by the Senate and House of Representa-*

2   *tives of the United States of America in Congress assembled,*

Continued on page 591

Legislation as
Received in the Senate

2

1 **SECTION 1. SHORT TITLE; PURPOSES; TABLE OF CON-**

2   **TENTS.**

3   (a) SHORT TITLE.—This Act may be cited as the

4 "Financial Services Act of 1999".

5   (b) PURPOSES.—The purposes of this Act are as fol-

6 lows:

7   (1) To enhance competition in the financial

8   services industry, in order to foster innovation and

9   efficiency.

10   (2) To ensure the continued safety and sound-

11   ness of depository institutions.

12   (3) To provide necessary and appropriate pro-

13   tections for investors and ensure fair and honest

14   markets in the delivery of financial services.

15   (4) To avoid duplicative, potentially conflicting,

16   and overly burdensome regulatory requirements

17   through the creation of a regulatory framework for

18   financial holding companies that respects the diver-

19   gent requirements of each of the component busi-

20   nesses of the holding company, and that is based

21   upon principles of strong functional regulation and

22   enhanced regulatory coordination.

23   (5) To reduce and, to the maximum extent

24   practicable, to eliminate the legal barriers preventing

25   affiliation among depository institutions, securities

26   firms, insurance companies, and other financial serv-

HR 10 PCS

15

§15.11 Legislation as Introduced in the Senate

S. 900 is an *original bill*, which means that it was not introduced and referred to the Senate Committee on Banking, Housing, and Urban Affairs, but rather was drafted in the committee and then reported to the Senate. The chair of the committee, Mr. Gramm, reported the measure on April 28, 1999. A committee report, S. Rept. 106-44, was also filed in the Senate. The measure was placed on the Senate calendar as the 94th item.

§ 15.11a

Legislation as
Introduced in the Senate

II

① Calendar
number

② Committee
report number

③ Original bill
reported from
committee

④ Official title

⑤ Enacting
clause

⑥ Short
(popular) title

① **Calendar No. 94**

106TH CONGRESS
1ST SESSION
S. 900

② **[Report No. 106–44]**

To enhance competition in the financial services industry by providing a
prudential framework for the affiliation of banks, securities firms, insurance companies, and other financial service providers, and for other
purposes.

IN THE SENATE OF THE UNITED STATES

APRIL 28, 1999

③ Mr. GRAMM, from the Committee on Banking, Housing, and Urban Affairs,
reported the following original bill, which was read twice and placed on
the calendar

A BILL

④ To enhance competition in the financial services industry
by providing a prudential framework for the affiliation
of banks, securities firms, insurance companies, and
other financial service providers, and for other purposes.

⑤ 1   *Be it enacted by the Senate and House of Representa-*

2 *tives of the United States of America in Congress assembled,*

3 **SECTION 1. SHORT TITLE; TABLE OF CONTENTS.**

⑥ 4   (a) SHORT TITLE.—This Act may be cited as the

5 "Financial Services Modernization Act of 1999".

15

§ 15.12 Senate Committee Report

The Committee on Banking, Housing, and Urban Affairs reported S. 900 to the Senate, by an 11-to-9 vote. A committee report was filed in the Senate on April 28, 1999, and numbered S. Rept. 106-44, the 44th Senate committee report filed in the 106th Congress. *Additional views* were also filed and included in the body of the report. The calendar number is repeated on the cover page of the Senate report. A section entitled *introduction* and another entitled *history of legislation* summarized the Senate Banking Committee's actions on the legislation.

§ 15.12a

Senate Committee
Report

1 Calendar number

2 Committee
report number

3 Reporting
committee

4 Measure reported

5 Additional views

---

1 Calendar No. 94

106TH CONGRESS 1st Session	SENATE	**2** REPORT 106–44

FINANCIAL SERVICES MODERNIZATION
ACT OF 1999

R E P O R T

OF THE

3 COMMITTEE ON BANKING, HOUSING,
AND URBAN AFFAIRS
UNITED STATES SENATE

TO ACCOMPANY

4 S. 900

together with

5 ADDITIONAL VIEWS

APRIL 28, 1999.—Ordered to be printed

———

U.S. GOVERNMENT PRINTING OFFICE
69–010   WASHINGTON : 1999

15

§15.13 Statement of Administration Policy (Senate)

On May 3, 1999, the Office of Management and Budget issued a Statement of Administration Policy on S. 900, the Senate bill, announcing the administration's opposition to S. 900. The statement indicated that the president would veto the Senate measure in its current form.

§ 15.13a

Statement of Administration Policy (Senate)

EXECUTIVE OFFICE OF THE PRESIDENT
OFFICE OF MANAGEMENT AND BUDGET
WASHINGTON, D.C. 20503

STATEMENT OF ADMINISTRATION POLICY
(THIS STATEMENT HAS BEEN COORDINATED BY OMB WITH THE CONCERNED AGENCIES.)

May 3, 1999
(Senate)

S. 900 - Financial Services Modernization Act of 1999
(Gramm (R) TX)

The Administration strongly opposes S. 900, which would revise laws governing the financial services industry. This Administration has been a strong proponent of financial modernization legislation that would best serve the interests of consumers, businesses, and communities, while protecting the safety and soundness of our financial system. Consequently, it supports the bill's repeal of the Glass-Steagall Act's prohibition on banks affiliating with securities firms and of the Bank Holding Company Act's prohibitions on insurance underwriting. Nevertheless, because of crucial flaws in the bill, the President has stated that, if the bill were presented to him in its current form, he would veto it.

In its current form, the bill would undermine the effectiveness of the Community Reinvestment Act (CRA), a law that has helped to build homes and create jobs by encouraging banks to serve creditworthy borrowers throughout the communities they serve. The bill fails to require that banks seeking to conduct new financial activities achieve and maintain a satisfactory CRA record. In addition, the bill's "safe harbor" provision would amend current law to effectively shield financial institutions from public comment on banking applications that they file with Federal regulators. The CRA exemption for banks with less than $100 million in assets would repeal CRA for approximately 4,000 banks and thrifts that banking agency rules already exempt from CRA paperwork reporting burdens. In all, these limitations constitute an assault upon CRA and are unacceptable.

The bill would unjustifiably deny financial services firms holding 99 percent of national bank assets the choice of conducting new financial activities through subsidiaries, forcing them to conduct those activities exclusively through bank holding company affiliates. Thus the bill largely prohibits a structure with proven advantages for safety and soundness, effectively denying many financial services firms the freedom to organize themselves in the way that best serves their customers.

The bill would also inadequately inform and protect consumers under the new system of financial products it authorizes. If Congress is to authorize large, complex organizations to offer a wide range of financial products, then consumers should be guaranteed appropriate disclosures and other protections.

The bill would dramatically expand the ability of depository institutions and nonfinancial firms to affiliate. The Administration has serious concerns about mixing banking and

Continued on page 597

§ 15.13a (continued)

Statement of Administration Policy (Senate)

commercial activity under any circumstances, and these concerns are heightened by the financial crises affecting other countries over the past few years.

The Administration also opposes the bill's piecemeal modification of the Federal Home Loan Bank System. The Administration believes that the System must focus more on lending to community banks and less on arbitrage activities and short-term lending that do not advance its public purpose. The Administration opposes any changes to the System that do not include these crucial reforms.

In addition, the Administration opposes granting the Federal Housing Finance Board independent litigation authority. Such authority would be inconsistent with the Attorney General's authority to coordinate and conduct litigation on behalf of the United States.

Pay-As-You-Go Scoring

S. 900 would affect direct spending and receipts. Therefore, it is subject to the pay-as-you-go requirement of the Omnibus Budget Reconciliation Act of 1990. OMB's pay-as-you-go scoring of this bill is under development.

15

§ 15.14 Legislation as Passed the Senate

The legislation was considered in the Senate by agreeing to a *motion to proceed to consideration*. Numerous amendments were offered and disposed of, either by being agreed to, rejected, withdrawn, or tabled. The measure passed the Senate by a vote of 54 to 44, on May 6, 1999.

The legislation is now designated as *An Act*, which is how the reader knows that the legislation has passed one chamber. This document is referred to as the *Senate engrossed bill*.

---

§ 15.14a

Legislation as Passed the Senate

106TH CONGRESS
1ST SESSION
S. 900

❶ No longer *A Bill* but *An Act* (engrossed measure)

❶ AN ACT

To enhance competition in the financial services industry by providing a prudential framework for the affiliation of banks, securities firms, insurance companies, and other financial service providers, and for other purposes.

1   *Be it enacted by the Senate and House of Representa-*

2   *tives of the United States of America in Congress assembled,*

3   **SECTION 1. SHORT TITLE; TABLE OF CONTENTS.**

4   (a) SHORT TITLE.—This Act may be cited as the

5   "Financial Services Modernization Act of 1999".

§15.15 Legislation Received in the House from the Senate

On July 20, 1999, the Senate bill, S. 900, was transmitted to the House, which considered it and amended it with its own version. This is evident from the language "strike out all after the enacting clause and insert."

The House and Senate took their first step toward reconciling differences—selecting one bill number, S. 900, to use as the legislative vehicle for further action.

---

§ 15.15a

Legislation Received in the House from the Senate

> ### *In the House of Representatives, U. S.,*
>
> *July 20, 1999.*
>
> *Resolved,* That the bill from the Senate (S. 900) entitled "An Act to enhance competition in the financial services industry by providing a prudential framework for the affiliation of banks, securities firms, insurance companies, and other financial service providers, and for other purposes", do pass with the following
>
> ### AMENDMENTS:
>
> ❶   Strike out all after the enacting clause and insert:
>
> 1   *SECTION 1. SHORT TITLE; PURPOSES; TABLE OF CON-*
> 2   *TENTS.*
> 3   *(a) SHORT TITLE.—This Act may be cited as the "Fi-*
> 4   *nancial Services Act of 1999".*
> 5   *(b) PURPOSES.—The purposes of this Act are as fol-*
> 6   *lows:*
> 7   *(1) To enhance competition in the financial serv-*
> 8   *ices industry, in order to foster innovation and effi-*
> 9   *ciency.*
> 10   *(2) To ensure the continued safety and soundness*
> 11   *of depository institutions.*

❶ House amendment to Senate bill (text of H.R. 10)

15

599

§15.16 Side-by-Side Comparative Print

Before convening a conference committee, it is customary for respective committee staff to prepare a side-by-side comparative print of the two versions of the measure to be reconciled in conference. This document enables conferees to see the differences between the two versions of a measure. A side-by-side often includes a fourth column—current law.

§ 15.16a

Side-by-Side
Comparative Print

COMPARISON OF

S. 900, FINANCIAL SERVICES MODERNIZATION ACT OF 1999

AND

H.R. 10, FINANCIAL SERVICES ACT OF 1999

September 1, 1999

COMPARISON OF H.R. 10 AND S. 900

September 1, 1999

	H.R. 10	S. 900
1. Title	"Financial Services Act of 1999" (p.1)	"Financial Services Modernization Act of 1999" (p.1)
2. Statement of purpose	Purposes of this Act are: (1) to enhance competition in the financial services industry, in order to foster innovation and efficiency; (2) to ensure the continued safety and soundness of depository institutions; (3) to provide necessary and appropriate protections for investors and ensure fair and honest markets in the delivery of financial services; (4) to avoid duplicative, potentially conflicting, and overly burdensome regulatory requirements through creation of a regulatory framework for financial holding companies that respects the divergent requirements of each of the component businesses of the holding company, and that is based upon principles of strong functional regulation and enhanced regulatory coordination; (5) to reduce and, to the maximum extent practicable, to eliminate the legal barriers preventing affiliation among depository institutions, securities firms, insurance companies, and other financial service providers and to provide a prudential framework for achieving that result; (6) to enhance the availability of financial services to citizens of all economic circumstances and in all geographic areas; (7) to enhance the competitiveness of US financial services providers internationally; and, (8) to ensure compliance by depository institutions with the provisions of the CRA of	No provision.

-1-

§ 15.17 Conference Chair's Letter to Conferees

Informal documents relevant to a measure's consideration in conference are often produced, such as letters to conference committee members and leadership memoranda. In this case, Representative Leach, the House Banking and Financial Services Committee chair and the chair of the conference, provided to all conferees a set of ground rules related to consideration of the measure in the conference. Senate conferees were appointed on July 23, 1999. House conferees were named on July 30, 1999. The appointment of conferees is reported in the *Congressional Record*.

§ 15.17a

Conference Chair's Letter to Conferees

JAMES A. LEACH, IOWA, CHAIRMAN

BILL McCOLLUM, FLORIDA
MARGE ROUKEMA, NEW JERSEY
DOUG BEREUTER, NEBRASKA
RICHARD H. BAKER, LOUISIANA
RICK LAZIO, NEW YORK
SPENCER BACHUS, III, ALABAMA
MICHAEL CASTLE, DELAWARE
PETER KING, NEW YORK
TOM CAMPBELL, CALIFORNIA
EDWARD ROYCE, CALIFORNIA
FRANK D. LUCAS, OKLAHOMA
JACK METCALF, WASHINGTON
ROBERT NEY, OHIO
BOB BARR, GEORGIA
SUE W. KELLY, NEW YORK
RON PAUL, TEXAS
DAVE WELDON, FLORIDA
JIM RYUN, KANSAS
MERRILL COOK, UTAH
BOB RILEY, ALABAMA
RICK HILL, MONTANA
STEVEN LATOURETTE, OHIO
DONALD A. MANZULLO, ILLINOIS
WALTER B. JONES, JR. NORTH CAROLINA
PAUL RYAN, WISCONSIN
DOUG OSE, CALIFORNIA
JOHN E. SWEENEY, NEW YORK
JUDY BIGGERT, ILLINOIS
LEE TERRY, NEBRASKA
MARK GREEN, WISCONSIN
PAT TOOMEY, PENNSYLVANIA

JOHN J. LaFALCE, NEW YORK
BRUCE F. VENTO, MINNESOTA
BARNEY FRANK, MASSACHUSETTS
PAUL E. KANJORSKI, PENNSYLVANIA
MAXINE WATERS, CALIFORNIA
CAROLYN B. MALONEY, NEW YORK
LUIS V. GUTIERREZ, ILLINOIS
NYDIA M. VELAZQUEZ, NEW YORK
MELVIN WATT, NORTH CAROLINA
GARY ACKERMAN, NEW YORK
KEN BENTSEN, TEXAS
JAMES H. MALONEY, CONNECTICUT
DARLENE HOOLEY, OREGON
JULIA CARSON, INDIANA
ROBERT A. WEYGAND, RHODE ISLAND
BRAD SHERMAN, CALIFORNIA
MAX SANDLIN, TEXAS
GREGORY MEEKS, NEW YORK
BARBARA LEE, CALIFORNIA
VIRGIL H. GOODE, JR., VIRGINIA
FRANK MASCARA, PENNSYLVANIA
JAY R. INSLEE, WASHINGTON
JAN SCHAKOWSKY, ILLINOIS
DENNIS MOORE, KANSAS
CHARLES A. GONZALEZ, TEXAS
STEPHANIE TUBBS JONES, OHIO
MICHAEL E. CAPUANO, MASSACHUSETT

BERNARD SANDERS, VERMONT

(202) 225-7502

U.S. HOUSE OF REPRESENTATIVES

COMMITTEE ON BANKING AND FINANCIAL SERVICES

ONE HUNDRED SIXTH CONGRESS

2129 RAYBURN HOUSE OFFICE BUILDING
WASHINGTON, DC 20515–6050

October 13, 1999

** CONFERENCE COMMITTEE **

To: House/Senate Conferees on S. 900
From: James A. Leach, Chairman

All conferences are unique, with rules less stringently observed than in other legislative contexts. The principal rule of conferences is that a majority of conferees in each body must sign the conference report before it can be considered by the full House and Senate.

In this conference, it is my intention to proceed title-by-title through the mark, alternating recognition to the extent practicable between House and Senate Members and Republicans and Democrats for purposes of offering amendments. As Members understand, in conference committees, each body has a single vote, but it will be my intention to assume that any amendment offered by a Member of the conference represents his or her body's position unless another Member of that body requests a vote of that body to determine whether that is in fact the case.

On the House side we have a particularly complex conference arrangement. Conferees will only be able to vote on and offer amendments to those provisions on which they are designated as conferees.

While precedents are mixed, it will be my intention to proceed on the basis that if an amendment is offered by a Member, it may only be amended by Members within the body of the offeror until it is formally presented to the other side, at which point it may be amended by that side. The original offeror, however, may accept suggestions from any member of the Conference and at his or her discretion modify an amendment before it is passed to the opposite side.

I have consulted with the parliamentarian, and while no firm rules apply in this area, the precedent is that each body determines how to proceed in the voting process. This means that on the House side, proxy voting will not be permitted, while in the Senate, it will be.

The first amendment to be offered at the mark-up may be a manager's amendment making certain technical and other revisions to the Chairmen's mark. Any Member who has a proposed technical amendment or other issue that fits a manager's amendment should contact the staffs of one of the relevant chairmen or ranking members.

15

§ 15.18 Conference Committee Amendment Proposed

Each conference committee conducts its work differently. Some conferences proceed through the engrossed measure *section-by-section;* others consider *full-text substitutes.* The document excerpted in § 15.18a, and the text of the substitute, provided a summary of a *chairmen's mark,* a full-text substitute considered by the conferees.

---

§ 15.18a

Conference Committee Amendment Proposed

Financial Services Modernization Act

Summary of Provisions of Chairmen's Mark

TITLE I - FACILITATING AFFILIATION AMONG BANKS, SECURITIES FIRMS, AND INSURANCE COMPANIES

- Repeals the restrictions on banks affiliating with securities firms contained in sections 20 and 32 of the Glass-Steagall Act.

- Creates a new "financial holding company" under section 4 of the Bank Holding Company Act. Such holding company can engage in a statutorily provided list of financial activities, including insurance and securities underwriting and merchant banking activities. The financial holding company may also engage in developing activities and activities which the Federal Reserve Board, subject to a Treasury coordinating process, determines are financial in nature or incidental to such financial activities. Complementary activities are also authorized. The nonfinancial activities of firms predominantly engaged in financial activities are grandfathered (subject to a 15% limitation) for at least 10 years, but no more than 15 years. Such financial holding companies must be well capitalized, well managed, and have at least a satisfactory CRA rating.

- Provides for state regulation of insurance, subject to certain specified state preemption standards.

- Provides that a bank holding company organized as a mutual holding company will be regulated on terms and subject to limitations, comparable to any other bank holding company.

- Liberalizes the restrictions governing nonbank banks.

- Provides for a study of the use of subordinated debt to protect financial system and deposit funds from "too big to fail" institutions and a study on the effect of financial modernization on the accessibility of small business and farm loans.

- Streamlines bank holding company supervisions by clarifying the regulatory roles of the Federal Reserve as the umbrella holding company supervisor and the state and Federal nonbank financial functional regulators.

§15.19 Conference Report

The conference report, H. Rept. 106-434, was filed in the House on November 2, 1999, by Mr. Leach, the chair of the conference committee. The measure was now officially called the Gramm-Leach-Bliley Act, after the three chairs of the committees that considered the legislation. Negotiations in conference resulted in the naming.

§ 15.19a

Conference Report

106TH CONGRESS *1st Session*	HOUSE OF REPRESENTATIVES	REPORT 106–434

GRAMM-LEACH-BLILEY ACT

NOVEMBER 2, 1999.—Ordered to be printed

Mr. LEACH, from the committee of conference,
submitted the following

CONFERENCE REPORT

[To accompany S. 900]

The committee of conference on the disagreeing votes of the two Houses on the amendments of the House to the bill (S. 900), to enhance competition in the financial services industry by providing a prudential framework for the affiliation of banks, securities firms, insurance companies, and other financial service providers, and for other purposes, having met, after full and free conference, have agreed to recommend and do recommend to their respective Houses as follows:

That the Senate recede from its disagreement to the amendment of the House to the text of the bill and agree to the same with an amendment as follows:

In lieu of the matter proposed to be inserted by the House amendment, insert the following:

SECTION 1. SHORT TITLE; TABLE OF CONTENTS.

(a) SHORT TITLE.—*This Act may be cited as the "Gramm-Leach-Bliley Act".*

(b) TABLE OF CONTENTS.—*The table of contents for this Act is as follows:*

Sec. 1. Short title; table of contents.

TITLE I—FACILITATING AFFILIATION AMONG BANKS, SECURITIES FIRMS, AND INSURANCE COMPANIES

Subtitle A—Affiliations

Sec. 101. Glass-Steagall Act repeals.
Sec. 102. Activity restrictions applicable to bank holding companies that are not financial holding companies.
Sec. 103. Financial activities.
Sec. 104. Operation of State law.
Sec. 105. Mutual bank holding companies authorized.
Sec. 106. Prohibition on deposit production offices.
Sec. 107. Cross marketing restriction; limited purpose bank relief; divestiture.

60–398

§ 15.20 Joint Explanatory Statement

A second conference document is appended to the conference report and is called the *joint explanatory statement*. This document explains in lay terms what was in the House text and the Senate text of the measure in conference and what is the agreement recommended by the committee on conference. A majority of conferees from each chamber must sign not only the conference report but also the joint explanatory statement.

§ 15.20a

Joint Explanatory Statement

JOINT EXPLANATORY STATEMENT OF THE COMMITTEE OF CONFERENCE

The Managers on the part of the House and the Senate at the conference on the disagreeing votes of the two Houses on the amendments of the House to the bill (S. 900), to enhance competition in the financial services industry by providing a prudential framework for the affiliation of banks, securities firms, insurance companies, and other financial service providers, and for other purposes, submit the following joint statement to the House and the Senate in explanation of the effect of the action agreed upon by the managers and recommended in the accompanying conference report:

The House amendment to the text of the bill struck all of the Senate bill after the enacting clause and inserted a substitute text.

The Senate recedes from its disagreement to the amendment of the House with an amendment that is a substitute for the Senate bill and the House amendment. The differences between the Senate bill, the House amendment, and the substitute agreed to in conference are noted below, except for clerical corrections, conforming changes made necessary by agreements reached by the conferees, and minor drafting and clerical changes.

TITLE I—FACILITATING AFFILIATIONS AMONG BANKS, SECURITIES FIRMS, AND INSURANCE COMPANIES

The legislation approved by the Conference Managers eliminates many Federal and State law barriers to affiliations among banks and securities firms, insurance companies, and other financial service providers. The House and Senate bills established an identical statutory framework (except for minor drafting differences) pursuant to which full affiliations can occur between banks and securities firms, insurance companies, and other financial companies. The Conferees adopted this framework. Furthermore, the legislation provides financial organizations with flexibility in structuring these new financial affiliations through a holding company structure, or a financial subsidiary (with certain prudential limitations on activities and appropriate safeguards). Reflected in the legislation is the determination made by both Houses to preserve the role of the Board of Governors of the Federal Reserve System (the "Federal Reserve Board" or the "Board") as the umbrella supervisor for holding companies, but to incorporate a system of functional regulation designed to utilize the strengths of the various Federal and State financial supervisors. Incorporating provisions found in both the House and Senate bills, the legislation establishes a mechanism for coordination between the Federal Reserve Board and the Secretary of the Treasury ("the Secretary") regarding the approval of new financial activities for both holding companies and national bank financial subsidiaries. The legislation

(151)

15

§ 15.21 Special Rule from the Rules Committee for Consideration of the Conference Report

Conference reports are *privileged* in the House and as such do not require a special rule for consideration. However, special rules are often sought for conference reports if *waivers* of existing rules are needed. H. Res. 355 was a special rule providing for the consideration of the conference report on S. 900. The special rule provided that the conference report be considered as read, and waived all points of order against the report and its consideration by the House. The special rule was reported on November 2, 1999.

§ 15.21a

Special Rule from the Rules Committee for Consideration of the Conference Report

❶ Calendar number

❷ Resolution number

❸ Committee report number

❹ Majority manager of special rule

❺ Special rule waiving points of order against the conference report (S. 900)

---

❶ House Calendar No. 147

106TH CONGRESS
1ST SESSION **❷ H. RES. 355**

❸ [Report No. 106–440]

Waiving points of order against the conference report to accompany the bill (S. 900) to enhance competition in the financial services industry by providing a prudential framework for the affiliation of banks, securities firms, insurance companies, and other financial service providers, and for other purposes.

IN THE HOUSE OF REPRESENTATIVES

NOVEMBER 2, 1999

❹ Mr. SESSIONS, from the Committee on Rules, reported the following resolution; which was referred to the House Calendar and ordered to be printed

---

RESOLUTION

❺ Waiving points of order against the conference report to accompany the bill (S. 900) to enhance competition in the financial services industry by providing a prudential framework for the affiliation of banks, securities firms, insurance companies, and other financial service providers, and for other purposes.

1   *Resolved,* That upon adoption of this resolution it
2   shall be in order to consider the conference report to ac-
3   company the bill (S. 900) to enhance competition in the

Continued on page 608

607

Special Rule from the Rules Committee for Consideration of the Conference Report

2

1 financial services industry by providing a prudential

2 framework for the affiliation of banks, securities firms, in-

3 surance companies, and other financial service providers,

4 and for other purposes. All points of order against the con-

5 ference report and against its consideration are waived.

6 The conference report shall be considered as read.

§ 15.22 Enrolled Measure

The conference report was agreed to by the Senate by a 90-to-8 vote on November 4, 1999. The House also agreed to the conference report on November 4, 1999, by a vote of 362-to-57. The measure was then cleared for the White House. It was printed on parchment paper and presented to the president on November 9, 1999.

---

§ 15.22a

Enrolled Measure

One Hundred Sixth Congress
of the
United States of America

AT THE FIRST SESSION

Begun and held at the City of Washington on Wednesday,
the sixth day of January, one thousand nine hundred and ninety-nine

An Act

To enhance competition in the financial services industry by providing a prudential framework for the affiliation of banks, securities firms, insurance companies, and other financial service providers, and for other purposes.

Be it enacted by the Senate and House of Representatives of the United States of America in Congress assembled,

SECTION 1. SHORT TITLE; TABLE OF CONTENTS.

(a) SHORT TITLE.—This Act may be cited as the "Gramm-Leach-Bliley Act".

(b) TABLE OF CONTENTS.—The table of contents for this Act is as follows:

Sec. 1. Short title; table of contents.

TITLE I—FACILITATING AFFILIATION AMONG BANKS, SECURITIES FIRMS, AND INSURANCE COMPANIES

Subtitle A—Affiliations

Sec. 101. Glass-Steagall Act repeals.
Sec. 102. Activity restrictions applicable to bank holding companies that are not financial holding companies.
Sec. 103. Financial activities.
Sec. 104. Operation of State law.
Sec. 105. Mutual bank holding companies authorized.
Sec. 106. Prohibition on deposit production offices.
Sec. 107. Cross marketing restriction; limited purpose bank relief; divestiture.
Sec. 108. Use of subordinated debt to protect financial system and deposit funds from "too big to fail" institutions.
Sec. 109. Study of financial modernization's effect on the accessibility of small business and farm loans.

Subtitle B—Streamlining Supervision of Bank Holding Companies

Sec. 111. Streamlining bank holding company supervision.
Sec. 112. Authority of State insurance regulator and Securities and Exchange Commission.
Sec. 113. Role of the Board of Governors of the Federal Reserve System.
Sec. 114. Prudential safeguards.
Sec. 115. Examination of investment companies.
Sec. 116. Elimination of application requirement for financial holding companies.
Sec. 117. Preserving the integrity of FDIC resources.
Sec. 118. Repeal of savings bank provisions in the Bank Holding Company Act of 1956.
Sec. 119. Technical amendment.

Subtitle C—Subsidiaries of National Banks

Sec. 121. Subsidiaries of national banks.
Sec. 122. Consideration of merchant banking activities by financial subsidiaries.

Subtitle D—Preservation of FTC Authority

Sec. 131. Amendment to the Bank Holding Company Act of 1956 to modify notification and post-approval waiting period for section 3 transactions.
Sec. 132. Interagency data sharing.

§15.23 Public Law

The president signed the Gramm-Leach-Bliley Act on November 12, 1999. The adoption of the *short title* was part of the conference committee agreement. It now was P.L. 106-102, 113 Stat. 1338.

---

§ 15.23a

Public Law

---

113 STAT. 1338   PUBLIC LAW 106–102—NOV. 12, 1999

Public Law 106–102
106th Congress

An Act

Nov. 12, 1999
[S. 900]

To enhance competition in the financial services industry by providing a prudential framework for the affiliation of banks, securities firms, insurance companies, and other financial service providers, and for other purposes.

Be it enacted by the Senate and House of Representatives of the United States of America in Congress assembled,

Gramm-Leach-
Bliley Act.
Inter-
governmental
relations.
12 USC 1811
note.

SECTION 1. SHORT TITLE; TABLE OF CONTENTS.

(a) SHORT TITLE.—This Act may be cited as the "Gramm-Leach-Bliley Act".

(b) TABLE OF CONTENTS.—The table of contents for this Act is as follows:

Sec. 1. Short title; table of contents.

TITLE I—FACILITATING AFFILIATION AMONG BANKS, SECURITIES FIRMS, AND INSURANCE COMPANIES

Subtitle A—Affiliations

Sec. 101. Glass-Steagall Act repeals.
Sec. 102. Activity restrictions applicable to bank holding companies that are not financial holding companies.
Sec. 103. Financial activities.
Sec. 104. Operation of State law.
Sec. 105. Mutual bank holding companies authorized.
Sec. 106. Prohibition on deposit production offices.
Sec. 107. Cross marketing restriction; limited purpose bank relief; divestiture.
Sec. 108. Use of subordinated debt to protect financial system and deposit funds from "too big to fail" institutions.
Sec. 109. Study of financial modernization's effect on the accessibility of small business and farm loans.

Subtitle B—Streamlining Supervision of Bank Holding Companies

Sec. 111. Streamlining bank holding company supervision.
Sec. 112. Authority of State insurance regulator and Securities and Exchange Commission.
Sec. 113. Role of the Board of Governors of the Federal Reserve System.
Sec. 114. Prudential safeguards.
Sec. 115. Examination of investment companies.
Sec. 116. Elimination of application requirement for financial holding companies.
Sec. 117. Preserving the integrity of FDIC resources.
Sec. 118. Repeal of savings bank provisions in the Bank Holding Company Act of 1956.
Sec. 119. Technical amendment.

Subtitle C—Subsidiaries of National Banks

Sec. 121. Subsidiaries of national banks.
Sec. 122. Consideration of merchant banking activities by financial subsidiaries.

Subtitle D—Preservation of FTC Authority

Sec. 131. Amendment to the Bank Holding Company Act of 1956 to modify notification and post-approval waiting period for section 3 transactions.
Sec. 132. Interagency data sharing.

Back of the Book

Analysis

Glossary

Account: Control and reporting unit for budgeting and accounting.

Act: Legislation that has been passed by both houses of Congress and signed by the president or passed over his veto, thus becoming law. Also, parliamentary term for a measure that has been passed by one chamber and engrossed.

Adjourn: Formal motion to end a day's session of a chamber of Congress.

Adjourn *Sine Die*: Final adjournment of a session of Congress.

Adjourn to a Day or Time Certain: Adjournment that fixes the next day and time of meeting for one or both chambers.

Adoption (Adopted): Usual parliamentary term for approval of conference report.

Agreed To: Usual parliamentary term for approval of motions, amendments, and simple and concurrent resolutions.

Amendment: Proposal of a member of Congress to alter the text of a measure.

Amendment in the Nature of a Substitute: Amendment that seeks to replace the entire text of the underlying measure. The adoption of such an amendment usually precludes any further amendment to that measure.

Amendment Tree: Diagram showing the number and types of amendments to a measure permitted by the chamber. It also shows the relationship among the amendments, their degree or type, and the order in which they may be offered and the order in which they are voted on.

Amendments between the Houses: Method for reconciling differences between the two chambers' versions of a measure by passing the measure back and forth between them until both have agreed to identical language; sometimes referred to in the media as the "ping pong" approach to reconciling differences in legislation. *Contrast to Conference Committee.*

Amendments in Disagreement: Provisions in dispute between the two chambers.

Amendments in Technical Disagreement: Amendments agreed to in a conference but not included in the conference report because they may violate the rules of one of the chambers and would open the conference report to a point of order.

Appeal: Member's challenge to a ruling made by the presiding officer or a committee chair.

Appropriated Entitlement: An entitlement for which budget authority is provided in annual appropriations acts.

Appropriation: Provision of law providing budget authority that permits federal agencies to incur obligations and make payments out of the Treasury. *See Budget Authority.*

Appropriations Bill: Bill that, if enacted as law, gives legal authority to spend or obligate money from the Treasury. *See Budget Authority.*

Authorization: Provision in law that establishes or continues a program or agency and authorizes appropriations for it.

Baseline: Projection of future revenues, budget authority, outlays, and other budget amounts under assumed economic conditions and participation rates without a change in current policy.

"Bigger Bite" Amendment: Although an amendment cannot amend previously amended language under House rules, a "bigger bite" amendment can be offered because it changes more of the measure or amendment than the original amendment.

Bill: Measure that becomes law when passed in identical form by both chambers and signed by the president or passed over his veto. Designated as *H.R.* or *S. See also Joint Resolution.*

Blue-Slip Resolution: House resolution ordering the return to the Senate of a Senate bill or amendment that the House believes violates the constitutional prerogative of the House to originate revenue measures.

Borrowing Authority: Spending authority that permits a federal agency to incur obligations and to make payments for specified purposes out of funds borrowed from the Treasury or the public.

Budget Authority: Authority in law to enter into obligations that normally result in outlays.

Budget Resolution: Concurrent resolution incorporating an agreement by the House and Senate on an overall budget plan; may contain reconciliation instructions.

By Request: A designation on a measure that appears next to the sponsor's name and indicates that a member has introduced the measure on behalf of the president, an executive agency, or a private individual or organization.

Byrd Rule: Bars the inclusion of extraneous matter in a reconciliation measure considered in the Senate.

Chairman's Mark/Staff Draft/Committee Print: Recommendation by committee (or subcommittee) chair of the measure to be considered in a markup, usually drafted as a bill.

Christmas-Tree Bill: Jargon for a bill containing many amendments (*see Rider*) unrelated to the bill's subjects; usually refers to Senate measures.

Clean Bill: New measure reported by a House committee incorporating all changes made in markup. Measure, with new number, is introduced by the chair and referred to the committee, which then reports that measure.

Closed Rule: Permits general debate for a specified period of time but generally permits no amendments.

Cloture: Process by which a filibuster can be ended in the Senate.

Cluster Voting: Allowance for sequential recorded votes on a series of measures or amendments that the House finished debating at an earlier time or on a previous date. The Speaker can reduce the minimum time for the second and subsequent votes in the series to five minutes each.

Colloquy: Discussion between members during floor proceedings, generally to put on the record a mutual understanding about the intent of a provision or amendment. The discussion is usually scripted in advance.

Committee of the Whole: The House in a different parliamentary form. Committee consisting of all members of the House, where measures are considered for amendment. The quorum is 100. Members are generally permitted to speak for five minutes. A chair presides in lieu of the Speaker.

Committee Report: Document accompanying a measure reported from a committee. It contains an explanation of the provisions of the measure, arguments for its approval, and other information.

Companion Bills: Identical or similar bills introduced in both chambers.

Concur: Agree to an amendment of the other chamber, either as is or with an amendment.

Concurrent Resolution: Used to express the sentiment of both chambers on some matter without making law, or to carry out the administrative business of both chambers. A concurrent resolution does not require presidential approval or become law, but requires passage in identical form by both houses to take effect between them. Designated as *H. Con. Res.* or *S. Con. Res.*

Conferees: Representatives from each chamber who serve on a conference committee; also referred to as managers.

Conference Committee: Temporary joint committee created to resolve differences between the chambers on a measure. *Contrast to Amendment between the Houses.*

Conference Report: Document containing a conference committee's agreements and signed by a majority of conferees from each chamber. *See also Joint Explanatory Statement of Managers.*

Cordon Rule: Senate rule that requires a committee report to show changes the reported measure would make in current law.

Cost Estimate: An estimate of the impact of legislation on revenues, spending, or both, generally as reported by a House or Senate committee or a conference committee; the 1974 Congressional Budget Act requires the Congressional Budget Office to prepare cost estimates on all public bills.

Credit Authority: Authority to incur direct loan obligations or make loan guarantee commitments.

Custody of the Papers: Custody of the engrossed measure and other documents that the two chambers produce as they try to reconcile differences in their versions of a measure. *See Papers.*

Deferral: Action or inaction that temporarily withholds, delays, or effectively precludes the obligation or expenditure of budget authority.

Deficit: Excess of outlays over revenues.

Degrees of Amendment: Designations that indicate the relationship of an amendment to the text of a measure and of one amendment to another. Amendments are permitted only in two degrees. *See Amendment Tree.*

Direct Spending: Spending controlled outside of annual appropriations acts, and specifically including the Food Stamp program; also referred to as mandatory spending. *See also Entitlement Program; contrast to Discretionary Spending.*

Disagree: To reject an amendment of the other chamber.

Discharge a Committee: Procedure to remove a measure from a House committee to which it was referred, to make it available for floor consideration.

Discretionary Spending: Spending provided in, and controlled by, annual appropriations acts. *Contrast to Direct Spending.*

Division Vote: A vote in which the committee chair or House presiding officer counts those members in favor and those in opposition to a proposition with no record made of how each voted. The chair can either ask for a show of hands or ask members to stand.

Earmark: For expenditures, an amount set aside within an appropriations account for a specified purpose.

Electronic Vote: A vote in the House using electronic voting machines. Members insert voting cards into one of the devices located throughout the House chamber.

En Bloc Amendment: Several amendments, affecting more than one place in a measure, offered as a group after obtaining unanimous consent.

Enacting Clause: Phrase at the beginning of a bill that gives it legal force when enacted: "Be it enacted by the Senate and House of Representatives of the United States of America in Congress assembled. . . ."

Engrossed Measure: Official copy of a measure as passed by one chamber, including the text as amended by floor action. Measure is certified by the clerk of the House or the secretary of the Senate.

Enrolled Measure: Final official copy of a measure as passed in identical form by both chambers and then printed on parchment. Measure is certified by the house of origin and signed by the Speaker of the House and the president pro tempore of the Senate before it is sent to the president.

617

Entitlement Program: Federal program that guarantees specific benefits to individuals, businesses, or units of government that meet eligibility requirements.

Executive Document: A document, usually a treaty, sent by the president to the Senate for its consideration and approval.

Executive Session: Meeting of the Senate devoted to the consideration of treaties or nominations. Also a term used to describe a chamber or committee session closed to the public.

Expenditures: Often a synonym for outlays; a general term to mean spending.

Fast-Track Procedures: Procedures that circumvent or speed up all or part of the legislative process. Some rule-making statutes prescribe expedited procedures for certain measures, such as trade agreements.

Federal Funds: All monies collected and spent by the federal government other than those designated as trust funds.

Filibuster: Tactic in the Senate to delay or defeat a measure by unlimited debate and other means.

First-Degree Amendment: Amendment offered to the text of a measure or a substitute offered to a first-degree amendment.

First Reading: Required reading of a bill or joint resolution to a chamber by title after its introduction.

Fiscal Year: The period from October 1 through September 30; fiscal year 2008 began October 1, 2007, and ends September 30, 2008.

Five-Minute Rule: House limit of debate on an amendment offered in the Committee of the Whole to five minutes for its sponsor and five minutes for an opponent. In practice, the Committee of the Whole permits the offering of pro forma amendments, each pro forma amendment allowing five more minutes of debate on an amendment. *See Pro Forma Amendment.*

Floor Manager: Member steering legislation through floor debate and the amendment process, usually a committee or subcommittee chair or ranking minority member.

General Debate: Term for period of time at the beginning of proceedings in the Committee of the Whole to debate a measure. The time is generally divided equally between majority and minority floor managers.

Germaneness: Rule in the House requiring that debate and amendments pertain to the same subject as the bill or amendment under consideration. In the Senate, germaneness is not generally required.

Hereby Rule: *See Self-Executing Rule.*

Hold: Senator's request to party leadership to delay or withhold floor action on a measure or executive business.

Hopper: Box on the Speaker's dais near the House clerk's desk where members place bills and resolutions to introduce them.

Impoundment: Action or inaction by an executive official that delays or precludes the obligation or expenditure of budget authority. *See Deferral and Rescission.*

Insert: Amendment to add new language to a measure or another amendment.

Insist: Motion by one chamber to reiterate its previous position during amendments between the chambers.

Instruct Conferees: Formal, although not binding, action by one chamber urging its conferees to uphold a particular position in conference.

Joint Explanatory Statement of Managers: Statement appended to a conference report explaining the conference agreement and the intent of the conferees. *See also Conference Report.*

Joint Resolution: Similar to a bill, though limited in scope (for example, to change a minor item in existing law). Becomes law when passed in identical form by both chambers and signed by the president. It also is the form of legislation used to consider a constitutional amendment. A constitutional amendment requires a two-thirds vote in each house but does not require the president's signature. Designated as *H. J. Res.* or *S. J. Res. See also Bill.*

Lame-Duck Session: Session of Congress held after the election for the succeeding Congress.

Law/Public Law/Private Law: Act of Congress signed by the president or passed over his veto.

Legislative Day: Time a chamber meets after an adjournment until the time it next adjourns.

Managers: Representatives from a chamber to a conference committee; also called conferees.

Mandatory Spending: *See Direct Spending.*

Mark: *See Vehicle.*

Markup: Meeting by a committee or subcommittee during which members offer, debate, and vote on amendments to a measure.

Minority, Supplemental, and Additional Views: Statements in a committee report presenting individuals' or groups' opinions on the measure.

Modified Closed Rule: Permits general debate for a specified period of time, but limits amendments to those designated in the special rule or the House Rules Committee report accompanying the special rule. May preclude amendments to particular portions of a bill. Also called a structured rule.

Modified Open Rule: Permits general debate for a specified period of time, and allows any member to offer amendments consistent with House rules subject only to an overall time limit on the amendment process and a requirement that amendments be pre-printed in the *Congressional Record.*

Morning Business: In the Senate, routine business transacted at the beginning of the Morning Hour, or by unanimous consent throughout the day.

Morning Hour: In the Senate, the first two hours of a session following an adjournment, rather than a recess.

Obligation: Binding agreement by a government agency to pay for goods, products, or services.

Official Objectors: House members who screen measures on the Private Calendar.

Official Title: Statement of a measure's subject and purpose, which appears before the enacting clause. *See also Popular Title.*

Omnibus Bill: A measure that combines the provisions related to several disparate subjects into a single measure. Examples include continuing appropriations resolutions that might contain two or more of the thirteen annual appropriations bills.

Open Rule: Permits general debate for a specified period of time and allows any member to offer an amendment that complies with the standing rules of the House.

Ordered Reported: Committee's formal action of agreeing to report a measure to its chamber.

Original Bill: A measure drafted by a committee and introduced by its chair when the committee reports the measure back to its chamber. It is not referred back to the committee after introduction.

Outlays: Payments to liquidate obligations.

Papers: Documents passed back and forth between the chambers, including the engrossed measure, the amendments, the messages transmitting them, and the conference report. *See also Custody of the Papers.*

Parliamentary Inquiry: Member's question posed on the floor to the presiding officer, or in committee or subcommittee to the chair, about a pending procedural situation.

619

Pass Over without Prejudice: A request in the House to defer action on a measure called up from the Private Calendar without affecting the measure's position on the calendar.

Passed: Term for approval of bills and joint resolutions.

PAYGO (Pay-As-You-Go): Process by which direct spending increases or revenue decreases must be offset so that the deficit is not increased or the surplus reduced. A statutory PAYGO requirement was in effect from 1991 through 2002; the House and Senate each have their own PAYGO rules.

Perfecting Amendment: Amendment that alters, but does not completely substitute or replace, language in another amendment. *See Amendment Tree.*

Pocket Veto: Act of the president in withholding approval of a measure after Congress has adjourned *sine die.*

Point of Order: Objection to a current proceeding, measure, or amendment because the proposed action violates a rule of the chamber, written precedent, or rule-making statute.

Popular Title: The name by which a measure is known. *See also Official Title.*

Postpone: There are two types of motions to postpone: to postpone (indefinitely) kills a proposal, but to postpone to a day certain merely changes the day or time of consideration.

Preamble: Introductory language in a bill preceding the enacting clause. It describes the reasons for and intent of a measure. In a joint resolution, the language appears before the resolving clause. In a concurrent or simple resolution, it appears before the text.

Precedence: Order in which amendments or motions may be offered and acted upon.

Precedent: Previous ruling by a presiding officer that becomes part of the procedures of a chamber.

President Pro Tempore: Presiding officer of the Senate in the absence of the vice president; usually the majority-party senator with the longest period of continuous service.

Previous Question: Nondebatable House (or House committee) motion, which, when agreed to, cuts off further debate, prevents the offering of additional amendments, and brings the pending matter to an immediate vote.

Private Bill: A measure that generally deals with an individual matter, such as a claim against the government, an individual's immigration, or a land title. Private bills are considered in the House via the Private Calendar on the first and third Tuesdays of each month.

Privilege: Attribute of a motion, measure, report, question, or proposition that gives it priority status for consideration.

Pro Forma Amendment: Motion whereby a House member secures five minutes to speak on an amendment under debate, without offering a substantive amendment. The member moves to "strike the last word" or "strike the requisite number of words." The motion requires no vote and is deemed automatically withdrawn at the expiration of the five minutes. *See also Five-Minute Rule.*

Proxy Vote: The practice of permitting a member to cast the vote of an absent colleague. Proxy voting is permitted only in Senate committees if committee rules allow them.

Public Debt: Amounts borrowed by the Treasury Department from the public or from another fund or account.

Public Law: Act of Congress that has been signed by the president or passed over his veto. It is designated by the letters P.L. and numbers noting the Congress and the numerical sequence in which the measure was signed; for example, P.L. 107-111 was an act of Congress in the 107th Congress and was the 111th measure signed by the president (or passed over his veto) during the 107th Congress.

Queen-of-the-Hill Rule: A special rule that permits votes on a series of amendments, usually complete substitutes for a measure, but directs that the amendment receiving the greatest number of votes is the winning amendment.

Quorum: Minimum number of members required for the transaction of business.

Quorum Call: A procedure for determining whether a quorum is present—218 in the House and 100 in the Committee of the Whole House on the State of the Union; a quorum in the Senate is 51.

Ramseyer Rule: House rule that requires a committee report to show changes the reported measure would make in current law.

Recede: Motion by one chamber to withdraw from its previous position during amendments between the chambers.

Recede and Concur: Motion to withdraw from a position and agree with the other chamber's position.

Recede and Concur with an Amendment: Motion to withdraw from a position and agree, but with a further amendment.

Recess: Temporary interruption or suspension of a committee or chamber meeting. In the House, the Speaker is authorized to declare recesses. In the Senate, the chamber may recess rather than adjourn at the end of the day so as not to trigger a new legislative day.

Recommit: To send a measure back to the committee that reported it. A motion to recommit without instructions kills a measure; a motion to recommit with instructions proposes to amend a measure. In the House, the motion may be offered just before vote on final passage. In the Senate, the motion may be offered at any time before a measure's passage.

Reconciliation: Process by which Congress changes existing laws to conform revenue and spending levels to the limits set in a budget resolution.

Reconsider: Parliamentary practice that gives a chamber one opportunity to review its action on a motion, amendment, measure, or any other proposition.

Refer: Assignment of a measure to committee.

Report/Reported: Formal submission of a measure by a committee to its parent chamber.

Reprogram: Shifting funds from one program to another in the same appropriation account. *Contrast to Transfer.*

Rescission: Cancellation of budget authority previously provided by Congress.

Resolution/Simple Resolution: Sentiment of one chamber on an issue, or a measure to carry out the administrative or procedural business of the chamber. Does not become law. Designated as *H. Res.* or *S. Res.*

Resolution of Inquiry: A simple resolution calling on the president or the head of an executive agency to provide specific information or papers to one or both chambers.

Resolution of Ratification: Senate vehicle for consideration of a treaty.

Resolving Clause: First section of a joint resolution that gives legal force to the measure when enacted: "Resolved by the Senate and House of Representatives of the United States of America in Congress assembled. . . ."

Revenues: Income from individual and corporate income taxes, social insurance taxes, excise taxes, fees, tariffs, and other sources collected under the sovereign powers of the federal government.

Rider: Colloquialism for an amendment unrelated to the subject matter of the measure to which it was attached.

Rise: In order only in the Committee of the Whole during the amendment stage, it has the effect of terminating or suspending debate on the pending matter.

Rise and Report: Term to refer to the culmination of proceedings in the Committee of the Whole. The Committee of the Whole sends the measure it has been considering back to the House for final disposition.

Roll-Call (Record) Vote: A vote in which members are recorded by name for or against a measure.

Scope of Differences: Limits within which a conference committee is permitted to resolve its disagreement.

Scorekeeping: Process for tracking and reporting on the status of congressional budgetary actions affecting budget authority, revenues, outlays, and the surplus or deficit.

Second: The number of members required to indicate support for an action, such as calling for a vote.

Second-Degree Amendment: An amendment to an amendment. Also called a perfecting amendment. *See Amendment Tree.*

Second Reading: Required reading of a bill or joint resolution to a chamber: in the House, in full before floor consideration in the House or Committee of the Whole (usually dispensed with by unanimous consent or special rule); in the Senate, by title only, before referral to a committee.

Self-Executing Rule: If specified, the House's adoption of a special rule may also have the effect of amending or passing the underlying measure. Also called a "hereby" rule.

Slip Law: First official publication of a law, published in unbound single sheets or pamphlet form.

Stage of Disagreement: Stage at which one chamber formally disagrees with an amendment proposed by the other chamber and insists on its own amendment. A measure generally cannot go to conference until this stage is reached.

Star Print: A reprint of a measure, amendment, or committee report to correct errors in a previous printing. The first page carries a small black star.

Strike: Amendment to delete a portion of a measure or an amendment.

Strike and Insert: Amendment that replaces text in a measure or an amendment.

Strike the Last Word/Strike the Requisite Number of Words: Also called a pro forma amendment. Means of obtaining time to speak on an amendment without actually offering a substantive change. *See Pro Forma Amendment.*

Structured Rule: Another term for a modified closed rule.

Substitute Amendment: Amendment that replaces the entire text of a pending amendment. *See Amendment Tree.*

Surplus: Excess of revenues over outlays.

Suspension of the Rules: Expeditious procedure for passing noncontroversial measures in the House. Requires a two-thirds vote of those present and voting, after forty minutes of debate, and does not allow floor amendments.

Table/Lay on the Table: Prevents further consideration of a measure, amendment, or motion, thus killing it.

Tax Expenditure: Loss of revenue attributable to an exemption, deduction, preference, or other exclusion under federal tax law.

Teller Vote: A House procedure in which members cast votes by passing through the center aisle of the chamber to be counted. Now used only when the electronic voting system breaks down and for ballot votes.

Third Reading: Required reading of bill or joint resolution to chamber before vote on final passage; usually a pro forma procedural step.

Transfer: Shifting funds from one appropriation account to another, as authorized by law. *Contrast to Reprogram.*

Trust Funds: Accounts designated by law as trust funds for receipts and expenditures earmarked for specific purposes.

Unanimous Consent Agreement/Time Limitation Agreement: Device in the Senate to expedite legislation by spelling out the process for considering a proposal.

Unprinted Amendment: Senate amendment not printed in the *Congressional Record* before its offering. Unprinted amendments are numbered sequentially through a Congress in the order of their submission.

Vehicle/Legislative Vehicle: Term for legislative measure that is being considered.

Veto: Disapproval by the president of a bill or joint resolution (other than a joint resolution proposing a constitutional amendment).

Views and Estimates: Annual report of each House and Senate committee on budgetary matters within its jurisdiction to respective chamber's Budget Committee; submitted in advance of Budget Committees' drafting of a concurrent resolution on the budget.

Voice Vote: A method of voting where members who support a question call out "aye" in unison, after which those opposed answer "no" in unison. The chair decides which position prevails.

Waiver Rule: A special rule in the House that waives points of order against a measure or an amendment.

Well: Open space in the front of the House chamber between members' seats and the podium. Members may speak from lecterns in the well.

Yea and Nay: A vote in which members respond "aye" or "no" on a question. Their names are called in alphabetical order.

Appendix One

Representatives Room and Telephone Directory
(As of April 22, 2007)

The telephone area code is 202. All House offices can be reached through the Capitol switchboard, 202-225-3121. Email addresses and individual members' web sites can be obtained through the House web site, *<www.house.gov>*.

All office addresses are in the Cannon, Longworth, and Rayburn House Office Buildings. The mailing address is the office address plus *Washington, DC 20515*. Any mail or packages go through a security screening process; delivery may be delayed by at least several days.

If a representative dies or resigns during a Congress, the successor who is elected occupies the former member's office suite through the end of that Congress.

Following a member's name is his or her party affiliation (D=Democrat, R=Republican, I=Independent), state, and district.

Neil Abercrombie, D-HI (1)
1502 Longworth 225-2726

Gary L. Ackerman, D-NY (5)
2243 Rayburn 225-2601

Robert B. Aderholt, R-AL (4)
1433 Longworth 225-4876

W. Todd Akin, R-MO (2)
117 Cannon 225-2561

Rodney Alexander, R-LA (5)
316 Cannon 225-8490

Thomas H. Allen, D-ME (1)
1127 Longworth 225-6116

Jason Altmire, D-PA (4)
1419 Longworth 225-2565

Robert E. Andrews, D-NJ (1)
2439 Rayburn 225-6501

Michael A. Arcuri, D-NY (24)
327 Cannon 225-3665

Joe Baca, D-CA (43)
1527 Longworth 225-6161

Michele Bachmann, R-MN (6)
412 Cannon 225-2331

Spencer Bachus, R-AL (6)
2246 Rayburn 225-4921

Brian Baird, D-WA (3)
2443 Rayburn 225-3536

Richard H. Baker, R-LA (6)
341 Cannon 225-3901

Tammy Baldwin, D-WI (2)
2446 Rayburn 225-2906

J. Gresham Barrett, R-SC (3)
439 Cannon 225-5301

John Barrow, D-GA (12)
213 Cannon 225-2823

Roscoe G. Bartlett, R-MD (6)
2412 Rayburn 225-2721

Joe Barton, R-TX (6)
2109 Rayburn 225-2002

Melissa L. Bean, D-IL (8)
318 Cannon 225-3711

Xavier Becerra, D-CA (31)
1119 Longworth 225-6235

Shelley Berkley, D-NV (1)
405 Cannon 225-5965

Howard L. Berman, D-CA (28)
2221 Rayburn 225-4695

Marion Berry, D-AR (1)
2305 Rayburn 225-4076

Judy Biggert, R-IL (13)
1034 Longworth 225-3515

Brian P. Bilbray, R-CA (50)
227 Cannon 225-0508

Gus M. Bilirakis, R-FL (9)
1630 Longworth 225-5755

Rob Bishop, R-UT (1)
124 Cannon 225-0453

Sanford D. Bishop, Jr.,
D-GA (2) 2429 Rayburn
225-3631

Timothy H. Bishop, D-NY (1)
225 Cannon 225-3826

Marsha Blackburn, R-TN (7)
509 Cannon 225-2811

Earl Blumenauer, D-OR (3)
2267 Rayburn 225-4811

Roy Blunt, R-MO (7)
217 Cannon 225-6536

John A. Boehner, R-OH (8)
1011 Longworth 225-6205

Jo Bonner, R-AL (1)
422 Cannon 225-4931

Mary Bono, R-CA (45)
104 Cannon 225-5330

John Boozman, R-AR (3)
1519 Longworth 225-4301

Madeleine Z. Bordallo, D-GU
(Delegate) 427 Cannon
225-1188

Dan Boren, D-OK (2)
216 Cannon 225-2701

Leonard L. Boswell, D-IA (3)
1427 Longworth 225-3806

Rick Boucher, D-VA (9)
2187 Rayburn 225-3861

Charles W. Boustany, Jr.,
R-LA (7) 1117 Longworth
225-2031

Allen Boyd, D-FL (2)
1227 Longworth 225-5235

Nancy E. Boyda, D-KS (2)
1711 Longworth 225-6601

Kevin Brady, R-TX (8)
301 Cannon 225-4901

Robert A. Brady, D-PA (1)
206 Cannon 225-4731

Bruce L. Braley, D-IA (1)
1408 Longworth 225-2911

Corrine Brown, D-FL (3)
2336 Rayburn 225-0123

Henry E. Brown, Jr., R-SC (1)
1124 Longworth 225-3176

Ginny Brown-Waite, R-FL (5)
414 Cannon 225-1002

Vern Buchanan, R-FL (13)
1516 Longworth 225-5015

Michael C. Burgess, R-TX (26)
1224 Longworth 225-7772

Dan Burton, R-IN (5)
2308 Rayburn 225-2276

G. K. Butterfield, D-NC (1)
413 Cannon 225-3101

Steve Buyer, R-IN (4)
2230 Rayburn 225-5037

Ken Calvert, R-CA (44)
2201 Rayburn 225-1986

Dave Camp, R-MI (4)
137 Cannon 225-3561

John Campbell, R-CA (48)
1728 Longworth 225-5611

Chris Cannon, R-UT (3)
2436 Rayburn 225-7751

Eric Cantor, R-VA (7)
329 Cannon 225-2815

Shelley Moore Capito, R-WV (2)
1431 Longworth 225-2711

Lois Capps, D-CA (23)
1110 Longworth 225-3601

Michael E. Capuano, D-MA (8)
1530 Longworth 225-5111

Dennis A. Cardoza, D-CA (18)
435 Cannon 225-6131

Russ Carnahan, D-MO (3)
1710 Longworth 225-2671

Christopher P. Carney,
D-PA (10) 416 Cannon
225-3731

Julia Carson, D-IN (7)
2455 Rayburn 225-4011

John R. Carter, R-TX (31)
408 Cannon 225-3864

Michael N. Castle, R-DE
(At Large) 1233 Longworth
225-4165

Kathy Castor, D-FL (11)
317 Cannon 225-3376

Steve Chabot, R-OH (1)
129 Cannon 225-2216

Ben Chandler, D-KY (6)
1504 Longworth 225-4706

Donna M. Christensen, D-VI
(Delegate) 1510 Longworth
225-1790

Yvette Clarke, D-NY (11)
1029 Longworth 225-6231

Wm. Lacy Clay, D-MO (1)
434 Cannon 225-2406

Emanuel Cleaver, D-MO (5)
1641 Longworth 225-4535

James E. Clyburn, D-SC (6)
2135 Rayburn 225-3315

Howard Coble, R-NC (6)
2468 Rayburn 225-3065

Steve Cohen, D-TN (9)
1004 Longworth 225-3265

Tom Cole, R-OK (4)
236 Cannon 225-6165

K. Michael Conaway, R-TX (11)
511 Cannon 225-3605

John Conyers, Jr., D-MI (14)
2426 Rayburn 225-5126

Jim Cooper, D-TN (5)
1536 Longworth 225-4311

Jim Costa, D-CA (20)
1314 Longworth 225-3341

Jerry F. Costello, D-IL (12)
2408 Rayburn 225-5661

Joe Courtney, D-CT (2)
215 Cannon 225-2076

Robert E. (Bud) Cramer, Jr.,
D-AL (5) 2184 Rayburn
225-4801

Ander Crenshaw, R-FL (4)
127 Cannon 225-2501

Joseph Crowley, D-NY (7)
2404 Rayburn 225-3965

Barbara Cubin, R-WY (At Large)
1114 Longworth 225-2311

Henry Cuellar, D-TX (28)
336 Cannon 225-1640

John Abney Culberson, R-TX (7)
428 Cannon 225-2571

Elijah E. Cummings, D-MD (7)
2235 Rayburn 225-4741

Artur Davis, D-AL (7)
208 Cannon 225-2665

Danny K. Davis, D-IL (7)
1526 Longworth 225-5006

David Davis, R-TN (1)
514 Cannon 225-6356

Geoff Davis, R-KY (4)
1108 Longworth 225-3465

Jo Ann Davis, R-VA (1)
1123 Longworth 225-4261

Lincoln Davis, D-TN (4)
410 Cannon 225-6831

Susan A. Davis, D-CA (53)
1526 Longworth 225-2040

Tom Davis, R-VA (11)
2348 Rayburn 225-1492

Nathan Deal, R-GA (9)
2133 Rayburn 225-5211

Peter A. DeFazio, D-OR (4)
2134 Rayburn 225-6416

Diana DeGette, D-CO (1)
2421 Rayburn 225-4431

William D. Delahunt,
D-MA (10) 2454 Rayburn
225-3111

Rosa L. DeLauro, D-CT (3)
2262 Rayburn 225-3661

Charles W. Dent, R-PA (15)
116 Cannon 225-6411

Lincoln Diaz-Balart, R-FL (21)
2244 Rayburn 225-4211

Mario Diaz-Balart, R-FL (25)
328 Cannon 225-2778

Norman D. Dicks, D-WA (6)
2467 Rayburn 225-5916

John D. Dingell, D-MI (15)
2328 Rayburn 225-4071

Lloyd Doggett, D-TX (25)
201 Cannon 225-4865

Joe Donnelly, D-IN (2)
1218 Longworth 225-3915

John T. Doolittle, R-CA (4)
2410 Rayburn 225-2511

Michael F. Doyle, D-PA (14)
401 Cannon 225-2135

Thelma D. Drake, R-VA (2)
1208 Longworth 225-4215

David Dreier, R-CA (26)
233 Cannon 225-2305

John J. Duncan, Jr., R-TN (2)
2207 Rayburn 225-5435

Chet Edwards, D-TX (17)
2369 Rayburn 225-6105

Vernon J. Ehlers, R-MI (3)
2182 Rayburn 225-3831

Keith Ellison, D-MN (5)
1130 Longworth 225-4755

Brad Ellsworth, D-IN (8)
513 Cannon 225-4636

Rahm Emanuel, D-IL (5)
1319 Longworth 225-4061

Jo Ann Emerson, R-MO (8)
2440 Rayburn 225-4404

Eliot L. Engel, D-NY (17)
2161 Rayburn 225-2464

Phil English, R-PA (3)
2332 Rayburn 225-5406

Anna G. Eshoo, D-CA (14)
205 Cannon 225-8104

Bob Etheridge, D-NC (2)
1533 Longworth 225-4531

Terry Everett, R-AL (2)
2312 Rayburn 225-2901

Eni F. H. Faleomavaega, D-AS
(Delegate) 2422 Rayburn
225-8577

Mary Fallin, R-OK (5)
1432 Longworth 225-2132

Sam Farr, D-CA (17)
1221 Longworth 225-2861

Chaka Fattah, D-PA (2)
2301 Rayburn 225-4001

Tom Feeney, R-FL (24)
323 Cannon 225-2706

Mike Ferguson, R-NJ (7)
214 Cannon 225-5361

Bob Filner, D-CA (51)
2428 Rayburn 225-8045

Jeff Flake, R-AZ (6)
240 Cannon 225-2635

J. Randy Forbes, R-VA (4)
307 Cannon 225-6365

Jeff Fortenberry, R-NE (1)
1517 Longworth 225-4806

Luis G. Fortuño, R-PR
(Resident Commissioner)
126 Cannon 225-2615

Vito Fossella, R-NY (13)
2453 Rayburn 225-3371

Virginia Foxx, R-NC (5)
430 Cannon 225-2071

Barney Frank, D-MA (4)
2252 Rayburn 225-5931

Trent Franks, R-AZ (2)
1237 Longworth 225-4576

Rodney P. Frelinghuysen,
R-NJ (11) 2442 Rayburn
225-5034

Elton Gallegly, R-CA (24)
2309 Rayburn 225-5811

Scott Garrett, R-NJ (5)
1318 Longworth 225-4465

Jim Gerlach, R-PA (6)
308 Cannon 225-4315

Gabrielle Giffords, D-AZ (8)
502 Cannon 225-2542

Wayne T. Gilchrest, R-MD (1)
2245 Rayburn 225-5311

Kirsten E. Gillibrand, D-NY (20)
120 Cannon 225-5614

Paul E. Gillmor, R-OH (5)
1203 Longworth 225-6405

Phil Gingrey, R-GA (11)
119 Cannon 225-2931

Louie Gohmert, R-TX (1)
510 Cannon 225-3035

Charles A. Gonzalez, D-TX (20)
303 Cannon 225-3236

Virgil H. Goode, Jr., R-VA (5)
1520 Longworth 225-4711

Bob Goodlatte, R-VA (6)
2240 Rayburn 225-5431

Bart Gordon, D-TN (6)
2310 Rayburn 225-4231

Kay Granger, R-TX (12)
440 Cannon 225-5071

Sam Graves, R-MO (6)
1415 Longworth 225-7041

Al Green, D-TX (9)
425 Cannon 225-7508

Gene Green, D-TX (29)
2335 Rayburn 225-1688

Raúl M. Grijalva, D-AZ (7)
1440 Longworth 225-2435

Luis V. Gutierrez, D-IL (4)
2266 Rayburn 225-8203

John J. Hall, D-NY (19)
1217 Longworth 225-5441

Ralph M. Hall, R-TX (4)
2405 Rayburn 225-6673

Phil Hare, D-IL (17)
1118 Longworth 225-5905

Jane Harman, D-CA (36)
2400 Rayburn 225-8220

J. Dennis Hastert, R-IL (14)
2304 Rayburn 225-2976

Alcee L. Hastings, D-FL (23)
2353 Rayburn 225-1313

Doc Hastings, R-WA (4)
1214 Longworth 225-5816

Robin Hayes, R-NC (8)
130 Cannon 225-3715

Dean Heller, R-NV (2)
1023 Longworth 225-6155

Jeb Hensarling, R-TX (5)
132 Cannon 225-3484

Wally Herger, R-CA (2)
2268 Rayburn 225-3076

Stephanie Herseth Sandlin,
D-SD (At Large) 331 Cannon
225-2801

Brian Higgins, D-NY (27)
431 Cannon 225-3306

Baron P. Hill, D-IN (9)
223 Cannon 225-5315

Maurice D. Hinchey,
D-NY (22) 2431 Rayburn
225-6335

Rubén Hinojosa, D-TX (15)
2463 Rayburn 225-2531

Mazie K. Hirono, D-HI (2)
1229 Longworth 225-4906

David L. Hobson, R-OH (7)
2346 Rayburn 225-4324

Paul W. Hodes, D-NH (2)
506 Cannon 225-5206

Peter Hoekstra, R-MI (2)
2234 Rayburn 225-4401

Tim Holden, D-PA (17)
2417 Rayburn 225-5546

Rush D. Holt, D-NJ (12)
1019 Longworth 225-5801

Michael M. Honda, D-CA (15)
1713 Longworth 225-2631

Darlene Hooley, D-OR (5)
2430 Rayburn 225-5711

Steny H. Hoyer, D-MD (5)
1705 Longworth 225-4131

Kenny C. Hulshof, R-MO (9)
409 Cannon 225-2956

Duncan Hunter, R-CA (52)
2265 Rayburn 225-5672

Bob Inglis, R-SC (4)
330 Cannon 225-6030

Jay Inslee, D-WA (1)
403 Cannon 225-6311

Steve Israel, D-NY (2)
432 Cannon 225-3335

Darrell E. Issa, R-CA (49)
211 Cannon 225-3906

Jesse L. Jackson, Jr., D-IL (2)
2419 Rayburn 225-0773

Sheila Jackson-Lee, D-TX (18)
2435 Rayburn 225-3816

William J. Jefferson, D-LA (2)
2113 Rayburn 225-6636

Bobby Jindal, R-LA (1)
1205 Longworth 225-3015

Eddie Bernice Johnson,
D-TX (30) 1511 Longworth
225-8885

Henry C. "Hank" Johnson, Jr.,
D-GA (4) 1133 Longworth
225-1605

Sam Johnson, R-TX (3)
1211 Longworth 225-4201

Timothy V. Johnson, R-IL (15)
1207 Longworth 225-2371

Stephanie Tubbs Jones,
D-OH (11) 1009 Longworth
225-7032

Walter B. Jones, R-NC (3)
2333 Rayburn 225-3415

Jim Jordan, R-OH (4)
515 Cannon 225-2676

Steve Kagen, D-WI (8)
1232 Longworth 225-5665

Paul E. Kanjorski, D-PA (11)
2188 Rayburn 225-6511

Marcy Kaptur, D-OH (9)
2186 Rayburn 225-4146

Ric Keller, R-FL (8)
419 Cannon 225-2176

Patrick J. Kennedy, D-RI (1)
407 Cannon 225-4911

Dale E. Kildee, D-MI (5)
2107 Rayburn 225-3611

Carolyn C. Kilpatrick, D-MI (13)
2264 Rayburn 225-2261

Ron Kind, D-WI (3)
1406 Longworth 225-5506

Peter T. King, R-NY (3)
339 Cannon 225-7896

Steve King, R-IA (5)
1609 Longworth 225-4426

Jack Kingston, R-GA (1)
2368 Rayburn 225-5831

Mark Steven Kirk, R-IL (10)
1030 Longworth 225-4835

Ron Klein, D-FL (22)
313 Cannon 225-3026

John Kline, R-MN (2)
1429 Longworth 225-2271

Joe Knollenberg, R-MI (9)
2349 Rayburn 225-5802

Dennis J. Kucinich, D-OH (10)
2445 Rayburn 225-5871

John R. "Randy" Kuhl, Jr.,
R-NY (29) 1505 Longworth
225-3161

Ray LaHood, R-IL (18)
1424 Longworth 225-6201

Doug Lamborn, R-CO (5)
437 Cannon 225-4422

Nick Lampson, D-TX (22)
436 Cannon 225-5951

James R. Langevin, D-RI (2)
109 Cannon 225-2735

Tom Lantos, D-CA (12)
2413 Rayburn 225-3531

Rick Larsen, D-WA (2)
107 Cannon 225-2605

John B. Larson, D-CT (1)
1005 Longworth 225-2265

Tom Latham, R-IA (4)
2447 Rayburn 225-5476

Steven C. LaTourette, R-OH (14)
2371 Rayburn 225-5731

Barbara Lee, D-CA (9)
2444 Longworth 225-2661

Sander M. Levin, D-MI (12)
1236 Longworth 225-4961

Jerry Lewis, R-CA (41)
2112 Rayburn 225-5861

John Lewis, D-GA (5)
343 Cannon 225-3801

Ron Lewis, R-KY (2)
2418 Rayburn 225-3501

John Linder, R-GA (7)
1026 Longworth 225-4272

Daniel Lipinski, D-IL (3)
1717 Longworth 225-5701

Frank A. LoBiondo, R-NJ (2)
2427 Rayburn 225-6572

David Loebsack, D-IA (2)
1513 Longworth 225-6576

Zoe Lofgren, D-CA (16)
102 Cannon 225-3072

Nita M. Lowey, D-NY (18)
2329 Rayburn 225-6506

Frank D. Lucas, R-OK (3)
2311 Rayburn 225-5565

Daniel E. Lungren, R-CA (3)
2448 Rayburn 225-5716

Stephen F. Lynch, D-MA (9)
221 Cannon 225-8273

Carolyn McCarthy, D-NY (4)
106 Cannon 225-5516

Kevin McCarthy, R-CA (22)
1523 Longworth 225-2915

Michael T. McCaul, R-TX (10)
131 Cannon 225-2401

Betty McCollum, D-MN (4)
1714 Longworth 225-6631

Thaddeus G. McCotter,
R-MI (11) 1632 Longworth
225-8171

Jim McCrery, R-LA (4)
242 Cannon 225-2777

Jim McDermott, D-WA (7)
1035 Longworth 225-3106

James P. McGovern, D-MA (3)
438 Cannon 225-6101

Patrick T. McHenry, R-NC (10)
224 Cannon 225-2576

John M. McHugh, R-NY (23)
2366 Rayburn 225-4611

Mike McIntyre, D-NC (7)
2437 Rayburn 225-2731

Howard P. "Buck" McKeon,
R-CA (25) 2351 Rayburn
225-1956

Cathy McMorris Rodgers,
R-WA (5) 1708 Longworth
225-2006

Jerry McNerney, D-CA (11)
312 Cannon 225-1947

Michael R. McNulty, D-NY (21)
2210 Rayburn 225-5076

Connie Mack, R-FL (14)
115 Cannon 225-2536

Tim Mahoney, D-FL (16)
1541 Longworth 225-5792

Carolyn B. Maloney, D-NY (14)
2331 Rayburn 225-7944

Donald A. Manzullo, R-IL (16)
2228 Rayburn 225-5676

Kenny Marchant, R-TX (24)
1037 Longworth 225-6605

Edward J. Markey, D-MA (7)
2108 Rayburn 225-2836

Jim Marshall, D-GA (8)
504 Cannon 225-6531

Jim Matheson, D-UT (2)
1323 Longworth 225-3011

Doris O. Matsui, D-CA (5)
222 Cannon 225-7163

Martin T. Meehan,* D-MA (5)
2229 Rayburn 225-3411

Kendrick B. Meek, D-FL (17)
1039 Longworth 225-4506

Gregory W. Meeks, D-NY (6)
2342 Rayburn 225-3461

Charlie Melancon, D-LA (3)
404 Cannon 225-4031

* Announced April 2, 2007, that he would resign Congress May 9, 2007, to become chancellor of the University of Massachusetts at Lowell, and leave the House on July 1.

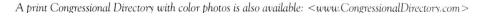

A print Congressional Directory with color photos is also available: <www.CongressionalDirectory.com>

John L. Mica, R-FL (7)
2313 Rayburn 225-4035

Michael H. Michaud, D-ME (2)
1724 Longworth 225-6306

Juanita Millender-McDonald,**
D-CA (37) 2233 Rayburn
225-7924

Brad Miller, D-NC (13)
1722 Longworth 225-3032

Candice S. Miller, R-MI (10)
228 Cannon 225-2106

Gary G. Miller, R-CA (42)
2438 Rayburn 225-3201

George Miller, D-CA (7)
2205 Rayburn 225-2095

Jeff Miller, R-FL (1)
1535 Longworth 225-4136

Harry E. Mitchell, D-AZ (5)
2434 Rayburn 225-2190

Alan B. Mollohan, D-WV (1)
2302 Rayburn 225-4172

Dennis Moore, D-KS (3)
1727 Longworth 225-2865

Gwen Moore, D-WI (4)
1239 Longworth 225-4572

James P. Moran, D-VA (8)
2239 Rayburn 225-4376

Jerry Moran, R-KS (1)
2202 Rayburn 225-2715

Christopher S. Murphy,
D-CT (5) 501 Cannon
225-4476

Patrick J. Murphy, D-PA (8)
1007 Longworth 225-4276

Tim Murphy, R-PA (18)
322 Cannon 225-2301

John P. Murtha, D-PA (12)
2423 Rayburn 225-2065

Marilyn N. Musgrave,
R-CO (4) 1507 Longworth
225-4676

Sue Wilkins Myrick, R-NC (9)
230 Cannon 225-1976

Jerrold Nadler, D-NY (8)
2334 Rayburn 225-5635

Grace F. Napolitano, D-CA (38)
1610 Longworth 225-5256

Richard E. Neal, D-MA (2)
2208 Rayburn 225-5601

Randy Neugebauer, R-TX (19)
429 Cannon 225-4005

Eleanor Holmes Norton,
D-DC (Delegate)
2136 Rayburn 225-8050

Charlie Norwood,*** R-GA (9)
2452 Rayburn 225-4101

Devin Nunes, R-CA (21)
1013 Longworth 225-2523

James L. Oberstar, D-MN (8)
2365 Rayburn 225-6211

David R. Obey, D-WI (7)
2314 Rayburn 225-3365

John W. Olver, D-MA (1)
1111 Longworth 225-5335

Solomon P. Ortiz, D-TX (27)
2110 Rayburn 225-7742

Frank Pallone, Jr., D-NJ (6)
237 Cannon 225-4671

Bill Pascrell, Jr., D-NJ (8)
2464 Rayburn 225-5751

Ed Pastor, D-AZ (4)
2465 Rayburn 225-4065

Ron Paul, R-TX (14)
203 Cannon 225-2831

Donald M. Payne, D-NJ (10)
2209 Rayburn 225-3436

Stevan Pearce, R-NM (2)
1607 Longworth 225-2365

Nancy Pelosi, D-CA (8)
235 Cannon 225-4965

Mike Pence, R-IN (6)
1317 Longworth 225-3021

Ed Perlmutter, D-CO (7)
415 Cannon 225-2645

Collin C. Peterson, D-MN (7)
2211 Rayburn 225-2165

John E. Peterson, R-PA (5)
123 Cannon 225-5121

Thomas E. Petri, R-WI (6)
2462 Rayburn 225-2476

Charles W. "Chip" Pickering,
R-MS (3) 229 Cannon
225-5031

Joseph R. Pitts, R-PA (16)
420 Cannon 225-2411

Todd Russell Platts, R-PA (19)
1032 Longworth 225-5836

Ted Poe, R-TX (2)
1605 Longworth 225-6565

Earl Pomeroy, D-ND
(At Large) 1501 Longworth
225-2611

Jon C. Porter, R-NV (3)
218 Cannon 225-3252

David E. Price, D-NC (4)
2162 Rayburn 225-1784

Tom Price, R-GA (6)
424 Cannon 225-4501

Deborah Pryce, R-OH (15)
320 Cannon 225-2015

Adam H. Putnam, R-FL (12)
1725 Longworth 225-1252

George Radanovich, R-CA (19)
2367 Rayburn 225-4540

Nick J. Rahall II, D-WV (3)
2307 Rayburn 225-3452

Jim Ramstad, R-MN (3)
103 Cannon 225-2871

Charles B. Rangel, D-NY (15)
2354 Rayburn 225-4365

Ralph Regula, R-OH (16)
2306 Rayburn 225-3876

** Died April 22, 2007. A special election is scheduled for June 26, 2007, and a runoff election, if needed, for August 21.
*** Died Feb. 13, 2007. A special election is scheduled for June 19, 2007, and a runoff election, if needed, for July 17.

A print Congressional Directory with color photos is also available: <www.CongressionalDirectory.com>

Dennis R. Rehberg, R-MT
(At Large) 516 Cannon
225-3211

David G. Reichert, R-WA (8)
1223 Longworth 225-7761

Rick Renzi, R-AZ (1)
418 Cannon 225-2315

Silvestre Reyes, D-TX (16)
2433 Rayburn 225-4831

Thomas M. Reynolds, R-NY (26)
332 Cannon 225-5265

Ciro D. Rodriguez, D-TX (23)
2458 Rayburn 225-4511

Harold Rogers, R-KY (5)
2406 Rayburn 225-4601

Mike Rogers, R-AL (3)
324 Cannon 225-3261

Mike Rogers, R-MI (8)
133 Cannon 225-4872

Dana Rohrabacher, R-CA (46)
2300 Rayburn 225-2415

Ileana Ros-Lehtinen, R-FL (18)
2160 Rayburn 225-3931

Peter J. Roskam, R-IL (6)
507 Cannon 225-4561

Mike Ross, D-AR (4)
314 Cannon 225-3772

Steven R. Rothman, D-NJ (9)
2303 Rayburn 225-5061

Lucille Roybal-Allard,
D-CA (34) 2330 Rayburn
225-1766

Edward R. Royce, R-CA (40)
2185 Rayburn 225-4111

C. A. Dutch Ruppersberger,
D-MD (2) 1730 Longworth
225-3061

Bobby L. Rush, D-IL (1)
2416 Rayburn 225-4372

Paul Ryan, R-WI (1)
1113 Longworth 225-3031

Tim Ryan, D-OH (17)
1421 Longworth 225-5261

John T. Salazar, D-CO (3)
1531 Longworth 225-4761

Bill Sali, R-ID (1)
508 Cannon 225-6611

Linda T. Sánchez, D-CA (39)
1222 Longworth 225-6676

Loretta Sanchez, D-CA (47)
1230 Longworth 225-2965

John P. Sarbanes, D-MD (3)
426 Cannon 225-4016

Jim Saxton, R-NJ (3)
2217 Rayburn 225-4765

Janice D. Schakowsky, D-IL (9)
1027 Longworth 225-2111

Adam B. Schiff, D-CA (29)
326 Cannon 225-4176

Jean Schmidt, R-OH (2)
238 Cannon 225-3164

Allyson Y. Schwartz,
D-PA (13) 423 Cannon
225-6111

David Scott, D-GA (13)
417 Cannon 225-2939

Robert C. "Bobby" Scott,
D-VA (3) 1201 Longworth
225-8351

F. James Sensenbrenner, Jr.,
R-WI (5) 2449 Rayburn
225-5101

José E. Serrano, D-NY (16)
2227 Rayburn 225-4361

Pete Sessions, R-TX (32)
1514 Longworth 225-2231

Joe Sestak, D-PA (7)
1022 Longworth 225-2011

John B. Shadegg, R-AZ (3)
306 Cannon 225-3361

Christopher Shays, R-CT (4)
1126 Longworth 225-5541

Carol Shea-Porter, D-NH (1)
1508 Longworth 225-5456

Brad Sherman, D-CA (27)
2242 Rayburn 225-5911

John Shimkus, R-IL (19)
2452 Rayburn 225-5271

Health Shuler, D-NC (11)
512 Cannon 225-6401

Bill Shuster, R-PA (9)
204 Cannon 225-2431

Michael K. Simpson, R-ID (2)
1339 Longworth 225-5531

Albio Sires, D-NJ (13)
1024 Longworth 225-7919

Ike Skelton, D-MO (4)
2206 Rayburn 225-2876

Louise McIntosh Slaughter,
D-NY (28) 2469 Rayburn
225-3615

Adam Smith, D-WA (9)
2402 Rayburn 225-8901

Adrian Smith, R-NE (3)
503 Cannon 225-6435

Christopher H. Smith, R-NJ (4)
2373 Rayburn 225-3765

Lamar Smith, R-TX (21)
2409 Rayburn 225-4236

Vic Snyder, D-AR (2)
1330 Longworth 225-2506

Hilda L. Solis, D-CA (32)
1414 Longworth 225-5464

Mark E. Souder, R-IN (3)
2231 Rayburn 225-4436

Zachary T. Space, D-OH (18)
315 Cannon 225-6265

John M. Spratt, Jr., D-SC (5)
1401 Longworth 225-5501

Fortney Pete Stark, D-CA (13)
239 Cannon 225-5065

Cliff Stearns, R-FL (6)
2370 Rayburn 225-5744

Bart Stupak, D-MI (1)
2352 Rayburn 225-4735

John Sullivan, R-OK (1)
114 Cannon 225-2211

Betty Sutton, D-OH (13)
1721 Longworth 225-3401

Thomas G. Tancredo, R-CO (6)
1131 Longworth 225-7882

John S. Tanner, D-TN (8)
1226 Longworth 225-4714

Ellen O. Tauscher, D-CA (10)
2459 Rayburn 225-1880

Gene Taylor, D-MS (4)
2269 Rayburn 225-5772

Lee Terry, R-NE (2)
1524 Longworth 225-4155

Bennie G. Thompson, D-MS (2)
2432 Rayburn 225-5876

Mike Thompson, D-CA (1)
231 Cannon 225-3311

Mac Thornberry, R-TX (13)
2457 Rayburn 225-3706

Todd Tiahrt, R-KS (4)
2441 Rayburn 225-6216

Patrick J. Tiberi, R-OH (12)
113 Cannon 225-5355

John F. Tierney, D-MA (6)
2238 Rayburn 225-8020

Edolphus Towns, D-NY (10)
2232 Rayburn 225-5936

Michael R. Turner, R-OH (3)
1740 Longworth 225-6465

Mark Udall, D-CO (2)
100 Cannon 225-2161

Tom Udall, D-NM (3)
1410 Longworth 225-6190

Fred Upton, R-MI (6)
2183 Rayburn 225-3761

Chris Van Hollen, D-MD (8)
1707 Longworth 225-5341

Nydia M. Velázquez, D-NY
(12) 2466 Rayburn 225-2361

Peter J. Visclosky, D-IN (1)
2256 Rayburn 225-2461

Tim Walberg, R-MI (7)
325 Cannon 225-6276

Greg Walden, R-OR (2)
1210 Longworth 225-6730

James T. Walsh, R-NY (25)
2372 Rayburn 225-3701

Timothy J. Walz, D-MN (1)
1529 Longworth 225-2472

Zach Wamp, R-TN (3)
1436 Longworth 225-3271

Debbie Wasserman Schultz,
D-FL (20) 118 Cannon
225-7931

Maxine Waters, D-CA (35)
2344 Rayburn 225-2201

Diane E. Watson, D-CA (33)
125 Cannon 225-7084

Melvin L. Watt, D-NC (12)
2236 Rayburn 225-1510

Henry A. Waxman, D-CA (30)
2204 Rayburn 225-3976

Anthony D. Weiner, D-NY (9)
1122 Longworth 225-6616

Peter Welch, D-VT (At Large)
1404 Longworth 225-4115

Dave Weldon, R-FL (15)
2347 Rayburn 225-3671

Jerry Weller, R-IL (11)
108 Cannon 225-3635

Lynn A. Westmoreland,
R-GA (3) 1213 Longworth
225-5901

Robert Wexler, D-FL (19)
2241 Rayburn 225-3001

Ed Whitfield, R-KY (1)
2411 Rayburn 225-3115

Roger F. Wicker, R-MS (1)
2350 Rayburn 225-4306

Charles A. Wilson, D-OH (6)
226 Cannon 225-5705

Heather Wilson, R-NM (1)
442 Cannon 225-6316

Joe Wilson, R-SC (2)
212 Cannon 225-2452

Frank R. Wolf, R-VA (10)
241 Cannon 225-5136

Lynn C. Woolsey, D-CA (6)
2263 Rayburn 225-5161

David Wu, D-OR (1)
2338 Rayburn 225-0855

Albert Russell Wynn, D-MD (4)
2470 Rayburn 225-8699

John A. Yarmuth, D-KY (3)
319 Cannon 225-5401

C. W. Bill Young, R-FL (10)
2407 Rayburn 225-5961

Don Young, R-AK (At Large)
2111 Rayburn 225-5765

Appendix Two

House Committees Room and Telephone Directory
(As of April 2, 2007)

The telephone area code is 202. All House offices can be reached through the Capitol switchboard, 202-225-3121. Email addresses and individual committees' web sites can be obtained through the House web site, <*www.house.gov*>.

All office addresses are in the Capitol and the Cannon, Ford, Longworth, and Rayburn House Office Buildings. The mailing address is the office address plus *Washington, DC 20515*. Any mail or packages go through a security screening process; delivery may be delayed at least several days.

Most committees' web sites contain information on their subcommittees. The majority and minority staffs of subcommittees can be reached through their parent committees' majority or minority offices. The names, addresses, and telephone numbers of the subcommittees of the Appropriations Committee are provided here because of the subcommittees' importance. (*See* § 9.80, *Authorization and Appropriation Processes.*)

Committee	Majority Office	Majority Phone	Minority Office	Minority Phone
Agriculture	1301 Longworth	225-2171	1305 Longworth	225-0029
Appropriations	H-218 Capitol	225-2771	1016 Longworth	225-3481

Subcommittees of Appropriations Committee[1]

Agriculture, Rural Development, Food and Drug Administration, and Related Agencies	2362 Rayburn	225-2638
Commerce, Justice, Science, and Related Agencies	H-309 Capitol	225-3351
Defense	H-149 Capitol	225-2847
Energy and Water Development, and Related Agencies	2362 Rayburn	225-3421
Financial Services and General Government	1040A Longworth	225-7245
Homeland Security	B307 Rayburn	225-5834
Interior, Environment, and Related Agencies	B308 Rayburn	225-3081
Labor, Health and Human Services, Education, and Related Agencies	2358 Rayburn	225-3508
Legislative Branch	H-147 Capitol	226-7252
Military Construction, Veterans Affairs, and Related Agencies	H-143 Capitol	225-3047
State, Foreign Operations, and Related Programs	HB-26 Capitol	225-2041
Transportation and Housing and Urban Development, and Related Agencies	2358 Rayburn	225-2141

1. Minority staff of the Appropriations Committee's subcommittees may be contacted through the full committee's minority staff office.

Committee	Majority Office	Majority Phone	Minority Office	Minority Phone
Armed Services	2120 Rayburn	225-4151	2340 Rayburn	225-8980
Budget	207 Cannon	226-7200	B-71 Cannon	226-7270
Education and Labor	2181 Rayburn	225-3725	2101 Rayburn	225-4527
Energy and Commerce	2125 Rayburn	225-2927	2322A Rayburn	225-3641
Energy Independence and Global Warming, Select	H2-250 Ford	225-4012	H2-346 Ford	225-0110
Financial Services	2129 Rayburn	225-4247	B-371A Rayburn	225-7502
Foreign Affairs	2170 Rayburn	225-5021	B360 Rayburn	225-8467
Homeland Security	H2-176 Ford	226-2616	H2-176 Ford	226-4817
House Administration	1309 Longworth	225-2061	1313 Longworth	225-8281
Intelligence, Permanent Select[2]	H-405 Capitol	225-7690	——	——
Judiciary	2138 Rayburn	225-3951	B351-C Rayburn	225-6906
Natural Resources	1324 Longworth	225-6065	1329 Longworth	225-2761
Oversight and Government Reform	2157 Rayburn	225-5051	B-350A Rayburn	225-5074
Rules	H-312 Capitol	225-9091	H-152 Capitol	225-9191
Science and Technology	2320 Rayburn	225-6375	H2-389 Ford	225-6371
Small Business	2361 Rayburn	225-4038	B-363 Rayburn	225-5821
Standards of Official Conduct[3]	HT-2 Capitol	225-7103	——	——
Transportation and Infrastructure	2165 Rayburn	225-4472	2163 Rayburn	225-9446
Veterans' Affairs	335 Cannon	225-9756	335 Cannon	225-3527
Ways and Means	1102 Longworth	225-3625	1139-E Longworth	225-4021

For links to House committees, see <*www.CongressLeaders.com*>.

2. Minority staff of the Permanent Select Intelligence Committee may be contacted through the majority office.
3. The Standards of Official Conduct Committee by tradition maintains a nonpartisan staff.

House Leadership Room and Telephone Directory
(As of April 2, 2007)

The telephone area code is 202. All House leadership offices can be reached through the Capitol switchboard, 202-225-3121. Email addresses and web sites for the leaders and party conference or caucus can be obtained through the House web site, *<www.house.gov>*.

All office addresses (except the parties' campaign committees) are in the Capitol and the Cannon, Longworth, and Rayburn House Office Buildings. The mailing address is the office address plus *Washington, DC 20515.* Any mail or packages go through a security screening process; delivery may be delayed by at least several days.

The principal leadership offices, such as Speaker, majority leader, and minority leader, have offices and staffs associated with those positions that are separate from their personal offices and staffs. Their personal offices usually remain the principal points of contact for the leaders' constituents.

A member in a subordinate leadership position might not have a leadership office and staff. He or she might rely on personal office staff to assist with leadership duties or share staff in another leader's office. In those instances, the office address and telephone number listed is for the member's personal office. (*For information on House leadership structure, see § 7.40.*)

House Democratic Leadership

Speaker	Nancy Pelosi, D-CA	H-232 Capitol	225-0100
Assistant to the Democratic Leader	Xavier Becerra, D-CA	1119 Longworth	225-6235
Majority Leader	Steny Hoyer, D-MD	H-107 Capitol	225-3130
Majority Whip[1]	James E. Clyburn, D-SC	H-329 Capitol	225-3210
Senior Chief Deputy Majority Whip	John Lewis, D-GA	H-330 Capitol	225-3210
Chief Deputy Majority Whip	G.K. Butterfield, D-NC	413 Cannon	225-3101
Chief Deputy Majority Whip	Joseph Crowley, D-NY	312 Cannon	225-3965
Chief Deputy Majority Whip	Diana DeGette, D-CO	1527 Longworth	225-4431
Chief Deputy Majority Whip	Ed Pastor, D-AZ	2465 Rayburn	225-4065
Chief Deputy Majority Whip	Janice Schakowsky, D-IL	1027 Longworth	225-2111
Chief Deputy Majority Whip	John Tanner, D-TN	1226 Longworth	225-4714

1. The parties have an extensive array of whips assisting the elected majority whip and minority whips. *(See § 7.43.)*

House Democratic Leadership

Chief Deputy Majority Whip	Debbie Wasserman Schultz	118 Cannon	225-7931
Chief Deputy Majority Whip	Maxine Waters, D-CA	2344 Rayburn	225-2201
Democratic Caucus Chair	Rahm Emanuel, D-IL	202A Cannon	225-1400
Democratic Caucus Vice Chair	John B. Larson, D-CT	1005 Longworth	225-2265
Democratic Steering and Policy Committee Chair	Nancy Pelosi, D-CA	H-204 Capitol	225-0100
Democratic Steering and Policy Committee Co-Chair (for Steering)	Rosa DeLauro, D-CT	H-204 Capitol	225-0100
Democratic Steering and Policy Committee Co-Chair (for Policy)	George Miller, D-CA	H-204 Capitol	225-0100
Democratic Congressional Campaign Committee Chair	Chris Van Hollen, D-MD	430 South Capitol St., SE Washington, DC 20003	863-1500

House Republican Leadership

Minority Leader	John A. Boehner, R-OH	H-204 Capitol	225-4000
Minority Whip[1]	Roy Blunt, R-MO	H-307 Capitol	225-0197
Chief Deputy Minority Whip	Eric Cantor, R-VA	H-307 Capitol	225-0197
Republican Conference Chair	Adam H. Putnam, R-FL	1420 Longworth	225-5107
Republican Conference Vice Chair	Kay Granger, R-TX	440 Cannon	225-5071
Republican Conference Secretary	John Carter, R-TX	408 Cannon	225-3864
Republican Steering Committee Chair	John A. Boehner, R-OH	H-204 Capitol	225-4000
Republican Policy Committee Chair	Thaddeus G. McCotter, R-MI	B-58 Cannon	225-6168
National Republican Congressional Committee Chair	Tom Cole, R-OK	320 First St., SE Washington, DC 20003	479-7000

For links and photographs of the top House leadership, see <*www.CongressLeaders.com*>.

Senators Room and Telephone Directory
(As of April 2, 2007)

The telephone area code is 202. All Senate offices can be reached through the Capitol switchboard, 202-224-3121. The Senate web site, *<www.senate.gov>*, links to individual senators' web sites and to their email addresses or email forms.

All office addresses are in the Dirksen, Hart, and Russell Senate Office Buildings. The mailing address is the office address plus *Washington, DC 20510*. Any mail or packages go through a security screening process; delivery may be delayed by at least several days.

In the list below, senators' names are followed by their party designations (D=Democrat, R=Republican, I=Independent) and their states.

Akaka, Daniel K., D-HI
SH-141 Hart 224-6361

Alexander, Lamar, R-TN
SD-455 Dirksen 224-4944

Allard, Wayne, R-CO
SD-521 Dirksen 224-5941

Baucus, Max, D-MT
SH-511 Hart 224-2651

Bayh, Evan, D-IN
SR-131 Russell 224-5623

Bennett, Robert F., R-UT
SD-431 Dirksen 224-5444

Biden, Jr., Joseph R., D-DE
SR-201 Russell 224-5042

Bingaman, Jeff, D-NM
SH-703 Hart 224-5521

Bond, Christopher S., R-MO
SR-274 Russell 224-5721

Boxer, Barbara, D-CA
SH-112 Hart 224-3553

Brown, Sherrod, D-OH
SR-455 Russell 224-2315

Brownback, Sam, R-KS
SH-303 Hart 224-6521

Bunning, Jim, R-KY
SH-316 Hart 224-4343

Burr, Richard, R-NC
SR-217 Russell 224-3154

Byrd, Robert C., D-WV
SH-311 Hart 224-3954

Cantwell, Maria, D-WA
SD-511 Dirksen 224-3441

Cardin, Benjamin L., D-MD
SH-509 Hart 224-4524

Carper, Thomas R., D-DE
SH-513 Hart 224-2441

Casey, Bob, D-PA
SR-383 Russell 224-6324

Chambliss, Saxby, R-GA
SR-416 Russell 224-3521

Clinton, Hillary Rodham, D-NY
SR-476 Russell 224-4451

Coburn, Tom, R-OK
SR-172 Russell 224-5754

Cochran, Thad, R-MS
SD-113 Dirksen 224-5054

Coleman, Norm, R-MN
SH-320 Hart 224-5641

Collins, Susan M., R-ME
SD-413 Dirksen 224-2523

Conrad, Kent, D-ND
SH-530 Hart 224-2043

Corker, Bob, R-TN
SD-185 Dirksen 224-3344

Cornyn, John, R-TX
SH-517 Hart 224-2934

Craig, Larry E., R-ID
SH-520 Hart 224-2752

Crapo, Mike, R-ID
SD-239 Dirksen 224-6142

DeMint, Jim, R-SC
SR-340 Russell 224-6121

Dodd, Christopher J., D-CT
SR-448 Russell 224-2823

Dole, Elizabeth, R-NC
SD-555 Dirksen 224-6342

Domenici, Pete V., R-NM
SH-328 Hart 224-6621

Dorgan, Byron L., D-ND
SH-322 Hart 224-2551

Durbin, Richard J., D-IL
SH-309 Hart 224-2152

Ensign, John, R-NV
SR-119 Russell 224-6244

Enzi, Mike, R-WY
SR-379A Russell 224-3424

Feingold, Russell D., D-WI
SH-506 Hart 224-5323

Feinstein, Dianne, D-CA
SH-331 Hart 224-3841

Graham, Lindsey O., R-SC
SR-290 Russell 224-5972

Grassley, Charles E., R-IA
SH-135 Hart 224-3744

Gregg, Judd, R-NH
SR-393 Russell 224-3324

Hagel, Chuck, R-NE
SR-248 Russell 224-4224

Harkin, Tom, D-IA
SH-731 Hart 224-3254

Hatch, Orrin G., R-UT
SH-104 Hart 224-5251

Hutchison, Kay Bailey, R-TX
SR-284 Russell 224-5922

Inhofe, James M., R-OK
SR-453 Russell 224-4721

Inouye, Daniel K., D-HI
SH-722 Hart 224-3934

Isakson, Johnny, R-GA
SR-120 Russell 224-3643

Johnson, Tim, D-SD
SH-136 Hart 224-5842

Kennedy, Edward M., D-MA
SR-317 Russell 224-4543

Kerry, John F., D-MA
SR-304 Russell 224-2742

Klobuchar, Amy, D-MN
SH-302 Hart 224-3244

Kohl, Herb, D-WI
SH-330 Hart 224-5653

Kyl, Jon, R-AZ
SH-730 Hart 224-4521

Landrieu, Mary L., D-LA
SH-724 Hart 224-5824

Lautenberg, Frank, D-NJ
SH-324 Hart 224-3224

Leahy, Patrick J., D-VT
SR-433 Russell 224-4242

Levin, Carl, D-MI
SR-269 Russell 224-6221

Lieberman, Joseph I., I-CT*
SH-706 Hart 224-4041

Lincoln, Blanche L., D-AR
SD-355 Dirksen 224-4843

Lott, Trent, R-MS
SR-487 Russell 224-6253

Lugar, Richard G., R-IN
SH-306 Hart 224-4814

Martinez, Mel, R-FL
SR-356 Russell 224-3041

McCain, John, R-AZ
SR-241 Russell 224-2235

McCaskill, Claire, D-MO
SH-717 Hart 224-6154

McConnell, Mitch, R-KY
SR-361A Russell 224-2541

Menendez, Robert, D-NJ
SH-317 Hart 224-4744

Mikulski, Barbara A., D-MD
SH-503 Hart 224-4654

Murkowski, Lisa, R-AK
SH-709 Hart 224-6665

Murray, Patty, D-WA
SR-173 Russell 224-2621

Nelson, Bill, D-FL
SH-716 Hart 224-5274

Nelson, E. Benjamin, D-NE
SH-720 Hart 224-6551

Obama, Barack, D-IL
SH-713 Hart 224-2854

Pryor, Mark, D-AR
SD-257 Dirksen 224-2353

Reed, Jack, D-RI
SH-728 Hart 224-4642

Reid, Harry, D-NV
SH-528 Hart 224-3542

Roberts, Pat, R-KS
SH-109 Hart 224-4774

Rockefeller IV, John D., D-WV
SH-531 Hart 224-6472

Salazar, Ken, D-CO
SH-702 Hart 224-5852

Sanders, Bernard,* I-VT
SD-332 Dirksen 224-5141

Schumer, Charles E., D-NY
SH-313 Hart 224-6542

Sessions, Jeff, R-AL
SR-335 Russell 224-4124

Shelby, Richard C., R-AL
SH-110 Hart 224-5744

Smith, Gordon, R-OR
SR-404 Russell 224-3753

Snowe, Olympia J., R-ME
SR-154 Russell 224-5344

Specter, Arlen, R-PA
SH-711 Hart 224-4254

Stabenow, Debbie, D-MI
SH-133 Hart 224-4822

Stevens, Ted, R-AK
SH-522 Hart 224-3004

Sununu, John E., R-NH
SR-111 Russell 224-2841

Tester, Jon, D-MT
SR-204 Russell 224-2644

Thomas, Craig, R-WY
SD-307 Dirksen 224-6441

Thune, John, R-SD
SR-493 Russell 224-2321

Vitter, David, R-LA
SH-516 Hart 224-4623

Voinovich, George V., R-OH
SH-524 Hart 224-3353

Warner, John W., R-VA
SR-225 Russell 224-2023

Webb, Jim, D-VA
SR-144 Russell 224-4024

Whitehouse, Sheldon, D-RI
SH-502 Hart 224-2921

Wyden, Ron, D-OR
SD-230 Dirksen 224-5244

* Independent who caucuses with the Democrats.

A print Congressional Directory with color photos is also available: <www.CongressionalDirectory.com>

A p p e n d i x   F i v e

Senate Committees Room and Telephone Directory
(As of April 2, 2007)

The telephone area code is 202. All Senate offices can be reached through the Capitol switchboard, 202-224-3121. Email addresses and individual committees' web sites can be obtained through the Senate web site, <*www.senate.gov*>.

All office addresses are in the Capitol and Dirksen, Hart, and Russell Senate Office Buildings. The mailing address is the office address plus *Washington, DC 20510*. Any mail or packages go through a security screening process; delivery may be delayed by at least several days.

Most committees' web sites contain information on their subcommittees. The majority and minority staffs of subcommittees can be reached through their parent committees' majority or minority offices. The names, addresses, and telephone numbers of the subcommittees of the Appropriations Committee are provided here because of the subcommittees' importance. *(See § 9.80, Authorization and Appropriation Processes.)*

Committee	Majority Office	Majority Phone	Minority Office	Minority Phone
Aging, Select	SD-G31 Dirksen	224-5364	SH-628 Hart	224-5364
Agriculture, Nutrition, and Forestry	SR-328A Russell	224-2035	SR-328A Russell	224-2035
Appropriations	S-131 Capitol	224-7363	S-112 Capitol	224-7292

Subcommittees of Appropriations Committee

	Majority Office	Majority Phone	Minority Office	Minority Phone
Agriculture, Rural Development, Food and Drug Administration, and Related Agencies	SD-129 Dirksen	224-8090	SD-190 Dirksen	224-5270
Commerce, Justice, and Science, and Related Agencies	SD-144 Dirksen	224-5202	SH-123 Hart	224-7277
Defense	SD-119 Dirksen	224-6688	SD-115 Dirksen	224-7255
Energy and Water Development	SD-186 Dirksen	224-8119	SD-118 Dirksen	224-7260
Financial Services and General Government	SD-184 Dirksen	224-1133	SD-142 Dirksen	224-2104
Homeland Security	SD-135 Dirksen	224-8244	SH-123 Hart	224-4319
Interior, Environment, and Related Agencies	SD-131 Dirksen	224-0774	SH-123 Hart	228-7233
Labor, Health and Human Services, Education, and Related Agencies	SD-131 Dirksen	224-9145	SH-156 Hart	224-7230
Legislative Branch	SD-135 Dirksen	224-3477	S-146A Capitol	224-7257

Subcommittees of Appropriations Committee

	Majority Office	Majority Phone	Minority Office	Minority Phone
Military Construction, Veterans' Affairs, and Related Agencies	SD-125 Dirksen	224-8224	SH-123 Hart	224-5245
State, Foreign Operations, and Related Programs	SD-127 Dirksen	224-7284	SD-142 Dirksen	224-2104
Transportation, Housing and Urban Development, and Related Agencies	SD-133 Dirksen	224-7281	SD-128 Dirksen	224-5310

Committee	Majority Office	Majority Phone	Minority Office	Minority Phone
Armed Services	SR-228 Russell	224-3871	SR-228 Russell	224-3871
Banking, Housing, and Urban Affairs	SD-534 Dirksen	224-7391	SD-534 Dirksen	224-7391
Budget	SD-624 Dirksen	224-0642	SD-624 Dirksen	224-0642
Commerce, Science, and Transportation	SD-508 Dirksen	224-5115	SD-508 Dirksen	224-1251
Energy and Natural Resources	SD-304 Dirksen	224-4971	SD-304 Dirksen	224-4971
Environment and Public Works	SD-456 Dirksen	224-8832	SD-410 Dirksen	224-6176
Ethics, Select[1]	SH-220 Hart	224-2981	——	——
Finance	SD-219 Dirksen	224-4515	SD-219 Dirksen	224-4515
Foreign Relations	SD-439 Dirksen	224-4651	SD-450 Dirksen	224-6797
Health, Education, Labor, and Pensions	SD-428 Dirksen	224-5375	SH-835 Hart	224-6770
Homeland Security and Governmental Affairs	SD-340 Dirksen	224-2627	SD-304 Dirksen	224-4751
Indian Affairs	SH-838 Hart	224-2251	SH-838 Hart	224-2251
Intelligence, Select[2]	SH-211 Hart	224-1700	——	——
Judiciary	SD-224 Dirksen	224-7703	SD-152 Dirksen	224-5225
Rules and Administration	SR-305 Russell	224-6352	SR-481 Russell	224-6352
Small Business and Entrepreneurship	SR-428A Russell	224-5175	SR-428A Russell	224-7884
Veterans' Affairs	SR-412 Russell	224-9126	SH-143 Hart	224-2074

For links to Senate committees, see <*www.CongressLeaders.com*>.

1. The Select Committee on Ethics by tradition maintains a nonpartisan staff.
2. The Select Committee on Intelligence by tradition maintains a nonpartisan staff.

Appendix Six

Senate Leadership Room and Telephone Directory
(As of April 2, 2007)

The telephone area code is 202. All Senate leadership offices can be reached through the Capitol switchboard, 202-224-3121. Email addresses and the leaders' and party conferences' web sites can be obtained through the Senate web site, <*www.senate.gov*>.

All office addresses (except the parties' campaign committees) are in the Capitol and the Russell, Dirksen, and Hart Senate Office Buildings. The mailing address is the office address plus *Washington, DC 20510*. Any mail or packages go through a security screening process; delivery may be delayed by at least several days.

The principal leadership offices, such as majority leader and minority leader, have offices and staff associated with those positions that are separate from the senators' personal offices and staffs. Their personal offices usually remain the principal points of contact for the leaders' constituents.

A senator in a subordinate leadership position might not have a leadership office and staff. He or she might rely on personal office staff to assist with leadership duties or share staff in another leader's office. In those instances, the office address and telephone number listed is for the senator's personal office. (*For information on the Senate leadership structure, see § 7.40.*)

In addition, some senators obtain separate Capitol offices, popularly referred to as "Capitol hideaways," based on seniority and other factors. These offices are not listed here.

President of the Senate

Vice President of the United States	**Richard B. Cheney**, R	[1]	224-2424
President Pro Tempore	**Robert C. Byrd**, D-WV	S-128 Capitol	224-2848

---

1. The vice president as president of the Senate maintains a ceremonial office on the Senate side of the Capitol, and an office in the Dirksen Senate Office Building, in addition to his principal offices in the White House and the Dwight D. Eisenhower Building (formerly known as the Old Executive Office Building).

Senate Democratic Leadership

Majority Leader	Harry Reid, D-NV	S-221 Capitol	224-2158
Assistant Majority Leader[2]	Richard Durbin, D-IL	S-321 Capitol	224-9447
Chief Deputy Whip	Barbara Boxer, D-CA	SH-112 Hart	224-3553
Democratic Conference Chair	Harry Reid, D-NV	S-221 Capitol	224-5556
Democratic Conference Vice Chair	Charles Schumer, D-NY	SH-313 Hart	224-6542
Democratic Conference Secretary	Patty Murray, D-WA	SR-173 Russell	224-2621
Democratic Policy Committee Chair	Byron Dorgan, D-ND	S-118 Capitol	224-5554
Democratic Steering and Outreach Committee Chair	Debbie Stabenow, D-MI	SH-712 Hart	224-9048
Committee Outreach Chair	Hillary Rodham Clinton, D-NY	SR-476 Russell	224-4451
Committee Outreach Vice Chair	Jeff Bingaman, D-NM	SH-703 Hart	224-5521
Democratic Senatorial Campaign Committee Chair	Charles Schumer, D-NY	120 Maryland Ave., NE Washington, DC 20002	224-2447

Senate Republican Leadership

Minority Leader	Mitch McConnell, R-KY	S-230 Capitol	224-3135
Minority Whip[2]	Trent Lott, R-MS	S-208 Capitol	224-2708
Chief Deputy Whip	John Thune, R-SD	SR-493 Russell	224-2321
Republican Conference Chair	Jon Kyl, R-AZ	SH-405 Hart	224-2764
Republican Conference Vice Chair	John Cornyn, R-TX	SH-517 Hart	224-2934
Republican Steering Committee Chair	Michael Crapo, R-ID	SD-239 Dirksen	224-6142
Republican Policy Committee Chair	Kay Bailey Hutchison, R-TX	SR-347 Russell	224-2946
National Republican Senatorial Committee Chair	John Ensign, R-NV	425 Second St., NE Washington, DC 20002	675-6000

For links and photographs of the top Senate leadership, see <*www.CongressLeaders.com*>.

2. The parties have an extensive array of whips assisting the elected majority and minority whips. (*See § 7.43.*)

Appendix Seven

Joint Committees Room and Telephone Directory
(As of April 2, 2007)

The telephone area code is 202. All joint committee offices can be reached through the Capitol switchboard, 202-225-3121 or 202-224-3121. Email addresses and individual committees' web sites can be obtained through the House and Senate web sites, <*www.house.gov*> and <*www.senate.gov*>, respectively.

Office addresses for the House and Senate office buildings are shown. The mailing address is the office address plus *Washington, DC 20515* for offices in House Buildings, and *Washington, DC 20510* for offices in Senate buildings. Any mail or packages go through a security screening process; delivery may be delayed by at least several days.

Economic	SD-G-01 Dirksen	224-0372
Library	SR-305 Russell	224-6352
Printing[1]	1309 Longworth	225-2061
Taxation	1015 Longworth	225-3621

---

1. At the start of the 109th Congress, contact information for the Joint Committee on Printing is the same as for the Senate Rules and Administration Committee.

Table of Web Sites

Name	URL	Section
109th Congress House Rules and Manual	www.gpoaccess.gov/hrm/index.html	12.40
110th Congress House Rules and Manual	www.rules.house.gov/ruleprec/110th.pdf	12.40
ABC	www.abcnews.go.com	13.51
Advocacy Tipsheet	www.advocacyguru.com/tipsheet.htm	13.43
Almanac of American Politics	http://nationaljournal.com/about/almanac	13.20
American Association for the Advancement of Science Fellowship	http://fellowships.aaas.org/02_Areas/02_Congressional.shtml	5.100
American Enterprise Institute for Public Policy Research	www.aei.org	13.52
American, The	www.american.com	13.53
American Journal of Political Science	www.ajps.org	13.54
American League of Lobbyists	www.alldc.org	4.21
American Planning Association Congressional Fellowship for Urban Planning and Community Livability	www.planning.org/fellowships	5.100
American Political Science Association Congressional Fellows	www.apsanet.org/section_165.cfm	5.100
American Political Science Review	www.apsanet.org/section_327.cfm	13.54
American Prospect, The	www.prospect.org	13.53
American Society of Association Executives	www.asaecenter.org	4.21
American Spectator, The	www.spectator.org	13.53
American University's Washington Semester Fellows	www.american.edu/washingtonsemester	5.100
Architect of the Capitol	www.aoc.gov	5.112; 5.121; 6.12; 6.15; 13.10
ASAE Gateway to Associations	www.asaecenter.org/Directories/AssociationSearch.cfm	13.50
Aspen Institute	www.aspeninstitute.org	13.52
Associated Press	www.ap.org	13.51
BBC News	http://news.bbc.co.uk	13.51
Bernan	www.bernan.com	13.30
Biographical Directory of the United States Congress	http://bioguide.congress.gov/biosearch/biosearch.asp	12.81; 13.20
Bloomberg	www.bloomberg.com/news	13.51
Brookings Institution	www.brookings.org	13.52
Brookings Institution LEGIS Fellows Program	www.brookings.edu/execed/fellows/legis_fellows.htm	5.100
Bureau of Engraving and Printing	http://moneyfactory.gov	3.112
Bureau of National Affairs	www.bna.com	13.30
Campaigns & Elections	www.campaignonline.com	13.30
Capitol Advantage	www.capitoladvantage.com	13.30

This table is available online: <www.HillWebsites.com>

Name	URL	Section
Capitol Hill Fellowship Program (Georgetown University)	www3.georgetown.edu/grad/gppi/gai/ programscourses/program/fellowship.html	5.100
Capitol Police	www.uscapitolpolice.gov	5.123
Capital Source, The	http://nationaljournal.com/about/capitalsource	13.50
Carl Albert Congressional Research & Studies Center	www.ou.edu/special/albertctr/cachome.html	13.52
Carnegie Endowment for International Peace	www.carnegieendowment.org	13.52
Carroll Publishing	www.carrollpub.com	13.30
Catalog of Federal Domestic Assistance	www.cfda.gov	3.10; 5.160; 10.200
Cato Institute	www.cato.org	13.52
CBS	http://cbsnews.com	13.51
Census Bureau	www.census.gov	2.13; 13.30
Census Bureau (apportionment)	www.census.gov/population/www/ censusdata/apportionment.html	2.13
Census Bureau (district maps)	www.census.gov/geo/www/maps/cd109/ cd109_mainPage.htm	2.13
Census Bureau (population)	www.census.gov/Press-Release/www/releases/ archives/population/004704.html	2.13
Center for American Progress	www.americanprogress.org	13.52
Center for Congressional and Presidential Studies	http://spa.american.edu/ccps	13.52
Center for Democracy & Citizenship Program	www.excelgov.org/index.php? keyword=a432929c8e1952	5.190
Center for National Policy	www.cnponline.org	13.52
Center for Responsive Politics	www.opensecrets.org	2.21; 13.30
Center for Strategic and International Studies	www.csis.org	13.52
Center on Budget and Policy Priorities	www.cbpp.org	13.52
Center on Congress	www.congress.indiana.edu	13.52
Chaplain of the House	http://chaplain.house.gov	5.110
Chief Administrative Officer	www.house.gov/cao	5.110; 5.112
Christian Science Monitor	www.csmonitor.com	13.51
City Journal	www.city-journal.org	13.53
Clerk of the House	http://clerk.house.gov	5.110; 11.10; 13.10
CNN	www.cnn.com	13.51
Columbia Books	www.columbiabooks.com	13.30
Commentary	www.commentarymagazine.com	13.53
Commission on Security and Cooperation in Europe	www.csce.gov	7.70; 10.170
Committee on House Administration	http://cha.house.gov	4.30; 7.60; 12.80
Congressional Accountability Act Office of Compliance	www.compliance.gov	5.150

Name	URL	Section
Congressional Apportionment	www.census.gov/population/www/ censusdata/apportionment.html	2.13
Congressional Black Caucus Fellowship Program	www.cbcfinc.org/Leadership%20Education/ Fellowships/congressional.html	5.100
Congressional Budget Office	www.cbo.gov	5.130; 9.50; 13.10; 13.43
Congressional Deskbook	www.CongressionalDeskbook.com	front
Congressional Digest	www.congressionaldigestcorp.com/pcp/pubs/cd	13.53
Congressional Directory	www.gpoaccess.gov/cdirectory/index.html	13.20
Congressional-Executive Commission on China	www.cecc.gov	7.70
Congressional Franking	http://cha.house.gov	12.80
Congressional Hispanic Caucus Institute Fellowship Program	www.chci.org/chciyouth/fellowship/ fellowship.htm	5.100
Congressional Information Service	www.lexisnexis.com/academic	12.10
Congressional Institute	www.conginst.org	5.190
Congressional Management Foundation	www.cmfweb.org	5.190; 13.30
Congressional Pictorial Directory	www.gpoaccess.gov/pictorial/index.html	13.20
Congressional Quarterly	www.cq.com	8.42; 8.52; 8.123; 8.161; 8.262; 13.30
Congressional Record	www.gpoaccess.gov/crecord/index.html	12.20
Congressional Research Service	www.loc.gov/crsinfo/whatscrs.html#about	5.130;
Congressional Staff Directory	http://csd.cq.com/scripts/index.cfm	13.20
Congressional Yellow Book	www.leadershipdirectories.com	13.20
Cornell University's Legal Information Institute	www.law.cornell.edu/uscode	11.50
Council of State Governments	www.csg.org	10.201
Council on Foreign Relations	www.cfr.org	13.52
CRS Reports	www.llrx.com/features/crsreports.htm	13.10
C-SPAN	www.c-span.org	8.42; 8.123; 8.161; 8.262; 13.30; 13.43; 13.51
CQ Weekly	www.cq.com	13.51
Department of Justice Foreign Agents Registration Unit	www.usdoj.gov/criminal/fara	4.21
Deschler-Brown Precedents of the House	www.gpoaccess.gov/precedents/ deschler/index.html	12.40
Dirksen Congressional Center	www.dirksencongressionalcenter.org	13.52
Economist, The	www.economist.com	13.51
Executive Calendar of the Senate	www.senate.gov/pagelayout/legislative/one_ item_and_teasers/exec_calendar_page.htm	12.20
Executive Orders and Proclamations	www.gpoaccess.gov/executive.html	11.50
Federal Business Opportunities	www.fedbizopps.gov	5.112
Federal Depository Libraries	www.gpoaccess.gov/libraries.html	5.140; 11.10

Name	URL	Section
Federal Election Commission	www.fec.gov	2.20; 2.21; 13.30
FederalNewsRadio.com	http://federalnewsradio.com	13.51
Federal News Service	www.fnsg.com	13.30
Federal Register	www.gpoaccess.gov/fr/index.html	9.42; 11.50
Federal Register (Public Laws)	www.archives.gov/federal-register/laws/current.html	8.300; 11.50
Federal Register Documents	www.archives.gov/federal-register	11.50; 13.30
FedStates	www.fedstats.gov	13.40
Floor Procedures in the U.S. House of Representatives	www.rules.house.gov/archives/floor_man.htm	12.60
Focus	www.jointcenter.org/publications_recent_publications/focus_magazine	13.53
Foreign Affairs	www.foreignaffairs.org	13.53
Foreign Policy	www.foreignpolicy.com	13.53
Fox News	www.foxnews.com	13.51
FY 2008 Budget	www.access.gpo.gov/usbudget	9.43
Gale	www.gale.cengage.com	13.30
Gallery Watch.com	www.gallerywatch.com	13.30
General Services Administration	www.gsa.gov	5.160; 5.172
Google News	http://news.google.com	13.50
Governing	www.governing.com	13.51
Government Accountability Office	www.gao.gov	5.130; 10.41; 13.10; 13.43
Government Printing Office	www.gpoaccess.gov	5.140; 6.15; 7.10; 9.42; 9.43; 10.80; 11.10; 11.12; 11.50; 12.10; 12.20; 12.40; 12.50; 12.60; 12.61; 13.30 13.10; 13.20
GovTrack.us	www.govtrack.us	13.30
GPOLISTSERV	http://listserv.access.gpo.gov	13.43
Grants.gov	www.grants.gov	5.160; 10.200
Guide to the Records of the United States House of Representatives, 1789-1989	http://archives.gov/legislative/finding-aids	12.80
Guide to the Records of the United States Senate, 1789-1989	http://archives.gov/legislative/finding-aids	12.80
Harvard Journal on Legislation	www.law.harvard.edu/students/orgs/jol	13.54
Heritage Foundation	www.heritage.org	13.52
Hill, The	www.thehill.com	13.30; 13.51
Hispanic Americans in Congress, 1822-1995	www.loc.gov/rr/hispanic/congress	12.81
History of the Senate Republican Policy Committee	www.access.gpo.gov/congress/senate/repub_policy	12.81

Name	URL	Section
Holocaust Museum	www.ushmm.org	3.112
Hoover Institution	www.hoover.org	13.52
House Budget Committee	www.budget.house.gov	9.50
House Democratic Caucus	www.dems.gov	12.70
House Democratic Whip	http://majoritywhip.house.gov	11.10; 12.70
House Ethics Committee	www.house.gov/ethics	4.21; 4.30;
House Ethics Manual	www.house.gov/ethics	4.30; 12.80
House Journal (1991-1999)	www.access.gpo.gov/hjournal/index.html	12.20
House Majority Leader	http://majorityleader.gov	12.70
House Minority Leader	http://republicanleader.house.gov	12.70
House Calendar	www.gpoaccess.gov/calendars/house/index.html	12.20
House of Representatives Telephone Directory	http://bookstore.gpo.gov	13.20
House Practice	www.gpoaccess.gov/hpractice/index.html	12.40
House Press Gallery	www.house.gov/daily/hpg.htm	3.22
House Republican Conference	www.gop.gov	12.70
House Republican Policy Committee	http://policy.house.gov	12.70
House Republican Whip	http://republicanwhip.house.gov	11.10; 12.70;
House Rules Committee Publications	www.rules.house.gov	12.40; 12.60
House Speaker	http://speaker.house.gov	12.70
How Laws are Made	http://thomas.loc.gov/home/lawsmade.toc.html	12.60
Hudson's Directory	www.hudsonsdirectory.com	13.30
Human Events	www.humanevents.com	13.53
Impeachment Records of President Clinton	www.gpoaccess.gov/serialset/cdocuments/106cat2.html	12.50
Inspector General	www.house.gov/IG	5.110; 12.80
Institute for International Economics	www.iie.com	13.52
Institute for Policy Studies	www.ips-dc.org	13.52
International City/County Managers Association	www.icma.org	10.201
James A. Baker III Institute for Public Policy	http://bakerinstitute.org	13.52
John F. Kennedy Center for the Performing Arts	www.kennedy-center.org/visitor/tours.html	3.112
Joint Center for Political and Economic Studies	www.jointcenter.org	13.52
Joint Committee on Taxation	www.house.gov/jct	9.50
Journal of Law & Politics	www.student.virginia.edu/~jalopy	13.54
Journal of Legislation	http://law.nd.edu/jleg	13.54
Journal of Politics, The	www.journalofpolitics.org	13.54
Law Library of Congress	www.loc.gov/law	5.130; 13.10
Law Librarians' Society of Washington, DC	www.llsdc.org	13.30
Leadership Directories	www.leadershipdirectories.com	13.30

Name	URL	Section
Legal Times	www.law.com/dc	13.51
Legislative Counsel (House)	http://legcoun.house.gov	5.110
Legislative Counsel (Senate)	http://slc.senate.gov	5.120
Legislative Resource Center	http://clerk.house.gov/about/offices_lrc.html	11.10
Legislative Studies Quarterly	www.uiowa.edu/~lsq	13.54
LegiStorm	www.legistorm.com	13.30
Lexis-Nexis	www.lexisnexis.com	12.10; 13.30
Library of Congress	www.loc.gov	3.112; 5.130; 6.15; 12.20; 13.10
Lobbying Disclosure Act Forms (House)	http://lobbyingdisclosure.house.gov/register.html	4.21
Lobbying Disclosure Act Forms (Senate)	www.senate.gov/pagelayout/legislative/ g_three_sections_with_teasers/lobbyingdisc.htm	4.21
Los Angeles Times	www.latimes.com	13.51
Memorandum.com	www.memorandum.com	13.50
Morris K. Udall Foundation Native American Congressional Internship	www.udall.gov/udall.asp?link=300	5.100
Mount Vernon	www.mountvernon.org	3.112
Nation, The	www.thenation.com	13.53
National Academy of Public Administration	www.napawash.org	5.190
National Academy of Sciences	www.nationalacademies.org	5.190
National Archives and Records Administration	www.archives.gov	8.300; 11.50; 13.30; 13.43
National Archives and Records Administration (Electoral College)	www.archives.gov/federal-register/ electoral-college	10.91
National Association of Counties	www.naco.org	10.201
National Association of State Budget Officers	www.nasbo.org	10.201
National Bureau for Economic Research	www.nber.org	13.52
National Center for Policy Analysis	www.ncpa.org	13.52
National Conference of State Legislatures	www.ncsl.org	10.201
National Governors Association	www.nga.org	10.201
National Journal	http://nationaljournal.com	8.42; 8.52; 8.123; 8.161; 8.262; 13.30; 13.51
National Law Journal	www.nlj.com	13.51
National League of Cities	www.nlc.org	10.201
National Press Club	http://npc.press.org	13.51
National Public Radio	http://news.npr.org	13.51
National Review	www.nationalreview.com	13.53
NBC News	www.msnbc.msn.com	13.51
New Republic, The	www.tnr.com	13.53

Name	URL	Section
New York Times	www.nytimes.com	13.51
NewsHour with Jim Lehrer	www.pbs.org/newshour	13.51
Newsweek	www.newsweek.com	13.51
Office of Compliance	www.compliance.gov	5.150
Office of the Law Revision Counsel	http://uscode.house.gov	5.110; 11.50; 13.10
Office of Management and Budget	www.whitehouse.gov/omb	5.180; 9.42; 9.43; 10.20; 13.30
Office of Management and Budget Legislative Coordination and Clearance	www.whitehouse.gov/omb/ memoranda/m01-12.html	10.20
OpenCongress.org	www.opencongress.org	13.30
Periodical Press Gallery (House)	http://periodical.house.gov	3.22
Periodical Press Gallery (Senate)	www.senate.gov/galleries/pdcl	3.22
Perspectives on Politics	www.apsanet.org/section_328.cfm	13.54
Photographers Press Gallery (Senate)	www.senate.gov/galleries/photo	3.22
Political MoneyLine/FECInfo	www.fecinfo.com and www.politicalmoneyline.com	2.21
Political Science Quarterly	www.psqonline.org	13.54
Politico	www.politico.com	13.30; 13.51
Politics in America	www.cqpress.com	13.20
Policy Review	www.hoover.org/publications/policyreview	13.53
PR Newswire	www.prnewswire.com	13.30
Progressive Policy Institute	www.ppionline.org	13.52
Progressive, The	www.progressive.org	13.53
PS: Political Science & Politics	www.apsanet.org/section_223.cfm	13.54
Public Affairs Council	www.pac.org	4.21
Public Forum Institute, The	www.publicforuminstitute.org	13.52
Public Leadership Education Network	www.plen.org/internships.html	5.100
Public Papers of the President	www.archives.gov/federal-register/ publications/presidential-papers.html	11.50
Radio-Television Correspondents Gallery (House)	http://radiotv.house.gov	3.22
Radio-Television Correspondents Gallery (Senate)	www.senate.gov/galleries/radiotv	3.22
Rand Corporation	www.rand.org	13.52
Readex	www.readex.com	13.30
Reason	www.reason.com	13.53
Refdesk.com	www.refdesk.com	13.40
Regulation	www.cato.org/pubs/regulation	13.53
Reuters	www.reuters.com	13.51
Riddick's Senate Procedure	www.gpoaccess.gov/riddick/index.html	12.50
Robert Wood Johnson Health Policy Fellowship	www.healthpolicyfellows.org	5.100

This table is available online: <www.HillWebsites.com>

Name	URL	Section
Roll Call	www.rollcall.com	13.30; 13.51
Secretary of the Senate	www.senate.gov/reference/office/secretary_of_senate.htm	5.120
Secretary of the Senate (office and its functions)	www.senate.gov/artandhistory/history/common/briefing/secretary_senate.htm	5.120; 13.10
Secretary of the Senate (public records)	www.senate.gov/pagelayout/legislative/one_item_and_teasers/opr.htm	13.10
Senate Assistant Majority Leader	http://durbin.senate.gov	12.70
Senate Assistant Minority Leader	http://lott.senate.gov	12.70
Senate Budget Committee	www.budget.senate.gov	9.50
Senate Budget Committee's Budget Bulletin	www.senate.gov/~budget/republican/NewBB.htm	9.50
Senate Calendar	www.senate.gov/pagelayout/legislative/d_three_sections_with_teasers/calendars.htm	11.10
Senate Chaplain	www.senate.gov/reference/office/chaplain.htm	5.120
Senate Democratic Conference	http://democrats.senate.gov	12.70
Senate Democratic Policy Committee	http://democrats.senate.gov/dpc	12.70
Senate Democrats	http://democrats.senate.gov	11.10
Senate Enactment of Law	http://thomas.loc.gov/home/enactment/enactlawtoc.html	12.60
Senate Ethics Manual	http://ethics.senate.gov	4.21; 4.30; 12.80
Senate Lobbyist Filings	http://sopr.senate.gov	13.10
Senate Manual	www.gpoaccess.gov/smanual/index.html	12.50
Senate Majority Leader	http://reid.senate.gov	12.70
Senate Minority Leader	http://mcconnell.senate.gov	12.70
Senate Press Gallery	www.senate.gov/galleries/daily	3.22
Senate Republican Conference	http://src.senate.gov/public	12.70
Senate Republican Policy Committee	http://rpc.senate.gov	12.70
Senate Republicans	http://republican.senate.gov/public/index.cfm?FuseAction=Home.MonthlyView	11.10
Senate Telephone Directory	http://bookstore.gpo.gov	13.20
Sergeant at Arms of the Senate	www.senate.gov/reference/office/sergeant_at_arms.htm www.senate.gov/artandhistory/history/common/briefing/sergeant_at_arms.htm	5.120
Smithsonian Institution	www.si.edu	3.112
Standing Rules of the Senate	http://rules.senate.gov/senaterules	12.50
Stennis Center for Public Service	www.stennis.gov	5.190
TheCapitol.Net	www.TheCapitol.Net	front; 13.30; 3.112
Budget process glossary	www.CongressionalGlossary.com	9.160
Capitol flags	www.capitolflags.us	3.112
Communication and advocacy training	www.CommunicationAndAdvocacy.com	4.21

This table is available online: <www.HillWebsites.com>

Name	URL	Section
Congressional Directory	www.congressionaldirectory.com	13.20
Current House leadership	www.CongressLeaders.com	7.42
Current Senate leadership	www.CongressLeaders.com	7.44
Grass-roots training	www.CapitolHillDay.com	4.11
Grass-roots training	www.AdvocacyCampaigns.com	4.11
Legislative process flowchart	www.CongressPoster.com	8.01
Legislative terms	www.CongressionalGlossary.com	8.11, 8.51, 8.91, 8.121, 8.261
Party alignment/control	www.PartyNumbers.com	7.14; 7.41
Thomas	http://thomas.loc.gov	5.130; 8.42; 8.52; 8.123; 8.161; 8.262; 11.00; 11.10; 11.11; 12.10; 12.20; 12.60; 13.10; 13.30
Thomson West	http://west.thomson.com	13.30
Time	www.time.com	13.51
Treaties and Other International Agreements	www.access.gpo.gov/congress/senate/senate11cp106.html	12.60
Truman Scholars	www.truman.gov	5.100
United Press International	http://about.upi.com	13.51
United States Government Manual	www.gpoaccess.gov/gmanual	13.20
Univ. of Michigan Documents Center	www.lib.umich.edu/govdocs	13.40; 13.50
Urban Institute	www.urban.org	13.52
U.S. Association of Former Members of Congress	www.usafmc.org	5.190
U.S. Capitol Historical Society	www.uschs.org	5.190; 6.15
U.S. Conference of Mayors	www.usmayors.org	10.201
U.S. Congress Votes database	http://projects.washingtonpost.com/congress	13.30
U.S. Congressional Bibliographies	www.lib.ncsu.edu/congbibs	13.20
U. S. Constitution, Analysis and Interpretation	www.gpoaccess.gov/constitution	12.60
U.S. Department of Commerce Office of General Counsel	www.ogc.doc.gov	5.173
U.S. Department of Health and Human Services	www.hhs.gov and www.grants.gov	5.160; 5.172
U.S. Department of State (tours)	http://receptiontours.state.gov	3.112
U.S. Department of Transportation Office of the General Counsel	www.dot.gov/ost/ogc	5.173
U.S. Department of the Treasury (tours)	www.ustreas.gov/offices/management/curator/tours.shtml	3.112
U.S. Geological Survey (district maps)	www.nationalatlas.gov/printable/congress.html	2.13

Name	URL	Section
U.S. House of Representatives	www.house.gov	4.21; 4.30 6.15; 8.42; 8.52; 8.123; 8.262; 11.10; 11.13; 12.40; 12.80; p 561; p 569; p 571; p 580
U.S. Marine Corps Evening Parade	www.mbw.usmc.mil/parades.asp	3.112
U.S. News and World Report	www.usnews.com	13.51
U.S. Newswire	www.usnewswire.com/publicinterest	13.51
U.S. Senate	www.senate.gov	4.21; 5.120; 6.15; 8.42; 8.52; 8.161; 8.262; 11.10; 11.14; 12.20; 12.50; p 573; p 575; p 577; p 580
U.S. Supreme Court	www.supremecourtus.gov	3.112
USDA Graduate School Congressional Fellowship Program	www.grad.usda.gov/index.php?option=com_content+task=view+id=214+Itemid=306	5.100
Vice Presidents of the United States, 1789-1993	www.senate.gov/artandhistory/history/common/briefing/Vice_President.htm	12.81
Virtual Chase, The	www.virtualchase.com	13.40
Voice of America News	www.voanews.com	13.51
Wall Street Journal, The	www.wsj.com	13.51
Washington Information Directory	www.cqpress.com	13.20
Washington Monthly, The	www.washingtonmonthly.com	13.53
Washington National Cathedral	www.cathedral.org/cathedral	3.112
Washington Post, The	www.washingtonpost.com	13.51
Washington Times	www.washingtontimes.com	13.51
Weekly Compilation of Presidential Documents	www.gpoaccess.gov/wcomp/index.html	11.50
Weekly Standard, The	www.weeklystandard.com	13.53
White House	www.whitehouse.gov	3.112; 11.50; 13.30; 13.43
William S. Hein & Co.	www.wshein.com	13.30
Women in Congress, 1917-2006	http://womenincongress.house.gov	12.81
Women in Government Relations	www.wgr.org	4.21
Women's Research and Education Institute	www.wrei.org/Fellows.htm	5.100
Woodrow Wilson International Center for Scholars	http://wilsoncenter.org	5.190; 13.52
World-newspapers.com	www.world-newspapers.com	13.50
WTOP	www.wtopnews.com	13.51
Yahoo! News	http://news.yahoo.com	13.50

Principal Index Terms

Index

A

ASAE Gateway to Associations, 13.50

Abraham Lincoln Bicentennial Commission, 7.70

Abraham, Spencer, 3.32

Academic journals, 13.54

Account. *See* Appropriations process

Act, when a bill becomes an, 11.40
  bill as passed by the House, annotated example, 15.09
  bill as passed by the Senate, annotated example, 15.14
  bill as received in the Senate, annotated example, 15.10

Activities reports (of House committees). *See* Congressional oversight

Adams, Henry, 6.10

Adams, John, 6.20

Adams, John, Building, 6.20

Adams, John Quincy, 6.10

Additional referral. *See* Referral

Additional views. *See* Committee reports

Adjourn sine die, 7.20, 111.20

Administrative Assistants Association (House), 7.30

Administrative counsel (House). 5.30, 5.110

Administrative Procedure Act, 10.10, 10.40, 11.50

Advise and consent. *See* Constitution, U.S.

Advisory Council on Historic Preservation, 5.121

Advocacy Tipsheet, 13.43

African Growth and Opportunity Act, 10.170

Age Discrimination in Employment Act, 5.150, 10.190

Aging Committee (Senate)
  category, 7.58
  chair, 7.57
  ratio, 7.52

Agriculture Committee (House), 5.130, 6.20, 10.170
  category, 7.56
  chair, 7.54
  history, 12.10
  ratio, 7.51

Agriculture, Nutrition, and Forestry Committee (Senate), 5.130, 6.20, 8.30, 10.170
  category, 7.58

chair, 7.57

history, 12.10

ratio, 7.52

Air Force Academy, 7.70

Alaska, 7.01, 7.41

Alito, Samuel A. Jr., 4.10

Allowances (for congressional office expenses). *See* Congressional officers, staff, and allowances; Members of Congress; Congressional ethics

Almanac of American Politics, 13.20, 13.30

Almanac of the Unelected, 13.30

Amendment in the nature of a substitute, 8.50, 15.02, 15.05

Amendment process (House)
  amendment in the nature of a substitute, 8.50, 15.02, 15.05
  amendment tree (House), 8.120, 8.122
  base text, 8.120
  bigger-bite amendment, 8.120
  committee amendments, 8.120
  Committee of the Whole, 8.120
  degrees, 8.50
  designating, 8.120
  en bloc amendment, 8.50, 8.120
  first-degree amendment, 8.120
  five-minute rule, 8.120
  germaneness, 8.50, 8.90, 8.120
  glossary, 8.121
  in committee, 8.50
  in House (Committee of the Whole), 8.120
  perfecting amendment, 8.120
  pro forma amendment, 8.120
  reading, 8.120
  second-degree amendment, 8.50, 8.120
  separate vote (in House), 8.120
  special rule and, 8.80, 8.90
  strike the last word/requisite number of words, motion to, 8.120
  substitute amendment, 8.120
  voting in the Committee of the Whole, 8.130

Amendment process (Senate)
  amendment tree, 8.220
  Christmas-tree bills, 8.220
  en bloc amendment, 8.220
  first-degree amendment, 8.220
  germaneness, 8.220
  glossary, 8.121
  in Senate, 8.220

insert/strike/strike and insert, 8.220
  perfecting amendment, 8.220
  printed/unprinted amendments, 8.220
  riders, 8.220
  second-degree amendment, 8.220
  substitute amendment, 8.220
  under cloture, 8.230

Amendments between the Houses, 8.70, 8.260, 8.270. *See also* Conference committee
  glossary, 8.261
  Keeping Up with Reconciling House-Senate Differences, 8.262

Amendments in true/technical disagreement, 8.270

Amendment tree, 8.122

American Association for the Advancement of Science, 5.100

American Dietetic Association, 4.11

American League of Lobbyists, 4.10, 4.21

American Pantheon: Sculptural and Artistic Decoration of the United States Capitol, 6.15

American Planning Association, 5.100

American Political Science Association, 5.100

American Samoa, 7.10

American Society of Association Executives, 4.13, 4.21, 13.50

American University, 5.100

American Youth Scholarship Foundation, 3.10

Americans with Disabilities Act, 5.150, 10.190

Annals of Congress, 12.20

Annual appropriations. *See* Appropriations process

Annual authorizations, 9.80

Anthony, Susan, 6.10

Antideficiency Act, 9.140, 9.150

Apotheosis of Democracy, 6.10

Apotheosis of George Washington, The, 6.10

Appointments (to executive and judicial positions), 10.80, 10.81, 10.121
  travel for senators' advisory groups, 5.40

Apportionment (budget authority), 9.130

Apportionment (House seats), 2.10, 2.13

Appropriations. *See* Appropriations process

Appropriations Committee (House).
See also Appropriations process; Budget process

appropriations measures and, 9.80

architect of the Capitol and, 5.121

budget decisions and, 9.50, 9.70, 9.71

calendar not published, 12.10

category, 7.56

chair, 7.54

Congressional Budget Office and, 5.130

federal aid to states and localities, 10.200

foreign policy and, 10.170

funding, 5.80

legislative veto, 10.51

originate appropriations measures, 9.80, 11.20

ratio, 7.51

reprogramming, 9.140

section 302(a) and (b) allocations/subdivisions, 9.50

subcommittees, 7.50, 9.82

Appropriations Committee (Senate).
See also Appropriations process; Budget process

Air Force Academy and, 7.70

appropriations measures and, 9.80, 11.20

architect of the Capitol and, 5.121

budget decisions and, 9.50, 9.70, 9.71

calendar not published, 12.10

category, 7.58

chair, 7.57

Congressional Budget Office and, 5.130

federal aid to states and localities, 10.200

foreign policy and, 10.170

funding, 5.90

history, 12.10

legislative veto, 10.51

ratio, 7.52

reprogramming, 9.140

section 302(a) and (b) allocations/subdivisions, 9.50

subcommittees, 7.50, 9.82

Appropriations process. *See also* Appropriations Committee (House); Appropriations Committee (Senate); Budget Process

account, 9.80

apportionment, 9.130

appropriated entitlements, 9.70, 9.71

appropriations legislation, 9.70, 9.71, 9.80, 9.84

appropriations legislation originates in House, 8.20, 9.00, 9.80

authorization legislation and, 9.80

budget authority, 9.02, 9.70, 9.110, 9.130

constitutional requirements, 9.00, 9.01, 10.50

continuing appropriations measures/resolutions, 9.80, 11.20

contract authority, 9.80

deferral, 9.80, 10.50

directive, 9.81

earmark, 9.80, 9.81, 9.85, 10.50

general appropriations measures, 9.80

general provision, 9.81

glossary, 9.160

House may begin consideration of appropriations bills, when, 9.50, 9.80

impoundment, 9.150, 10.50

justification, 9.80

legislation in an appropriations measure, 9.80

limitation, 9.80, 9.81, 10.50

line item veto, 9.150

multiyear appropriations, 9.80

no-year appropriations, 9.80

obligation, 9.80, 9.130

offsetting collections, 9.40

omnibus appropriations measure, 9.80

one-year appropriations, 9.80

outlays, 9.02, 9.110

permanent appropriations, 9.40, 9.80

process, 9.80

program and finance schedule, 9.40, 9.44

reappropriation, 9.80

regular appropriations measures, 9.80

report language, 9.80

reprogramming, 9.140, 10.50

rescission, 9.80, 10.50

section 302(a) and (b) allocations/subdivisions, 9.50, 9.80

sequence of appropriations measures through Congress, 9.84

special rules and, 9.80

status table, 12.20

supplemental appropriations measures, 9.80,

transfer, 9.40, 9.80, 9.140, 10.50

unanimous consent agreements and, 9.80

unauthorized appropriations, 9.80

Approval of the Journal (House), 14.10

Approval terminology, 8.141

Archbald, Robert, 10.100

Architect of the Capitol, 5.30, 5.40

architects of the Capitol and construction during their tenure, 6.10

bibliography on Capitol, 6.15

duties, 5.121, 6.20

procurement, 5.112

projects at Capitol, 6.12

research and, 13.10

Archivist of the United States. *See* National Archives and Record Administration

Arizona, 7.10

Armed forces, 10.81, 10.140, 10.160

Armed Services Committee (House), 6.20, 10.170

category, 7.56

chair, 7.54

ratio, 7.51

Armed Services Committee (Senate), 7.70, 10.160, 10.170

category, 7.58

chair, 7.57

ratio, 7.52

Armey, Richard, 1.55

Arms Export Control Act, 10.20, 10.151

Army Corps of Engineers, 10.190

Art in the United States Capitol, 6.15

Articles of Confederation, 12.50

Ashcroft, John, 3.20, 3.32

Association of Former Members of Congress, 5.190

Associations Unlimited, 13.30

Attending physician, 5.30, 5.40, 5.122

Audit of the Financial Statements (by House inspector general), 12.80

August recess. *See* Constituents

Authorization process, 9.80. *See also* Appropriations process; Budget process

Ayes and noes. *See* Voting

B

Baker, Richard, 12.61

Balanced Budget and Emergency Deficit Control Act of 1985, 9.10, 9.30, 9.100

Banking and Financial Services Committee. *See* Financial Services Committee (House)

Banking, Housing, and Urban Affairs Committee (Senate), 10.170, 11.20

category, 7.58

chair, 7.57

history, 12.10

ratio, 7.52

Baptism of Pocahontas, 6.10

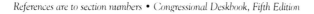

About Us

TheCapitol.Net is the exclusive provider of Congressional Quarterly (CQ) Executive Conferences.

We are a non-partisan business that came out of Congressional Quarterly in 1999.
CQ had offered many of our courses since the 1970s.

Our courses and workshops cover the legislative process, budget process, congressional operations,
how public policy and foreign policy are developed, advocacy and media training,
business etiquette, business writing, and our Capitol Hill Workshop.

The 150-plus experts who teach and write for us are all independent, subject matter experts,
and include senior government executives, former members of Congress, Hill and agency staff,
editors and journalists, lobbyists, lawyers, nonprofit executives, scholars, and other experts.

All of our courses, seminars and workshops can be tailored to meet educational objectives
for your organization, and presented on-site at your location. We have worked with hundreds
of clients to develop and provide a wide variety of custom, on-site training and consulting.

We publish hands-on books for practitioners, written by subject matter experts. All of our booklets
and audio courses on CD, and many of our publications, can be customized with your logo.

Our 2,000-plus clients include Congressional offices, federal and state agencies, the military,
news media, NGOs, and large and small organizations across the country.

Our blog: Hobnob Blog—hit or miss ... give or take ... this or that ...

TheCapitol.Net

Non-partisan training and publications that show how Washington works.™

www.TheCapitol.Net
PO Box 25706, Alexandria, VA 22313-5706 202-678-1600

CPSIA information can be obtained at www.ICGtesting.com
Printed in the USA
LVOW022203010112

261947LV00001B/2/A